THE JEWISH NATIONAL HOME IN PALESTINE

COMMITTEE ON FOREIGN AFFAIRS

SOL BLOOM, New York, *Chairman*

LUTHER A. JOHNSON, Texas
JOHN KEE, West Virginia
JAMES P. RICHARDS, South Carolina
JOSEPH L. PFEIFER, New York
PETE JARMAN, Alabama
W. O. BURGIN, North Carolina
WIRT COURTNEY, Tennessee
THOMAS S. GORDON, Illinois
HOWARD J. McMURRAY, Wisconsin
WILL ROGERS, Jr., California
J. W. FULBRIGHT, Arkansas
MIKE MANSFIELD, Montana
JAMES A. WRIGHT, Pennsylvania

CHARLES A. EATON, New Jersey
EDITH NOURSE ROGERS, Massachusetts
ROBERT B. CHIPERFIELD, Illinois
JOHN M. VORYS, Ohio
FOSTER STEARNS, New Hampshire
KARL E. MUNDT, South Dakota
BARTEL J. JONKMAN, Michigan
FRANCES P. BOLTON, Ohio
JAMES W. WADSWORTH, New York
CHARLES L. GERLACH, Pennsylvania
ANDREW C. SCHIFFLER, West Virginia

BOYD CRAWFORD, *Clerk*

II

THE JEWISH NATIONAL HOME
IN PALESTINE

HEARINGS

BEFORE THE

COMMITTEE ON FOREIGN AFFAIRS
HOUSE OF REPRESENTATIVES

SEVENTY-EIGHTH CONGRESS
SECOND SESSION

ON

H. Res. 418 and H. Res. 419

RESOLUTIONS RELATIVE TO THE JEWISH
NATIONAL HOME IN PALESTINE

FEBRUARY 8, 9, 15, and 16, 1944

**WITH APPENDIX OF DOCUMENTS RELATING TO THE
JEWISH NATIONAL HOME IN PALESTINE**

Printed for the use of the Committee on Foreign Affairs

Introduction by
BEN HALPERN

KTAV PUBLISHING HOUSE, INC.
NEW YORK
1970

This volume was first printed in 1944 by the United States
Government Printing Office, Washington, D.C. for the use
of the Committee on Foreign Affairs.

NEW MATTER
© COPYRIGHT 1970
KTAV PUBLISHING HOUSE, INC.

SBN 87068-050-1

Library of Congress Catalog Card Number: 72-106509
Manufactured in the United States of America

INTRODUCTION

The ordeal of the Jews during World War II, already the subject of extensive study, discussion, and agonized polemics, will continue to try men's conscience for centuries to come. European writers, and American writers of European background, historians, dramatists, and philosophical publicists, have raised painful issues of the guilt, by silence or active complicity, of Western leaders and Western societies. The conduct of the Jews has come under fierce and bitter examination, especially by Jews themselves.

The history of the Final Solution will continue to be analyzed, as it has already been picked over again and again, for unattainable answers to ultimate questions: How should the victims have acted? How should the totally helpless have confronted the totally ruthless? Did they not share in the guilt for the manner of their deaths when herded into ghettos, concentration camps, labor camps, crematoria? Why did they not resist? Or, why was their resistance foredoomed to be useless? Was not their rescue sabotaged by the cowardly inaction of Jews on the outside; in Palestine, in the United States? Were not Poles, Lithuanians, Ukrainians, and others active accomplices in the slaughter? And did not the Pope and the International Red Cross, or the British government, or the American presidency and executive establishment bear responsibility for acts of commission and omission that consigned Jews to the furnaces?

The political struggle over the future of Palestine, running through the whole period of Hitler's rule is, of course, inseparably part of the history of the Holocaust. Underlying any attempt to dissect the body of interrelated actions and motives that produced the State of Israel, there must be a constant awareness of the grim issues and ethical dilemmas of the Genocide. This is certainly true also of the history of American involvement in the Palestine problem and of the efforts of American Jewry to influence American policy during World War II. But the literature on this problem has, so far, been slanted in a rather different direction. Apart from some general histories which were written close to the events and broadly reflected their major features,[1] discussion has concentrated in a peculiar way upon a special issue: the impact of American Jewish lobbying upon American policy towards the Palestine problem.

A major source for this discussion has been the memoirs and biographies of top American officials, from President Truman on down.[2] It is easily understandable that, when the men in charge of policy tell the story, a constant theme should be the complaint about the pressure American Jews brought to bear upon them. Another type of literature, consisting of the studies by political scientists of the American and U.N. policy on Palestine in the 1940's, examines in detail techniques by which, purportedly, organized American Jewry swayed decisions at critical moments.[3]

Such memoirs and studies give only a very limited, biased account of the events. Officials who recall the immediate pressures upon themselves cannot be expected to reproduce faithfully and with true empathy on each occasion the whole moral background of the importunities which so annoyed them. Special studies of Jewish lobbying, in their academic concentration on the mechanisms of political pressure, often fail to convey the decisive, all-pervading influence of wartime traumas upon Jewish political activism. Not only such studies, but the partisan records of one or another of the Jewish political-action groups,[4] give a distorted picture when they focus upon particular organizations without taking sufficient account of the whole force-field of turbulent emotions among Jews at that time. The internal pressures thus generated are an essential element in understanding the positions taken by Jewish leaders and the tactics they used; and also in appreciating their impact upon the political scene.

The "Hearings before the Committee on Foreign Affairs"

in February 1944 on the resolutions H. Res. 418 and H. Res. 419, relative to the Jewish National Home in Palestine, may well illustrate these points. In itself this is a record of the response of a group of legislators to pressing demands of their constituents, brought to bear by Jewish organizations and sympathetic non-Jewish bodies. The participants in the hearings were a limited representation of the major, but not all, Jewish pro-Zionist bodies; of the most outspoken, but not quite all, Jewish anti-Zionist bodies; and of organized pro-Arab organizations and some, but hardly all, of their sympathizers.

What the Congressmen said may often reflect their specific concern for reelection. The statements of the parties on ideological issues and particular immediate controversies may sometimes represent positions adopted for their immediate effect. But underlying the spoken record, and appearing in a choice of words or inflections, are latent arguments and attitudes responding to the pressures of many who were not directly represented at the open sessions. Whether present or not, the whole range of political pressures and organized or unorganized opinion relating to the issues at stake was effective, and is a necessary element in understanding this document of the times.

American Jews, like emancipated Jews in other Western countries, have been organized for political action on behalf of Jews abroad for over a century. Since World War I, two opposed views have been held by rival sets of American Jewish organizations on the appropriate principles and methods for conducting such activity.

On one side were an interconnected group of philanthropic communal agencies, locally active wherever substantial numbers of Jews resided in American cities, and conducting extensive relief and welfare operations, through the American Jewish Joint Distribution Committee, in all overseas countries where Jews were in need or oppressed and where Jewish organizations were permitted by governments to work. The wealthy men who were the top leadership of this network were likely to be associated with the American Jewish Committee, and through this organization engaged in a wide range of political and public-relations activities in the general interest of Jews everywhere.

In spite of efforts, from its origin, to make the American Jewish Committee more generally representative, it remained at the outbreak of World War II a small, self-constituted committee of wealthy and influential men disproportionately recruited from the relatively tiny old-established German Jewish segment of the community.[5] The Committee generally preferred methods of quiet, confidential intercession to mass-pressure tactics. It maintained close contact with the permanent officials of the government, particularly the State Department, and regularly consulted the Department before defining positions on major, potentially controversial questions. Committee activities of a more diffuse kind, directed to a wider public, were primarily defensive and intended to promote favorable views about the Jews and counteract anti-Semitic agitation.

The main ideological rival of the American Jewish Committee was the American Jewish Congress. It was originally organized, following World War I, in direct opposition to the American Jewish Committee and its methods. Thus it was intended to be a broadly representative body reflecting the mood and opinions of all American Jews, overwhelmingly Eastern European in origin, and utilizing methods of mass pressure in the political defense of Jews in all countries. In fact, however, it was not successful in uniting American Jewry for these purposes, and became merely one among numerous politically active Jewish organizations. It nevertheless continued to symbolize the conception of mass political action broadly responsive to Jewish popular opinion. Its contacts with government were not, like the Committee's, primarily through permanent officials and top political appointees of the executive branch, but with party leaders and elected officials, both legislative and executive, especially in the Democratic Party. This should not be interpreted to mean that the American Jewish Committee failed to cultivate relations with elected officials or the American Jewish Congress with government departments; but the structure and traditions of each made it relatively more successful in one or the other type of political contact.

As the American Jewish Committee stood as the head and political-action front of an array of local, national, and internationally active American Jewish philanthropic agencies, so the American Jewish Congress, too, was associated with and backed by a wide variety of other organizations with a similar clientele or membership to its own, and with the same general tradition and political approach. Foremost among these were the several American Zionist organizations, representing ideological variants of Zionism, different sources of recruitment (men, women, youth, labor, the religiously Orthodox), and different functional interests. The Congress also attracted affiliates among the folk organizations of American Jews of Eastern European origin—*landsmanshaftn,* veterans' groups, and so on.

But the relationship between the Congress and its associated organizations differed from that between the Committee and its associates. The Zionist organizations, in particular, did not regard the Congress as their representative and leader in all political and Jewish public-relations issues. There was, rather, a division of areas of jurisdiction. The Zionist parties, directly and through the World Zionist Organization, were active on questions concerning Palestine, and the Congress dealt with political and public-relations problems in America and, to a lesser extent, with overseas Jewries other than the community in Palestine.

Organized American Jewry was blessed with additional establishments that fell under neither of the two rival heads, but pursued independent lines, including political action and public-relations work, with no less authority, sometimes, than the Committee or the Congress. As a religious community, the American Jews' public image was most suitably represented among non-Jews by its three "denominations"; and the lay and rabbinic organizations of American Orthodox, Conservative, and Reform Judaism were natural instruments of political and public-relations activity. A group of powerful

needle-trades unions, originally built by Jewish workers and
still led in the 1930's by politically influential Jewish liberals
and radicals, worked on their own lines, supported by the
major Yiddish newspaper, the *Forverts*. Jewish fraternal organizations traditionally conducted political action as inher-
ently related to their welfare work on behalf of Jews. Among
them, the B'nai B'rith, together with its affiliated agency, the
Anti-Defamation League (ADL), rivaled the American Jewish Committee and the American Jewish Congress as the leading public-relations and political-action agency of American
Jewry.

This large and complicated Jewish establishment represented only a part of the American Jews, and that part only
partially. What vast untapped responsiveness to Jewish need
and to political crisis existed in the community was repeatedly discovered during the successive traumas of the Hitler era.
The reports of atrocities and unexampled horror from abroad
were coupled with a sharp and increasingly violent rise of
anti-Semitic incidents in American cities. Strong popular reactions of American Jews, unforeseen in their character and
intensity, exerted pressure on all the Jewish organizations to
adopt more militant, more ethnically defined attitudes on
the current issues: defense against Hitler and local anti-Semites; efforts to protect, or rescue, European Jews; and the
critical questions of the immediate and future status of Jews
in the Jewish National Home in Palestine.

Such pressure came from previously passive constituents
or associates of the existing organizations, especially those
with some mass base, like the American Jewish Congress and
the Zionist organizations, the B'nai B'rith, and the lay and
rabbinic synagogue councils. It came also from the European
or Palestinian Zionist or other organized groups united with
American Jews in Jewish international bodies. In a sharply
challenging form, it came from new organizations, drawing
on supporters and leaders previously inactive in the community, that sprang up overnight whenever the tactics of the establishment fell short of the drastic measures the popular
mood required.

The American Jewish Committee felt this pressure less
powerfully in a direct way, owing to its structure and composition; though this could not be said of some of its "corporate members"—for example, the women's Zionist organization, Hadassah—and its associated agencies directly concerned with overseas Jewish relief. In an indirect way, however, the Committee was more critically affected by the pressure of the times than were ethnically oriented organizations,
better able to swim with this tide. One of the demands of
the period of crisis, as had also been the case during the First
World War, was aimed primarily against the Committee: the
clamor for uniting Jewish defense and political-action agencies in a single body effectively responsible to the community
at large. To yield to this demand, as the Committee to an
extent was forced to do, not only meant abandoning the
autonomous and unchallenged authority that was considered
a basic principle of the Committee's operations; it meant
risking what, in the event, the Committee was also compelled
to witness: the secession of some of its more hidebound members who could not make any compromise whatever with the
ethnically oriented attitudes of the mass of American Jews.

The new mood began to show its effects shortly after Hitler
came to power, in the agitation for an anti-Nazi boycott and
other mass-protest action.[6] The American Jewish Committee,
in line with the requests of established Jewish communal
leadership in Germany itself, sought to confine American
Jewish reactions to quiet pressures through American official
channels. The Congress, while inclined to more public methods of mass protest, took a cautious attitude toward militant proposals like an anti-Nazi boycott. It only agreed to
them, in the end, under pressure from its own constituents
and from other quarters, which had not been notably active
in Jewish affairs recently or were drawn into activity for the
first time by the boycott agitation. Men like the Yiddish pub-
licist, Abraham Coralnik, the lawyer, Samuel Untermyer,
and the rabbi, Dr. Abba Hillel Silver, all leaders who had
become rather quiescent in Jewish politics, built a new organization, ultimately named the Nonsectarian Anti-Nazi

League, drawing on new sources of Jewish and Gentile support, and using militant boycott tactics. The Congress, under the pressure of relatively minor constituents, like the Jewish War Veterans and the smaller Zionist parties, and of a second-rank leader like Dr. Joseph Tenenbaum, head of the *landsmanshaft* of Polish Jews, had to undertake its own boycott activity, and eventually set up a Joint Boycott Council with other Jewish organizations, primarily the new Jewish Labor Committee organized by the needle-trades unions.

Such already established activities as Jewish defense against local anti-Semitism and aid for refugees, especially in Palestine, were also forced into new and broader channels, necessitating efforts for greater unity and central control. With great difficulty and much conflict, Jewish fund-raising campaigns for Palestine and other overseas and refugee needs were brought together in a United Jewish Appeal. The challenge of local anti-Semitism produced a series of new local Jewish community councils, activating new leaders and expressing the mood of wider Jewish constituencies. It also created pressure for greater coordination, if not unity, among those organizations, the Committee, Congress, ADL, and the new Jewish Labor Committee, who claimed the right to defend American Jewry against anti-Semitism on a national scale.[7]

The shock of war in 1939 brought to a boiling head such simmering pressures upon American Jewish organizations. Previously passive elements in the community grew increasingly active and vocal, both within and beyond the established framework. Among the recognized Jewish organizations demands rapidly mounted for broader unification, based on a distinctly more militant program of action. This led to a heightening of inner tensions, especially in the more conservative agencies. In addition, a new element was injected when the threat of war propelled a wave of refugees, as well as a number of active European leaders, into the American scene.

By 1940 most of the major American Jewish political-action agencies, and a number of newly created ones, had begun to organize for postwar planning and also for immediate action for the protection and rescue of European Jews. In this activity European refugee leaders, scholars, and experts, sometimes explicitly representing the communities whose future and very survival were at stake, assumed prominent, responsible positions. The American Jewish Committee created a Research Institute on Peace and Postwar Problems led by Central European scholars. The American Jewish Congress, together with the new World Jewish Congress founded in 1936, sponsored a parallel agency, the Institute of Jewish Affairs, primarily organized and staffed by East Europeans who had been leaders in the World Jewish Congress and in the European Zionist parties. The Jewish Labor Committee similarly organized new research and rescue agencies, drawing on Eastern European refugee Socialist leaders with whom it had ideological affinities. The ultra-Orthodox anti-Zionist Agudat Israel, an insignificant group hitherto, drew on its qualified European refugee leaders to create similar rescue and postwar planning agencies that highlighted its presence in the Jewish community and also, to an extent, on the general scene of American politics.

A similar irruption of overseas leadership had a marked effect upon the Zionist establishment in the United States, and thus upon major bodies concerned with political action on Palestine, as well as the rescue of European Jews. The fear that global war would disrupt the international functioning of the Zionist movement, especially in the belligerent countries, led, as in the First World War, to the creation of an emergency Zionist organization in the United States. Dr. Chaim Weizmann, President of the World Zionist Organization and the Jewish Agency, not only appointed representatives of the Jewish Agency to serve on this body, chiefly constituted by the major American Zionist organizations; he spent considerable periods in the United States himself, in connection with his wartime scientific research. The Chairman of the Jewish Agency Executive, David Ben-Gurion, also found it necessary, at crucial moments, to come to America and participate in the local Zionist emergency activities. Dr. Nahum Goldmann, who had represented the Jewish Agency

Executive in Geneva and who headed the World Jewish Congress, transferred his base of operations to America in 1940, upon the Nazi invasion of Holland and Belgium. He worked on efforts to rescue European Jewry through the joint organization of the World and American Jewish Congress, and on Palestine issues jointly for the Jewish Agency Executive and the Zionist emergency committee in America.

Apart from such European leaders of the recognized World Zionist Organization and Jewish Agency, the dissident Zionist Revisionist leadership also transferred its Diaspora headquarters from Europe to America. Vladimir Jabotinsky worked from a New York base on his campaign for a "Jewish Army" of American and other Jewish volunteers, from the time he arrived in March, 1940, until his death in August of that year. He was aided in this effort by a group of young activists including Peter H. Bergson (Hillel Kook), Aryeh Ben-Eliezer, Samuel Merlin, some of whom, together with Jabotinsky's son Eri, had already organized the "American Friends of a Jewish Palestine" in 1939 to support the refugee smuggling of the Irgun Tz'vai Leumi. Upon Vladimir Jabotinsky's death the latent internal cleavages of the Revisionist movement, in America as elsewhere, came to the surface. The old-line Revisionists of Jabotinsky's New Zionist Organization continued in his footsteps. The younger men took up a free-lance activity, aligned with the independent actions of the Revisionist youth movement and the paramilitary organization, Irgun Tz'vai Leumi. They were able to achieve a remarkable public relations impact in America. They developed techniques previously neglected by others, in particular the use of full-page political advertisements in newspapers, and other ways of exploiting the mass media. They also reached out to new circles of Gentile support for Jewish (or, as they came to say, Hebrew) nationalism, and involved types of influential Jews, particularly in the entertainment industry, who had not been as widely or as intensively involved by the established Jewish agencies.

The beginning of war in September, 1939, had sealed the doom of European Jewry, but it led, at first, to a pause and slackening of the militant activism Jews engaged in during the immediately preceding period. The voluntarily organized popular anti-Nazi boycott, until then gathering steam, was now superseded by blockades and other measures of war executed by sovereign states against Germany. Jewish agitation against the British anti-Zionist policies signalized by the 1939 White Paper now took a different direction: instead of seeking to effect an immediate policy change by mass pressures, Jews concentrated their political action on measures suitable for influencing the ultimate policy Britain might adopt after the war ended. The negotiations for a Jewish Army, by both the established World Zionist Organization and the Revisionists' New Zionist Organization, while expressing the direct, overpowering need of Jews to fight in their own name against their archenemy, Hitler, also kept in mind the question of Britain's ultimate position on the status of the Jewish National Home.

The issue that aroused the greatest, most furious energies of Jewish activists before the war was the plight of Jewish Hitler refugees and the bars against their admittance, everywhere, but above all in the Jewish National Home. Opposition to the 1939 British White Paper was common to all Jewish opinion. Not content with vocal opposition, both the Jewish Agency and its militant opponents, the Revisionists, had activated clandestine organizations that tried, with varying success, to bring Jewish refugees into Palestine through the British blockade. Rescue operations by such paramilitary organizations were being supported publicly, in direct or indirect fashion, by mass agitation conducted by the official and dissident Zionist bodies. But this issue, too, subsided in the immediate aftermath of Hitler's invasion of Poland, when Zionist attention focused on the demand to obtain recognition of Jewish military contingents in the anti-Nazi war.

As time passed grim reports of the gathering Holocaust began to mount up. The clamor for action to rescue the doomed Jews now beat helplessly against the barred doors of British officialdom, who saw in every such demand a threat to their anti-Zionist policy in Palestine. The Jewish establishment,

Zionist as well as non-Zionist, was bound by its reliance on the good will of the American government and their hope that Churchill might eventually alter the British attitude. Their restraint was severely strained by a succession of pressures, one upon the other: upon the American Jewish Committee, by the Zionists; upon the official Zionists and their associates, by their own aroused constituencies; and upon the entire establishment, by the free-lance ex-Revisionist agitators, who knew how to echo and respond to the turmoil of anger and grief that convulsed the mass of Jews and also touched all compassionate Gentiles.

During 1940 and 1941 the primary aim of militant Jewish nationalists was to gain authorization for a Jewish military force to fight Hitler. The Jewish Agency Executive sought to achieve this by dealing with British authorities. The Revisionists' effort was conducted in America by mass pressure tactics, especially after Jabotinsky died and the young dissidents associated with the Irgun Tz'vai Leumi took the lead.

Unlike Jabotinsky, they found both ideological and tactical reasons, which they made increasingly evident, for sharply detaching their nationalist demands from any connection with American Jewry. He had called for volunteers from the free American Jewish community, as part of the Jewish people, in spite of fears (very timely in 1940) that Jews would be branded warmongers. The new ex-Revisionist lobby, organizing successively a "Committee for a Jewish Army," an "Emergency Committee to Save the Jewish People of Europe," and a "Hebrew Committee of National Liberation," now stressed that they proposed an army made up only of Palestinians meaning the Irgun Tz'vai Leumi—and stateless, refugee European Jews. Ideologically, this meant disavowing any national tie with those Jews who, like many in America, defined themselves strictly as a religious and not an ethnic group. Tactically, this helped them avoid any opposition that could be provoked, among Jews or Gentiles, by asserting an ethnic obligation of American Jews toward Jewish refugees or the Jewish National Home. The plea to rescue the oppressed European Hebrews and allow them to fight, together with the Irgun Tz'vai Leumi, in Palestine was based on universal human sentiments. As a result, the ex-Revisionist group was able to set up, not only a "Hebrew Committee of National Liberation" and even a "Hebrew Embassy" composed of their tight cadre, but also a number of broad nonsectarian front-organizations in support, made up of Americans without distinction of Jew and Gentile. In 1941 this lobby made its first approach to Congress when Representative Andrew L. Somers of New York introduced a resolution, on November 28, intended to secure American action requesting Britain to authorize "all-Jewish military units in Palestine."

Approaches to Gentile laymen and clergy, Congressmen, Senators, and Presidents were part of the traditional activity of American Zionists since World War I. These activities were conducted in routine manner in the early war years, too. But attention was chiefly concentrated at that time on efforts to organize the entire American Jewish community in support of new postwar demands appropriate to the altering situation.

The 1939 White Paper had convinced many Zionists that the future admission of masses of displaced Jews would depend on a clear political decision in favor of a Jewish state. But the American Jewish Committee and other non-Zionists, while committed to the fight against the White Paper, would still go no further than demanding the restoration of the *status quo ante*. This seemed chimerical in 1941, when Axis advances in North Africa and pro-Axis Arab coups in West Asia led Britain to intensify its efforts to retain Arab support. There was much planning of a postwar pan-Arab bloc sponsored by Britain; and sacrificing the Jewish stake in Palestine was the obvious price to pay. Under British urging, State Department officials, too, began to press for sharp reductions in Jewish demands on Palestine, to the point of suggesting postwar evacuation of Palestinian Jews to Africa. These were circumstances which imperatively required Zionists to seek a clear redefinition of the Jewish political claim to Palestine, broadly supported by the entire Jewish community, in order to counteract anti-Zionist pressures in high British and American quarters.

A definitive step in this direction was taken by the Extraordinary Zionist Conference convened by the American Emergency Committee for Zionist Affairs in New York's Hotel Biltmore on May 6–11, 1942. With Weizmann's and Ben-Gurion's active participation, the American Zionists adopted a program demanding

> that the gates of Palestine be opened; that the Jewish Agency be vested with control of immigration into Palestine and with the necessary authority for upbuilding the country, including the development of its unoccupied and uncultivated lands; and that Palestine be established as a Jewish Commonwealth integrated in the structure of the new democratic world.

This was a challenge that undoubtedly helped to produce an anti-Zionist turn in the American Jewish Committee's policies. Maurice Wertheim, who was negotiating with the Zionists for a common stand, had been under increasing pressure by an anti-Zionist Committee faction, led by Judge Joseph M. Proskauer. This relative novice in Jewish leadership was one of a group of laymen whose advice and support were sought by Reform rabbis who were in revolt against the pro-Zionist turn of their own Central Conference at its 1942 annual meeting. Beginning with a rabbinical conference of anti-Zionists in June, a month after the Biltmore meeting, the rabbinical uprising developed by the end of 1942 into a general anti-Zionist organization, the American Council for Judaism. At the January 31, 1943 annual meeting of the American Jewish Committee, Wertheim relinquished the presidency to Proskauer. Elected as a unity candidate capable of holding anti-Zionists with leanings toward the American Council for Judaism within the Committee's fold, Proskauer now had to reconcile this assignment with another task: to negotiate with the Zionists for a consensus position to keep American Jewry from splintering. But on the Zionist side, 1942 had ended with sharply increased demands for more militancy; and instead of being deterred by the prospect of a clash with the Committee, Zionist leaders were compelled to undertake the unification of the whole community around their own position.

All established Jewish agencies, including the Zionists, suffered a violent blow to their credibility and prestige because of their loyalty to the White House and the State Department in 1942. Reports from the World Jewish Congress office in Geneva gave definite information of the scope and nature of Hitler's "Final Solution," already being systematically carried out. At the request of Sumner Welles, the Jews' friendliest contact in the State Department, Stephen S. Wise and other established American Jewish leaders refrained from making public, or from acting publicly on this supreme emergency for three whole months until, on November 25, 1942, a release was authorized. The fury of the Jewish public against American officialdom and their own establishment rose to a desperate intensity, and broke out in outcries against "moral bankruptcy" from the ranks. Those outside the establishment observed no bounds in their expressions of contempt.[8]

The year 1943 was climactic. It was marked by an evasive response of the American government, in collaboration with Britain, which finally filled the Jews' cup of moral outrage to overflowing. In that year B'nai B'rith, responding to mounting pressures of its members and led by its deeply angered president Henry Monsky, joined the Zionists in relentless demands for a united Jewish, militant, corporate voice. The character of the American Jewish Conference, convened after country-wide elections on August 29–September 1, 1943, was decisively affected by the bitter mood that American official behavior had produced.

On April 19, 1943 the American and British governments conferred in Bermuda on a problem defined as that of "political refugees . . . not confined to persons of any particular race or creed." The circumlocution, avoiding the mention of Jews, was paralleled by the careful omission throughout the conference of the issue of Palestine. The proceedings, patently futile as to the substance of the problem, were conducted in such a way as to cause maximum abrasion of already frayed Jewish sensitivities. Congressman Sol Bloom, chairman of the House Foreign Affairs Committee, earned personal opprobrium by explaining that proposals by Jewish agencies, which had been denied access to the conference, would not be considered, coming as they did from "pressure groups." The callous attitudes of Bermuda were voiced repeatedly through 1943, when various official excuses were found for rejecting one after another specific, concrete proposals to rescue groups of Jews from imminent extermination in Europe. Even a promise to allow an extension for the use of those 1939 White Paper Palestine immigration certificates remaining unused at the terminal date of March 31, 1944, a step which Congressman Bloom, in these hearings, said had been agreed on in Bermuda in April, was not made public until the month of November.

At the American Jewish Conference's constituent session at the end of summer, efforts were still being made to reduce Jewish pressure on American policy. Weeks before the August 29 opening of the Conference, some Zionist leaders had been negotiating with the American Jewish Committee to manage the Conference agenda in such a way as to produce a "moderate" resolution, denouncing the White Paper but not echoing the Biltmore program, with its specific demand for a Jewish Commonwealth. In correspondence between Proskauer and Stephen Wise the American government's desire for such an outcome was made clear. But earlier that month, Dr. Abba Hillel Silver had finally been brought, at Weizmann's urging and with strong support from the smaller Zionist parties, into the Zionist emergency committee's leadership, as co-chairman with Wise. Mounting the rostrum, he swept the session in a furious address that lifted the frustrated delegates to their feet in roaring support. The Conference voted a resolution, with only four dissenting votes out of over five hundred delegates, calling for "the fulfillment of the Balfour Declaration and of the Mandate for Palestine, whose intent and underlying purpose . . . was to reconstitute Palestine as the Jewish Commonwealth."

In the aftermath, the Zionist Emergency Committee was reorganized, under the new name of the American Zionist Emergency Council, and brought under the powerful, direct control of Abba Hillel Silver. The budget of the Emergency Council rapidly expanded and activities swiftly spread and deepened into every significant local community and all conceivable avenues of influence. On the other side, only the American Jewish Committee seceded from the American Jewish Conference in direct reaction to the Jewish Commonwealth resolution; the Jewish Labor Committee dropped out later over another matter. Proskauer's secession from the American Jewish Conference brought the resignation of the Zionist corporate members from the American Jewish Committee, which came under a flood of bitter and violent criticism. In the ensuing period, the public voice of the Committee was muted while it devoted itself to examining its own crisis. But the American Council for Judaism more than made up for this decline in the force of anti-Zionism. With the powerful financial support of Lessing Rosenwald, who became president of the Council in April, 1942, and with public attention generously bestowed upon it by Council member Arthur Hays Sulzberger's *New York Times,* the new anti-Zionist body greeted the American Jewish Conference in August, 1943, with a campaign of vociferous opposition uninhibited by any such concern to remain within a Jewish consensus as might restrain the American Jewish Committee. But in the Jewish community their voice was drowned out in the roar of fury against them.

In the last months of 1943, the rising pressure of Jewish opinion had still had no marked effect on the organs of government. In October, 1943, Senators Guy M. Gillette, Elbert D. Thomas, and Edwin C. Johnson who had all (like the then Senator Harry S. Truman) been original national sponsors of the maverick Committee for a Jewish Army, introduced a resolution recommending "the immediate creation by the President of an Agency to Save the Jewish People of Europe." It was to be "composed of military, economic and diplomatic experts," and to function initially under the

Secretary of State and later as a "United Nations Agency," with "full authority to determine and effectuate a realistic and stern policy of action to save the lives and preserve the dignity of the ancient Jewish people of Europe . . ." In December the Senate Foreign Relations Committee gave unanimous support to this resolution. In the House, however, the Foreign Affairs Committee, under Sol Bloom's chairmanship, called on Assistant Secretary of State Breckinridge Long for advice and counsel. In the face of his obdurate denial that anything could be done for the Jews and his negative attitude to any reference to Palestine (proposed as an emendation in testimony by Stephen Wise), the House committee dropped the matter without action on December 26.

But the atmosphere had nevertheless changed. Not only had Jewish anger been made widely and powerfully evident, and brought effectively to the attention of the public and of political officials, but the conscience of men in power was moved. The Secretary of the Treasury, Henry Morgenthau, Jr., was deeply and painfully aroused. His "Personal Report to the President" in January, 1944, was followed, on January 22, by an Executive Order, setting up a War Refugee Board, composed of the Secretaries of State, Treasury, and War. It was instructed to take specific actions, in the spirit of the Gillette resolution, and in line with innumerable elaborate projects pressed upon the government in vain throughout 1943 by the several Jewish organizations desperately concerned with proposals for rescue.

By February, Congressman Sol Bloom's House Committee on Foreign Affairs, too, was prepared to consider a new resolution in the Jewish interest. For Bloom there was a serious problem of recovering the support his previous attitudes had cost him among his New York constituents. Other committee members, as for example, Will Rogers, Jr. of California, had long been active supporters of the more militant pro-Jewish lobbyists. The resolutions proposed reflected accurately the position of the American Jewish consensus, established by the Biltmore program and the September 1, 1943 resolution of the American Jewish Conference.

They echoed the language of these documents in proposing:

> . . . that the United States shall use its good offices
> and take appropriate measures to the end that the doors
> of Palestine shall be opened for free entry of Jews into
> that country, and that there shall be full opportunity
> for colonization, so that the Jewish people may ultimate-
> ly reconstitute Palestine as a free and democratic
> Jewish Commonwealth.

Those offering testimony in favor of the resolution, apart
from a long list of Congressmen wishing to be placed on
record individually, were Zionist-minded, established leaders
who had demonstrated their authority to voice the American
Jewish consensus. They appeared representing officially the
several rabbinical organizations, the general American Jewish
Conference, as well as the specifically Zionist, American
Zionist Emergency Council and its four major constituent
parties. But there was no doubt that it was the Zionist establishment, and especially the effective organization personified
and commanded by Abba Hillel Silver, which, with the cooperation of the chairman, dominated the proceedings.
Christian pro-Zionists who testified were also men who supported the activities of the Zionist Emergency Council. The
maverick pro-Jewish militants, whose influence had been
evident in the Gillette resolution, did not participate.

The Hearings also gave full scope to advocates of anti-
Zionist positions. Arab views were represented by K. S.
Twitchell, a consulting engineer to the government of Saudi
Arabia, and two Lebanese Americans, Professor Philip Hitti
of Princeton and a Boston lawyer, Faris S. Malouf, President
of the Syrian and Lebanese American Federation of the
Eastern States. The Arabs spoke and were questioned at
sufficiently great length to balance the proceedings, as Congressman Bloom took pains several times to point out. Jewish
anti-Zionists were represented in numbers more than double
that of the Arabs. The American Jewish Committee put in a
quite perfunctory appearance, not even making a verbal
statement. But the minuscule American Council for Judaism

was represented by no less than four speakers, including three Reform rabbis.

The Hearings were so organized in division of speakers, questioners, and interwoven and appended documentation, supplied both by the witnesses and the chairman, as to make it an extraordinarily comprehensive running argument covering all controversial issues connected with Palestine and the Jewish problem. These very issues are in many cases the ones raised over again in our times.

This was a Committee hearing on Palestine thoroughly Zionist in its fundamental tone and emphasis, notwithstanding the courteous attention given to anti-Zionist sentiments. The pro-Zionist legislative consensus in committee was unmistakable, but the outcome was an anticlimax. On March 17, 1944, Secretary of War Stimson wrote to the committee chairman that military considerations, in his view, made adoption of the proposed resolution inadvisable. On this advice from the Executive, whose officers had not publicly testified, all action was promptly dropped. But in the election campaigns which began in Spring, 1944, first the Republicans and then the Democratic party and the respective candidates for President issued ringing declarations in favor of Zionist-sounding objectives. The pattern thus set was maintained in the following period.[9] But events also illuminated with increasing clarity the rather paradoxical outcome of Jewish pro-Zionist political action.

The Spring, 1944 lobbying for pro-Zionist planks in the Republican and Democratic party platforms had caused the development of a rift between Zionist leaders. The Republicans, naturally, had used the occasion of their pro-Zionist statement to attack President Roosevelt's inadequate record on this issue. Silver tried to persuade the Zionists to endorse the Republican position, including the partisan attack on FDR, and was defeated. Wise and other Zionists with Democratic ties tried hard to retain good relations with the Administration, especially after the elections. They were compelled to fight Silver and even to disavow positions he took.

On October 13, Secretary Stimson withdrew the objections

he had voiced earlier, and a campaign was launched for a new resolution. However, when Secretary of State Stettinius was consulted, he expressed reservations in the name of President Roosevelt. Disregarding a decision not to proceed without State Department approval, Silver sent Congressman Bloom, at the latter's demand, a written request for a new resolution. The result was a resolution so watered down in the House committee that Lessing Rosenwald expressed his approval of it, while Wise advised Stettinius that the Zionists, who in the majority regarded the proposed text as a defeat, would agree to defer action. But Silver thought otherwise, feeling that even this resolution would count as a Zionist victory; and upon his unilateral insistence the resolution passed the House. The Emergency Council majority now instructed Silver to forestall passage in the Senate Committee, but he again acted on his own, refusing to intervene with the Senate leadership. The Senate Foreign Relations Committee then rejected the proposed resolution, by a vote of twelve to eight on December 11, 1944, upon the expressed opposition of the State Department.

In the storm that then blew up, Silver and Wise resigned, following which Wise was elected sole chairman of the Emergency Council, with the support of Hadassah and the Zionist Organization of America against the opposition of the two smaller Zionist parties, the labor and religious Zionists. But, whatever the merits of this particular dispute and of its occasion, the ill-starred Congressional resolution, Silver's established image was by then that of the militant, and Wise's that of the moderate. A powerful reaction, stimulated by a strong campaign by Silver's friends, immediately set in; and by July, 1945, Silver was back in control of American Zionist public relations and political work. He was thus able to exercise a militant force in America, backing the militancy of Ben-Gurion and others in Palestine, during the crucial years when Truman and Bevin clashed over the future of Palestine and the displaced Jews.

If one were to strike a balance of the foregoing record of Zionist lobbying, one could hardly call it an unmitigated or even a substantial success. If the State Department or another Department of the Administration is cast in the role of the Zionists' opponent, then the anti-Zionist side has a consistent record of victory in virtually every encounter. In the case of the Hearings here presented, a mere brief note by the Secretary of War was sufficient, without the trouble of a public appearance, to overthrow the entire practical effect of the well-prepared, cogent, and extensive Zionist testimony and all its laborious background lobbying.

The record also highlights another feature of the problem in pressure politics which has rarely, if ever, been sufficiently noticed in this connection. Rather than Jews swaying government, the plain fact, repeatedly substantiated in our narrative, is that government proved capable of swaying Jews, and decisively affected the position some of them took in the inner politics of their own community. Here, however, what the story shows is a rapid, decisive liberation of the organized Jewish community from such influences. There grows up, indeed, a defiance, increasingly impatient, of all such hints and pressures from above and a headstrong insistence of the Jewish community on responding to its own rage, fear, grief, and rebellious pride. This, and not any game theory analysis of Jewish pressure tactics in the war years, is the most obvious reason for most of what happened in that anguished time.

Ben Halpern
Brandeis University
Waltham, Mass.

April, 1970

INTRODUCTION

NOTES

1 J. C. Hurewitz, *The Struggle for Palestine* (1950) and Frank E. Manuel, *The Realities of American-Palestine Relations* (1949) are good studies of this kind.

2 For the most embittered, personal involvement, see *The Forrestal Diaries* (1951) edited by Walter Millis.

3 The best study is Samuel Halperin, *The Political World of American Zionism* (1961).

4 Isaac Zaar's, *Rescue and Liberation* (1954) is useful despite its fictionalized frame. A serious study is the late Joseph B. Schechtman's, *The United States and the Jewish State Movement* (1966).

5 For a contemporary analysis, see Ben Halpern, "The American Jewish Committee," *Jewish Frontier* (Dec. 1943).

6 The material on this subject is collected in Moshe Gottlieb's unpublished 1967 doctoral dissertation at Brandeis University, *The Anti-Nazi Boycott Movement in the American Jewish Community.*

7 See Harry Lurie, *A Heritage Affirmed* (1961).

8 See in particular Ben Hecht, *Perfidy* (1961).

9 Detailed analysis and accounts of the whole subject in Samuel Halperin, *op. cit.;* Irwin Oder's unpublished Columbia University doctoral dissertation, *The United States and the Palestine Mandate, 1920–1948: A Study of Public Opinion and Policy Making* (1956); and an unpublished Brandeis University master's thesis by Doreen Bierbrier, *The American Zionist Emergency Council: An Analysis of a Pressure Group* (1968).

THE JEWISH NATIONAL HOME IN PALESTINE

TUESDAY, FEBRUARY 8, 1944

House of Representatives,
Committee on Foreign Affairs,
Washington, D. C.

The committee met at 10 a. m., pursuant to notice, Hon. Sol Bloom, chairman, presiding, for consideration of House Resolutions 418 and 419, which are as follows:

[H. Res. 418, 78th Cong., 2d sess.]

RESOLUTION

Whereas the Sixty-seventh Congress of the United States on June 30, 1922, unanimously resolved "that the United States of America favors the establishment in Palestine of a national home for the Jewish people, it being clearly understood that nothing shall be done which may prejudice the civil and religious rights of Christian and all other non-Jewish communities in Palestine, and that the holy places and religious buildings and sites in Palestine shall be adequately protected"; and

Whereas the ruthless persecution of the Jewish people in Europe has clearly demonstrated the need for a Jewish homeland as a haven for the large numbers who have become homeless as a result of this persecution: Therefore be it

Resolved, That the United States shall use its good offices and take appropriate measures to the end that the doors of Palestine shall be opened for free entry of Jews into that country, and that there shall be full opportunity for colonization, so that the Jewish people may ultimately reconstitute Palestine as a free and democratic Jewish commonwealth.

[Note.—H. Res. 419 is an identical resolution.]

Chairman Bloom. The committee will kindly come to order.

Mr. Eaton. Mr. Chairman.

Chairman Bloom. Representative Eaton.

Mr. Eaton. I would like to call the attention of the members of the committee to a very constructive and useful compilation on the history of this proposition which has been prepared by Chairman Bloom, and which, as I understand, is, and ought to be before us. Note this little book. It is a very concise and comprehensive statement, and I want to thank the chairman for preparing it for us. I have read it carefully, and it is filled with information which we will need in order to intelligently discuss these resolutions. Thank you, Mr. Chairman.

Chairman Bloom. Thank you, Dr. Eaton.

The committee has under consideration House Resolution 418, introduced by Mr. Wright, and House Resolution 419, introduced by Mr. Compton. They are identical resolutions, so we will consider both of them at the same time. You also have before you the booklet that is referred to by Mr. Eaton, and this booklet will give to you full information with reference to the legislation that we have under consideration.

Mr. Jarman. Does it include a report from the State Department, Mr. Chairman?

Chairman Bloom. There is no report from the State Department. I will say to the gentleman that this is merely a House resolution, and

1

there is no report here from the Department. The resolution simply calls for an expression of opinion of the House of Representatives. A similar resolution was introduced in the Senate. The resolution introduced in the House and in the Senate has the approval of the majority leader and of the minority leader of the House and of the majority leader of the Senate and the acting minority leader of the Senate, Senator Barkley and Senator White.

The resolution is a simple resolution, and the resolution part of it is:

Resolved, That the United States shall use its good offices and take appropriate measures to the end that the doors of Palestine shall be opened for free entry of Jews into that country, and that there shall be full opportunity for colonization, so that the Jewish people may ultimately reconstitute their Palestine as a free and democratic Jewish commonwealth.

I will say for the benefit of the committee that the information that is contained in this pamphlet which is before you, and which has been compiled for your information and consideration, contains the history of Palestine going back hundreds of years, and also the expression of thought with reference to this matter, especially the commonwealth idea, of President Wilson, President Harding, and President Coolidge.

It also contains speeches made in the House of Lords and the House of Commons in opposition to the British white paper on Palestine.

Your chairman thought that we would listen to the witnesses who wish to testify on these resolutions, and then if we want any further advice, or any further information, in addition to what is contained in this document, why, of course, it is very easy for us to get it and to consider it in executive session.

Mrs. ROGERS. Are you going to ask the State Department for a report on this, Mr. Chairman?

Chairman BLOOM. The Chair just finished stating that if we want any further information we would be very glad to ask them.

Mrs. ROGERS. I introduced a resolution some time ago and the committee insisted that the State Department be asked for an opinion on it.

Chairman BLOOM. When was the resolution introduced?

Mrs. ROGERS. Oh, it was some time ago, a year ago. The committee would not act upon it without an opinion from the State Department.

Chairman BLOOM. The Chair would like to state, that with the ever changing situation throughout the world, what might have been considered appropriate and the best thing to do a year ago, might be changed today, so that if it is necessary, and if the committee feels that they want to get further information, why, there is no reason we ought not to get it.

Mrs. ROGERS. You would have no objection?

Chairman BLOOM. Oh, no; none at all. We want to get all the information we possibly can.

Mr. EATON. I have been asked by a number of people about this resolution. Who wrote it; who prepared this resolution; is it the child of our two distinguished leaders, the majority leader and the minority leader, or who is the author of it?

Chairman BLOOM. The author of the idea goes back 2,000 years, if I remember.

Dr. EATON. Let us bring it down to date—February 1944.

Chairman BLOOM. As to the idea contained in both of these resolutions, I do not know by whom it was suggested. The chairman merely had these resolutions referred to your committee through regular channels. If you wish to find out who the actual authors are I would be glad to try to find out for you.

Dr. EATON. I have to answer these constituents of mine.

Chairman BLOOM. I am not afraid, Dr. Eaton, of your answer, and I know the answer will be the correct one. I know your constituents will know, whichever way you vote, that you are voting according to the dictates of your heart.

We have with us this morning the majority and minority leaders of the House. I would like to call on Mr. John McCormack, first, to express his views to the committee, and then Mr. Martin, and then the Chair would like to state that we will call Members of the Congress immediately after Mr. McCormack and Mr. Martin. We would like to go along until about half-past 12, and then recess until 2 o'clock, because there are some witnesses here from out of town, and they would like to get away, because they cannot get accommodations here in Washington. So that we will run along until 12:30, and then recess until 2 o'clock, and go along from 2 to 4.

Mrs. BOLTON. Have we secured permission from the House to sit this afternoon, Mr. Chairman?

Chairman BLOOM. We will receive it. There is nothing on the floor of the House anyway, but we will receive permission, because there is only general debate. Is there any objection to that? The Chair hears none.

Mr. McCormack.

STATEMENT OF THE HONORABLE JOHN W. McCORMACK, A REPRESENTATIVE IN CONGRESS FROM THE STATE OF MASSACHUSETTS

Mr. McCORMACK. Mr. Chairman, and members of the committee, the resolution before this committee, which I support, is a clarification of the historic American policy established by the joint resolution of the Sixty-seventh Congress, adopted in 1922.

In fact, before the Balfour Declaration was accepted by the Allied and Associated Powers in the First World War, the approval of the United States was sought and secured.

President Woodrow Wilson, on March 3, 1919, speaking of the Balfour Declaration, said, and I quote:

I have before this expressed my personal approval of the declaration of the British Government regarding the aspirations and historic claims of the Jewish people in regard to Palestine. I am, moreover, persuaded that the Allied Nations, with the fullest concurrence of our Government and people, are agreed that in Palestine shall be laid the foundations of a Jewish commonwealth.

A study of the record discloses that it was intended in due time when the Jewish people shall attain a majority in Palestine they shall reconstitute their Palestine as a Jewish commonwealth. This was the way Mr. Churchill himself, the then British Secretary of State for War, hailed the Balfour Declaration when on February 8, 1920, Mr. Churchill said:

If, as may well happen, there should be created in our own lifetime by the banks of the Jordan a Jewish state under the protection of the British Crown which might comprise three or four millions of Jews, an event will have occurred in the history of the world which would from every point of view be beneficial, and would be especially in harmony with the truest interests of the British Empire.

It may be worthy of mention that in the resolution adopted by the legislature of the Commonwealth of Massachusetts in favor of the Jewish National Home in Palestine on the 13th day of February 1919, it is declared that—

* * * There should be established such political, administrative, economic conditions in Palestine as will assure the development of Palestine into a Jewish commonwealth.

I am persuaded that the original intention of the Balfour Declaration was to afford to the Jews the opportunity to immigrate into Palestine and to develop that country. It was contemplated that this will in due time lead to the establishment of a Jewish commonwealth.

In the face of the terrible tragedy of the Jewish homelessness in Europe today and which will follow the inevitable victorious conclusion of the war by the United Nations, it is appropriate to point to Palestine as the one country which was publicly and legally set apart as the Jewish national home for this dark hour, in order that it might receive and absorb a large number of these victims of Nazi persecution.

I will not undertake to describe the plight of the Jewish people in Europe. Language is inadequate for that purpose except to say that they have been driven about like the last dying leaves before the chill winds of winter.

Where shall they go?

There is nothing on the European horizon to which they may look with hope. Where is the country which is extending an invitation to the Jews to come, except Palestine?

It is the Jewish pioneers themselves with the help of American Jewry and other Jewries of the world who rebuilt the land of their forefathers, reclaimed its soil, and made it a decent place for all the inhabitants to live in, without injury to anyone.

Mr. Malcolm MacDonald as the British Secretary of State for the Colonies in a statement in the House of Commons on February 24, 1938, said:

* * * Their (the Jews') achievement has been remarkable. They have turned sand dunes into orange groves. They have pushed ever farther into waste land the frontiers of cultivation and settlement. They have created a new city, housing today 140,000 souls, where before there was only bare seashore. There is no knowledge where their achievement might end if Palestine were empty of all other populations and could be handed over to them in full ownership. The Jews are in Palestine not on sufferance but by right, and today, under the lash of persecution in central Europe, their eagerness to return to their own homeland is multiplied a hundred times. The tragedy of a people who have no country has never been so deep as it is in this week. The sympathy of our own countrymen, their anxiety to do everything they can to help the persecuted Jews has never been so firm as it is today. * * *

Mr. Chairman and members of the committee, this resolution is expressive not only of the historic American policy with reference to Palestine, but it is in line with the highest ideals of humanity and the basic principles for which this war is being fought.

If, as we hope and expect, that order shall be established in this world out of the present chaos, it is indeed imperative that the problem of Jewish homelessness should be solved in the interest of world order and of justice, which we believe will eventually come into being.

We cannot close our eyes from the point of view of the enlightened self-interest of the non-Jewish world to the cruel spectacle of 2,000,000 Jews roaming over Europe in search for a home. It is a challenge to all kinds of justice, particularly Christian justice.

We can do no less than to declare our views in favor of free entry of Jews into their National Home and full freedom of opportunity for Jewish colonization and resettlement in Palestine.

It is important for the Jewish people to know that in the course of time when they shall constitute a majority in Palestine then, with the sanction of the nations of the world, Palestine shall become a free and democratic Jewish commonwealth.

I know that every decent-minded person, without regard to race, color, or creed, has a deep feeling not only of sympathy, but far beyond sympathy for the unfortunate plight of all persecuted peoples, of peoples who have been maltreated by the Nazi horde, and particularly those of the Jewish faith who have undergone vicious persecution in the past several years. It is the cry of humanity that I have referred to, the cry of justice, and particularly a challenge to Christian justice that this problem be met. They are human beings just like you and I. They have their hopes and their aspirations. They have their little families, the men have their wives, and the wives have their husbands, and they have their children as God has blessed them. They are human beings seeking a home, some place where they can live without fear of future persecution.

The least that the Congress and the House of Representatives can do is to go on record in the direction which shows that they think along not only constructive but human lines. I think this resolution is the foundation for action on our part which will be an adequate expression of the feelings of the members of this committee and of the House of Representatives.

May I at this time to you, Mr. Chairman, and to the committee express my congratulations and my thanks for this fine, historical compilation, and to the chairman, Congressman Bloom, whom we all admire and respect, a man who enjoys the deep respect of every colleague of his, a great American, may I express my appreciation for your courtesy, and may I compliment you for this fine publication of the documents which are of great value and which will remain a source of intelligent information.

Chairman BLOOM. Thank you very much, Mr. McCormack. Are there any questions the members of the committee want to ask?

Mrs. ROGERS. He made a very forceful statement.

Chairman BLOOM. Mr. McCormack, Mrs. Rogers agrees with you.

Mr. McCORMACK. I am very happy to know that.

Chairman BLOOM. We now have another gentleman from the Commonwealth of Massachusetts, our beloved friend, the minority leader, and a former member of this committee, as I was reminded by my good friend, Mr. Johnson, here.

The thought occurred to me that we are talking about a commonwealth in this resolution, and here we have two gentlemen from a commonwealth of this country, the Commonwealth of Massachusetts, Mr. McCormack and Mr. Martin, representing both of the major parties from the same Commonwealth. The thought occurred to me that where we have leaders of the two major political parties from one commonwealth in this great country of ours working in harmony on these resolutions, could it not be possible that in that other commonwealth that we are discussing here today that the people would be able to live in harmony and peace and good will the same as in the Commonwealth of Massachusetts.

I now call upon our very good friend, Mr. Martin.

STATEMENT OF THE HONORABLE JOSEPH W. MARTIN, A REPRESENTATIVE IN CONGRESS FROM THE STATE OF MASSACHUSETTS

Mr. MARTIN. Mr. Chairman and members of the committee, it is almost like coming home for me to come up to this little room. It seems natural to see it crowded, as, indeed, it always is at these hearings of the Foreign Affairs Committee. I spent 12 very pleasant years as a member of this committee, and I have often wished I was still a member.

Chairman BLOOM. We also wish you were back with us, Mr. Martin.

Mr. MARTIN. For more than 20 years I have been in sympathy with the resolution which is presented here today. I have believed that it was the solution of one of the great problems that must be solved some day if we are going to have a happy and contented world. This resolution is an expression of the sympathy of the people of the United States with Jewish aspirations for the restoration of their national life in Palestine. It is a reassertion of the historic attitude of the United States as embodied in the Lodge Palestine resolution which was adopted by Congress in 1922.

The tragedy of the Jewish people has never been so deep as it is today. The terrible persecution and mass murder of the Jews of Europe is so ghastly that no true Christian heart can withhold its sympathy. But, all will not be destroyed. That is the hope and prayer of all civilized men. Those Jews who will escape Nazi extermination will face cruel homelessness, except for Palestine.

Following the victorious conclusion of the war the only country which will be capable of receiving and absorbing large number of these unfortunate people will be Palestine, which country was made ready for that very purpose.

During the past two decades the Jewish pioneers in Palestine have turned sand dunes into orange groves. They have pushed farther into the waste land frontiers of cultivation and settlement. They have developed industries and made Palestine a better place to live in for all of its inhabitants regardless of race or creed.

The 600,000 Jews of Palestine have made a magnificent contribution to the war effort of the United Nations. Thousands of their sons have volunteered in the armed service of Great Britain and gave a good account of themselves on the field of battle.

It is nothing but elementary justice to enable the homeless Jews of Europe, the victims of the Nazi tyranny, to enter Palestine, not on sufferance, but as a matter of right.

This resolution is a reaffirmation of the established policy of the United States in favor of a Jewish national home in harmony with the new and terrible realities with which the Jews of Europe are faced today.

Mrs. ROGERS. That is a splendid statement.

Chairman Bloom. I am very happy to say, Mr. Martin, that Mrs. Rogers agrees with you also.

Mr. Martin. I am delighted at this.

Dr. Eaton. Mr. Chairman, we have one more reason for having faith in Massachusetts.

Chairman Bloom. Yes, Dr. Eaton.

Mr. Martin. Because the distinguished Representative of New Jersey's ancestors came from there.

Dr. Eaton. For which I am very grateful.

Chairman Bloom. Thank you very much, gentlemen. Representative Rolph.

STATEMENT OF THE HONORABLE TOM ROLPH, A REPRESENTATIVE IN CONGRESS FROM THE STATE OF CALIFORNIA

Mr. Rolph. Mr. Chairman, and members of the committee, I want to say that it is a decided privilege and a pleasure to be here today and to attend a meeting that is under the chairmanship of a former San Franciscan. There are people who do not know that Sol Bloom lived in San Francisco years ago. The people of San Francisco are very proud of the job he has been doing here in the House of Representatives, and it is an honor and a privilege to serve with him.

The people of San Francisco, Mr. Chairman, and members of the committee, are very much in favor of this legislation.

Last June a great mass meeting was held in our Civic Auditorium, and 11,000 people attended that meeting. The gathering endorsed a resolution which I would like to read. This resolution represents the sentiment not only of the people of San Francisco but of the entire State of California. With your permission, Mr. Chairman, I would just like to read these resolutions. They were adopted Thursday evening, June 17, 1943. They were offered by State Senator Jack Shelley, who represents the San Francisco district in the California Legislature. [Reading:]

This assembly, representing a great cross section of citizens of northern California, convened in the Civic Auditorium of San Francisco on June 17, 1943, voices its sympathy and encouragement to the persecuted peoples under the yoke of Nazi oppression. We honor the memory of the dead; we honor the memory of the innocent and helpless martyrs of all peoples and the millions of Jews who fell victims to a madness unparalleled in history.

Whereas silence and inaction on our part in the face of such monstrous conditions would betray the sacred obligations of brotherhood, as well as the humanitarian ideals to which the United Nations are dedicated; and

Whereas the holocaust of mass murder of civilian populations, especially Jews, continues unabated: Now, therefore, be it

Resolved, That—

1. The United Nations should approach neutral governments with a view to having them intercede for the release of Jewish and other minority victims; and

2. The United Nations should, without delay, take steps to designate and establish a number of sanctuaries in Allied and neutral countries to accommodate substantial numbers of Hitler's victims and to serve as havens of refuge for those whose release from captivity may be arranged, or who may find their way to freedom through efforts of their own.

3. We urge that the doors of Palestine be opened to Jewish immigration.

4. The administration of immigration laws to the United States be liberalized to permit the filling of the established quotas.

That resolution was adopted unanimously, and I am very pleased to insert it in the record with my enthusiastic endorsement.

Recently I made an address on the floor of the House of Representatives along the lines of this legislation, and read a resolution which was submitted by the Men's Club of the Temple Sherith Israel. Since that time I have received a number of similar resolutions. One, from San Francisco Lodge, No. 21, of B'nai B'rith I should like to insert in the record.

(The resolution referred to is as follows:)

Whereas the White Paper issued by the British Government in May 1939 under the leadership of Prime Minister Chamberlain stops the immigration of Jews into Palestine after March 31, 1944, and imposes unfair restrictions on the rights of Jews in Palestine; and

Whereas the ruthless persecution of the Jewish people in Europe and the resultant existence of hordes of refugees in Nazi-occupied countries has clearly demonstrated the need for a haven for the large numbers who have become homeless because of this persecution; and

Whereas such White Paper is a vestige of an appeasement policy which has been repudiated by Great Britain under the leadership of Winston Churchill and by the other United Nations; and

Whereas the terms of said White Paper in closing immigration constitute a flagrant breach of the provisions of the mandate accepted by Great Britain as to Palestine, which provisions were approved by the Congress of the United States together with 52 nations; and

Whereas millions of lives are now dedicated to assure the preservation of freedom for all peoples, and equality of rights throughout the world: Now, therefore, be it

Resolved, By San Francisco Lodge, No. 21, B'nai B'rith, that it calls upon the present government of Great Britain to abrogate immediately and before the effective date of March 31, 1944, the White Paper and that it requests the Government of the United States through its State Department, its Senate and its House of Representatives to urge that the doors of Palestine may be kept open for free entry of Jews into that country and that there shall not be any restrictions on the opportunity for land purchase or colonization in Palestine.

SAN FRANCISCO LODGE, No. 21, B'NAI B'RITH,
SAMUEL L. FENDEL, Secretary.
Dated: JANUARY 24, 1944.

Mr. ROLPH. I also request permission to give the names of other organizations that have endorsed this proposition.

Chairman BLOOM. Give anything that you wish to have inserted in the record to the stenographer, and, if you will, just read the other names of those from whom you have received messages.

Mr. ROLPH. I will comply with that; yes, Mr. Chairman.

Chairman BLOOM. Without objection it is so ordered.

RESOLUTIONS AND TELEGRAMS RECEIVED FROM SAN FRANCISCO IN CONNECTION WITH THE ABROGATION OF THE CHAMBERLAIN WHITE PAPER AND URGING THE ESTABLISHMENT OF A JEWISH HOMELAND IN PALESTINE, PURSUANT TO HOUSE RESOLUTION 418 AND HOUSE RESOLUTION 419

JEWISH LEGISLATION

Resolutions

San Francisco Emergency Committee for the Abrogation of the White Paper, Eugene Block, executive secretary, 110 Sutter Street, Room 706.
Beth Israel Sisterhood, 1839 Geary Street.
Temple Sherith Israel Men's Club, California and Webster Streets.
Zionist Organization of America, 369 Pine Street, San Francisco.
San Francisco Chapter, National Home for Jewish Children, 733 Thirty-first Avenue.
Jewish Educational Society, William Weiss, secretary, 745 Buchanan Street.
Pacific Hebrew Orphan Asylum and Home Society, 1600 Scott Street.
B'nai B'rith, California Lodge, No. 163, 1087 Market Street.
B'nai B'rith, San Francisco Lodge, No. 21, 703 Market, 1607 Central Tower.
National Home for Jewish Children, San Francisco Chapter, 733 Thirty-first Avenue.

Telegrams

Mrs. Louis Bloch; Mrs. Jessie Gans; Mrs. Henry Sahlein; Mrs. Carl Jacob; Mrs. Maurice Heppner, president, San Francisco chapter of Hadassah; Prof. Sam Lepkowsky; Prof. Zev Hassid; Prof. Michael Goodman; Prof. Ben Bernstein; Prof. Jacob Traum; Mrs. Richard M. Neustadt; Mrs. Henry Harris.

Mr. ROLPH. I sincerely hope that this legislation is voted out of your committee unanimously, and that it passes the House unanimously.

Chairman BLOOM. The Chair would like to ask that there be no demonstrations by guests of the committee. It is something that we prefer not to have, if you do not mind.

Chairman BLOOM. Representative Talbot, of Connecticut.

STATEMENT OF JOSEPH E. TALBOT, A REPRESENTATIVE IN CONGRESS FROM THE STATE OF CONNECTICUT

Mr. TALBOT. Mr. Chairman, and members of the committee, I want to take only a minute of your time. First, I would like to express my own approval of this resolution, and I hope that it comes out of the committee unanimously.

Second, I would like to express the appreciation of Mr. Compton, the sponsor of this resolution, who, unfortunately, was called back to New Haven last night, and who has asked me to express to you, Mr. Chairman, his regrets, and his hope that on some other day he might appear before this committee.

Third, I would like to present and have included in the record some telegrams from Jewish citizens in my district, representing some five thousand or six thousand people in the State of Connecticut. I sincerely trust that this resolution will be approved unanimously.

Mr. JOHNSON. Will the gentleman yield for a question?

Chairman BLOOM. Mr. Johnson.

Mr. JOHNSON. Do you mean to incorporate the body of all of those telegrams in the record, or just the names of the senders? I was thinking of the size of the record of you put them all in.

Mr. TALBOT. I will say to the gentleman that I have placed on top of the pile three or four telegrams which I think should be included in the record. As to the rest of them they are similar and the names would be sufficient.

Chairman BLOOM. The Chair would like to state that all telegrams and petitions and matters of that kind will be left to the discretion of the committee. After they have examined them they will determine what to do with the telegrams, as to whether they shall go into the record.

Mrs. ROGERS. We have all had a good many telegrams on this matter.

Chairman BLOOM. Yes.

Mr. JOHNSON. If we put in all of the telegrams the size of the record might be unduly large and repetitious.

Chairman BLOOM. That will await further discretion of the committee. Congressman Eberharter, of Pennsylvania. Mr. Eberharter is a former member of this committee.

STATEMENT OF THE HONORABLE HERMAN P. EBERHARTER, A REPRESENTATIVE IN CONGRESS FROM THE STATE OF PENNSYLVANIA

Mr. EBERHARTER. Mr. Chairman, and gentleman of the committee, I appreciate the opportunity of appearing before this very distinguished committee, a committee which will have before it in the next few years to come the most important questions that will come before the Congress. I am happy that my service on this committee for some years which terminated just a few months ago, has given me an opportunity to know and value its true worth and also to know that any of the problems that do come before it will be considered in a nonpartisan and statesmanlike manner, having simply the best interests of the country in mind.

I am thankful for this opportunity to make a few extemporaneous remarks in respect to these resolutions. Members of the committee will recall that on a previous occasion in a public hearing this very subject came up and at that time I expressed my interest in it and my hearty approval of the principle that is set forth in these resolutions.

I could, of course, Mr. Chairman, develop a very lengthy argument this morning in support of my reasons for being very vitally interested in the passage of these resolutions, but there are many others who will appear before the committee who have practically lived with this subject for many years, and I know that they are more able to present logically what I deem to be unanswerable reasons why this committee and the Congress should pass these resolutions unanimously.

The chairman, of course, I feel is to be commended very highly for his wisdom and foresight in having prepared in advance for study by members of the committee this pamphlet which contains the important and relevant facts relative to this very difficult problem, and yet it is not so difficult but that if it were tackled in the right way I believe it could be solved to the satisfaction of the world and all mankind.

Mr. JOHNSON. Will the gentleman yield for a question?

Chairman BLOOM. Mr. Johnson.

Mr. JOHNSON. I want to concur in what you said with reference to the chairman's compilation of these documents in this pamphlet, and it is not only valuable for the use of this committee, but it has historical data and knowledge in it which will cause many of us to want to preserve it.

Mr. EBERHARTER. Thank you, Mr. Johnson. In that connection I might add that we have so often seen the chairman, Mr. Bloom, go above and beyond the call of duty in this manner that we almost come to expect such extra effort on his part as a matter of course. He has been extraordinarily diligent and conscientious in seeing that the committee is fully informed on the matters under consideration, particularly those somewhat akin to the subject now before you, while at the same time exhibiting and acting in a strictly impartial manner. The committee is fortunate in this respect, as are the witnesses who have appeared in the past and will appear in the future.

I think I might now call particular attention of the committee to the fact that when the White Paper was issued in 1939 there was very, very strong opposition to it in the Parliament of Great Britain, and that opposition was heard and presented what I deem to be very compelling arguments as to the wrong position then being taken by the dominant party in Great Britain at that time, and if I might be permitted, I would just like to read a few lines from the address on May 23, 1939, in the House of Commons by the Right Honorable Stanley Morrison when he was opposing the approval of this White Paper in the House of Commons.

Chairman BLOOM. Will you give the page number from which you are reading?

Mr. EBERHARTER. This is on page 70 of the pamphlet to which I have referred. Speaking of this White Paper he said:

> If we do this thing today we shall have done a thing which is dishonorable to our good name, which is discreditable to our capacity to govern, and which is dangerous to British security, to peace, and to the economic interest of the world in general and of our own country. Moreover, it will not work.

Mr. CHIPERFIELD. Will the gentlemen yield at that point?

Mr. EBERHARTER. Yes; I shall be glad to.

Chairman BLOOM. Mr. Chiperfield.

Mr. CHIPERFIELD. Do you feel, then, that the White Paper is in violation of the convention between the United States and Great Britain, and especially article 7, where it says:

> Nothing contained in the present convention shall be affected by any modification which may be made in the terms of the mandate, as recited above, unless such modification shall have been assented to by the United States.

Mr. EBERHARTER. I think it is absolutely in violation of the mandate under which Great Britain was given mandatory powers over Palestine. I think it is not only in violation of the mandate of the Council of the League of Nations, but it is also in violation of the convention to which the gentleman has just referred. I think it is absolutely illegal. Other gentlemen will present in a very clear and concise manner proof of the illegality of this White Paper by Great Britain.

I believe this, Mr. Chairman, that the passage of these resolutions by the Congress will be helpful to Great Britain itself in the solving of this problem.

I also believe that the passage of these resolutions by the Congress of the United States is a proper move on our part, particularly in view of the terms of the convention of 1925 between Great Britain and the United States, and of the patent illegality of the White Paper, and I think it is proper also because the United States is looked upon as a leader in the world, insofar as humanitarian principles are concerned. It is the humane and moral thing for this country to do toward solving this great problem.

I think the whole world will approve of the passage of these resolutions, and the whole world will also approve of the setting up of not only what may be called a Jewish national home in Palestine, but also of the commencement of moves for the ultimate establishment of a Jewish commonwealth in Palestine, which will fit in with the aspirations of the Jews of the entire world.

Thank you very much, Mr. Chairman.

Chairman BLOOM. Thank you, Mr. Eberharter.

Congressman Celler, of New York.

STATEMENT OF THE HONORABLE EMANUEL CELLER, A REPRESENTATIVE IN CONGRESS FROM THE STATE OF NEW YORK

Mr. CELLER. Mr. Chairman and members of the committee, I want, at the outset, to thank you for this high privilege of presenting a statement this morning on H. R. 418, introduced by our distinguished colleague, the gentleman from Pennsylvania, Mr. Wright, and H. R. 419, introduced by our distinguished colleague from Connecticut, Mr. Compton.

I shall occupy but 10 minutes of your valuable time, ladies and gentlemen, trying to cramp into that space my views on this most momentous question.

The resolutions before this committee are in the spirit of the humanitarian Presidential directive setting up the War Refugee Board, to rescue helpless and hopeless Jews and other refugees from the charnel house of Hitler's Festung Europa.

The resolutions seek at long last to have definite action taken by way of urging Great Britain to abrogate the Malcolm Macdonald White Paper of 1939, and to reestablish Palestine as a haven and national homeland for the Jews, in accordance with the principles laid down by the famous Balfour Declaration of 1917.

Now, since this White Paper of 1939 limits immigration into Palestine to 75,000, (and up to this point there are only thirty-odd thousand certificates of entrance left), and thereafter by April 1 next precludes the entrance of Jews except by will of the Arab majority, we have a paper which violates the Balfour Declaration guaranteeing Palestine as a national homeland, which declaration was abbetted and approved by 52 nations, including our own.

It violates the concurrent resolution of Congress adopted in 1922, favoring the said Balfour Declaration as the basis for ceding of Palestine to Great Britain as a mandatory power.

It violates the Anglo-American treaty in 1924, wherein the said Balfour Declaration was reaffirmed, and wherein it was mutually agreed:

(a) that there could be no unilateral infraction of the treaty by either party, and

(b) that there could be no discrimination as to immigration into Palestine of peoples on the grounds of race or religion.

Aside from the moral and spiritual ties, thus there is a legal nexus between the United States and Palestine. Thus far our administration has not given any expression of opinion anent this so-called White Paper. Our State Department has been strangely silent. In my humble opinion, there were ample grounds for vigorous protest, since this White Paper was a unilateral infraction of the Treaty of 1924, and further involves discrimination as to immigration into Palestine on the grounds of religion and race. Congress should not be silent.

Be it remembered that once before there was such a violation of the Treaty of 1924. In 1937 there was an exchange of notes between our then British Ambassador, Robert W. Bingham, and the British Foreign Office concerning the partition of Palestine with the slicing off of Transjordan, and Ambassador Bingham reminded Anthony Eden, then Foreign Secretary, that no change in the political status of Palestine could take place without the previous consent of the

Government of the United States, and I quote the Ambassador, "having regard to the terms of the American-British Convention of December 3, 1924."

America has not consented to the so-called white paper

In a note of July 7, 1937, from the British Foreign Office to our American Ambassador at London, the British Government states:

The United States Government has accepted the provisions in article 27 of the mandate, which lays down that the mandate may be altered with the consent of the Council of the League of Nations.

Great Britain submitted the White Paper in 1939 to the Permanent Mandates Commission of the League of Nations as a condition precedent to seeking approval of the Council of the League of Nations, but the Permanent Mandates Commission which contained a British member, not only refused to accept the terms of the White Paper limiting immigration as well as the purchase of land by the Jews, but in very forceful language repudiated the terms of the Macdonald White Paper.

The exigencies of the war precluded England's presenting the White Paper for approval to the Council of the League of Nations.

Thus, then, the White Paper is stripped of all legality. It has no legal justification whatsoever. By its own admission, Britain states it cannot alter the terms of the mandate given to it by the League of Nations without the consent of the Council of the League of Nations, and that consent has not been obtained.

Upon Britain's announcement of its change of policy, as contained in the White Paper, President Roosevelt was asked to take action in protest by a petition signed by 51 Senators, 194 Representatives, and 30 Governors. The President expressed his sympathy and promised to do "all in his power" to prevent curtailment of Jewish immigration to Palestine.

On May 17, 1939, despite animadversions against it from all over the world, the British Government published its White Paper, which, in effect, as of April 1st next, would freeze the Jewish minority in Palestine as a permanent ghetto, and if I might say, in common parlance, then their homeland "will be sold down the river."

Also, at that very time, 1939, 15 members of this Foreign Affairs Committee urged our State Department to protest and termed the White Paper a clear repudiation of the 1924 Anglo-American convention.

That the British Cabinet itself felt that its proposed solution for the future of Palestine was not based on the merits of the case but rather on political expediency of the moment is evidenced from a statement reputedly made by Lord Halifax, then Secretary of State for Foreign Affairs, now British Ambassador here, that "there are times when ethical considerations must yield to practical necessity." That is a fine bit of sophistry. If such practical necessity may be deemed just, I say, "There is a point beyond which even justice becomes unjust."

Now, in the House of Commons in the debate on the White Paper, which has been referred to by our distinguished colleague from Pennsylvania, Mr. Eberharter, Leopold S. Amery, formerly First Lord of the Admiralty, and formerly Secretary of State for the Colonies, and who was closely associated with the discussion which preceded the Balfour Declaration when he was Secretary to the War Cabinet, said, "The Jews were to be in Palestine as of right, and on sufferance."

Reference has already been made to the remarks of Herbert Morrison, now Home Secretary, Minister of Home Security in this historic debate on the White Paper in the House of Commons.

The Archbishop of Canterbury, in the House of Lords, on May 23, 1939, said:

When I come to the actual policy as outlined in this White Paper, then I am bound in honesty to say that I have very grave misgivings. I cannot feel that it holds out a prospect of reasonable justice to the Jews.

The views of many other distinguished men, like Lord Wedgewood, Lloyd George, and General Smuts, are reflected in the following views uttered by Winston Churchill, who, on the occasion of the debate on the White Paper, said:

I say quite frankly that I find this a melancholy occasion. I feel bound to vote against the proposals of His Majesty's Government. As one intimately and responsibly concerned in the earlier stages of our Palestine policy, I could not stand by and see solemn engagements into which Britain has entered before the world set aside for reasons of administrative convenience or—and it will be a vain hope—for the sake of a quiet life. Like my honorable friend, I should feel personally embarrassed in the most acute manner if I lent myself, by silence or inaction, to what I must regard as an act of repudiation.

He finally continued by saying that the White Paper was equivalent to filing a petition in moral and physical bankruptcy.

In a little over 1 month, Jews will be bar locked from Palestine. How ill have the Jews used Palestine that now the one open door must be slammed shut in their search for dignity and security? Indeed, they husbanded its arid soil, made it rich in the fruits of the earth. They built hospitals for Jews and Arabs alike. They brought music and science that had been left behind in civilization's march.

The British Colonial Office says, "Let the Jews go elsewhere." That is said in mocking parallel to, "Let them eat cake."

Many suggestions have been made for havens for Jews. How fruitful were these suggestions is revealed by the attitude tersely expressed by the Australian delegate at Evian. "Gentlemen," he said, "we in Australia have no racial problem, thank God. We do not intend to have one started." That summation is brilliant in its brevity, finality and tragedy.

Palestine is the only place where the Jews are not unwanted. Now, the White Paper even precludes. Palestine must be opened as a temporary as well as a permanent shelter. It has an absorptive capacity for 2,000,000 more Jews.

Be it remembered, also, that shortly before the signing of the mandate, a statement of policy was issued on June 3, 1922, by Winston Churchill, then Secretary for Colonies, in which the principle of absorptive capacity was set up as the sole criterion for immigration into Palestine. The White Paper sets up another but illegal, amoral standard.

Jews trapped by the Nazi jackals will manage to escape if they know Palestine is open. The underground will help them, just as our underground railway helped escaping slaves to the North before and during the Civil War.

Jews will make the anabasis to Palestine. No matter how perilous the trek may be, they will make it. Their nostalgia for their homeland will sustain them and they will go rejoicing and singing into Zion.

Among the real pleasures of Winston Churchill was his tender care for his 10,000 tropical fish which he maintained in seven ponds on his estate at Chartwell Manor. In peaceful times, he used to watch them for hours, feed them, and call some of them by name. He remembered them when Hitler's attacks on man and beast in England grew ever more ruthless. As First Lord of the Admiralty, he took care to have them removed to safer ponds.

I petition Churchill to have the White Paper, a real cataract of disaster to humans, abrogated so as many as possible of the Jews be taken from Hitler's cesspools of iniquity and death and removed to safer "ponds" in Palestine.

Finally, Cato in the Roman Senate terminated all his speeches with the famous statement, "Delenda est Carthago." "Carthage must be destroyed." I, too, terminate my remarks with the phrase "Delenda est Charta Blanca," "The White Paper must be destroyed."

It will be destroyed by your favorable consideration of these resolutions.

Chairman BLOOM. Thank you very much, Mr. Celler.

We are honored this morning by a former member of this committee, a gentleman you all know, Representative Hamilton Fish from New York.

STATEMENT OF HON. HAMILTON FISH, A REPRESENTATIVE IN CONGRESS FROM THE STATE OF NEW YORK

Mr. FISH. Mr. Chairman and members of the Committee on Foreign Affairs, it is a great honor and privilege for me to come back here to this committee table around which I sat for some 20 years as a member of your distinguished committee.

I know very well that any words that I may add to this subject will not be at all persuasive to those of you who have studied this question, but it does not do any harm I believe to look at the record. I am not quite sure whether you, Mr. Chairman, were a member of your committee in 1922 when we adopted the so-called Zionist resolution, or the Fish-Lodge resolution in favor of establishing a homeland for the Jews in Palestine. And I would like to ask you, Mr. Chairman, were you a member of the committee at that time in 1922?

Chairman BLOOM. No.

Mr. FISH. Therefore, nobody on the committee was a member then?

Chairman BLOOM. That is right.

Mr. FISH. And perhaps that is the reason, Mr. Chairman, because I have the highest regard for you personally, that you overlooked the little fact in this pamphlet which I read last night, and which I think has been so ably written entitled "The Jewish National Home in Palestine," and failed to mention the fact that a member of this committee, your committee, the Committee on Foreign Affairs, introduced in 1922 a resolution endorsing the Balfour resolution, and as a matter of record, and I am very proud of the record, I was the sponsor of that resolution.

It was known then as the Fish-Lodge resolution, and it merely placed the approval of Congress upon the Balfour resolution for the establishment of a homeland in Palestine for Jews with certain restrictions as to religion.

To have the record correct, it so happened that both the Lodge resolution and the Fish resolution passed our respective Houses, but in the parliamentary mix-up the Fish resolution was the only one that went through and was signed by President Harding. It was an act of Congress and not a proclamation of the President, who merely signed the resolution.

I have noticed in recent years, and I say it with the utmost good humor, that some of the Zionists have perhaps unintentionally over-looked the fact that the author of this resolution, who happened to be a noninterventionist before the war, and proud of it, has been perhaps deliberately overlooked as the sponsor of the resolution, but I want to go on record as saying that does not make a particle of difference to me. I do not change my views after I make up my own mind if I believe in a thing and they are my convictions. I stand by it just the same whether anybody is against me or everybody is against me.

I was a Zionist back in 1922, I am a Zionist today, and I am more of a Zionist than ever before now because there is more need for Zionism today to take care of these homeless Jewish people in Palestine, who are the victims of persecution, hatred, and bigotry, than ever before, so that these hunted and persecuted Jews of central and western Europe may find a refuge in Palestine, which was their original homeland.

This is no new matter, Mr. Chairman, for your committee, not since 1922, because we have had this matter up many times.

In looking over my files yesterday I came across some telegrams, and I came here not only by the prompting of my own mind and own heart but also was instigated, I am glad to say, by many Jewish organizations in my district as well as many prominent Jewish people. Perhaps before I go any further I should read you just one of the telegrams that I have received. It is addressed to me:

On behalf of 3,500 Jewish citizens of Newburgh I urge your immediate public endorsement of House Resolutions 418 and 419 and ask that you notify the Foreign Affairs Committee of your stand. I recall your sponsorship of the Lodge-Fish resolution a quarter century ago, one of the finest actions taken during your lengthy public service. Today as never before it is vital that the United States publicly and officially stand back of Prime Minister Churchill, who has always been a friend of world Jewry in voiding the dastardly White Paper which threatens cessation of immigration into Palestine March 31, 1944. Alleged suspension of the White Paper as reported in the press is a subterfuge. It merely extends visa rights to several thousand immigrees but closes the door to multithousands who, if denied entry where wanted, will die the Hitlerian death. Establishment of a Jewish commonwealth as urged in the Lodge-Fish resolution in 1922 is paramount today. Palestine has been in the vanguard of the United Nations, only land in the Near East heart and soul with us in winning the war. Palestine welcomes all the Nazi victims who can be transported, and remember the Mediterranean today is ours. I urge your valiant effort in this matter. Enlist your friends and have them notify the Foreign Affairs Committee of their attitude on this nondebatable humanity-saving proposal.

It is signed "Seymour S. Cohen, president of the Newburgh Jewish Community Council."

I sent them this telegram:

SEYMOUR COHEN,
    President, Newburgh Jewish Community, Newburgh, N. Y.

In compliance with your friendly and ably worded request as president of the Newburgh Jewish Community Council and that of Freda F. Miller of the Newburgh Chapter of Hadassah and Louis Leis of the Walden Jewish Community Center and numerous others, I have spoken to Chairman Bloom and arranged with his complete accord and cooperation to appear before the Foreign Affairs Committee this Tuesday morning in behalf of the Wright-Compton bill urging that Palestine be opened up to Jewish immigration in accordance with the terms of the Lodge-Fish resolution adopted by Congress 21 years ago. I agree it is more important than ever to provide a homeland in Palestine for the Jewish victims of Nazi brutality and persecution.

Now, Mr. Chairman, this as I said before is no new matter for the Committee on Foreign Affairs.

In looking over my files last evening in preparing a speech to deliver in the Congress at some little length so I would not take up the committee's time unnecessarily, I found an original resolution back in 1939, signed by most of the members of the committee who are here, including the chairman, on this very question. This is the original with the signatures, and I think I can better read it in the corrected form.

We, the undersigned members of the Committee on Foreign Affairs, desire to call to the attention of the House and the State Department a declaration of the British Government announced last Wednesday, May 17, which is a clear repudiation of the convention between the United States and Great Britain with respect to Palestine, dated December 3, 1924.

I hate to go all over this matter because I assume Mr. Celler and others have discussed it at some little length.

Article 7 of that treaty provides:
"Nothing contained in the present convention shall be affected by any modification which may be made in the terms of the mandate, as recited above, unless such modifications shall have been assented to by the United States."

The convention contains as a part thereof the Balfour ¡Declaration and the League of Nations mandate. Both the Balfour Declaration and the mandate recite the solemn pledges of the British Government "to facilitate the establishment of a Jewish National Home in Palestine."

In this connection we further call to your attention joint resolution of the Senate and the House, passed unanimously on June 30, 1922, known as the Lodge-Fish resolution, which recites: "That the United States of America favors the establishment in Palestine of a National Home for the Jewish people."

Last Wednesday's declaration of the British Government is a repudiation o the Balfour Declaration, the mandate of the League of Nations, and of direct concern to us, a violation of article 7 of the treaty between the United States and Great Britain, in that the contemplated action of the British Government proposes to restrict further immigration of Jews into Palestine and to reduce the Jewish people in Palestine to a permanent minority status. On neither of these matters has our Government been consulted, as required by the treaty.

We desire to point out to the Members of the House and to call to the attention of the State Department that Americans have invested over $100,000,000 in Palestine, relying upon the treaty between Great Britain and our Government, and upon which treaty they had the right to rely. It is the duty of the American Government to protect these rights by proper protest and to see to it that the treaty is carried out in good faith.

As members of the Foreign Affairs Committee, we respectfully request the State Department to advise the British Government that the contemplated action, if carried out, will be regarded as a violation of the British-American convention and will be viewed with disfavor by the American people.

I happen to have written this statement. And I was a member of this committee and that is why I have the original in my files.

And it is signed by Sol Bloom of New York; Luther A. Johnson of Texas; John Kee of West Virginia; James P. Richards of South Carolina; James A. Shanley of Connecticut; Edward V. Izac of California; Robert G. Allen of Pennsylvania; W. O. Burgin of North Carolina; Hamilton Fish of New York; George Holden Tinkham of Massachusetts; Edith Nourse Rogers of Massachusetts; Bruce Barton of New York; Robert J. Corbitt of Pennsylvania; John M. Vorys of Ohio; and Andrew C. Shiffler of West Virginia, all of whom were members of this committee, and many of whom are still members of this committee, and this is exactly what you are discussing today.

This was the original white paper that we were protesting back in 1939. We saw the meaning of it at that time and we protested, and we are still protesting it because we know if that is carried out it will be the end of immigration into Palestine and it is in defiance and repudiation of the Balfour Declaration and the Mandate Convention between the United States and Great Britain and the end of the establishment of a homeland for the Jews in Palestine which Congress has gone on record unanimously for.

I am going to make a statement, and will hand it to the press if they want it because it is very short. I shall deliver a speech this afternoon in Congress on the whole subject and in some detail.

As the author of the Zionist resolution for a homeland for the Jewish people in Palestine, enacted into law on September 21, 1922, I urge that there be no retreat, surrender, or compromise with the British betrayal of the promises and pledges given in the Balfour resolution. There can be no compromise with such a perfidious proposal to repudiate her plighted word as set forth in the white paper to practically stop Jewish immigration into Palestine on March 31, 1944.

I hope that the Zionists all over the world will not yield to this proposed breach of trust in order to cajole the Arabs by double-crossing the Jewish people in Palestine and elsewhere and selling them out for a mess of porridge.

I urge the President, the State Department, and the Congress to demand that there shall be no modification of our treaty rights in Palestine without our consent.

The proposed disgraceful and shocking repudiation of the Balfour pledges, under which vast sums of money have gone from America to Palestine to rebuild and establish it as a place of refuge for hundreds of thousands of Jewish people of central Europe, must be vigorously opposed. There never was a time when there was more need for such a homeland. There must be no compromise, otherwise all past efforts will have been in vain.

Now, Mr. Chairman and members of the committee, I am going to ask your indulgence for a few minutes more to make a statement that I do not know whether I have ever made publicly or not until this day.

Chairman BLOOM. Proceed, Mr. Fish.

Mr. FISH. But it has a bearing on this subject.

I agree with everything the gentleman from New York, Mr. Celler, had to say, except as to one thing, and possibly there my Zionist friends will not agree with me.

I have stated my views openly, clearly, and they have never been changed. I believe in keeping Palestine open for Jewish immigration in peace and war, and more today than ever before, but I do not go to the extent possibly referred to by the gentleman from New York, Mr. Celler, that there must be no other homelands, or, rather, places of refuge and haven, for Jewish persecuted people throughout the world. But he may have just carried that inference or I may have even misunderstood him.

However, I want to make a statement to the committee that I do not know whether I have ever made before.

In 1939 I was president of the congressional group, the Interparliamentary Union, composed of 24 Members of the House and 4 Members of the Senate. And one of my main purposes at that time of going abroad was to try to find if there was not some other place besides Palestine for a refugee haven, because eventually even if you put 1,000,000 or so in Palestine there might be a need for a place for more Jewish and those from Spain and elsewhere, and the aim was to see if we could not find some healthy place that would be an additional home and refuge. And men of great wealth and philanthropies were behind this idea and urged me to take the lead in it, which I did not mind because I was sponsor of this resolution.

In my trips to Europe I spoke to Lord Halifax in London on August 4, 1939, and he was very receptive and cooperative even to the extent of having the land set up in the British Empire or sphere of influence or even on British territory. I then saw the French Prime Minister, Mr. Bonet. Then I also saw the French Colonial Minister—Monsieur Mandel—who himself was a Jewish victim, one of the victims of Hitlerism and I believe was killed. But I met him in Mr. Bullitt's office. I had to talk French to him, and it took me considerable time to persuade him it should be placed in the northern part of Africa and in the highlands so as to take in as many as 10,000,000 people. Finally I convinced him. He arranged for me to come back. I was to telegraph him in advance on September 1 which was the day on which war was declared. He was to call in by air the Governors of Equatorial, West, and North Africa, and the purpose was to find the proper place, and then to start immediately a colony to see how it worked out. The money was already available for that purpose. And he was cooperative, they were all cooperative, to that extent. And so it was decided that Palestine alone even if it took 1,000,000 refugees would not be large enough for this problem.

It has always been a deep regret to me this conference could not be held on account of the war and that it should not have been tried out in some healthy undeveloped part of Africa. I say that so that people might know the record.

I want to say the British were entirely cooperative and so were the French in every possible way, and I believe it would have gone through. I say that because there are Zionists who believe we should not permit the Jews to go anywhere but Palestine. I am liberal in my view because I believe in sending as many there as it will hold, but there is a limit to everything. This was not of course only for Jewish but for refugees from Spain and also any part of Europe.

Mr. Chairman, I am very glad to come here. I am sorry to take up so much of your time. I want to endorse the resolution. I think it is very proper that the Congress of the United States should take action. It is in accordance with action taken in the past. It is entirely up to the committee. But I do believe in the principles of the resolution; I do believe in a homeland for the Jews.

Of course, Mr. Chairman, we do not expect many Jews from America to go to Palestine. This is meant for the persecuted Jews of central and western Europe. There are more of them today than ever before. There is no place for them to go. Mr. Chairman, I believe we should pass a resolution without delaying too long. Every day we delay hundreds of Jews, maybe thousands of Jews, are finding no place to go, dying of starvation and persecution by Hitler and the Nazis.

The tragedy of this war, the greatest single tragedy of the war, is the beastly, inhuman, and barbaric treatment of the Jews in central Europe. There are more Jews who have died in this war than all the armies probably fighting together through sheer persecution, hunger, and famine.

It is little enough for us to do to simply express our desires to the British that they keep their plighted word.

Mr. Chairman, I am of British origin. I admire the British. Nobody admires Winston Churchill more than I do. I know him personally. He always put the interests of the British Empire first. I believe in that kind of philosophy. But I also admire him in view of the fact that he is for Zionism and for a homeland for the Jewish people. I see no reason why we should not help him. Whenever there is opposition in England, and there is a great deal of opposition in England, why should not we Americans help Winston Churchill? Why should we not pass a resolution so he can get up in Parliament and say, "Here is a resolution from our greatest friends and allies in favor of keeping immigration open to the Jews"? Because they know and we know if you shut the doors now it is the end of aspirations thousands of years old and a breach of faith by the British Government. We cannot in this war repudiate what we did in the last war and serve notice on the Jews of this war their aspirations are at an end and they can no longer hope for anything in the way of establishing a homeland in Palestine.

Therefore I just want to add my voice and to cooperate with you in any properly worded resolution in placing the Congress of the United States and the Government of the United States on record in favor of a homeland for the Jews in Palestine and permitting Jews to continue to immigrate and thus establish this homeland.

Mr. CHIPERFIELD. Will the gentleman yield?

Mr. FISH. I certainly do.

Mr. CHIPERFIELD. We have heard a great deal lately about standing up and being counted. Before these hearings are over do you not think the State Department ought to say whether it is for or against this resolution?

Mr. FISH. You and I know each other pretty well. I did not come here to give any views whatever to the committee on matters on which they are the sole judges.

As long as you put the matter up to me in that way I can say I should certainly ask and demand the State Department, which is your right as a member of this committee, to send a representative to this committee to state their views to you without evasion.

Mr. CHIPERFIELD. Or equivocation?

Mr. FISH. That is all I can say at the moment.

Mr. WRIGHT. Would the gentleman yield?

Mr. FISH. I yield with pleasure.

Mr. WRIGHT. I just want to remind the gentleman from New York, Mr. Celler did not say he wished to have immigration restricted to Palestine. He said he did not wish to have it interfered with.

Mr. FISH. I am glad to hear that.

Mr. CELLER. In other words, the resolution provides for havens, not one haven, but Palestine or elsewhere.

Chairman BLOOM. Mr. Fish, did you look on page 5, and did you see your resolution that you spoke about of September 21, 1922, which you said was not in there?

Mr. FISH. No; I thought I read it with great care, and I thought it was an excellent document, but I did not see my name anywhere. [Laughter.]

Chairman BLOOM. Oh, I see.

Mr. FISH. I did not see my name there, Mr. Chairman, because in the first page of the resolution it refers to the Wright resolution. My resolution is incorporated in it. But I want to say I see the names of at least 50 Britishers in your pamphlet and a great many Americans and others, but the author of the resolution was somewhat overlooked. Of course, I know you were not a member of the committee at the time and probably did not know it.

Chairman BLOOM. Mr. Fish, the Chair would like to state, because I have been very, very careful to try to have this pamphlet correct, as you know when you report acts signed by the President the name of the sponsor of the resolution is never mentioned. Of course, we have your resolution right before us, Resolution 307, and your joint resolution. There are several. There is 322. Your resolution is here. But when it becomes an act I am sure you will remember that the name of the sponsor is not carried with it into the statute books. I am sorry that your name is not here, but it is absent simply because it is a literal and correct copy of the act as signed by President Warren G. Harding. I am sure you would not have wanted me to show it in its preliminary form as it was before it reviewed the favorable action of the Sixty-seventh Congress. This was copied completely from the records of the State Department where we got the reports from. I am very sorry that the official copy does not bear your name.

Mr. FISH. That is why I wanted to impress you about my having been the author of the original resolution 22 years ago on which the pending resolutions are both based.

Chairman BLOOM. I am sure, Mr. Fish, we are going to have a reprint, and I will see that your name is in there.

Mr. FISH. I am very happy. It was worth while my coming here, if you will, Mr. Chairman.

Chairman BLOOM. The Chair will. And the Chair would like to state I tried to do the best I could with this pamphlet. It was difficult to get in things necessary to print for the information of those interested. I tried to get certain information from the libraries and I could not get it. We have in this pamphlet almost everything that has been called to our attention in the way of essential facts relating to the Jewish national home in Palestine.

I would like to state to the committee or to anyone listening that if there is anything wrong with this pamphlet or anything which should be inserted I would like to have the attention of the Chair called to it so we can correct.

Mr. Fish, you said there were 24 Members of the House and 4 Members of the Senate in the Interparliamentary Union.

Mr. FISH. They were delegates to the Interparliamentary Union in 1939.

Chairman BLOOM. You said "members." I think it should be corrected. The reporter will kindly correct it.

Mr. FISH. I meant to refer to the delegates.

Chairman BLOOM. Thank you, Mr. Fish.

Mr. FISH. I am delighted to come back here.

Chairman BLOOM. I assure you it will bear your name.

Mr. FISH. I have waited a number of years to come back, but I am very glad I came here today.

Chairman BLOOM. I can assure you we appreciate your coming here.

Mr. FISH. I do hope you will take favorable action.

Chairman BLOOM. On your name? [Laughter.]

Mr. FISH. On my name; yes. I would prefer the resolution, but I hope you will take care of my name also.

Mrs. ROGERS. There is just one question. Do you remember what action the State Department took regarding that statement we all signed in 1939?

Mr. FISH. I do not know what definite action they took because the White Paper still exists. I think they would probably have to communicate it to the British Government.

Mr. CELLER: Mr. Chairman, may I answer that question?

Chairman BLOOM. Mr. Celler may answer the question if he knows.

Mr. CELLER. I was told verbally by the Secretary of State with reference to the resolution of this distinguished committee the matter as far as the White Paper was concerned in the langauge of Mr. Hull was still unfrozen, if you know what that means.

Chairman BLOOM. It is a little bit cold.

Mr. SCHIFFLER. Mr. Chairman, I might add something to that because at that time I had a conversation with the Secretary of State and he advised me there had been a protest filed against the White Paper.

Chairman BLOOM. Thank you very much.

Mrs. ROGERS. My recollection was something of the sort.

Chairman BLOOM. The committee will find out and get the correct information.

Mr. Celler, Representative Eaton desires to ask you a question, if you do not mind.

Mr. CELLER. I would be glad to try to answer it.

Dr. EATON. I would like to ask the very erudite and distinguished colleague of mine, for the benefit of our committee, to elaborate somewhat on his use of the word "right" of the Jewish immigration into Palestine, upon what that right is based? It would help our committee if you would elucidate that a little.

Mr. CELLER. Of course, the right goes back to Biblical times when Isaac said, "The race of Abraham, Isaac, and Jacob would again go singing into Zion."

Dr. EATON. I want to go on record as recognizing the authenticity of that passage.

Mr. CELLER. As to legalities it was mentioned repeatedly in the Balfour resolution as to settling up a homeland for Jews, which, as I stated before, was accepted not only by our own Nation but by 52 other nations as a condition precedent for letting England have trusteeship or the stewardship involved in that.

There can be no national homeland if immigration is summarily cut off as of April 1 next.

You now have in Palestine a population of about one-third Jews and two-thirds Arabs. Arabs may come into Palestine in unlimited numbers after April 1, but Jews may not come in. So you will have a status which will be equivalent substantially to what we commonly term a ghetto. Jews will be a homeless minority.

The right I speak of also stems from the so-called Fish resolution of 1922 which reaffirms that Balfour Declaration.

It likewise stems from the treaty solemnly entered into by the United States and Great Britain in 1924, which in one of its articles, as set forth in this very fine document prepared by your chairman of the committee, states that there can be no discrimination with reference to immigration into Palestine on grounds of race or religion. If

Jews are discriminated against then they are discriminated against under race or religion. And the diplomatic correspondence between our own State Department and its accredited representatives and the British Foreign Minister and its accredited representatives clearly indicate that there can be no change in the political status——

Chairman BLOOM. Just a second. Let us have no talking because it disturbs the witness.

Mr. CELLER (continuing). In the political status, no change in the terms of the mandate without the consent of the Council of the League of Nations and without the consent of the United States Government. The British Government sought to obtain the consent of the League of Nations. The procedure is to first apply to the Permanent Mandates Commission. It did so apply. Its proposal was turned down in very harsh terms, terms which are equivalent to repudiation. The United States has not consented to a change in the political status of Palestine, as indicated by my reference to the correspondence between Ambassador Bingham and British Minister for Foreign Affairs, then Anthony Eden. We have not consented, unless the State Department has covertly consented, and I doubt whether that would be the case because there has been no change in that treaty of 1924. One of the specific provisions of that treaty is there can be no unilateral change by either side of the treaty, without the consent of the other. Since we have not consented and since this White Paper is a change in the terms of the mandate, a change in the terms of the political status, it is equivalent beyond peradventure of a doubt to a change in that treaty.

Upon all of that I base the right of the Jews to go into Palestine without let or hindrance which Winston Churchill stated shall be economic absorption capacity. Now, the economic experts, I am sure those who will follow today and possibly tomorrow, will indicate from their testimony the expert opinion that Palestine has still an absorptive capacity economically of at least the entrance of 2,000,000 more Jews.

Chairman BLOOM. Mr. Cellar, thank you very much for that. Go ahead, Dr. Eaton.

Dr. EATON. Mr. Chairman, I would like to make one correction in the gentleman's statement, which was very illuminating. Do not put the word "so-called" before the Fish amendment in there.

Mr. CELLER. I accept that.

Mrs. ROGERS. Mr. Chairman, the State Department could not take action without Congress taking action.

Chairman BLOOM. Just a minute. The Chair would like to say that there is a gentleman here who wanted to be heard by at least 10:30. He is here, and he wishes to get away as soon as possible. If you want to call any witnesses back to cross examine them you may do so, which the Chair would like very much, but we have Rabbi Abba Hillel Silver here, who is chairman of the executive committee of the American Zionist Emergency Council. Dr. Silver, I think knows all the answers to any questions that you would want to ask him. Rabbi, please proceed.

STATEMENT OF DR. ABBA HILLEL SILVER, CHAIRMAN OF THE EXECUTIVE COMMITTEE, AMERICAN ZIONIST EMERGENCY COUNCIL

Dr. SILVER. Thank you very much, Mr. Bloom. I am indeed very grateful for this opportunity to speak a word in endorsement of these resolutions which have been introduced in the House. I am very grateful for your courtesy, Mr. Bloom. You know what we think of you.

Chairman BLOOM. Do I know? Better tell the committee what you think of me. Tell these people around the table.

Mr. EATON. Mr. Chairman, I think that would be very appropriate, considering the dead cats and bricks that have been hurled at you unnecessarily and unjustly.

Chairman BLOOM. You and I have talked it over and you know, I fall back on that saying of my dear sainted mother, that one with God is a majority, so I do not care about those brickbats or dead cats when I know that I am in the right.

Dr. EATON. I agree with you.

Dr. SILVER. May I say, at the outset, that nothing is further from the minds of those for whom I speak—and I believe I speak for millions of Jewish citizens of the United States—who through the representatives of their national organizations and the elected delegates of their respective communities gathered at the great American-Jewish conference last September and voiced overwhelmingly their endorsement of the Jewish commonwealth in Palestine and called for the abrogation of the White Paper than to embarrass our great and gallant ally Great Britain, whose heroic defense of civilization against Nazi barbarism in the dark days when she stood alone will remain an epic of high courage and spiritual grandeur to inspire all future generations. We have no quarrel with Great Britain. We can never forget that it was Great Britain which, first among the nations, gave recognition to the national aspirations of the Jewish people in the issuance of the Balfour Declaration. But a wrong and unjustifiable political policy affecting the Jewish national home which this very declaration welcomed and committed His Majesty's Government to its achievement, is about to be consummated. It would to all intents and purposes liquidate the Jewish national home. It is this policy, which has been sharply criticized by the foremost statesmen of Great Britain herself, that we ask to be rescinded. We retain our strong confidence in the integrity and the abiding good will of Great Britain that this will be done.

We feel that this very resolution when adopted will, as was pointed out here a moment ago, strengthen the hands of our many friends in Great Britain who wish to see this wrong, unwise, and illegal policy abrogated.

May I also be permitted to give a brief historical background to the movement to reconstitute the Jewish commonwealth in Palestine, perhaps a subject which will not be covered by the other people who will speak here? It is not a recent movement. It did not begin with modern Zionism, nor with the first Zionist colonies which were established in Palestine 65 years ago. The ideal of national restoration dates from the year of the destruction of Jerusalem and of the Temple in the year

A. D. 70, and from the beginning of the widespread dispersion of the Jewish people.

Throughout the following centuries the hope of rebuilding their national home was never absent from among our people. Modern Zionism is only the latest expression of that undeviating will to national restoration which has persisted throughout the ages.

For fifteen centuries and more prior to the time of the great Dispersion, the Jewish people lived in Palestine as a nation. undergoing all the changing political vicissitudes which all nations, large or small, are bound to experience over a long period of time.

During some of those centuries they made their greatest contribution to civilization in the religious field. They gave the Bible to the world and formulated the great spiritual and ethical ideals of mankind. In Palestine and from the Jewish Nation came both Judaism and Christianity.

Whenever disaster threatened their national existence, they found strength to surmount it. The destruction of the first temple in the sixth century B. C., and the exile of the best part of Israel to Babylonia did not result in the death of the nation. By the rivers of Babylon they sat down and wept as they remembered Zion, and in their exile they vowed: "If I forget thee, O Jerusalem, may my right hand forget her cunning."

In the second pre-Christian century, the Jews revolted against their Syrian overlords and regained their political independence. A century later they lost it again to the Romans. When the oppression of the Romans became too great, they revolted again. This great revolt lasted for 6 years, until 70 A. D., when Jerusalem and the temple was destroyed. But the Jewish Nation did not perish then. In 115 the Jewish people revolted again. And in 135 they revolted a third time. Determinedly they resisted the greatest empire of the earth in defense of their national life and liberties.

In the following centuries and as a result of persecution, Jewish life in Palestine sharply declined from its high levels, but it continued in a relatively large scale up to the seventh century, when we again hear of Jews fighting for their freedom. Jews clung to Palestine all through Roman, Byzantine, Arab, Christian, and Turkish domination, to this very day. "Throughout the ages, even in the darkest periods of the Crusades, the protracted wars of the Middle Ages, and in modern times, the Jews never entirely left the soil of Palestine." They never surrendered the hope that some day they would rebuild their national life there. The bitter experiences of 2,000 years of exile, outlawry, ghettos, and massacres only served to reinforce that hope.

The effort to return to Palestine was unremitting through the ages. The living bond with Palestine was never broken. The hope of return became part of the Jews' creed. It echoed through the pages of his prayer book. His festivals were redolent of memories and hopes of Palestine. The Messianic hope which sustained the spirits of our people throughout the bleak centuries was essentially the hope of Israel's return to Palestine. All through the Middle Ages, when traveling was most difficult and dangerous, Jews found ways singly or in groups, to return to Palestine.

In the nineteenth century this age-old national aspiration finally entered the phase of political organization and practical action.

Orthodox rabbis and lay leaders, moved by convictions both religious and national, were among the first to advocate planned and concerted colonization projects to Palestine.

A strong urge towards political action for national emancipation came also from the circles of Jews of western Europe who had become disillusioned with the results of the nineteenth century enlightenment and emancipation. Sudden and violent outbursts of anti-Semitism in unexpected places forced upon these Jews who had so sanguinely awaited the early liquidation of the Jewish problems, the necessity of taking stock of their position anew.

They realized that the problem of the national homelessness of the Jewish people was the principal source of the Jewish millennial tragedy and that it remained as stark and as menacing as ever. It simply could not be circumvented by wishful thinking or pleasant daydreaming.

These Jews began to look for the basic solution of the problem and they soon discovered it. Fundamentally the root of all the trouble was that the Jewish people was a national homeless people in the world and the only solution for national homelessness is a national home.

Great thinkers from among the intellectual circles of westernized Europe Jewry formulated this new insight and conviction. The theme common to all was emancipation through national restoration. Not that all Jews should return to Palestine any more than that all Englishmen in all parts of the world should return to England, or all Frenchmen to France, or all Germans to Germany. Every nation today has many of its former nationals, citizens of other countries. The Jews in other parts of the world will remain as heretofore loyal citizens of the country which will permit them to remain equal citizens of those countries, and the American Jews, who have served their country so faithfully both in peace and in war, intend to remain citizens of the United States, and their relationship with the Jewish commonwealth will be no different from that of other American citizens with respect to their ancestorial homes. But, just as there is an England, a France, and a Germany, so must there be a Land of Israel in order that the status of the Jewish people might be normalized throughout the world. Politically the Jewish people as a people must become, like every other people, possessed of an independent life in a national home.

In 1897, Theodore Herzl convoked the first Zionist Congress at Basle, Switzerland. There the official Zionist platform was adopted: "The aim of Zionism is to create for the Jewish people a home in Palestine secured by public law."

Within 20 years of the organization of modern political Zionism, the movement received formal approval at the hands of the greatest empire on earth—Great Britain.

On November 2, 1917, Arthur James Balfour, then Secretary of State for Foreign Affairs, issued the famous declaration in the name of the British Government

His Majesty's Government views with favor the establishment in Palestine of a national home—

note the term "national"—

for the Jewish people, and will use their best endeavors to facilitate the achievement of this object, it being clearly understood that nothing shall be done which may prejudice the civil and religious rights of existing non-Jewish communities in Palestine, or the rights and political status enjoyed by Jews in any other country.

The Balfour Declaration, which represents a turning point in the history of the Jewish people, was not, as has sometimes been represented, a purely British formulation of policy. It was for many months the subject of long and earnest negotiation between the principal Allied Powers. In February and March of 1918 the French and Italian Governments, respectively, issued parallel statements in support of the Balfour Declaration. President Wilson had followed the negotiations, and had encouraged the issuance of that declaration, and our Government insisted on having a hand in the drafting of the mandate.

At a meeting of the Supreme Council of the Allied Powers, held at San Remo in April 1920, the Balfour Declaration was unanimously adopted and embodied in the Mandate for Palestine which was offered to Great Britain.

On July 24, 1922, the Council of the League of Nations unanimously ratified the British mandate, with the incorporated declaration as an integral part. That same year the Congress of the United States adopted the resolution which has been read to you this morning:

Resolved by the Senate and House of Representatives of the United States of America in Congress assembled, That the United States of America favors the establishment in Palestine of a national home for the Jewish people, it being clearly understood that nothing shall be done, etc.—

And then occurs the rest of the Balfour Declaration.

The preamble to the mandate contains this significant clause, and I would like to call it to your attention:

Whereas recognition has hereby been given to the historical connections of the Jewish people with Palestine and the grounds for reconstituting their national home in that country * * *.

These are the words of the preamble of the mandate. In other words, the creation, or reconstitution, of a Jewish homeland in Palestine was thus accepted as a world policy. It was also regarded as an act of restitution. It was a recognition both of the present need of the Jewish people and of the continuity of its claim to its homeland, a continuity unbroken by the vicissitudes of 2,000 years of history.

What did the framers of the Balfour Declaration and the Palestine mandate have in mind when they spoke of the establishment of a national home for the Jewish people in Palestine? Their utterances leave no doubt as to their clear intent. They meant a Jewish state, a Jewish commonwealth.

Lloyd George, Prime Minister of Great Britain at the time of the issuance of the Balfour Declaration, writes in his memoirs:

It was not their [the British Cabinet's] idea that a Jewish state should be set up immediately by the peace treaty without reference to the wishes of the majority of the inhabitants. On the other hand, it was contemplated that when the time arrived for according representative institutions to Palestine, if the Jews had meanwhile responded to the opportunity afforded them by the idea of a national homeland and had become a definite majority of the inhabitants, then Palestine would thus become a Jewish commonwealth. The notion that Jewish immigration would have to be artificially restricted in order to ensure that the Jews should be a permanent minority never entered into the head of anyone engaged in framing the policy. That would have been regarded as unjust and as a fraud on the people to whom we were appealing.

General Smuts, still one of Great Britain's foremost statesmen, perhaps next to Churchill the most powerful political figure in the British Empire, who, in 1919 was a member of the Imperial War Cabinet, declared that he envisaged an increasing stream of Jewish immigration into Palestine and in generations to come a great Jewish state rising there once more and that he is convinced today, no less than he was in 1917 of the necessity of establishing a Jewish state in Palestine; and he expressed the hope and confidence that there could and would be peace and cooperation between the Jewish state and other neighboring states.

Winston Churchill, when he was Secretary of State in 1920, declared:

> If, as may well happen, there should be created in our lifetime by the banks of the Jordan a Jewish State under the protection of the British Crown, which might comprise 3,000,000 or 4,000,000 Jews, an event will have occurred in the history of the world which would from every point of view be beneficial and would be especially in harmony with the truest interests of the British Empire.

President Wilson, in 1919, declared:

> I am persuaded that the Allied nations, with the fullest concurrence of our Government and our people, are agreed that in Palestine shall be laid the foundations of a Jewish commonwealth.

Our then Secretary of State, Charles E. Hughes, writing to Lord Balfour in January 1922, concerning the mandate for Palestine, which was a subject of extensive negotiation between our Government and Great Britain, and which negotiations resulted in substantial modifications in the draft of the mandate, assumes that what was being planned in Palestine was a Jewish State. There were three or four drafts. (See p. 60, Mandate for Palestine—prepared in the Division of Near Eastern Affairs—publication of the Department of State, Washington, 1931.)

Chairman BLOOM. Would you mind an interruption there? The resolution favoring that was also approved by Charles Evans Hughes, at that time Secretary of State, which you read a few moments ago.

Dr. SILVER. That is correct.

Chairman BLOOM. And that was in his own words?

Dr. SILVER. That is right. And he in that letter to Lord Balfour assumed that what was being planned in Palestine was a Jewish state.

It is, therefore, historically accurate, and in view of what has transpired since those years, politically sound, for the resolutions which have been introduced in the House, to speak of a free and democratic Jewish commonwealth. It is not a new concept. It is exactly what was originally contemplated. Attempts have been made to whittle down the meaning of the terms, "a national home," employed in the Balfour Declaration and the mandate. It has been asserted that a Jewish national home already exists in Palestine and that a permanent Jewish minority within a Palestine state, such as the White Paper envisages, is quite consistent with the avowed purposes of the mandate. This, of course, is not the case. It is well, therefore, to stress the true objective of the mandate which was the reconstitution of the Jewish commonwealth, which presupposes a Jewish majority in the country, as Mr. Lloyd George correctly points out. The experiences of the last 25 years indicate that no such majority will ever be attained unless the control of immigration is vested with the Jewish agency, which alone is interested in the creation of absorptive capacity and in the intensive agricultural and industrial development of the land in order to absorb rapidly large numbers of immigrants and provide them with the means of earning a livelihood.

It was not contemplated to set up two states in Palestine, or to set up a Palestine state in which Jews would be a permanent minority. The mandate made Great Britain "responsible for putting into effect the declaration officially made on November 2, 1917, by the Government of His Britannic Majesty," i. e., the Balfour Declaration. The mandatory was charged with the responsibility "for placing the country under such political, administrative and economic conditions as will secure the establishment of the Jewish national home" (art. 2). The mandate nowhere speaks of the establishment of an Arab national home in Palestine.

The mandate calls for the recognition of "an appropriate Jewish agency as a public body for the purpose of advising and cooperating with the administration of Palestine in such economic, social and other matters as may affect the establishment of the Jewish national home * * * and to assist and take part in the development of the country." The mandate nowhere speaks of the recognition of an Arab agency, for it was not required, inasmuch as it was not contemplated to set up in Palestine an Arab national state.

Under the terms of the mandate the Zionist organization of the world was invited "to secure the cooperation of all Jews who are willing to assist in the establishment of the Jewish national home" (art. 4).

The mandatory was charged with the duty of "facilitating Jewish immigration" into Palestine and of encouraging "in cooperation with the Jewish agency" close settlement by Jews on the land, including State lands and waste lands not required for public purposes (art. 6)

It was called upon to enact a nationality law—

so as to facilitate the acquisition of Palestinian citizenship by Jews who take up their permanent residence in Palestine (article 7).

There are no provisions in the mandate for facilitating Arab immigration into Palestine or their close settlement on the land.

The administration of Palestine was asked to—

arrange with the Jewish agency to construct or operate any public works, services, and utilities, and to develop any of the national resources of the country (article 11).

What do all those clear provisions mount up to? That Palestine was to be built up as a Jewish national state—and that for the transition period, until a Jewish majority is achieved and the country is ready for self-governing institutions, Great Britain was entrusted by the principal Allied Powers with a mandate to administer the country upon terms and powers clearly defined in the mandate by the Council of the League of Nations.

Was the proposed reestablishment of the Jewish commonwealth in Palestine unfair to the Arabs? May I be permitted to quote the words of the Right Honorable Alfred Duff Cooper, former First Lord of the British Admiralty, spoken here in Washington in the spring of 1940:

In 1914 there was hardly any territory which the Arabs could call their own. They were almost throughout the Near East subject to Turkish suzerainty. Since 1914, they have acquired vast tracts of territory where they are independent; the whole of Arabia; Transjordania, which was taken away from the original conception of Palestine; Syria, where again they exercise semi-independent rights. No nation in the world has so little ground for complaining of what the Germans call lack of lebenstraum as the Arab race. They have vast spaces in which to expand. They have been amongst the greatest beneficiaries of the World War, and now they are subject to no particular evils.

Realizing that the Arabs would have their nàtional aspirations satisfied after the war by the establishment of a number of Arab national states, and that these states would have land areas so large that it would take them centuries to develop them, and realizing also that the Jews stood in desperate need of a place of refuge, for their people, the Allies reserved "the tiny notch" of Palestine, as Balfour called it—just 10,000 square miles for the Jewish people. The Arab lands cover more than a million square miles and they are under-populated and largely undeveloped.

Provision, of course, was made in the Balfour Declaration and in the mandate for the political equality of all citizens and for the civil and religious rights of existing non-Jewish communities. These rights have been fully protected. The Palestine Arab has not been exploited. In fact, there are no Arabs on the face of the earth today more prosperous than the Arabs of Palestine.

The establishment of the Jewish National Home in Palestine will, we believe, be a great boon to the entire Near East and to all the Arab peoples. Jews are bringing scientific skill, technical knowledge, material resources, and high enthusiasm to the upbuilding of Palestine. Palestine is destined to become the hub of a great and rapid economic development of the entire Near East. The prosperity of Palestine will stimulate, and, in the course of time will come to depend upon the prosperity of all adjacent Arab countries.

Chairman BLOOM. Would you mind an interruption there? I thought it would be good to get into the record at this point the amount of money that has been expended in Palestine for development. I understand it was around $600,000;000, or something like that.

Dr. SILVER. The Jews have invested in private and public funds over $600,000,000 in the development of the country.

Dr. EATON. I would also like to ask a question.

Dr. SILVER. Certainly.

Dr. EATON. Was Palestine ever looked upon as an Arab state like Syria or Arabia?

Dr. SILVER. At no time was there an Arab state. I will put it this way: Palestine never was an Arabian state, but a part of some empire, very often regarded as the hinterland of Syria. There was never an independent Arab state of Palestine.

Dr. EATON. After the Turks relinquished their hold on Palestine, what form of government or political set-up did Palestine have?

Dr. SILVER. The mandate given the British Government to build it up as a national home for Jewish people.

Mr. EATON. It had no political entity, except only as a dwelling place for certain peoples?

Dr. SILVER. It was only at that time that the territorial boundaries of Palestine were established.

Chairman BLOOM. Proceed, Doctor.

Dr. SILVER. It has been alleged that promises were also made to the Arabs during the last war to the effect that Palestine was to be included in the area in which Arab independence would be established. Sir Henry McMahon, then His Majesty's High Commissioner in Egypt, who negotiated with the Sherif of Mecca, later King Hussein, is alleged to have made such a promise. The British Government has consistently maintained that Palestine was definitely excluded from McMahon's pledge.

McMahon, himself, in a letter to the Times, London, July 23, 1937, stated:

I feel it my duty to state, and I do so definitely and emphatically, that it was not intended by me in giving this pledge to King Hussein, to include Palestine in the area in which Arab independence was promised.

I also had every reason to believe at the time that the fact that Palestine was not included in my pledge was well understood by King Hussein.

During the years 1917 to 1921 no claims to Palestine were raised by the Arab representatives. Indeed, they did in various ways explicitly agree to Palestine being treated differently from Arab territories.

Emir Feisal, son of Hussein, afterward King of Iraq, the leader of the Arabs, in the crucial war years, stated in December 1918:

The two main branches of the Semitic family, Arabs and Jews, understand one another, and I hope that as a result of interchange of ideas at the Peace Conference, which will be guided by ideals of self-determination and nationality, each nation will make definite progress toward the realization of its aspirations. Arabs are not jealous of Zionist Jews, and intend to give them fair play, and the Zionist Jews have assured the Nationalist Arabs of their intention to see that they too have fair play in their respective areas.

And in January 1919, Emir Feisal, for the Arab Kingdom of Hedjaz, and Dr. Chaim Weizmann, on behalf of the Zionist Organization, signed a treaty of friendship which clearly shows that Feisal regarded Palestine as a land reserved for Jewish national settlement. He also submitted to the Peace Conference a memorandum on the Arab claims in which he asked for the independence of a number of Arabic areas with the explicit exception of Palestine.

If I may be permitted, Mr. Chairman, I should like to read into the record the documents to which I have referred.

(The documents referred to are as follows:)

DOCUMENTS RELATING TO THE McMAHON LETTERS

(Published by the Jewish Agency for Palestine, 77 Great Russell Street, London, W. C. 1. March 1939)

ARAB TERRITORIES AND PALESTINE

"So far as the Arabs are concerned . . . I hope they will remember that it is we who have established an independent Arab sovereignty of the Hejaz. I hope they will remember it is we who desire in Mesopotamia to prepare the way for the future of a self-governing, autonomous Arab State, and I hope that, remembering all that, they will not grudge that small notch—for it is no more than that geographically, whatever it may be historically—that small notch in what are now Arab territories being given to the people who for all these hundreds of years have been separated from it."

—[Lord Balfour, Albert Hall, July 12th, 1920.]

The map [1] shows only those Arab territories which were under Turkish domination or suzerainty before the World War. The extensive Arab territories of Lybia, Tunis, Algeria, Morocco and Egypt are not indicated.

The map shows the frontiers of Palestine and Trans-Jordan as drawn after the Peace Conference. The parts of historic Palestine in the North up to the Littany River (which Great Britain had first proposed should be included in Western Palestine) and in the North-East (Bashan and Hauran now included in Syria)

---

[1] Not printed.

are not demarcated.   Nor is the enlargement of the Trans-Jordan territory by a section of the Syrian Desert in the East indicated.   The Sanjak of Alexandretta was recently severed from the rest of Syria by the Franco-Turkish Agreement.

It is almost impossible to give exact figures of area and population of some of the principal Arab countries, as no reliable land survey or census has ever been taken.   The following data appear nearest the truth:

	Approximate area in square miles	Approximate population
Syria (including Lebanon, Jebel Druze, Latakia)	58,000	3,600,000
Iraq	116,000	2,860,000
Saudi Arabia	900,000	4,500,000
Yemen	75,000	3,500,000
Transjordan	35,000	300,000
Total	1,184,000	14,760,000
Western Palestine	10,500	[1] 1,450,000

[1] 1,000,000 Arabs, 450,000 Jews.

His Majesty's Government have now published the McMahon letters.   Had any promises been contained in these letters such as the Arabs now allege, and had claims been raised on that basis at the Peace Conference, even then an international Treaty and an international Mandate would cancel the legal validity of previous declarations and agreements.   But from the documents published below, emerges the fact that during the crucial years 1917–1921 no claims to Palestine were raised by the Arab representatives on the basis of the McMahon correspondence.   Indeed, they did in various ways explicitly agree to Palestine being treated differently from Arab territories.

The McMahon correspondence is historical material, and the claims built up upon it are political afterthoughts.

The Balfour Declaration

Foreign Office,
November 2nd, 1917.

Dear Lord Rothschild: I have much pleasure in conveying to you, on behalf of His Majesty's Government, the following declaration of sympathy with Jewish Zionist aspirations which has been submitted to, and approved by, the Cabinet.

"His Majesty's Government view with favour the establishment in Palestine of a national home for the Jewish people, and will use their best endeavours to facilitate the achievement of this object, it being clearly understood that nothing shall be done which may prejudice the civil and religious rights of existing non-Jewish communities in Palestine, or the rights and political status enjoyed by Jews in any other country."

I should be grateful if you would bring this declaration to the knowledge of the Zionist Federation.

Yours sincerely,

Arthur James Balfour.

British Government's Message to King Hussein

"Through Sir Mark Sykes and Colonel Lawrence we informed the Arab leaders, King Hussein and his son, Feisal, of our proposals.   We could not get in touch with the Palestinian Arabs as they were fighting against us * * *."

In January 1916 the British Government's policy in regard to Palestinian Holy Places and Zionist colonisation was officially communicated in the following message to Hussein:

"That so far as Palestine is concerned, we are determined that no people shall be subjected to another, but in view of the fact:

"(a) That there are in Palestine, Shrines, Wakfs, and Holy Places, sacred in some cases to Moslems alone, to Jews alone, to Christians alone, and in others to two or all three, and inasmuch as these places are of interest to vast masses of people outside Palestine and Arabia, there must be a special regime to deal with these places approved of by the world.

"(b) That as regards the Mosque of Omar, it shall be considered as a Moslem concern alone, and shall not be subjected directly or indirectly to any non-Moslem authority.

"That since the Jewish opinion of the world is in favour of a return of Jews to Palestine, and inasmuch as this opinion must remain a constant factor, and further, as His Majesty's Government view with favour the realisation of this aspiration, His Majesty's Government are determined that in so far as is compatible with the freedom of the existing population, both economic and political, no obstacle should be put in the way of the realisation of this ideal."

"The Arab leaders did not offer any objections to the declaration so long as the rights of the Arabs in Palestine were respected. Pledges were given to the non-Jewish population of Palestine who constituted the great majority of its inhabitants, as well as to the Jews. These were the results of conversations which we had with such Arab leaders as we could get in touch with. There was a two-fold undertaking given to them, that the establishment of a Jewish National Home would not in any way, firstly, affect the civil or religious rights of the general population of Palestine; secondly, would not diminish the general prosperity of that population. Those were the only pledges we gave to the Arabs." (*The Truth About the Peace Treaties* by David Lloyd George (Gollancz, 1938, Vol. II, pp. 1140–1142.))

KING HUSSEIN ON ARAB-JEWISH COOPERATION

Mr. George Antonius in *The Arab Awakening* (p. 269) refers to an article from "Al Qibla" (Mecca) No. 183, of March 23, 1918, which he says appears to have been written by Hussein himself, "calling upon the Arab population in Palestine to bear in mind that their sacred books and their traditions enjoined upon them the duties of hospitality and tolerance, and exhorting them to welcome the Jews as brethren and co-operate with them for the common welfare."

It should be added that this article also refers to the remarkable achievements of the Jewish people in Palestine as worthy of imitation by the Arabs and states that "the resources of the country are still virgin soil," and will be developed by the labour and capital of the Jewish immigrants. "One of the most amazing things till recent times," the article goes on, "was that the Palestinian used to leave his country, wandering over the high seas in every direction. His native soil could not retain him, though his ancestors had lived on it for over a thousand years. And, at the same time, we saw the Jews from foreign countries streaming to Palestine from Russia, Germany, Austria, Spain, America. * * * The cause of causes could not escape those who had the gift of a deeper insight; they knew that that country was for its original sons (abna'ihi-l-asliyin), for all their differences, a sacred and beloved homeland. Experience has proved their capacity to succeed in their energies and their labours. * * * The return of these exiles (jaliya) to their homeland will prove materially and spiritually an experimental school for their brethren [i. e., the Arabs] who are with them in the fields, factories, trades, and in all things connected with toil and labour."

DR. WEIZMANN'S VISIT TO EMIR FEISAL

When * * * the Emir Feisal came to London and Paris [December 1918] he was persuaded not merely to accept but to welcome the policy of the Balfour Declaration. At his camp east of the Jordan in the previous summer he had met Dr. Chaim Weizmann, who had done great service by his chemical discoveries to the Allied cause in the War and had taken a leading part in the Zionist movement and the discussion of the Balfour Declaration. He had been able to convince the Emir of the benefits which the Jewish National Home would bring to Palestine as a whole. (From the *Report of the Palestine Royal Commission*, p. 26.)

THE BRITISH GOVERNMENT'S "DECLARATION TO THE SEVEN ARABS"

Mr. George Antonius in *The Arab Awakening*, Appendix D., reproduces his "own rendering of the Arabic text which is in the possession of one of the seven memorialists." He quotes their names—Rafiq al-'Azm, Shaikh Kamel al-Qassab, Mukhtar al-Sulh, Abdul-Rahman Shahbandar, Khaled al-Hakim, Fauzi al-Bakri, Hasan Himadeh—, but does not indicate which of them is the owner of the document. It is not clear whether this is an original or a copy. There is no reproduction of the document, and no way of checking the accuracy of the translation.   For the sake of completeness the passage relating to Palestine is nevertheless reproduced below:

"With regard to the territories occupied by the Allied armies, His Majesty's Government invite the attention of the memorialists to the proclamations issued by the commander in chief on the occasions of the capture of Baghdad (March 19, 1917), and of the capture of Jerusalem (December 9, 1917).   These proclamations define the policy of His Majesty's Government towards the inhabitants of those regions, which is that the future government of those territories should be based upon the principle of the consent of the governed.   This policy will always be that of His Majesty's Government.

"With regard to the territories in the fourth category, it is the desire of His Majesty's Government that the oppressed peoples in those territories should obtain their freedom and independence."

EMIR FEISAL'S INTERVIEW WITH REUTER

The Emir Feisal, in a statement made to a representative of Reuter's Agency, published in *The Times* of December 12, 1918, said, on the subject of Zionist aspirations in regard to Palestine:

"The two main branches of the Semitic family, Arabs and Jews, understand one another, and I hope that as a result of interchange of ideas at the Peace Conference, which will be guided by ideals of self-determination and nationality, each nation will make definite progress towards the realisation of its aspirations.   Arabs are not jealous of Zionist Jews, and intend to give them fair play, and the Zionist Jews have assured the Nationalist Arabs of their intention to see that they too have fair play in their respective areas.   Turkish intrigue in Palestine has raised jealousy between the Jewish colonists and the local peasants, but the mutual understanding of the aims of Arabs and Jews will at once clear away the last trace of this former bitterness, which indeed had already practically disappeared even before the war by the work of the Arab Secret Revolutionary Committee, which in Syria and elsewhere laid the foundation of the Arab military successes of the past two years."

EMIR FEISAL'S MEMORANDUM TO PEACE CONFERENCE

In a memorandum circulated to the delegates of the Peace Conference under date January 1st, 1919, the Emir Feisal set forth the Arab claims.   After describing the national aspirations of the Arabs and claiming independence for the Arabic-speaking countries generally, the memorandum proceeds as follows:

"In Palestine the enormous majority of the people are Arabs.   The Jews are very close to the Arabs in blood, and there is no conflict of character between the two races.   Nevertheless, the Arabs cannot assume the responsibility of holding level the scales in the clash of races and religions that have, in this one province, so often involved the world in difficulties.   They would wish for the effective super-position of a great trustee, so long as a representative local administration commended itself by actively promoting the material propserity of the country." (David Hunter Miller: *My Diary of the Peace Conference*, Vol. IV, pp. 297–299 (Document 250).)

AGREEMENT BETWEEN EMIR FEISAL AND DR. WEIZMANN

His Royal Highness the Emir Feisal, representing and acting on behalf of the Arab Kingdom of Hedjaz, and Dr. Chaim Weizmann, representing and acting on behalf of the Zionist Organisation,

mindful of the racial kinship and ancient bonds existing between the Arabs and the Jewish people, and realising that the surest means of working out the consummation of their national aspirations is through the closest possible collaboration in the development of the Arab State and Palestine, and being desirous further of confirming the good understanding which exists between them,
have agreed upon the following Articles:

ARTICLE I

The Arab State and Palestine in all their relations and undertakings shall be controlled by the most cordial goodwill and understanding, and to this end Arab and Jewish duly accredited agents shall be established and maintained in the respective territories.

ARTICLE II

Immediately following the completion of the deliberations of the Peace Conference, the definite boundaries between the Arab State and Palestine shall be determined by a Commission to be agreed upon by the parties hereto.

ARTICLE III

In the establishment of the Constitution and Administration of Palestine all such measures shall be adopted as will afford the fullest guarantees for carrying into effect the British Government's Declaration of the 2d of November 1917.

ARTICLE IV

All necessary measures shall be taken to encourage and stimulate immigration of Jews into Palestine on a large scale, and as quickly as possible to settle Jewish immigrants upon the land through closer settlement and intensive cultivation of the soil. In taking such measures the Arab peasant and tenant farmers shall be protected in their rights, and shall be assisted in forwarding their economic development.

ARTICLE V

No regulation nor law shall be made prohibiting or interfering in any way with the free exercise of religion; and further the free exercise and enjoyment of religious profession and worship without discrimination or preference shall forever be allowed. No religious test shall ever be required for the exercise of civl or political rights.

ARTICLE VI

The Mohammedan Holy Places shall be under Mohammedan control.

ARTICLE VII

The Zionist Organisation proposes to send to Palestine a Commission of experts to make a survey of the economic possibilities of the country, and to report upon the best means for its development. The Zionist Organisation will place the aforementioned Commission at the disposal of the Arab State for the purpose of a survey of the economic possibilities of the Arab State and to report upon the best means for its development. The Zionist Organisation will use its best efforts to assist the Arab State in providing the means for developing the natural resources and economic possibilities thereof.

ARTICLE VIII

The parties hereto agree to act in complete accord and harmony on all matters embraced herein before the Peace Congress. |

ARTICLE IX

Any matters of dispute which may arise between the contracting parties shall be referred to the British Government for arbitration.

Given under our hand at London, England, the third day of January, one thousand nine hundred and nineteen.

CHAIM WEIZMANN.
FEISAL IBN-HUSSEIN.

RESERVATION BY THE EMIR FEISAL

If the Arabs are established as I have asked in my manifesto of January 4th addressed to the British Secretary of State for Foreign Affairs, I will carry out what is written in this agreement. If changes are made, I cannot be answerable for failing to carry out this agreement.

FEISAL IBN-HUSSEIN.

(Copy of note in Colonel Lawrence's handwriting—translation of Arabic note at end of Treaty.)

EMIR FEISAL'S STATEMENT BEFORE THE COUNCIL OF FIVE

On February 6th, 1919, the Arab case was laid before the Council of Five by the Emir Feisal as the head of a Hedjaz Delegation comprising, in addition to himself, Colonel Lawrence, Rustum Haidar, Nuri Said, and Auni Bey Abdul Hadi.[1] In the official note of the meeting the Emir is reported to have referred to Palestine as follows:

"Palestine, for its universal character he left on one side for the mutual consideration of all parties interested. With this exception, he asked for the independence of the Arabic areas enumerated in his memorandum." (David Hunter Miller: *My Diary of the Peace Conference*, Vol. IV., p. 226 (Document 250).)

[Quoted in *The Truth about the Peace Treaties* by David Lloyd George. (*Gollancz* 1938. Vol. II, p. 1042).]

[*Note:* Mr. Antonius' reproduction of Emir Feisal's Statement breaks off before reaching this passage while leaving the reader under the impression that the complete statement has been given (Compare *The Arab Awakening*, page 286 to 287, with D. H. Miller, from which Mr. Antonius claims to quote it).]

STATEMENT OF THE SYRIAN DELEGATION TO THE PEACE CONFERENCE

On Thursday, February 13th, 1919, at 3 p. m. there was a meeting of the Supreme Council, at which Mr. A. J. Balfour and Viscount Milner represented the British Empire; President Wilson and Mr. R. Lansing the United States of America; Monsieur Clemenceau and Monsieur Pichon, France; Signor Orlando and Baron Sonnino, Italy; and M. Matsui, Japan. There were also present Major the Hon. W. Ormsby Gore and Mr. A. J. Toynbee.

This meeting received the members of the Syrian Commission, consisting of the following:

M. Chekri Ganem_ _ _ _ _ _ _ _ _ _ _ _ _ _ _ _ _ _	The Chief Representative of the Central Syrian Committee.
M. Anis Schehade_ _ _ _ _ _ _ _ _ _ _ _ _ _ _ _ _	Orthodox Greek.
Jamil Mardam Bey [2]_ _ _ _ _ _ _ _ _ _ _ _ _ _ _	Moslem.
Dr. Georges Samne_ _ _ _ _ _ _ _ _ _ _ _ _ _ _ _	Greek Melchite.
Nejil Bey Maikarzel_ _ _ _ _ _ _ _ _ _ _ _ _ _ _	Maronite.
Dr. Tewfik Farhi_ _ _ _ _ _ _ _ _ _ _ _ _ _ _ _	Hebrew.

[2] Jamil Mardam Bey was until recently Prime Minister of Syria.

M. Chekri Ganem read a long statement occupying 16 pages of the Diary, in which he pleaded for the constitution of Syria, within its natural frontiers, into a democratic State distinct from the other Arabic-speaking countries. He argued against the annexation of Syria to Arabia on political, geographical, and moral grounds (describing the Syrians as an educated people and the population of the Hejaz as a "race less advanced"), and repudiated the right of Emir Feisal to exercise any authority in Syria.

In the concluding part of his statement M. Chekri Ganem said: "May we say one word as regards Palestine—although the subject is said to be a thorny one?

"Palestine is incontestably the Southern portion of our country. The Zionists claim it. We have suffered too much from sufferings resembling theirs, not to throw open wide to them the doors of Palestine. All those among them who are oppressed in certain retrograde countries are welcome. Let them settle in Palestine, but in an autonomous Palestine, connected with Syria by the sole bond of federation. Will not a Palestine enjoying wide internal autonomy be for them a sufficient guarantee?

"If they form the majority there, they will be the rulers. If they are in the minority, they will be represented in the Government in proportion to their numbers.

"Is it necessary, in order to establish them, to dismember Syria, to take from it its means of access and its historic safeguard against any invasion (which always took that route), and to constitute a State in the midst of a country which, as a consequence, would be hostile to them." (David Hunter Miller: *My Diary of the Peace Conference*, Vol. XIV, Minutes of the Supreme Council. pp. 389–415.)

(Quoted in part by David Lloyd George: *Truth about the Peace Treaties*, Vol. II, p. 1057.)

---

[1] General Nuri Said, at present Prime Minister of Iraq, and Auni Bey Abdul Hadi, a Palestine Arab leader, are both members of the Arab Delegations to the London Conferences.

FEISAL-FRANKFURTER CORRESPONDENCE

DELEGATION HEDJAZIENNE, *Paris, March 3, 1919.*

DEAR MR. FRANKFURTER: I want to take this opportunity of my first contact with American Zionists to tell you what I have often been able to say to Dr. Weizmann in Arabia and Europe.

We feel that the Arabs and Jews are cousins in race, having suffered similar oppressions at the hands of powers stronger than themselves, and by a happy coincidence have been able to take the first step towards the attainment of their national ideals together.

We Arabs, especially the educated among us, look with the deepest sympathy on the Zionist movement. Our deputation here in Paris is fully acquainted with the proposals submitted yesterday by the Zionist Organization to the Peace Conference, and we regard them as moderate and proper. We will do our best, in so far as we are concerned, to help them through: we will wish the Jews a most hearty welcome home.

With the chiefs of your movement, especially with Dr. Weizmann, we have had and continue to have the closest relations. He has been a great helper of our cause, and I hope the Arabs may soon be in a position to make the Jews some return for their kindness. We are working together for a reformed and revived Near East, and our two movements complete one another. The Jewish movement is national and not imperialist. Our movement is national and not imperialist, and there is room in Syria for us both. Indeed I think that neither can be a real success without the other.

People less informed and less responsible than our leaders and yours, ignoring the need for cooperation of the Arabs and Zionists have been trying to exploit the local difficulties that must necessarily arise in Palestine in the early stages of our movements. Some of them have, I am afraid, misrepresented your aims to the Arab peasantry, and our aims to the Jewish peasantry, with the result that interested parties have been able to make capital out of what they call our differences.

I wish to give you my firm conviction that these differences are not on questions of principle, but on matters of detail such as must inevitably occur in every contact of neighbouring peoples, and. as are easily adjusted by mutual goodwill. Indeed nearly all of them will disappear with fuller knowledge.

I look forward, and my people with me look forward, to a future in which we will help you and you will help us, so that the countries in which we are mutually interested may once again take their places in the community of civilised peoples of the world.

Believe me,

Yours sincerely,

(*Sgd.*) FEISAL.

5TH MARCH, 1919.

ROYAL HIGHNESS:

Allow me, on behalf of the Zionist Organisation, to acknowledge your recent letter with deep appreciation.

Those of us who come from the United States have already been gratified by the friendly relations and the active cooperation maintained between you and the Zionist leaders, particularly Dr. Weizmann. We knew it could not be otherwise; we knew that the aspirations of the Arab and the Jewish peoples were parallel, that each aspired to reestablish its nationality in its own homeland, each making its own distinctive contribution to civilisation, each seeking its own peaceful mofe of life.

The Zionist leaders and the Jewish people for whom they speak have watched with satisfaction the spiritual vigour of the Arab movement. Themselves seeking justice, they are anxious that the just national aims of the Arab people be confirmed and safeguarded by the Peace Conference.

We knew from your acts and your past utterances that the Zionist movement— in other words the national aims of the Jewish people—had your support and the support of the Arab people for whom you speak. These aims are now before the Peace Conference as definite proposals by the Zionist Organisation.! We are happy indeed that you consider these proposals "moderate and proper," and that we have in you a staunch supporter for their realisation. For both the Arab and the Jewish peoples there are difficulties ahead—difficulties that challenge the united statesmanship of Arab and Jewish leaders. For it is no easy task to rebuild two great civilisations that have been suffering oppression and misrule for centuries. We each have our difficulties we shall work out as friends, friends who are animated by similar purposes, seeking a free and full development for the two neighbouring peoples.   The Arabs and Jews are neighbours in territory; we cannot but live side by side as friends.

Very respectfully,

(Sgd.) FELIX FRANKFURTER.

His Royal Highness Prince Feisal.

BRITISH GOVERNMENT PRONOUNCEMENTS

No formal Treaty was concluded between His Maejsty's Government and the King of the Hejaz in 1915.   His Majesty's Government, however, gave certain undertakings to the Arabs through King Hussein to support their efforts to gain their independence subject to reservations as to British and French interests and as to boundaries.   These undertakings were embodied in a long and inconclusive correspondence; and on certain points no specific agreement was reached.   (*Under Secretary of State for Foreign Affairs (Mr. Harmsworth), House of Commons, October 24, 1921.   (H. C. Official Report, October 24, 1921, col.461.*)

It is not the case, as has been represented by the Arab Delegation, that during the War His Majesty's Government gave an undertaking that an independent national government should be at once established in Palestine.   This representation mainly rests upon a letter dated the 24th October, 1915, from Sir Henry McMahon, then His Majesty's High Commissioner in Egypt, to the Sherif of Mecca, now King Hussein of the Kingdom of the Hejaz.   That letter is quoted as conveying the promise to the Sherif of Mecca to recognise and support the independence of the Arabs within the territories proposed by him.   But this promise was given subject to a reservation made in the same letter, which excluded from its scope, among other territories, the portions of Syria lying to the west of the district of Damascus.   This reservation has always been regarded by His Majesty's Government as covering the *Vilayet* of Beirut and the independent Sanjak of Jerusalem.   The whole of Palestine West of the Jordan was thus excluded from Sir H. McMahon's pledge.   (*Statement of British Policy in Palestine, June 3, 1922 (Cmd.* 1700, 1922, p. 20.)

No pledges were made to the Palestine Arabs in 1915.   An undertaking was given to the Sherif of Mecca that His Majesty's Government would recognise and support the independence of the Arabs within certain territorial limits, which specifically excluded the districts of Mersina and Alexandretta, and the portions of Syria lying to the west of the districts of Damascus, Homs, Hama and Aleppo.   It was also stipulated that the undertaking applied only to those portions of the territories concerned in which Great Britain was free to act without detriment to the interests of her Allies.   His Majesty's Government have always regarded, and continue to regard Palestine as excluded by these provisos from the scope of their undertaking.   This is clear from the fact, to which the hon. Member refers, that in the following year they concluded an agreement with the French and Russian Governments under which Palestine was to receive special treatment.

So far as I am aware, the first suggestion that Palestine was included in the area within which His Majesty's Government promised to recognise and support the independence of the Arabs was made by the Emir Feisal, now King of Iraq, at a conversation held in the Foreign Office on 20th January, 1921, more than five years after the conclusion of the correspondence on which the claim was based.   On that occasion the point of view of His Majesty's Government was explained to the Emir, who expressed himself as prepared to accept the statement that it had been the intention of His Majesty's Government to exclude Palestine.

When I assumed responsibility for Middle Eastern Affairs I went carefully into the correspondence referred to, and my reading of it is the same as that of the Foreign Office, as was recently stated in the Declaration of British Policy in Palestine, which has been published and laid before the House.   I am quite satisfied that it was as fully the intention of His Majesty's Government to exclude Palestine from the area of Arab independence as it was to exclude the more northern coastal tracts of Syria.   (*Secretary of State for the Colonies (Mr. Winston Churchill), House of Commons,* July 11, 1922 (*H. C. Official Report,* July 11, 1922, col. 1032/34).)

I have not been content merely to accept those statements as they appeared, but since I have been at the Colonial Office I have, to the best of my ability and power, most carefully investigated the subject for myself, and I certainly see no reason, on broad grounds, to dissent from the interpretation which the late Government has placed upon the promises. Whether they were expressed in the best terms or not, it is perhaps not for me to say, but undoubtedly there never was any intention, when the pledge was given, to recognise the independence of the Arabs so as to include Palestine. I think that is perfectly clear, and in my own mind I am certain of it. Although the terms may not have been expressed in the clearest possible language, I think it was the intention of both Sir H. McMahon and the Government at the time, when those pledges were given, that Palestine should not be included. (*Secretary of State for the Colonies* (*Duke of Devonshire*), *House of Lords,* March 1, 1923. (*H. L. Official Report,* 1.3.1923, col. 233.*))

I served in 1916 in the Arab Bureau in Cairo on Sir Henry McMahon's staff, and I wish myself to testify to the fact that it never was in the mind of anyone on that staff that Palestine west of the Jordan was in the area within which the British Government then undertook to further the cause of Arab independence. And, after all, the whole sequel proves the case. Immediately after the Arab revolt and in successive months, the then British Government, before the right hon. gentleman the Member for Carnarvon Boroughs (Mr. Lloyd George) became Prime Minister, was advised in these matters largely by the late Sir Mark Sykes, and immediately after the McMahon correspondence and the outbreak of the revolt in the Hedjaz he was instructed by the then Government to get into touch with the French and other Allied Governments in regard to the future of that part of the world. Negotiations were long, with the results that England and France, France then having claimed the whole of Palestine, acceded to an arrangement which is set out very fully on page 21 of the Report [of the Royal Commission for Palestine].

* * * When the preliminary negotiations took place leading up to the Balfour Declaration—and it was at least a year after the first adumbration of a desire on the part of the Allied Governments to make some approach to the Jewish people had first been thought of—I remember myself serving in the Arab Bureau helping to edit a thing called the "Arab Bulletin" in the autumn of 1916, putting into that "Bulletin" information regarding Jewish colonies and Jewish aspirations in Palestine; and all through the early days of 1917 His Majesty's Government and the other Governments were becoming increasingly aware of this factor in the Near Eastern problem, and the Balfour Declaration, which was not issued until November, 1917, was the result of prolonged weeks of controversy—I say that advisedly—in this country, because some people put forward views vigorously opposed to it, after negotiations with France and Italy, and after, as the Commission bring out for the first time, President Wilson was consulted as to its precise terms. It was a most deliberate act. * * * It was not only Sir Mark Sykes but others brought to the attention of the Government the fact that undertakings of a general character had been given to the Arabs, and the McMahon correspondence was fully in the mind of His Majesty's and the Allied Governments when the Balfour Declaration was made. I say it was opposed, but let me make it clear that the Cabinet as a whole were absolutely determined, and the idea that this was a particular nostrum of Lord Balfour or any other individual is quite out of the question. * * *

This further fact should be known, that the draft as originally put up by Lord Balfour was not the final draft approved by the War Cabinet. The particular draft assented to by the War Cabinet, and afterwards by the Allied Governments, and by the United States, expressed in the Resolution of Congress and finally embodied in the Mandate, happens to have been drafted by Lord Milner. The actual final draft had to be issued in the name of the Foreign Secretary, but the actual draftsman was Lord Milner.

I want it clearly and finally understood that His Majesty's Government, neither then nor now, can or will admit that Palestine west of the Jordan was included in the pledge given to the Sherif, and that they have always in mind that special considerations must obtain in regard to the future government of the Holy Land. The unique character of Palestine was recognised by the Arab Delegates to the Peace Conference. It is recognised all over the world. (*Secretary of State for the Colonies* (*Mr. Ormsby-Gore, House of Commons,* July 21, 1937 (*H. C. Official Report,* July 21, 1937, col. 2249/50).))

STATEMENTS BY BRITISH NEGOTIATORS

SIR HENRY MCMAHON

Sir: Many references have been made in the Palestine Royal Commission Report and in the course of the recent debates in both Houses of Parliament to the "McMahon Pledge," especially to that portion of the pledge which concerns Palestine and of which one interpretation has been claimed by the Jews and another by the Arabs.

It has been suggested to me that continued silence on the part of the giver of that pledge may itself be misunderstood.

I feel, therefore, called upon to make some statement on the subject, but I will confine myself in doing so to the point now at issue—i. e., whether that portion of Syria now known as Palestine was or was not intended to be included in the territories in which the independence of the Arabs was guaranteed in my pledge.

I feel it my duty to state, and I do so definitely and emphatically, that it was not intended by me in giving this pledge to King Hussein to include Palestine in the area in which Arab independence was promised.

I also had every reason to believe at the time that the fact that Palestine was not included in my pledge was well understood by King Hussein.

    Yours faithfully,

                                 A. HENRY MCMAHON.

5, Wilton Place S.W. 1.,"July 22.
(Letter to *The Times*, July 23, 1937.)

SIR GILBERT CLAYTON, THEN CHIEF SECRETARY OF THE PALESTINE GOVERNMENT, IN A NOTE TO THE HIGH COMMISSIONER, SIR HERBERT SAMUEL, 12TH APRIL, 1923

I was in daily touch with Sir Henry McMahon throughout the negotiations with King Hussein, and made the preliminary drafts of all the letters. I can bear out the statement that it was never the intention that Palestine should be included in the general pledge given to the Sherif. The introductory words of Sir Henry's letter were thought at the time, perhaps erroneously, clearly to cover the point. It was, I think, obvious that the peculiar interests involved in Palestine precluded any definite pledges in regard to its future at so early a stage. (*Quoted by Lord Samuel, House of Lords*, 20th July, 1937. [(*H. L. Official [Report*, July 20, 1937, col. 629.))

COLONEL C. E. VICKERY

Sir: Since it has been decided to publish the letter addressed by Sir Henry McMahon to Sherif Hussein in 1915 it may be of interest to record my impressions of the interview that I had with the late King Hussein in 1920 under instructions from Cairo to read personally the original copy of this letter held by the King. My information was that no copy existed at Cairo, but as to that I am not in a position to say whether this was so or not.

It happened that the King had arrived at Jeddah the day before I received my instructions, and I asked for my audience, which was at once accorded. It was not my custom to take an interpreter with me for these audiences and I was received by the King alone on the top storey of his Jeddah house. For an hour or more I listened to the bitter complaints of King Hussein of the way he had been treated in defiance of pledged and written word; again and again I brought the discussion round to the 1915 letter and tried to provoke the Sherif into showing it to me. It must have been after midday when I had been with him over three hours, for on looking down from my seat in the bow window there was no shadow in the street and the sun was suspended like some sword over the city, that the King suddenly clapped his hands and bade the slave who came in to bring his portfolio. This was done and unlocked by Hussein himself; he fumbled through some papers and finally threw one at me. "Read yourself, O light of my eye." he said. I read the letter through very slowly; it was not written in very scholarly Arabic and had no English translation in the margin, and it was quite evident that Palestine was not included in the proposals to the King.

I can say most definitely that the whole of the King's demands were centred round Syria and only round Syria. Time after time he referred to that vineyard, to the exclusion of any other claim or interest. He stated most emphatically that he did not concern himself at all with Palestine and had no desire to have suzerainty over it for himself or his successors. He did, however, frequently and vehemently, point out to me the following excerpt of the letter, and as it is to be published, the accuracy of my memory can be established. *"Bil niabah el hakumah el britannieh el azimah ana aqbil bi kull motalibkum."* "On behalf of the great British Government I accept all your demands." This may have been worded unfortunately, for there was no doubt in my mind that it referred to the requests for munitions of war which he demanded with great frequency. Nothing would persuade the Sherif Hussein that it did not refer to everything that he had asked for in the acquisition of territories to form the Arabian Empire which inspired every waking moment of his life.

So many are the historians of the Arab revolt and so many are the stories of events which one person had from another who knew a third who was present, that I venture to send you this account of an interview at which there were only two people present and one has long since passed to that paradise that the great prophet promised to the faithful.

I am, Sir,
Your obedient servant.

C. E. Vickery.

Whorlton Grange, Barnard Castle, Co. Durham.
(Letter to *The Times*, February 21, 1939.)

T. E. Lawrence

Draft Preface, dated 18th November, 1922, to an abridgment (not published) of the Oxford Text of *Seven Pillars of Wisdom*.

The book dates itself to 1919, when powerful elements in the British Government were seeking to evade their war-time obligations to the Arabs. That stage ended in March 1921, when Mr. Winston Churchill took charge of the Middle East. He set honesty before expediency in order to fulfil our promises in the letter and in the spirit. He executed the whole McMahon undertaking (called a treaty by some who have not seen it) for Palestine, for Trans-Jordania, and for Arabia. In Mesopotamia he went far beyond its provisions, giving to the Arabs more, and reserving for us much less, than Sir Henry McMahon had thought fit. In the affairs of French Syria he was not able to interfere, and the Sherif of Mecca can fairly complain that the settlement there is not yet in accordance with the Anglo-French agreement of 1916, or with our word to him. I say "not yet" advisedly, since the McMahon proposals (being based on racial and economic reasons) were likely to have imposed themselves eventually, even if Mr. Churchill's progressive British military withdrawal from Mesopotamia had not come to prejudge the future of all the Arab areas.

I do not wish to publish secret documents, nor to make long explanations: but must put on record my conviction that England is out of the Arab affair with clean hands. Some Arab advocates (the most vociferous joined our ranks after the Armistice) have rejected my judgment on this point. Like a tedious Pensioner I showed them my wounds (over sixty I have, each scar evidence of a pain incurred in Arab service) as proof I had worked sincerely on their side. They found me out-of-date: and I was happy to withdraw from a political milieu which had never been congenial. (*The Letters of T. E. Lawrence.* Edited by D. Garnett. Cape, 1938 p. 345.)

It is my deliberate opinion that the Winston Churchill settlement of 1921–1922 (in which I shared) honourably fulfils the whole of the promises we made to the Arabs, insofar as the so-called British spheres are concerned. (From a letter to Professor William Yale, dated October 22, 1929. *The Letters of T. E. Lawrence,* p. 671.)

Mr. Winston Churchill was entrusted by our harassed Cabinet with the settlement of the Middle East; and in a few weeks, at his conference in Cairo, he made straight all the tangle, finding solutions, fulfilling (I think) our promises in letter and spirit (where humanly possible) without sacrificing any interest of our Empire or any interest of the people concerned. So we were quit of the war-time Eastern adventure, with clean hands, but three years too late to earn the gratitude which peoples, if not states, can pay. (Footnote to p. 276 of *Seven Pillars of Wisdom* (1935).)

(Documents submitted for the record by Dr. A. H. Silver: (1) Statements of the Emir Feisal, leader of the Arab delegation at the Peace Conference at Paris in 1919, excluding Palestine from the Arab domain and agreeing to cooperate with the Zionists for the establishment of a Jewish Palestine. (2) Statements on progressing Palestine since the initiation of the Jewish National Home. (3) Excerpts from the Royal Commission Report concerning beneficial effects of the Jewish National Arab progress in Palestine.)

STATEMENTS OF THE EMIR FEISAL, LEADER OF THE ARAB DELEGATION AT THE PEACE CONFERENCE AT PARIS IN 1919, EXCLUDING PALESTINE FROM THE ARAB DOMAIN AND AGREEING TO COOPERATE WITH THE ZIONISTS FOR THE ESTABLISHMENT OF A JEWISH PALESTINE

EMIR FEISAL'S MEMORANDUM TO PEACE CONFERENCE

In a memorandum circulated to the delegates of the Peace Conference under date January 1st, 1919, the Emir Feisal set forth the Arab claims. After describing the national aspirations for the Arabs and claiming independence for the Arabic-speaking countries generally, the memorandum proceeds as follows:

"In Palestine the enormous majority of the people are Arabs. The Jews are very close to the Arabs in blood, and there is no conflict of character between the two races. Nevertheless, the Arabs cannot assume the responsibility of holding level the scales in the clash of races and religions that have in this one province, so often involved the world in difficulties. They would wish for the effective superposition of a great trustee, so long as a representative local administration commended itself by actively promoting the material prosperity of the country."— (David Hunter Miller: *My Diary of the Peace Conference*.)

EMIR FEISAL'S STATEMENT BEFORE THE COUNCIL OF FIVE

On February 6th, 1919, the Arab case was laid before the Council of Five by the Emir Feisal as the head of a Hedjaz Delegation comprising, in addition to himself, Colonel Lawrence, Rustum Haidar, Nuri Said and Auni Bey Abdul Hadi. In the official note of the meeting the Emir is reported to have referred to Palestine as follows:

"Palestine, for its universal character he left on one side for the mutual consideration of all parties interested. With this exception, he asked for the independence of the Arabic areas enumerated in his memorandum." (David Hunter Miller: *My Diary of the Peace Conference*.)

LETTER OF EMIR FEISAL TO PROFESSOR FRANKFURTER

DELEGATION HEDJAZIENNE,
Paris, March 3, 1919.

DEAR MR. FRANKFURTER: I want to take this opportunity of my first contact with American Zionists to tell you what I have often been able to say to Dr. Weizmann in Arabia and Europe.

We feel that the Arabs and Jews are cousins in race, having suffered similar oppressions at the hands of powers stronger than themselves, and by a happy coincidence have been able to take the firts step towards the attainment of their national ideals together.

We Arabs, especially the educated among us, look with the deepest sympathy on the Zionist movement. Our deputation here in Paris is fully acquainted with the proposals submitted yesterday by the Zionist Organization to the Peace Conference, and we regard them as moderate and proper. We will do our best, in so far as we are concerned, to help them through: we will wish the Jews a most hearty welcome home.

With the chiefs of your movement, especially with Dr. Weizmann, we have had and continue to have the closest relations. He has been a great helper of our cause, and I hope the Arabs may soon be in a position to make the Jews some return for their kindness. We are working together for a reformed and revived Near East, and our two movements complete one another. The Jewish movement is national and not imperialist. Our movement is national and not imperialist, and there is room in Syria for us both. Indeed I think that neither can be a real success without the other.

People less informed and less responsible than our leaders and yours, ignoring the need for cooperation of the Arabs and Zionists have been trying to exploit the local difficulties that must necessarily arise in Palestine in the early stages of our movements. Some of them have, I am afraid, misrepresented your aims to the Arab peasantry, and our aims to the Jewish peasantry, with the result that interested parties have been able to make capital out of what they call our differences.

I wish to give you my firm conviction that these differences are not on questions of principle, but on matters of detail such as must inevitably occur in every contact of neighbouring peoples, and as are easily adjusted by mutual goodwill. Indeed nearly all of them will disappear with fuller knowledge.

I look forward, and my people with me look forward, to a future in which we will help you and you will help us, so that the countries in which we are mutually interested may once again take their places in the community of civilized peoples of the world.

Believe me,
Yours sincerely,

(Sgd.) FEISAL.

AGREEMENT BETWEEN EMIR FEISAL AND DR. WEIZMANN

His Royal Highness the Emir FEISAL, representing and acting on behalf of the Arab Kingdom of Hedjaz, and Dr. CHAIM WEIZMANN, representing and acting on behalf of the Zionist Organization,
mindful of the racial kinship and ancient bonds existing between the Arabs and the Jewish people, and realizing that the surest means of working out the consummation of their national aspirations is through the closest possible collaboration in the development of the Arab State and Palestine, and being desirous further of confirming the good understanding which exists between them have agreed upon the following Articles:

ARTICLE I

The Arab State and Palestine in all their relations and undertakings shall be controlled by the most cordial goodwill and understanding, and to this end Arab and Jewish duly accredited agents shall be established and maintained in the respective territories.

ARTICLE II

Immediately following the completion of the deliberations of the Peace Conference, the definite boundaries between the Arab State and Palestine shall be determined by a Commission to be agreed upon by the parties hereto.

ARTICLE III

In the establishment of the Constitution and Administration of Palestine all such measures shall be adopted as will afford the fullest guarantees for carrying into effect the British Government's Declaration of the 2nd of November 1917.

ARTICLE IV

All necessary measures shall be taken to encourage and stimulate immigration of Jews into Palestine on a large scale, and as quickly as possible to settle Jewish immigrants upon the land through closer settlement and intensive cultivation of the soil. In taking such measures the Arab peasant and tenant farmers shall be protected in their rights, and shall be assisted in forwarding their economic development.

ARTICLE V

No regulation nor law shall be made prohibiting or interfering in any way with the free exercise of religion; and further the free exercise and enjoyment of religious profession and worship without discrimination or preference shall forever be allowed. No religious test shall ever be required for the exercise of civil or political rights.

ARTICLE VI

The Mohammedan Holy Places shall be under Mohammedan control.

ARTICLE VII

The Zionist Organization proposes to send to Palestine a Commission of experts to make a survey of the economic possibilities of the country, and to report upon the best means for its development. The Zionist Organization will place the aforementioned Commission at the disposal of the Arab State for the purpose of a survey of the economic possibilities of the Arab State and to report upon the best means for its development. The Zionist Organization will use its best efforts to assist the Arab State in providing the means for developing the natural resources and economic possibilities thereof.

ARTICLE VIII

The parties hereto agree to act in complete accord and harmony on all matters embraced herein before the Peace Congress.

ARTICLE IX

Any matters of dispute which may arise between the contracting parties shall be referred to the British Government for arbitration.

Given Under Our Hand At London, England, The Third Day of January, One Thousand Nine Hundred and Nineteen.

CHAIM WEIZMANN.
FEISAL IBN HUSSEIN.

RESERVATION BY THE EMIR FEISAL

If the Arabs are established as I have asked in my manifesto of January 4th addressed to the British Secretary of State for Foreign Affairs, I will carry out what is written in this agreement. If changes are made, I cannot be answerable for failing to carry out this agreement.

FEISAL IBN HUSSEIN.

STATEMENTS ON PROGRESS IN PALESTINE SINCE THE INITIATION OF THE JEWISH NATIONAL HOME

FIRST HIGH COMMISSIONER IN 1921

"It is obvious to every passing traveller, and well known to every European resident, that the country was before the War and is now undeveloped and underpopulated. The methods of agriculture are for the most part primitive; the area of land now cultivated could yield a far greater product. There are in addition large cultivable areas that are left untilled * * *. The Jordan and Yarmuk offer an abundance of water power, but it is unused * * * the markets of Palestine and the neighbouring countries are supplied almost wholly from Europe. The seaborne commerce, such as it is, is loaded and discharged in the open roadsteads of Haifa and Jaffa; there are no harbours. The country is underpopulated because of this lack of development." (*Interim Report on the Civil Administration of Palestine, July 1st, 1920, to June 30th, 1921.* Cmd. 1499, 1921, p. 4.)

TREASURER OF THE GOVERNMENT OF PALESTINE, W. J. JOHNSON, IN 1936

"During the last fifteen years the population is estimated to have nearly doubled; the urban areas of Jerusalem, Haifa, Jaffa and Tel-Aviv, in particular, have developed beyond the most optimistic expectations, and there is little, if any, unemployment; most of the cultivable land is tilled although in recent years drought and low prices have largely counteracted this; stocks of cattle and horses have been replenished and increased, although the supply falls short of the very much increased demand; millions of trees have been planted by the Government Forest Service and privately; new orange groves have been established which place Palestine among the first five citrus producing countries of the world, and commerce and industry have been developed so as to enable them to support more than one-third of the present total population of the country." (*Palestine Post*, Commercial Section, May 26th, 1936, p. 10.)

*   *   *   *   *   *   *

PROGRESS FROM 1922 TO 1937

The total population of the country in 1922 was 752,048. In 1937 it grew to 1,383,305, an increase of over 80 percent. The agricultural production of winter crops in 1922 amounted to 143,996 tons, and in 1937 it went up to 216,237 tons; the summer crops of 1922 amounted to 97,811 tons, and in 1937 it reached the 420,749-ton mark, an increase of about 340 percent. In 1928 the country produced 341,836 kilos of tobacco, while in 1936 it rose to 1,236,749 kilos. The export trade of 1923 amounted to L. P. 1,172,548, while in 1937 it rose to L. P. 5,813,535; thus the export trade of 1937 was almost five times that of 1923. The import trade of 1923 amounted to L. P. 4,948,907, while that of 1937 amounted to L. P. 15,905,66; thus the imports of 1937 were only 3.3 times that of 1923. The Palestine currency in circulation in 1930 was L. P. 1,672,664, while in 1937 it rose to L. P. 4,829,134. In 1922 Palestine had 2,255 teachers and 52,162 pupils, while in 1937 there were 6,126 teachers and 145,420 pupils, an increase of 170 percent in both teachers and pupils. In 1924 only 1,167 motor vehicles were registered, while in 1937 there were registered 15,641, an increase of 1,240 percent. (*Palestine Government Blue Book, 1937.*)

On the Growth of Arab Population

Statement by Mr. Malcolm MacDonald, British Secretary of State for the Colonies (Parliamentary Debates, House of Commons, November 24, 1938, Vol. 341, Col. 1994).

"* * * The Arabs cannot say that the Jews are driving them out of their country. If not a single Jew had come to Palestine after 1918, I believe the Arab population of Palestine would still have been round about the figure 600,000 at which it had been stable under Turkish rule. It is because the Jews who have come to Palestine bring modern health services and other advantages that Arab men and women who would have been dead are alive today, that Arab children who would never have drawn breath have been born and grown strong. It is not only the Jews who have benefited from the Balfour Declaration. They can deny it as much as they like, but materially the Arabs in Palestine have gained very greatly from the Balfour Declaration."

Excerpts from Palestine Royal Commission Report (Cond. 5479) July 1937 (Pp. 125–129) Concerning Beneficial Effects of the Jewish National Home on Arab Progress in Palestine

"In Arab as in Jewish Palestine the most striking fact is the growth of population. It has risen since 1920 from about 600,000 to about 950,000 and in this case, unlike the Jewish, the rise has been due in only a slight degree to immigration. No accurate estimate can be made of the number of Arabs who have come into Palestine from neighbouring of Arab lands and settled there, but, it may be reckoned that roughly nine-tenths of the growth has been due to natural increase, and it has been a growth of over 50 percent, in 17 years."

*   *   *   *   *   *   *

"* * * a steadily increasing number of *effendi* and other educated Arabs have obtained posts in the Government service since the British Occupation, and some of them high-salaried posts. Apart from that, it is difficult to detect any deterioration in the economic position of the Arab upper class. Landowners have sold substantial pieces of land at a figure far above the price it could have fetched before the War. * * * Partly, no doubt, as the result of land-sales the *effendi* class has been able to make substantial investments of capital. Some of this has gone towards increased production, especially of fruit, from the land they have retained. At least six times more Arab-owned land is now planted with citrus than in 1920. Arab citrus plantations in the Maritime Plain now cover 135,000 *dunums*, and represent an investment of £6,500,000."

*   *   *   *   *   *   *

"Some of the capital has been directed to building houses for lease or sale or to industrial enterprise. The development of Arab industry, though not comparable, of course, with that of Jewish industry, has made progress. It appears from the Government Report for 1933 that the number of Arab "industrial undertakings," which was about 1,200 before the War, had risen to about 2,200. Among relatively large-scale industries are soap, flour milling, bricks and tiles, cigarettes and tobacco, cotton, wool and silk weaving, salt quarrying, stone and lime, bedsteads, nails, wearing apparel, confectionery, and alcoholic liquor. No official statistics are available as to the amount of capital invested in this industrial field as a whole; but it has certainly increased in the course of the last few years, as has the amount of Arab bank deposits."

*   *   *   *   *   *   *

"It is the condition of the *fellaheen*, still the great majority of the Arab population, that must be regarded as the dominant factor in any estimate of the economic progress of Arab Palestine. It cannot, unhappily, be questioned that the standard of living among the *fellaheen* is still low. Like other agricultural communities they have suffered from the world-wide fall in prices. They have suffered, too, from severe and repeated droughts and consequent bad harvests. Some of the obstacles to their progress have been partially removed. Some of the cramping *mash'a* system of land tenure has been replaced by individual ownership. Their burden of debt has been eased. The Government has done much to relieve them by reducing and remitting taxation and providing loans. Tithe was reduced, commuted, and finally replaced by a more equitable tax on rural property. The development of cooperation has been slow and somewhat discouraging, but at least a beginning has been made and over 60 Arab Cooperative Societies are now in existence. There is evidence, moreover, that some *fellahee* are at any rate on the way to becoming better cultivators. If the great majority are still wedded to their old, primitive ways, there are some who are learning better methods, using better seed and better tools, under official guidance and inspection."

* * * * * * * *

"* * * the rate of wages has steadily gone up. The daily wage paid to an Arab for skilled labour is now from 250 to 600 mils, and for unskilled labour from 100 to 180 mils. In Syria the wage ranges from 67 mils in older industries to 124 mils in newer ones. Factory labour in 'Iraq is paid from 40 to 60 mils.'

"Nor is it only in the towns that the landless *fellah* finds a livelihood. The Government's programme of public works means a continuous demand for labour, and a large number of Arabs are employed on roads and bridges and the like. Moreover, the great expansion of citrus cultivation, Arab as well as Jewish, has greatly increased the demand for agricultural labour; and for that, too, the rate of wages has risen. For general agricultural work it was 80 to 120 mils a day in 1931, and 100 to 150 mils in 1935. For tree-planting and nursery work it was 100 to 150 mils in 1931, and 150 to 200 mils in 1935."

* * * * * * *

"* * * The whole range of public services, the initiation of which we described in the preceding chapter, has steadily developed, to the benefit of the *fellaheen*. Except in periods of 'disturbance,' their lives and property have been reasonably safe. Their civil rights have been safeguarded by the Courts. The growth in their numbers has been largely due to the health services, combating malaria, reducing the infant death rate, improving water supply and sanitation. Education, if as yet it only meets half the demand, has to that extent enabled the rising generation to profit more easily from the technical instruction given in the Arab Agricultural College or by official advisers in the villages. Better roads and quicker transport have meant higher returns on market produce. In sum, it may be said that though much more could have been done if more money had been available, the equipment of Palestine with social services is more [advanced than that of any of its neighbours, and far more advanced than that of an Indian province or an African colony."

It remains to examine the validity of the Jewish claim that this advance has been largely due to the establishment of the National Home. After considering the evidence submitted to us, both orally and in writing, by the Jewish representatives on this question, we have come to the following conclusions:

(i) The large import of Jewish capital into Palestine has had a general fructifying effect on the economic life of the whole country.

(ii) The expansion of Arab industry and citriculture has been largely financed by the capital thus obtained.

(iii) Jewish example has done much to improve Arab cultivation, especially of citrus.

(iv) Owing to Jewish development and enterprise the employment of Arab labour has increased in urban areas, particularly in the ports.

(v) The reclamation and antimalaria work undertaken in Jewish "colonies" have benefited all Arabs in the neighbourhood.

(vi) Institutions, founded with Jewish funds primarily to serve the National Home, have also served the Arab population. *Hadassah*, for example, treats Arab patients, notably at the Tuberculosis Hospital at Safad and the Radiology Institute at Jerusalem, admits Arab countryfolk to the clinics of its Rural Sick Benefit Fund, and does much infant welfare work for Arab mothers.

(vii) The general beneficent effect of Jewish immigration on Arab welfare is illustrated by the fact that the increase in the Arab population is most marked in urban areas affected by Jewish development. A comparison of the Census returns in 1922 and 1931 shows that, six years ago, the increase per cent. in Haifa was 86, in Jaffa 62, in Jerusalem 37, while in purely Arab towns such as Nablus and Hebron it was only 7, and at Gaza there was a decrease of 2 percent.

"The further claim, based on the Jewish contribution to revenue, seems to us indisputable.   Arab witnesses could not deny that such public services as had in fact been provided had benefited their people; nor could they deny that the revenue available for those services had been largely provided by the Jews.   It is impossible to calculate with anything like precision what share of taxation is borne by the Jews.   But it is certain that much the greater part of the customs duties are paid by them, and the rising amount of customs revenue has formed from 1920 to the present day the biggest item in the rising total revenue."

A Survey of the Diplomatic Negotiations and Relevant Circumstances Bearing on the Right of the United States to Participate in Any Disposition of Palestine

The United States was one of the Principal, Allied and Associated Powers whose common efforts resulted in the common victory which made possible the severance from Germany and Turkey of their territories outside Europe.   In the disposition of those territories, in their allocation for administration under mandate, and in the formulation of the standards which the administering powers are obligated to observe in the government of such territories, the United States successfully asserted, as of right, a claim to an equal voice with the other principal powers.   The dispositions of former German and Turkish territories to which the United States gave its consent by treaties with the mandatory Powers were limited and temporary dispositions.

The earnest controversy with the Principal Allied Powers concerning the right of the United States to participate in the disposition of former Turkish territory originated in British interference with the Standard Oil Company in Palestine. Protest was made against British failure to respect the acquired rights of that company.[1]   Since it was not yet clear in 1919 that the United States would not ratify the Peace Treaty, the question did not arise whether the United States was legally justified in invoking the principle of trusteeship which the Powers had agreed to apply to former German and Turkish territories, outside Europe.   In the correspondence during 1919 and 1920 the assumption was constantly made that such principle enured to the benefit of the United States.[2]

Evidence of the intention of the Principal Allied Powers to exclude American nationals from commercial opportunities in the territories severed from Germany and Turkey continued, however, to accumulate.[3]

On May 12, 1920, Ambassador Davis invoked the mandate principle:

The Government of the United States desires to point out that during the Peace negotiations at Paris leading up to the Treaty of Versailles, it consistently took the position that the future Peace of the world required that as a general principle any Alien territory which should be acquired pursuant to the Treaties of Peace with the Central Powers must be held and governed in such a way as to assure equal treatment in law and in fact to the commerce of all nations. It was on account of and subject to this understanding that the United States felt itself able and willing to agree that the acquisition of certain enemy territory by the victorious powers would be consistent with the best interests of the world.   The representatives of the principal Allied Powers in the discussion of the Mandate principles expressed in no indefinite manner their recognition of the justice and farsightedness of such a principle and agreed to its application to the Mandates over Turkish territory.[4]

In an instruction of July 26, 1920, the ground of American remonstrance was broadened still further:

It is the opinion of this Government that the treatment of the economic resources of the regions which will be held under mandate by Great Britain or other nations involves *a question of principle transcending in importance questions relating merely to the commercial competition of private interests or to control for strategic purposes of any particular raw material.*[5]

---

[1] See the correspondence in *For. Rel.* 1919, Vol. 2, pp. 250–262, and 1920, Vol. 2, pp. 649–675.
[2] "Great Britain as *trustee* cannot legally allow discrimination in favor of her own or other nationals"; see *For. Rel.*, 1920, Vol. 2, p. 650. Polk to Wright, March 17, 1920.
[3] *Ibid.*, p. 655 and note 68 on the same page, the Cadman-Berthelot agreement of April 24, 1920.
[4] *Ibid.*, pp. 651-655, Davis to Curzon, May 12, 1920.
[5] *Ibid.*, p. 658, Colby to Davis, July 26, 1920.

By note of August 9, 1920, Lord Curzon challenged the right of the United States to make protest against the economic partition of former Turkish territories. Lord Curzon wrote:

> 15. The draft mandates for Mesopotamia and for Palestine, which have been prepared with a view to secure equality of treatment and subjects, of all states who are members of the League of Nations, will, when approved by the Allies interested, be communicated to the Council of the League of Nations. In these circumstances His Majesty's Government, while fully appreciating the suggestion for discussing with the United States Government the various propositions mentioned by you, with which they are in full sympathy, are none the less of the opinion that the terms of the mandates can only properly be discussed at the Council of the League of Nations by the signatories of the Covenant.[6]

In Secretary Colby's reply of November 20, 1920, the right of the United States to participate in the disposition of former German and Turkish territories was emphatically asserted. It was said that—

> Such powers as the Allied and Associated nations may enjoy or wield, in the determination of the governmental status of the mandated areas, accrued to them as a direct result of the war against the Central powers. The United States, as a participant in that conflict and as a contributor to its successful issue, cannot consider any of the Associated powers, the smallest not less than itself, debarred from the discussion of any of its consequences, or from participation in the rights and privileges secured under the mandates provided for in the treaties of peace.
> This Government notes with interest your statement that the draft mandates for Mesopotamia and for Palestine, which have been prepared with a view to secure equality of treatment and opportunity for the commerce, citizens and subjects of all states which are members of the League of Nations, will, when approved by the interested Allied powers, be communicated to the Council of the League of Nations. The United States is, undoubtedly, one of the powers directly interested in the terms of the mandates, and I therefore request that the draft mandate forms be communicated to this Government for its consideration before their submission to the Council of the League.[7]

The controversy had in the meantime broadened to include the disposition of the island of Yap and the distribution of the cables taken from Germany. In the distribution of the former German cables the United States was again faced by the denial of its equal right with the Principal Allied Powers to participate in determining the consequences of the common victory. In February 1920, the Government of the United States had issued invitations to a conference for the settlement of international questions relating to communications by telegraph, telephone, cable, wireless, etc. On July 9, 1920, the French Government rejected the invitation on the ground that although—

> * * * under the Treaty of Versailles, Germany relinquished her rights to her cables in favor of the Principal Allied and Associated Powers * * * * * * inasmuch as the United States, one of the principal Allied and Associated Powers, has not, up to date, ratified the treaty with Germany, the Government of the Republic doubts whether the American Government is in a position to enter upon a useful discussion of that question at the present time.[8]

Nevertheless, on August 18, 1920, the French Government informed Secretary Colby that it would attend the conference.[9]

At the conference, however, the French and British Delegates sought to exclude the United States from an equitable share in the distribution of the former German cables on the ground of an agreement entered into before the United States declared war on Germany.

On November 5, 1920, Secretary Colby wrote:

> that the five Principal Allied and Associated Powers have title to the German cables acquired under the treaty is fully admitted. Unanimous consent is essential, not only to a division of ownership in this joint property, but also to the use of it by any one power.[10]

6 *Ibid.*, p. 663, Davis to Colby, August 11, 1920.
7 *Ibid.*, pp. 670–672, Colby to Curzon, November 20, 1920.
8 *For. Rel.*, 1920, vol. 1, pp. 124–125, Bearn to Colby, July 9, 1920.
9 *Ibid.*, p. 128, Bearn to Colby, Aug. 18, 1920.
10 *Ibid.*, p. 137, Colby to Wright, Nov. 5, 1920.

On December 8, 1920, Acting Secretary Davis wrote to the British Senior Delegate to the Communication Conference as follows:

> In the early stages of this Conference you stated that by a gentleman's agreement with France, made before the entry of the United States into the war, the British delegation felt at least a moral obligation to support the French claims. I need not restate in detail my views as to the validity of such understanding which must or should have been automatically cancelled by the subseqnent entrance of the United States into the war and its prosecution thereof in association with the Allies * * * [11]

On December 14, 1920, the Department of State was able to make public announcement that tentative agreement for an equitable distribution of ownership and operation of the former German cables had been reached and that pending the final settlement, those cables were to be operated for the financial account of the five powers.[12]

Contemporaneously with the settlement of the cables controversy, the first steps were being taken by the United States to make clear that there could be no valid allocation to Japan of the mandate for the island of Yap without its consent.[13] The Japanese Government, nevertheless, proceeded with the presentation to the Council of the League of a draft mandate for the former German islands in the North Pacific, which was approved by the Council on December 17, 1920.[14] It had become clear [15] that only by obtaining express recognition of its entire legal equality with the Principal Allied Powers in the disposition of former German and Turkish territories, could the United States protect its rights and interests.

By note of February 21, 1921, Secretary Colby transmitted to the Council of the League of Nations a copy of his note of November 20, 1920, copies of which had also been transmitted to the Governments of France and Italy. Secretary Colby invited the attention of the Council of the League of Nations particularly to the request made in the note of November 20, 1920, that the draft mandate forms intended to be submitted to the League of Nations be communicated to the Government of the United States for its consideration before submission to the Council |of the League, in order that the Council might thus have before it an expression of the opinion of the Government of the United States on the form of such mandates—

> and a clear indication of the basis upon which the approval of this Government, which is essential to the validity of any determination which may be reached, might be anticipated and received.[16]

Emphatic protest was made against the allocation to Japan of the mandate for the former German islands in the North Pacific, which purported to be made in the name of the Principal Allied and Associated Powers, although the United States had never given its consent.

On March 1, 1921, the Council replied as follows:

> The most fundamental contention brought forward by the American Note is that the "approval of the United States of American is essential to the validity of any determination which may be reached" respecting the Mandates which have been, or may be, submitted to the judgment of the Council. The United States was one of the leading actors, both in the war and in the negotiations for peace. The rights which it acquired are not likely to be challenged in any quarter. But the American Government will itself recognise that the situation is complicated by the fact that the United States, for reasons which the Council would be the last to question, has so far abstained from ratifying the Peace Treaty, and has not taken her seat on the Council of the League of Nations.

[11] *Ibid.*, pp. 143–144, Davis to Brown, Dec. 8, 1920.
[12] *Ibid.*, p. 147.
[13] *For. Rel.*, 1921, vol. 2, pp. 265–268, Davis to Davis, Dec. 4, 1920.
[14] *Official Journal of the League of Nations*, 1921, p. 82.
[15] See the account of Secretary Hughes' conversation with M. Viviani of Mar. 30, 1921, *For. Rel.*, 1921, vol. 1, pp. 946–967.
[16] *For. Rel.*, 1921, vol. 1, p. 89, Colby to Wallace, Feb. 21, 1921.

The Council had already determined on February 21, before the receipt of the American Note, to postpone the consideration of the "A" Mandates for former Turkish possessions, including Mesopotamia. No conclusions will therefore be reached with regard to "A" Mandates until the United States Government has had an opportunity to express its views.

The Council had expected to approve finally at the Session now being held the "B" Mandates for the former Central African Colonies for of] Germany. In view of the desire expressed by the United States, the Council is, however, deferring its consideration of these Mandates until its next Session which will probably take place in May or June. * * *

The Council invites the United States to take part in the discussions at its forthcoming meeting when the final decisions as to the "A" and "B" Mandates will, it is hoped, be taken. * * *

The Council of the League of Nations would remind Your Excellency that the allocation of all the Mandated territories is a function of the Supreme Council and not of the Council of the League. The League is concerned, not with the allocation but with the administration of these territories. Having been notified in the name of the Allied and Associated Powers that all the Islands North of the Equator had been allocated to Japan, the Council of the League merely fulfilled its responsibility of defining the terms of the Mandate.

Consequently, if a misunderstanding exists as to the allocation of the Island of Yap, that misunderstanding would seem to be between the United States and the Principal Allied Powers rather than between the United States and the League. However, in view of the American contention the Council of the League has hastened to forward the American Note to the Governments of France, Great Britain, Italy and Japan.[17]

On June 15, 1921, the Acting President of the Council informed the Principal Allied Powers that—

* * * the Council of the League of Nations prefers not to exercise the functions conferred upon it by article 22.of the Covenant so long as the conditions requisite to the exercise of those functions have not been completely fulfilled, and particularly so long as the title of the mandatory Powers to exercise this mandate has not been accepted and defined as the result of a complete agreement between the Principal Allied and Associated Powers.

I therefore venture to ask the Principal Allied Powers to be good enough to make every effort to arrive at a solution of the points under discussion between them and the United States, so as to enable the Council of the League to settle the whole question of mandates before the next meeting of the Assembly.[18]

As a result of the protest of the United States, the Japanese Government was brought to reopen the entire question of the validity of its mandate for the former German islands in the North Pacific and to admit the necessity for American consent thereto. Conversations on the Japanese mandate were begun by Secretary Hughes and Ambassador Shidehara in June 1921. In reply to the Japanese inquiry whether the United States claimed an interest in all the former German islands in the Pacific, Secretary Hughes said that—

* * * the principle was of general application to all the overseas possessions of Germany, and that there was no reason why the United States should be denied an equal participation. The Secretary, however, said that while he would maintain this general principle, if it were contested, still the United States had no desire to advance the principle for the purpose of obtaining territory or of increasing its possessions, but merely for the purpose of protecting its interests. * * * The Secretary said he did not see upon what grounds it could be maintained, after we had entered the war and participated in obtaining the victory, that those associated with us should attempt to deprive us of equal privileges in what were German possessions wherever we had interests to safeguard.

17 For. Rel., 1921, vol. 1, pp. 94–95.
18 Official Journal of the League of Nations, 1921, p. 441. At the meeting of the Council on June 17, 1921, consideration of the A and B mandates was deferred "in order that the United States might be able to concur in any modifications which might be necessary;" Official Journal, 1921, p. 641. On June 25, 1921, the Council decided that the mandatory powers might transmit the texts of the draft mandates to the United States without the consent of the Council; Quincy Wright, Mandates under the League of Nations, Chicago, 1930, p. 54, n. 86. The texts appear to have been transmitted officially to the United States by the proposed mandatories in June or July, 1921. The B mandates were not approved by the Council until it had been officially informed that American approval of the terms of those mandates had been obtained, July 20, 1922; Official Journal, 1922, pp. 791–793, 810, 847. The A mandates were not approved until July 24, 1922, after announcement had been made that agreement had been reached with the United States; ibid., 1922, pp. 546, 823.

* * * The Secretary said that if there was anything that the islands could be used for aside from cables, he saw no reason why the United States should not have its equal opportunity for such a use. He asked the Ambassador whether Japan desired to fortify the island. The Ambassador said that Japan did not * * *.

The Secretary said the type "C" mandate made the mandated territory part of the territory of the mandatory and that the United States could not consent to having Japan, as a sovereign power in possession of the territory, granting or withholding such licenses as it might see fit as a sovereign to grant or withhold; that *the United States desired that whatever Power or Powers had administration of the Island their authority should be subject to the equality of right, and administration should be maintained under suitable terms which would assure the maintenance of the privileges, not as those granted by a sovereign power* which was in possession of the islands, *but as privileges in which all the Powers were entitled to share and subject to the exercise of which the island was administered.*

The Ambassador again asked whether the United States would be satisfied if an attempt was made to internationalize the islands for cable purposes, and again suggested that his Government might be willing to go that far. The Secretary repeated that there should be equality in the enjoyment of all privileges afforded by the island, but that if these were secured, he thought there would not be any trouble with regard to a suitable arrangement for the civil administration; after a full consideration of what uses the island served, there should be no difficulty in arriving at an agreement with respect to the manner of administration.[19]

On June 18, 1921, Ambassador Shidehara proposed—

* * * that the United States shall have free access to the Island of Yap on the footing of entire equality with Japan or any other nation, in all that relates to the landing and operation of the existing Yap-Guam cable, or of any cable which may hereafter be laid by the United States or its nationals.[20]

In conversation of August 19, 1921, Secretary Hughes observed that—

* * * in view of the position taken by the United States in the Yap note, he supposed that it would be desirable that the legal situation should be cleared up; that this could appropriately be done by a Convention between the Principal Allied and Associated Powers in whose favor Germany had renounced her title and interest in the Island of Yap * * *.

In a memorandum of the same date, he added that—

Such convention should also contain suitable provisions relating to the administration, such as are found in articles 3, 4, and 5 of the mandate purporting to have been granted on behalf of the Principal Allied and Associated Powers, but to which the United States has not agreed.[21]

By memorandum of September 8, 1921, the Japanese Embassy indicated that the proposals of the United States were acceptable to it and proceeded upon—

the assumption that upon these rights of the United States being recognized by Japan, there will be no objection on the part of the American Government to the assignment to Japan of the Mandate for the Island of Yap or for any of the former German possessions in the Pacific lying north of the Equator.[22]

Secretary Hughes' memorandum in reply of September 15, 1921, expressly claimed the benefit of all the engagements set forth in the mandate and required, *in addition*, that agreement be "reached with respect to the additions to, or qualifications of, the Mandate, which are deemed necessary to give suitable protection to the interests of the United States." Only if such agreement was reached was the assumption true that there would be no objection on the part of the United States to the assignment to Japan of a mandate for the islands. Secretary Hughes wrote:

(a) As the United States is not a member of the League of Nations or a party to the Mandate, there should be a general provisions in the Convention that the United States should have the benefit of the engagements set forth in the Mandate * * *

[19] *For. Rel.*, 1921, vol. 2, p. 287, Memorandum of a conversation between Secretary Hughes and Ambassador Shidehara, June 3, 1921.
[20] *Ibid.*, p. 291.
[21] *Ibid.*, p. 295, Memorandum of August 19, 1921, from the Department of State to the Japanese Embassy.
[22] *Ibid.*, p. 295, Memorandum of September 8, 1921, from the Japanese Embassy to the Department of State.

* * *   The mandate in its present form could easily be recited in the Convention, and the provisions [23] indicated above might thereafter be inserted in appropriate clauses of the Convention.

It is understood that the administration by Japan of the mandated islands will be subject to the Convention with the United States, and that the terms of the Mandate which are recited in the Convention and of which the United States is to have the benefit will not be modified without the express consent of the United States. It is also desired that, as the United States is not a member of the League of Nations, a report will be made to the United States similar to that which is to be made by Japan to the Council of the League of Nations, as provided in article 6 of the Mandate.[24]

The Japanese Government acquiesced, by memorandum of October 17, in the American proposals. Objection was made, however, to the proposal that the Japanese Government should submit to the United States an annual report on the administration of the mandated islands.[25] Secretary Hughes replied on October 18, 1921, that—

In paragraph 6 of the Embassy's memorandum it is requested that specific reference to the question of transmitting to the Government of the United States an annual report regarding the mandate be withheld in the Convention, the Japanese Government not feeling itself at liberty to enter into any binding engagement in the matter apart from and in advance of other nations similarly placed. While it may be remarked that it is, as surmised in the Embassy's memorandum, the intention of this Government to make a similar suggestion to all the mandatories, the American Government cannot perceive that the settlement of that point, rather than any of the other matters concerning the mandate which the Japanese Government has found appropriate for adjustment in the present direct negotiations between the United States and Japan, should require reference to the other mandatory Powers.

Inasmuch therefore, *as the Japanese Government has indicated its acceptance of the principle that the United States should have the benefit of the engagements set forth in the Mandate,* the Government of the United States thinks it proper that, in the event of its assenting to the administration by the Japanese of the Islands in accordance with the terms of the Convention *it should be placed in a position not inferior to that of the other Principal Allied and Associated Powers which under the terms of the Mandate are to receive an annual report submitted through the Council of the League,* by having addressed to it by the Japanese Government a duplicate of such report.[26]

By memorandum of December 12, 1921, the Japanese Government yielded its objections and undertook to transmit to the United States a duplicate of the annual report to be made to the Council of the League regarding its administration of the mandated territory.[27] The treaty defining the rights of the United States and Japan in the former German islands in the North Pacific was signed on February 11, 1922.[28]

Shortly after the conclusion of the Yap Treaty, Professor George H. Blakeslee, of Clark University, Technical Adviser to the American Delegation to the Washington Conference, wrote:

The Treaty should satisfy both Japan and the United States, for each secures its essential needs and desires. Japan has gained a clear title as Mandatory. The United States has obtained: (1) equal cable rights in Yap; (2) a definite guarantee, given both in the original Mandate and repeated in the present treaty, that "no military or naval bases shall be established or fortifications erected in the territory," a provision which, in largest part, does away with the menace of these islands remaining in Japan's possessions; (3) protection for American missions and American traders; and (4) a recognition of its rights as one of the original trustees of the Mandate—shown especially by Japan's agreement to send annually to the United

[23] The provisions referred to related to the qualifications of and additions to the Mandate, contained in paragraphs b, c, d, and e of the memorandum. They concerned the rights of missionaries, monopolistic concessions, the application to the mandated islands of American-Japanese treaties, and respect for vested American property rights.
[24] *Ibid.,* p. 297, Hughes to Shidehara, September 15, 1921.
[25] *Ibid.,* p. 301, Memorandum of Japanese Embassy to the Department of State, October 17, 1921.
[26] *Ibid.,* p. 303, Memorandum of October 18, 1921.
[27] *Ibid.,* p. 306, Shidehara to Hughes, Memorandum of December 12, 1921.
[28] *Treaty Series,* No. 664.

States a duplicate of the report on its administration which is to be made to the Council of the League of Nations.

The legal status of Japan's title as Mandatory, as a result of the new treaty, is an interesting one. The title is derived in part from Great Britain, France, Italy, and Japan, as four of the Principal Allied and Associated Powers, and is granted by the Mandate, ratified by the League of Nations; but it is also derived in part from the United States, as the remaining Principal Allied and Associated Power, and is granted by the present treaty, which ratifies the Mandate and stipulates for certain additional advantages. The essential parts of the Mandate cannot be modified without the consent both of the Council of the League and of the United States; the necessity for the consent of the Council is stipulated for in the terms of the Mandate; while the consent of the United States is assured by a provision in the present treaty. As Japan derives its title from two sources, given by two differing legal documents, so it is also responsible for its administration to two trustees: (1) the Council of the League, for administering in accordance with the terms of the Mandate; and (2) the United States, for administration in accordance with the terms of the Treaty of February 11, 1921.[29]

The Japanese Government appears to have consulted with the Principal Allied Powers in the course of the negotiations with the United States, so that the results of those negotiations may be said to represent the consensus of the powers, and to have a direct bearing upon the meaning of the identical provisions in the Palestine Treaty.[30] In support of the demands made on the British Government, repeated appeal was made to the Japanese Treaty, which was the model after which the Palestine Treaty was expressly patterned. Both treaties reflect the entire legal equality of the United States with the Principal Allied Powers in the disposition of former German and Turkish territories, outside Europe.[31]

The negotiations with Great Britain concerning the mandates to be allocated to that Power were begun by memorandum of August 24, 1921, transmitted by Ambassador Harvey to Lord Curzon,[32] identic memoranda being transmitted to the Governments of France, Italy, and Japan,[33] containing the observations of the United States concerning the various classes of mandates and the alterations in the draft texts which it proposed. These memoranda were considered in concert by the Powers addressed, and identic notes sent in reply.[34]

Two distinct, if related, claims were advanced by the United States. The first was a claim of right to participate in the discussion of the terms of the mandate. The other, upon which the first was founded, was that the consent of the United States was indispensable for any valid determination concerning the disposition of these territories. The logical consequence of this latter fundamental assertion of right was the demand that the legal status of the United States in relation to the *future* regime should not be inferior to that of its late associates.

The memorandum of August 24, 1921, opened with a restatement of the general principles involved. It was laid down that the right to dispose of the overseas possessions of Germany was acquired only through the common victory and that there could be no valid or effective disposition of them without the assent of the United States. It was asserted that this position was not opposed, but was confirmed by the Treaty of Versailles, and that the Government of the United States perceived no possible basis for a claim to exclude the United States from full participation. Nor was any such claim understood to have been made.

[29] George H. Blakeslee: "The Mandates of the Pacific," *Foreign Affairs* (September, 1922), vol. 1, No. 1, pp. 104–105.

[30] Cf. the note from the French Government of April 5, 1921, *For. Rel.*, 1921, vol. 2, p. 288; the memorandum of a conversation between Secretary Hughes and Ambassador Geddes of April 12, 1921, *ibid.*, p. 284; the Italian note of April 29, 1921, *ibid.*, p. 287; the Japanese memorandum of December 2, 1921, *ibid.*, p. 304.

[31] Secretary Hughes wrote in the memorandum of August 24, 1921, that "it is not the intention of the Government of the United States to raise objection to allocation or terms of mandates for the purpose of seeking additional territory or for any other purpose than to safeguard the interests of the United States and the fair and equal opportunities which it is believed the United States should enjoy in common with the other powers." That limitation does not support a restrictive interpretation of the Palestine *treaty* and was not designed to assure mere equality of commercial opportunity as is shown by the fact that *the subsequent offer of assurances of such equality, which was coupled with a challenge to American equality of right, was rejected as giving inadequate recognition to the entire legal equality of the United States with the Principal Allied Powers and their successors*, see *infra*, p. 20.

[32] *For. Rel.*, 1921, vol. 2, p. 106.

[33] *For. Rel.*, 1921, vol. 1, p. 922, and vol. 2, p. 106, n. 57.

[34] The British reply of December 22, 1921, *For. Rel.*, 1921, vol. 2, p. 111; the French reply of December 22, 1921, *For. Rel.*, 1921, vol. 1, p. 925. It was perhaps not without importance that these replies were not sent until after the conclusion of the negotiations with Japan relating to the Pacific mandate allocated to that Power. The Japanese Government appears to have consulted with the Allies as the suggestion that the British Delegates to the Washington Conference be invited to discuss certain points relating to the Japanese mandates shows: Memorandum of December 2, 1921, from the Japanese Embassy to the Department of State, *For. Rel.*, 1921, vol. 2, p. 304.

It was declared that the right of the United States could not be made the subject of such disposition as was proposed without its consent, and that under the constitutional system, the giving of that assent was not exclusively within the authority of the President. It was thought, however, that there would be no difficulty in negotiating an appropriate treaty if the terms of the mandates were defined in the line of the suggestions that followed. The same principles were regarded as applicable to former Turkish territories.[35]

Without attempting to restate the general principles governing mandates, which had been the subject of earlier correspondence between the two governments, the memorandum then commented upon those provisions of the mandate drafts which bore upon capitulatory rights, monopolistic concessions, missionary activities, and economic discrimination which, it was proposed, should be extended by collective definition to embrace the United States. *It was, finally, understood that the consent of the United States should be necessary to any modification of a mandate after it had been agreed to.*

The reply of the British Government of December 22, 1921,[36] which dealt with the African mandates, disclaimed any intention to deprive the United States of the fruits of a victory to which it had contributed so generously. The British Government was quite willing to meet the wishes of the United States as regarded the British mandates. Detailed consideration of the general considerations in the American note seemed, therefore, unnecessary. The following general observations were, however, made:

The cooperation of the United States in the making of peace was a necessary corollary of their cooperation in the war and in the victory. The treaty of Versailles was the outcome of the cooperation. It was entered into by the Allied powers upon the assumption that it represented the common views of all those who had taken part in its preparation after their combined effort to achieve the victory. It was upon the faith of this assumption that the Allied powers undertook obligations not only towards Germany, but also towards each other, and from which it is now impossible for them to escape.

The decision of one of the Allied and Associated powers not to ratify the treaty does not modify the obligations which that treaty imposed upon those who have ratified it, nor release them from the pledges it contains; nor can they now enter into new engagements which would be inconsistent with its terms.

What is said above is preeminently true with regard to the overseas territories which formerly belonged to Germany. By the treaty of Versailles Germany renounced all her sovereignty over them; that renunciation was intended, as pointed out in the American note, to be indivisible; no part of that sovereignty remains to Germany today. But Germany parted with her sovereignty upon the terms laid down in the treaty. Among the conditions so laid down was the assurance that these territories would in future be administered by mandatories on behalf of, and subject to, the general control of the League of Nations in connection with the mandates over these territories; they can consent to no arrangement with any power which is inconsistent with the pledges they have given.

It was in these circumstances and because—

* * * the aim of the mandatory system is to make the mandatory Power permanently responsible for the fulfillment of certain duties to those States which have adhered to the covenant of the League of Nations [that] His Majesty's Government find it difficult, therefore, to accept a proposal that the terms of the mandate should refer to any other States, whether by name or by collective definition.

---

[35] "It is important to note that this claim was preferred by the United States not against Turkey, but against its enemies with which the United States was aligned in the general conflict. To the United States the method by which the sovereignty was transferred from the Ottoman possessor was of slight concern. The significant fact, from an American point of view, was not only that some time before the conclusion of any treaty of peace Turkey had been ousted from actual control, but also that its victorious enemies had decided that there must be a new sovereign." Charles Cheney Hyde, "Charles Evans Hughes," *American Secretaries of State*, New York, 1929, vol. 10, p. 434. In this connection it is of interest to note that the fundamental contentions of the United States with respect to former German territories had been advanced before the date of the treaty with Germany of August 25, 1921. Cf. Secretary Hughes' instruction to Chargé Bell of April 2, 1921, *For. Rel.*, 1921, vol. 2, p. 279: *"the right accruing to the Allied and Associated Powers through the common victory is shared by the United States and that there could be no valid or effective disposition of the overseas possessions of Germany, now under consideration, without the assent of the United States."*
[36] *For. Rel.*, 1921, vol. 2, p. 111.

It appeared to His Majesty's Government that—

the best way to meet the wish expressed in the American note would be for the British Government to give to the Government of the United States a guarantee that citizens of the United States shall enjoy in all respects in the mandated territory the same rights and privileges as citizens of States members of the League of Nations, it being understood that they will be subject to the same conditions.

This undertaking might be embodied in an exchange of notes which might also include guarantees of the freedom of missionaries to exercise their vocation.

To the wish expressed by the Government of the United States that the consent of the United States should be obtained before any alteration was made in the text of the mandates, the British Government made objection that—

It would be difficult to insert in the mandate itself a provision of this nature as between the League of Nations and a Power which is not a member of the League. There is, however, nothing to prevent the mandatory giving a separate undertaking to this effect.

In these circumstances the best method of satisfying the desire of the United States would appear to be that His Majesty's Government, as mandatory, should give the American Government an undertaking that they will not propose nor accept any modifications in the terms of the mandate without previous *consultation* with the Government of the United States.

The terms of the British note of December 29, 1921,[37] which dealt with the Middle East, were the same, *mutatis mutandis*, as those of the note of December 22, 1921.

The general observations of the British Government were marked by reluctance to admit that the failure of the United States to approve the peace settlement had not deprived if of the rights derived from the common victory. This reluctance was reflected in the inadmissible proposal that the disposition of American rights be dealt with by an exchange of notes, instead of treaty.

There was apparent failure to distinguish between the mandate principle and the machinery for its enforcement. That principle was not inseparably bound up with the League of Nations, although the existence of that body made it possible to assure the regular scrutiny of mandatory administration. Conventional limitations even on sovereignty in an altruistic behalf are not unknown.[38]

This confusion of the mandate principle and of the method of its enforcement resulted in a misunderstanding of the relation between American substantive contention and the American suggestion that the provisions of the mandate be extended by collective definition to embrace the United States. If that suggestion was inacceptable, it was only because the mandate purported to define the relations between the League of Nations and the mandatory, thus making mention of the United States inappropriate.[39] The principle, however, to which the suggestion was intended to give effect, was the entirely valid one that as the United States had been an equal partner in the victory, its equality in the disposition of the fruits of that victory should be recognized by providing that the engagements of the mandatory should run to it also and that it should have an equal voice in the modification of the terms of administration, although it was not a member of the League of Nations and hence could not be a member of the Council.

The British Government was not left uncertain as to the inadequacy of its proposals. The presence of Mr. Balfour, as he then was, at the Washington Conference on the Limitation of Armaments afforded an opportunity for the exploration of the questions at issue. Mr. Balfour was informed that—

An undertaking on the part of the British Government that it will not propose nor accept any modification in the terms of the mandate without

[37] *For. Rel.*, 1921, vol. 2, p. 115, Crowe to Harvey, Dec. 29, 1921.

[38] One example is the British reservation of the right to safeguard the welfare of the aboriginal inhabitants of Queensland and New Guinea, title to which had been transferred to Australia, Temperley, *History of the Peace Conference*, vol. 2, p. 236. A more striking example is offered by the treaty of Managua of January 28, 1860, whereby Great Britain resigned its protectorate and recognized the sovereignty of Nicaragua over the Mosquito Indians. Article 3 of the treaty provided, however, that "The Mosquito Indians, within the district designated in the preceding Article, shall enjoy the right of governing, according to their own customs, and according to any regulations which may from time to time be adopted by them, not inconsistent with the sovereign rights of the Republic of Nicaragua, themselves, and all persons residing within such district. Subject to the above-mentioned reserve, the Republic of Nicaragua agrees to respect and not to interfere with such customs and regulations so established, or to be established within the said district;" *British and Foreign State Papers*, vol. 60, p. 96. By agreement between the parties, the question of the right of Great Britain to interpose to assure to the Mosquito Indians the performance of Article 3 of the Treaty of Managua was presented to the Emperor of Austria for decison. He held for Great Britain. See Award, July 2, 1881, in H. La Fontaine; *Pasicrisie Internationale, Histoire Documentaire des Arbitrages Internationaux*, Berne, 1902, pp. 385–393.

[39] Note, however, that the Council of the League of Nations had found no difficulty in inviting the United States to meet with it to discuss the terms of the mandates.

previous *consultation* with the Government of the United States would not, I fear, adequately meet the wish expressed in the memorandum of August last, that the consent of the United States shall be obtained before any alteration is made in the text of the mandates.[40]

The determination of the Government of the United States that its position should be in no way inferior to that of the other Principal Powers was revealed further by Secretary Hughes in the proposal that the treaty to be concluded should provide for the submission to the United States of a duplicate of the annual report to the League of Nations. A copy, Mr. Balfour was informed, would not be sufficient. Secretary Hughes wrote:

> A provision to this effect is incorporated in the treaty with Japan, relating to the mandated islands north of the Pacific, and the same provisions should be included in the treaty relating to Palestine, inasmuch as Japan has been promised that the same undertaking will be secured in the case of other mandate forms.[41]

On April 5, 1922, formal communication was made to the British Government of the views which had already been made known to it through the informal exchange with Mr. Balfour. It was stated that the Government of the United States had observed Lord Curzon's statement in the note of December 22, 1921, that it would be difficult to insert in the mandate itself a provision that the consent of the United States should be obtained before any alteration was made in the text of the mandate, and that it was not believed that such an insertion was necessary, in view of the fact, to which Lord Curzon had adverted, that there was "nothing to prevent the Mandatory giving a separate undertaking to this effect." Such an undertaking might be embodied in the proposed treaty. It would not, however, it was said, "be deemed by my Government to be sufficient to provide merely for consultation with the United States."

Mention was again made of the agreement of the Japanese Government to furnish a duplicate, not a copy, of its annual report to the League of Nations on the administration of mandated territories, and the request was made that a similar provision should be included in the treaty relating to the mandate for Palestine.[42]

By note of April 29, 1922, the British Government signified its acquiescence in the American proposals and was thereupon informed that there would be no objection to the submission of the draft mandate to the Council of the League for approval at its forthcoming meeting—

> providing that it is understood that the approval of the Mandate given by the Council of the League shall not be deemed to be binding upon the United States, but shall be subject to the assent of the United States upon the terms and conditions which have been set forth in our correspondence upon this subject.[43]

By note of June 20, 1922, the British Foreign Office transmitted to the American Ambassador at London, a draft treaty regarding the Palestine mandate. The preamble recited the Turkish renunciation of all rights and titles to Palestine, the purport of Article 22 of the Covenant of the League of Nations, Article 95 of the Treaty of Sèvres, the entrusting of the mandate to His Britannic Majesty by the Principal Allied Powers, the terms of the mandate, the issuance of the mandate upon the coming into force of the Treaty of Sèvres, the contribution of the United States to the defeat of Turkey and the Turkish renunciation of title, the desire of the President of the United States to concur in the mandate for Palestine, and the desire of His Britannic Majesty to ensure to the United States and its citizens the same rights as they would enjoy if the United States were a member of the League of Nations.[44]

The preamble of the British draft was not acceptable to the United States, because it was deemed not to be expressive of the reasons for the negotiation of the treaty, and because the United States was not a signatory of the unratified treaty of Sèvres. Hence it was suggested that there should be no reference to the treaty of Sèvres in the preamble of the treaty and that the preamble of the mandate, because of its reference to the treaty of Sèvres, should be omitted. By way of substitute, it was suggested that recitals similar to those in the other mandate conventions then in course of negotiation should be inserted.[45]

---

[40] Department of State: *Mandate for Palestine*, Washington, 1931, p. 59, Hughes to Balfour, Jan. 27, 1922.
[41] *Ibid.*
[42] *Ibid.*, pp. 61, 64–65, Harvey to Curzon, April 5, 1922.
[43] *Ibid.*, p. 67, Wheeler to Curzon, May 10, 1922.
[44] *Ibid.*, p. 70, British Foreign Office to Harvey, June 20, 1922.
[45] *Ibid.*, p. 75, Memorandum from the Department of State to the British Embassy, July 12, 1922.

Difference appears to have existed between the two Governments over the word "concurs" in Article 1 of the British draft. It was apparently felt by the Government of the United States that the word "concurs" gave inadequate recognition to the necessity for its consent to any valid determination concerning the mandated territory. This question may have been the subject of an unpublished memorandum of July 8, 1922, to which reference is made in the memorandum of July 12, mentioned above. On July 14, 1922, Ambassador Harvey wrote that while the Government of the United States desired to have the word "consents" used in the conventions relating to the African mandates—

> * * * It seems particularly appropriate that it should be used in the convention with respect to the mandate for Palestine, in view of the fact that my Government was not at war with Turkey but is interested in the disposition of former Ottoman territories, because of its participation in the war against Germany which contributed to her defeat and the defeat of her allies.[46]

On October 2, 1922, Lord Curzon informed Ambassador Harvey that the British Government

> * * * accepted the word "consents" instead of "concurs" in Article 1 of the convention, subject to the reservations already made on this point by His Majesty's representative at Washington in connection with the African mandate.[47]

The phrase "including therein equality as regards commercial opportunity", which appeared in Article 2 of the British draft, was expunged as unnecessary, since the article placed the United States and its nationals on a footing of entire equality with the members of the League of Nations and gave them the benefit of *all* the engagements of the British Government defined in the mandate.

As signed on December 3, 1924, the treaty reflected the view maintained by the United States on all important points. The preamble recited Turkey's renunciation of her rights and titles over Palestine (thus indicating merely that Turkey was no longer sovereign), the purport of Article 22 of the Covenant of the League, and the agreement of the Principal Allied Powers to entrust the mandate for Palestine to His Britannic Majesty. Then followed the text of the mandate, including the preamble, mention of the effective date of the mandate, recital of the contribution of the United States to the defeat of Germany and of her allies and to the renunciation of title by the latter, and recital of the desire of the Governments of the United States and Great Britain *"to reach a definite understanding with respect to the rights of the two governments and their respective mationals in Palestine."*

Article I of the treaty recorded the "consent" of the United States, subject to the provisions of the convention, to the administration of Palestine by the British Government, pursuant to the mandate. Article 2 gave to the United States and its nationals all the rights and benefits secured under the terms of the mandate to members of the League of Nations and their nationals, notwithstanding the fact that the United States was not a member of the League. Article 3 enjoined respect for and forbade impairment of vested American property rights in the mandated territory. Article 4 obligated the British Government to furnish to the United States a duplicate of the annual report which it was under obligation to make to the Council of the League. Article 5 accorded to American nationals the right to establish and maintain educational, philanthropic and religious institutions in the mandated territory, to receive voluntary applicants and to teach in the English language. Article 6 dealt with the application to Palestine of treaties of extradition and consular rights between the United States and Great Britain. Article 7 read:

> Nothing contained in the present convention shall be affected by any modification which may be made in the terms of the mandate, as recited above, unless such modification shall have been assented to by the United States.

In short, every aspect of the treaty reflected American equality with the Principal Allied Powers in all determinations affecting Palestine, and the necessity for American consent to such determinations was expressly recognized in Articles 1 and 7 of the treaty.

---

[46] *Ibid.*, p. 77, Harvey to Balfour, July 14, 1922.

[47] *Ibid.*, p. 82, Curzon to Harvey, Oct. 2, 1922. It appears probable that the reservation related to the position of the British Government under the Treaty of Versailles. The triumph of the American contention indicates, however, that it was conceded that, whatever the agreement of the Principal Allied Powers with respect to their own interests in former enemy territories, they could not, without the consent of the United States, deal with the interests of the latter.

Elucidation of the legal consequences of Articles 1 and 7 requires some analysis of the nature of a mandate [48] and of the relations between the League, the Mandatory and the United States. As authoritatively interpreted in the note of March 1, 1921, from the President of the Council of the League of Nations to Secretary of State Colby, a mandate "defines the responsibilities and limits the powers of the governments entrusted with the administration of various territories, outside Europe, formerly in the possession of Germany and Turkey." [49] In other words, a mandate lays down the terms upon which, and the purposes for which, a limited transfer of rights of jurisdiction is made, and creates an international responsibility to bring about the realization of the declared purposes of the mandate by application of its provisions.

The mandates are not themselves instruments of transfer.[50] The transfers of former German and Turkish territories were made by the Principal Allied and Associated Powers, in whom the right to make such transfers lodged by virtue of their common victory over the former sovereigns of the territories transferred. Thus, the agreement of the Principal Allied Powers to transfer Palestine to Great Britain for administration under mandate was reached at the meeting of the Supreme Council at San Remo on April 24, 1920.[51] The agreement of the United States to such transfer was given by Article 1 of the Treaty of December 3, 1924.

The determination whether the transfers of former German and former Turkish territories should be absolute or limited, in sovereign fee or for international purposes, rested with the states which had won the victory. Preliminary agreement had been reached by the Council of Ten of the Peace Conference at the meeting of January 30, 1919, that the transfers should be limited and for purposes of international concern; the subsidiary questions of allocation (transfer) of territory for administration under mandate and of definition of the terms of administration were postponed.[52] The agreement to make such limited transfers for purposes of international concern was recorded in Article 22 of the Treaty of Versailles as follows:

> To those colonies and territories which as a consequence of the late war have ceased to be under the sovereignty of the States which formerly governed them and which are inhabited by peoples not yet able to stand by themselves under the strenuous conditions of the modern world, there should be applied the principle that the well-being and development of such peoples form a sacred trust of civilization and that securities for the performance of this trust should be embodied in this Covenant.
>
> The best method of giving practical effect to this principle is that the tutelage of such peoples should be entrusted to advanced nations who by reason of their resources, their experience, or their geographical position can best undertake this responsibility, and who are willing to accept it, and that this tutelage should be exercised by them as Mandatories on behalf of the League.

In the case of Palestine, it had been announced by the British Government as early as November 2, 1917, that the future administration of that country should be directed to the realization of the purposes set forth in the declaration issued on that date, which read:

His Majesty's Government view with favour the establishment in Palestine of a national home for the Jewish people, and will use their best endeavors to facilitate the achievement of this object, it being clearly understood that nothing shall be done which may prejudice the civil and religious rights of existing non-Jewish communities in Palestine, or the rights and political status enjoyed by the Jews in any other country.

The adoption of that declaration by the other Allied Powers and its approval by President Wilson and by the Congress of the United States transformed it into an expression of purposes of international concern to be realized in the future administration of Palestine.[53]

The agreement of the Principal Allied Powers to transfer the right to exercise jurisdiction in Palestine to Great Britain was conditioned on the employment of

---

[48] See Quincy Wright, *Mandates Under the League of Nations*, Chicago, 1930, p. 364, n. 48, for an analysis of the uses of the term "mandate".

[49] Department of State, *Mandate for Palestine*, Washington, 1931, p. 43

[50] See report by M. Hymans to the Council, *Assembly Document* No. 161, Dec. 6, 1920, p. 17.

[51] Cf. Articles 95 and 96 of the Treaty of Sèvres, of August 10, 1920.

[52] Baker, *Woodrow Wilson and the World Settlement*, Garden City, 1921, vol. 1, p. 272.

[53] By France on February 9, 1918, by Italy on February 25, 1918, by Japan in December 1918, by President Wilson in a letter to Rabbi Stephen S. Wise of August 1918, again by him on March 2, 1919, and by the Congress of the United States by Joint Resolution signed by President Harding on September 21, 1922, Public, No. 73, 67th Congress.

that right to give effect to the Balfour Declaration, and the transfer was made in order that the right might be so exercised. The consent of the United States to the administration of Palestine by Great Britain which was granted in Article 1 of the Treaty of December 3, 1924, was likewise so conditioned:

> Subject to the provisions of the present convention the United States consents to the administration of Palestine by His Britannic Majesty, pursuant to the mandate recited above.

The consent of the United States was thus a consent to a limited exercise of rights of jurisdiction, that is, to an exercise of such rights *"pursuant to the mandate"* which was designed to give effect to the common policy of the Principal Allied and Associated Powers expressed in the Balfour Declaration.

The legal consequence of such limited transfer, as Professor Wright points out, is that—

> as the Mandatory is incompetent to act beyond the scope of the Mandate, a treaty [or other act] which violated that instrument would be void.[54]

There was no transfer to the mandatory of title to the territory, of sovereignty over the territory, or of the right to use such powers as were granted for any other purposes or in any other manner than was prescribed in the instrument of direction and definition, the mandate.

As Professor Brierly observes—

> * * * The mandatory's rights, like the trustee's, have their foundation in his obligations; they are tools given to him in order to achieve the work assigned to him; he has "all the tools necessary for such end, but only those." [55]

As was stated by M. Van Rees, the Dutch member of the Permanent Mandates Commission, in an early memorandum:

> * * * That which has "passed" or been "transferred" to the governor has been handed over to him as governor and not as State; consequently, there has been no final alienation, and no real rights have been acquired by that State; the territory, property, possessions and rights * * * do not belong to the mandatory State but have merely been placed at its disposal; it has been granted their use in order that it may carry out its duties as governor with which it has been entrusted.[56]

Professor Wright points out that—

> * * * The mandatories have usually recognized in the form of their legislation, that their authority flows not from territorial sovereignty but from jurisdictional rights in foreign territory and consequently that the mandated territories are not within the national domain * * *.[57]

These conclusions have been judicially sanctioned. In 1926 the Supreme Court of Palestine declared:

> To hold that the petitioners are British subjects would involve holding that the crown having accepted responsibility to govern Palestine as a mandatory has acquired sovereignty, a view for which no authority has been cited.[58]

Nor has there been any transfer of sovereignty to the League: it has neither title to the territory nor may it exercise jurisdiction therein. By Lord Balfour, speaking in the Council of the League in 1922, the powers of the League were defined in terms of obligation as follows:

> * * * The duty of the League * * * was first to see that the terms of the mandates were in conformity with the principles of the Covenant and, secondly, that these terms would, in fact, regulate the policy of the Mandatory Powers in the mandated territory.[59]

Sir John Fischer Williams has described the position of the League as follows:

> The League itself * * * is not the owner of the sovereignty; the position of the League is rather analogous to that of the judicial authority— in England, in past times, the Lord Chancellor and now the appropriate division of the High Court of Justice—which supervises the execution of the trust.[60]

[54] Wright, *op. cit.*, p. 482.
[55] *British Yearbook of International Law*, 1929, p. 219.
[56] Permanent Mandates Commission, *Minutes of the Third Session*, P. 221.
[57] Wright, *op. cit.*, p. 401.
[58] *A. J. I. L.* (1926), vol. 20, p. 771.
[59] *Official Journal of the League of Nations*, 1922, 0. 546.
[60] Williams, *Aspects of the Covenant of the League*, London, 1932, pp. 208–209.

Professor Arnold McNair, the learned editor of Oppenheim, writes:

> Article 22 of the Covenant   *   *   *   defines the terms upon which the Allied Powers, who signed and ratified the Peace Treaties and as victors could all claim some interest in the future of the territories acquired from their enemies, assented to the disposition and government of those territories, and entrusted to the League the supervision of the scheme embodied in that article   *   *   *.[61]

M. Rolin's conclusion was that—

> Article 22 does not imply the transfer of any portion of that sovereignty to the League of Nations.[62]

Since there has been no transfer to the mandatory or to the League of ultimate possession of the mandated territory, or of any rights in excess of those defined in the mandate, the question of the ultimate disposition of such territory remains to be determined by the Principal Allied Powers or their successors. In the case of the Principal Allied Powers, the right to a voice in the ultimate disposition of the territory appears to have been surrendered to the Council and the Assembly of the League of Nations, although one writer at least is of opinion that—

> *   *   *   As the treaties stand the ultimate disposition of the Mandated Territories rests with the Principal Allied and Associated Powers.[63]

However it may be with the rights of the Principal Allied Powers, whether they have transferred to the mandatory one part of their rights and have conveyed to the League of Nations all the rest, there has been no surrender by the United States of its right to a voice in determination affecting the mandated territory. The consent of the United States to the administration of Palestine by Great Britain, *pursuant to the mandate*, did not involve the transfer of any American rights to the League of Nations, and the League's powers of supervision are therefore exercised only within the ambit of the rights formerly possessed by the Principal Allied Powers. The United States, therefore, retained the right to require the mandatory to restrain its exercise of rights of jurisdiction within the limits by which American consent to British administration of Palestine was qualified.

In providing that the conditions by which American consent to British administration of Palestine was limited should not be altered without American consent, it was necessary, since the mandate in which those conditions were defined was in form an instrument of League provenance, to avoid any suggestion of interference in the relations between the League and the mandatory Power. It would have been inappropriate, as the British Government had previously indicated,[64] to provide in the mandate itself that a nonmember of the League should give its consent to an alteration in the terms of the mandate. It would have been equally inappropriate to declare in the treaty that the consent of the United States should be necessary to an alteration in the relations between the League of Nations and one of its members.

The same technical problem had arisen earlier in the negotiations between Japan and the United States relating to the mandate for the former island possessions of Germany in the North Pacific. The American requirement was that no change should be made in the terms of the mandate without the express consent of the United States. In a memorandum of October 17, 1921, the Japanese Government acceded to this demand in the following language:

> It is proposed in the last paragraph of the Memorandum of the Secretary of State that the terms of the Mandate which are to be recited in the proposed Convention between the United States and Japan, and of which the United States is to have the benefit, shall not be modified without the express consent of the United States. The Japanese Government understand it to be the meaning of this proposal that nothing contained in the new American-Japanese Convention shall be affected by any modification which may be made in the terms of the Mandate recited in the Convention, unless and until such modification shall have been expressly assented to by the United States. They are prepared to accept the insertion of a provision in this sense.[65]

Accordingly, in the treaty with Japan of February 11, 1922, the fifth paragraph of Article 2 read:

---

[61] Oppenheim, *International Law* (4th ed.), London, 1928, vol. 1, p. 203.
[62] Rolin, "Le système des mandats coloniaux", *Revue de Droit Internationa let Legislation Comparèe* (1920), 3ème sér,. tome 1, p. 347.
[63] Freda White, *Mandates*, London, 1926, pp. 165-166.
[64] *For. Rel.*, 1921, vol. 2, p. 111.
[65] *For. Rel.*, 1921, vol. 2, p. 301.

Nothing contained in the present Convention shall be affected by any modification which may be made in the terms of the Mandate as recited in the Convention, unless such modification shall have been expressly assented to by the United States.

The provision in the Japanese treaty was used without change in the Palestine Convention. Thereby the rights enjoyed by the United States as a result of the victory and its rights under Article 2 of the treaty were placed beyond the possibility of impairment without its consent, while all suggestion of entanglement with the League was avoided.

It is believed that the foregoing analysis justifies the following conclusion. The failure of the mandatory Power to adhere to the provisions of the mandate in any respect involves a "disposition" of the territory in excess of that made under the terms of the treaty of December 3, 1924. To the extent of such excess, the mandatory Power is acting *ultra vires*, since the directions of the mandate as to the manner in which, or the purposes for which, the mandatory's rights of jurisdiction are to be exercised are integral conditions of the exercise of jurisdiction. Any departure from the directions of the mandate, therefore, is tantamount to a tacit enlargement of the rights of jurisdiction to the exercise of which the United States consented, and modifies the conditions upon which that consent was given. Such a modification is a clear violation of Article 7 of the treaty.

Quite apart, therefore, from any question whether, in failing to adhere to the terms of the mandate, the mandatory Power has been guilty of a violation of its affirmative obligations to the United States under Article 2 of the treaty, it is manifest that the United States has undoubted legal authority, by reason of Articles 1 and 7 of the treaty, for protesting against the failure of the mandatory Power to respect the limitations by which American consent to British administration of Palestine was conditioned, and for protesting against modification of the terms of the mandate without the consent of the United States, as it had for its original insistence that no valid determination could be made concerning Palestine without its concurrence.

These conclusions are confirmed by the interpretation subsequently placed by the parties themselves upon the meaning of Article 7 of the treaty of December 3, 1924, and upon the parallel articles in other conventions relating to mandated territories.

In 1922 the British Government had invited the Council of the League to give effect to Article 25 of the mandate by declaring that the second and third recitals in the preamble of the mandate, parts of Articles 2, 7, and 11, bearing on the establishment of the Jewish National Home, and Articles 4, 6, 13, 14, 22, and 23 in their entirety were not applicable to Trans-Jordan.[66]

On April 30, 1924, before the signing of the Treaty, the Government of the United States addressed a note to the British Government, which read in part as follows:

My Government's attention has been called to a note of the Secretary General of the League of Nations dated September 23, 1922 (C667 M396, 1922 V. I.), relating to Article 25 of the Palestine mandate, which indicated that the Council of the League of Nations had approved a memorandum submitted by the British representative outlining the provisions of the mandate for Palestine which are not to be applicable to the territory known as Trans-Jordan, as therein defined. In this memorandum it is stated that His Majesty's Government accept full responsibility as mandatory for Trans-Jordan, and that such provision as may be made for the administration of that territory in accordance with Article 25 of the mandate shall be in no way inconsistent with those provisions of the mandate which are not by the resolution declared inapplicable.

Upon the conclusion of the convention between the United States and Great Britain with respect to Palestine, it is my Government's understanding that the convention will be applicable to such territory as may be under British mandate to the East, as well as to the West of the River Jordan, and that, in view of the provisions of Article 7 as proposed, no further change will be made with respect to the *conditions of the British administration* of the territory known as Trans-Jordan without the previous assent of my Government. I am instructed to inquire whether the British Government is in accord with this view.[67]

Apparently misinterpreting the phrase "conditions of the British Administration," the British Government replied on July 17, 1924, as follows:

[66] Note of the Secretary-General of the League of Nations, Sept. 23, 1922, *Cmd.* 1785, p. 10.
[67] Department of State, *op. cit.*, p. 87, Kellogg to MacDonald, April 30, 1924.

3. As regards the penultimate paragraph of your note, His Majesty's Government agree that the present convention shall be applicable to such territory as may be under British mandate to the East as well as to the West of the River Jordan. They regret, however, that they can not concur in the interpretation put by the United States Government on Article 7 of the draft convention as regards changes in the administration of Trans-Jordania, as it is essential that they be allowed latitude to make changes in the administration of that territory in such manner as may appear necessary, *provided that such action does not conflict with the terms of the mandate.*

By note of September 2, 1924, Ambassador Kellogg replied that it had not been the intention of his Government to suggest the necessity of consultation in matters relating to minor administrative changes in Trans-Jordania:

* * * It is my Government's view, as briefly set forth in my communication of April 30, last, that it would be entirely consistent with the general policy which is followed by states enjoying mandatory administration over territories relinquished by the Central powers as a result of the late war to consult with this Government as well as with the states represented on the Council of the League of Nations in connection with any general changes in the form of the mandatory administration of Trans-Jordania.

4. My Government had, however, noted the statement contained in your communication that the Palestine convention shall be applicable to territory under British mandate to the East as well as to the West of the River Jordan and the further statement that *the changes which may be made in the administration of the territory will not be of a character to conflict with the terms of the mandate.* My Government is not therefore disposed to delay the conclusion of the Palestine convention for the purpose of entering into a further discussion of the questions relating to Trans-Jordania, since the essential points in which my Government is interested, appear to be safeguarded by the assurances already given, which are understood also to embody the undertaking that the changes which may be made in the administration of the territory will not be of such a character as to conflict with the terms of the convention.[68]

On November 10, 1924, the British Government gave the assurance that it would consult the United States, as well as the powers represented on the Council of the League of Nations, regarding any alteration in the administration of Trans-Jordania for which the British Government might decide to seek the approval of the Council.[69]

Much the same question arose in connection with the Iraq mandate. By Article 6 of the Convention and Protocol of January 9, 1930, between the United States, Great Britain and Iraq, it was provided that—

No modification of the special relations existing between His Britannic Majesty and His Majesty the King of Iraq, as defined in Article 1 (other than the termination of such special relations as contemplated in Article 7 of the present Convention) shall make any change in the rights of the United States as defined in this Convention, unless such change has been assented to by the Government of the United States.

Article 7 provided that upon the termination of the special relations mentioned in Article 6, the United States and Iraq were to negotiate a treaty in regard to their future relations and the rights of the nationals of each in the territories of the other. Pending the conclusion of such an agreement, each state was to enjoy most-favored-nation treatment in the territory of the other.

When the question of the termination of the Iraq mandate arose in 1932, the Government of the United States informed the British Government that while the right of the United States to consultation with respect to the termination of the "special relations" between Great Britain and Iraq had been waived, *the right to consultation with respect to the conditions under which Iraq was to be administered upon the cessation of the mandatory relationship had not been waived.* It was said that—

Since the termination of a regime in a mandated territory necessarily involves the "disposition"[1] of that territory and affects the interests of American nationals therein, the right of the United States to be consulted with respect to the conditions under which the territory is subsequently to be administered is on precisely the same basis as its right to be consulted with regard to the establishment of a mandatory regime.

[68] *Ibid.*, p. 93, Kellogg to MacDonald, September 2, 1924.
[69] *Ibid.*, p. 95, Chamberlain to Kellogg, November 10, 1924.

In its reply of April 1, 1932, the British Government observed that the termination of the mandate was expressly excepted from the operation of Article 6 and was dealt with by Article 7, which laid down what was to happen upon the termination of the mandate. The provisions of the treaty did not confer on the United States any right to be consulted—

> as to the obligations which the League of Nations may require Iraq to undertake as conditions of the termination of the mandatory regime, and of her election as a member of the League of Nations.

Nevertheless, His Majesty's Government was happy to keep the United States informed of the progress of events in regard to the termination of the mandatory regime in Iraq. The United States was informed that, on January 28, 1932, the Council had declared itself ready in principle to pronounce the termination of the mandate, provided that Iraq gave certain assurances, the purpose of which was solely to discharge the responsibilities of the League, as trustee, to minorities in Iraq and to legitimate foreign interests in the country. Those assurances were still in process of elaboration at the date of writing and His Majesty's Government would be glad to communicate them to the Government of the United States as soon as it was possible to do so.

In an aide-memoire of July 8, 1932, reply was made that, from information which it had already received from other sources, the Government of the United States was satisfied that the assurances to be given by Iraq, to the benefits of which American nationals would be entitled under the provisions of Article 7 of the Tripartite Convention of January 9, 1930, would afford adequate protection to legitimate American interests in Iraq. No useful purpose would be served, therefore, by continuing the discussions with the British Government concerning the right of the United States to be consulted with respect to the future conditions of administration of Iraq. At the same time the Government of the United States declared that it could not fully accept the British interpretation of the position of the United States vis-a-vis Iraq.

> *   *   * while the American Government concedes that by the terms of the Tripartite Convention it waived its right to consultation with respect to the actual termination of the mandate, it considers that *the right was retained to be consulted with respect to the conditions under which Iraq is to be administered upon such termination.* This Government is therefore of the opinion that *in addition to the most-favored-nation treatment,* which, by virtue of the provisions of the Tripartite Convention of January 9, 1930 it will enjoy in Iraq upon the termination of the special relation, *it is also entitled to a voice in the determination of the conditions upon which that most-favored-nation treatment is to be used.*
>
> Accordingly the American Government desires to make a full reservation of its position in this matter and, with a view to avoiding any possible misconception which may arise in the future, to make clear that its action *in refraining from insisting upon a fulfillment of its rights in the case of Iraq is not be be construed as an abandonment of the principle established in 1921 that the approval of the United States is essential to the validity of any determination which may be reached regarding mandated territories.*[70]

The foregoing exchange indicates conclusively that it is the American view that in negotiating the treaties relating to the mandated territories the United States neither diminished nor surrendered any of the rights which accrued to it by reason of the participation in the common victory. The treaty was, as the note of July 8, 1932, indicated, not an act of surrender, but an act of consent which left untouched such rights as were not expressly or by necessary implication given up.

The Belgian Mandate for East Africa also affords evidence that the consent of the United States is required for any valid modification of a mandate once agreed to. By treaty signed at Brussels on April 18, 1923, the United States consented to the Belgian administration of East Africa under mandate. After the signing of the treaty, the Belgian Government applied to the Government of the United States for its assent to a modification of the boundaries of the mandated territory which was given by a protocol signed at Brussels on January 21, 1924. The preamble of the protocol recites the modification of the boundary and its approval by the Council of the League, the requirement of Article 5 of the treaty between

---

[70] Department of State, *Press Releases*, Nov. 5, 1932, pp. 300–306. Because of the wish of the United States that its position in the matter should be made clear to the members of the League, the British Foreign Office, by letter of October 11, 1932, transmitted to the Secretary General of the League copies of the correspondence paraphrased above; *Official Journal of the League of Nations*, 1933, pp. 152–154.

the United States and Belgium relating to the assent of the United States to modifications in the mandate and the fact that the Government of the United States perceived no objection to the modification in question. The operative provision reads:

Article 1 of the mandate recited in the preamble of the Treaty signed April 18, 1923, shall be replaced by the following [there follows the new description]. [71]

PALESTINE'S ROLE IN THE SOLUTION OF THE JEWISH PROBLEM

By Chaim Weizmann [72]

Almost half the Jews in the world find themselves today under the Nazi heel It is impossible to determine the rate at which their physical destruction is proceeding. Nor is it possible to visualize the condition in which the Jewish masses of Poland, Rumania, occupied Russia, and even Hungary will be found when the pall of darkness is finally lifted from Nazi-occupied Europe. Tragic as is the position of the Polish peasant, he is rooted in his native soil—at least where he has not been dragged away from it and made to slave in an armament factory. The Jew in his Ghetto, on the other hand, finds himself despoiled of everything. Deprived of his meagre possessions, driven from his home, torn from his family, he has become the most abject of all the abject victims of the terror. In the reconstruction of a new and—let us hope—a better world, the reintegration of the Jew will thus present a peculiarly difficult problem, and one which is likely to tax both the energies and the good will of the countries of Eastern and Central Europe.

The experience of the past twenty years, and the vexed problem of "minorities" which has caused so much trouble in Europe, hardly give much ground for hope of a satisfactory solution on the spot. No doubt many Jews will return and readapt themselves to the new conditions; but there will be vast masses which will have to emigrate. It would probably be unduly optimistic to assume that countries like the United States, Canada, and some of the South American republics, will radically change their immigration policy after this war—particularly in the strained economic conditions then to be expected. The hunted and disinherited will once more be faced with the eternal question: "Whither"? And little promise can be held out for them unless decisive steps are taken towards a radical solution of their problem.

It is a complex problem, which means that it will have to be faced with courage, imagination, and sympathy. After the agonizing experiences through which European Jewry has passed in the last eight years, no makeshift or temporary expedients can suffice, and indeed such would be unworthy of the spirit of the Atlantic Charter and the principles so often enunciated by the leaders of the democracies. Responsibility for the solution will rest with those charged with the task of reconstruction, and also with the Jewish communities which have escaped the fate of their European brethren. Of the latter, it is estimated that the Jews in the Western Hemisphere number about five millions; in the British Empire about half a million; in Palestine about half a million; and there are smaller communities in Turkey, Egypt, Syria, Iraq, India, and French North Africa, totalling perhaps a further half-million (though some of them can hardly be ranked as "free" communities).

The Nazi attack on the Jews came at first as a rude shock to the outside world. But its effects soon wore off. Many European statesmen and politicians found it convenient to treat the whole business as a purely internal German affair; they felt it more "politic" not to consider its darker implications. Persecution of the Jews, as practised by the Nazis, has served many useful purposes of the persecutors. They have succeeded in ridding themselves of a group which, by reason of its longstanding liberal democratic traditions, could never have made real peace with the new régime. They have enriched themselves considerably from the wealth of their victims, and have thus been able to increase the "wages of sin" available for payment to their friends and adherents. They have flooded neighboring countries with tens of thousands of refugees who, though generously received and

---

[71] *Treaty Series*, No. 704; see also Permanent Mandates Commission, *Minutes of the Fourth Session*, p. 65.
[72] Dr. Weizmann is the president of the World Jewish Agency for Palestine. The article appeared in *Foreign Affairs*, January 1942.

befriended, were almost bound—once the first emotional wave of pity and indignation had subsided—to cause difficulties and create problems and friction, contributing thereby to the bedevilment of relations between Jew and Gentile even in tolerant and free countries like England or pre-war France or Switzerland. This part of the Nazi scheme has not fully succeeded. It has, however, made the West "Jew-conscious"—aware of one more complexity in a life already overcrowded with urgent problems.

As the numbers of refugees swelled, it became obvious that their problems required a fresh approach and coordinated effort on the part of the Powers. The President of the United States, animated by humanitarian considerations and generous implulses, initiated two conferences. The intention was that representatives of Europe and America should devise ways and means of assisting the wanderers, of enabling them to begin a new life without becoming a burden on the communities which had offered them temporary shelter.

The Evian Conference achieved something, but on the whole, the measures there adopted were mere palliatives. Attempts naturally were made to find a radical solution—e. g. the delimitation of a territory somewhere on the earth's surface to which the stream of immigration could be diverted, a territory vast enough to allow the refugee to begin a new life without having to insinuate himself into the pores of an already mature organism. Many countries were mentioned, and even seriously considered. The Polish Government sent a Commission of Experts to Madagascar; the British Government sent one to British Guiana; Alaska was named as a possible "territory;" so was Santo Domingo, as also a remote part of Southern California bordering on Mexico. There is no reason why these geographical exercises should not be continued indefinitely. But the countries under discussion had all to be admitted to be either too hot or too cold; none could be discovered in the temperate zone.

Curiously enough, a *mot d'ordre* seemed to have gone out to pass over in silence the possibilities of Palestine. This was the more remarkable in view of the contribution which Palestine had even then making to the solution of the refugee problem. Refugees had flocked to this small country in tens of thousands, and had been absorbed with great advantage to themselves and to the country. New settlements had sprung up, old settlements had been expanded, new industries had arisen. Up to the beginning of the war, about 100,000 refugees from Greater Germany had found homes in Palestine. The reason for this studied silence was no doubt the British Government's desire not to emphasize Palestine in the role of a country of mass-immigration, since to do so might, in their view, complicate the already rather disturbed internal conditions prevailing there. But apart from this there was always the opinion (shared by many participants in the Evian Conference) that Palestine was too small to meet the pressing need. This view was fostered by the advocates of the various utopias who gathreed on the fringe of the Conference, and in particular by certain Jewish philanthropic (and perhaps anti-Zionist) groups, who were prepared to send their fellow-Jews to almost any country in the world, provided only that it was not Palestine. Even now one has still to contend with the recurrent argument that Palestine lacks sufficient size. Admittedly the argument is one which has to be answered—and answered it can be.

Two great colonizing experiments have been made by Jews in the past fifty or sixty years, one in the Argentine and the other in Palestine. Colonization in the Argentine was begun under the best possible auspices. Practically unlimited areas of fertile soil were at the disposal of the settlers; a benevolent government placed no obstacles in their way. The price of land was moderate, and the committee conducting the operations had great resources at its disposal (something like £10,000,000 in gold, which, fifty years ago, represented a vast sum of money). The Jewish Colonization Association was a body of most competent men, commanding great authority in the Jewish world, and devoted to their work. They acquired some 1,500,000 acres of land for agricultural settlement. But after fifty years of colonization, no more than 30,000 people have been settled there. Moreover, the younger generation of the settlers shows little disposition to remain on the land.

The first modern settlers to arrive in Palestine, on the other hand, were mostly poor young students who had abandoned Russian universities in search of a free, independent, and simple life. This they intended to make for themselves on the soil of Palestine. They entered upon their task without experience, without funds, unaided and untutored. The leaders of the Jewish communities looked askance at this quixotic undertaking, and prophesied its early and dismal failure. Moreover, the Turkish Government placed every imaginable difficulty in the way of the first pioneers. It was an upstream passage for them. But the men who set out on it were inspired by a sacred faith in a future. They were the men of destiny, called upon to blaze the trail—however narrow and steep—on which later generations were to tread. Their awareness of a great mission sustained them, and gave them the endurance and spirit of sacrifice which laid the foundations of the first Jewish settlements—chiefly in the coastal plain. Small in their beginnings, these villages have grown gradually and continually. They have a place—and a very honorable place—in the development of Jewish life in Palestine, and with them will always be associated the name of their founder—Baron Edmond de Rothschild—a man whose heart and power of vision were as great as his wealth. At first it was a mere trickle of new settlers which came to join them, rising after 1905, and in full tide since 1919.

Today there are in Palestine some 250 Jewish rural settlements, with a population of more than 140,000. Towns have been built up and industries established. The country has been awakened from its age-long neglect. The ancient Hebrew tongue has been revived, and is heard today in the fields and orchards of Palestine, in the streets and workshops, as well as in the schools and the University. The total acreage of land in Jewish hands—acquired by slow degrees by purchase in the open market—is now approximately 400,000 acres. On this land a close-knit, well-organized, modern Jewish community of over half-a-million souls has arisen. It is normal in every way—in its structure, its occupational distribution—and the whole edifice, moral, social, and intellectual, has been built up in a comparatively short space of time by the efforts of the Jews themselves on the neglected land of Palestine. Jewish labor, highly organized and creative, has played a leading part in this performance.

It should be realized that the labor movement in Palestine is not just a copy of the labor or trades-union movements in other countries. Its object is to create a Jewish working class by fostering Jewish immigration and the absorption of the immigrants into the expanding economy of the country. Its field of activity and the structure of its organization are shaped accordingly. Apart from purely trades-union activities, it comprises agricultural settlements, building guilds, industrial cooperatives, transport cooperatives, cultural institutions, and so on. It unites all workers in town and country who live by labor without exploiting the labor of others, i. e., hired laborers, members of guilds and cooperatives, independent small-holders, and collective settlement groups. Sir Arthur Wauchope, for seven years British High Commissioner for Palestine, speaks of the last-named in the following terms:

These 30,000 Jewish settlers have not only in theory, but in actual practice, solved the problem of the equal distribution of wealth, by the simple, if drastic, method of having none. * * * During the last 20 or 30 years the Jewish immigrants have proved most successful farmers. The villagers generally prefer mixed farming. They own many herds of dairy cattle, the number of their sheep and poultry increases every year. * * * In over 80 well established settlements the land is held in common, and not only the land, but also the produce, the means of production and transport, are all owned by the community as a whole.[73]

There is, of course, no compulsion about these communal settlements nor any state control (as in Russia). The farms are run by mutual agreement among their members, and communal organization of the settlement's economic life does not interfere with the freedom of the individual or of the family.

The passing of Palestine from Turkish to British rule, and the policy of the Balfour Declaration and the Mandate (grudgingly and halfheartedly though they were applied), have provided the indispensable background for this development. But the decisive factor has been the character of the immigrant, and his consciousness of returning to his homeland. The Balfour Declaration was a call to Jewish honor and dignity, and it was answered with all the sacred zeal latent in an oppressed people.

From the last 20 years of trial and error certain conclusions can be drawn about the possibilities of Palestine in connection with future mass-immigration. Two salient facts emerge.

A Jewish family can live on five acres (20 dunams) of irrigated land—in some cases on even less—provided the scientific principles of modern mixed farming are applied. Many such settlements have been established in recent years, where people live by the labor of their hands, employ no hired labor, and lead lives of modest toil. They have acquired a sense of security; modern social institutions provide them with many amenities of life; they can give their children a sound

[73] Address delivered at the Overseas League, London, April 8, 1941.

education, and pay back the investment in easy instalments over a period of 30 years or so. The repayments go to the Jewish Agency, which employs the funds for further colonization. Most of the settlers also find themselves in a position to put by something for a rainy day. In the case of nonirrigable land, some 15 acres (60 dunams) are needed for a family.

It is not easy to establish with precision the area of land available. Much of the land which figures in surveys as "uncultivable" is so described by the Government because account has been taken only of the standards and methods of the average Arab cultivator, and not of modern methods of cultivation. Adding together the large uncultivated area south of the Gaza-Beersheba line, the irrigable free stretches in the Jordan and other valleys, and the Maritime Plain, and allowing for some intensification of agriculture in the hills, it is hardly over-optimistic to say that at least 100,000 more Jewish families can be settled on the land. Experience shows, further, that for every family which settles on the land, three others are absorbed in urban pursuits—industry and commerce. Room can therefore be created for something like 400,000 families, or nearly two million souls. This is likely to be approximately the number of people whom Palestine will in fact have to take care of very rapidly after the war in order to relieve to some extent the terrible misery in the distressed areas of Europe.

But is an appreciable industrial development to be reckoned on in a country with very limited natural resources? Compare Palestine with Switzerland. This is another small country, also poor in natural resources; yet the Swiss people have built up a firmly-founded and varied industry, including engineering, electrical, chemical, and textile industries, food products, manufacture of watches and other instruments of precision, which enjoys an excellent reputation in the world market for quality products. The country is prosperous; the standard of life high; all in all, it is one of the most orderly and stable of European democracies. Two causes have contributed to this result. First, the character of the Swiss people, moulded by their hard struggle with nature. In carrying their civilization up to the snow-line, they have had to contend for every inch of ground and extract out of it the maximum of subsistence. A sturdy and disciplined race has grown up, with a deep belief in, and respect for, moral and intellectual values. The second element in Switzerland's success is her central geographical position, which affords her easy access to the great European markets.

Roughly similar conditions obtain in Palestine. There, too, the population has to face a hard struggle with a soil neglected for centuries, denuded of vegetation, and so eroded that its reconstruction involves great expenditure of energy. But Jews have been trained in the school of adversity, and are patient and persevering. Besides, they have no choice: they must succeed or go under. The Jews also have a long tradition of intellecutal training and are learning rapidly to apply it to the problems of their new life. Palestine's geographical position is even more favorable than that of Switzerland, lying as it does on the sea and at the cross-roads of the great trade routes of the Old World—a bridge between East and West. There are already in Palestine considerable industrial achievements. There are the great electric works on the Jordan; the Dead Sea works near Jericho, which produce potash, bromine, etc., and are capable of further expansion into an important basic heavy chemical industry; oil and soap works, a modern cement factory, and an iron foundry in Haifa; a textile industry (cotton and silk); a clothing industry; canned fruit, jam, furniture, drug, and shoe factories; various small engineering works with modern workshops, in which repairs are now being effectively carried out for the British Army; and a number of minor industries. In all, Palestinian Jewish industry employs today some 35,000 persons and has an annual output valued at some £13,000,000. In the first year of the war it supplied the Army with goods to the value of £1,000,000, and with as much again in the first five months of the second year. This industrial war effort is due entirely to the initiative of the Jews themselves; it could be greatly intensified if afforded reasonable encouragement and opportunity. Just as Palestine could now do much more for the war effort, so after the war it can make— given suitable economic and political conditions—a much greater contribution than so far it has been allowed to make.

The financial responsibility of the Jewish people in connection with the absorption of some millions of new settlers in Palestine will be heavy. Jewish money sunk in Palestine so far amounts to roughly $500,000,000, of which public funds account for some 15 percent while the rest is private investment. This represents an investment of about $1,000 per settler. The immigration and settlement of each 100,000 persons would accordingly require $100,000,000. Only a fraction of this sum could be expected from voluntary contributions.

The financing of such a large-scale operation over a period of years would necessitate the raising of state loans. These would have to be repaid from the revenue of the country. But this would demand a radical modification of the Palestinian fiscal system. The very conspicuous increase in its state income has been due almost entirely to the rapid development initiated by the Jews; but financial control has been vested in the Government of Palestine, and the Jewish Agency has had to rely entirely on private contributions. Today the impoverishment of the Jewish masses of Europe is so complete that one can no longer count on any substantial contributions from European Jewry.

In 1937 a Royal Commission under the late Lord Peel came to the conclusion that the present form of administration in Palestine had outlived its usefulness.[74] It recommended the partition of the country into two states—a Jewish state in the west and North, embracing the Maritime Plain and Galilee, and an Arab state to the east and south. Without entering here into the question of how far such a second limitation of the area of the Jewish National Home (already truncated in 1922 by the severance of Transjordan) could be justified, I merely record the fact that the Jews, dissatisfied as they were with the area actually allotted to the Jewish state, were nevertheless prepared to try and negotiate a settlement on the basis of the principles laid down in the Peel Report. But the plan, though at first accepted by the British Government, was subsequently abandoned under Arab pressure. Arab states like Iraq and Egypt, which had no *locus standi* in Palestinian affairs, were first allowed, and later encouraged, to exercise a powerful influence, and the Arabs were lined up in a united front against the Jewish National Home. The Government held a conference in London with the Arabs and the Jews; and, after much manoeuvering, it laid down its own policy in the White Paper of May 1939. The principal features of this policy were: complete stoppage of Jewish immigration after another five years (during which period the total Jewish immigration was not to exceed 75,000); Jewish acquisition of land to be restricted to certain diminutive areas (the first modern case of discrimination against the Jews under the British flag); and the establishment of a "Palestinian" state in which the Arabs, artificially secured of a two-to-one majority, would naturally have administrative control of the country. This policy was opposed by Labor and Liberal leaders in the House of Commons, and by leading Conservatives, foremost Mr. Churchill, who severely criticized it in his famous speech of May 23, 1939. It was condemned by the Mandates Commission as incompatible with the spirit and letter of the Mandate. In fact, its sole purpose was to appease the Arabs. But events in Egypt, Iraq, and elsewhere, and the attitude of many Arabs even in Palestine and Syria during the persent war, have sufficiently illustrated the failure also of this dose of appeasement.

The Palestine Administration applied itself to the enforcement of the White Paper of 1939 with an energy and promptitude which contrasted strangely with its hesitations and vacillations in putting the policy of the Mandate into effect during the past 20 years. The Jews have refused, and continue to refuse, to accept the White Paper, since it is contrary to their historic rights and to the spirit of the Balfour Declaration, and is a breach of a solemn agreement concluded by the British Government, sanctioned by British public opinion, by the League of Nations, and by the United States of America.

This attempt to degrade the promise of a National Home for the Jewish people to minority status in an Arab Palestine is mainly due to the peculiar relationship between the British and the Arabs on the one side, and the British and the Jews on the other. The British in Palestine have never clearly explained to the Arab population the real meaning and implications of the Balfour Declaration; at best they have been rather apologetic about the policy they were appointed to carry out; at worst, some of them have been openly hostile to it. Among British administrators and politicians in the Near and Middle East, there is a school of thought which is all too ready to ascribe every difficulty encountered by British policy in Egypt, India or elsewhere to the Jewish National Home in Palestine. The Arabs have been quick to seize on this evidence of weakness, and, with the help of the Axis Powers, have succeeded in whipping up an agitation which at times has assumed threatening dimensions. The Arabs had to be pacified at any price, and the Jews had to foot the bill. To the Palestinian administrator the Arab presents no problems: ye is a "native," and the methods which have proved their efficacy in various backward British dependencies can be applied to him with their usual success. The Jew does not fall into the same

---

[74] *Editor's Note:* See "The Palestine Report: Alternatives to Partition," by Viscount Samuel, and "The Arabs and the Future of Palestine," by H. St. J. Philby, both in FOREIGN AFFAIRS, October 1937.

category. He has come to Palestine to construct there a modern civilization, and has brought with him a number of new, complex and baffling problems. He is "difficult," critical, always anxious to be trying something new, and he does not fit into the time-honored framework of administrative routine which has proved serviceable in Nigeria or Iraq.

This is reflected in the attitude of the British Government and of the Palestine Administration towards the Jewish war effort today. At the outbreak of the war, all the available Jewish manpower of Palestine offered itself for war service. Many were men with some training and a thorough knowledge of the country. Technical and industrial assistance could also be made available, and these, too, were offered. But the zeal of the Jews was somewhat blunted by the cold politeness which greeted their readiness to serve. They were allowed, it is true, to enlist in limited numbers in the British Forces, but—so far as fighting units were concerned—only *pari passu* with Arab volunteers, who showed little disposition to come forward. The "parity" principle was eventually dropped, under pressure of circumstances, a short while ago, and about 10,000 Jew now form part of the Nile Army, as combatants or in auxiliary services. They have given a good account of themselves in Libya, Crete, Greece and Syria, but even now they are not allowed to fight under their own name and flag; and their presence with the British Forces is camouflaged under the description "Palestinian." One wonders why, shipping difficulties being what they are, the British authorities should find it necessary to bring men and material from Australia and New Zealand instead of utilizing what is available on the spot.

This peculiar and—to the Jews—disheartening attitude is presumably designed to demonstrate to the Arab world that the Jews have no particular status or stake in Palestine. Even after the bitter experiences of the present war this idea seems to be a fixation, ineradicable from certain minds. The vain effort to obliterate the very name of a highly active community in Palestine is a tragic anomaly, due to a total lack, in quarters responsible for Middle Eastern policy, of a real sense of the values involved in the present life-and-death struggle.

In any settlement of Middle Eastern problems, account must be taken of the Arab Nationalist Movement, inspired by pan-Arab ideas on the one side, and by exaggerated local chauvinism on the other. These two aspects are, curiously enough, not mutually exclusive; they coexist in a state of unstable equilibrium. So far, with the exception of Sa'udi Arabia, Arab Nationalist energies have not been directed into constructive channels; they are devoted to weilding the Sword of Islam rather than the spade or the ploughshare. The movement is emotional, turbulent, made heady by the unexpected political gains which have vicariously accrued to it since the last war. It is fashioning itself on the totalitarian pattern; young Arabs stand in awe before the achievements of Germany and Italy, and still believe in their coming victory. Groups of Arab students from Iraq, Syria and Palestine were encouraged before the war to make pilgrimages to Berlin, Nuremberg, and Rome, and there worship at the Nazi and Fascist shrines. There they were indoctrinated with "modern" ideas, which they have now transplanted into their respective countries. The Rashid Ali revolt (accompanied by a regular pogrom in the best Berlin-Bucharest manner) testifies to the success of Nazi-Fascist teaching, and no doubt rejoices the hearts of the tutors. The Baghdad pogrom (120 killed, 850 wounded) was perpetrated on an ancient native Jewish community resident there for centuries. These happenings, incidentally, belie the idea, so assiduously spread by Arab propagandists, that their people have always lived in harmony with their native Jewish populations, and that their animosity is directed only against incoming "foreign" Jewish immigrants. Of these there are none in Baghdad.

It is to be hoped that this state of mind among the Arabs will prove transitory. A great opportunity awaits the Arab peoples—to rebuild their countries, to bring happiness and prosperity to the oppressed fellaheen. This will be the acid test of Arab Nationalism. Pride in a glorious past is of value only if it serves as a spur to the hard task of rebuilding a happier future.

In the early stages of our work in Palestine there were distinct possibilities of reaching a reasonable *modus vivendi* with the Arabs. In 1918, at the suggestion of His Majesty's Government, and with the approval and encouragement of General Allenby, I went to Transjordan on a visit to the Emir Feisal, then Commander in Chief of the Arab forces. We had a frank discussion in which I clearly stated the aims and aspirations of the Jews. He expressed himself prepared to give them his full consent, after consultation with his father, then Sheriff of Mecca. A year later, in London, a treaty of friendship was concluded between us, embodying the main points of this conversation in the desert. Lawrence of

Arabia—often erroneously quoted as an anti-Zionist—helped in the drafting and negotiation of this treaty and acted as interpreter. Articles III and IV read as follows:

> In the establishment of the Constitution and Administration of Palestine all such measures shall be adopted as will afford the fullest guarantees for carrying into effect the British Government's Declaration of November 2nd, 1917.
> All necessary measures shall be taken to encourage and stimulate immigration of Jews into Palestine on a large scale and as quickly as possible to settle Jewish immigrants upon the land through closer settlement and intensive cultivation of the soil. In taking such measures the Arab peasant and tenant farmers shall be protected in their rights and shall be assisted in forwarding their economic development.

Developments in Syria prevented the implementation of the Treaty, and after Feisal's death things in Iraq went from bad to worse. With him an important link between the Jews and the Arab world was broken. Nevertheless, even in Palestine, where relations between Arabs and Jews were of late rather acute, there remained among the Arabs some who were ready to discuss terms of coöperation. After all, though our work in Palestine has for its object primarily the welfare of the Jews, the benefits derived from it by the Arabs are incontestable. The Arab population of Palestine has increased—by natural growth and through immigration—far more rapidly than in Transjordan, or even than in wealthy Egypt. The increase has been greatest in precisely those parts of Palestine where Jewish activity has been most intense. Arab wages are higher in Palestine than in any Arab country, and this accounts for a very considerable Arab influx.

But the Mufti of Jerusalem assumed the leadership of the extreme Nationalist party. He is an implacable enemy of both the Jews and the British. Supported by powerful outside influences (and sometimes even favored by the British Administration), he has gained a great ascendancy over the Palestine Arabs, and, by terrorizing the moderates, has succeeded in frustrating all attempts at reconciliation. Even so, the Mufti has never-represented the whole of the Palestine Arabs, and there is some ground for thinking that, had the Government made a determined attempt to implement the Royal Commission's proposals, many Arabs would have acquiesced in them, and a Jewish state in a part of Palestine might today have been a going concern. I believe I am not too bold in adding that in that case the military situation on this front might have been more favorable than it is.

For Palestine's strategic importance cannot be forgotten. The countries which stretch from the Euphrates to the Nile constitute a vast and greatly under-populated region. In ancient times they were great centers of civilization. But though they fell on evil days their geographical importance remains unchanged—in fact it is, if anything, greater than ever. These countries are a bridge between the three continents of the Old World. The Suez Canal is the gateway to the Far East and India, and thus, in a sense, one of the approaches to the Pacific; its fate may even affect the interests of the Western Hemisphere. Small wonder, then, that the predatory countries have long sought, and still seek, to obtain a foothold in this part of the world. They will continue to regard it with covetous eyes so long as it remains weak, undeveloped, unstable, and a prey to political intrigue. Once these countries have been rebuilt, and raised to a higher level of culture and administration, this undesirable situation will show a rapid change for the better. Their reconstruction, however, cannot be brought about by capitalist activity, but only through the energies and efforts of their own inhabitants. On the first stages along this road they will certainly need to be guided by nations like England or America; in return, I believe that a Jewish Palestine will be able to contribute much to their progress and prosperity. But if Palestine plays such a rôle there is a countervailing obligation on the Arabs to acknowledge Jewish rights there.

Whatever the Arabs gained—and it was a great deal—as a result of the last war; whatever they may gain—and they have already gained something, and will gain more—as a result of this one, they owe, and will owe, entirely to the democracies. It is therefore for the democracies to proclaim the justice of the Jewish claim to their own commonwealth in Palestine. There is nothing new in this principle. It was implicit in the Balfour Declaration; it was reaffirmed by the Peel Commission. And we have now acquired the invaluable experience of the last 20 years, which has proved beyond doubt that when the Jew is reunited with the soil of Palestine energies are released in him which have been stored up and suppressed for thousands of years—energies which, given an outlet, can create values which may be of service even to richer and more fortunate countries.

To sum up. The Arabs will greatly profit from a British victory by obtaining independence in Syria and Libya, and as large a measure of national unity as they themselves are capable of achieving. On the other hand, it is essential to obtain such a settlement in Palestine as will help to solve the Jewish problem—one of the most disturbing problems in the world. The Arabs must, therefore, be clearly told that the Jews will be encouraged to settle in Palestine, and will control their own immigrations; that here Jews who so desire will be able to achieve their freedom and self-government by establishing s state of their own, and ceasing to be a minority dependent on the will and pleasure of other nations.

In that state there will be complete civil and political equality of rights for all citizens, without distinction of race or religion, and, in addition, the Arabs will enjoy full autonomy in their own internal affairs. But if any Arabs do not wish to remain in a Jewish state, every facility will be given to them to transfer to one of the many and vast Arab countries. Considering the strategic and economic importance of Palestine, the inclusion of the Jewish state within the British Commonwealth of Nations would be to the interest of both. But we should also be ready, if necessary, to consider joining, under proper safeguards, in federation with Arab states.

A Jewish state in Palestine would be more than merely the necessary means of securing further Jewish immigration and development. It is a moral need and postulate, and it would be a decisive step towards normality and true emancipation. I believe that after the war Jews everywhere can gain in status and security only through the rise of a Jewish state, and this would be especially the case if that state is a part of the British Commonwealth. Anti-Semites, determined to reduce the Jews to slavery or drive them into exile, have not waited for the excuse of the establishment of a Jewsih state in order to proceed against them. The latest manifestation of Nazi ingenuity is the decree by which every Jew under Nazi rule must bear on his breast a so-called "badge of shame"—the Shield of David. We wear it with pride. The Shield of David is too ancient and too sacred a symbol to be susceptible of degradation under the pagan Swastika. Hallowed by uncounted ages of suffering, of martyrdom patiently and unrevengefully borne, it will yet shine untarnished over Zion's gates, long after the horrors of our present night are forgotton in the light of the new day that is to come.

RESOLUTIONS ADOPTED BY VARIOUS STATE LEGISLATURES RELATIVE TO THE JEWISH NATIONAL HOME IN PALESTINE

(Submitted by Dr. Abba Hillel Silver)

AMENDMENT

Offered by Senator Mortensen of the Second District to Substitute for Senate Joint Resolution, No. 155. File No. 736. In lines 5, 9 and 20 strike out the words "Jewish National Homeland" and insert in lieu thereof, the following, viz.: "Jewish Commonwealth".

[Endorsement]

AMENDMENT

Schedule A. File No. 736. Substitute for Senate Joint Resolution No. 155. Senate, _____ 1943.
(Adopted)
——— ——— *Clerk.*

H. of R., _____ 1943.
(Adopted)
——— ——— *Clerk.*

State of Connecticut: Senate, May 11, 1943, Passed—R. S. Trans.
CLARENCE F. BALDWIN, *Clerk.*

State of Connecticut: House of Representatives, May 14, 1943, Passed—R. S. Trans.
CHARLES DUNNINGTON, *Clerk.*

Serial No. 94.   (Not printed.)   Legislative Journal Page —.

By Messrs. Irvin and Leonard

CONDEMNATION OF NAZI RELIGIONS PERSECUTION AND RACIAL HATRED,
DEVELOPMENT OF JEWISH NATIONAL HOME IN PALESTINE

In the HOUSE OF REPRESENTATIVES, *May 7, 1943.*
Whereas, the persecution and attempted extermination by Nazi Germany of the Jews in occupied Europe have outraged the conscience of the civilized world and emphasized the tragedy of the Jewish problem in Europe, and
Whereas, at the conclusion of the war great numbers of Jews in Europe will find themselves homeless, despoiled, and desperately in need of a refuge where they may reconstruct their shattered lives, and
Whereas, pursuant to the treaties of peace terminating the first World War, a Mandate was issued approved by fifty-two nations including the United States, to facilitate the establishment of a Jewish National Home in Palestine; and
Whereas, this policy was concurred in by a Joint Resolution adopted unanimously by both Houses of the Congress of the United States on June 30, 1922, and approved by the President on September 21, 1922; therefore, be it
Resolved (if the Senate concurs) that we of the Commonwealth of Pennsylvania express our most profound sympathy toward the victims of Nazi religious persecution and racial hatred; and
Be it Further Resolved that we urge the fullest cooperation of the United Nations in punishing those responsible for this horrible crime against humanity, and in all alleviating suffering through an international rescue agency; and
Be it Further Resolved that we favor the continued development of the Jewish National Home in Palestine for the absorption of as many Jews as may be required by the urgent needs of the Jewish people and the full development there of a Jewish Homeland in the democratic world order in accordance with the principles for which the United Nations are now fighting; and
Be it Further Resolved, That a copy of this Resolution be forwarded to the President and to the Secretary of State of the United States, the President of the United States Senate, and to the Speaker of the House of Representatives.
Adopted, May 7.

By Mr. Key of Jasper and Mrs. Mankin of Fulton

A RESOLUTION

Whereas on Nov. 2, 1917 His Majesty's Government issued the Balfour Declaration viewing with favor the establishment in Palestine of a national home for the Jewish people and
Whereas this policy was concurred in by the United States in a joint Congressional Resolution adopted on June 30, 1922 and implemented by the Anglo-American treaty of December 3rd, 1924 and
Whereas the sufferings of the Jews in Europe under the heels of the Axis dictators cry out to the enlightened conscience of the United Nations and the need for a Jewish homeland for the stricken and persecuted Jewish masses after the war has become not merely a matter of justice but of dire necessity,
Now therefore be it resolved by the Senate and House of Representatives of the State of Georgia, That the establishment of a Jewish homeland in Palestine and its further development for the absorption of as many Jewish refugees as may be called for by the exigencies of the situation be commended to the considered judgment of the United Nations, not only as an act of justice to the Jewish people, but as an integral part of a new democratic world order in which every people shall have the right to self-government and self-determination in accordance with the principles for which we now fight, and

Be it further resolved, That a copy of this resolution be forwarded to the President of the United States, to Senators Wagner and McNary, cochairman of the American Palestine Committee, and to the British Embassy in Washington for transmission to the proper authorities in London.

Roy V. Harris,
Speaker of the House of Representatives.
P. T. McCutchen, Jr.,
Clerk of the House of Representatives.
Frank C. Gross,
President of the Senate.
Henry W. Neinie
Secretary of the Senate.

No. 2002

State of Connecticut,
  Office of the Secretary, ss.

I, Frances Burke Redick, Secretary of the State of Connecticut, and keeper of the seal thereof, and of the original record of the Acts and Resolutions of the General Assembly of said State, do hereby certify that I have compared the annexed copy of Resolution favoring the continued Development of a Jewish National Home in Palestine being Senate Joint Resolution No. 155 of the 1943 General Assembly of Connecticut with the original record of the same now remaining in this office, and have found the said copy to be correct and complete transcript thereof.

And I further certify, that the said original record is a public record of the said State of Connecticut, now remaining in this office.

In Testimony Whereof, I have hereunto set my hand and affixed the Seal of said State, at Hartford, this twenty-fifth day of May, 1943.

[seal]   Arthur F. Brown,
                                                   Deputy Secretary.

State of Connecticut, General Assembly,
January Session, A. D., 1943.

Resolution Favoring the Continued Development of a Jewish National Home in Palestine

Resolved by this Assembly:

Whereas the persecution and attempted extermination by Nazi Germany of the Jews in Occupied Europe have outraged the conscience of the civilized world and have manifested the urgent necessary of continued maintenance and development of a Jewish National Homeland; and

Whereas pursuant to the treaties of peace terminating the first World War a mandate was issued approved by fifty-two nations including the United States, to facilitate the establishment of a Jewish National Home in Palestine; and

Whereas this policy was concurred in by a Joint Resolution adopted by both Houses of the Congress of the United States on June 30, 1922, and approved by the President on September 21, 1922;

Now, therefore, be it resolved: That the Senate and House of Representatives, as the representatives of, and in the name of, the people of the State of Connecticut express our most profound sympathy toward the victims of Nazi religious persecution and racial hatred; and

Be it further resolved: That we favor the continued development of a Jewish National Home in Palestine for the absorption of as many Jews as may be required by the urgent need of the Jewish people, as an integral part of the new democratic world order in accordance with the principles for which the United States are now fighting; and

Be it further resolved: That a copy of this Resolution be forwarded to the President, to the Secretary of State of the United States, to the President of the United States Senate and to the Speaker of the United States House of Representatives. Committee Bill, Federal Relations, Apr. 21, 1943.

[Endorsement]

Senate Joint Resolution No. 155: Resolution favoring the continued Development of a Jewish National Home in Palestine.
Examined:

JOHN M. BAILEY,
Revision Commissioner.

Federal Relations Committee, committee bill introduced by Senator ———— of the ——————— District ———, File No. 736.

State of Connecticut: Senate, May 5, 1943, tabled for calendar and printing.

CLARENCE F. BALDWIN, *Clerk.*

Connecticut: Senate, May 11, 1943, passed as amended by schedule "A." R. S. & T.

CLARENCE F. BALDWIN, *Clerk.*

State of Connecticut: House of Representatives, May 12, 1943, tabled for calendar.

CLARK DEARINGTON, *Clerk.*

State of Connecticut: House of Representatives, May 14, 1943, passed—A. S. Trans. As amended by Sched. "A."

CLARK DEARINGTON, *Clerk.*

STATE OF MISSOURI

DEPARTMENT OF STATE

To all to Whom these Presents shall Come:

I, Dwight H. Brown, Secretary of State of the State of Missouri, hereby certify that the annexed pages contain a full, true and complete copy of House Concurrent Resolution Number 10 as the same appears on file and of record in this office.

In Testimony Whereof, I hereunto set my hand and affix the seal of my office. Done at the City of Jefferson, this first day of December A. D., Nineteen Hundred and Forty-three.

[SEAL]

DWIGHT H. BROWN,
Secretary of State.
GEO. E. CROW,
Chief Clerk.

HOUSE CONCURRENT RESOLUTION NO. 10

Whereas the conscience of the civilized world has been outraged by the continued persecution and extermination of many peoples in the conquered countries of Europe; and

Whereas at the conclusion of this war a great number of the oppressed and downtrodden people of Europe will find themselves homeless, despoiled and desperately in need of a refuge to reconstruct their shattered lives; and

Whereas the Jewish people of Europe are victims of Nazi oppression and attempted extermination not only in occupied Europe, but also within Nazi Germany; and

Whereas, pursuant to the treaties of peace terminating the first World War, a Mandate was issued and approved by fifty-two nations, including the] United States, for a Jewish National Home in Palestine; and

Whereas this policy was concurred in by a Joint Resolution adopted unanimously by both Houses of the Congress of the United States on June 30th, 1922, and approved by the President on September 21st, 1922; now, therefore be it

Resolved, That the House of Representatives of the 62nd General Assembly of Missouri, the Senate concurring therein, express its most profound sympathy towards the victims of Nazi religious persecution and racial hatred; and be it further

Resolved, That we urge the fullest cooperation of the United Nations in punishing those responsible for this horrible crime against humanity and to alleviate suffering through an international rescue agency; and be it further

Resolved, That we favor the continued development of a Jewish National Home in Palestine for the absorption of as many Jews as may be required by the urgent need of the Jewish people and the development there of a Jewish Commonwealth as an integral part of the new democratic world order in accordance with the principles for which the United Nations are now fighting; and be it further

Resolved, That a copy of this resolution be forwarded to the President of the United States, the Secretary of State; the President of the United States Senate and to the Speaker of the House of Representatives.

HOWARD ELLIOTT,
Speaker, Missouri House of Representatives.
LEONARD E. NEWTON,
Chief Clerk, Missouri House of Representatives.

Approved May 12, 1943 at 11:46 a. m.

FORREST C. DONNELL, *Governor.*

SOUTH CAROLINA

Introduced by Mr. Blatt

A CONCURRENT RESOLUTION COMMENDING FOR THE CONSIDERATION OF THE UNITED NATIONS THE ESTABLISHMENT OF A JEWISH HOMELAND IN PALESTINE

Whereas on November 2, 1917, His Majesty's Government issued the Balfour Declaration viewing with favor the establishment in Palestine of a national home for the Jewish people and,

Whereas this policy was concurred in by the United States in a joint Congressional Resolution adopted on June 30, 1922, and implemented by the Anglo-American treaty of December 3, 1924, and,

Whereas the suffering of the Jews in Europe under the heels of the Axis dictators cry out to the enlightened conscience of the United Nations and the need for a Jewish homeland for the stricken and persecuted Jewish masses after the war has become not merely a matter of justice but of dire necessity: Now, therefore,

Be it resolved by the House of Representatives, the Senate concurring: That the establishment of a Jewish homeland in Palestine and its further development for the absorption of as many Jewish refugees as may be called for by the exigencies of the situation be commended to the considered judgment of the United Nations, not only as an act of justice to the Jewish people, but as an integral part of a new democratic world order in which every people shall have the right to self-government and self-determination in accordance with the principles for which we now fight, and,

Be it further resolved, That a copy of this Resolution be forwarded to the President of the United States, to Senators Wagner and McNary, Co-Chairmen of the American Palestine Committee, and to the British Embassy in Washington for transmission to the proper authorities in London.

IN THE HOUSE OF REPRESENTATIVES,
May 5, 1943.

I hereby certify that the foregoing is a true and correct copy of a Resolution adopted by the House of Representatives and concurred in by the Senate on April 14, 1943.

(Signed) INEZ WATSON, *Clerk of the House.*

TEXAS

H. C. R. No. 85

HOUSE CONCURRENT RESOLUTION

Whereas, The persecution and attempted extermination of the Jews in Occupied Europe by Nazi Germany have outraged the conscience of the civilized world; and

Whereas, On the basis of authentic information in the hands of the United States Department of State, at least two million Jews have been ruthlessly annihilated, and the remainder of the Jewish communities in Europe stand in immediate danger of similar extermination unless prompt action is taken by the United Nations to provide havens of refuge for them; and

Whereas, Tens of thousands of Jews are stranded in European ports desperately seeking rescue; and

Whereas, The Balfour Declaration of November 2, 1917, guaranteeing the establishment of a Jewish National Homeland in Palestine was approved by fifty-two Nations, including the United States, and incorporated into the treaties of peace terminating the First World War; and

Whereas, This policy was concurred in by a Joint Resolution adopted by both Houses of the Congress of the United States on June 30, 1922, and approved by the President on September 21, 1922, and implemented by the Anglo-American treaty of December 3, 1924; therefore, be it

Resolved by the House of Representatives, the Senate concurring, That we express our most profound sympathy toward the victims of Nazi religious persecution and racial hatred; and be it further

Resolved, That the United Nations be urged to take steps to find even temporary havens of refuge, through an international rescue agency, for those homeless and hounded Jews who can be rescued immediately; and be it further

Resolved, That we urge that all barriers on Jewish immigration into Palestine be now removed so that those Jews who can find escape from Axis-dominated Europe have permanent haven in the Land of Israel in their urgent need; and we view with favor the absorption of all Jews into Palestine after the war who need or desire to go there, not only as an act of justice to the Jewish people, but as an integral part of a new democratic world order in which every people shall have the right to self-government and self-determination in accordance with the principles for which we now fight; and be it further

Resolved, That copies of this Resolution be forwarded to the President of the United States, Mr. Cordell Hull, Secretary of State, the President of the United States Senate, the Speaker of the National House of Representatives, and to the British Embassy in Washington for transmission to the proper authorities in London.

> JOHN LEE SMITH,
> *President of the Senate.*
> PRICE DANIEL,
> *Speaker of the House.*

I hereby certify that H. C. R. No. 85 was adopted by the House on April 2, 1943.

> CLARENCE JONES,
> *Chief Clerk of the House.*

I hereby certify that H. C. R. No. 85 was adopted by the Senate on April 6, 1943.

[SEAL]

> BOB BARKER,
> *Secretary of the Senate.*

ILLINOIS

OFFICE OF THE SECRETARY OF STATE

UNITED STATES OF AMERICA,
   State of Illinois, ss:

I, Edward J. Hughes, Secretary of State of the State of Illinois, do hereby certify that the following is a true copy of *Senate Joint Resolution No. 17 of the Sixty-third General Assembly of the State of Illinois*, the original of which is now on file in my office.

In witness whereof, I hereunto set my hand and affix the Great Seal of State. Done at the City of Springfield, this 17th day of May A. D. 1943.

[SEAL]

> EDWARD J. HUGHES,
> *Secretary of State.*

EXECUTIVE DEPARTMENT

UNITED STATES OF AMERICA,
State of Illinois, ss:
I, Dwight H. Green, Governor of the State of Illinois, do hereby certify that Edward J. Hughes, who signed the foregoing certificate, was at the time of signing the same, and is now, Secretary of State of the State of Illinois, duly elected and qualified to that office, and that full faith and credit are due his official attestations; that he is the custodian of the above documents and authorized by law to certify to same, and that the same is in due form and by the proper officer; and that he is the custodian of the Great Seal of State of the State of Illinois.
In witness whereof, I hereunto set my hand. Done at the City of Springfield, this 17th day of May, 1943.

DWIGHT H. GREEN, *Governor.*

OFFICE OF THE SECRETARY OF STATE

UNITED STATES OF AMERICA,
State of Illinois, ss:
I, Edward J. Hughes, Secretary of State of the State of Illinois, hereby certify that Dwight H. Green, who signed the foregoing certificate, was at the time of signing the same, and is now, Governor of the State of Illinois, duly elected and qualified, and that as such, full faith and credit is, and ought to be, given to his official attestations; and I further certify that under the Constitution and laws of the State of Illinois, the Secretary of State is the custodian of the Great Seal of State, and that the Governor has no official seal. And I further certify that the foregoing signature is the genuine signature of Dwight H. Green, Governor, and that the foregoing certificate signed by him is in due form.
In Testimony Whereof, I hereunto set my hand and cause to be affixed the Great Seal of State. Done at the City of Springfield, this 17th day of May 1943.
[SEAL]   EDWARD J. HUGHES,
                                                   Secretary of State.

SENATE JOINT RESOLUTION NO. 17

Whereas, The ruthless persecution of the Jews in Occupied Europe by Nazi Germany has resulted in the extermination of at least two million members of that race, and the remnants of Jewish population in Europe stand in immediate danger of similar extermination unless havens of refuge are made available to them; and
Whereas, Thousands of Jews are massed in European ports clinging desperately to hopes of salvation; and
Whereas, The United Nations are faced with the solemn obligation, in the interests of humanity and justice and in accordance with the principles for which this war is being waged, to undertake steps which will facilitate the immediate removal of Jews from Europe and to provide them with a permanent haven after the termination of the war; therefore, be it
Resolved, By the Senate of the Sixty-third General Assembly of the State of Illinois, the House of Representatives concurring herein, That we express our profound sympathy to the victims of Nazi religious persecution and racial hatred; and
Resolved, Further, That we respectfully urge the United Nations to act immediately, through an international rescue agency, in finding even temporary havens of refuge for those homeless and persecuted Jews who can now be rescued; and
Resolved, Further, That we urge that all barriers on Jewish immigration into Palestine be now removed so that those Jews who can find escape from Axis-dominated Europe have permanent haven therein in accordance with the spirit and intent of the Balfour Declaration; and we view with favor the absorption of all Jews into Palestine after the war who need or desire to go there, not only as an act of justice to the Jewish people, but as an integral part of a new democratic world order in which every people shall have the right to self-government and self-determination; and, be it further

Resolved, That copies of this Resolution be forwarded by the Secretary of State to the President of the United States, Mr. Cordell Hull, Secretary of State, the President of the United States Senate, the Speaker of the National House of Representatives, and to the British Embassy in Washington for transmission to the proper authorities in London.

Adopted by the Senate, April 20, 1943.

> HUGH W. CROSS,
> *President of the Senate.*
>
> EDWARD H. ALEXANDER,
> *Secretary of the Senate.*

Concurred in by the House of Representatives, April 21, 1943.

> ELMER J. SCHACKENBERG,
> *Speaker of the House of Representatives.*
>
> R. R. RANDOLPH,
> *Clerk of the House of Representatives.*

Filed 2:45 p. m., May 4, 1943.

> EDWARD J. HUGHES,
> *Secretary of State.*

FREDERIC W. COOK
Secretary of the Commonwealth

THE COMMONWEALTH OF MASSACHUSETTS
OFFICE OF THE SECRETARY
BOSTON

RESOLUTIONS MEMORIALIZING CONGRESS RELATIVE TO THE JEWISH NATIONAL HOME IN PALESTINE

Whereas, Recognition has been given by the nations of the world to the historical connection of the Jewish people with Palestine and to the grounds for reconstituting their National Home in that country; and

Whereas, The United States of America has given its approval to the reestablishment of the Jewish National Home in Palestine, as embodied in a resolution adopted by the Congress of the United States known as "The Lodge Resolution"; and

Whereas, The General Court of Massachusetts deplores the persecution of peoples in any land based upon racial bigotry and religious intolerance and has on previous occasions expressed its sympathetic interest in the Jewish National aspirations; therefore be it

Resolved, That the General Court of Massachusetts expresses its concern in the welfare of the Jewish National Home and its admiration of the progress made in Palestine by the efforts of the Jewish Pioneers;

That it is inspiring to behold an ancient people return to the land of its origin for the purpose of being able to live its own life, to develop their own culture and civilization and to mold its national destiny; and

That it views with favor the achievements of the Jewish pioneers in Palestine where opportunities were created for tens of thousands of Jews to return to the land of their fathers as of right and not on sufferance; and be it further

Resolved, That the United States of America be and is respectfully solicited to use its good offices for the purpose of safeguarding the integrity of the Balfour Declaration and the interest of the Jewish National Home, in accordance with the terms of the Palestine Mandate, and to the end that the doors of Palestine may be opened for the purpose of admitting the homeless Jewish vicitims of racial bigotry and religious intolerance, where they may find the opportunity of rebuilding their broken lives; and be it further

Resolved, That copies of these resolutions be forwarded by the Secretary of the Commonwealth to the President of the United States, to the Vice President of the

United States, to the Speaker of the House of Representatives, and to the Representatives in Congress from this Commonwealth.
In Senate, adopted, May 11, 1939.

IRVING N. HAYDEN, *Clerk.*

In House of Representatives, adopted, in concurrence, May 12, 1939.

LAWRENCE R. GROVE, *Clerk.*

A true copy.
Attest:
[SEAL]

F. W. COOK,
Secretary of the Commonwealth.

STATE OF CALIFORNIA

OFFICE OF THE SECRETARY OF STATE

I, Frank M. Jordan, Secretary of State of the State of California, do hereby certify:
That I have compared the annexed transcript with the record on file in my office, of which it purports to be a copy, and that the same is a full, true and correct copy thereof.
In Witness Whereof, I hereunto set my hand and affix the Great Seal of the State of California this 25th day of May, 1943.
[SEAL]

FRANK M. JORDAN,
Secretary of State.

CHAPTER 131

Assembly Concurrent Resolution No. 56—Relative to settlement of Jewish refugees in Palestine

Whereas, The intolerable sufferings of the Jewish people in Europe at the hands of the ruthless dictators of the Axis Powers make an irresistible appeal to the Christian world and to the enlightened conscience of the United Nations, and make clear the need for a homeland where stricken and persecuted Jewish people may settle in peace: and

Whereas, The favor with which Great Britain viewed the establishment in Palestine of a national home for the Jewish people was evidenced by the Balfour Declaration of November 2, 1917; and

Whereas, The United States of America expressed concurrence in this policy by joint congressional resolution adopted on June 30, 1922, and by the provisions of the Anglo-American Treaty of December 2, 1924; now, therefore, be it

Resolved by the Assembly of the State of California, the Senate thereof concurring, That we favor the continued establishment of a Jewish homeland in Palestine and its further development for the absorption of as many Jewish refugees as may be called for by the exigencies of the situation be commended to the considered judgment of the United Nations, not only as an act of justice to the Jewish people, but as an integral part of a new democratic world order in which every people shall have the right to self-government and self-determination in accordance with the principles, to perpetuate which we are now engaged in the fiercest struggle of all time; and be it further

Resolved, That a copy of this resolution be forwarded to the President of the United States, to Senators Wagner and McNary, Co-chairmen of the American Palestine Committee, and to the British Embassy in Washington for transmission to the proper authorities in London, to the Secretary of State of the United States, to the President of the United States Senate, and to the Speaker of the House of Representatives of the United States.

Adopted in Assembly May 5, 1943.

ARTHUR A. OHNIMUS,
Chief Clerk of the Assembly.

Adopted in Senate May 5, 1943.

J. A. BEEK,
Secretary of the Senate.

This resolution was received by the Governor this 5th day of May 1943 at 2 o'clock p. m.

HELEN R. MACGREGOR,
Private Secretary of the Governor.

Endorsed: Filed in the office of the Secretary of State of the State of California, May 12, 1943 at 5 o'clock p. m.

FRANK M. JORDAN,
Secretary of State.
By CHAS. J..HAGERTY, *Deputy.*
CHARLES W. LYON,
Speaker of the Assembly.
FREDERICK F. HOUSER,
President of the Senate.

Attest:
[SEAL]

FRANK M. JORDAN,
Secretary of State.

[Endorsement]

FLORIDA

HOUSE MEMORIAL NO. 10

Joint Memorial of the Legislature of the State of Florida, to Honorable Franklin D. Roosevelt, President of the United States, and to Honorable Cordell Hull, Secretary of State of the United States

Whereas, the Government of Great Britain did in the year 1917 declare it to be the policy of that government that a Jewish Homeland be established in Palestine, and did declare in the Balfour Declaration that that government would assist in its establishment, and

Whereas, the Jews of the United States, along with sympathizers everywhere, did cooperate to develop Palestine, and in its development did spend countless millions of dollars, and have sacrificed thousands of lives, and have made, through their efforts a habitable and fruitful nation out of a desert waste, and

Whereas, Palestine has been the last hope of millions of homeless refugees, who, because of religious and political persecution, are without a resting place or home, and

Whereas, the Government of the United States, through Congress, as well as the League of Nations, did subscribe to the Balfour Declaration, is morally, at least, responsible for its execution, and

Whereas, it is in the interest of Democracy that the promises and pledges of democratic governments be not regarded as mere scraps of paper, and

Whereas, humanitarian motives should impell the government of the United States to call upon the government of Great Britain to abide by its pledges contained in its Balfour Declaration, therefore, be it

Resolved by the Legislature of the State of Florida, That a copy of this resolution be conveyed to Hon. Franklin D. Roosevelt, President of the United States, and the Hon. Cordell Hull, Secretary of State of the United States, and that they be advised hereby that it is the considered opinion of the Legislature of the State of Florida, that proper representations should be made by the Government of the United States to the Government of Great Britain, urging the latter Government to abide by its pledges contained in the Balfour Declaration, and approved by our Government.

Approved by the Governor May 30, 1939.

Filed in Office, Secretary of State, May 31, 1939.

STATE OF FLORIDA

OFFICE OF SECRETARY OF STATE

I, R. A. Gray, Secretary of State of the State of Florida, do hereby certify that the above and foregoing is a true and correct copy of House Memorial No. 10, regular session, 1939, as approved by the Governor and filed in this office on May 31, 1939.

Given under my hand and the Great Seal of the State of Florida at Tallahassee, the Capital, this the 30th day of November A. D. 1943.

[SEAL]   R. A. GRAY,
                                                      Secretary of State.

_____

FLORIDA

HOUSE MEMORIAL No. 4

A MEMORIAL TO THE CONGRESS OF THE UNITED STATES REQUESTING THE ESTABLISHMENT IN PALESTINE OF A NATIONAL HOME FOR THE JEWISH PEOPLE

Whereas on November 2, 1917, His Majesty's Government issued the Balfour Declaration viewing with favor the establishment in Palestine of a national home for the Jewish people, and

Whereas, this policy was concurred in by the United States in a joint Congressional Resolution adopted on June 30, 1922, and implemented by the Anglo-American treaty of December 3d, 1924, and

Whereas the sufferings of the Jews in Europe under the heels of the Axis dictators cry out to the enlightened conscience of the United Nations and the need for a Jewish homeland for the stricken and persecuted Jewish masses after the war, has become not merely a matter of justice but of dire necessity,

Now, therefore, be it resolved by the Senate and House of Representatives of the State of Florida, That the establishment of a Jewish homeland in Palestine and its further development for the absorption of as many Jewish refugees as may be called for by the exigencies of the situation be commended to the considered judgment of the United Nations, not only as an act of justice to the Jewish people, but as an integral part of a new democratic world order in which every people shall have the right to self-government and self-determination in accordance with the principles for which we now fight; and

Be it further resolved, That a copy of this resolution be forwarded to the President of the United States, to Senators Wagner and McNary, Co-chairman of the American Palestine Committee, and to the British Embassy in Washington for transmission to the proper authorities in London.

Approved by the Governor April 27, 1943.
Filed in Office Secretary of State April 27, 1943.

STATE OF FLORIDA

OFFICE OF SECRETARY OF STATE

I, R. A. Gray, Secretary of State of the State of Florida, do hereby certify that the above and foregoing is a true and correct copy of House Memorial No. 4, as passed by the Legislature of the State of Florida, Regular Session 1943, approved by the Governor and filed in this office.

Given under my hand and the Great Seal of the State of Florida at Tallahassee, the Capital, this the 7th day of May A. D. 1943.

[SEAL]   R. A. GRAY,
                                                      Secretary of State.

_____

THE COMMONWEALTH OF MASSACHUSETTS

in the year one thousand nine hundred and nineteen

RESOLUTIONS RELATIVE TO THE ESTABLISHMENT OF A JEWISH HOME LAND IN PALESTINE AND THE PROTECTION OF JEWISH RIGHTS AND LIBERTIES IN THE SETTLEMENT OF THE EUROPEAN WAR

Whereas, The future prosperity and peace of the world depend upon a just settlement of the European war whereby every nationality, however small, shall be granted the right to determine its own destiny and the opportunity of living its own life; and

Whereas, The government of the United States is recognized as an ardent exponent of the rights of the small nations; therefore be it

Resolved, That, in the opinion of the House of Representatives of The Commonwealth of Massachusetts, the national aspirations and historic claims of the Jewish people with regard to Palestine should be recognized at the peace conference, and that, in accordance with the British government's declaration of November second, nineteen hundred and seventeen, there should be established such political, administrative, and economic conditions in Palestine as will assure the development of Palestine into a Jewish commonwealth, and that the American representatives at the peace conference should use their best endeavors to accomplish this object; and be it further

Revolved, That in the opinion of the House of Representatives of Massachusetts, express provision should be made at the peace conference for granting to the Jewish people in every land the complete enjoyment of life and liberty, and the opportunities for national development, to the end that justice may be done to that people which, in the long course of history, has suffered more than any other on earth; and be it further

Resolved, That a copy of these resolutions be transmitted by the Secretary of Commonwealth to the President of the United States.

In House of Representatives, adopted, February 13, 1919.

THE COMMONWEALTH OF MASSACHUSETTS

In the year one thousand nine hundred and twenty

AN ORDER RELATIVE TO THE OFFICIAL RECOGNITION BY THE POWERS OF THE RIGHT OF THE JEWISH PEOPLE TO A NATIONAL EXISTENCE IN PALESTINE

Ordered, That the Massachusetts House of Representatives greets with profound satisfaction the official recognition by the Powers of the right of the Jewish People to a National existence in Palestine, and that it deeply rejoices to see the National liberation of the Children of Israel who will once more shed lustre on our civilization; that it hails the Jewish National restoration to the ancestral soils as a triumph of justice for which all mankind should be grateful; that it urges the Government of the United States of America to use its best endeavors to facilitate the speedy development of Palestine into a Jewish National Homeland, for only on its own soil can the Jewish people live its own life and make, as it has made in the past, its characteristic and specific contribution to the spiritual treasure of humanity; and be it further

Ordered, That copies of this order be forwarded by the Secretary of the Commonwealth to the President of the United States, to the Senators and Representatives in Congress from this Commonwealth, and to the Zionist Organization of America.

In House of Representatives, adopted, May 5, 1920.

A true copy. Attest:

ALBERT P. LANGTRY,
Secretary of the Commonwealth.

THE COMMONWEALTH OF MASSACHUSETTS

Whereas, The Supreme Council of the Allied Peace Conference meeting at San Remo recognized the right of the Jewish nation to spiritual existence in Palestine and conferred upon Great Britain a mandate over Palestine; and

Whereas, The various great nations of the World have approved the establishment of the national homeland for the Jews in Palestine; and

Whereas, The people of the United States individually and through their spokesmen in Congress, and by leading men in all walks of life, have expressed their gratification at the realization of the national hopes of the Jews; and

Whereas, The General Court of Massachusetts views with pleasure the progress of the Jewish people in Palestine, in developing the economic resources of the country, in founding institutions of learning and in creating a spiritual centre, so that it may the better serve mankind; therefore be it

Ordered, That the General Court of Massachusetts urges the government of the United States of America formally to recognize the present status of the Jewish people in Palestine and thus to approve the fulfillment of its yearning desire for a national home in the land of its forefathers; and be it further

Ordered, That copies of this order be sent by the Secretary of the Commonwealth to the President of the United States, to the presiding officers of both branches of Congress, to each of the Senators and Representatives in Congress from Massachusetts, and to the Zionist Organization of America.

H. R., March 29, 1922.   Adopted.   Sent up for concurrence.

JAMES W. KIMBALL, *Clerk.*

Senate, March 29, 1922.   Adopted, in concurrence.

                                 WILLIAM H. SANGER, *Clerk.*

A true copy.   Attest:

                                  ALBERT P. LANGTRY,
                         Secretary of the Commonwealth.

RHODE ISLAND

JANUARY SESSION, 1939

No. 58, S 150, Approved, March 3, 1939

JOINT RESOLUTION respectfully and earnestly praying the administrative government of Great Britain not to repudiate the Balfour declaration with relation to the establishment of Palestine as a Jewish national home.

Whereas, It appears that under the mandate of the league of nations and by the Balfour declaration, Great Britain has undertaken the establishment of Palestine as the Jewish national home; and

Whereas, It appears that Great Britain has indicated a possible repudiation of the Balfour declaration; now therefore be it

Resolved, That the members of the general assembly of the State of Rhode Island and Providence Plantations of the United States of America do respectfully and earnestly pray the administrative government of Great Britain not to repudiate the Balfour declaration with relation to the establishment of Palestine as a Jewish national home; and be it further

Resolved, That a duly certified copy of this resolution be transmitted by the secretary of state of the State of Rhode Island and Providence Plantations to the secretary of state of the United States to be forwarded in turn by him to the United States ambassador to the court of Saint James for transmission to the proper authority in the administrative government of Great Britain.

STATE OF RHODE ISLAND AND PROVIDENCE PLANTATIONS

DEPARTMENT OF STATE

Office of the Secretary of State

PROVIDENCE

I, Armand H. Cote, Secretary of State of the State of Rhode Island and Providence Plantations, hereby certify the foregoing to be a true photostatic copy of Resolution No. 58, entitled, "Joint resolution respectfully and earnestly praying the administrative government of Great Britain not to repudiate the Balfour Declaration with relation to the establishment of Palestine as a Jewish National Home"; the same being passed by the General Assembly at the January Session, A. D. 1939 and approved by the Governor on the third day of March, A. D. 1939.

In Testimony Whereof, I have hereunto set my hand and affixed the seal of the State of Rhode Island, this sixth day of December, in the year of our Lord nineteen hundred and forty-three.

[SEAL]   ARMAND H. COTE,
                                       Secretary of State.

OHIO

UNITED STATES OF AMERICA,
  STATE OF OHIO,
    Office of the Secretary of State.

I, Edward J. Hummel, do hereby certify that I am the duly elected, qualified and acting Secretary of State of the State of Ohio, and I further certify that the attached is a true and correct copy of House Joint Resolution No. 45, as adopted April 15th, 1919, as same appears in the Laws or Ohio, Volume 108, Part 2, as passed by the Eighth-third General Assembly of the State of Ohio.

In Testimony Whereof, I have hereunto subscribed my name and affixed my official seal at the City of Columbus, Ohio, this first day of December, A. D. 1943.
[SEAL]   ———— ———— *Secretary of State.*

HOUSE JOINT RESOLUTION No. 45

Joint Resolution Relative to the rights of the Jewish people

Whereas, The future prosperity and peace of the world depends upon a just and equitable settlement of the European war whereby each and every nationality, however small, shall be granted the liberty to determine its own destiny and the opportunity of living its own life; and
Whereas, The government of the United States of America is recognized as an ardent exponent of the rights of small nations; therefore be it
Resolved, By the General Assembly of the State of Ohio:
That in its opinion the national aspirations and historic claims of the Jewish people with regard to Palestine should be recognized at the peace conference, in accordance with the British government's declaration of November second, nineteen hundred and seventeen, that there be established such political, administrative and economic conditions in Palestine as will assure the development of Palestine into a Jewish commonwealth, and that the American representatives at the peace conference should use their best endeavors to facilitate the achievement of this object; be it further
Resolved, That it is the opinion of the general assembly of the State of Ohio, that express provisions be made at the peace conference for the purpose of granting the Jewish people in every land the complete enjoyment of life, liberty, and the opportunities for national development to the end that justice may be done to one of the most suffering people on earth, the Jewish people; and be it further
Resolved, That the secretary of state be and he is hereby directed to send duly certified copies of this resolution to each of the representatives of this State in the Senate and House of Representatives of the United States and to each of the representatives of the United States in attendance as members of the Peace Conference assembled at Paris.

CARL R. KIMBALL,
Speaker of the House of Representatives.
CLARENCE J. BROWN,
President of the Senate.

Adopted April 15, 1919.

NEW YORK

STATE OF NEW YORK

OFFICE OF THE CLERK OF THE SENATE

ALBANY

STATE OF NEW YORK,
County of Albany, ss:
I, William S. King, Clerk of the Senate of the State of New York, do hereby certify that I have carefully compared the annexed copy of Senate concurrent resolution No. 38 by Senator John J. Dunnigan which was adopted in the Senate and concurred in by the Assembly on March 8, 1943 relative to Memorializing the President of the United States and Congress, favoring the continued development of a Jewish National Home in Palestine with the original thereof on file in my office, and that the same is a true and correct copy thereof.
In Witness Whereof, I have hereunto set my hand and affixed the official seal of the Senate, this third day of May 1943.
[SEAL]

WILLIAM S. KING.

STATE OF NEW YORK

IN SENATE RESO. NO. 38

ALBANY, *March 8, 1943.*

By Mr. Dunnigan:

Whereas the persecution and attempted extermination by Nazi Germany of the Jews in occupied Europe have outraged the conscience of the civilized world and have manifested the necessity of continued maintenance and development of a Jewish National Homeland; and

Whereas, pursuant to the treaties of peace terminating the first World War, a mandate was issued, approved by fifty-two nations including the United States, to facilitate the establishment of a Jewish National Home in Palestine; and

Whereas this policy was concurred in by a joint resolution unanimously adopted by both Houses of the Congress of the United States on June 30, 1922, and approved by the President on September 21st, 1922; now, therefore be it

Resolved (if the Assembly concur), That we of the State of New York express our most profound sympathy toward the victims of Nazi religious persecution and racial hatred; and be it further

Resolved (if the Assembly concur), That we urge the fullest cooperation of the United Nations in punishing those responsible for this horrible crime against humanity and in alleviating suffering through an international rescue agency; and be it further

Resolved (if the Assembly concur), That we favor the continued development of a Jewish National Home in Palestine, for the absorption of as many Jews as may be required by the urgent needs of the Jewish people, as an integral part of the new democratic world order in accordance with the principles for which the United Nations are now fighting; and be it further

Resolved (if the Assembly concur) That a copy of this resolution be forwarded to the President and to the Secretary of State of the United States, the President of the United States Senate and to the Speaker of the House of Representatives.

By Order of the Senate.

WILLIAM S. KING, *Clerk.*

In Assembly March 8, 1943. Concurred in without amendment. By order of the Assembly.

ANSLEY B. BORKOWSKI, *Clerk.*

_____

JANUARY SESSION, 1919

No. 26. (H. 821.) Approved Mar. 26, 1919

RESOLUTION favoring the establishment of a Jewish Home Land in Palestine and the protection of Jewish rights and liberties in the settlement of the European war.

Whereas, The future prosperity and peace of the world depend upon a just settlement of the European war whereby every nationality, however small, shall be granted the right to determine its own destiny and the opportunity of living its own life; and

Whereas, The government of the United States is recognized as an ardent exponent of the rights of the small nations; therefore be it

Resolved, That the General Assembly of the State of Rhode Island endorses the national aspirations and historic claims of the Jewish people with regard to Palestine and hopes that they be recognized at the peace conference, and that, in accordance with the British government's declaration of November second, nineteen hundred and seventeen, there should be established such political, administrative and economic conditions in Palestine as will assure development of Palestine into a Jewish commonwealth, and that the General Assembly of Rhode Island requests the American representatives at the peace conference that they use their best endeavors to accomplish this object; and be it further

Resolved, That in the opinion of the General Assembly of Rhode Island, express provision should be made at the peace conference for securing for the Jewish people of every land the complete enjoyment of life and liberty, and the opportunities for national development, to the end that justice may be done to that people which, in the long course of history, has suffered more than any other on earth; and be it further

Resolved, That a copy of these resolutions be transmitted by the Secretary of State to the President of the United States.

STATE OF RHODE ISLAND AND PROVIDENCE PLANTATIONS

DEPARTMENT OF STATE

Office of the Secretary of State

PROVIDENCE

I, Armand H. Cote, Secretary of State of the State of Rhode Island and Providence Plantations, hereby certify the foregoing to be a true photostatic copy of Resolution No. 26, entitled, "Resolution favoring the establishment of a Jewish home land in Palestine and the protection of Jewish rights and liberties in the settlement of the European war"; the same being passed by the General Assembly at the January Session, A. D. 1919 and approved by the Governor on the twenty-sixth day of March, A. D. 1919.

In The Testimony Whereof, I have hereunto set my hand and affixed the seal of the State of Rhode Island, this sixth day of December, in the year of our Lord nineteen hundred and forty-three.

[SEAL]   ARMAND H. COTE,
                                              Secretary of State.

THE STATE OF WISCONSIN

DEPARTMENT OF STATE

To All to Whom These Presents Shall Come:

I, Fred R. Zimmerman, Secretary of State of the State of Wisconsin and Keeper of the Great Seal thereof, do hereby certify that the annexed copy of Enrolled Joint Resolution No. 34 of the Wisconsin Legislative Session of 1919, has been compared by me with the original enrolled joint resolution, on file in this Department, and that the same is a true copy thereof, and of the whole of such joint resolution.

In Testimony Whereof, I have hereunto set my hand and affixed the Great Seal of the State at the Capitol, in the city of Madison, this 6th day of January, A. D. 1944.

[SEAL]   FRED R. ZIMMERMAN,
                                              Secretary of State.

                                              Rec'd. March 11, 1919   3:00 P. M.
[Jt. Res. No. 40, S.]

JOINT RESOLUTION Relating to the establishment of a Jewish State of Palestine and for the granting of complete liberty to the Jewish people in all countries

The peace of the world depends upon a just and equitable settlement of the war just ended, and whereby each and every nationality, however small, be granted liberty to determine its own destiny and opportunity of living its own life.   The people of the United States of America are recognized as ardent supporters of the rights of small nations to exist.

On November 3rd, 1917, the government of the British Empire, declared in favor of the establishment in Palestine, of a national home for the Jewish people and pledged its best endeavors to facilitate the achievement of a Jewish state, with the provision that in the establishment of the same, nothing shall be done that shall prejudice the civil and national rights of non-Jewish communities in Palestine or the rights and political status enjoyed by the Jewish people in other countries.

That the establishment of a Jewish state is essential to the millions of people who have been faithful and loyal subjects of the several nations of which they are citizens and have been for centuries oppressed, through racial prejudice, and left without a parent country for their race; therefore be it

Resolved by the senate, the assembly concurring, That the national aspiration and historic claims of the Jewish people with regard to establishment of a state in Palestine be recognized at the Peace Conference, in accordance with both the American and British declarations. That there shall be established such political and economical conditions in Palestine as will insure the development of a Jewish commonwealth in that country; that the American Representatives at the Peace Conference shall use their best endeavors to promote same and that the Jewish people in every land be granted complete enjoyment of life, liberty, and opportunities for national development to the end that delayed justice may be done to one of the most suffering people of the earth; be it further

Resolved, That a copy of these resolutions properly signed by the presiding officer of both houses and duly attested by the chief clerks thereof be forwarded to the President of the United States, with the purpose of having the same presented in a formal manner to the Representatives of the Nations of the World, now sitting at the Great Peace Conference in France.

RILEY S. YOUNG,
Speaker of the Assembly.
C. E. SHAFFER,
Chief Clerk of the Assembly.
EDWARD F. DITTMAR,
President of the Senate.
O. G. MUNSON,
Chief Clerk of the Senate.

ALABAMA

THE STATE OF ALABAMA

DEPARTMENT OF STATE

I, Howell Turner, Secretary of State of the State of Alabama, do hereby certify that the pages hereto attached, contain a true, accurate and literal copy of Act No. 144, Senate Joint Resolution No. 4 by Simpson, approved June 10, 1943, as the same appears on file and of record in this office.

In Testimony Whereof, I have hereunto set my hand and affixed the Great Seal of the State, at the Capitol, in the City of Montgomery, this 29th day of November One Thousand Nine Hundred and Forty-three.

[SEAL]

HOWELL TURNER,
Secretary of State.

(No. 144) (S. J. R. 4—Simpson)

SENATE JOINT RESOLUTION

Be it resolved by the Senate, the House of Representatives concurring, that;

Whereas, The policy of the Axis powers to exterminate the Jews of Europe through mass murder cries out for action by the United Nations representing the civilized world and emphasizes the urgent need for a Jewish homeland: and

Whereas, On November 2, 1917, the British Government issued the Balfour Declaration viewing with favor the establishment in Palestine of a national home for the Jewish People and offering to facilitate such an endeavor; and

Whereas, On June 30, 1922, a resolution was adopted by a joint session of the Congress of the United States which approved the Balfour Declaration and it was included in the Anglo-American treaty of December 3, 1924: Now, therefore, be it

Resolved by the Senate and House of Representatives of the State of Alabama, That the establishment of a Jewish homeland in Palestine and facilities for its further development for receiving the maximum number of Jewish refugees who have been uprooted from their homes be commended to the considered judgment of the United Nations, not only as an act of justice to the Jewish people and the righting of an ancient wrong, but as an integral part of the new democratic world order in which every people shall have the right to self-government and self-determination in accordance with the principles for which we are now waging war; and be it further

Resolved, That a copy of this resolution be forwarded to the President of the United States, to Senators Wagner and McNary, Co-chairmen of the American Palestine Committee, and to the British Embassy in Washington for transmission to the proper authorities in London.

Approved June 10, 1943.

Chairman Bloom. Proceed, please.

Dr. Silver. The record, then, of what was intended for Palestine and what was undertaken is quite clear. The civilized world recognized the right of the Jewish people to rebuild their national home in Palestine. Great Britain accepted a mandate to facilitate its consummation. The Jews of the world set themselves to the task of upbuilding.

Thus a new era in Jewish history was ushered in. The Jewish people threw themselves into the work of upbuilding with incomparable zeal and enthusiasm. The task was enormous—untrained hands, inadequate means, overwhelming difficulties. The land was stripped and poor—neglected through the centuries. European Jewry was shattered and impoverished by the war and could not be quickly rallied to the work of reconstruction. Plans had to be improvised and carried through piecemeal. Nevertheless, the record of pioneering achievement of the Jewish people in Palestine in the 20 years between the two world wars, the story of their heroic labors and sacrifices and their courageous experimentation have received the acclaim of the entire world. A veritable miracle of colonization was performed. The Jewish population increased from 55,000 to 600,000. Close to 300 colonies have been established. Social vision and high human idealism went into the planning and structure of many of them. Some 2,000 factories and 4,000 small workshops were opened. The waters of the Jordan were harnessed for electric power. The Dead Sea was made to yield up its vast chemical resources. Barren hills and valleys were reforested. Marshes were drained. A splendid educational system was developed, crowned by the Hebrew University on Mount Scopus. A modern health service was established throughout the country, available to Jews, Mohammedans, and Christians alike.

I hope you will have the privilege of hearing later on one of the great experts of our country, Dr. Lowdermilk, tell you of what has been accomplished in Palestine.

It was fortunate indeed that Palestine was available, readied and prepared by the labor of these Jewish pioneers, when the horrible Hitler persecutions swept over European Jewry. For that little country was able to absorb more than 300,000 refugees from Germany and Central Europe, a country so small that it could hide itself in one of the great States that you represent. Today Jewish Palestine is again vindicating its claim to full life and national freedom by the extraordinary contributions which it is making to the war effort of the United Nations. Some 23,000 young Palestinian Jews out of that small population have volunteered for service in the armies of the United Nations, have fought bravely, many of them with rare distinction. The civilian population is engaged in an all-out effort to back up the fighting armies in the Near East by providing them with many vital supplies and services; 50,000 Palestinian Jews are engaged in defense work.

And here we come to the point back of this resolution. The administration of Palestine has unfortunately not always been conducted on a plane corresponding to the high intentions of the framers of the Balfour declaration, nor did it reflect the good will and unflagging sympathy of the English people whose historic friendship the Jewish people will never forget. Local British officials, though of high integrity, have shown little understanding of the processes involved in the building of a Jewish homeland, and there are always great difficulties associated with the upbuilding of a new homeland. They have not grasped the implications of the organic relationship between the Jewish people outside of Palestine, to whom the Balfour declaration was issued, and the land which they administered. The rebuilding of the Jewish homeland implies a dynamic outlook. The outlook of British officials has been in the main static, based on the tacit assumption that Palestine alone, and not the integration of large numbers of immigrants with an evolving Jewish homeland, was their concern.

They have, therefore, tended to look upon the local difficulties associated with the upbuilding of the Jewish homeland as unnecessary disturbances of the status quo, instead of a natural part of the task assigned to them. No corrective to this attitude was applied by the home government in London. No consistent attempt was made to bring home to the Arabs of Palestine the fact that the Balfour Declaration was an interallied policy, and later, that the mandate was international law, and the first evidence of recalcitrance on their part—namely, the riots of May 1921—was rewarded by a temporary suspension of Jewish immigration.

Concession led to concession. The White Paper issued in 1922 declared that—

the terms of the Balfour Declaration do not contemplate that Palestine as a whole should be converted into a Jewish national home, but that such a home should be established in Palestine.

This was the beginning of reinterpretation. It introduced an element of ambiguity into what had been quite clear till then.

The Palestine contemplated in the mandate had consisted of Transjordan and cis-Jordan. In the year 1922, Transjordan—three times the area of cis-Jordan—was closed to Jewish immigration.

In subsequent years, Palestine's British officials took the view that they were not primarily concerned with the facilitation of the creation of a Jewish homeland, but with the administration of the country in its existing condition.

This view has dominated the policies and actions of the Palestine administration ever since. The national rights of the Jewish people in relation to Palestine which had been internationally acknowledged and which alone gave legal basis for the mandatory presence there at all were progressively and consistently sacrificed.

Following the disturbances of 1936, a Palestine Royal Commission was sent to Palestine to investigate. Its report proposed to partition the country, to create an Arab and a Jewish state, and an area reserved for British administration.

A technical commission was then set up to work out the details of a partition plan. It finally declared that the partition plan was unworkable.

Following discussions in London in 1939, to which representatives of Arabs and Jews were invited and which brought no positive results, the British Government of the late Mr. Chamberlain prepared the White Paper of May 17, 1939. The House of Commons reluctantly consented to it during a tense period of international complications, only after the Government insisted on acceptance as a vote of confidence. The White Paper was formally disapproved by the Permanent Mandates Commission. It was never submitted for approval to the Council of the League of Nations, although article 27 of the mandate clearly states that—

the consent of the Council of the League of Nations is required for any modifications of the terms of the mandate.

It was thus denied legal validity. However, despite all this, it was put into effect.

Under the terms of this White Paper, Jewish immigration was limited to 10,000 a year for the next 5 years. A bonus immigration of an additional 25,000 was allowed in consideration of the plight of Jewish refugees. However, after March of this year, 1944, Jewish immigration is to be discontinued entirely "unless the Arabs of Palestine are prepared to acquiesce in it."

The White Paper likewise grants the High Commissioner of Palestine general powers to prohibit and regulate transfers of land. Regulations have been issued according to which Jews are allowed the right of free purchase in only 2.6 percent of the total area of Palestine—260 square miles! A total prohibition on transfer of land to Jews was imposed in about two-thirds of the country; in the remaining area transfer is permissible only under severe restriction and subject to the consent of the High Commissioner. Thus discriminatory laws against Jews were introduced in their own national home!

Thus the Jews were left to build their national home without men and without land, just as their ancestors in Egypt were expected to make brick without straw.

The White Paper is by no stretch of the imagination the fulfillment of the national aspirations of the Jewish people recognized in the mandate. It is their total liquidation. This White Paper when it was issued in 1939, in the disastrous Munich appeasement era and as part of that tragic political and spiritual debacle of those days, aroused the bitterest opposition. It was denounced both at home and abroad. It was violently opposed by some of the foremost statesmen of Great Britain. I would just like to quote this sentence from the great statement of Winston Churchill which he made in the House of Commons when the policy of the White Paper was being discussed. He said:

We are now asked to submit, and this rankles most with me, to an agitation which is fed with foreign money and ceaselessly inflamed by Nazi and by Fascist propaganda.

Chairman BLOOM. Rabbi, would you mind an interruption there? I would like to call to your attention that the Secretary of State in his letter to Lord Balfour, addressed to him from Washington, January 27, 1922, signed by Charles Evans Hughes, said this—they were referring to the mandate—

An undertaking on the part of the British Government that it will not propose or accept any modification in the terms of the mandate without previous consultation with the Government of the United States would not, I fear, adequately meet the condition expressed in the memorandum of August last that the consent of the United States shall be obtained before any alteration is made in the text of the mandate.

Dr. SILVER. That is correct, Mr. Bloom. It was suggested by Great Britain that our Government should be consulted about changes in the mandate, but our Government insisted that our consent be received before any changes are made.

Chairman Bloom. I wish to state that that is from the document issued by the State Department. It is on pages 60 and 61 of the document of the State Department entitled "Mandate for Palestine."

Dr. Eaton. I wonder if the Rabbi could in a word or two outline the reasons that actuated the issuance of the White Paper. What were the circumstances that made that apparently necessary by the British Government?

Dr. Silver. The White Paper was a product, Dr. Eaton, of the same appeasement era as Munich was.

Dr. Eaton. Who were they appeasing?

Dr. Silver. The Arabs.

Dr. Eaton. Have they appeased them?

Dr. Silver. They have not, I am afraid, and the events of the last few years have shown that the Arabs were not appeased. And when England found itself in war it received no help from the Arabs. As you well know, the Iraqi revolted against Great Britain and that revolt had to be put down by force. The Arabs today have not moved a finger to help the Allies. This policy proved as bankrupt as the Munich policy proved bankrupt in relation to Mr. Hitler.

Dr. Eaton. Is the attitude of the Arabs at this time as recalcitrant as it was when the White Paper was issued?

Dr. Silver. I would not be in a position to say as to that. At present there is an element which is working for the Axis. The Mufti is in Berlin at the moment.

Dr. Eaton. How large is that element?

Dr. Silver. We have no way of knowing. We do know that those who instigated the riots in previous years were relatively few in relation to the total population. The official figures were some 1,500 brigands who carried on all of the rioting during all of that period.

Dr. Eaton. Have you any reason to believe that the Arabs would not create a disturbance now in a large degree making possible a very serious situation in this present war?

Dr. Silver. I do not think so. I will give you my reasons for it. The thought that the Arabs must be appeased lest they will do this or that is not borne out by facts. I will give you an illustration of what I have in mind.

When our forces landed in north Africa they found that the Cremieux laws had been abrogated by the Vichy government. The Cremieux laws had given citizenship to the Jews of Algeria some 75 years ago. The Vichy government had abrogated those laws. When that part of north Africa was taken over by our forces we naturally asked our Government to see that the Cremieux laws be reinstated as part of our program of freedom for oppressed peoples. And the first reaction was, oh, no, you must not do anything to disturb the Arabs. We pressed for it.

Chairman Bloom. You say "we pressed for it." Please say who pressed for it.

Dr. Silver. The Jews of America.

Chairman Bloom. That is right.

Dr. Silver. And the Cremieux laws were reinstated. There was not a peep out of the Arabs and nothing happened.

Dr. Eaton. Then your belief is if we show sufficient force the Arabs will behave?

Dr. SILVER. That is exactly my position.

Dr. EATON. Who will furnish the force?

Dr. SILVER. The Government which is charged with the responsibility of the mandate.

Dr. EATON. That is Great Britain?

Dr. SILVER. That is Great Britain. And it is well able to handle the job if it has a mind to. There will be no disturbances in Palestine if the British Government does not want them.

Chairman BLOOM. Rabbi, have you finished your statement?

Dr. SILVER. I can in 2 minutes.

Dr. EATON. I just want to ask if that is Great Britain's job why should we mix up in it?

Dr. SILVER. Because Palestine is an international obligation which Great Britain assumed for us and for the 52 other nations.

May I be permitted to finish, Mr. Chairman?

CHAIRMAN BLOOM. Yes, please.

Dr. SILVER. If the White Paper was found odious and morally unjustifiable in 1939, before the Second World War and before the appalling disasters swept over the Jewish communities of Europe, driving hundreds of thousands of Jews helpless and impoverished from their homes to wander over the face of the earth, how utterly insupportable and insufferable is it today?

The last 5 years have been the blackest in Jewish history. They climaxed 5 other years which the Nazi regime ushered in, during which one Jewish community after another in central and eastern Europe was broken and myriads of Jews were driven into exile from countries and homes where they had known dignity, honor, and where they and their ancestors had lived for centuries. Myriads of them crowded the highways of the world in quest of refuge and sanctuary and finding most doors barred against them. But a worse fate awaited those who could not escape in time. For them Hitler has decreed total extermination—systematic, ruthless annihilation—in gas chambers, by machine guns, in human slaughter pens. Two million perished. Some who managed to escape, and after months of wandering finally reached the shores of Palestine—the shores of the Jewish national home—were turned away. They were refused admission. They had no certificates. The last door of hope was shut to them. Many tried to enter illegally. Hundreds of them were apprehended, sent to concentration camps, and later forcibly evacuated to the island of Mauritius in the Indian Ocean where they are rotting to this day. Many perished in Haifa Bay; 760 souls perished in the Black Sea on the ill-fated *Struma*, because permission to enter Palestine was refused to them. But for this infamous White Paper they might have been saved. Had the doors of Palestine been wide open these last years of Nazi terror and had the mandatory government fully cooperated in the task tens of thousands of additional refugees might have been saved from Hitler's mass execution.

In March of this year, the pitifully restricted immigration schedule permitted under the White Paper will come to an end. Only the 30,000 unused visas—unused, principally because of the administrative difficulties put in the way by Palestine officials—remain. Thereafter no more Jews will be permitted to Palestine except on Arab sufferance and consent. This confronts the Jewish people and the whole civilized world with an appalling prospect. It is self-evident that Jewish homelessness will be widespread after the war. There will be hundreds of thousands of Jews, perhaps millions, who will seek new homes in a world which will be inhospitable to immigration. The struggle for existence in a ravaged post-war Europe will be harsh and bitter. Famine, poverty, and misery will stalk over the face of that war-riven continent. There will be ruined economies, worthless currencies, social collapse and revolutions in every defeated country—just as after the last war. The youth of half of half the world which has been indoctrinated with the racial and nationalistic mythologies of Nazi-Fascist dictatorship will be spiritually lost and unsuited to a democratic way of life which they have been taught to hate and despise—and they will be virulent Jew haters. Jews will again be eyed sullenly as unwelcome economic competitors by millions of job-hungry and career-hungry men. Economic hostility will once again be rationalized into the well-known and quite serviceable anti-Semitic thesis.

No doubt the Jews of Europe, following an Allied victory, will be restored to their political rights and to equality of citizenship. But they possessed these rights after the last war—even minority rights in some of the countries of Central and Eastern Europe; and anti-Semitism was never so rampant and so vicious as after the last war.

Can Europe, can the world, can America, which is for all time to come so inextricably bound up with the rest of the world, permit this menacing situation to continue indefinitely after the war?

The Jewish people must be permitted and helped to develop their homeland in Palestine in such a way as to be able to drain off, in a relatively short time, two or three million Jews from the crowded and economically tensioned centers of central and eastern Europe. This will ease the pressures upon the Jews who will remain there, who will then cease to be foci of irritation, conflict, and unrest.

And this brings me back to what Mr. Hamilton Fish said. He told a fine story of what he tried to do and earnestly tried to do, about the establishment of other colonies, but you heard the conclusion of it. Nothing was done. We have had experience with other colonies. There was one recently founded in Santo Domingo in which we placed very high hopes but which perhaps will take care only of a few thousand souls, perhaps only of a few hundred souls.

There are no other opportunities for mass emigration of Jews anywhere else in the world. There will be none. We wish it were otherwise, but wishes are not horses. Feeble trickles of immigration will be permitted in this or that country, but waves will be fiercely resisted; but it is with waves and not with trickles that we must concern ourselves. We Zionists are not opposed to Jewish immigration to any country in the world. Quite the contrary. We hope and pray all countries will open their doors to our refugees. But those things do not happen.

We must not forget the experiences of Jewish refugees in the last 10 years. These experiences will be no different after the war. They may be even more difficult; for nations will then be in the grip of vast economic dislocations and they will be thinking in terms of helping their own people over the extremely formidable transition period when their national economies will be passing from a wartime to a peacetime footing. They will refuse to complicate their lives with large influxes of impoverished immigrants. The Jewish colonies are ready to expand and take in Jewish immigrants.

Mr. RICHARDS. Mr. Chairman, may I ask a question?

CHAIRMAN BLOOM. Mr. Richards.

Mr. RICHARDS. Rabbi, what is the maximum absorptive capacity of Palestine? What figure would you say?

Dr. SILVER. Our best Palestine experts have estimated an additional three or four million people.

Dr. EATON. That does not include Transjordania?

Dr. SILVER. No. That has room for five to eight million people. It was in ancient times the granary of the Roman Empire.

Dr. EATON. In settling this vexed question are we to call on any other governments or do we intend to do it ourselves?

Dr. SILVER. It may be done as in 1926 in the case of the Greeks who were repatriated. There will naturally be some assistance from friendly governments who will want to help in this enterprise. But the Jewish agency is prepared to take on the maximum burden in this task.

Mr. RICHARDS. You would consider it advisable to take Transjordania and open that along with western Palestine to the Jews?

Dr. SILVER. I do not think it is necessary to evacuate the Arabs from any territory. In that territory there are only 300,000 Arabs. They can remain. We do not want to transfer anybody.

Mr. RICHARDS. Some of these Arabs could not exist very well then, could they?

Dr. SILVER. They will adjust themselves to rural life. The Arab lands in the Near East are vast and are nearly two-thirds as large as Europe.

Mr. RICHARDS. Palestine you mentioned as having 12,000 square miles a while ago?

Dr. SILVER. 10,000 square miles.

Mr. RICHARDS. That is about the distance from here to Richmond squared. No; it is not quite that. You were referring then to western Palestine?

Dr. SILVER. That is right.

Mr. RICHARDS. You did not go across the river there at all?

Dr. SILVER. No; just western Palestine. A free and open Palestine is the indispenable condition not only for a peaceful solution of this most obdurate problem of Europe, but also for the pacification of Europe and the world.

Statesmen should clearly understand this. If the problem of mass Jewish emigration and of the national homelessness of the Jewish people is not clearly faced and solved after the war, it will return over and over again to harass and unsettle the world. Reaction will exploit the situation again and again. The defenseless position of the Jews was exploited by the Nazis to rise to power. They employed it as a weapon to achieve the distintegration of Europe. Fascist adventurers after the war will continue to exploit it. The Jewish problem is quite as much the word's problem as it is that of the Jews.

What the world will do concerning the Jewish people and concerning the restoration of its national life in Palestine after the war will be the true index of the nature and character of the entire program of world reconstruction. The world patterns of reconstruction will unerringly reflect the decisions which will be made concerning the Jewish people and its national status. If in the case of the Jewish people, which possesses no armies or navies, and which will emerge from the World War the most shattered of all peoples, the United Nations will act in a spirit of justice, vision, and true statesmanship, then there is hope that by the same spirit the entire world will be healed and saved.

Surely, the Jewish people are no less deserving than other peoples whose national independence and freedom have been guaranteed by the United Nations. They have been the worst victims of Nazi brutality, and their casualties have been proportionately the heaviest. The Jewish people desperately needs Palestine for its homeless millions now and after the war, and for its national security, dignity, and normalcy. Jews have shown a remarkable capacity for pioneering, for labor and sacrifice. They have built worthily and well in Palestine. They have made Palestine their own again by their heroic labor, by their blood and sweat. Nearly all is hopeful, promising, and progressive in that country today, the Jews have created.

What has been called the noblest enterprise of our time must not now be cruelly sapped and undermined.

These resolutions which have been introduced in the House and in the Senate, and which have received the endorsement of the leaders of both political parties, ask our Government to use its good offices, as it did once before, to assist a sorely tried and harassed people in accomplishing the task of rebuilding its national life in its ancestral home—a task approved of by our Government and our people and by 52 other nations at the close of the last war—a task, however, which cannot be accomplished without the free entry of Jews into the country and without the fullest opportunities for colonization and economic development. The reconstitution of Palestine as a Jewish commonwealth would be to us men of faith a fulfillment of prophecy and to all an act of historic justice to an ancient and long-martyred people.

Chairman BLOOM. The Chair wishes to state that permission has been obtained for the committee to sit during the sessions of the House, so we will come back at 2:30. And I would like to ask the members of the committee to please get your questions ready, and this afternoon we will have Dr. Abba Hillel Silver for questioning, to be followed by Dr. Israel Goldstein and Mr. Lessing J. Rosenwald.

We will recess at this time.

(Whereupon, at 12:55 p. m., a recess was taken until 2:30 p. m., of the same day.)

AFTER RECESS

The committee reconvened at 2:30 p. m., pursuant to the taking of recess, for further consideration of House Resolution 418 and House Resolution 419, the Honorable Sol Bloom, chairman, presiding.

Chairman BLOOM. The committee will kindly come to order.

Mr. WRIGHT. I understand that you have a statement to make, so while we are waiting for the members to come would you mind making your statement for the record now?

Mr. WRIGHT. I would be very happy to, Mr. Chairman. I shall make it brief, because I know you have a good many more witnesses to hear this afternoon.

Chairman BLOOM. We have just one or two more.

STATEMENT OF THE HONORABLE JAMES A. WRIGHT, A REPRESENTATIVE IN CONGRESS FROM THE STATE OF PENNSYLVANIA

Mr. WRIGHT. I might say, Mr. Chairman, that I am very proud to be the cosponsor of this resolution which your committee is considering today, and I am also very happy that in this approach to this problem, which is a national rather than a partisan problem, I had the cosponsorship of my distinguished colleague from Connecticut, Mr. Compton.

Now, I think that the United States should give evidence of its post-war intent by assuring Jews of full opportunities for creation of a national homeland in Palestine. The British White Paper would force Jewry into a minority status in the country set aside by mandate as its homeland.

We have moral, treaty, practical, and strategic obligations in this matter. Unless we enunciated the principles of the "four freedoms" with our tongues in our cheeks, we cannot close our eyes to the problem of the Jews.

If we bypass this issue, we are failing to live up to all the principles we profess when we say the right of minorities should not be denied. This is not only a Jewish problem, but a problem of western civilization.

We have treaty rights in this matter, as witnessed by the Convention of 1924 between Great Britain and the United States. We have likewise an interest in preserving the peace and stability of the world.

From the long-term point of view, it is definitely to our political advantages, as Americans, to pass this resolution, to do what we can to see that the rights of free immigration are restored.

The Jews are pacific and democratic by nature. By aiding them at this time we would be building a friendly relationship in the future with whatever commonwealth they might establish. Any movement in the Jews' behalf must be bipartisan to safeguard it against the fate of previous international causes, such as the League of Nations.

Now, victory will come to the United Nations. It is my prayer that it may come soon. We are fighting a war for the purpose of making this world a better place for our posterity to live in and to obtain conditions for a peaceful and orderly developmeEt of mankind.

One of the most tragic problems of humanity is the Jewish problem. This was recognized during the last World War when Palestine was designated by the Allied and Associated Powers, including our own country, as the Jewish national home.

On the basis of this pledge and inspired by this hope, the Jews began to return to Palestine for the purpose of rebuilding their national life. There are today about 600,000 Jews in Palestine. By their own efforts they have prepared the soil of Palestine to enable the country to absorb the large number of homeless Jews in Europe today.

The victory of the United Nations must not be followed by disillusionment and despair. We must not permit conditions to be maintained which would make possible the rise of another Hitler to use the Jewish tragic position in the world as a vehicle for his evil designs.

The Palestine resolution that was adopted 22 years ago by the Sixty-seventh Congress was a recognition of the need of helping to solve the most painful problem of mankind—the Jewish problem. This resolution asserts that since Palestine is the Jewish national home, the Jews should have the right to enter freely into that home and to develop it agriculturally and industrially.

If these rights be denied to the Jewish people, then it would be mockery to call Palestine the Jewish national home.

This resolution affirms the fact that freedom of enjoyment of the home is indispensable to the very existence of the home.

I feel that this problem is not only a Jewish problem. It is not only even an American problem, although it is a distinct problem for America as the foremost exponent of democracy and liberal ideas, but it is a world problem, and I feel certain that in order to establish stability in the world after the war, some solution as the one now proposed must be found. Thank you, Mr. Chairman.

The CHAIRMAN. Thank you very much, Mr. Wright.

The next witness is Dr. Carl J. Friedrich, professor of government and director of the School for Overseas Administration at Harvard University.

STATEMENT OF DR. CARL J. FRIEDRICH, PROFESSOR OF GOVERNMENT AND DIRECTOR OF THE SCHOOL FOR OVERSEAS ADMINISTRATION, HARVARD UNIVERSITY, CAMBRIDGE, MASS.

Dr. FRIEDRICH. Mr. Chairman, would you like to have me stand or sit?

Chairman BLOOM. Suit your own pleasure, Doctor. I think it will be more comfortable for you to sit down.

Dr. FRIEDRICH. As I understand it, Mr. Chairman, I am here in the uncomfortable position of an expert, the most dubious kind of being since he is supposed to be on tap and not on top, I was inclined to feel that the thing to do was to answer questions rather than to make an ex cathedra statement, particularly in view of the admirable statements that have already been made developing the background of the resolution that is before the committee.

I do not speak for any organization or interest, and I might add that I am not a Jew. I am associated with Christian organizations that have interested themselves in the problem of Palestine, as we have interested ourselves in the problem of the plight of the Jewish people in Europe.

I have been asked repeatedly, in speaking before public audiences, what is America's interest in Palestine? My answer is that America's interest in Palestine is very real, practical, and concrete. We are, of course, also motivated by the humanitarian sentiments that have been expressed, but there is more to foreign policy than riding around the globe as Sir Galahad.

Of primary importance to our foreign policy is the establishment and maintenance of peace. General Sherman once said that free men fight wars only in order to establish a better peace. I do not see how a better peace can be established unless a solution is found to the Jewish problem in Europe.

The Jewish problem in Europe has become what it is as the result of Nazi persecution. But if we face the facts frankly it has become what it is also because of the general slackness and indifference on the part of non-Jewish people as they faced the situation.

For quite a number of years I struggled with the problem, as a well intentioned American might, without getting into the problem of Palestine, because I thought there must be a solution for it in Europe.

I have now come to the conclusion, Mr. Chairman, that that is not the case. Nazi persecution of the Jews, unfortunately, is only the most extreme expression of a sentiment which is widespread among other Europeans, and I think it is perfectly fantastic to expect Jewish people to go back to the places in which they have been persecuted to any appreciable extent.

Jewish people see Palestine as a refuge. My impression is that Palestine is not only a refuge, but Palestine is the place where most Jewish people want to go if they want to go to any other place. However, it does not preclude their going to other places.

Now, there is usually the objection raised that the Arabs are already there. I think myself that there is a perfectly clear line of American policy that cuts across these legalistic and historical arguments that are advanced by the proponents of views opposed to the National Home.

There is no suggestion in the policy, as contained in this resolution, that the Arabs are to keep out of Palestine. As a matter of fact, the Arabs have been perfectly free to move into Palestine, and they have been moving into Palestine over the past 25 years. The Arab population of Palestine, as my researches show, is larger today by far than it was 25 years ago.

Mr. CHIPERFIELD. Would the Doctor yield at that point for a question?

Dr. FRIEDRICH. Certainly.

Chairman BLOOM. Mr. Chiperfield.

Mr. CHIPERFIELD. What is the percentage of Jewish population, as compared with the Arab population in Palestine; do you have those figures, Doctor?

Dr. FRIEDRICH. There are reported to be in Palestine about 550,000 Jews and about 1,000,000 to 1,100,000 Arabs.

Chairman BLOOM. That is about one-third to two-thirds Arabs. Do you mind interruptions, Doctor?

Dr. FRIEDRICH. No, sir; I do not mind interruptions.

Chairman BLOOM. I thought you had a statement, and it might be better not to interrupt you until you had concluded.

Dr. FRIEDRICH. I have a few notes, but not a statement.

Mr. CHIPERFIELD. I did not mean to interrupt your statement.

Dr. FRIEDRICH. I do not mind at all.

Mr. McMURRAY. May I ask the Doctor a question, Mr. Chairman.

Chairman BLOOM. Mr. McMurray.

Mr. McMURRAY. In relation to the percentage of Arab population in Palestine, do you happen to recall, roughly, what the Arab population of Palestine today is as compared with that of 25 years ago?

Dr. FRIEDRICH. As I remember it, it was roughly about 600,000 25 years ago, and it has grown to over a million today.

Mr. McMURRAY. It has almost doubled?

Dr. FRIEDRICH. Yes. Of course, not all of that is immigration into Palestine. A good deal of it has come about because the Jewish people have brought better health and sanitation to Palestine, and, consequently, the infant mortality among the Arabs has greatly decreased. It is also due to the fact that a lot of Arabs that were poor and dilapidated tenants have moved into the prosperous Jewish towns and have been able to do better after they got there.

So, I think there is no suggestion that the Arabs be kept out of Palestine, nor is there any suggestion, as you may perhaps assume, if you read some of the Arab stuff that the Arabs are forced to sell their land to the Jews. They have never been forced to sell their land at all, but they have been given the opportunity to sell it. Nor, on the other hand, is there any suggestion made that the Arabs be prevented from leaving. In other words, as far as I can see, sound American policy would seek to have a very great measure of freedom for the international movement of people and goods and capital.

There is, therefore, a definite intention here to secure freedom of opportunity to the Jews to move to Palestine to develop the country and to buy land, and as I have said before all of these aspects seem to me to be vital to the United States, because in it we have a solution of the Jewish problem.

Chairman BLOOM. I hope you have read Mr. Churchill's speech which was made in the House of Commons?

Dr. FRIEDRICH. Yes, certainly, many times.

Chairman BLOOM. I believe I state it fully and correctly in substance when I say that he said the Jewish problem, the problem of Palestine was not a problem of the Jews in Palestine, but it was the problem of the Jews outside of Palestine, and the problem of the Jews of the world—is that correct?

Dr. FRIEDRICH. Yes, sir; that is correct, and he said, also—and it is important since he was a member of the Cabinet—that the promises involved in the Balfour Declaration were made not to the Jews of Palestine, but to all Jews.

Chairman BLOOM. Of the world?

Dr. FRIEDRICH. Yes, sir; of the world.

Chairman BLOOM. I think in his speech he used the expression "the world" about a half a dozen times, which emphasized that, in his thought, he was talking not of the problem of the Palestine Jews, but the Palestine of the world.

Dr. FRIEDRICH. That is correct. Mr. Chairman, I think a good deal of erroneous information has been handed out suggesting, that the problem of Palestine is a purely local problem, whereas actually, it has ramifications, and the British official documents are full of indications, that it is a problem of the world.

Chairman BLOOM. Since you qualified yourself as an expert, I wanted to bring that out.

Dr. FRIEDRICH. Well, I am on tap, Mr. Chairman, but that is about all.

Chairman BLOOM. Proceed; you are doing very well, Doctor.

Dr. FRIEDRICH. I think I should say that if the Congress of the United States should, as I sincerely hope it will, adopt this resolution unanimously or otherwise, that it will see to it that it becomes something more than a resolution. Reference has been repeatedly made to the resolution of 1922, and to the convention of 1924. As I understand the American foreign policy, I cannot help saying that I feel our policy has been theoretical, it has been a policy of big words, and very few deeds, indeed.

One of the gentlemen this morning made reference to the fact that protests were made. There is very little on the record that shows any genuine, active support for the policy involved in the resolution of 1922, and I think it will bear continuous watching to see to it that the policy now adopted be implemented by effective action.

Mrs. BOLTON. Mr. Chairman, may I ask a question?

Chairman BLOOM. Yes; Mrs. Bolton.

Mrs. BOLTON. Do you mean by that that it should be implemented with military action?

Dr. FRIEDRICH. No, not necessarily military action. In fact, I had not thought of that at all, but implemented by concrete and practical steps. Let me give you an illustration of what I mean by that. The Congress has voted, and the President has signed, as I understand it, although I am not sure about the latter, an appropriation for the United Nations Relief and Rehabilitation Administration.

Chairman BLOOM. Pardon me, an authorization was made by the House, and the legislation is now before the Senate. The House has passed it and it is now in the Senate.

Mr. FRIEDRICH. I see.

Chairman BLOOM. And then after it passes the Senate it goes to the President for signature to the enabling legislation, and then it comes back again to the House and Senate for an appropriation. This is merely an authorization for the appropriation.

Dr. FRIEDRICH. Well, it sounds like a long story to me, and I hope you can make it short. But the point I would like to make in that connection in answer to your question is this: here you have an administration which is going to spend a very substantial amount of funds coming from the American taxpayer, to provide for relief and rehabilitation for those who have been uprooted by the Nazi terror. Well, among them are first and foremost the Jews, and if the Jews go home to Palestine, appropriations under United Nations Relief and Rehabilitation should be made available to these people, even though they have gone to Palestine, and yet, at the present time, the United Nations Relief and Rehabilitation Administration does not include Palestine amongst the territories to which their activities will extend. I think the Congress should see to it that Palestine is so included. That is the kind of thing I mean by practical and concrete action to implement the resolution.

Mrs. BOLTON. Of course, you realize that Congress can make no changes in the United Nations Relief and Rehabilitation agreement; that is up to the 44 nations that signed it, and it is not a matter for congressional action.

Dr. FRIEDRICH. They cannot immediately, but they can do a lot informally, since they provide the appropriations for it.

Chairman BLOOM. Yes, there is no question about that. You see, the U. N. R. R. A. merely applies to those countries that have been occupied, and they can only come in after the military authorities are out. Now, it is only that part of the country that has been occupied to which those funds apply. In other words, if they went into China, the U. N. R. R. A. would apply only to that part of China which has been occupied by the enemy, and it would not apply to Palestine, because it has not been occupied by the enemy at all.

Dr. FRIEDRICH. Well, there has been talk about India being included.

Chairman BLOOM. It is not included; you can leave India out right now.

Dr. FRIEDRICH. I know Mrs. Bolton is correct regarding the technical point she made. But a powerful appropriating commonwealth like the United States Government and the Congress can vitally affect the decision of an organization like the United Nations Relief and Rehabilitation Administration.

Chairman BLOOM. Let us get back to the resolution, please, as that has nothing to do with it.

Dr. FRIEDRICH. It seems to me that we must try to avoid being satisfied with purely general expressions of sentiment in this field. In other words, I would be prepared to back more than the present resolution indicates in the way of concrete action to implement what the resolution indicates.

In order to illustrate that more fully, I think I can just briefly state what I consider the especially pertinent parts of a new American policy with respect to the national home which would, in my own personal view, be involved in making real the legislation which you are asking the opportunity to vote upon:

First, as the resolution itself provides, the removal of present restrictions on the movement of people into and out of Palestine. Everybody speaks merely of the White Paper. There were very onerous restrictions imposed, as I am sure the members of the committee know, on the movement of people before the publication of the White Paper. The White Paper is only the most extreme and the last step in continuing the policy of restricting the movement of people into Palestine, and I myself feel that the removal of present restrictions on that movement should go beyond the removal of those restrictions envisaged by the White Paper.

Second, the removal of restrictions on the settlement and reclamation of land, such as restrictions on land purchases, and I believe that is also obviously involved in No. 1. There is no point in removing restrictions on the movement of people into Palestine if you do not also, at the same time, remove restrictions on enabling them to live there.

Third, the removal of restrictions on the movement of goods into and out of Palestine, as far as practical.

Fourth, a program of rapid, large-scale economic development, including basic reclamation and irrigation works, industrial development and the like, with a view to maximizing absorptive capacity. I believe your resolution involves steps along this line because people who do not want to open the gates of Palestine, always bring forward the argument that its absorptive capacity is very restricted. Twenty-five years ago they said none could go to Palestine, and then more went there, and then the limit was supposed to be 300,000, and now we have 550,000 people there, and these same people say that that is about all that can go there. They have always argued in terms of the absorptive capacity of Palestine. As the history of the United States shows, absorptive capacity is something that is vitally related to pioneering effort on the part of the people. The Jews have been the pioneers in going to Palestine in the last 25 years, as far as I can make out, and it is up to them to develop the absorptive capacity of Palestine. They must be given an opportunity to increase absorptive capacity, and hence I make this point No. 4 for a program of rapid and large-scale economic development.

The fifth point would be opposition to all efforts to use political maneuvers, especially the terror, for the purpose of preventing the development of the Jewish majority, should the Jew throughout the world continue to back development in Palestine and thus bring this about.

One of the worst features of the policy of the British mandatory in Palestine was the vaccilation. It was never clear-cut. And as a result confusion ensued and terror, and I think there is no object in initiating the kind of policy in this resolution——

Mr. CHIPERFIELD (interposing). If I understand you correctly, you would have the wording in this resolution:

That the United States shall use its good offices and take appropriate measures to the end * * *—

and then include your final point,

Dr. FRIEDRICH. I approve of the wording.

My sixth point is:

Participation in such international authorities, including an international police force, as may be required to insure an unimpeded progress of the above-stated measures.

That is my sixth point, and then I have done.

You are quite correct. The reason I feel justified in putting these six suggestions before you in the light of experience, and a sorry one in the last 25 years, is this very phrasing of the resolution:

* * * shall use its good offices and take appropriate measures * * *.

In stating them, I know I am stepping on all kinds of peoples' toes.

Chairman BLOOM. You are stepping on their necks; you are going far afield there.

Dr. FRIEDRICH. But I myself feel, Mr. Chairman, there is no point in not facing the facts. I do not see much object in initiating a policy in Palestine or anywhere else in the world which is merely the pro-creator of trouble, and if you are going to have the type of thing that this resolution suggests, you have got to be prepared to enforce it. If you are not prepared to enforce it you are just going to create for yourself a vast amount of trouble. That is my honest conviction as a student of these matters and I think, as was said this morning, that such a policy would be actually welcomed by the British.

There are very large numbers of people in Britain who have been very much distressed about the course of the British policy and I think they have been looking for support from the United States but they have not been getting it and I do not think it is a reflection of the British on the United States at all. It is a question of the forward-looking people both in Britain and in the United States against the small reactionary group in both countries they want to prevent the Jew opening up and democratizing that part of the world, and that is why we ought to be for this resolution and we ought to be for the things that are embraced in the resolution, Mr. Chairman.

Chairman BLOOM. Mrs. Rogers, do you have any questions?

Mrs. ROGERS. Do you feel that it should have the backing of the State Department in order to be effective?

Dr. FRIEDRICH. Well, Mrs. Rogers, I think the State Department ought to do what the people of the United States want them to do and, therefore, what I am asking is that we support this policy and then make the State Department support it. The State Department is not our master; we are theirs.

Mrs. ROGERS. Yes; but I mean it is customary to ask the opinion of the State Department.

Dr. FRIEDRICH. Oh, surely.

Mrs. ROGERS. It would be very helpful, naturally, to have their backing.

Dr. FRIEDRICH. Yes, madam.

Chairman BLOOM. Mr. Vorys, have you any questions?

Mr. VORYS. In regard to your sixth point, Dr. Friedrich, as to the international police force, wouldn't that answer Mrs. Bolton's question? That is, you believe that under the appropriate measures which should be taken we should be prepared to use our force to enforce the other five planks in your platform. Isn't that correct?

Dr. FRIEDRICH. Well, you are putting it a little differently than I would. I said:

Participation in such international authorities, including an international police force, as may be required to insure an unimpeded progress of the above-stated measures.

Let me point out that I said "Including an international police force."

Mr. VORYS. We cannot by congressional resolution enforce international policies by getting others to participate. Now, would you feel if we could not get others to join us that we should use our forces to enforce our views or take appropriate measures that would have to be taken under this resolution?

Dr. FRIEDRICH. I do not think we could under the present set-up. Although the position of the British mandatory is somewhat complex, to say the least, the League being in the position it is in, they are developing, of course, a de facto sovereignty, and I do not see how we could at the present time go in there and use force. All we can do is to use our good offices to aid new and effective international authority that would clarify the situation and themselves be the authority.

Chairman BLOOM. Would you mind an interruption there?

Mr. VORYS. No, Mr. Chairman.

Chairman BLOOM. Dr. Friedrich, in your last statement you said "international authority." Now, don't you mean that international authority that would apply to all nations, not to the United States employment of the police force?

Dr. FRIEDRICH. I said, Mr. Chairman, participation in such international authorities as may be required.

Chairman BLOOM. That is of all nations, is it not?

Dr. FRIEDRICH. Not necessarily all nations but more than one nation.

Chairman BLOOM. But you said "international authority," which would apply to all nations that came in under the authority.

Dr. FRIEDRICH. That is right.

Chairman BLOOM. Is that right?

Dr. FRIEDRICH. Yes, sir.

Chairman BLOOM. You do not mean that the United States should take it upon themselves to do the things that you suggested with reference to a police force?

Dr. FRIEDRICH. No; not at all.

Chairman BLOOM. I wanted to get that clear in the record. You may proceed, Mr. Vorys.

Mr. VORYS. The reason I asked the question was in your preliminary statement you said some policies should be deeds and not words and should be implemented by effective action and I just wanted to see what you had in mind as to deeds and effective action. That is all.

Chairman BLOOM. Mr. Chiperfield, have you any questions?

Mr. CHIPERFIELD. You would not want to intimate that a person could not favor the passage of this resolution without agreeing to all your six points, would you?

Dr. FRIEDRICH. No; I think the resolution is a very desirable entering wedge by itself.

Mr. CHIPERFIELD. It is a sort of a first step?

Mrs. BOLTON. You said "an entering wedge." An entering wedge to what?

Dr. FRIEDRICH. It would be an entering wedge to what I consider the right thing.

Mrs. BOLTON. That is far beyond the homeland; what do you envisage in connection with that?

Dr. FRIEDRICH. No, these are essential concomitants of a sound policy toward the Jewish National Home in Palestine. You will see very largely this sort of thing: They go a little further than I do. I favor a consistent American policy with reference to the Jewish National Home in Palestine and have held to it right along.

Mr. CHIPERFIELD. I am glad to find out what our foreign policy is.

Mr. SCHIFFLER. May I ask a question?

Chairman BLOOM. Mr. Schiffler.

Mr. SCHIFFLER. Pursuing further the questions that were asked by Mrs. Bolton and Mr. Vorys, I think that your idea is not that we should oppose England on this matter, but we should cooperate with England and probably with the United Nations whenever the time is suitable to say that the Jews have a program acceptable and which intends to develop policy. You do not contemplate a break with England but only cooperation. Is that it?

Dr. FRIEDRICH. That is right.

Chairman BLOOM. Mrs. Rogers, have you any questions?

Mrs. ROGERS. Dr. Friedrich, you have quite a good many soldiers, have you not, in Palestine?

Dr. FRIEDRICH. Yes; and we also have, as I understand it, quite a few soldiers in Italy.

Mrs. ROGERS. They are Jewish people, also?

Dr. FRIEDRICH. Yes; they are Jewish people.

Mrs. ROGERS. How many are there?

Dr. FRIEDRICH. I understand that we have a whole division fighting on the Italian front. I stated at the outset when you were not here, that I am not a Jew, but I am interested in them.

Mrs. ROGERS. I see you have made quite a study of this.

Dr. FRIEDRICH. Yes; and as I understand it, the contribution—and this has been said by British authority—the contribution of the Jewish people toward the progress of the war in the Mediterranean theater has been very substantial; and the school that was referred to at Harvard, in one part of it, was devoted to the Mediterranean theater of the war and we had many favorable reports on their work, whereas on the other hand the Arabs, far from having made a contribution, have been a very great obstacle and some like the celebrated Mufti of Jerusalem are reported to be in the Elite Guards of Hitler. That is where they indeed belong, and that is the place where their philosophy would lead them.

Mrs. ROGERS. Do you say they have gotten on very amicably with the Jewish people or that Jewish people have gotten along very amicably with them in Palestine?

Dr. FRIEDRICH. With whom?

Mrs. ROGERS. The Arabs.

Dr. FRIEDRICH. No; I would not be able to say that, Mrs. Rogers. I think that situation is very complicated. The difficulty arises from the fact that the social organization of the Arabs is clearly and definitely of a feudalist kind. The Arab people themselves, in other words, have not received genuine self-expression in the way in which we think of it in this country.

Mrs. ROGERS. They are not united?

Dr. FRIEDRICH. Not the Arabs, even in Palestine; there are all kinds of different groups and there have been very definitely differences between the Jewish people and the Arabs. Among the Arabs, there are a group of people who have a point of view and a philosophy very similar to that of the Nazis.

Mrs. ROGERS. Is that recently?

Dr. FRIEDRICH. They have had that point of view right along and that has been more than just repeated rumors; nobody can say for sure, but very high authority has stated, Mr. Winston Churchill, who is taken pretty seriously nowadays.

Mrs. ROGERS. What do they say?

Dr. FRIEDRICH. That this movement has been financed by the Nazis. In the famous speech which you will find in this admirable collection of documents, even if it does not contain Hamilton Fish's name, you will find a very remarkable passage on this point that you are now raising, Mrs. Rogers. I think it is on page 85, although I am not sure.

Chairman BLOOM. I am sorry, Doctor, but we have to go ahead with some other witnesses. Your 15 minutes was up 15 minutes ago and we will have to get on.

Mrs. ROGERS. This is an important contribution.

Chairman BLOOM. You have it in the book, even if you do not think it is correct. As far as Mr. Hamilton Fish's name may not be in the book, it is not supposed to be there because no Senators or Members of the House have their names on any resolutions. We might as well have that understood. It would not have been correct if we had included Mr. Fish's name.

Dr. FRIEDRICH. Mr. Chairman, I appreciate the time you have given me.

Chairman BLOOM. I want to ask you a question. I yielded to Mrs. Rogers a moment ago.

Dr. FRIEDRICH. I want to read what Winston Churchill said:

Now, we are asked to decree that all this is to stop and all this is to come to an end. We are now asked to submit—and this is what rankles most with me—to an agitation which is fed with foreign money and ceaselessly inflamed by Nazi and by Fascist propaganda.

Mrs. ROGERS. He feels that the Arabs were used by the Nazis?

Dr. FRIEDRICH. Yes, indeed. That is why he used that language.

Mrs. ROGERS. I think we want to work out a happy and abiding solution of the whole problem. Do you feel that the passage of this resolution would in any way stir up the Arabs and make it hard for the Jewish people in Palestine? I think you or some other witness said there were more Arabs than Jewish people in Palestine. I do not want any more harm to come to the Jewish people.

Dr. FRIEDRICH. I do not think it would do harm to the Jewish people; far from it. I do think you will have protests from people who will represent themselves as speaking in behalf of the Arabs, and you will want to bear that in mind—and my opinion is that there is something to Mr. Schiffler's opinion that these people have an ax to grind and that you will hear from them. They will make a great deal of the fact that the Arabs want this and the Arabs object to that, and it is very important to inquire what Arabs are being represented by those particular people who make those statements.

Mrs. ROGERS. I mean it may lead to bloodshed there.

Dr. FRIEDRICH. Not under the British policy as it is carried on right now. At present the British policy is firm. However, from 1936 to 1939 there was terror in Palestine because the Arab nationalists stirred up trouble, but then in 1939 on the outbreak of the war the British decided to take a firm position and they used a firm hand and, curiously enough, when war broke out in Europe, peace was established in Palestine.

Mrs. ROGERS. You feel if there was bloodshed it would be curbed by the British troops, or should our troops go in?

Dr. FRIEDRICH. I am firmly of the conviction, but I may be entirely wrong, that the way to deal with the Fascist type of individual or groups is firmness and determination and I think if this policy is carried forward with firmness and determination the Arab elements of that type are going to be quiet, but if it is just talked of and at the same time they have a feeling that if they make themselves a nuisance as Nazis or Fascists, they would get something, they would go ahead; but if they are faced with a firm and determined policy they will back down.

Mrs. ROGERS. You feel we should have the backing of the State Department?

Dr. FRIEDRICH. Yes; that is why I made these points.

Mrs. ROGERS. Thank you, I get your point of view.

Chairman BLOOM. Doctor, you mentioned the six points. You do not object to this resolution as it is written here, do you?

Dr. FRIEDRICH. Not at all.

Chairman BLOOM. The six points are your own ideas that you would want to see enacted in some kind of legislation. That is your own idea, is that it?

Dr. FRIEDRICH. That is correct.

Chairman BLOOM. But the resolution itself that we have before us meets with your whole-hearted approval?

Dr. FRIEDRICH. That is correct, Mr. Chairman.

Chairman BLOOM. Thank you very much.

STATEMENT OF HON. ARTHUR G. KLEIN, A REPRESENTATIVE IN CONGRESS FROM THE STATE OF NEW YORK

Mr. KLEIN. Mr. Chairman and members of the committee, it is not my purpose and I do not propose to take up the time of the committee by going into the advantages of this resolution. I know other witnesses have done that, and I suppose still other witnesses will.

My purpose in being here is to say that the district which I represent, which is the lower East Side of New York, a great majority or, I might say, they are practically unanimous in support of this resolution.

I have had many delegations call on me and I have received many telephone calls and letters from hundreds of people who are in favor of this resolution. I also feel, Mr. Chairman, that I speak for a majority of the New York City delegation here in Congress. I have taken this matter up with them, and I know they all feel the way I do.

We in New York City, particularly, and I hope the feeling is the same throughout the country, firmly believe that the most important step that we could take at the present time is to pass this resolution and pass it unanimously.

Chairman BLOOM. Thank you Mr. Klein. We will now hear from Representative Herter.

STATEMENT OF HON. CHRISTIAN A. HERTER, A REPRESENTATIVE IN CONGRESS FROM THE STATE OF MASSACHUSETTS

Mr. HERTER. Mr. Chairman and members of the committee, I appear here favoring the resolution. I must confess at the outset that I cannot pose as an expert on the situation in the Near East, but I followed with tremendous interest the, to my mind, very extraordinary progress that has been made in the Jewish homeland, the development there in the last 20 years; and the White Paper, naturally, came as a great surprise and as a great blow to those who were interested in the development of Palestine as the Jewish homeland.

Last September I had a group of Jewish people from my district come to see me to discuss the whole situation. At that time I asked the specific question whether or not a reaffirmation of the so-called Fish-Lodge resolution would be of help in the existing picture. I was told that it would be of great help, and at that time I drafted a resolution which I sent to that group for the purpose of submitting it to the national committee, and I think it eventually led to the particular resolution which is now before you, although I would not claim authorship of that.

I happen to have a copy of that original resolution that I drafted at that time.

Chairman BLOOM. Are you referring to the 1922 resolution?

Mr. HERTER. No; Mr. Chairman; this is the one I drafted in September.

Chairman BLOOM. Of last year?

Mr. HERTER. Yes; I drafted this in September of 1943. If I might insert it in the record, perhaps some of the language might be of help to you in case your consider changing the terminology of the present resolution.

Chairman BLOOM. Was your proposed resolution introduced?

Mr. HERTER. It was not introduced. It was merely submitted at that time by me to this group, and I now merely suggest that it be put in the record. Perhaps some of the language would amplify the present language.

Chairman BLOOM. Without objection, I will insert it in the record.

Mr. HERTER. That is all I have to say.

Chairman BLOOM. Is that all?

Mr. CHIPERFIELD. Mr. Herter, does the resolution you are submitting state the views as to the way to proceed in this matter?

Mr. HERTER. It is very much like the present resolution. I would be glad to read it.

Chairman BLOOM. Suppose you read it.

Mr. HERTER. The resolution reads as follows [reading]:

Whereas the Congress by joint resolution passed without a dissenting vote and approved September 21, 1922, affirmed that the United States of America favors the establishment in Palestine of a national home for the Jewish people;

Whereas the British mandate over Palestine adopted in 1920, ratified by the League of Nations in 1922, was formally recognized by the United States in the Palestine convention of December 3, 1924, between this Government and Great Britain;

Whereas the record of the Jewish people in Palestine since 1923 is one of notable achievement, with deserts reclaimed, modern cities established, and health, educational, and recreational facilities provided;

Whereas, the despoliation of the Jews in western Europe and the unspeakable cruelties which they have suffered at the hands of the Nazis, bringing death to millions, and leaving other millions homeless and penniless, has evoked the sympathy of all decent mankind everywhere;

Whereas, as a consequence of the Nazi savagery toward the Jewish people is to create conditions which make the maintenance and expansion of the Jewish homeland in Palestine in the post-war era an even more pressing necessity than ever before: Now, therefore, be it

Resolved, by the Senate and the House of Representatives of the United States in Congress assembled, That the long-established policy of the United States in favor of the establishment in Palestine of a national home for the Jewish people is hereby expressly reaffirmed, and that no barriers should be interposed to Jewish immigration into Palestine, and further Jewish acquisition of lands there.

Chairman BLOOM. Mr. Herter, that was a joint resolution.

Mr. HERTER. Yes; but while it is in the form of a joint resolution, I have not introduced it.

Chairman BLOOM. You have read a joint resolution and the resolution under consideration before this committee at this time is simply a house resolution. The present resolution under consideration merely expresses the will of the House itself.

Mr. HERTER. I understand so.

Chairman BLOOM. And this resolution which you just read would have to be passed by both Houses and be signed by the President. Is that right?

Mr. HERTER. That is correct.

Chairman BLOOM. It expresses the same idea; the only thing, that is a law and this is merely a suggestion.

Mr. HERTER. Correct.

Chairman BLOOM. It goes further than this resolution; it does not use the word "commonwealth" but uses the word "homeland."

Mr. HERTER. That is right.

Chairman BLOOM. Did you think of the word "commonwealth" when you used the word "homeland"?

Mr. HERTER. I was not conscious of choosing between the two.

Chairman BLOOM. Thank you, Mr. Herter.

STATEMENT OF HON. WILLIAM B. BARRY, A REPRESENTATIVE IN CONGRESS FROM THE STATE OF NEW YORK

Mr. BARRY. Mr. Chairman, I wish to go on record in support of House Resolution 418, which proposes in substance that the United States shall use its best efforts to persuade the British Government to live up to the obligations of the Balfour Declaration of November 2, 1917, so that the doors of Palestine shall be opened for free entry of Jews, and the Jewish people may ultimately reconstitute Palestine as a Jewish commonwealth.

On April 25, 1920, the Allied Supreme Council allotted a mandate for Palestine to Great Britain for the express purpose of putting the Balfour Declaration into effect. The draft of the Palestine Mandate was submitted to the United States Government, and at its request, minor alterations were made in it. At the same time in the interest of the Jewish national home, the United States expressly gave up certain economic rights which it had in Palestine. On June 30, 1922, Congress adopted a joint resolution which was signed by President Harding on September 21, 1922, favoring the establishment in Palestine of a national home for the Jewish people. Finally in 1924, the terms of the Palestine Mandate were ratified by the treaty of December 3 between Great Britain and the United States. That treaty cites the terms of the mandate in full. Article 1—

subject to the provisions of the present convention, the United States consents to the administration of Palestine by His Britannic Majesty pursuant to the mandate recited above. * * * Nothing in the treaty shall be affected by any modifications which may later be made in the terms of the mandate unless such modifications shall have first been assented to by the United States.

It is, therefore, clear that the assent of America was regarded as necessary in the disposition of Palestine by the Associated Powers.

The United States never agreed to the Palestine White Paper which provides (1) total stoppage of Jewish immigration into Palestine after March 1944; (2) rigorous restrictions on land purchase by Jews, and (3) the ultimate establishment of an independent Palestine state, in which Jews should constitute not more than one-third of the population.

The White Paper was issued in May 1939 to appease the Arabs. Whatever conditions existed then impelling the British to take the position they did do not exist now. The Arabs contributed nothing to the victories in Syria, north Africa, Ethiopia, whereas the Palestine Jews sent into the fight 30,000 volunteers, which is a high percentage for their Palestine population. Furthermore, the Jews have many members of their religion and race fighting in armies of the United States, the British Empire, and other United Nations. There never was a time in the history of the Jewish people when they needed a place of refuge more than they do now.

I feel that it is, therefore, our right and our duty to use every reasonable method of persuasion to have the British Government repudiate the White Paper and to permit unlimited Jewish colonization of Palestine.

STATEMENT OF DR. ISRAEL GOLDSTEIN, PRESIDENT OF THE ZIONIST ORGANIZATION OF AMERICA, AND OF THE SYNAGOGUE COUNCIL OF AMERICA, COCHAIRMAN OF THE INTERIM COMMITTEE OF THE AMERICAN JEWISH CONFERENCE, AND HONORARY PRESIDENT OF THE JEWISH NATIONAL FUND OF AMERICA

Dr. GOLDSTEIN. Mr. Chairman and members of the committee, I am deeply gratified for the courtesy extended me to appear before this committee. I am especially grateful to my friend, Mr. Bloom, whom perhaps I may in a sense claim as a communicant, because I happen to be administering to the community in which he is a resident.

Mr. Chairman and members of the committee, my subject is the interest of the American Jews in the development of Palestine as a Jewish national home and as a Jewish commonwealth.

As a matter of history, the interest of American Jews in Palestine dates back to the earliest Jewish settlements in America 300 years ago, for ever since the destruction of the Jewish state and the dispersion of the Jewish people nineteen centuries ago, the yearning for Zion has accompanied Jews in all their wanderings.

In modern times the sentimental yearning for the restoration of Jews and Palestine to one another began to find embodiment in practical planning. This is modern Zionism, which is nearly a hundred years old. One of the forerunners was a great American Jew, Mordecai Noah, New York patriot, jurist, journalist, and playwright, who in 1825 had an idea about establishing a training center here where Jews from all over could be prepared, in the atmosphere of American democracy, for the tasks of self-government in Palestine.

For the past 45 years the Zionist Organization of America, which it is my privilege to head, together with its sister organizations, has been fostering the Zionist ideal on the American scene and giving expression to the interest of American Jewry in the rebuilding of Palestine as the Jewish national home. Among the earlier presidents of the Zionist Organization of America have been outstanding American Jews such as Prof. Richard H. Gottheil, of Columbia University; Dr. Harry Friedenwald, of Baltimore; Justice Louis D. Brandeis, Judge Julian W. Mack, and Rabbi Stephen S. Wise. Quite apart, however, from the strictly organizational aspects of the Zionist movement, American Jewry has felt and exercised its interest in Palestine along the broadest possible lines, animated by a variety of motivations.

First was the underlying religious motivation. The devout Jew in his daily prayers repeats three times a day the prayer, "Oh, may our eyes behold Thy return in mercy unto Zion." Bible prophecy nourishes his hope that the prayer would be answered and sheer self-respect stirs him to cooperate with God's purpose. I have had occasion to observe, as president of the Synagogue Council of America, scores of synagogues enrolling their membership en masse in the Zionist Organization of America as a register of their religious interest in Palestine's restoration.

Other American Jews have been prompted by philanthropic considerations to interest themselves in Palestine as a refuge for persecuted Jews in European lands. Palestine's record in the tragic decade since 1933, when it took in more Jewish refugees than all the other lands combined, and its exceptional suitability after the war for great numbers who will need and want to settle there, place that country in a class by itself even from the purely humanitarian point of view. Therefore, all American Jews have been interested in contributing funds to its development, and all American Jews without exception are protesting against the White Paper policy which imposes unjust restrictions upon its availability and development as a home for the homeless.

Many leading American Jews have interested themselves, through the Palestine Economic Corporation and the American Economic Committee for Palestine, in the economic aspects of its upbuilding, bringing to bear American principles of economic enterprise upon the development of Palestine's industry and commerce, advising American Jews regarding investments in Palestine, and helping businessmen and business enterprises there with expert advice and with loans. Bernard Flexner, Robert Szold, and the late Felix M. Warburg and Justice Louis D. Brandeis have been pioneers in this field. Justice Brandeis defined the objective when he stated—

There rests upon the Jews of America the duty of aiding in the upbuilding of Palestine by making careful studies of the economic opportunities, by necessary capital outlays and by efficient leadership.

A few thousand American Jews have settled in Palestine and have invested a portion of their capital there.

While a number of leading American Jews have encouraged private initiative in Palestine, the greater portion of American Jewry have made their contribution through public funds which go toward the building of the national institutions and maintaining Jewish public services. The oldest of these public funds is the Jewish National Fund, which I have had the honor to head for the past 10 years. This fund purchases land in Palestine and prepares it for colonization. Much of the land when purchased requires either drainage or irrigation. Thus, habitable acres are virtually added to the country. Arabs who are living on the land, even if they are only squatters, are provided with other homesteads at the expense of the Jewish National Fund. The land is expensive, costing twice and thrice as much as similar land in New York State. Having been made fit for colonization, this land is then given on 49-year leaseholds at nominal rentals to those who are ready to work on it. Thus, the return of many thousands of Jewish families to the soil has been made possible, and the social idealism of the Old Testament land code has been revived. Only about 6 percent of the land in Palestine west of the Jordan is now in Jewish possession. The Jewish National Fund is the people's fund beginning with the coin which the Jewish housewife drops into the blue and white box just before she blesses the candles as she ushers in the Sabbath in the Jewish home. American Jews have contributed approximately $20,000,000 to this fund, which is the major portion of its total resources. It is the most popular of all Jewish funds, claiming the largest number of individual contributors next to the Red Cross.

Upon the land thus purchased and prepared colonization takes place. The cost of the colonization is defrayed by a sister fund of the Jewish National Fund, which bears the name, Palestine Foundation Fund. It is likewise a public fund. It provides not only for housing, farming equipment, and livestock, but also for education, as education is considered an indispensable necessity as much as land and buildings. Toward this fund American Jews have contributed the sum of $25,000,000, which is the major portion of its total resources. In these ways Americans, too, have helped to develop the economic absorptive capacity of Palestine.

These two public funds have built the foundations for Jewish agriculture in Palestine. Nearly 25 percent of the Jewish population live on the soil and are the most vital, the most idealistic, and the most civilized peasantry to be found anywhere.

Of special interest from the American point of view is the fund raised and expended by Hadassah, the women's Zionist Organization of America, which is an exclusively American organization. Hadassah devotes itself to the establishment of hospitals and health stations where Arab and Jew alike are cared for, and to the settlement in Palestine of Jewish children who can be saved from Europe's infernos.

A fair estimate of American funds, public and private, invested in Palestine, would place the figure at an amount in excess of $100,000,000. No amount of money, however, could measure the prayers and the hopes, the tears, the love, and the labors which American Jews have poured into the alma mater of their religion, the haven of their persecuted kin, and the cornerstone of their future as a people. All these would be hurt and outraged if the White Paper policy would be permitted to stand. All these would be encouraged and fulfilled if Palestine would be constituted as a Jewish commonwealth, as was envisaged by the Balfour Declaration.

American Jewry's interest and pride in Jewish achievements in Palestine has been increased manifold during the war. Having plighted our resources, our lives, and the lives of our children in defense of our country, we derived tremendous satisfaction from the record of Palestinian Jewry in this war. Without being subject to conscription, 10 percent of its male population have enlisted for military duty, a percentage nearly as great as that in countries where conscription obtains, while 25 percent of the total population have registered for war service in all categories. Palestine agriculture and industry have produced vitally necessary foods, commodities, medicaments, materials, machine parts, and precision instruments. The skill and fortitude of the Jewish soldiers, many of whom lie dead in Greece and Crete, have evoked the commendation of General Wavell and Prime Minister Churchill. Thus the small Jewish community has made a greater contribution to the victory of the United Nations in the Near and Middle East than all the Arab states put together. This record has thrilled the Jews of America and has made them feel proud of their part in the building of that Jewish community.

And as American Jewry looks to the post-war world in which it is hoped the ideals of democracy will win ever increasing adherence, it derives considerable satisfaction from the knowledge that the Jewish community of Palestine will be a leaven for democracy in that part of the world. It looks to the Jewish commonwealth of tomorrow to be that kind of free and democratic commonwealth, and it has reason to expect it on the basis of what the Jews of Palestine have built up since the Balfour Declaration.

They have given ample demonstration that they can be entrusted with the responsibilities of democratic self-government. We are reassured, moreover, as American Jews, to know that in the Jewish commonwealth to be established as soon as the Jews are the majority of the population, Arabs will have the same religious, cultural, economic, and civic rights as are enjoyed by Jewish citizens of the United States. Indeed, Jews in the one land where they are the majority, seeing that in other lands they are the minorities, will want to set an example to the world of how a majority treats a minority.

One final consideration makes American Jews feel a special link with the status of Palestine, namely the recognition by the British Government in article 4 of the Mandate that Jewish rights to Palestine are the concern of the entire Jewish people.

Who are the entire Jewish people today? Millions perhaps have been murdered. American Jews today constitute the largest single unit of the Jewish people and, therefore, feel a correspondingly great concern and responsibility in reference to this problem. And they feel that they have a moral right to look to the Government of the United States, in which they are proud and happy to be loyal citizens, to use its best offices to bring about that dispensation which holds for the surviving remnant of European Jewry the greatest promise of life, liberty, and happiness.

All these considerations have led up to a clear and unequivocal statement which stands as the official word of American Jewry on this subject.

You gentlemen of the committee and you ladies of the committee want to know, of course, what does American Jewry think. This official word has been registered by the American Jewish Conference, which was and is the only all-embracing democratically elected body in American Jewish life. At its session some months ago it adopted by a vote of more than nine to one—and we Americans know that very often the most important questions are adopted by the Congress by a vote of two to one, or just a majority—but by a vote of nine to one, the democratically elected delegates of American Jewry, representing every shade of opinion and every part of this country, adopted a resolution which I have the honor to submit as one of the two chairmen of the interim committee of the American Jewish Conference. If there are among American Jews voices of dissent from this resolution, be they ever so loud or oft repeated, or emanating from men of ever such great wealth or high social position, they must always be evaluated in their true proportion, namely as representing less than 10 percent of American Jewry. Representatives of America will know how to evaluate that phenomenon. The great masses of American Jews have spoken through the following resolution of the American Jewish Conference. I will read only the resolution part. It was adopted September 1, 1943 [reading]:

We call for the fulfillment of the Balfour Declaration, and of the Mandate for Palestine, whose intent and underlying purpose, based on the "historical connection of the Jewish people with Palestine," was to reconstitute Palestine as the Jewish commonwealth.

We demand the immediate withdrawal in its entirety of the Palestine White Paper of May 1939, with its unwarranted restrictions on Jewish immigration and land settlement. The White Paper is a violation of the rights accorded to the Jewish people under the mandate for Palestine. It was characterized by Mr. Winston Churchill in the House of Commons as "a breach and a repudiation of the Balfour Declaration." The Permanent Mandates Commission of the League of Nations refused to recognize its legality or its moral validity.

The conference demands that the gates of Palestine be opened to Jewish immigration, and that the Jewish agency, recognized under the Mandate as the authorized representative of the Jewish people, be vested with authority to direct and regulate immigration into Palestine, to develop to the maximum the agricultural and industrial possibilities and the natural resources of the country, and to utilize its uncultivated and unoccupied lands for Jewish colonization and for the benefit of the country as a whole.

The measures here urged constitute the essential prerequisites for the attainment of a Jewish majority and for the re-creation of the Jewish commonwealth.

In the pursuit of its objective of a Jewish commonwealth, the Jewish people has steadfastly held before it the ideals which shall integrate Jewish Palestine within the new democratic world structure. The Jewish people pledges itself to scrupulous regard for and preservation of the religious, linguistic, and cultural rights of the Arab population of Palestine, and to the civil and religious equality of all its inhabitants before the law. The inviolability of the holy places of the various religions shall be guaranteed. The Jewish people reaffirms its readiness and desire for full cooperation with its Arab neighbors in Palestine and, in the work of its own national redemption, welcomes the economic and political development of the Arab peoples of the Near East.

On the basis both of the part it has played in the history of civilization, and its present achievement in Palestine, the Jewish people believes that the Jewish commonwealth to be established will represent another fundamental contribution to the social and political ideals of the world. It will finally answer the agonized cry of the most martyred of peoples, and enable it to take its rightful place in that progressive order of mankind which, we pray, may issue from the present struggle.

The resolution on which you are now conducting this hearing would, if passed, rejoice the heart of the Jews of America because it would lift the hopes of the surviving remnant of European Jewry. It would be in the best American tradition, coupling Bible prophecy with realistic statesmanship.

Chairman BLOOM. Mr. Johnson, have you any questions?

Mr. JOHNSON. I have no questions.

Chairman BLOOM. Mrs. Rogers, have you any questions?

Mrs. ROGERS. That was a very fine statement of yours, Rabbi, and while you are considering a homeland or commonwealth for Jewish people in Palestine, have you considered setting up a homeland or commonwealth in any other country?

Dr. GOLDSTEIN. Unfortunately, the past events of recent years have helped to answer that question. The Jews of European lands will have to find new lands, as you can well recognize. We believe that the immigration of approximately 2,000,000 Jews from European lands into Palestine in the course of the next few years will solve that problem because, perhaps, there may not be many more who would be sufficiently able bodied to undertake the venture of readjustment; and, on the other hand, we are convinced that Palestine, especially its Jewish enterprise—and only under Jewish enterprise, because Jews have this deep passion for it—would be capable of absorbing that number of Jews. And so, no matter how much we look around the rest of the world, we do not find any offers coming forth. We do not see any place where the foundations have already been laid. Here is a chance to utilize the work that has been done over the past 25 years, or even a longer number of years. Everything is ready; the land is there; we know how to treat the land.

Chairman BLOOM. You have done a marvelous work.

Dr. GOLDSTEIN. The land is there and of all the Jewish people of the world, the Jews of Palestine are the most eager to share their homes and their bread with the less fortunate. So, when a new Jew comes into the country it is a holiday, it is a cause for rejoicing. Then, too, you have the cultural background. They very well know of the historical associations of the land, where Hebrew is the language and their whole kin is there. So that politically, geographically, and economically, psychologically, religiously, Palestine is the one and easily qualified place for the solution of that problem.

Mrs. ROGERS. I saw it before the war and I would like to see it again.

Dr. GOLDSTEIN. I think you will. I think this resolution will help.

Mrs. ROGERS. Tell me how Jewish persons go there. How can they be taken in there? Is there any board that passes upon their admittance? I am very much interested in it.

Dr. GOLDSTEIN. Well, that is quite a crucial question, as to how they shall get in. They will not get in merely by our say-so; there will have to be provided the instrumentality for regulating immigration, and we feel that the Jewish agency for Palestine which has been charged with considerable responsibility in the past and which is recognized under the mandate, is the proper body to determine the question of immigration; because no one will be more careful not to overtax the possibilities of Palestine than Jewish organizations themselves. They are the ones who will look at this thing from the standpoint of the immediate desperate necessity and also from the long-range or permanent solution viewpoint.

Mrs. ROGERS. I read some figures in a publication the other day and I wish I had it with me, as I would like to ask you some questions about it.

I gather you are ready to take over the work and do not feel satisfied entirely with what has been done under U. N. R. R. A.

Dr. GOLDSTEIN. U. N. R. R. A. is a temporary problem, to take care of readjustments during the war and immediately after the war. In regard to U. N. R. R. A. our feeling is there is a great opportunity to absorb that capacity by having U. N. R. R. A. give to Palestine its proper share of what is needed for the manufacture of materials and for the provision of goods that will be necessary for relief and rehabilitation work even in the European countries.

Chairman BLOOM. You do not need legislation for that.

Dr. GOLDSTEIN. I think that is something that will be done by wise administrators, and I have confidence when this matter is brought to their attention they will see the wisdom of it from their own standpoint; so that instead of importing materials, for example, from this country across the Atlantic and using much-needed ship space, they have the opportunity of getting materials from Palestine and getting it into Europe even overland without the use of shipping. So I think the administrators will see the wisdom of using Palestine manufactured goods for the purpose.

Mrs. ROGERS. I also understand that they have units of Jewish soldiers fighting on the various fronts. I recall having heard of them being on the Italian front. I understand that they are being kept together as a unit, just as General Pershing kept our American boys together in the last war. I remember certain countries wanted to have our soldiers used for replacements in filling in different companies. I understand that the Jewish people have been keeping their soldiers together.

Dr. GOLDSTEIN. I think perhaps that would be the preferred way, but whether that is actually being done is something which is subject to the military conditions; which are, after all, determined by the people in command and, naturally, the Jewish soldiers are at the disposal of the commands as they are given. But if they have their choice, I am sure they would prefer to do that chiefly for the reasons of efficiency, because where there is homogeneity and compactness in a military unit, there is maximum efficiency.

Mrs. ROGERS. And when you are creating a nation you would want them together.

Dr. GOLDSTEIN. Yes, of course.

Chairman BLOOM. Mr. Kee, have you any questions?

Mr. KEE. Dr. Goldstein, prior to the issuance of the White Paper, how was the immigration into Palestine regulated by the Jewish commission?

Dr. GOLDSTEIN. It was not regulated by a Jewish commission, but the Jewish agency served in an advisory capacity to the British authorities. The Jewish agency would indicate, for example, how many certificates of immigration they believed ought to be granted, bearing in mind the opportunities in the land for the absorption of those immigrants.

Mr. KEE. Did that same commission have any authority since the White Paper was issued to control the quota under the White Paper?

Dr. GOLDSTEIN. One of our disappointments has been that the ageny never had the authority which we hoped and believed would be given under the mandate, but even such authority as it had at the beginning was whittled down drastically so that it became in effect inoperative toward the end, and that is one of our deepest disappointments. We feel that the Jewish agency being there, knowing the situation, and having the interest at heart, was in the best position to determine what would be a fair amount of immigration.

Mr. KEE. The withdrawal of the White Paper would automatically restore the authority to the Jewish agency that it had before.

Dr. GOLDSTEIN. Well, if it only restored what it had before, it would not restore very much. We trust that the expression of opinion regarding the White Paper and its injustice will have a tonic effect in bringing about a new orientation based on considerations of justice and humanity.

Mr. KEE. I agree with you that it ought to be.

Chairman BLOOM. Mr. Vorys, have you any questions?

Mr. VORYS. Rabbi, I was very much interested in your description of the religious background for the desire of American Jewry for a Jewish national homeland. As I understand it, you said the Jewish national fund, of which you are the head, is the most popular of the Jewish charitable funds.

Dr. GOLDSTEIN. Yes, that is right. It has the greatest number of individual contributors, because may of those contributions are very small coins, a penny, a nickel, or a dime.

Mr. VORYS. What I wondered about was the very touching prayer that you mentioned as being said three times a day. It might have just a spiritual connotation. We Methodists have songs about Zion in our hymnal, but, as I understand, you refer to it in prayers, and so forth, and you have in mind a physical return to Zion and the restoration of this homeland as a religious matter; is that right?

Dr. GOLDSTEIN. Yes; of course, all prayers are subject to the process of sublimation, depending on who does the praying. The Jews who pray for that pray for it devoutly and also realistically. They have in mind directly the restoration and their hope is that it may come in their time. There have been periods in Jewish history when the spiritual prospect was so desperate or almost so hopeless that they began to postpone that time to Messianic age; and it was the great Rabbi Hillel who handed down his precept, teaching us: "If I do not help myself, who will help me? And if I am only for myself who am I?" And so the Jew feels it is his duty to cooperate with God's purpose in doing what he can to speed that day.

Chairman BLOOM. Mr. Jarman, have you any questions?

Mr. JARMAN. Rabbi, this Jewish commission, does it sit in Palestine or London?

Dr. GOLDSTEIN. The Jewish agency has its central headquarters in Palestine.

Chairman BLOOM. Will you explain what the Jewish agency is and how it was organized?

Dr. GOLDSTEIN. The mandate provides in article IV the establishment of a Jewish agency which will advise and cooperate with the mandatory in all matters pertaining to the upbuilding of Palestine in accordance with the provisions of the mandate. The head of the Jewish agency is Dr. Weizmann, whose name has been mentioned in the hearing and who lives in Palestine and who at the present time happens to be in London.

Our chairman really has no end of surprises. Now he is handing me the Haggadah. I really should have brought it down and handed it to him. Absolutely I do not need it. We say at every Passover, as we celebrate the Passover here now, "May we next year be privileged to celebrate it in the land of Israel," which carries out the same yearning that I referred to before as a part of our religious tradition.

Mr. JARMAN. As I understand "Zionism" has just one purpose, the reestablishment of the Jewish homeland; is that correct?

Dr. GOLDSTEIN. That is the essential purpose of Palestine—the restoration of Zion to the Jewish people.

Mr. JARMAN. Thank you.

Chairman BLOOM. Mrs. Bolton, have you any questions?

Mrs. BOLTON. Rabbi, I was very much interested in your presentation. I was just wondering whether if in the immigration of 1,000,000 to Palestine you had decided upon any proportion of professional people or agricultural people? What method is followed in regard to immigration and what happens to them when they get in? Does everybody have a job to do?

Dr. GOLDSTEIN. Yes, I will be very glad to answer your question. May I, however, preface it by stating that the Jewish agency does not control or determine the number of certificates of immigration. It only guides the distribution of those certificates and that leads up to a question. Of course it advises the Government in Palestine as to how many citizens it thinks Palestine is ready for, but its advice is not usually taken.

Now, when the number is determined then the agency itself tries to achieve a certain balance and there are always people in various parts of Europe who are craving for the opportunity to come in. The demand inevitably exceeds the supply and so we find that there are some people in Poland that have been waiting for years; not only have they been waiting but they have been preparing themselves by being trained on farms so that when they get to Palestine they do not have to go through the process of adjustment but are immediately placed to take their place in these agricultural cooperatives; and such training centers have existed in virtually all the lands of Europe, so that in this way the maximum use is made of the ability and of the efficiency of the people going into Palestine.

Mrs. BOLTON. Is the ratio of professional people to agriculturalists different from what it is in this country or is it largely the other way around?

Dr. GOLDSTEIN. Yes, it is different, and that difference is itself one of the glories of the achievements in Palestine. We ourselves never had a way of knowing how we could adapt ourselves economically to an agricultural mode of life. We knew from our Bible that we were farmers, but we were afraid that perhaps we had lost that gift in the course of centuries during which we were denied the opportunity in most lands of even living on the soil and therefore it meant a good deal to our own self-confidence when we saw that within a few years university graduates were able to take care of the land and women with degrees as physicians and lawyers considered themselves privileged to clean the stables in Palestine and to build the roads because it was a driving idealism and a passion and is that which makes it impossible to speak of any other country in the same breath. The Jewish people will never be able to do in any other land outside of Palestine what they are able to do there under the impulse of the idealistic drive that has its roots in centuries of history.

Mrs. BOLTON. You propose to maintain control of a number that are in the professional group?

Dr. GOLDSTEIN. Yes; our proposal is to keep a proper balance between agriculture, commerce, and the professions. I suppose there are accepted standards for that. I do not know what the standard is in this country. We feel at the present time that a reasonable basis would be that for every family settled on the land there should be about four in industry and the professions. We think that is a fairly wholesome proportion and to the extent we can control it, we suppose we shall endeavor to do that.

Mrs. BOLTON. Thank you.

Chairman BLOOM. Mr. McMurray, have you any questions?

Mr. McMURRAY. I should like to check roughly on some figures. There are in the neighborhood of 600,000 Jewish people in Palestine?

Dr. GOLDSTEIN. Somewhat less than that.

Mr. McMURRAY. And your estimates are that there will be about 2,000,000 more people that will want to leave Europe and go to Palestine if Palestine is available and that Palestine can absorb them under a condition of high economic development?

Dr. GOLDSTEIN. Yes; through a highly efficient and intelligent economic enterprise; both would contribute.

Mr. McMURRAY. That would involve both agricultural and industrial?

Dr. GOLDSTEIN. There has to be motivation; it has to be dynamic and not static and that is the importance of placing it in the hands of the Jewish people who are deeply interested in it.

Mr. McMURRAY. Is it your opinion that you can drain off those 2,000,000 people from Europe that they could stay in Palestine and be absorbed there?

Dr. GOLDSTEIN. It would make the problem considerably easier, I believe, as Dr. Silver pointed out.

Mr. McMURRAY. Have you any idea how many Jewish people that would leave in Europe?

Dr. GOLDSTEIN. Well, it it difficult to make estimates.

Mr. McMURRAY. I realize that.

Dr. GOLDSTEIN. We do not know; every day there are new disasters, but we believe that 2,000,000 will probably represent about 40 percent.

Mr. McMURRAY. Forty percent?

Dr. GOLDSTEIN. Forty percent.

A VOICE. It is more than 40 percent.

Dr. GOLDSTEIN. Perhaps my estimates of survivors are more optimistic.

Chairman BLOOM. Mr. Schiffler, have you any questions?

Mr. SCHIFFLER. I listened with intense interest to your very interesting discourse and I want to compliment you on your very able presentation; but I have only one criticism. Among those from whom I have heard have been Baptists, Methodists, representatives of the Presbyterian Church of Princeton, and many other groups, as well as a number of laymen whose nationalities I think are quite diffused. The tenor of all their statements is that this is not entirely a Jewish problem. I find interest manifested in this resolution among all groups, not only the group you represent.

Dr. GOLDSTEIN. I am sure of that.

Mr. SCHIFFLER. I have found their interest as great as your own Jewish people.

Dr. GOLDSTEIN. May I say I was too literal in self-limitation. The theme assigned me was the Interest of the American Jews in the Building of Palestine. But I could have spent at least as much time in dealing with the interest of American Christians, because of my capacity as head of the Synagogue Council I am with them all the time. I also know from talks with most devout Christians that they are also in favor of it, and I am glad you brought it out.

Mr. SCHIFFLER. I have had this brought to my attention by very many who were very intensely interested in this subject and who are wholeheartedly backing this resolution. As I understand from your testimony and also the testimony of the preceding witnesses, as a practical matter, if this White Paper is ever abrogated you hope there will be more cooperation with this group than there was before the White Paper was promulgated, so that the number of immigrants permitted could be increased; is that right? However, you do not propose immediately to have a commonwealth?

Dr. GOLDSTEIN. No; we could not propose it as an immediate step, because we realize there would have to be a Jewish majority in the land before we could act for the implementation of a commonwealth, and the achievement of a Jewish majority will undoubtedly take some time, but we do hope that in the interim period there will be not only a more liberal interpretation but an interpretation which is premised upon the recognition of the objective, and that makes all the difference. When the administering power knows that its mandate is to bring about a Jewish state in the nearest possible time the whole gait and the whole tempo of its work will be determined accordingly and that is the importance of defining in the resolution what is the goal which we are seeking. This part of the resolution serves really as the directive with respect to the whole administration during its interim period.

I thank you.

Mr. JOHNSON. With reference to the agencies of immigration you have got in Palestine, is there any rule about that, or are there some agents of the Jewish people who have gone back to Palestine?

Dr. GOLDSTEIN. I think you will find, sir, that the Palestinian Jewish community is probably the foremost in its general association as in any community anywhere, for reasons which, of course, are obvious. The Jewish agency was to get in those who could make the greatest contribution to the building of the country.

Mr. JOHNSON. And one reason would be, Rabbi, that the younger men would probably adjust themselves after they were brought in, to either cultivation of the land or business, whereas the older men would find it more difficult to adjust themselves?

Dr. GOLDSTEIN. Undoubtedly that is a fundamental consideration.

Mr. JOHNSON. What has been the experience with reference to those who have come in? Have you ever found any who did not like it and wanted to leave?

Dr. GOLDSTEIN. Incidentally, Mr. Chairman, when I was in Texas on behalf of the Jewish national fund they told me they had a new project, to establish what they called "Texas." Now they have in Texas a "Palestine" and so why not have a Texas in Palestine? This ties up what you said, sir, about the interest of the American Christians, because I found in so many communities there are Christians wanting to do something to register their love and their appreciation of Palestine and the way they specified to do that was the establishment of some community or some activity to bear the name of the State or the county or the city.

Chairman BLOOM. If there are no further questions, Rabbi, it has been a great pleasure to have you before the committee.

Now I would like to ask the committee: We have here Mr. Lessing J. Rosenwald, and I promised him that he would be heard today. Do you want to come in the morning, Mr. Rosenwald, or continue now?

Mr. ROSENWALD. If it meets with the pleasure of the committee, I would be glad to make my presentation now.

Chairman BLOOM. We will now hear from Mr. Lessing J. Rosenwald, of Philadelphia.

STATEMENT OF LESSING J. ROSENWALD, PRESIDENT, AMERICAN COUNSEL FOR JUDAISM, INC., PHILADELPHIA, PA.

Mr. JOHNSON. I thought Mr. Rosenwald came from Chicago.

Mr. ROSENWALD. My residence is now Jenkintown, Pa.

Mr. Chairman and members of the committee, ladies and gentlemen, I appreciate this opportunity to appear before you in regard to the resolutions on Palestine that you are now considering. I am deeply grateful for the spirit that has animated you and your fellow Congressmen to take up this cause of the suffering, dispersed, and persecuted Jews of Europe. The consideration that you are giving to that problem is one more testimony of the fine American tradition of sympathy with, and help for, the unfortunates of all faiths. It is of a pattern with the recent action of our President naming a War Refugee Board and with the formation in this city of a committee headed by such distinguished public figures as Justice Murphy, Vice President Wallace, Governor Goodland of Wisconsin, Governor May of Utah, and others, to counter the dread cancer of bigotry in our national life.

I appear here both in my own capacity as an American citizen of Jewish faith and as president of the American Council for Judaism, Inc.

This organization, let me explain, was founded only recently to enlist support among like-minded Americans of Jewish faith in our stress on the religious character of the Jews and in resistance to the forces of racialism which we believe to be false doctrines in Judaism.

It may interest you to know that in the brief period of a few months, we have enlisted an active membership of close to 2,500 leading Jews all over the country and the interest and approval of many, many more. We are still, as you see, a young organization, but I dare say, we are probably the most rapidly growing organization in the Jewish community in the United States.

With this brief introduction, I beg to call to your attention the following, relative to the resolution now before both Houses of Congress; That should be just the House. I understand——

Chairman BLOOM (interposing). There is a similar resolution now in the Senate and you are right either way.

Mr. ROSENWALD. Thank you.

The text of the resolution calls upon the United States to use its good offices for two purposes. I ask you to note that there are two purposes, that they are distinct and different and that they are, therefore, properly subject to different reactions.

One part of the resolution calls for taking "appropriate measures to the end that the doors of Palestine shall be open for the free entry of Jews." I do not wish here to linger over the phrasing of this part of the resolution; I do want to say that the purpose of this part of the resolution is plainly humanitarian, consistent with American humanitarian traditions and characteristic of our desire to expand democratic processes wherever they can be expended.

As you know, this resolution has as its background the White Paper issued in 1939 by the British Government as the mandatory power for Palestine which, among other provisions, shuts the immigration doors of Palestine to Jews and restricts their acquisition of land in that country.

In a recent statement issued by the organization which I have the privilege of heading, we said as follows:

We of the American Council for Judaism record our unqualified opposition to those provisions. In behalf of the substantial section of American Jews whose views on Jewish problems coincide with ours, we petition our Government to use its best offices to prevail upon the British Government not to proceed with so prejudicial and unjust a policy.

We base our attitude on this fundamental fact: That proposals which exclude Jews, as Jews, from right of entry and restrict Jews, as Jews, from the acquisition of land, do violence to the fundamental concept of democratic equality and thus to the very purposes and ideals to which the United Nations are pledged.

The American Council for Judaism is dedicated to the view that Jews, as religious community, shall have, as of right and not on sufferance, full equality all over the world. As stated in our declaration of principles, "For our fellow Jews we ask only this: Equality of rights and obligations with their fellow nationals." This means equality in the countries in which we live and choose to remain; equality to return to those lands from which Jews have been forcibly driven; equality to migrate wherever there is an opportunity for migration.

We ask for no special privilege for Jews anywhere in the world. We will resist to the utmost the imposition of any disabilities on Jews anywhere in the world. There is no compromise on this basic demand.

This is the position of our membership and we believe that this viewpoint is supported by all American citizens of the Jewish faith and by an overwhelming body of our fellow Americans of Catholic and Protestant faiths.

We are, therefore, in hearty accord with the purpose of the first part of the resolution. We feel that it seeks to express the profound and invaluable sympathy of the American people for those driven from their lands by tyranny and terror.

There is, however, a second section of the resolution on which we feel obliged to convey to you, frankly and fully, our questions and our doubts as to its wisdom. It now reads:

* * * so that the Jewish people may ultimately reconstitute Palestine as a free and democratic Jewish commonwealth.

I urge you gentlemen to read and reflect on this part of the resolution with the utmost care. This is no longer designed to serve a solely humanitarian purpose. This brings you, and through you the American people, at once into a field of international political controversy, and into a subject that has deeply divided the Jewish community in this country.

The proposal, you will note, speaks of the establishment of a free and democratic "Jewish" commonwealth. I stress the word "Jewish." It does not say the establishment of a free and democratic "commonwealth." It specifically uses the word "Jewish," a word which has essentially a religious connotation only, although it has been used in a racial sense by the Nazi enemies of the Jews and of democracy.

But the concept of the theocratic state is long past. It is an anachronism. The concept of a racial state—the Hitlerian concept—is repugnant to the civilized world, as witness the fearful global war in which we are involved. We have reached a point of civilization where nations and states have their proper recognition without regard to the religious composition of their populations. I urge that we do nothing to set us back on the road to the past. To project at this time the creation of a Jewish state or commonwealth is to launch a singular innovation in world affairs which might well have incalculable consequences.

It may well be that this was in the mind of the King-Crane Commission in its report to President Woodrow Wilson and the State Department in the years after the last war.

You will recall that President Wilson, disturbed by the problems of the Near East, dispatched a commission there in 1919 for a careful survey. This commission, known as the King-Crane Commission, was to submit a report which would be of assistance in the final formulation of the peace treaties. With regard to Palestine, that commission reported that "a national home for the Jewish people is not equivalent to making Palestine a Jewish State." No doubt, your predecessors of the Sixty-seventh Congress of the United States had this report at hand when they adopted the resolution which forms a preamble to your present resolution.

I ask you to look at your present resolution again and, especially, at that part of it which reads: "* * * so that the Jewish people may ultimately reconstitute Palestine as a free and democratic Jewish commonwealth."

The language of the resolution thus makes "the Jewish people" the agency for the establishment of a free and democratic commonwealth. Here are some serious considerations on that section:

The accepted procedure of democracy is to have a commonwealth established with the participation of all of its people or citizens. It is a self-contradiction to speak of a democratic state organism which is the creation of only a part of the population within the country. The population in Palestine is made up of Christian, Mohammedan, and Jew. I believe you will agree with me, gentlemen, that true democratic developments in that country can only come about as the result of the efforts and with the participation of all of the elements of the population. All of Palestine must share in the establishment of a democracy. Any exclusion is undemocratic in character and defeats the very purpose that your resolution may seek to achieve.

Moreover, the language of the resolution places the responsibility for creating a commonwealth at the door of "Jewish people," presumably those outside of Palestine as well as those in Palestine. Yet I wonder whether the authors of this resolution actually intended this to be the case. The "Jewish people" are not organized politically, are not and do not want to be a political unit. They are nationals, loyal citizens of the various countries in which they live. They are to be found in all classes, in all political parties, in all economic levels. They are united only in their common derivation from a great religion and in their natural resistance to those who would destroy them. This being the case, it must be clear why the language of the second part of the resolution can only create confusion and encounter, perhaps, insurmountable difficulties. Jews in the United States and the world over, not being a national group but essentially a religious community, it is clear that they cannot assume responsibility anywhere as a political unit.

The development of such institutions, in the last analysis, must be the responsibility only of those in Palestine at the time such institutions are developed. All sections of the country—Jews, Christians, and Mohammedans, Palestinians all—whose proper concern is the welfare of their country, will determine and be responsible for their institutions.

In the statement of principles issued by the American Council for Judaism, we expressed the following views on Palestine:

Palestine has contributed in a tangible way to the alleviation of the present catastrophe in Jewish life by providing a refuge for a part of Europe's persecuted Jews. We hope it will continue as one of the places for such resettlement, for it has been clearly demonstrated that practical colonizing can be done, schools and universities built, scientific agriculture extended, commerce intensified and culture developed. This is the record of achievement of eager, hard-working settlers who have been aided in their endeavors by Jews all over the world, in every walk of life and thought.

We oppose the effort to establish a national Jewish state in Palestine or anywhere else as a philosophy of defeatism, and one which does not offer a practical solution of the Jewish problem. We dissent from all those related doctrines that stress the racialism, the nationalism, and the theoretical homlessness of Jews. We oppose such doctrines as inimical to the welfare of Jews in Palestine, in America, or wherever Jews may dwell. We believe that the intrusion of Jewish national statehood has been a deterrent in Palestine's ability to play an even greater role in offering a haven for the oppressed, and that without the insistence upon such statehood, Palestine would today be harboring more refugees from Nazi terror.

Palestine is a part of Israel's religious heritage, as it is a part of the heritage of two other religions of the world. We look forward to the ultimate establishment of a democratic, autonomous government in Palestine, wherein Jews, Moslems, and Christians shall be justly represented; every man enjoying equal rights and sharing equal responsibilities; a democratic government in which our fellow Jews shall be free Palestinians whose religion is Judaism, even as we are Americans whose religion is Judaism.

I earnestly commend these views for your consideration. I believe that your own compassionate purposes will be fully served by retaining only the first part of the resolution or by modifying its second provision so that it reads as follows:

* * * and there there shall be full opportunity for colonization in Palestine, ultimately to be constituted as a free and democratic commonwealth.

I have a few documents I should like to file with this report and if I may ask to have it done likewise, I should like to have a copy of the King-Crane report likewise made a part of these proceedings. I have no copy but it is available and it can be considered.

Chairman BLOOM. Without objection, so ordered. What are these various documents that you wish to have included?

Mr. ROSENWALD. The first is a "Statement of the American Council for Judaism, Inc., Interpretive Pamphlet No. 1." Then there are the information bulletins of the American Council for Judaism, Inc., under dates October 15 and December 31, 1943, and January 15 and 31, 1944, and also an article by me entitled "Reply to Zionism—Why many Americans of Jewish Faith are Opposed to the Establishment of a Jewish State in Palestine."

Chairman BLOOM. They may be made a part of the record.

Mr. ROSENWALD. Thank you, sir.

(The data above referred to and the King-Crane report are as follows:)

[Interpretive Pamphlet No. 1]

STATEMENT OF THE AMERICAN COUNCIL FOR JUDAISM, INC.

The American Council for Judaism, Inc., was organized to present the views of Americans of Jewish faith on problems affecting the future of their own lives and the lives of world Jewry in the present hour of world confusion.

The Council reaffirms the historic truth that the Jews of the world share common traditions and ethical concepts which find their derivation in the same religious source. For countless generations, "Hear, O Israel, The Lord our God, the Lord is One," has been the universal cry that has united all Jews in trial and tribulation, in suffering, hunger, and want, in despair—and in achievement. It is still the concept which distinguishes Jews as a religious group.

Racist theories and nationalistic philosophies, that have become prevalent in recent years, have caused untold suffering to the world and particularly to Jews. Long ago they became obsolete as realties in Jewish history; they remain only as a reaction to discrimination and persecution. In the former crises of Israel in ancient Palestine, the Prophets placed God and the moral law above land, race, nation, royal prerogatives, and political arrangements. Now, as then, we cherish the same religious values which emphasize the dignity of man and the obligation to deal justly with him no matter what his status.

As Americans of Jewish faith we believe implicitly in the fundamentals of democracy, rooted, as they are, in moralities that transcend race and state, and endow the individual with rights for which he is answerable only to God. We are thankful to be citizens of a country and to have shared in the building of a nation conceived in a spirit which knows neither special privilege nor inferior status for any man.

For centuries Jews have considered themselves nationals of those countries in which they have lived. Whenever free to do so, they have assumed, and will again assume, full responsibilities of citizenship in accordance with the ancient

Jewish command, "The law of the land is the law." Those countries in which Jews have lived have been their homes; those lands their homelands. In those nations where political action was expressed through minority groups, the Jew, following the law of his land, accepted minority status, thereby frequently gaining an improvement over previous conditions of inferior citizenship. Such East European concepts, however, have resulted in a misunderstanding, shared by Jews and non-Jews, a misunderstanding which we seek to dispel. American Jews hope that in the peace for which all of us pray, the old principle of minority rights will be supplanted by the more modern principle of equality and freedom for the individual. The interest of American Jews in the individual Jew in countries where the minority right principle prevailed is not to be confused with acceptance of this East European political concept.

As a result of the bigotry, sadism, and ambitions for world conquest of the Axis powers, millions of our co-religionists who had homes in and were nationals of other lands have been violently deported and made victims of indescribable barbarism. No other group has been so brutishly attacked and for one reason only—on the false claims that there are racial barriers or nationalistic impulses that separate Jews from other men.

The plight of those Jews together with millions of oppressed fellow men of all faiths, calls for the profoundest sympathy and the unbounded moral indignation of all freemen. The restoration of these broken lives to the status and dignity of men endowed by God with inalienable rights, is one of the primary objectives of the peace to come as expressed in the Atlantic Charter and the Four Freedoms of President Roosevelt. We believe that the Jew will rise or fall with the extension or contraction of the great liberal forces of civilization. By relying upon the broad, religious principles inherent in a democracy and implementing them wherever possible, we join our forces with those of all lovers of freedom; strengthened, in that we do not stand segregated and alone upon exclusive demands.

We ask that the United Nations secure the earliest feasible repatriation or resettlement under the best possible conditions of all peoples uprooted from their homes by the Axis powers, and that even in the face of obvious and discouraging obstacles the United Nations persevere in their efforts to provide immediate sanctuary for refugees of all faiths, political beliefs, and national origins. We believe that wherever possible the forced emigres should be repatriated in their original homelands under conditions which will enable them to live as free, upstanding individuals.

For our fellow Jews we ask only this: Equality of rights and obligations with their fellow nationals. In our endeavors to bring relief to our stricken fellow Jews, and to help rebuild their lives on a more stable basis, we rely wholly upon the principles of freedom, justice, and humanity, which are fundamental to both democracy and religion, and which have been declared as the principles which shall prevail in the better world for which the United Nations are fighting. We ally ourselves with those who believe this war will not have been fought in vain, that the mistakes of the last peace will not be duplicated.

Palestine has contributed in a tangible way to the alleviation of the present catastrophe in Jewish life by providing a refuge for a part of Europe's persecuted Jews. We hope it will continue as one of the places for such resettlement, for it has been clearly demonstrated that practical colonizing can be done, schools and universities built, scientific agriculture extended, commerce intensified, and culture developed. This is the record of achievement of eager, hard-working settlers who have been aided in their endeavors by Jews all over the world, in every walk of life and thought.

We oppose the effort to establish a National Jewish State in Palestine or anywhere else as a philosophy of defeatism, and one which does not offer a practical solution of the Jewish problem. We dissent from all those related doctrines that stress the racialism, the nationalism, and the theoretical homelessness of Jews. We oppose such doctrines as inimical to the welfare of Jews in Palestine, in America, or wherever Jews may dwell. We believe that the intrusion of Jewish national statehood has been a deterrent in Palestine's ability to play an even greater role in offering a haven for the oppressed, and that without the insistence upon such statehood, Palestine would today be harboring more refugees from Nazi terror. The very insistence upon a Jewish Army has led to the raising of barriers against our unfortunate brethren. There never was a need for such an army. There has always been ample opportunity for Jews to fight side by side with those of other faiths in the armies of the United Nations.

Palestine is a part of Israel's religious heritage, as it is a part of the heritage of two other religions of the world. We look forward to the ultimate establishment of a democratic, autonomous government in Palestine, wherein Jews, Moslems, and Christians shall be justly represented; every man enjoying equal rights and sharing equal responsibilities; a democratic government in which our fellow Jews shall be free Palestinians whose religion is Judaism, even as we are Americans whose religion is Judaism.

We invite all Jews to support our interpretation of Jewish life and destiny in keeping with the highest traditions of our faith. We believe these truths provide the basis for every program of a more hopeful future put forth by freemen. To proclaim those views at this time, we believe, is to express the abiding faith, shared by a great number of our fellow Jews, that in the fruits of victory of the United Nations all, regardless of faith, will share alike. It is also, we believe, to render a service to the task of clarifying the hopes and the purposes for which this war is being fought by freemen everywhere.

The above statement was issued August 31, over the signatures of the officers of the Council and representative Jews from all sections of the country.

[Information Bulletin of the American Council for Judaism, Inc., No. 1, Philadelphia, Pa., October 15, 1943]

By Way of Introduction

This is the first of a series of semimonthly bulletins to be issued by the American Council for Judaism. These bulletins are intended to convey the views of the Council on problems affecting Jews in the United States and the world over; and in that way to contribute to a full, free public discussion of these problems.

This issue follows by a few weeks the public appearance of the statement of views of the members of the American Council for Judaism upon the occasion of its initial organization. The publication of this statement had one primary purpose: That of informing Americans of the existence of these views among Americans of the Jewish faith. This, it was felt, was all the more necessary at a time when there was a deliberate, skillfully organized attempt to convey the impression that all American Jews were united in support of a partisan, nationalistic political platform.

At the same time that this statement became public, the American Jewish Conference was in session, a conference, representative in a measure, of other views held by others of America's Jews.

The effect upon the conference of the issuance of a simple statement of views was extraordinary.

The same conference whose resolutions paid tribute to the Four Freedoms (which include freedom of speech) at once brought out four rabbinical spokesmen to denounce, calumniate, and, to all appearances, excommunicate those who expressed a dissenting view.

The same Conference which reverently mentioned the Atlantic Charter (that includes a pledge of freedom of expression) stormed that one New York newspaper gave full space ot the views of the Council just as it did to the views of the Conference.

Why all the excitement? Why the characterization of the statement as "unsportsmanlike," as if what is involved is a parlor game, with fastidious rules? Why all this denunciation, this overwhelming attention to a statement of the Council at the same time that it is characterized as expressive of the views of only a hundred American Jews?

WHY?

Is it perhaps that in that clear, unambiguous statement by Americans of Jewish faith, a statement based on the highest traditions of our religion and of our democratic faith, the nationalistic leaders could see their entire pretentious balloon collapse? Is it perhaps that the nationalistic leaders knew very well that behind the hundred signatories there were many more hundreds, and thousands, even millions, who agree with those views and who, shown a course for helping their fellow Jews without involvement in international political manipulations, would willingly identify themselves with that course?

The statement itself pretended to nothing more than it was: an expression of views of some American Jews, on problems affecting all Jews. It may be that those who subscribe to the principles of the Council are in the minority, although that remains to be seen. But if they are in a minority, would it not have been more in accord with the best of our democratic traditions if a conference of Jews, themselves a minority, rallied to defend the right of any group to express its views?

Long ago, an American, persecuted, insulted, scorned in his day, who has since found his way into the pantheon of great American spirits, wrote: "I am in earnest; I will not equivocate; I will not excuse; I will not retreat a single inch; and I will be heard."

This is also the declaration and intention of the American Council for Judaism.

WHAT OTHERS SAY

THE CHRISTIAN CENTURY

(September 15, 1943)

By an overwhelming majority, the American Jewish Conference at its recent New York convention adopted a resolution in favor of making Palestine "the (sic!) Jewish commonwealth," demanding withdrawal of the British White Paper of 1939 which restricted Jewish immigration and landholding, and calling for unrestricted Jewish immigration into the Holy Land. In other words, the conference, which claimed to be a democratically chosen body representing all American Jewry, went all-out Zionist. The effect was somewhat lessened, however, by two incidents. In one, after the conference had voted, Joseph M. Proskauer, former New York supreme court justice and representative of the American Jewish Committee, announced that that body would not be bound by the resolution. In the other, publication of an anti-Zionist statement by the American Council for Judaism brought on that body an attack of almost unparalleled vituperation, with almost equally severe strictures aginst the New York Times for giving anti-Zionist views space in its news columns. The council opposed the idea of making Palestine a Jewish state, and declared that it should be given a democratic, autonomous government in which "Jews, Moslems and Christians shall be justly represented." Not content simply to uphold the opposing view, the New York body listened while four rabbis branded signers of the non-Zionist statement as "unsportsmanlike," "impertinent," as guilty of an "attempt to sabotage," of "outrageous action," of "misrepresentation," of "treachery to the cause of Israel," men who had "placed themselves outside the pale of Israel." With such divisions revealed inside Jewry, and such emotional excess manifested by the majority at any sign of dissent, there is little likelihood that the United Nations will deliberately incur the hazards of trouble with the Arabs at this juncture by adopting the policy demanded in the New York gathering.

(EDITOR's NOTE.—The Christian Century's attitude to Jews was illustrated the preceding week in its editorial as follows:)

Statistics concerning European Jewry require constant revision to keep them abreast with the appalling reality. Figures were given out last week in a report, compiled after careful study, by the Institute of Jewish Affairs representing the American Jewish Congress and the World Jewish Congress. In round numbers, there were, in the European countries now under Axis control, 8,000,000 Jews when Hitler came into power ten years ago. There now remain 3,000,000. What has happened to the other 5,000,000? Three million have been murdered, and 2,000,000 have migrated. Of the migrants, nine-tenths have gone to Russia. The murdered include 1,700,000 who have perished owing to the planned rigors of deportation, and nearly a million who have died by starvation or epidemics resulting from inhuman treatment. Almost a quarter of a million have been killed in actual war. If this were the final report of a completed chapter of barbarism, it would evoke horror, pity, determination to punish the perpetrators, and equal determination to find the means of preventing a recurrence of such frightfulness. These are all appropriate reactions. But since this is only a report of nazi progress toward the announced goal of the complete extermination of the race, it calls also for a search for measures which will, with all possible promptness, stop the slaughter. The fact that it will be impossible to put an immediate and complete end to this reign of terror so long as the nazi regime remains in force should not discourage steps to mitigate its horrors. Four types of action should be taken as quickly as possible: first, send food to the starving wherever it can be sent; second, provide place of asylum and escape for those who can get away, with special consideration of the admission of more refugees to the United States and to Palestine; third, make it known to every Axis soldier and administrator, so far as radio and leaflets can carry the word, that those guilty of specific crimes against Jews or other helpless civilians will be held criminally accountable for their deeds; fourth, defeat the Axis.

THE NATION

(September 11, 1943)

The American Jewish Conference, which met in New York City last week, registered an overwhelming vote in favor of the Zionist idea. The conference was made up of some 500 delegates elected from every section of the country. Only four voted against the resolution calling for a Jewish Commonwealth in Palestine, and these four votes seemed to indicate disagreement principally on the question of timing. The conference's spirited demand for the opening of Palestine to Jewish immigration under control of the Jewish Agency and for immediate nullification of the White Paper of 1939 reflects the tremendous increase of support for the Zionist program among American Jews as a result of events in Europe. Recent reports seem to bear out the assumption that by the end of the war no more than a million and a half—at most two million—Jews will be left alive in Europe. The delegates to the conference apparently made the further assumption that anti-Semitism has been so systematically and widely propagated by the Nazis that the Jews who survive will find it impossible to resume a normal life in Europe. Palestine, on the other hand, now offers, in their opinion, a final solution. Observers recently returned claim that with the development of the system of irrigation and hydroelectric power a million additional Jews can be absorbed into agriculture—and this in turn would open the way for a million new workers in industry. Certainly the emigration and settlement of those Jews who wish to turn their backs on Europe should be facilitated and the United Nations, acting in concert, should assume the responsibility of working out a permanent policy for Palestine which will take into account the interests and welfare of all concerned. But we cannot accept—and we think it dubious strategy for any minority to accept—the proposition that Jews will not be able to live in Europe after a war fought and won in the name of democracy and racial equality.

(EDITOR'S NOTE: We agree. That is one of the basic considerations of the American Council.)

THE NEW REPUBLIC

(September 13, 1943)

A sharp dispute has broken out between two sections of the Jewish community in the United States. The question is whether they should work for a strictly Jewish state in Palestine, or should be content to live in a state without any definite Jewish coloration. The American Council for Judaism opposes the Jewish state and the American Jewish Conference, which has been meeting in New York City, favors it.

Whatever may be the merits on either side of this question, it is a disaster that the dispute should have broken out publicly at the present time. The one great problem before the Jews of the world is how to rescue their remaining co-religionists in Europe before they are all massacred. Already this has happened to 3,000,000 and there are only 3,000,000 left. There is a definite and concrete program through which action can be taken immediately to save a large part of these innocent victims. Until it has been carried out, there should be a moratorium on all disputes over long-range policy. We do not mean to suggest of course that the rescue of the Jews is a responsibility of the Jewish community only. It is a charge on the conscience of every person in the world who dares to call himself civilized.

(EDITOR'S NOTE.—We, too, feel that it is important to concentrate on practical plans for immediate rescue. The obstacles are raised by those who insist on linking a fifty-year-old political program with the contemporary urgency of rescuing the remaining Jews of Europe.)

SAN ANTONIO EXPRESS

(September 12, 1943)

* * * *the Lord, our God, is one Lord.* (*Deuteronomy vi: 4*)

Out of this war should grow an International Bill of Rights that might become the Magna Carta of all minority peoples the world over. Such an instrument—effectuated by the nations—would guarantee to all peoples "the protection of life and liberty, equality under the law."

That proposal lately emanated from the American Jewish Conference, which met in New York to consider means to rescue persecuted co-religionists from the clutches of the savage, ruthless enemy—so far as possible.

Intelligent, humane-minded men in all the free world—regardless of crede or race—can approve and support that purpose. They likewise will agree with the conferees that justice and the world's future safety demand that the perpetrators of those foul crimes against Jews and other defenseless, unoffending peoples be tried and punished. The Conference's suggestion that those Jews who can reach Palestine—their ancestral homeland—be allowed to make their homes there, also is well founded.

At the same time, a clear-cut contribution toward solving the vexed Palestine problem comes from the American Council for Judaism, in Philadelphia. That body would set up no national Jewish state, but a democratic autonomous government in which Christian, Jew, and Moslem would have a voice, "every man enjoying equal rights and bearing equal responsibilities." In effect, that proposal would make Palestine a free country, as America is free—and the Bill of Rights would be the law of that land.

The underlying principles are older than the American Constitution, or the Declaration of Independence. They were written into the Mosaic Law: "The stranger that dwelleth with you shall be unto you as one born among you."

The Prophet Malachi spoke an identical truth: "Have we not all one Father? Hath not one God created us?"

The Council justifiably, therefore, may assert that "racist theories" and exaggerated nationalism such as have brought the present calamity upon mankind, "long ago became obsolete in Jewish history?" True religion—as Moses and the prophets taught it—equally with veritable democracy, "endows the individual man with rights for which he is answerable only to God."

The tragedy of European Jewry—a record of persecution, eviction, robbery and massacre that fills one of history's most hideous pages—thus has its root in the utterly baseless theory (better called a delusion) "that racial barriers or nationalistic impulses separate Jews from other men."

The plight of those unoffending victims of the Nazi hate-storm, and many million oppressed fellowmen of other faiths and national origins, should arouse all free men to "profoundest sympathy and unbounded moral indignation." Possessing humane sensibilities, the statesmen who shall write the peace must recognize their obligation to restore those persecuted peoples "to the status and dignity of men endowed by God with inalienable rights."

In seeking such reparation—so far as it may be had for wrongs which are without measure—for the stricken Jews, Czechs, Netherlanders, Poles, Norwegians, and all the other war-victims, the Council properly relies upon "the principles of freedom, justice and humanity to both democracy and religion." Those are the principles "which shall prevail in the better world for which the United Nations are fighting."

BRIEFS

"DEMOCRACY" IN CLEVELAND

Several weeks ago arrangements were made for a meeting in Cleveland to which representative Jews of the community were invited to hear a presentation of the views of the American Council for Judaism. Lessing J. Rosenwald was scheduled as speaker at that meeting. In advance of the meeting to which no general publicity was given and which was designed only to acquaint Jews with the Council's position, the Cleveland Jewish Community Council through its president, Philmore J. Haber, released a statement to the general and Jewish press condemning in advance the appearance of the Council's spokesman, and expressing "great shock and chagrin" that such a meeting should be arranged for.

In response to this demonstration of "democracy," Mr. Rosenwald wrote the following letter:

SEPTEMBER 23, 1943.

Mr. PHILMORE J. HABER,
President, Cleveland Jewish Community Council,
Cleveland, Ohio.

MY DEAR MR. HABER: During my short stay in Cleveland I saw the statement which was reported to have been released by you to the press and which was published on the morning of September 20.

This letter contains no personal animus, nor does it wish in any way to criticize the beliefs expressed by you as those held by the Cleveland Jewish Community Council.

The writer views with alarm that a body such as you represent is "deeply shocked and chargrined" because a person having sincere convictions at variance with those held by the Community Council expresses his views on the subject. Have your co-religionists in the fair city of Cleveland so far forgotten the rights of citizenship and of free speech that they utilize such means to proclaim themselves against one of the basic tenets of our Constitution?

I venture to suggest that if Palestine should ever become a National Jewish Commonwealth such as you advocate, it will never become the center of culture which you hope for unless the principle of free speech is wholeheartedly granted, and unless honest and divergent viewpoints can be thoroughly discussed in a spirit which will ultimately produce wise and sound courses of action.

Very truly yours,

LESSING J. ROSENWALD.

To date no reply has been received.

[Information Bulletin of The American Council for Judaism, Inc., No. 5, Philadelphia, Pa, December 31, 1943]

WHAT DOES THE BALFOUR DECLARATION MEAN?

By Rabbi Elmer Berger

EDITOR'S NOTE.—The review by Rabbi Berger of the history of the efforts to interpret the meaning of the Balfour Declaration is here published as a contribution to the public knowledge of a heatedly-debated and all-too-little known subject.   From time to time the "Information Bulletin" will publish similar studies of related subjects.

The confusion over a wise and just policy for Palestine has been inherent in the Palestinian, and indeed in the whole Near Eastern, situation for the last 25 years.

This confusion of interests is reflected in the McMahon letters to the Arabs, the Sykes-Picot agreement, involving Britain, France, and Russia and in the Balfour Declaration.

The McMahon letters and the Sykes-Picot agreement preceded the Balfour Declaration.   They provided the background against which the Declaration was issued.

The McMahon Correspondence is an exchange of letters between Husain ibn'-Ali, Grand Sharif of Mecca, and Sir Henry McMahon, then High Commissioner of Egypt.   Eight letters comprise this correspondence.   The first is dated July 14, 1915, the last January 30, 1916.   In these eight letters, Husain and McMahon discuss the terms upon which the Arabs would throw in their lot with Britain and France against Turkey and Germany in the vitally important war area of the Near East.

The goal of the Arabs was independence.   The goal of Great Britain was the winning of an ally and protection of her vital communication links in that part of the world.   The eight letters represent the attempts of spokesmen of both parties to agree upon terms.   The letters gave birth to the first controversy involving Palestine.   In discussing the boundaries of the proposed independent Arab territory, these letters never reached a definitive answer as to the fate of Syria, which was then considered to include Palestine.   England contended that Syria was never included in the promises made by McMahon to the Arabs. The Arabs insisted that they had never forfeited their claim to the territory but that, to expedite the alliance with Britain, Husain had been willing to postpone settlement of this disputed question.   In support of this contention, Husain's fourth letter to McMahon is quoted.   That letter, dated January 1, 1916, contains this sentence.   "* * * We shall deem it our duty, at the earliest opportunity after the conclusion of the War, to claim from you Bairut and its coastal regions which we will overlook for the moment on account of France." McMahon had pleaded that he could make no disposition of Syria (Bairut) because of other commitments that England had with France.

Thus it is clear that there never was any agreement upon this question, clearly understood and unqualifiedly accepted by both parties.

Against this first confusion of interests over the disposition of Syria (including Palestine) there was projected, in April-May 1916, the Sykes-Picot Agreement. Involved in the negotiations which led to the formulation of this document, were the governments of Great Britain, France, and Russia.   Only those parts of the agreement involving British and French interests are pertinent to the history of the Balfour Declaration, for the portions of the Turkish Empire, in which Russia had an interest, did not involve the Arab world.

The Sykes-Picot Agreement is of simpler construction than the McMahon Correspondence. It pledges France and England "to recognize and uphold an independent Arab State or a Confederation of Arab States * * * under the suzerainty of an Arab Chief." That section of the Near East which roughly corresponds to modern Palestine was to be under "an international administration, of which the form shall be decided upon after consultation with Russia, and after subsequent agreement with the other Allies and representatives of the Sharif of Mecca." In northern Syria, France was to be "at liberty to establish such direct or indirect administration or control" as she "may desire," or as she might "deem fit to establish after agreement with the Arab State or Confederation of Arab States." The same provision was made for English control in what was later to be known as Iraq.

A new element of confusion was thus injected. In the McMahon Correspondence the fate of Syria (including Palestine) had been left undetermined. Now, in the Sykes-Picot Agreement, that fate was decided and Palestine, separated from northern Syria, was to be placed under international control, to be agreed upon by the now four interested parties.

ARAB CLAIM TO SYRIA

The source of confusion was that the Arabs had never forfeited their claim to Syria and for eighteen months, knew nothing of the existence of the Sykes-Picot Agreement. Information of the existence of this document first reached Husain in December of 1917, when the Bolshevik party in Russia began to publicize secret documents found in the archives of the Czarist regime. The texts of the Sykes-Picot Agreement were sent to Husain by the Turks, who hoped to convince Husain that he had been duped. Accompanying the revelation was an offer of a separate Turkish-Arab peace. Husain rejected the peace offer at the exhortation of the British government, which sought to assure him that the agreement had been only "provisional" and that "the striking success of the Arab Revolt, as well as the withdrawal of Russia, had long ago created an altogether different situation."

The Arabs were not the only ones who were perturbed by the Agreement. It caused consternation in Zionist circles, after the issuance of the Balfour Declaration. For the agreement envisaged an internationalization of the Holy Land, in consultation with France, Russia, the Arabs as well as England. The Balfour Declaration, on the other hand, represented predominantly British interests. Russia had been eliminated from the war. But the previous commitment to France required that Britain and the Zionists deal with her with the greatest circumspection. That Arab agreement was ever invited in the preliminaries preceding the issuance of the Declaration, has never been established.

But the Sykes-Picot Agreement was an indispensable forerunner to the Balfour Declaration. Without it, England could not have made any further disposition of Palestinian interests.

THE BALFOUR DECLARATION

The text of this now famous document was contained in a letter written by the Secretary of State for Foreign Affairs in the British cabinet. Arthur James Balfour, to Lord Rothschild which reads as follows:

FOREIGN OFFICE,
November 2d, 1917.

DEAR LORD ROTHSCHILD:

I have much pleasure in conveying to you, on behalf of His Majesty's Government, the following declaration of sympathy with Jewish Zionist aspirations which has been submitted to, and approved by, the Cabinet.

"His Majesty's Government view with favour the establishment in Palestine of a national home for the Jewish people, and will use their best endeavours to facilitate the achievement of this object, it being clearly understood that nothing shall be done which may prejudice the civil and relgious rights of existing non-Jewish communities in Palestine, or the rights and political status enjoyed by Jews in any other country."

I should be grateful if you would bring this declaration to the knowledge of the Zionist federation.

A. W. JAMES BALFOUR.

The letter is called "a statement of policy" by the British Royal Commission's report in 1937. The Balfour Declaration became a part of the peace settlements at the end of World War I only in 1920, when the Treaty of Sevres made final disposition of the former Turkish provinces, placing them, through the system of Mandates, under the supervision of France and England which were, in turn, responsible to the Permanent Mandates Commission of the League of Nations.

The years between 1917 and 1920 saw the beginnings of the controversy about the meaning of the Balfour Declaration; a controversy that was to widen in scope and deepen in intensity with the passing of years. For the document used language without precedent in diplomatic history. The language of the Declaration was ambiguous because the Declaration sought to satisfy a multiplicy of unharmonious interests. Moreover, the term, "a national home" was an innovation in international affairs.

That the vaguely phrased letter of Arthur Balfour to Lord Rothschild should have been a source of constant and vexatious speculation as to meaning is not surprising, when it is remembered what varied interests it sought to satisfy with a single stroke. It sought to reconcile the following often incompatible groups: Arabs, Zionists, non-Zionists, France, England, Christians, Moslems, Jews; and, according to Dr. Weizmann, it was so worded as "to prevent anti-Semites from seizing upon the Balfour Declaration as a weapon whereby to bring about the disfranchisement of the Jews." (Dr. Weizmann himself was not unmindful of such a possibility.) Added to all these interests was Woodrow Wilson's insistence upon the right of self-determination of peoples in the construction of the post-war world.

It is not necessary to review here the interpretations placed upon the Declaration by all of these interested groups. Some of the differences have been reconciled. Others remain as serious irritants in the unsettled politics of the Near East.

THE FEISAL-WEIZMANN AGREEMENT

Before the public intrusion of the concept of Jewish National Statehood there seems to have been agreement between representative Arabs and Zionists on the meaning of the Balfour Declaration.

Weizmann himself tried to dispel Arab fears of Zionist aspirations for a Jewish State when in March of 1918, he and W. Ormesby-Gore stopped off in Cairo en route to Palestine. So convincingly did Weizmann make protestations of moderate aspirations that one of Cairo's leading Arabic newspapers took up the task of attempting to allay Arab apprehensions. The paper, al-Muqattam, was owned by Dr. Faris Nimr Pasha, one of the earliest and most vigorous Arab nationalists.

In January, 1919, Emir Feisal and Chaim Weizmann signed an agreement, the main provisions of which were that in the future "constitution and administration of Palestine all such measures shall be adopted as will afford the fullest guarantees for carrying into effect the British Government's Declaration of the 2nd of November, 1917" (The Balfour Declaration). Jewish immigration and close settlement on the land were to be facilitated. There were to be no religious tests for civil or political rights. "Mohammedan Holy Places shall be under Mohammedan control." [1] To this Feisal-Weizmann agreement was added a clause, signed by both men, in which the Arab representative qualified this agreement by these terms: "Provided that the Arabs obtain their independence as demanded by my Memorandum dated the 4th of January, 1919, to the Foreign Office of the Government of Great Britain, I shall concur in the above articles. But if the slightest modification or departure were to be made (sc. in relation to the demands in the Memorandum) I shall not then be bound by a single word of the present agreement which shall be deemed void and of no account or validity, and I shall not be answerable in any way whatsoever.

"FEISAL IBN HUSAIN,
"CHAIM WEIZMANN."

On both of these occasions then, for whatever reasons of policy or expediency, Weizmann, as official representative of the Zionists, seems to have spoken in terms of such moderation as to satisfy Arab nationalists. Whatever their unspoken thoughts, the Zionists, from the evidence at hand, did not then publicly interpret the Balfour Declaration to imply sanction for a Jewish National State.

---

[1] Compare with American Jewish Conference Resolution: "The Jewish people pledges itself to scrupulous regard for and preservation of the religious, linguistic and cultural rights of the Arab population of Palestine, and to the civil and religious equality of all its inhabitants before the law. The inviolability of the Holy Places of the various religions shall be guaranteed."

CLASHING NATIONALISMS

Yet, six months after the conclusion of the Feisal-Weizmann agreement, relationships between the Arabs and Jews began to deteriorate. Despite the official and public utterances which refrained from mentioning a Jewish State, it was becoming apparent that there were considerable elements among the Zionists that viewed the Balfour Declaration as a green light to the realization of such a project. This situation is, at least, implicitly reflected in an event of July 2, 1919. On that date, the General Syrian Congress una nimously passed a series of resolutions, designed to express the wishes of "Moslem, Christian, and Jewish inhabitants" of the lands involved in the Near Eastern negotiations. These resolutions, ten in number, were premised upon "the basic principles proclaimed by President Wilson in condemnation of secret treaties and cause us to enter an emphatic protest against any agreement providing for the dismemberment of Syria and against any undertaking envisaging the recognition of Zionism in southern Syria (Palestine); and we ask for the explicit annulment of all such agreements and undertakings." Accordingly, the sixth resolution denied the right of France to any part of Syria and resolution seven rejected "the claims of the Zionists for the establishment of a Jewish commonwealth in that part of southern Syria which is known as Palestine. * * * Our Jewish fellow-citizens shall continue to enjoy the rights and to bear the responsibilities which are ours in common."

One element of current interest becomes clear in this recitation of history of the early years of the Balfour Declaration. Arab nationalism has been a real factor in the Near Eastern area. Part of the language of the Balfour Declaration was in acknowledgment of the existence of Arab nationalism.

THE "FOUNDATIONS" FOR A COMMONWEALTH

And the moderation with which Zionists spoke publicly of their aspirations showed that they were aware of the resistance to any attempt to use the Balfour Declaration as the opening wedge for the establishment of a Jewish State in Palestine.

Before the great powers could stabilize the Near Eastern situation by a definitive peace, there were, nevertheless, a considerable number of statements pertaining to the Declaration, which used the terms "Jewish Commonwealth" and "Jewish State." So, in March of 1919, Woodrow Wilson could say, "I am persuaded that the Allied nations, with the fullest concurrence of our own government and people, are agreed that in Palestine shall be laid the foundations for a Jewish commonwealth." And in November of the same year, Jan Smuts could say, "in generations to come a Jewish state" might rise in Palestine "once again."

There is no reason not to believe that Wilson and Smuts had anything other in mind that an eventual Palestine population, predominantly Jewish, much the same as Italy is composed of a people whose religion is predominantly Catholic. Moreover, it is obvious, that even such an understanding of the Declaration envisaged this the consequence of a natural, evolutionary process, over a period of a great many years. There is, on the other hand, every reason to question the use of names like Wilson and Smuts as having sanctioned a program which would impose political control by a minority of Palestine's population.

As the specific problems of the Near East crystallized, President Wilson was apparently so disturbed by the dangerous potentialities of the situation that in June 1919, he dispatched a commission to the Near East for a careful survey. This commission, known as the King-Crane Commission, was to submit a report which would be of assistance in the final formulation of the peace treaties.

THE KING-CRANE REPORT

With regard to Palestine, the King-Crane Commission gave the following interpretation and definition, "A national home for the Jewish people is not equivalent to making Palestine into a Jewish state." The commission further reported that in its estimation, the establishment of such a state would gravely "trespass upon the civil and religious rights of existing non-Jewish communities in Palestine" and even ventured the opinion after studying Zionist literature "that the Zionists looked forward to a practically complete dispossession of the present non-Jewish inhabitants of Palestine by various forms of purchase." Moreover, the Commission reported that despite wide varieties of opinion on other matters, the entire Arab world was in great opposition to a Jewish state. And the report concluded with the affirmation that if the creation of such a State was to be the interpretation put upon the Balfour Declaration, that interpretation would have to be implemented with force.

"No British officer, consulted by the Commissioners," the report says, "believed that the Zionist programme could be carried out except by force of arms." What use President Wilson and our State Department made of this report is unknown. It is significant, however, that while the Presidents since Wilson have endorsed the Balfour Declaration, none has endorsed the idea of a Jewish State in Palestine. There is every reason to believe that the resolution adopted by the Congress of the United States in 1922, endorsing the Balfour Declaration, was predicated on the interpretation given in the report of the King-Crane Commission.

Subsequently the British Government made several attempts to clarify the meaning of the Balfour Declaration. The divergence between the Declaration and Zionist demands for a Jewish state is emphasized in such a statement as this, issued by the Haycraft Commission in 1921. "Much we feel might be done to allay the existing hostitlity between the races if responsible persons on both sides could agree to discuss the questions arising between them in a reasonable spirit on the basis that the Arabs should accept implicity the declared policy of the Government on the subject of the Jewish National Home and that Zionist leaders should abandon and repudiate all pretensions that go beyond it."

THE FIRST OFFICIAL INTERPRETATION

The next year, 1922, Winston Churchill, then Secretary of State for the Colonies, gave the official attitude of the British Government in a Command Paper, as follows:

"When it is asked what is meant by the development of the Jewish National Home in Palestine, it may be answered that it is not the imposition of a Jewish nationality upon the inhabitants of Palestine as a whole, but the further development of the existing Jewish community, with the assistance of Jews in other parts of the world, in order that it may become a center in which the Jewish people [2] as a whole may take, on grounds of religion and race, an interest and a pride. But in order that this community should have the best prospect of free development and provide a full opportunity for the Jewish people to display its capacitites, it is essential that it should know that it is in Palestine as of right and not on sufferance. That is the reason why it is necessary that the existence of a Jewish National Home in Palestine should be internationally guaranteed, and that it should be formally recognized to rest upon ancient historic connection.

"This, then, is the interpretation which His Majesty's Government place upon the Declaration of 1917, and, so understood, the Secretary of State is of opinion that it does not contain or imply anything which need cause either alarm tb the Arab population of Palestine or disappointment to the Jews."

This statement of the man who is now Prime Minister, is one of the definitive documents in the history of the Balfour Declaration. We find here, in that clear and precise language for which Mr. Churchill is renowned, an authoritative explanation of the disputed term "national home."

Such was also the interpretation put upon the Balfour Declaration in the White Paper of 1939, which says of Mr. Churchill's definition, "H. M. Government adhere to this interpretation of the Declaration of 1917 and regard it as an authoritative and comprehensive description of the character of the Jewish National Home in Palestine." The 1939 statement says further, "But, with the Royal Commission, His Majesty's Government believe that the framers of the Mandate, in which the Balfour Declaration was embodied, could not have intended that Palestine should be converted into a Jewish state against the will of the Arab population of the country. That Palestine was not to be converted into a Jewish state might be held to be implied in the message from the Command Paper of 1922 which reads as follows:

UNAUTHORIZED STATEMENTS DENOUNCED IN 1922

"Unauthorized statements have been made to the effect that the purpose in view is to create a wholly Jewish Palestine. Phrases have been used such as 'Palestine is to become as Jewish as England is English.' His Majesty's Government regard any such expectation as impracticable and have no such aim in view. Nor have they at any time contemplated the disappearance or subordination of the Arabic population, language or culture in Palestine. They would draw

---

[2] In the same statement Churchill defined "national" when he described the Jewish community in Palestine as: "This community, then, with its town and country population, its political, religious, and social organizations, its own language, its own customs, its own life, has in fact 'national' characteristics."

attention to the fact that the terms of the (Balfour) declaration referred to do not contemplate that Palestine as a whole should be converted into a Jewish national home, but that such a home should be founded in Palestine." What then, does the Balfour Declaration mean? That it did not contemplate the establishment of a Jewish state by any artificial means such as directed immigration or immigration controlled solely by Jews, as a sovereign right, is obvious. That it did not contemplate absolute cessation of immigration of Jews, may be fairly presumed.

Moreover the Royal Commission Report of 1937 suggests that the Declaration was issued upon the basis of one indispensable assumption: namely, that Zionist aspirations would not encounter Arab resistance. "It is clear," the report says, "that the policy of the Balfour Declaration was subjected to the operation of the Mandate System in 1919 in the belief that the obligations thereby undertaken towards the Arabs and the Jews respectively would not conflict."

"It must have been obvious from the outset that a very awkward situation would arise if that basic assumption should prove false * * *. To foster Jewish immigration in the hope that it might ultimately lead to the creation of a Jewish majority and the establishment of a Jewish state with the consent or at least the acquiescence of the Arabs was one thing It was quite another thing to contemplate, however remotely, the forcible conversion of Palestine into a Jewish state against the will of the Arabs. For that would clearly violate the spirit and intention of the Mandate System. It would mean that national self-determination had been withheld when the Arabs were a majority in Palestine and only conceded when the Jews were a majority. * * * The international recognition of the right of Jews to return to their old homeland did not involve the recognition of the right of Jews to govern Arabs in it against their will."

The ever-increasing demands of Jewish nationalists, seeking to interpret the document as sanction for the creation of a Jewish National State, despite the official definitions of the original language have long proved an irritant in a troubled world area. It is clear that neither Britain nor America is in any way committed to the establishment of a Jewish State. Jewish Nationalists have, time and again, been served notice as to the meaning of the promise for "a national home." If, despite such notice, they led and continue to lead Jews to assume fantastic interpretations an already agonized Jewry will be pushed further down the long, heart-breaking path to disillusionment and frustration.

[Information Bulletin of the American Council for Judaism, Inc., No. 6, Philadelphia, Pa., January 15, 1944]

THE BRITISH WHITE PAPER ON PALESTINE

Cutting across the broad issues relating to the future of Jews all over the world is the widespread, immediate concern in regard to the British White Paper of 1939. This official document, having taken cognizance of the tense situation created by two conflicting nationalist aspirations, attempts a resolution of the problem by proposals that include the stoppage of immigration of Jews into Palestine after a fixed quota of immigrants has been exhausted and restrictions on their further acquisition of land in that country.

We of the American Council for Judaism record our unqualified opposition to those provisions. In behalf of the substantial section of American Jews whose views on Jewish problems coincide with ours, we petition our Government to use its best offices to prevail upon the British Government not to proceed with so prejudicial and unjust a policy.

We base our attitude on this fundamental fact: That proposals which exclude Jews, as Jews, from right of entry and restrict Jews, as Jews, from the acquisition of land, do violence to the fundamental concept of democratic equality and thus to the very purposes and ideals to which the United Nations are pledged.

The American Council for Judaism is dedicated to the view that Jews, a religious community, shall have, as of right and not on sufferance, full equality all over the world. As stated in our Declaration of Principles "For our fellow Jew we ask only this: Equality of rights and obligations with their fellow nationals." This means equality in the countries in which we live and choose to remain; equality to return to those lands from which Jews have been forcibly driven; equality to migrate wherver there is an opportunity for migration.

We ask for no special privileges for Jews anywhere in the world. We will resist to the utmost the imposition of any disabilities on Jews anywhere in the world. There is no compromise on this basic demand.

The tragic plight of Jews in various parts of the world is the consequence of the break-down or inadequate implementation of the democratic concept which accords equality of rights and expects equality of obligations. Hope for post-war Jews and, indeed, for all mankind is that inequalities which have obtained in the past shall be permanently removed; and that national and international provisions and sanctions will make impossible a continuation or revival of differential treatment. Yet this very objective, for which in part this war is being fought, is violated in the White Paper.

There is yet time to correct this injustice and to reaffirm in ringing terms the principle of equality of opportunity. Sympathy for the victims of Nazi terror calls for the cancellation of so grievous a discrimination. Fidelity to the traditions of democracy and equality which animate the British people, the American people, and freedom-loving peoples everywhere, calls for the abrogation of a document that projects into the future the very evils and inequities against which the whole civilized world has risen in arms.

We are not unmindful of the nationalist conflict that led to the issuance of the White Paper. Our Statement of Principles declared, "We believe that the intrusion of Jewish national statehood has been a deterrent in Palestine's ability to play an even greater role in offering a haven for the oppressed, and that without the insistence upon such statehood, Palestine would today be harboring more refugees from Nazi terror."

The part played by Jewish nationalism, by the Zionist contention for political power, is made clear in the very White Paper that we oppose. Those who read the White Paper in its entirety will find the record of a long history of controversy deriving from nationalist claims, although the British Government time and again, made it clear that a "national home" was not synonymous with a Jewish National State. In the face of such declarations, Zionists extended rather than modified their demands that the rights of Jews in Palestine be based upon acceptance of a so-called "Jewish State." This was done in the Biltmore Platform and again in the Palestine Resolution of the American Jewish Conference. Such demands have only exacerbated an already serious situation.

We stand at a cross roads of decision, at a time of indescribable tragedy for our co-religionists in Axis Europe. Are we to be occupied with the creation of a Jewish National State? Or are we to be concerned with human lives, the lives of harassed and driven Jews?

We believe it a crucial wrong to confuse the two. One is a contention for a political ideology. The other is a battle for the elementary rights of men.

At the same time that we appeal that the unjust provisions of the White Paper be annulled, we call upon American Jews to organize in strength, out of deep concern for oppressed Jews everywhere, behind a non-nationalistic program to deal with the total Jewish problem. Beyond the abrogation of the White Paper lies the need for a basic solution. That solution, we believe, can come only when there is world wide recognition of the rights of Jews to full equality. It can come in Palestine only when the pretentions to Jewish Statehood are abandoned and we seek instead freedom of migration opportunity based on incontestable rights and not on special privilege. The declaration of our Statement of Principles is beyond challenge from any quarter. "We look forward to the ultimate establishment of a democratic autonomous government in Palestine, wherein Jews, Moslems and Christians shall be justly represented; every man enjoying equal rights and sharing equal responsibilities; a democratic government in which our fellow Jews shall be free Palestineans whose religion is Judaism even as we are American whose religion is Judaism."

BRIEFS

R. L. Duffus in a review in the New York Times of The Forgotten Ally by Pierre Van Paassen.

"Laying aside all Mr. Van Paassen's excesses of statement, and all in which one might wish to agree with him, the old question still remains: Is the Jew a race? Or are the Jews, in the plural, a diversified people adhering to a single religion of a number of sects. with many elements of common culture and tradition?

"Many of us in these days believe in humanity rather than in races and would rather fight for justice in all cities than set aside a few cities of refuge. The idea is not inconsistent with the encouragement of immigration to Palestine for those of the Jewish faith or community who want to go there. But Palestine is no final solution. If democracy is to survive, then the kind of stupid intolerance of which anti-Semitism is an example must die; and if democracy does not survive, the Jewish people will be no safer in Palestine than in Germany. Nor will any of us who respect ourselves and our neighbors be safe.

"No one can read Mr. Van Paassen and doubt his disinterested zeal to help the poor and heavy laden. One can read him and gravely doubt, as the present reviewer does, that his book will advance the cause of tolerance in this world one bit."

Zivion in the Forward (December 11): "The Jewish Conference is alive only when there is something in the air which has to do with a commonwealth in Palestine and is asleep when it concerns rescue work for the Jews in the Diaspora * * * Rabbi Wise knew very well that his demand could not become a part of the resolution, and Congressman Rogers told him specifically that the inclusion of the Palestine demand would mean the doom of the resolution, because the American Government now wants to avoid any public statements concerning Palestine and that the House Committee for Foreign Affairs will not adopt any resolutions dealing with the political problems of Palestine."

A JTA report from London quotes Andre MacLaren, a Laborite member of Parliament, as saying that "* * * the Arabs feel that the Zionists have prevented any approach to self-government by insisting that it cannot be granted until the Arabs are a minority." Declaring that Palestine has already made a notable contribution to the solution of the Jewish problem, he asserts that Palestine, in itself, cannot solve that problem. Both moderate Arabs and Jews, he concludes, desire a policy which will replace the present turmoil, and possible bloodshed, with peace and "traditional quiet."

Major Edgar Dessen (in a private communication sent from the Middle East): "The gay and beautiful city of Tel-Aviv is loaded to the gunwales with German Jews, Austrian Jews, Slavic Jews, Jews of all nations. And what do they dream of day and night and speak of incessantly—of returning to Berlin, to Vienna, to Warsaw, to all of their native hearths—and that, mind you, despite the terrible stories that most of them can tell about the circumstances of their leaving. Finish the war, establish the peace—and then watch the exodus.

"Deep thinkers in Palestine who know a great deal more of the situation than I do, such as Dr. Davidowitz, formerly an American rabbi, concede this point. Secondly, the same thinkers are not sure of the advisability of establishing a Jewish state, of associating a religion with a political ideology and thus lending credence to the babblings of the anti-Semite."

From the pamphlet "The Races of Mankind," by Ruth Benedict and Gene Weltfish of the Public Affairs Committee: "Jews are people who practice the Jewish religion. They are of all races, even Negro and Mongolian. European Jews are of many different biological types; physically they resemble the populations among whom they live. The so-called 'Jewish type' is a Mediterranean type, and no more 'Jewish' than the South Italian. Wherever Jews are persecuted or discriminated against, they cling to their old ways and keep apart from the rest of the population and develop socalled 'Jewish' traits. But these are not racial or 'Jewish'; they disappear under conditions where assimilation is easy."

[Information Bulletin of The American Council for Judaism, Inc., No. 7, Philadelphia, Pa., January 31, 1944]

NATION OR RELIGION, WHICH?

Much more than the immediate disposition of the uncertain political future of Palestine is involved in the present controversy over Jewish nationalism. The fate of Jewish nationalistic aspirations in Palestine is an aspect—important, but only one aspect—in a conflict between two fundamentally opposed and irreconcilable interpretations of Jewish life and destiny.

On the one hand there is the Zionist-Nationalist school which contends that the normal status of Jews is that of a national group. Jews, the Zionist claims, are a nation—abnormalized (and therefore a problem) because unlike all other nations they have no territory in which to exercise the sovereign authority of political statehood. This is the fundamental concept; this is the Zionist interpretation of Jewish history. On that basis the Zionists agitate for a solution of the Jewish problem in terms of the creation of a Jewish State.

Not always is the explicit language used. That varies from time to time, depending upon immediate, political expediencies. It is as bold as it dares to be and as cautious as it has to be. At its boldest, the Zoinist speaks clearly of a Jewish Nation and of Palestine as a Jewish State. When prudence indicates a need for circumspection there is drawn into use a vocabulary of milder, substitute words: "nationhood," "nationality," "national group," "people," "peoplehood" and, in speaking of Palestine, the term "Jewish homeland."

Yet in historic perspective, the aim of Jewish nationalism is clear and classic. It is now, as it was in the days of Herzl, the establishment of Jewish political Statehood in some area of the earth and as a necessary instrument for that purpose—the identification of Jews as members of a national group.

Whatever the circumlocutions used, the sense of the Zionist ideology is clear: that Jews are essentially a nation and that like other nationals, Jews are entitled to have and must possess a sovereign territory.

There is another viewpoint in Jewish life; the viewpoint of the American Council for Judaism and of myriads of other like-minded Jews here and in other countries of the world. That viewpoint holds that Jews are essentially a religious community and that their normal status is as members of the Jewish faith. This viewpoint holds that Judaism long ago outgrew and shed its nationalistic implications; that the genius of the Jew is inherent in his perception of a religion of universal values.

As members of a religious community, Jews are entitled to the civic and political equality of their conationals in all of [the countries in which they live or to which they choose to go.

This viewpoint considers the tragic plight of the Jews as the product of anti-democratic forces which, among other devices, exaggerate the nationalistic definitions of Jewish life, and exploit them to serve their own reactionary ends. So Nazi philosophy seizes upon mythical claims of race and nationality to divide the Jew from his fellows and to drive a wedge into democratic life. Thus a Mosley of England chatters about Jews as a foreign element. Thus the cry of the French anti-Semite is "on your way to Jerusalem."

The viewpoint of the American of Jewish faith is pivoted on the extension of the benefits of emancipation. It holds that only as a religious community can Jews have the status of equal citizens in their homelands and continue to remain Jews. It rejects the defeatist philosophy that anti-Semitism represents the norm of civilized life from which there is escape by isolation into a petty national state.

The difference is thus clear. What is perhaps not as clear is that programs for relief of Jews, for political and religious equality and for our spitirual development follow different patterns as a result of these basic viewpoints. For both of these philosophies of Jewish life are dynamic and the many institutions and organizations of Jewish life take on, inevitably, the coloration of either the nationalistic or antinationalistic philosophy. Between the two there is no neutral ground for any Jew concerned selflessly with the destiny of Jewry or out of enlightened self-interest with his own status in his own milieu.

It is clear then why a fuller study of these viewpoints is imperative. The differences are so challenging and immediate that every Jew must find it necessary to declare himself. In so profound a division there is no escape from the necessity of choice. There can be no halfway house. The so-called non-Zionist, the so-called neutral will, if he is sincerely concerned !with his role as a Jew, have to ask himself what he believes, where he stands and give the unequivocal answer that he has not yet given.

We are, therefore, gratified to notice that along with the discussion over the political fate of Palestine, there is emerging this process of reexamination [of the character and destiny of Jewish life. For a time it seemed as if the Zionist-Nationalist doctrine would go unchallenged. In the natural community of concern with Jewish suffering—on which all Jews are united—in the passionate outpouring of sympathy for victims of brutality, we ran the risk of losing sight of a fundamental issue in Jewish life. We all but overlooked a difference in viewpoint, serious in its immediate significance and compact with meaning for the survival and future fate of Jews.

That difference is real and cannot be thoughtlessly submerged. It must be known and upon the basis of that knowledge, each Jew must make his choice. Only with such full knowledge of the differences involved can the Jews of America and elsewhere even hope to shape their future with wisdom, against the broad perspective of history. Upon the answer given depends the healthy continuance of Jewish life here and abroad and the world's outlook upon Jews for an indefinite period in the future.

An interesting article by Erika Mann, daughter of Thomas Mann, who has just returned from a visit to Palestine, appears in the January 8 issue of Liberty Magazine. Her article is entitled "The Powder Keg of Palestine," and contains among other material describing the conflict in Palestine, the following interesting section:

"In the building owned in Jerusalem by the Jewish Agency I talked with the head of the Political Department, Mr. Moshe Shertok. Was there any compromise solution he might be willing to accept?

"Vehemently he shook his head. 'Look here,' he exclaimed. 'This is no matter for bargaining. This is a matter of life or death for our people. Why, even if I wanted to, I couldn't possibly sign away their rights. Even if I did, Jews would continue to come to Palestine. The absorbing capacity of this country is far from exhausted. In order to exploit all possibilities, we'll need more people; and, as matters stand, more and more Jews will need to come here. Just how many Palestine will be able to absorb I could not say. Perhaps two million, perhaps four——'

" 'But the Arabs?" I ventured.

" 'Indeed!' he said. 'The Arabs! They keep fighting against the very nature of things. And why? We have done nothing to alarm them. None of their rights has been injured. Nor would we ever prejudice any of their legitimate interests. This they ought to know, since we've always scrupulously avoided exploiting our skills to their disadvantage. We've been trying, not without success, to teach them how to run their own business effectively and to the benefit of the whole. So what are they afraid of?'

" 'They are afraid of your nationalism'."

Premier John Curtin of Australia, a member of the Australian Labor Party, is reliably reported to have opposed the adoption of a resolution asking for Jewish representation at the Peace Table. The resolution was also to have registered the opposition of the Australian Labor Conference to anti-Semitism and its condemnation of Nazi atrocities.

A spokesman for Premier Curtin maintained that exception was taken only to that part of the resolution dealing with Jewish representation at the Peace talks. "We have condemned anti-Semitism on more than one occasion," one of the labor leaders said, "but we are not willing to commit ourselves on the issue of recognizing the Jewish race as a nation."

The American Council for Judaism formally announced its opposition to the White Paper in a statement issued by Lessing Rosenwald, president of the Council. In the statement he declared:

"We of the American Council for Judaism record our unqualified opposition to these provisions. In behalf of the substantial section of American Jews whose views on the Jewish problem coincide with ours, we petition our government to use its best offices to prevail upon the British Government not to proceed with so prejudicial and unjust a policy. Opposition is based in the fundamental fact that proposals which exclude Jews, as Jews, from right of entry and restrict Jews, as Jews, from acquisition of land, do violence to the fundamental concept of democratic equality and thus to the very purposes and ideals to which the United Nations are pledged."

This foregoing statement is as clear and unequivocal as any that has been issued by any group that favors Jewish migration and settlement in Palestine. It makes collaboration possible among all elements and sections of American Jewry.

Will the hard bitten factionists who are opposed to the Council, because it believes in a Palestinian state in which Jews, Arabs, and Christians have equal political rights, refuse to make some effort to get united action on this vitally important matter of the abrogation of the White Paper?

Would it not be infinitely better if all factions, elements and selections of American Jewry made united representations to the Government of the United States, to the end that the British be persuaded to change its policy, than to continue to assail other organizations as not entitled to speak for American Jewry?

We do not expect men to compromise on fundamental convictions, but because they will not or cannot do this is no good reason why they cannot unite on those things on which they do agree.

There are times when differences should be forgotten, and this is one of those times. The immediate abrogation of the White Paper is of greater importance than any ideological programs that may or may not be realized in the future.

Unity on this matter may mean the saving of thousands of lives of men, women and children now living in the inferno of Europe. The saving of a human life is a positive achievement.

Ideologies have been and are changed and even abandoned and repudiated. The tragic history of mankind is a long tale of ideologies warmly embraced and then rejected for a different one. But a human life once lost cannot be restored or another one substituted for it.

The fight to abrogate the White Paper is an opportunity for united action. Let us not miss the opportunity.

—From the Detroit Jewish Chronicle, January 14, 1944.

William Zukerman, a well-informed journalist, writes the following in an article in the January issue of *New Currents*, in an appraisal of the American Jewish Conference:

"For the last generation a struggle has been going on in most Jewish communities in the world, including also the American, between two fundamental Jewish philosophies and ways of life.   One holds that the present and future of the Jews in most countries of the world lies in the places where they were born, live, work, and contribute their energies; that the homes and the real interests of the Jews are in the countries of their birth, or immigration, such as the United States, Great Britain, France, Russia, where Jews have lived for generations and centuries. Another view holds that the real home of the Jews is Palestine; that all other places of Jewish abode are merely temporary residences; that the real problems of Jewry are in Palestine, and that all Jewish interests should, therefore, be focused there.

"In most European countries before the war, this controversy between Palestine and the Diaspora was a vital issue of Jewish life, and it was fought with much passion.   In this country, fortunately, the controversy was never acute and it never reached the dimensions it did in Europe.   American Jews, non-Zionists and Zionists alike, have found a middle road on this question.   They assumed almost overwhelmingly that the United States was, in the nationalistic sense, different from most countries in Europe, and that here the Jews can find a home and have a future.   On the other hand, they also realized that there were Jewish communities in Europe which were not as fortunate as we are, and that these Jews needed a home in Palestine.   American Jews have, therefore, always given generously of their sympathy and financial aid to the upbuilding of Palestine, but at the same time they steered clear of the political nationalistic aspects of Zionism which were the chief interest of the European Zionists.

"But with the rise of Naziism and anti-Semitism in Europe, stronger national istic tendencies have begun to stir among European Zionists and have also reached the United States.   The financial and moral support which American Jews have given Palestine has become insufficient, and a persistent effort has been started to draw American non-Zionist Jews into the political and nationalistic issues of Zionism.   Chief among these at the present moment is the question of a Jewish Commonwealth, i. e., a Jewish State immediately after the war."

A. C. J. NOTES

In the six weeks since its inception, the San Francisco Section of the American Council for Judaism has obtained a membership more than double that of the local chapter of the National Zionist Organization.

A mailing list of approximately 2,000 names was obtained without recourse to official lists of organizations.   An envelope containing a copy of Rabbi Irving F. Reichert's Yom Kippur Sermon, "Where Do You Stand," a reprint of the Council's statement of principles from the New York Times) (August 30), a membership application, self-addressed envelope, a letter from the membership chairman, Mr. Harry F. Camp, and a request for names of interested people was sent to the mailing list.   Over 10 percent of those solicited joined within sixty hours and our mailing list was augmented by about 300 names.   Signed membership application averaging 20 a day continue to arrive at our office and our mailing list now contains over 3,500 names.

An office was opened under the supervision of Mrs. Joseph Ehrman, Jr., with a paid Executive Secretary, and volunteers who assist in addressing envelopes and sending out our literature.   The office is open daily.   The Rabbi, the Membership Chairman and members of his committee are always available for consultation and information.

The membership committee continues to be in the process of formation. This group, and their guests, meet every Thursday evening at Council headquarters. Rabbi Reichert gives a fifteen minute informal talk on our aims and principles. Questions and general discussion follow. Everyone is urged to contribute to the discussion. Attendance at these meetings is between thirty and fifty.

The membership committee represents a cross section of San Francisco Jewry. Small luncheon and dinner meetings have been held which have been most successful. Rabbi Reichert or Mr. Camp speak informally at these meetings and our literature is distributed. A Speaker's Bureau has been given an indoctrination course by Rabbi Reichert, and members of this group are always available to speak at these meetings.

A letter will be sent to the Board of Directors of all Jewish Organizations requesting permission to have a speaker appear at one of their open meetings to give information about the American Council.

Membership on our Board of Directors has been accepted by fifty men and women representing various groups in San Francisco. The Executive Committee of seven, meets weekly. Plans are now being made for a large meeting for our members and guests to be held late in January or February.

JEAN MEIER EHRMAN,
Vice Chairman, Membership Committee.

REPLY TO ZIONISM

WHY MANY AMERICANS OF JEWISH FAITH ARE OPPOSED TO THE ESTABLISHMENT OF A JEWISH STATE IN PALESTINE

(By Lessing J. Rosenwald)

In Life's article of May 31 His Majesty, Ibn Saud, gave expression to the Arabs' viewpoint of the Jewish problem in Palestine.

Great numbers of Americans of Jewish faith do not consider the establishment of a National Jewish State in Palestine, or elsewhere, to be a part of a constructive or desirable solution of the post-war Jewish problems. In the United States this opinion is held by an organization known as the American Council for Judaism, Inc., while in England an organization maintaining a similar viewpoint is known as the Jewish Fellowship.

It is doubtful if the Palestine question will be settled on the basis of complicated historical claims to the land; practical considerations will undoubtedly play the leading role. Those of Jewish faith who oppose the creation of a National Jewish State hold that it embraces the very racist theories and nationalistic philosophies that have become so prevalent in recent years, that have caused untold suffering to the world, and particularly to the Jews. Those who hold this view contend that race and nationality long ago became obsolete as realities in Jewish history; that they remain now only as a reaction to discrimination and persecution. Exception is taken to those doctrines related to the efforts to establish a Jewish political state which stress the racialism, the nationalism, and the homelessness of the Jews as Jews.

The Jews of the world share common traditions and ethical concepts which find their derivations in the same religious source. Under normal conditions they share no universal craving for either Jewish statehood, or even for Palestine itself. Between the years 1920 and the rise of Hitlerism, 1933, the Jewish population increase in Palestine (immigration less emigration) was negligible. The truth of history is that for centuries Jews have considered themselves nationals of those countries in which they have lived. Whenever free to do so, they have assumed, and will again assume, full responsibilities of citizenship. Those countries in which the Jews have lived have been their homes; those lands their homelands. They have been successful in integrating their lives into their environments; they have maintained their distinctiveness only in the field of religion.

As a result of the bigotry, sadism and ambition for world conquest of the Axis Powers, millions of Jews who had homes in and were nationals of other lands have been violently deported and made victims of indescribable barbarism. No other group has been so brutally attacked, and for one reason only—on the false claim that there are racial barriers or nationalistic impulses that separate Jews from other men. Likewise, millions of non-Jews have been torn from their homes, but for entirely different reasons.

Repatriation of this uprooted humanity to their own homelands, with the status and dignity of men endowed by God with inalienable rights, is one of the primary objectives being sought for the peace which will follow this war. The problem of the Jew is part of the total human problem. It must be solved as such, and it must be solved in those places where it exists. In attempting to reach a solution of these problems it is likely that many people of all faiths may not be repatriated. Many, through necessity, or from their own choice, will seek to locate in other lands. It will be imperative to find adequate areas in the less densely populated portions of the globe where men can start life anew, under conditions where they can carve out their own destinies as free men, with the assurance that their new homelands will provide for them "Life, Liberty and the Pursuit of Happiness." In fact, this has been contemplated in the Atlantic Charter and the Four Freedoms.

Unquestionably Palestine has contributed in a tangible way to the alleviation of the present catastrophe in Jewish life by providing refuge for some of Europe's Jews. It has been clearly demonstrated that practical colonizing can be done, schools and universities built, scientific agriculture intensified, and culture developed. These achievements have been wrought by the hard-working settlers, who have been aided in their endeavors by Jews all over the world, Zionists and non-Zionists alike. This development has occurred largely under the British Mandate, and has proven beneficial both to Jewish settlers and to the Arabs. Under proper auspices Palestine is capable of absorbing even more settlers, to the advantage of themselves and their Mohammedan neighbors.

In discussing the settlement of Jews in Palestine the term "Jewish Homeland" is frequently used. This phraseology has been a bone of contention since its inception. The official Zionist platform demands that a Jewish body "be vested with control of immigration into Palestine, and with the necessary authority for upbuilding the country, including the development of unoccupied and uncultivated lands, and that Palestine be established as a Jewish Commonwealth integrated in the structure of the new democratic world." A "homeland" does not necessarily carry with it the implication of independent statehood. Certainly there is no historical or organic relationship between Judaism as a world religion and national statehood. Palestine has been, and still is, a "homeland" for those who have settled there in the real sense that, comparatively, the settlers have been enjoying the security, and the contentment that one properly associates with the word "home." The demands for a National Jewish State today exceed by far anything that was contemplated under the Balfour Declaration of 26 years ago. The success which has attended the efforts of the settlers under British Mandate does not necessarily indicate that such results would have been secured in the past, or are they likely to accrue in the future under a "Jewish Commonwealth." It must be recognized that the number of settlers that Palestine can accommodate is limited, and that this limitation will prevent Palestine alone from offering any adequate relief when the whole resettlement problem is conidered.

For centuries Palestine has been a Holy Land to three great religions—Mohammedan, Christian, and Jewish. Shrines sacred to each of them are located there. It appears obvious that any arrangement which sets up a National State under any one of the three religions is bound to create turmoil and strife between it and the other two. How is it possible to set up an autonomous religious state under the conditions that prevail? The setting up of a National Jewish State in Palestine may be extremely hazardous to the present Jewish population, might undo the splendid accomplishments of generations of Jewish settlers and probably would hinder proper Jewish settlement in the future, when it is most needed.

A National Jewish State carries with it, also, dangers to Jews now living outside of Palestine and particularly to those located in central European countries. Should such a State ever prevail, both Palestine and Jewish residents of these European countries would be between the upper and nether millstones. Migration pressures would militate against both. On the one hand, Palestine may be called upon to accept more Jews and at a faster rate than the land can possibly accommodate. Confusion and suffering would inevitably result, with the probability that such a Jewish State itself would be forced to stop or limit immigration. On the other hand, pressures may be placed upon these Central European Jews to force them, against their will, to migrate to Palestine. Being unable to do so, they would be left in a deplorable condition, without status, without assistance and without hope.

Many Americans of Jewish faith oppose the establishment of a National Jewish State upon still another consideration. Such a State would always be a small nation and could never hope to be a decisive force in the diplomacies of the world.

It would forever be in one bloc or another. Jewish citizens of other nations of the world would forever be embarrassed either by its decisions or by its neutrality upon issues of world politics. Men of Jewish faith in some nation or group of nations of the world would be, of a necessity, either opposed to or called upon to defend secular, political action. The result must inevitably be that here in America, or for Jews elsewhere, the question of dual allegiances will be raised by men who, in critical times, lack discrimination and understanding. This would be particularly unfortunate in America, where the Jew has found a security greater than has ever been known in all the long history of Israel. The only sure way to avoid such a misunderstanding is to avoid the creation of a National Jewish State. Palestine has made a great record. Palestine's achievement should not be wasted. Palestine should be one of the countries selected for resettlement. But a National Jewish State not only is not essential to such a purpose; it will be a detriment to such a service. In all probability, little if any difference of opinion exists regarding the desirability of considering Palestine as a place of settlement. It is very likely that it is the demand for a National Jewish State in Palestine that engenders the opposition of King Ibn Saud and many others.

It is hoped that Palestine can look forward to the ultimate establishment of a democratic, autonomous government wherein Jews, Moslems and Christians shall be justly represented; every man enjoying equal rights and sharing equal responsibilities; a democratic government in which Jews will be free Palestinians whose religion is Judaism, even as we in this country are Americans whose religion is Judaism. It is further hoped that such a program, embodying the spirit of the Atlantic Charter and the Four Freedoms, would be one to which Moslem and Christian would subscribe together with the Jew, and that Palestine might be another demonstration to the world that men of all faiths can live together in mutual respect for one another, and that such high regard of man for man is the cornerstone of lasting peace.

(Copyright 1943 by Time Inc.)

Chairman BLOOM. Mr. Johnson, have you any questions?

Mr. JOHNSON. As I understand, Mr. Rosenwald, the resolution quoted in the preamble of the pending resolution was a resolution adopted by the Sixty-seventh Congress, and which as set out in the preamble eliminates and does not have the feature you have pointed out as objectionable.

Do you think that perhaps the present resolution should either be in the language of the resolution of the Sixty-seventh Congress, or if the present language is retained it should be changed to conform to the suggestion you have made? Is that right?

Mr. ROSENWALD. If you gave me any alternative I should say I should like the present resolution with the elimination I mentioned in the body of my report, leaving out—

* * * so that the Jewish people may ultimately reconstitute Palestine as a free and democratic Jewish commonwealth.

Mr. JOHNSON. What about that clause in the resolution by the Sixty-seventh Congress which says—

It is clearly understood that nothing shall be done which may prejudice the civil and religious rights of Christian and all other non-Jewish communities in Palestine.

That, I assume, was inserted in order that it might not give offense to other people living in that country. It was done, I suppose, with that purpose in mind. I was not a member of the committee when that resolution was passed but I assume that was the purpose for which it was incorporated in the resolution. Do you think some similar language might be necessary now?

Mr. ROSENWALD. Sir, I think that was taken from the Balfour Declaration, if I am not mistaken; and it was included for that reason. I see no reason for leaving it out.

Mr. JOHNSON. Yes; it just occurred to me in order not to give offense to others, I was just wondering about the wisdom of incorporating it now.   In the statement you made you quoted quite extensively from the resolution in the Crane-King report.

Mr. ROSENWALD. That was the King-Crane report.

Mr. JOHNSON. What was the King-Crane report?

Mr. ROSENWALD. In 1919 President Woodrow Wilson established a Commission headed up by Mr. King and Mr. Crane, who went to Palestine, and it is my understanding, but I am not sure about this, that this was a commission which was to report back to him primarily.

Mr. JOHNSON. To President Wilson?

Mr. ROSENWALD. Yes, sir, to President Wilson.   The Commission went to Palestine and other places in the Near East and made quite an extensive report on the situation in Palestine.   The Commission returned to this country, and it returned just prior to President Woodrow Wilson's departure on a trip.   So consequently he never saw that report in full, although he had seen part of it.   On that trip President Wilson died, so that it is questionable whether he ever saw the King-Crane report in detail, or not.

Chairman BLOOM. I would like to call your attention, Mr. Rosenwald, to a statement made by President Wilson.   It is found on page 43 of the committee print, entitled "Jewish National Home in Palestine."   It is near the end of the page.   President Wilson, stating the case for America, said:

> I am persuaded that the Allied Nations, with the fullest concurrence of our Government and our people, are agreed that in Palestine shall be laid the foundations of a Jewish commonwealth.

Those are President Wilson's own words.

Now, if I may be permitted, I will have the clerk read from the memorandum of the Jewish Agency for Palestine on the legal aspects of the British White Paper on Palestine.   It is found on page 88 of the report.   The Royal Commission first quotes Mr. Lloyd George, whose evidence is reproduced as follows:

> The CLERK (reading).   The idea was, and this was the interpretation put upon it at the time, that a Jewish state was not to be set up immediately by the peace treaty without reference to the wishes of the majority of the inhabitants.   On the other hand, it was contemplated that when the time arrived for according representative institutions to Palestine, if the Jews had meanwhile responded to the opportunity afforded them by the idea of a national home and had become a definite majority of the inhabitants, then Palestine would thus become a Jewish commonwealth.

The report then proceeds:

> His Majesty's Government evidently realized that a Jewish state might in course of time be established, but it was not in a position to say that this would happen, still less to bring it about of its own motion.   The Zionist leaders, for their part, recognized that an ultimate Jewish state was not precluded by the terms of the declaration, and so it was understood elsewhere.   "I am persuaded," said President Wilson on March 3, 1919, "that the Allied Nations, with the fullest concurrence of our own Government and people, are agreed that in Palestine shall be laid the foundations of a Jewish commonwealth."

Chairman BLOOM. I just called that to your attention, Mr. Rosenwald, because that is the record.

Mr. ROSENWALD. This Commission, Mr. Chairman, I understood was the official Commission of the United States Government.

Chairman BLOOM. The clerk has been instructed to get copies of that report so we will have it available for the meeting tomorrow.

Mr. ROSENWALD. I have it in a book here.

Chairman BLOOM. If you will give it to us I will have copies made.

Dr. BURTON. Mr. Chairman, may I make a statement?

Chairman BLOOM. If Mr. Rosenwald will yield. He has the floor at this time.

Mr. ROSENWALD. I have no objection.

Dr. BURTON. A full and complete copy of the King-Crane report does not appear in the book that the gentleman refers to.

Mr. ROSENWALD. The confidential part is there.

Dr. BURTON. That part was just put out for the use of the Americans only and that is quite an insight into the whole character of the report. It was published in December 1922, in the New York Times. I believe it was in July.

Chairman BLOOM. It was published in July 1922?

Dr. BURTON. It was published in July in the magazine called Editor and Publisher, December 2, 1922, and that has a complete report of the King-Crane committee. There were also two minority reports by Dr. William Yale and Dr. Montgomery, who differed considerably with the recommendations. The Commission was a part of an international commission, the statement of which was never clear. It was never acted upon. The report was filed, as a routine matter, in the State Department. The recommendations were never accepted and they did not have to do particularly with Palestine, but with Syria and Iran as a Near East problem.

Chairman BLOOM. Thank you. The Chair wishes to state this, that Mr. Rosenwald has asked the committee's permission to insert in the record certain material and that permission was granted. Other witnesses are privileged to submit any data that they may have for the record, and that applies to Rabbi Goldstein or anyone else who would like to insert in the record any part of any other commission report. If they ask permission the committee will take it under consideration. However, Mr. Rosenwald has received permission to put in the record any part of that report that he wishes.

Mr. SCHIFFLER. Mr. Chairman, in view of the fact that Mr. Rosenwald's testimony differs greatly from that of other witnesses, I would like to interrogate him.

Chairman BLOOM. It is up to Mr. Rosenwald. We will stay here as long as you want. If you take this report that I have had read from and what we have put in the record I am sure it will answer your question.

Mr. VORYS. Mr. Chairman, I regret that I cannot remain any longer today, as I have to attend other matters.

Mr. McMURRAY. Mr. Chairman, I regret I cannot stay and hear all of this today, but I must leave to attend another meeting.

Chairman BLOOM. Mr. Rosenwald, do you mind coming back in the morning?

Mr. ROSENWALD. No. I will be glad to, Mr. Chairman.

Chairman BLOOM. All right. The committee will recess until 10:30 tomorrow morning.

(Thereupon the committee recessed at 5:10 p. m., until Wednesday, February 9, 1944, at 10:30 a. m.)

(Excerpts from King-Crane Report, taken from pages 448 and 449 of The Arab Awakening by George Antonius:)

E. We recommend, in the fifth place, serious modification of the extreme Zionist programme for Palestine of unlimited immigration of Jews, looking finally to making Palestine distinctly a Jewish State.

(1) The Commissioners began their study of Zionism with minds predisposed in its favour, but the actual facts in Palestine, coupled with the force of the general principles proclaimed by the Allies and accepted by the Syrians have driven them to the recommendation here made.

(2) The Commission was abundantly supplied with literature on the Zionist programme by the Zionist Commission to Palestine; heard in conferences much concerning the Zionist colonies and their claims; and personally saw something of what had been accomplished. They found much to approve in the aspirations and plans of the Zionists, and had warm appreciation for the devotion of many of the colonists, and for their success, by modern methods, in overcoming great natural obstacles.

(3) The Commission recognised also that definite encouragement had been given to the Zionists by the Allies in Mr. Balfour's often-quoted statement, in its approval by other representatives of the Allies. If, however, the strict terms of the Balfour Statement are adhered to—favouring "the establishment in Palestine of a national home for the Jewish people", "it being clearly understood that nothing shall be done which may prejudice the civil and religious rights of existing non-Jewish communities in Palestine"—it can hardly be doubted that the extreme Zionist programme must be greatly modified.

For a national home for the Jewish people is not equivalent to making Palestine into a Jewish State; nor can the erection of such a Jewish State be accomplished without the gravest trespass upon the civil and religious rights of existing non-Jewish communities in Palestine. The fact came out repeatedly in the Commission's conferences with Jewish representatives, that the Zionists looked forward to a practically complete dispossession of the present non-Jewish inhabitants of Palestine, by various forms of purchase.

*   *   *   *   *   *   *

It is to be noted also that the feeling against the Zionist programme is not confined to Palestine, but shared very generally by the people throughout Syria, as our conferences clearly showed. More than seventy-two per cent—1,350 in all—of all the petitions in the whole of Syria were directed against the Zionist programme. Only two requests—those for a united Syria and for independence—had a larger support. This general feeling was duly voiced by the General Syrian Congress in the seventh, eighth, and tenth resolutions of the statement.

The Peace Conference should not shut its eyes to the fact that the anti-Zionist feeling in Palestine and Syria is intense and not lightly to be flouted. No British officer, consulted by the Commissioners, believed that the Zionist programme could be carried out except by force of arms. The officers generally thought that a force of not less than 50,000 soldiers would be required even to initiate the programme. That of itself is evidence of a strong sense of the injustice of the Zionist programme, on the part of the non-Jewish populations of Palestine and Syria. Decisions requiring armies to carry out are sometimes necessary, but they are surely not gratuitously to be taken in the interests of serious injustice. For the initial claim, often submitted by Zionist representatives, that they have a "right" to Palestine, based on an occupation of 2,000 years ago, can hardly be seriously considered.

*   *   *   *   *   *   *

(Statement submitted by Rabbi Herbert S. Goldstein:)

WEST SIDE INSTITUTIONAL SYNAGOGUE,
New York City, February 7, 1944.

COMMITTEE ON FOREIGN AFFAIRS,
Washington, D. C.
(Att.: Hon. Sol Bloom.)

GENTLEMEN: Allow me to take this means to present the following to your Committee in reference to House Resolutions 418 and 419:

Certainly this is the time to reaffirm the Balfour Declaration declaring Palestine as a Homeland for the Jewish people. Palestine cannot be a Homeland to the

Jewish people if its doors of entry are closed against them. In view of the indescribable sufferings the Jewish people together with others are bearing, it certainly seems to be the debt of humanity to give them as well as others a haven for living.

On the other hand, there need be no fear on the part of any concerning the future of the Holy Land when one day it shall become a Jewish Commonwealth for the Prophet Micah, in describing that day said, "Every man shall walk by the name of the Lord his God and we shall walk by the name of the Lord our God." In other words the Messianic Era for the Jew is not that we shall have one religion but that all shall be able to serve their own God, every one sitting under his fig and his vine tree with none to make him afraid.

At this time House Resolutions 418 and 419 if passed unanimously by the Foreign Affairs Committee will undoubtedly bring a note of hope and of courage to the millions who look forward to the United States as a nation who will answer in the affirmative, "Am I my brother's keeper?"

May God soon send to all mankind, even our enemies, a healing peace and to the United Nations a speedy victory and a Holy peace.

Sincerely yours,

Rabbi HERBERT S. GOLDSTEIN,
Honorary President,
Union of Jewish Orthodox Congregations of America.

THE JEWISH NATIONAL HOME IN PALESTINE

WEDNESDAY, FEBRUARY 9, 1944

House of Representatives,
Committee on Foreign Affairs,
Washington, D. C.

The committee met at 10:30 a. m., pursuant to adjournment, Hon. Sol Bloom (chairman) presiding.

Chairman Bloom. The committee will kindly come to order.

The Chair would like to state at this time we will hear from the representatives of those organizations that merely want to present petitions and statements.

Is the American Federation of Labor representative here?

Mr. Hines. Yes, sir. I want to make a very brief statement.

Chairman Bloom. Very well; will you please be seated and give your name to the reporter?

STATEMENT OF LEWIS G. HINES, NATIONAL LEGISLATIVE REPRESENTATIVE, AMERICAN FEDERATION OF LABOR

Chairman Bloom. The Chair wishes to announce that we will hear these witnesses briefly and then resume with Mr. Rosenwald who has completed his principal statement, I understand.

You may proceed, Mr. Hines.

Mr. Hines. I will take but a moment, Mr. Chairman, to bring you a message from William Green, president of the American Federation of Labor, in reply to your program inviting him to attend this meeting. Unfortunately, he is out of the city at this time. He desires me to give you this message:

The American Federation of Labor desires to express itself as being in full accord with the intents and purposes of House Resolution 418 and House Resolution 419 which call upon the Government of the United States to use its good offices and take appropriate measures to the end that the doors of Palestine shall be opened for free entry of the Jews in that country, both now and in the post-war period.

President William Green, of the American Federation of Labor, has just recently stated that—

Our Government and the British Government agreed to this plan and the League of Nations approved it. In 1922 Congress unanimously endorsed the establishment of Palestine as the Jewish national homeland and it has reaffirmed this action several times subsequently.

Unfortunately, the British Government has seen fit to change its former policy. It has issued regulations which will, in effect, forbid further immigration of Jews into Palestine. This action comes at a time when the need of a haven for the victims of Hitler's barbarous persecution is greater than ever before.

The American Federation of Labor, which has always been a stanch supporter of the establishment of Palestine as a Jewish national homeland, believes it is proper and just for our Government to exert its influence in behalf of that cause.

149

We feel that the good faith of the United Nations in this war would be impaired if Great Britain is allowed to break its solemn pledge to the Jews which was made after the last war. We hope that passage of this resolution will be instrumental in prevailing upon the British Government to live up to the Balfour Declaration, thereby inspiring greater confidence in the justice and fairness of the post-war decisions the United Nations will be called upon to make.

Mr. Chairman, there is nothing I can add. I might state in passing that representatives consisting of some six and one-half million members of the American Federation of Labor heartily approve this.

Chairman BLOOM. My compliments.

Is there any other representative who wishes to present a short statement?

Mrs. EPSTEIN. Yes; Mr. Chairman.

STATEMENT OF MRS. JUDITH EPSTEIN, PRESIDENT OF HADASSAH, NEW YORK, N. Y.

Chairman BLOOM. I would like to present Mrs. Judith Epstein, president of Hadassah, from New York.

Would you kindly explain for the benefit of the committee and also for the record just what the Hadassah means and just what it represents?

Mrs. EPSTEIN. I would be very happy to.

Hadassah is the Women's Zionist Organization of America with a membership of 125,000 Jewish women organized in 600 chapters throughout the country.

Its purposes are: One, to foster understanding of Zionist principles, and two, to maintain, initiate, and support important and specific tasks for the upbuilding of Palestine as the Jewish National Home.

In recent years Hadassah has played an increasingly important role on the American scene. It has taken its place in all activities that further the war effort; it has raised more than $50,000,000 through the sale of War bonds; it is cooperating to the fullest as a unit with the Red Cross, United Service Organizations, Office of Price Administration, and all other groups functioning in the war effort. It is deeply concerned with the problems of the preservation of the American democratic forms and has an active educational program to foster the democratic ideal.

For the first phase of our work we have organized the American Jewish women both in senior and junior bodies throughout this country and we have helped create those conditions which have made it possible to facilitate settlement of the Jews in Palestine.

Hadassah was organized in 1912 and undertook in 1913 a very limited medical project, namely, the sending of two American-trained nurses to the country to make an attempt to meet the scourge of trachoma and other ills which beset the country.

Before the end of the war, Hadassah sent to Palestine the American Zionist Medical Unit of trained doctors, nurses, sanitary engineers, and so forth, whose purpose was to meet the very serious situation which disease and epidemics were causing in that country. Health conditions were so bad that they were affecting not only the civilian but also the military population.

In order to stress as effectively as I can what Hadassah has accomplished in a very short period of time, I would like to contrast has situation of Palestine when the Hadassah medical unit was sent there in 1917, while the war was still raging in the country, with the present situation. There was no machinery set up for the operation of this unit. The nurses, sanitary engineers, and doctors had to improvise everything on the spot. In World War No. 2 the large number of people, troops, visitors, and medical corps stationed in Palestine have found a completely different scene, and I think we can say with justifiable pride that Hadassah has played an important part in creating the conditions as they exist today.

There is in Palestine today a medical center. It was opened by Hadassah in May 1939 and consists of a nurses' training school, a postgraduate medical school, a completely modern hospital equipped with the latest scientific equipment and manned by men from lands from which they had been expelled and whose medical history they have helped make. These men have brought into Palestine their training and knowledge and a completely modern approach to the medical and health problems, of not only Palestine, but the whole East.

The medical center is utilized for civilians, but it has been able to care for special military cases. In addition, it has been able to offer service to the military medical branches of the United Nations through weekly conferences held at the hospital where clinical discussions, based on the needs of the troops, have taken place. Our laboratories have been put at the disposal of the military, and we are happy to say that we have been helpful by making available to them vaccines and other scientific help.

A dramatic contribution was the utilization of a wound-healing powder which was evolved through the cooperation of the Hadassah and Hebrew University laboratories and put at the disposal of the British Army. So successful was the use of this new wound-healing product that it was also offered to the Russian Government.

A second example of the change that has been wrought in Palestine is the condition of the youth population. When the armies entered Palestine in World War No. 1, they found a population whose health condition was at the lowest ebb. Children wandered about uncared for, beset by serious disease, and so seriously undernourished that their future health was jeopardized. A survey of the youth population today will show that in a quarter of a century, six or seven centuries have been bridged, and the standards of the twentieth century introduced into a land that had been living on the level of the thirteenth century.

The large oriental population in the country had accepted the fact that it was the will of Allah that children should die in infancy. With the opening of the Hadassah child-welfare centers, it became clear that prophylactics could change that fate. Therefore, we believe that what we have brought into Palestine through Hadassah's health program is important, not only for the Jewish population alone, but also for the Arab population of Palestine, and indeed, for the Near East as a whole, bringing there health standards that evolved in the western world and which bear the imprint of the twentieth century. Such standards carry with them potentialities for a completely new approach to public health and bring a new scientific era to that part of the world.

I want to say one word on the effect of our work on the Arab population, both direct and indirect. Arabs have benefited directly by taking advantage of our hospitals and our out-patient departments.

Chairman BLOOM. Do they pay?

Mrs. EPSTEIN. In the out-patient department, very few pay even the small fee scheduled. In the hospital, those who can afford to pay according to their means, an established scale, while many receive free treatment. Many distinguished Arab potentates come to our hospital for treatment. I have here a very interesting picture of the son and son-in-law of Ibn Saud seated on a bench under a large relief map of the United States. These are only two of the many important Arabs who have come into Palestine for treatment, and who have been very much impressed by the hospital and its services. A tribute from the son of Ibn Saud was sent on to us in a letter, one sentence of which I would like to read.

"You see," he [Prince Mansour] said, "when Prince Fahd fell ill there was a consultation of some 18 to 20 physicians in Cairo, and it was suggested that he be flown to London. I was asked my opinion and I said: 'Nonsense. Why should he be taken to London if there is Hadassah in Jerusalem—take [him there.' And you see, I was right. Now nobody will go anywhere but to Jerusalem. Your hospital is famous throughout the Middle East."

Hadassah's health program has been a very real factor in bringing Arabs and Jews closer together. The Arabs are beginning to understand that the contribution which Jewish colonization brings to the country, can do much to bridge the difference between the East and West and to introduce into that part of the world, the scientific standards which the twentieth century has made possible.

Another field in which Hadassah has brought about better health conditions, not only for the Jews, but also for other inhabitants of the country, is malaria control. At the beginning of the war, Hadassah voted on annual subsidy for intensifying malaria-control services in Palestine, particularly in the newly established colonies where such services were lacking. This work is carried on under the direction of Prof. I. J. Kligler, head of the department of hygiene of the Hebrew University. An interesting letter received by him, written in Arabic, reads in part:

The undersigned, the Muchtar, notables, and residents of the village of Mulacha, near Hule, hereby tender their deep thanks for the help given them during the last 15 years, when treatments were given to all the people of our village, young and old, who suffered from malaria.

Last year you established a malaria station in our village. This year, despite the spread of the disease among our children, and despite the increased cost of drugs and the higher cost of travel, instructions have not yet been issued to reopen this station.

Although insufficient funds had closed this station, Professor Kligler, as a result of this letter, was able to hurry along the necessary subsidies. The station was reopened and is now functioning.

I would like to add one word about the effectiveness of this malaria-control program on the health of the troops stationed in Palestine. I quote from Dr. Kligler's latest report:

It is a source of satisfaction that our control work has benefited the forces stationed in Palestine. The contrast between malaria incidence among the troops stationed in Palestine during the last war, or among those now stationed in Syria, with that among the forces at present in Palestine, is so striking that no comment is required. Twenty years of malaria control have rendered Palestine the only country in this part of the world in which this infectious disease is of minor significance as a factor in troop morbidity.

In addition to actual malaria control, efforts were invested also in the training of personnel. As a matter of fact, a group of malariologists trained by Professor Kligler are now serving with the armed forces not only in Palestine but also on other near eastern fronts. Another important indirect effect of Jewish colonization on the general health conditions of the Arabs is brought about by the use of state revenue for health conditions. It is a fact that the participation of the Jews in state revenue is higher than their proportion in the population, and this revenue serves to build up social services in the country. Since the Jews take care of their own health needs to the largest extent themselves, revenue is allocated almost entirely for the benefit of the Arabs.

According to Dr. Ruppin, the Jews in Palestine already contributed in 1932 40 percent of the state revenue, while their share in the population was only 17 percent. The percentage is much higher today.

The Royal Commission for Palestine confirmed that the social services in Palestine could be made "more advanced than that of any of its neighbors" as a result of this state revenue based on the Jewish contribution. At the same time, the Arab population benefited from the health services of the Jewish organizations.

We quote from the Palestine Royal Commission Report, July 1937 (p. 129):

(v) The reclamation and antimalaria work undertaken in Jewish colonies have benefited all Arabs in the neighborhood.

(vi) Institutions, founded with Jewish funds primarily to serve the National Home, have also served the Arab population. Hadassah, for example, treats Arab patients, notably at the Tuberculosis Hospital at Safad and the Radiology Institute at Jerusalem, admits Arab countryfolk to the clinics of its rural sick benefit fund, and does much infant welfare work for Arab mothers.

(vii) The general beneficent effect of Jewish immigration on Arab welfare is illustrated by the fact that the increase in the Arab population is most marked in urban areas affected by Jewish development. A comparison of the census returns in 1922 and 1931 shows that, 6 years ago, the percent in Haifa was 86, in Jaffa 62, in Jerusalem 37, while in purely Arab towns such as Nablus and Hebron it was only 7, and at Gaza there was a decrease of 2 percent.

33. The further claim, based on the Jewish contribution to revenue, seems to us indisputable. Arab witnesses argued that the Government could have spent more money in social services if the National Home had not, on the one hand, necessitated a more elaborate and costly administration than was needed for the Arabs, and if it had not, on the other hand, involved so large an expenditure on security to protect it from attack. But they could not deny that such public services as had in fact been provided had benefited their people, nor could they deny that the revenue available for those services had been largely provided by the Jews. It is impossible to calculate with anything like precision what share of taxation is borne by the Jews. But it is certain that much the greater part of the customs duties are paid by them, and the rising amount of customs revenue has formed from 1920 to the present day the biggest item in the rising total revenue.

We also quote from the Palestine Partition Commission, London, October 1938 (p. 27):

It would seem that the growth of the population must be due mainly to a lower death rate, brought about not so much by a change in personal habits (although in this region also the effect of education and advice by Government medical officers and clinics is beginning to be seen), as by general administrative measures, such as antimalarial control, under an efficient and enlightened government * * *. We thus have the Arab population reflecting simultaneously two widely different tendencies—a birth rate characteristic of a peasant community in which the unrestricted family is normal, and a death rate which could only be brought about under an enlightened modern administration, with both the will and the necessary funds at its disposal to enable it to serve a population unable to help itself. It is indeed an ironic commentary on the working of the mandate, and perhaps on the science of government, that this result, which so far from encouraging has almost certainly hindred close settlement by Jews on the land, could scarcely have been brought about, except through the appropriation of tax revenue contributed by the Jews.

I would like to add one word about other health services that are not under the aegis of Hadassah. Hadassah has been a standard bearer in Palestine and other Jewish groups have followed the lead. The labor group in Palestine has a highly organized health system of workmen's compensation and sick benefit which cares for the health needs of a large part of the population and assures good health conditions for the workers of the country.

In concluding this portion of my testimony, I would like to point out that if one judges the cultural level of a country by the health education and social service standards, then the level of Palestine has been raised very much higher than that of neighboring Arab countries. Inevitably, this higher standard must affect not only the population of Palestine, but must affect the Arabs of neighboring countries. When an Arab woman who has borne 20 children and is able to raise only 2 to manhood, accepting this condition as inevitable, sees a neighbor, a Jewish woman, bring up the children she has borne, in health and well-being, she will ultimately demand for her own children those conditions which have safeguarded the health of her neighbor's children.

Chairman BLOOM. You mean if the Arab woman had 20 and lost 2?

Mrs. EPSTEIN. No; I mean, lost 18.

Chairman BLOOM. What have these facts to do with the resolution which is before us today?

Mrs. EPSTEIN. I was asked to present a particular facet of the upbuilding program of the Jewish national home. The 125,000 Hadassah women functioning through Hadassah are motivated by the belief that the solution of the 2,000-year-old Jewish problem demands the reestablishment of Palestine as the Jewish commonwealth—a center where the Jews may be the majority section of the population and where they may live a normal national existence. Since the support of the resolution, calling for this objective, has been so ably expressed by others, I have not stressed it in my presentation, but I want to make it clear here that the large program which Hadassah carries is undertaken and motivated by the belief that we must create the facts which will make possible the speedy establishment of the Jewish commonwealth. At the same time, we are determined that the Jews returning to Palestine shall be supported and sustained on the level which we think this century with its great opportunities should make available to all people.

What I have tried to stress here in presenting the health work in some detail, is the effective weapon which I believe it to be for bridging the gap between Arab and Jew and supplying the means to bring two sections of the population together for the common good of the country and the whole population.

Mr. EATON. Will the lady tell the committee the meaning of the word "Hadassah"?

Mrs. EPSTEIN. It is the Hebrew word for Esther.

Mr. EATON. Esther was a queen and she seems to have some descendants.

Chairman Bloom. Tell me how many members the Hadassah has.

Mrs. Epstein. In the senior group we have about 110,000.

Chairman Bloom. That is all over the United States?

Mrs. Epstein. That is all over the United States from the Atlantic to the Pacific, very active and articulate women groups.

There is another part of Hadassah's program that is not directly connected with our health undertakings, but which is very important and has direct connection with the resolution before the House. That is the Youth Aliyah program (youth immigration program) for which Hadassah is the sponsor in America—a program which has been successful in bringing over 10,000 young girls and boys from central and eastern Europe to Palestine in the last 10 years. These children have been instructed and reeducated and made ready for a new life in their new home. They have been integrated into the country, have become useful citizens and are creating opportunities for new builders and new youth who will follow them. An interesting commentary is the fact that 1,500 Youth Aliyah graduates have volunteered their services and are fighting under British command on many fronts.

Hadassah alone has not been responsible for bringing over all of these children, but it has played a large part, and we are grateful to the American community that has made it possible for us to save such a large group of young people who would otherwise have perished and who now have the opportunity for a creative and useful life.

Chairman Bloom. Any questions, Mrs. Bolton?

Mrs. Epstein. I would like to quote for the record a letter from Dr. Parran which has a direct bearing on the report which I have brought here today:

Hadassah is especially to be commended for the wartime performance of the medical and public health units sponsored by it in the Middle East. There is a particular reason to rejoice that basic health and welfare facilities have been developed in Palestine over a period of 30 years. Decade-long encounters with illness in its entirety have made it possible for these units to hold the lines against disease and to sustain the armed forces of the United Nations in the present war crisis.

Chairman Bloom. Does that conclude your statement?

Mrs. Epstein. Yes, sir.

Chairman Bloom. Are there any questions?

Mr. Wright. Mr. Chairman, I am going to spoil the record and ask a question.

Chairman Bloom. All right, I will freely give you opportunity.

Mr. Wright. Is there any particular woman's group which reacts adversely to the proposition?

Mrs. Epstein. There is certainly no organized woman's group and I cannot imagine such a group is in formation or is possible.

The woman we have approached have understood very well the purposes of Hadassah.

Mrs. David de Sola Pool. Mr. Chairman, I would like to interpose a word here. There is a conference committee of national Jewish women's organizations which comprises every national Jewish women's organization in the country, and on a number of occasions they have gone on record as opposing the white paper and supporting the Balfour Declaration. There has been no group which has excepted itself from that position.

Mrs. Epstein. I want to add a few words. Hadassah women have been deeply interested as women in the services that we have been able to give to the men, women, and children of Palestine who otherwise would not have received them, but the motivation for working for a project 6,000 miles away is the determination to provide for the Jewish National Home those conditions that shall make possible the absorption of the largest possible number of Jews in the shortest possible time. They have worked for the preservation of the health of those who are in the land and those who are coming into the land in order to establish good and firm foundations for the future Jewish Commonwealth.

We are an integral part of the Zionist movement, the objective of which is the reestablishment of Palestine as a Jewish Commonwealth. Toward the achievement of that objective all our work and efforts are dedicated.

Chairman BLOOM. Any further questions? (No response.) Thank you very much and we appreciate your coming here.

I would like to call on two representatives, one from Brooklyn and one from New York, Mr. Delaney from Brooklyn.

STATEMENT OF HON. JOHN J. DELANEY, A REPRESENTATIVE IN CONGRESS FROM THE STATE OF NEW YORK

Mr. DELANEY. Mr. Chairman, I came in to get some education because as a member of the Rules Committee I thought you might want to come to us——

Chairman BLOOM. You do not want to go on record saying you are in favor of it.

Mr. DICKSTEIN. Surely he is.

Chairman BLOOM. Thank you, Mr. Dickstein.

STATEMENT OF HON. SAMUEL DICKSTEIN, A REPRESENTATIVE IN CONGRESS FROM THE STATE OF NEW YORK

Mr. DICKSTEIN. Mr. Chairman and gentlemen, I am in hearty support of House Resolution 418 and I see House Resolution 419 is along the same lines. I am in full support of both and I will do everything I can. I think in part the resolution came too late because some action ought to be taken and England ought to wake up and understand we have something to say about the Palestine question. I hope that some future date we will discuss it on the floor.

The Balfour Declaration is a sort of a Magna Carta for the Jewish people of Europe, especially at this time when most of the nations saw fit to indulge in a campaign of extermination and when Hitler and his satellites are doing everything in their power to destroy the Jewish people.

The only place which these people can find to reestablish their lives and to make a new home is Palestine. Palestine is not a British possession. Britain was only given a mandate by the League of Nations, a mandate which makes it a trustee for the benefit of the people of Palestine and which is based on Britain's declaration that "His Majesty's Government will facilitate the establishment in Palestine of a Jewish Home Land."

In 1924 our Government became a "contracting" party to the Palestine mandate. This was effected by a convention signed between the United States and Great Britain, in which there appeared these significant articles:

First. That no discrimination shall be made among the inhabitants of Palestine on the grounds of race or religion or language and that no person should be excluded from Palestine because of his religious beliefs.

Second. This convention could not be modified except with the consent of the United States.

Notwithstanding these specific provisions of our convention with Great Britain, the British Government without consulting us and without obtaining permission from this country issued what is known as the Palestine White Paper.

Under this so-called White Paper, it was provided among other things that Jewish immigration to Palestine should be limited to not more than 75,000 and that this total must be reached by March 31, 1944, after which no Jews would be allowed to enter Palestine. In other words, the Jewish Home Land would be the only place from which Jews would be absolutely barred as Jews—in spite of the fact that Britain solemnly pledged herself to establish a Jewish Home Land in Palestine.

Our Government cannot permit that a friendly government like that of Great Britain should thus flout its own solemn pledge in favor of the Jewish Home Land in Palestine.

It is also of importance to note that while most of the countries in the Near East are straddling and "sitting on the fence," not giving the United Nations the slightest help or cooperation in the war, it is the Jews of Palestine who participate in this war to the fullest extent. They have written a vivid chapter of brilliant, eager, and courageous participation in the war on the side of the United Nations.

Their self-sacrifice and courage have excited the admiration of the British and American officers under whom these men and women have served.

Pierre von Paassen has called the Jewish participation in the war and the extraordinary heroism displayed by the Jews in Palestine during all of the campaigns in the Near East as "the best-kept secret of this war."

But, the secret is out. There is no question that Britain is entirely unjust in closing the doors of Palestine to Jewish refugees at a time when they need it most.

The New York Times has published an editorial which I am submitting to the committee. The Times is by no means a paper which favors Zionism, nevertheless it has taken the sound view that the British White Paper is at the present time a tremendous mistake.

On the basis of Britain's pledges, as well as for humanitarian reasons which we must not lose sight of, I respectfully urge that the committee recommend favorably the resolution requesting Great Britain to abrogate the White Paper.

(The editorial from the New York Times is as follows:)

THE WHITE PAPER

According to the original provisions of the white paper issued by the British Government on May 17, 1939, Jewish immigration into Palestine was limited to 75,000 for a 5-year period and was due to be stopped completely on March 31, 1944. Even that small quota was not filled because of war conditions, and the terms were modified last November to permit the entry of immigrants who were unable to reach the country before the deadline. But a mere extension of the time limit is not enough. As the end of the 5-year period draws near it is clearer than it was in 1939 that the ban imposed by the British after years of disorder and the failure of the abortive round-table conference was a stopgap rather than a solution of a complex and burning problem.

The case for American intervention in this question is stronger than it was 5 years ago. The presence of our troops and supply depots in the Near East and our vital concern in peace and order in this strategic area give us a greater right to urge that the white paper should now be abrogated. At the time it was published this newspaper opposed the rigid limitation on the flow of immigrants into Palestine as unjust and unacceptable, and everything that has happened since confirms and strengthens that opinion. The increasingly desperate state of those of Jewish faith in Europe has made it more than ever evident that in these tragic years the doors of any place or refuge, instead of being closed to a crack, should have been opened wider.

On the future political status of Palestine there is room for wide and deep divergences of view. This question remains, and promises to remain for a long time to come, one of the most complex and highly charged problems of post-war statesmanship. But it is significant that Jews and non-Jews no matter how much they differ on this point, stand solidly in support of that part of the current congressional resolution that advocates American initiative in seeking to obtain the resumption of immigration. The hearings before the House Foreign Affairs Committee reveal general agreement on the justice and necessity of removing the white paper ban. This is a fair reflection of public opinion in this country. The final settlement of the Palestine problem fits into the framework of the general peace. It depends on the code of justice and security the victors are able to establish. Meantime there can be no question that humanity and a sense of reality demand that the arbitrary ban should be lifted and immigration should be permitted on the most generous terms possible.

Chairman Bloom. Thank you, Mr. Dickstein.

Chairman Bloom. We will now hear from our distinguished colleague from Vermont, Congressman Charles A. Plumley.

STATEMENT OF HON. CHARLES A. PLUMLEY, MEMBER OF CONGRESS FROM THE STATE OF VERMONT

Mr. Plumley. Mr. Chairman, and members of the Foreign Affairs Committee, I just desire to place myself on record as being wholeheartedly in favor of the resolution now under consideration which call for the reopening of Palestine to Jewish immigration so that the purpose and intent of the Balfour Declaration may be realized.

I believe that a careful study of the documents compiled in the pamphlet arranged by Chairman Bloom, which contains the remarks in opposition to the British white paper on Palestine which were made in the British Parliament in 1939, will show that House Resolutions 418 and 419 merit the support of the Congress. I hope that you ladies and gentlemen of the committee will soon report this matter favorably to the House so that steps may be taken to reopen this ancient homeland of the Jews so that it may become a true haven of refuge for the persecuted members of their faith who have endured and suffered so terribly under Nazi and Fascist tyranny and oppression.

Chairman Bloom. Mr. Rosenwald, I understand you completed your statement yesterday.

Mr. Rosenwald. That is right, sir.

Chairman Bloom. Mr. Johnson, were you here?

Mr. Johnson. Yes; I asked Mr. Rosenwald all the questions I cared to ask him yesterday, Mr. Chairman.

Chairman Bloom. Dr. Eaton?

Dr. Eaton. I was not here, I am sorry to say, but I have no questions at the moment. I am like Mr. Delaney who came here for education.

Chairman BLOOM. Mr. Jarman?

Mr. JARMAN. Just one question, Mr. Chairman.

ADDITIONAL STATEMENT OF LESSING J. ROSENWALD

Chairman BLOOM. You may proceed, Mr. Rosenwald.

Mr. JARMAN. Mr. Rosenwald, for the possible correction of the record you referred yesterday to President Wilson having appointed some committee which reported to him just before he left town on the trip during which he died. You must have meant President Harding.

Mr. ROSENWALD. No. He never did report to President Wilson in full because President Wilson had left the Capitol.

Mr. JARMAN. You mean he had gone out of office.

Mr. ROSENWALD. It may have been that way, I understand that he did not receive this report in full although he had a brief of it prior to that time.

Mr. JARMAN. If that was in error I wanted to correct it.

Mr. ROSENWALD. It was President Wilson.

Chairman BLOOM. Any further questions, Mr. Jarman?

Mr. JARMAN. That is all.

Chairman BLOOM. Mrs. Rogers, do you wish to ask Mr. Rosenwald any questions on his testimony of yesterday?

Mrs. ROGERS. No; I am very sorry I had to leave. I wonder if he would tell me briefly.

Chairman BLOOM. That is just a question it would not take too long to answer. Mrs. Rogers would like to know how you feel about the resolution.

Mrs. ROGERS. I am very sorry I was not here to hear your testimony yesterday.

Mr. ROSENWALD. If I could describe it briefly, Mrs. Rogers, I advocate the first part of the resolution which requests that the doors of Palestine be opened again for immigration and that the restrictions on purchases of land be removed and the ground that it was placed upon was that I felt that it was inadvisable to make such restrictions on Jews as Jews.

The second part of the resolution which had to do with the establishment of a national Jewish commonwealth or state in Palestine I opposed on the ground that I thought inimical to the Jewish people in Palestine as well as to the Jewish people outside of Palestine.

In brief I think that is as well as I can give it to you. The statement which I gave was not very long. I think it takes 10 or 15 minutes to read.

Mrs. ROGERS. Have you a copy of the statement?

Mr. ROSENWALD. I gave the only copy to the secretary.

Chairman BLOOM. The reporter will have it up here today.

Mrs. ROGERS. I will see it there.

Chairman BLOOM. Any further questions, Mrs. Rogers?

Mrs. ROGERS. Then I gather you do not favor the creation of a Jewish commonwealth.

Mr. ROSENWALD. A national Jewish state?

Mrs. ROGERS. Yes.

Mr. ROSENWALD. I think it would be more advisable to have an independent, democratic Palestine nation established with all the inhabitants of the country having equal rights and equal obligation, where all the inhabitants would be Palestinians regardless of their respective faiths, Jews in Palestine being Palestine citizens of Jewish faith even as we in the United States are American citizens of Jewish faith.

Mrs. ROGERS. Like our own Government.

Chairman BLOOM. Dr. Eaton, do you want to ask a question?

Dr. EATON. Mr. Rosenwald is a very practical businessman and I want to ask him his views, when the Jew follows out this idea and becomes a very large majority in Palestine it will then become practically a Jewish state; would it not?

Mr. ROSENWALD. Doctor, I cannot answer that yes or no. I would like to say a few words on the subject.

Dr. EATON. Certainly; that is what I want you to do.

Mr. ROSENWALD. I should say, Doctor, that it seems to me that the purpose of democracy almost precludes the fact that you take a minority population and artificially build it up by restriction so that that minority then becomes a majority and after that you declare that you are going to have a democratic state which shall be exclusively a democratic state of that majority, even if that should come to pass where the Jews are in the majority. I still feel there should be a democratic state of Palestine in which the citizens of the majority as well as the minority should be citizens of a Palestine state which would mean each would have their own rights and own responsibilities, being citizens of Palestine.

Dr. EATON. And share in the government?

Mr. ROSENWALD. And share in the government and in the responsibilities as well as the benefits of such a government.

Dr. EATON. Rabbi Silver raised the question of Trans-Jordan. There is no use considering that. You have a vast territory across the dark Jordan. Your idea sounds very statesmanlike to me; that is to have joint action of the nations to create a new nation, throw that nation open to immigration so that the Jewish people of the world will be free to go there and keep and develop this territory east of the Jordan. That would solve the problem of a Jewish home and eventually would solve the problem of their dominance in the home of their fathers, do you not think?

Mr. ROSENWALD. Doctor, may I suggest the language of your resolution I do not believe contemplates anything more than the limits of Palestine as it now exists, and do you not think that would apply to Trans-Jordan? If such land were available it would offer that much more haven of refuge for all the pressed people—Jews, political exiles, and all those who might desire to emigrate to Palestine as a place of refuge. I do not believe that part of the country is included in the resolution as indicating Palestine.

Dr. EATON. What is the capacity of this limited territory?

Mr. ROSENWALD. I do not have that.

Dr. EATON. Could it accommodate much beyond double the present population? How many millions could you squeeze into that little cubbyhole?

Mr. KEE. The testimony is they can absorb about 4,000,000 in addition to what they have now.

Dr. EATON. But the resolution provides that there shall be full opportunity for colonization. In your judgment does this small territory give full opportunity for colonization?

Mr. ROSENWALD. I think it gives additional opportunity for colonization, but to what extent I am not prepared to testify.

Mr. JOHNSON. Some of the members were not here yesterday and did not hear Mr. Rosenwald's objection. His objection to the resolution began with the last clause which says that there shall be full opportunity for colonization, so that the Jewish people may ultimately reconstitute Palestine as a free and democratic Jewish community; that is the last two lines.

Those were the lines of the resolution to which you objected?

Dr. EATON. You want Palestine to be a nation without the name of any particular race dominating.

Mr. ROSENWALD. Yes, sir.

Dr. EATON. But you take it for granted the dominant population will be Jewish.

Mr. ROSENWALD. I do not take it for granted.

Dr. EATON. But it might happen that way.

Mr. ROSENWALD. But it might happen that way. We happen to have certain sections of this country where I think such is the case, but we are still American citizens and citizens of this country, rather than having an isolated religious-political state, which I believe is not in the best interest of the Jews themselves.

Chairman BLOOM. Will the gentleman yield to me.

Mr. ROSENWALD. Certainly, Mr. Chairman.

Chairman BLOOM. I would like to have Mr. Johnson read from the mandate on page 11, the second article, will you kindly read that Mr. Johnson?

Mr. JOHNSON. At the request of the chairman I read from a document entitled "Excerpts from State Department Publication No. 153," page 11, second article.

(The matter referred to is as follows:)

ARTICLE 2

The Mandatory shall be responsible for placing the country under such political, administrative and economic conditions as will secure the establishment of the Jewish national home, as laid down in the preamble, and the development of self-governing institutions, and also for safeguarding the civil and religious rights of all the inhabitants of Palestine, irrespective of race and religion.

Dr. EATON. Mr. Chairman, may I ask Mr. Rosenwald to interpret for me his point of view on another word or two in this resolution.

What do you understand by the phrase "Appropriate measures," for our Government to take. "Good offices" are one thing, but what are "appropriate measures"? Have they got a bayonet on the end of them?

Mr. ROSENWALD. My point of view is I think that is something the committee must decide for themselves. From my own point of view it would be very hazardous to pass a resolution which carried with it an implication we are going to back up this by force of arms.

Dr. EATON. What would be your definition of "appropriate measures"?

Mr. ROSENWALD. First of all this committee should render its opinion. That opinion should be of great practicable value or only of moral effect. The moral effect would probably weigh considerably with our ally, Great Britain. On the other hand Great Britain may take the point of view if you are going to recommend such action and are wholeheartedly undertaking it, that by the very reason of your action we expect you to do what is necessary in carrying out the recommendation which you are proposing; namely, to see that this state you are recommending is established, and if necessary, aid by force of arms to keep it so established at least until such time as it can establish itself on a permanent foundation.

Dr. EATON. I think your position is eminently sound. Of course you could not expect this committee to make recommendation as to "appropriate measures" and have no idea what that would mean. We have to have some definite concept of what "appropriate measures" mean or else we should not make the recommendation.

Chairman BLOOM. May I answer that question?

Dr. EATON. I think Mr. Rosenwald knows more about it than the chairman.

Chairman BLOOM. He knows from his point of view.

Mr. ROSENWALD. I was only expressing my own views.

Dr. EATON. I am fully acquainted with the chairman's views.

Chairman BLOOM. I would like to say that "appropriate measures," would be embodied in legislation which would have to come before this committee. And now I would further like to state, my good friend, that we are not asking for anything more than what is today on the statute books. All of these things have been said time and time again and we have agreements, mandates, and resolutions and pledges. Now we are only saying this, we would like to have the things we have already agreed upon carried out. That goes from President Wilson down to the present day.

Dr. EATON. All right, but this resolution distinctly says that the United States shall use its good offices and take appropriate measures. I am interested in having this thing definitely made possible. Do you consider it wise at the present juncture when we have the world in flames, and a great possibility of an inflammatory movement in the Middle East beginning, to start creating a new state in Palestine under the auspices of the United States Government or the auspices of the British Government backed by the United States Government, because if we pass this resolution we are committed to stand by Great Britain.

Mr. ROSENWALD. Doctor, I do not believe it is in the mind of anyone that such a state could be established now during the heat of present turmoil, and I think the present resolutions do not call for that.

Dr. EATON. It does call for just that. It lays down policies. We will have to connect the cause with the effect.

Mr. ROSENWALD. My point of view is it should not be established in the future, but I do not believe it is contemplated during the heat of battle.

Mrs. ROGERS. Why do you think the resolution is not proper at this time, Mr. Rosenwald?

Mr. ROSENWALD. There seem to be many Jewish people in this country with sentiment in favor of this. A great number of people are conscientiously in favor of this resolution and what the resolution stands for and have so expressed themselves and it is my opinion the reason it is brought up at this time is probably in accordance with the wish of a great many Jewish citizens of the United States.

Mrs. Rogers. That are anxious just as I am to work out a specific solution. I realized the sentiment was there. I was in the Holy Land on my honeymoon, so I saw how people felt about this.

Dr. Eaton. One motive that must be dominant is the unbelievable persecution of the Jew in Europe going on at the present time and this is an attempt to relieve that impossible situation.

Chairman Bloom. I would like to say this, that of course Mr. Rosenwald, you said something about the feelings of the Jewish people. I would like to add to that, Mr. Rosenwald, the feeling of the non-Jewish people throughout the country in a great percentage, if not all Jewry, is in favor of this resolution.

Mrs. Rogers. To go back to the point of the bayonet, I suppose you would have to have a large Army if you have a Jewish nation or Jewish state, would you not?

Mr. Rosenwald. I cannot talk on this from any personal knowledge. In the report made in 1919, which was 25 years ago, you must bear in mind that at that time conditions were very very different especially in regard to the relative population of the Jews in Palestine and Arabs in Palestine. The Jews were a very much smaller percentage at that time. What relative importance you place on that I do not know, but one must be fair in keeping that in mind, it was estimated in this report, and indeed, such a program as this would require a standing army of not less that 50,000 soldiers.

Mrs. Rogers. That would be difficult to maintain.

Chairman Bloom. The Chair is about to rule we cannot go back and go over all of the things which were taken up yesterday. We took up that report and it is going to be published. I want to get on because we have many more questions and many more witnesses.

Mr. Burgin?

Mr. Burgin. Do you favor the passage of this resolution with a minor amendment?

Mr. Rosenwald. I favor the passage of this resolution with one or two amendments, either strike out the words after the word "colo-nization," ending on line five entirely, or by substituting, and I would have to get my papers to give you the exact words but I can give you the meaning of it, so that Palestine may be reconstituted as a democratic commonwealth, leaving out the Jewish people and leaving out the word "Jewish commonwealth. Have I made that point clear?

Mr. Burgin. You feel ultimately that would be to the best interest of the Jews?

Mr. Rosenwald. That is it exactly.

Dr. Eaton. The gentleman would not object if it became a republican commonwealth.

Chairman Bloom. The Chair will have to rule that question out of order. Mr. Vorys.

Mr. Vorys. Mr. Rosenwald, I am beginning to be perplexed by the meaning of the word "Jewish" as we use it in this resolution and apparently as we use it in conversation. Does that refer to a race, religion, or nationality?

Now yesterday Rabbi Goldstein told of the longing of Jews to return to Zion and stated that one very temporal result of that longing was the great popularity of the Jewish national fund, which would bring in the word nationality, and that the Jewish national fund was for the purpose of creating a Jewish National Home, but that the reason for it was a religious connotation.

Are the Jews a race, religion, or nationality, or all three in your judgment, or is there any expert decision on that?

Mr. ROSENWALD. I can only answer this. I think in trying to be fair by giving you both sides of the picture, there is one group of Jews in this country who consider Judaism not only a religion but as a race as well. That is not the group I happen to belong to, but that group conscientiously believes it. I do not think that I should talk for them, but I think they would agree with me. On the other hand there is a substantial body of Americans of Jewish faith who believe Jews are held together by religion only, and that there is no such thing as a Jewish race or Jewish nation. We believe we are simply, for example, Americans of Jewish faith, even as you are an American of Methodist faith as you said yesterday, and that we are bound together purely by religion. Now within Jewry itself there is that very great fundamental difference of opinion. I cannot give you any authority and I doubt if anybody could give you an authoritative statement which embodies that question appealing to all Jews throughout the United States or throughout the world.

May I ask Dr. Goldstein if he subscribes to what I have said as far as the position taken by Jews as to whether Judaism is a religion, race, or nation?

Rabbi GOLDSTEIN. May I answer?

Chairman BLOOM. Yes; Rabbi Goldstein.

Rabbi GOLDSTEIN. This is a very broad and great question. I wonder whether the Chair and whether the gentlemen and ladies of the committee would not agree that on a question of this kind the best kind of testimony should be offered by the representatives who represent the American Jewish Community. Now we have their opinions on record. The orthodox rabbinate have gone on record completely without exception in opposition to Mr. Rosenwald's point of view.

Mr. VORYS. Just what percentage is that?

Chairman BLOOM. What percentage is that?

Rabbi GOLDSTEIN. I would say the orthodox rabbinate consists of a majority of rabbis in this country. Their point of view is that Jews are historically a nation and have lost some of the physical factors of nationhood by virtue of force; that the destruction of Judea has deprived them of the soil which is one of the functions of nationhood, but they have never given up their hope for the restoration of that soil and therefore in their prayers in imploring God's favor for restoration of their soil they are affirming their sense of nationhood, so that whether they may not have the characteristics of a nation actually in being they have all the characteristics of a nation in the remaking and in the rebirth of Zionism and therefore in the rebirth of that Jewish nationhood in Palestine which was ended by the Roman destruction.

Now again I say, as I think I said yesterday in response to another question, that the Jewish people in Palestine want to be reconstituted a nation; that that will not in the slightest affect the status of Mr. Rosenwald or of anybody else in American Jewry; the status of the American Jew is determined by their citizenship in these United States.

Now proceeding again to the rabbinical beliefs, because it is a source of embarrassment to me as a rabbi, ladies and gentlemen, that questions of this kind should be subjects for lay testimony.

I might say that Mr. Rosenwald has tried to deal fairly with this matter and really in some humility, but I am confident if it were a

Protestant or Catholic being asked questions of that kind, he would say "I refer those questions to my spiritual authorities."

Now the rabbinate I have described, the conservative rabbinate of which I happen to be a member has gone on record 100 percent along the same line of the orthodox rabbinate.

It is in the reformed rabbinate there is some difference of opinion, where the minority share Mr. Rosenwald's view and the majority oppose that view. Therefore, I would say that the sentiment expressed in the resolution of the American Jewish Conference to which I referred, which was the democratic elected body of American Jewry, that the sentiment is more than 9 to 1 in favor of what is involved in this resolution; that that sentiment also measures the opinion of the rabbinate in America and that view I trust will be brought out somewhat later by other witnesses, but here is one of them, a distinguished orthodox rabbi, Rabbi Gold, and the other a reformed rabbi.

Dr. EATON. Would you yield for just one question?

Mr. VORYS. Yes, sir.

Dr. EATON. Do I understand from Rabbi Goldstein that the rabbis of your faith have supreme authority in spiritual affairs only?

Rabbi GOLDSTEIN. The rabbis of my faith have supreme authority with regard to Jewish laws and Jewish practices as they have had for some thousands of years, but I was going on to say that in my faith unfortunately perhaps not all of the laity defer to the authority of the rabbinate.

Dr. EATON. And if that is true, would you consider a resolution in Congress a spiritual matter for rabbinical attention?

Rabbi GOLDSTEIN. I believe this resolution, if passed, sir, would be consistent with the highest spiritual aspirations not only of the Jewish people but of American democracy because the relationship between that democratic idealism and the founding of this Republic is one which I think is fundamental to all students of the American history.

I suppose, Dr. Eaton, that the reconstitution of Palestine as a Jewish commonwealth would represent a spiritual gain for civilization because it would enable the Jewish people to function normally in the tradition of its own democratic spirit which I think you would be the first to admit has represented a spiritual milestone of the history of the race as it now exists.

May I say in the leadership of the Zionist movement and its organizations, rabbis predominate, Rabbi Wise is co-chairman with Rabbi Silver, of the American Zionist Emergency Council; Rabbi Heller is chairman of the United Palestine Appeal; Rabbi Gold is chairman of the Mizrachi Organization of America.

I do not think you will find any instance in American life in which the clergy prodominates as much as they do in the Zionist movement, and I submit that that is not accidental. This is in keeping with a place for Zionism in the religious traditions of our people.

Mrs. ROGERS. Will the gentleman yield?

Then I gather you feel the church is much stronger than the state. I am an Episcopalian and they do not believe that.

Rabbi GOLDSTEIN. It is just the contrary. Just because in Jewish life we do not commit the authority as Jewish rabbis comparable to that committed by other denominations it is all the more significant in such a situation the rabbis come to the leadership of organized Jewish activities.

Chairman BLOOM. Mr. Vorys, thank you very much for allowing the interruption.

Mr. VORYS. I am very glad to have Rabbi Goldstein's comment. As a Methodist I do not permit my preacher to determine anything about my nationality or my race, but I am very much interested in having the comment of the rabbi on his views and his desires.

Now on the matter of race, as I understand it, the Arabs are Semitic and the ·Jews are Semitic in racial stock, that is, according to biblical nomenclature they are the sons of Shem, and that branch of the human race is Semitic, is that your understanding?

Mr. ROSENWALD. I understand they are both Semitic. I am not an authority on that, however.

Mr. VORYS. But isn't that not well understood?

If I may, I would again refer to Rabbi Goldstein to ask whether my understanding is correct on the matter of race or racial background of both the Arabs and Jews.

Rabbi GOLDSTEIN. That is correct.

Mr. VORYS. Now on the question of immigration into Palestine, no matter what the white paper would say, I wonder what would be the proposal under the mandate, which says nothing shall be done, and I am quoting from page 11:

That nothing should be done which might prejudice the civil and religious rights of existing non-Jewish communities in Palestine, or the rights and political status employed by the Jews in any other country.

In my country, the United States of America, in grappling with the perplexing question of immigration, and the melting pot, before I came to Congress, our Government determined upon a policy of permitting immigration approximately in proportion to the racial and national strains of the people who were already here.

Now, how could immigration be arranged into Palestine as reconstituted except following that principle? Would not any other arrangement tend to prejudice the rights of those who were already there?

Mr. ROSENWALD. May I ask you a question, sir?

Mr. VORYS. Yes.

Mr. ROSENWALD. In this country is the immigration done by any racial basis? Is it not purely on a national basis?

Mr. VORYS. Yes; I think you are right. It is done by referring to the national origins of those who are here. You are correct.

Now that is the way we decided to do it in this country. I wonder what you suggest there as to how you would work it out in a reconstituted Palestine.

Mr. ROSENWALD. First of all may I say in answer to your question I think the great danger of the white paper as now constituted does introduce one factor that excludes Jews as Jews either as a religious community or race. I think that would constitute a very dangerous precedent.

Mr. VORYS. I agree with you. Suppose the white paper is torn up and you have a reconstituted Palestine on any basis you want, how would you go about handling immigration?

Mr. ROSENWALD. Well, immigration apparently was being handled more or less satisfactorily, and this was subject to a good deal of debate under the British mandate prior to the white paper on lines which apparently were serving a useful purpose.

It has been conceded the population increased from 1933 until the white paper very, very substantially. The figures are not in my mind, but as far as the Jewish population was concerned it increased very rapidly, but likewise it must be said the Arab population increased during that time and while the percentage of Jewish population was greater in 1939 than it was hitherto, the number of people that came in, both the Arabs and the Jews were not greatly different in number. Just what procedure you would adopt to get an equitable solution, I do not know. I believe a haven of refuge should be established in Palestine for the persecuted of Europe, and likewise for an increase in the Arab population. I see no reason why Palestine should not be utilized as a haven of refuge for all people. Then, if you decide to have a Palestine constituted as a nation all the population should be represented. It is of no great importance whether the Jews are in the majority or the minority, they will be duly represented. Each will be a citizen of the Palestine Government. To my mind it holds greater promise and greater merit than trying to determine in advance that one particular portion of the population should have what you might call almost absolute say in the conduct of the affairs of that particular country.

Mr. JOHNSON. Could I inquire?

Chairman BLOOM. Mr. Johnson.

Mr. JOHNSON. The present population of Palestine is what portion Arabic?

Mr. ROSENWALD. About one-third of the population is Jewish and about two-thirds is Arab, about 550,000 Jews and 1,100,000 Arabs.

Chairman BLOOM. Mr. McMurray?

Mr. McMURRAY. Perhaps I need only to say that Mr. Rosenwald has raised some very interesting questions on the theory of the state, particularly in regard to the theocratic state. I should like to discuss them with him but I do not think I should take the time of this committee.

Chairman BLOOM. Mrs. Bolton?

Mrs. BOLTON. I would like to pursue a little bit the question Mr. Vorys has asked the witness.

I am particularly interested in a viewpoint that is rather new to me that has been raised. Mr. McMurray also has touched upon it.

We here in this country have based our democratic way and freedom upon the complete cleavage between the church and state. This raises a question in my mind whether we would be reversing our entire thinking and feeling were we to proceed to set up a state which would be a theocratic state. It would be very definitely a theocratic state if as has been suggested the Jews are a religious entity.

I think it is a matter which perhaps should be thrashed out more fully by the committee before taking any action on this whole matter.

I am interested in the point of view that has been expressed—both as it relates to religions and as it relates to minorities. Should we give ourselves to an insistence that any special group must prevail in any given community it would seem that we would be denying a fundamental tenet of democracy. This question of minorities is going to come up many times in these next months and perhaps in the next years, as we have to deal with the points of view of minorities all over the world. Because of that I think perhaps the committee should give it more thorough study at this time because it might set a precedent in the action of this country in matters pertaining to our foreign policy. If we are going to have every minority group that exists in this country expect their particular minority to be given the backing of this country to establish itself again I think it is something that calls for consideration.

I am not saying it is my point of view, but I think it has been put forth in an interesting way and I am particularly interested in Mr. Rosenwald's very quiet and, as Rabbi Goldstein suggested, his very humble way of presenting a situation which is very far reaching. I think we will have to give it very serious thought and will perhaps want to discuss more fully, even outside of the committee, some of the points involved.

I am personally grateful to Mr. Rosenwald for the quiet and intelligent and intellectual fashion in which he has given us these facts.

Chairman BLOOM. The Chair would like to ask permission for Rabbi Silver to make a statement at this time if Mr. Rosenwald has no objection and it meets with the approval of the committee.

Mr. ROSENWALD. No objection.

Dr. SILVER. I should like to make just one or two observations principally because I was unfortunately unable to come back yesterday afternoon to be cross-examined by the members of the committee.

There were so many statements made this morning which I am afraid may tend to becloud the real issue involved in these resolutions.

Now, whether the Jews are a nation, race, or religion is largely in my humble judgment an academic question that you and I will not be able to decide this week.

In Jewry all of these concepts are involved in an intricate pattern. The Jews were a people of old and have continued to be a people to this day. Just what factors went into the composition of this group and to what extent each has determined it has been and continues to be a subject of debate. But the fact of the matter is—and that is the sole important consideration—that we are a people—the Jewish people—recognized as such by all the world. In some parts of the world Jews possess distinct nationality rights recognized as such by the law of the land. Following the last war the Jews of Poland and Lithuania were recognized as distinct nationality groups, among a number of other nationality groups, and were given specific group status.

In the Soviet Union where 3,000,000 Jews live today, Jews, like many other groups, are recognized as belonging to a definite nationality and in those regions where they are in the majority they are encouraged to exercise all the attributes of nationality, their own language, culture, schools, and their own literature. You may recall that the Soviet Union some years ago endeavored to set up an autonomous Jewish republic in the Soviet Union. This was certainly not motivate by the consideration that the Jews constituted a religious group in the Soviet Union.

Mr. VORYS. Would you pardon an interruption right there?

Chairman BLOOM. Mr. Vorys.

Mr. VORYS. In this country national distinctions are not stressed in that many of us feel we are all Americans and nothing else.

In the United States nationality distinctions are not stressed. Here we all stress our common American citizenship. In this country where nationality rights and differentiations are not and need not be emphasized, although they do exist, Jews naturally do not press for nationality status. They carry on as a historic community whose chief attribute is its distinctive religious culture. In Palestine, on the other hand, and in Palestine alone, the Jewish people have sought and do seek a complete national life of their own, with its full political complement.

Dr. SILVER. Yes.

Mrs. ROGERS. Suppose England should ask that we hold——

D.. SILVER. I will reach that when I come to Palestine. The Jewish people unlike every other people in the world unfortunately lost their national territory. In time Jews came to the United States and became United States citizens and completely identified themselves with America, just as did the Irish or the English or the Germans who came to these United States. But there still remained an Ireland, an England, and a Germany. The Jewish people, however, lacked a national territorial center. Throughout the ages they have endeavored to reestablish it in order that the Jewish people might become like every other people.

During the last war we took our problem to the Allied Nations who were fighting for the liberation of all small nations and for human rights generally. We told them of our aspirations and they regarded them as valid. Great Britain was the first among the great nations of the world to recognize our legitimate claims to Palestine. Subsequently 52 other nations, including our own, acknowledged the right of the Jewish people to reconstitute its national life in its ancestral home. We are now in 1944 and not in 1917. We are not at the beginning of a discussion of the problem but at the final stage of the consummation of its solution. These men who are opposing the resolutions would take you back to the days before the Balfour Declaration and the Palestine mandate and would reopen again the political discussions which were closed when the Palestine mandate was established.

The Jewish National Home—the right of the Jews freely to enter Palestine and to colonize it and to prepare for the full establishment of a Jewish Commonwealth—is now part of international law.

Unfortunately we are confronted today with a situation which threatens to liquidate all that has been achieved in the last 25 years. A quarter of a century ago, Great Britain undertook to facilitate Jewish immigration into Palestine; it now threatens to prohibit it. A quarter of a century ago, Great Britain undertook to make possible the close settlement of the Jews upon the soil of Palestine; today it threatens to prohibit it. In other words, the Jewish National Home which has been in process of fulfillment is now in danger of liquidation. The white paper is the instrumentality by which this Jewish National Home is to be liquidated.

I should like to make this point very clear. The Jewish people are not planning to set up a theocratic state in Palestine. The Jewish people are not planning to set up a racial state in Palestine. Zionism is a secular concept. We want Palestine to be as Jewish as England is English, as France is French. If France were inhabited two-thirds by Germans it would not be France. The white paper would compel the Jewish National Home to be inhabited two-thirds by Arabs. This is a contradiction in terms.

The whole crux of the matter is that if the nations of the world really want to see a Jewish National Home established in Palestine, they must make possible in the shortest time the creation of a Jewish majority in that country. Our right to free immigration into Palestine is predicated upon our right to build our national home there.

Mr. VORYS. At that point.

Chairman BLOOM. Mr. Vorys.

Mr. VORYS. The question that has perplexed me was how under the mandate, and I have been reading it over, if the white paper were torn up and the Zionists had it all their way but still felt the mandate should be carried out, how would the Jewish population be increased in a way that would not prejudice the rights of those who are now there?

Dr. SILVER. All the evidence of the last 25 years indicates that the coming of Jews into Palestine has in no way prejudiced the rights or the opportunities of the Arabs or of any other non-Jewish group living in that country. Their civil and religious rights have in no way been impaired. Their standard of living has risen tremendously and the Arab population of Palestine has nearly doubled in the last 25 years.

Mr. EATON. Mr. Chairman.

Chairman BLOOM. Dr. Eaton.

Mr. EATON. I would like to ask my old friend, Rabbi Silver, whom I have known so many years, how are you going to get rid of the Arabs?

Dr. SILVER. We do not want to get rid of them. The coming of 600,000 Jews into Palestine in the last 25 years has not forced a single Arab to leave the country but it has doubled the Arab population.

Mr. EATON. The white paper is evidently based on an objection the Arabs made to Jewish immigration. How are you going to meet that objection, by moral suasion or force or what?

Dr. SILVER. In the first place no arrangement that will be made after the war for any national settlement, whether it is Poland or any country in eastern or southern Europe, no arrangement which will be made, Mr. Eaton, will be satisfactory to everybody concerned. It is important to see that whatever arrangement is made is a just and moral one, and if so, the collective organization which we hope to establish after the war must see to it that that arrangement is preserved. Otherwise there will be chaos again.

Chairman BLOOM. Mr. Wright.

Mr. WRIGHT. If Palestine were allowed self-government, I do not say now because that is impracticable with the war going on, but after the war, were the Arabs in their present majority and Jews in the present minority do you think any more Jewish immigration would be allowed into Palestine?

Mr. ROSENWALD. I do not. The Arabs who are opposed to the Balfour Declaration are opposed to the immigration as well.

Chairman BLOOM. Mr. Wadsworth, I understand you want to ask a question.

Mr. WADSWORTH. Not just now. I would rather have the rabbi continue.

Dr. SILVER. I conclude now, and ask for a reaffirmation of the position which our Government has consistently followed for the last 25 years. Why do we ask for this? Because Jewish Palestine is in danger of being sacrificed through the instrumentality of the white paper. In order to avert a great wrong we call upon the same body which in 1922 endorsed the Balfour Declaration to reaffirm it, to express again the sentiments of the American people that it is in favor of:

A. Establishment of a national home for the Jewish people in Palestine;

B. That it would like to see those opportunities created which will make that national home possible, namely, free entry of Jews into Palestine and full opportunities for colonization. Back of the Balfour Declaration is the recognition the two factors that the Jews are a people and that they have an historic connection with Palestine.

Mrs. BOLTON. My very good friend and constituent, Rabbi Silver, has put words in my mouth. Let me make it clear that the only thing I am concerned about is that every member of this committee shall give the deepest study possible to this very important and far-reaching problem; that this committee do its utmost best to uphold that which is American as well as that which is also America with the utmost sympathetic understanding.

Chairman BLOOM. Mrs. Rogers?

Mrs. ROGERS. What is the position of Rabbi Silver or Mr. Justice Frankfurter our distinguished Massachusetts member of the Supreme Court. You spoke of Mr. Justice Brandeis.

Dr. SILVER. I can only refer to the articles which Justice Frankfurter has written championing the cause of Zionism and the Jewish National Home. Justice Frankfurter has been for many, many years a great advocate of that.

Chairman BLOOM. The Chair would like to thank Mr. Rosenwald very much. He has been very patient.

Mrs. ROGERS. I assume, Rabbi Silver, you would have no objection to some of the Syrians appearing before the committee. I have some Syrians around.

Chairman BLOOM. Now, Mrs. Rogers, if any Syrians or anyone else wants to appear before this committee, I think you know the rules; they should make application in the proper way through the Chairman.

What has Rabbi Silver to do with that?

Mrs. ROGERS. I think he is very powerful.

Chairman BLOOM. While I have the highest regard for my good friend, Dr. Silver, he has nothing to do with me as far as this committee is concerned.

Mr. EATON. Mr. Chairman, in order to break the stress that seems to have settled on us so suddenly I would like to go off the record.

Chairman BLOOM. The committee will stand in recess until 2 o'clock this afternoon.

(Whereupon, at 12:25 o'clock, the committee recessed until 2 p. m. this day.)

AFTERNOON SESSION

(The hearing was resumed at 2 p. m., at the expiration of the recess.)

Chairman BLOOM. The committee will kindly come to order. The committee will resume hearings on House Resolution 418 and House Resolution 419. We have the great honor and privilege of having several of our colleagues here. Mr. Harry Sauthoff, of Wisconsin, wishes to say a few words.

STATEMENT OF HON. HARRY SAUTHOFF, A REPRESENTATIVE IN CONGRESS FROM THE STATE OF WISCONSIN

Mr. SAUTHOFF. Mr. Chairman and members of the committee, I wanted to be recorded in favor of these resolutions, which I see are identical. Because there are many people here from out of the city and because I intend to take the floor on this subject, I shall not take any more of the time of the committee. Thank you very much for your courtesy.

Chairman BLOOM. Thank you, Mr. Sauthoff. It is a great pleasure to have you here. If you wish to put a statement in the record, you may do so.

Mr. SAUTHOFF. Thank you.

STATEMENT OF HON. JAMES M. FITZPATRICK, A REPRESENTA- TIVE IN CONGRESS FROM THE STATE OF NEW YORK

Chairman BLOOM. We will next hear from Mr. James M. Fitz- patrick of New York.

Mr. FITZPATRICK. Mr. Chairman and members of the committee, I am in sympathy with House Resolutions 418 and 419 introduced by Hon. James A. Wright and Hon. Ranulf Compton to establish a Jewish National Home in Palestine. I believe the British Govern- ment should, under all circumstances, grant this request.

I hope that your committee will report these resolutions out favor- ably in order that justice will be extended to the Jewish people.

Chairman BLOOM. Thank you, Mr. Fitzpatrick.

STATEMENT OF HON. DANIEL ELLISON, A REPRESENTATIVE IN CONGRESS FROM THE STATE OF MARYLAND

Chairman BLOOM. Mr. Ellison, the Committee would be pleased to hear from you.

Mr. ELLISON. Mr. Chairman, I wish to be recorded in support of House Resolutions 418 and 419.

The white paper issued by the Chamberlain government in 1939 was in direct violation of Great Britain's solemn pledges, and in contra- vention of the terms of the mandate.

Moreover, from the humanitarian point of view favorable action on these resolutions would be in line with our unbroken policy since the Balfour Declaration of favoring the establishment of Palestine as a Jewish national homeland.

I, therefore, hope that your committee will report favorably on these resolutions.

STATEMENT OF HON. HUGH D. SCOTT, JR., OF PENNSYLVANIA

Chairman BLOOM. We will now hear from Mr. Hugh D. Scott, Jr., of Pennsylvania.

Mr. SCOTT. Mr. Chairman, I wish to join with my many colleages in urging favorable action on the Wright and Compton resolutions asking for abrogation of the British white paper and the establishment of a Jewish national homeland in Palestine.

The ruthless persecution of Jews in certain sections of Europe should bring home to all of us the urgency of establishing such a haven for the large numbers who have become homeless as a result of this persecution. Constant mortal danger still faces these people and I can think of no greater assistance that can be rendered them at this time than an open door to Palestine. This is a matter which I believe fully merits immediate and effective action.

Chairman BLOOM. I wish to say to the committee that the Chair has received letters from several Representatives who are unable to be present, but who wish to place their views on record. Without objection, their letters will be placed in the record at this point.

HOUSE OF REPRESENTATIVES,
Washington, D. C., February 7, 1944.

Hon. SOL BLOOM,
Chairman, Committee on Foreign Affairs,
House of Representatives, Washington, D. C.

MY DEAR COLLEAGUE: It is my understanding that House Resolutions 418 and 419, urging the abrogation by Great Britain of the so-called white paper, will come up for public hearings before the committee on Tuesday, February 8, 1944. I shall appreciate it if you will record me as favoring the passage of these resolutions in the printed hearings.

Sincerely yours,

FRED J. DOUGLAS.

HOUSE OF REPRESENTATIVES,
Washington, D. C., February 8, 1944.

Hon. SOL BLOOM,
Chairman, House Foreign Affairs Committee,
House of Representatives, Washington, D. C.

DEAR SOL: For many months, I have entertained the wish to see something done about the establishment of a Jewish national homeland in Palestine. I have also wondered why the British have failed thus far to abrogate the white paper in connection with this whole matter.

In these days of strife and upheaval, it seems only logical and right that the persecuted Jews of Europe and elsewhere should be permitted to seek refuge and haven in at least one place which they may call home.

In my opinion, House Resolutions 418 and 419 which call for the establishment of Palestine as a Jewish national homeland and urge the British to take this action, ought to be reported favorably out of the House Foreign Affairs Committee immediately. It is my hope that favorable action by the Congress will follow directly thereafter.

I want you to know that I join with other Members of the House in expressing the hope that your committee will accomplish this as soon as possible.

With kindest personal regards, I remain,

Your colleague,

EDWIN A. HALL.

HOUSE OF REPRESENTATIVES,
Washington, D. C., February 9, 1944.

Hon. SOL BLOOM,
House Office Building, Washington, D. C.

My DEAR COLLEAGUE: I am very much interested in and endorse the Wright-Compton resolution now pending before the Foreign Relations Committee, and I hope that you will be able to report it out favorably in the near future. With usual good wishes,
Sincerely yours,

PHILIP J. PHILBIN.

P. S.—This is but plain simple justice for a people already sorely overburdened with persecution, grief, and sorrow and I hope you will act.

P. J. P.

HOUSE OF REPRESENTATIVES, COMMITTEE ON PATENTS,
Washington, D. C., February 9, 1944.

Hon. SOL BLOOM,
Chairman, Foreign Affairs Committee,
House of Representatives, Washington, D. C.

My DEAR COLLEAGUE: I want you to know that you have my full support of the Palestine Resolutions 418 and 419. Please let me know when, where, and how I can help on this.
Sincerely yours,

FRANK W. BOYKIN.

HOUSE OF REPRESENTATIVES,
Washington, D. C., February 8, 1944.

Hon. SOL BLOOM,
Chairman, Foreign Affairs, Committee,
House of Representatives, Washington, D. C.

My DEAR COLLEAGUE: I wish to advise you of my approval with reference to House Resolutions 418 and 419, which bills will receive my complete support.
I will be thankful if you will kindly acknowledge receipt of this communication.
Thanking you for your cooperation, I am
Sincerely yours,

WILLIAM T. BYRNE.

HOUSE OF REPRESENTATIVES,
Washington, D. C., February 8, 1944.

Hon. SOL BLOOM,
Chairman, House Committee on Foreign Relations,
House of Representatives, Washington, D. C.

DEAR COLLEAGUE: Two resolutions are now pending before your committee, House Resolutions 418 and 419. I know that you are thoroughly familiar with these resolutions and the purposes sought to be carried out through them.

I, personally, believe that these resolutions should receive early attention from your committee and the active support of the United States Government. I believe that the United States Government has a direct interest in the manner in which the affairs of Palestine are conducted.

I am sure that a majority of our people favor the removal of the restrictions recently placed by the British Government on immigration of Jewish people to Palestine. I feel that these restrictions should be removed and that the original purposes intended to be carried out at the time that Great Britain assumed the mandate over this area should be actively pursued.

I have written to President Roosevelt and to other officials in the administration on this subject favoring such action. I hope your committee will consider these resolutions favorably in the near future.
Very sincerely yours,

CHARLES R. CLASON.

House of Representatives,
Washington, D. C., February 8, 1944.

Hon. Sol Bloom,
Chairman, Committee on Foreign Affairs,
House Office Building, Washington, D. C.

My Dear Colleague: Referring to House Resolution 418 and House Resolution 419, I am today in receipt of a telegram from the Honorable Earl Riley, mayor of the city of Portland, Oreg., urging passage of these two resolutions. am enclosing herewith a copy of his wire for your information and that of the committee.

I have also received many telegrams and communications from other citizens in my district urging passage of these resolutions and lifting the ban against immigration of the Jewish people into Palestine and redeeming the Balfour pledge. I believe this is the only humane and just course and I believe these resolutions should be adopted, and I hope that your committee will soon vote out favorably the resolutions so they may be brought up for consideration.

Sincerely yours,

Homer D. Angell, *Member of Congress.*

February 8, 1944.

Hon. Homer D. Angell,
House of Representatives, Washington, D. C.:

I earnestly urge you to use your influence and support of House resolutions 418 and 419. It is essential in justice to thousands of human beings of the Jewish faith that the gates of Palestine remain open. We should, as freedom-loving citizens of America, reaffirm our pledge and support of the Balfour Declaration. Please make your position known as favoring the above with the House Foreign Affairs Committee.

Earl Riley,
Mayor, City of Portland.

STATEMENT OF W. C. LOWDERMILK, ASSISTANT CHIEF, SOIL CONSERVATION SERVICE, UNITED STATES DEPARTMENT OF AGRICULTURE, WASHINGTON, D. C.

Chairman Bloom. We will now hear from Dr. Lowdermilk, of the Department of Agriculture.

Dr. Lowdermilk. Mr. Chairman and members of the committee, I come not as representing any specific interest except possibly that of the land.

Chairman Bloom. Will you tell us a little about yourself, Doctor, so that the committee and those who read the record will have an idea who you are. Of course, I know who you are. Don't be bashful.

Dr. Lowdermilk. The way I have come to be interested in this problem is that the Appropriations Committee asked us, as we were presenting our claims for considerable moneys to control erosion in the United States, if we had examined lands of the old countries to see what they had been doing about this problem of soil erosion. Upon our saying that we had not done so yet, it was suggested that we do so. About 3 years later, the Department of Agriculture selected me to survey the use of land in the Old World, to see what we could learn for the benefit of our own farmers and our own stockmen, and for our country as a whole in our national program to save our soils from soil erosion.

In 1938 and 1939 I made a survey of southern Europe, north Africa, and the Near East. In addition to 26,000 miles by car, I traveled

18,000 miles on the highways and byways of north Africa and the Near East. The findings of that survey have been reported and are to be reported more fully a little later. We found, from Oran in Algeria, to the borders of Persia, except in Egypt, a general condition of neglect and of wasted lands, underused lands, and misused lands. We found ruins of cities buried by the products of erosion, both by wind and by water. In the place of beautiful cities of the past, we found wretched villages of illiterate people of the present—an obvious decline, both in the prosperity and in the culture and in the number of people, from ancient times to the present.

Let me cite a couple of examples. We spent some time at the ruins of Babylon, which was once the mistress of the ancient world, the center of culture and of political power, which is now a heap of salty desolation. Believe it or not, the only living thing I saw in the ruins of Babylon was a gray wolf shaking his head as if he might have had a tick in his ear, as he loped along to his lair, in the ruins of one of the seven wonders of the ancient world, the Hanging Gardens of Babylon, where air conditioning was used, in principle, 2,600 years ago. This was the center of a population estimated by archeologists at more than 30,000,000 of people. Now there are less than 4,000,000 of people in Iraq including ancient Mesopotamia.

In Iraq the climate has not changed, soils are still there, and the two rivers run full of water. The principal problem in times past was the control of silt. We found silted-up canals all through the area, and recently when I flew to China I saw from the air those herringbone marks of silted-up canals. The problem of keeping the canals clean of silt was a tremendous one. Rulers of Babylon brought in war captives for this purpose; now we understand why the captive Jews sat down by the waters of Babylon and wept, because they were called in to clean the silt out of these canals.

I also was present at the opening of the Kut Barrage, the guest of our American Minister and the guest of the King of Iraq, just a short time before he was accidentally killed. This barrage diverted waters of the Tigris out over an area in excess of 500,000 acres. It looked like a fine thing to do, and I asked the Minister of Agriculture of Iraq if they were going to do more of this. He said "We do not have farmers enough to make use of the lands that are now being irrigated."

There are very few farmers in Iraq. It has one of the greatest possibilities of supporting people, of any portion of that part of the world, with modern irrigation structures built with reinforced concrete, and with power machinery to dig canals and keep them clear. It will be possible, according to Willcocks, the great British irrigation authority, to support 50,000,000 of people in Iraq.

My computations on the basis of water now available, a somewhat lesser number may be sustained. But I think we can be sure that fully tenfold the people now living in Iraq can be supported in a state of civilization and prosperity in that area.

Mr. Chairman, I am afraid I will take too much time.

Chairman Bloom. Go right ahead. The Chair promised to notify you, if you did.

Dr. Lowdermilk. Another area is that of the ancient forest of the Cedars of Lebanon. You will recall that Solomon made arrangements with the King of Tyre to furnish him timbers out of the great forest, to build the Temple at Jerusalem. I wanted to see what had happened. According to the record, there were 60,000 lumberjacks, not called that in the record, cutting timber out of this forest. And there were 80,000 skidders, or bearers of burden, as they were called in the record. So it must have been quite a timbering or logging operation, in this ancient forest. We found, of that forest which possibly covered 2,000 square miles, only 4 small groves as remnants. The principal one is the Tripoli grove of cedars, which now has about 400 trees in it. It had been reduced to about 44 at one time. Then it was fenced around with stone walls to keep out the goats. As soon as the goats were kept out, seed from old trees began to grow up into a fine forest.

This was evidence that not change of climate had been the cause of the disappearance of this forest, but with protection against the goats, it would be possible to restore this forest over most of the area it once covered, especially in those areas where the soil had not been completely washed away.

Another area of special interest today is Palestine. I came to Palestine without much knowledge of this question of Zionism. I had heard of the colonists, but not very much about them.

CHAIRMAN BLOOM. What year was that, Doctor?

Dr. LOWDERMILK. That was in 1939.

So many of the things told me, at first I did not understand; I did not understand the implications. But the British Government was good to me; they furnished me armored cars so that I could travel over the country, in spite of the terrorists; and furnished me an airplane and permitted me to take pictures from the air, which was quite a courtesy. So I flew over a good portion of the country, especially the Negeb, and had an opportunity to study the country both from above and also from the ground, except that I did have difficulties in collecting samples of soil, because officers would not permit me to get too far off the road.

We found that Palestine had suffered a similar fate. We found the soils of the uplands had washed off to bedrock on a considerable portion of the area. The soil had been washed off the slopes and fields, into valleys, forming marshes; and in times past those had been malaria marshes. But in the midst of this desolation, I ran onto something that was new, something new under the sun. And it is this discovery that has aroused my interest in this problem of Palestine.

Let me, if you please, quote from my report. This is the first report, a fuller report comes out later. This is the first report I sent back to the Department and which Justice Louis D. Brandeis asked to see, and which I think he later discussed with some higher officials of the Government.

Chairman BLOOM. It is a Government report?

Dr. LOWDERMILK. Yes, sir. [Reading:]

The urge of Jewish people to build a national home in Palestine is an outstanding and fascinating phenomenon of our times. Agricultural colonization in Palestine is the most remarkable devotion to, and reclamation of, land that I have seen in any country of the New or Old World. The Jewish colonies were a refreshing balm to a soil conservationist after many months of travel in old lands revealing centuries of neglect and abuse of the soil.

The land of Palestine today is—

a sorry commentary on man's occupation and exploitation of a once fruitful country. The barren rocky hills, from which soils have been swept by rains and winds during centuries of neglect, are now taken for granted. The gullies, gouging out the remaining soils in the valleys, the destructive goats of the Fellaheen and

Bedouin, the poverty and low standards of living of the native population of Palestine, are accepted as inevitable by those who fail to read the tragic story of land wastage and exploitation, inscribed deeply in the landscape. Decadent native populations and political and social decay are the usual offspring of landscapes impoverished by erosion. It is not sufficiently recognized that the process of soil erosion, which has swept bare the fertile soils from the rocky hills, is still at work. Gone with the rain are more soils from the slopes. The outstanding exception to this dreary picture is the remarkable work of Jewish reclamation of lands. Their lands appear as gardens blossoming in a barren wilderness.

Then I say, further along in the report:

The possible absorptive capacity of the lands of Palestine for increased population is a subject under lively discussion. The best answer is to be found in the Jewish colonies. A 2 months' survey of land use made clear the extent to which the lands of Palestine have seriously deteriorated from their criginal condition, and furthermore that they can never be restored to that original condition. The soil has been washed thin and to bedrock over too large an area of the highlands. Soils have been deposited in valley floors and in the plains where it is or may still be as productive as of old; but the total area of good soils is much restricted.

This does not say, however, that the present land resources will not support a greater population. In the Jewish colonies we find evidence of far greater productivity of the land now than under the primitive methods of Arab farming. Capital, however, is required to bring about increased production in a short time. Besides marketing of the new production above subsistence needs must be developed to sustain more intensive agriculture. In any case, progress must be made with mixed farming which provides, first, subsistence and than a surplus or a money crop for sale.

If these conditions are met, it is my opinion, based on the splendid pioneering by the Jewish colonists, in reclamation and adjustment of uses to the characteristics of land, that the land of Palestine will support a considerable larger population. This opinion is further reinforced by archaeological evidence of denser population, due to highly developed measures of water and soil conservation which were in use during the Roman and Byzantine periods. Moreover, there are greater possibilities for irrigation under appropriate irrigation works in restricted areas. There is much yet to do to bring Palestine up to its carrying capacity for a human population.

May I add further: Possible increase in absorption capacity by reclaiming the land is in addition to industrialization. This report was written in Syria and revised 4 years ago. Justice Louis D. Brandeis was much interested in our findings and wanted to have the report published as it was. He was pleased that someone had caught the spirit of the colonists in their love of the land and devotion to redeem the land of Israel. But this old report, some parts of which have been called for, does not contain the greater possibilities of agriculture and industry, when irrigation and power are developed to their full possibilities in this specially favored corner of the vast region of the Near East.

Chairman BLOOM. Would you kindly give the title of that report, for the record?

Dr. LOWDERMILK. "Jewish Colonization."

Chairman BLOOM. Yes; I would like to have the record show that.

Dr. LOWDERMILK. The discovery I made in Palestine was this remarkable attachment for and love of the land; and I said:

This is what we need in the United States toward our land, to save it from destruction and the wastage it is undergoing at the present time.

Chairman BLOOM. Then you think it would be a good idea to bring these Jews over to this country? Is that the idea? [Laughter.]

Dr. LOWDERMILK. Certainly, if they will bring with them some of that love of the land.

From our studies we also realize in the final analysis land is not an economic commodity; it is part of the Nation.

In the case of Palestine, the land is also a refuge, as we have heard, and as such it is badly needed—but I shall not dwell upon that.

The colonization work is a hope of the future for the Near East, as we will develop a little later. These settlements now number nearly 300. There were something near 250 when I was there, and visited a number of them. Tracts of land were bought from Arabs. They were marshy areas that could not be used by the Arabs; they were rocky hills from which much of the soil had been washed away; and sites of that sort. I was astounded at the prices paid for them, being far too much for the land as we would consider it in California. I might point out that there is a considerable similarity between Palestine and California.

Mrs. ROGERS. The Californians love California.

Dr. LOWDERMILK. Yes; I am a Californian myself. I have been studying water problems there for years.

There are many kinds of settlements which were a great inspiration to me, and I examined quite a number of them. I am going to mention only a few. The colony at Hadera is one of the oldest; it was laid out in a marsh which was so infested with malaria that it was reclaimed with great difficulty, and cost the lives of many people, in in this period of reclamation. But finally they got the area drained, and put in orange groves and vegetable gardens and fruit orchards and fields; and now it looks like one of our orange groves in southern California. As we traveled one day along beside that colony, on one side was unreclaimed land, with the black tents of the seminomads, a very crude condition; and across this road was this orange grove with modern machinery, in a fine state of production, showing a sharp contrast between the use of the land in the two cases.

Another area was in the Emek, where there was also the malarial problem, and where a number of lives were lost in the reclamation work. One of the most interesting colonies I visited was Nahallal. I would like to speak of that a little later in another connection; but it was very successful. It was in the form of a wheel [indicating] and at the place of the hub were located the local community structures. Then at the upper portion were these various lots in the circle laid out for houses and gardens of the members of the colony. Then around that was the productive area, which was farmed cooperatively in large tracts, where up-to-date machinery could be put in use.

Another colony, which had just been established a short time before we arrived, was up in the hills of Galilee where young people had set up the colony, Hanita, right on the border between Palestine and Lebanon. They had set it up between sundown and sunrise, for fear of the terrorists. They had cut all pieces of their fortification wall, their barracks, and their watchtower, and all in readiness. At sundown they carried up the parts and had the buildings practically set up by morning and were ready then for any attack of terrorists.

When we went into the dining room of that colony, we saw a number of pictures on the wall, of young men, and I asked "Who are these young men?"

They said they had been killed from ambush as they had been clearing the fields about the colony. But that did not deter these people. They went establishing a colony in those inhospitable areas.

Mrs. ROGERS. By whom were they killed?

Dr. LOWDERMILK. By the so-called terrorists.

Mrs. ROGERS. Who are they?

Dr. Lowdermilk. Well, I am not in a position to know.

Chairman Bloom. If you know; I would not want the record to show, unless you really know.

Dr. Lowdermilk. I don't know, and I don't suppose the colonists knew.

Mrs. Rogers. Yes; I was interested in the whole picture.

Dr. Lowdermilk. Bands of terrorists were attacking them from time to time.

Mrs. Rogers. Did they have many soldiers there?

Dr. Lowdermilk. They had guards, yes; and certain of the young women had their guns, too. Here were young heroes and heroines who seemed to be working along together.

Mrs. Rogers. Pioneer work?

Dr. Lowdermilk. Yes; pioneering, very much as in America when the redskins used to pick our pioneers off, with the same spirit.

I understand this colony now is quite prosperous and that it has become very successful and self-supporting; but I have not seen it since 1939. Also, down in the Jordan Valley, above the Dead Sea, was a colony just in formation, which established itself on saline soil, salty soil, which ordinarily we would classify as unsuitable for farming. But they led out the water of the Jordan River and beached the soil very much as the Dutch have done in the Zuyder Zee project.

I was talking recently with a gentleman just back from Palestine, and he said they are growing fields of tomatoes on that very land, which has become self-supporting, I am told, furnishing vegetables and milk and beef and butter and eggs for the employees of the potash works.

Now, this is a costly venture, and I was asked over and over again, "Does it pay?"

I would not say that I would advise anyone to invest money and expect to get 10 percent interest on the investment. But it pays in other values. It pays in the redemption of the land and the redemption of people, because after all we are concerned in the conservation of soils and waters, because we are concerned with the conservation of human values and human people.

We found these settlements were supported and prepared for carefully by scientific research. The agricultural experiment station at Rehovoth was one of the best I had seen in my travels. They were attacking the problems the colonists were faced with, in the treatment of soils; the fertilizers needed; the type of crops they should grow. Economic questions were very carefully worked out.

They also carried on a number of livestock breeding experiments, which were rather interesting. For instance, the native Arab hen is small, producing only about 70 eggs a year. But by crossing that hen with the Leghorn they had increased the production of eggs on the average to 140 a year.

The Arab cow is a very poor animal, but it is hardy and able to survive under the conditions of that country. The Holstein could not stand the climate; so they crossed the two, and instead of getting 800 quarts of milk on the average per year, they get from 3,500 to 4.000 quarts from the mixed breed.

And while I was in Palestine, I heard there had been a call from India for that particular strain that had been developed in Palestine as an animal that could survive those conditions and produce a greater yield of milk and cream.

Chairman BLOOM. All of this work, Doctor, was done by the Jewish colonists and farmers you speak of?

Dr. LOWDERMILK. Yes; entirely.

Now, to make the record straight, there were a number of agricultural experiment stations established by the Palestine Government. Most of those, 7 out of 11, as I recall, had been destroyed by terrorists. I visited a number of them, and they were not functioning very well. But Rehovoth was in the midst of a pretty-well-settled community and it was protected from the raids of the terrorists.

The training of these young agricultural settlers interested me very much. I examined the school of Mikvah Israel, established way back in 1880, I think—1878. The plan of that school was to give book learning one-half of the day and the other half was spent in work on the farm, with the whole activity of the farm carried on by these students. These young people, after they had graduated, would be sent out as probationers to the colonies; and, after they had worked some time at the colonies, they would be permitted to group themselves and apply for a colony to be established on their own.

This type of training was most practical. It also trained people who had been accustomed to city life, in carrying out the practice of practical farming, so that it had made them quite effective.

Interesting enough, they found that unless the girls, the wives, were also trained in farming, the colonies would not be a success. So young women were trained in farming just as were the young men. They had common interests that contributed to the success of the colonies, we were told. We met quite a number of these charming farmerettes, as they worked with the menfolk out in the fields.

The social organization of these colonies was interesting to me because one of our greatest problems in this country and in the world today is the adjustment of a population to the land resources of the earth. I like to speak of it as a lasting adjustment; or sometimes, when I speak to religious people, I say it is a righteous adjustment of the people to their land resources. And until we do work that out, we are going to continue to have war. I consider this one of the chief and most important problems not only before our country but before the world today. So I am interested in any case where I find people who have worked out a way of gaining their livelihood and cultural satisfactions, from any organization dealing with the land. Here they had worked that out, by an experimental range. When we experiment we like to deal with extremes to detect the forces that are at work. The colonies had a range of organization, from everything privately owned to an arrangement practically collective. But the most successful and to me the most attractive was a cooperative type of organization such as we found at Nahallal, where each one had his own house and lot, where he could have his garden and chicken yard, and so on, and his orchard, and paint his house yellow or green or black, whichever suited his own particular fancy. But the land was farmed in large units on a cooperative basis, which permitted the use of machinery to accomplish the higher farming efficiency, which gave them purchasing power to enjoy the good things of life. By this means they were setting the stage for adjusting themselves quickly and at the same time opening up this colony to the possibility of taking in new members of the colony. That is why these colonies can absorb refugees so easily.

Chairman BLOOM. I think, Doctor, you have laid the foundation for a great many questions that I feel some of the members are going to ask you, because we have a really professional farmer in this committee and I know he is very much interested in what you are saying. When it gets down to him, I think he is going to ask you some questions; I hope he will. I think we have gone on pretty far, now, Doctor, and, as I say, I think you have laid the foundation of it; so that unless there is something to be presented in addition to what you have already said, I would like to give the committee a chance.

Dr. LOWDERMILK. May I have 2 minutes more?

Chairman BLOOM. Yes; you may have all the time you want. Go right ahead.

Dr. LOWDERMILK. I am sorry to take so much time.

Chairman BLOOM. That is all right; it is very interseting.

Dr. LOWDERMILK. In addition to speaking of agricultural colonies, industries had developed on quite a large scale when I was there. Many of these refugees had brought in skills and trades with them, and some of them had brought in tools, so that industries had developed right along with this agricultural colonization. And, since the war, these industries have multiplied manyfold, I have been informed.

Now the question arises, what is the absorptive capacity of Palestine? This, I think, is one of the crucial problems before your committee, and I would like briefly to sketch my approach to this. There is, of course, a need for these persecuted of Europe to find refuge, and the question is what is the absorption capacity of Palestine.

It has been stated that the economic, absorptive capacity should not be exceeded; but what do we mean by "economic, absorptive capacity"? When you examine it, it does not give us very much to tie to.

This is the analysis that I have been using for a number of years in attempting to work out what is the carrying capacity of land for social organization. Out West we have an expression, "The carrying capacity of the range for livestock."

After all, the carrying capacity of the earth for the human race follows just about the same principle, but it is a little more complex. It is based upon food production. Of all our needs, food is primary, and all things are purchased with food. When food fails, all else fails. So we can judge the carrying capacity of an area by the food supply. And until we have an ample food supply, we cannot count on any other source of organization.

But when food enough is produced for a whole population—and this is important, as we think of it—then the standard of living in that social group is dependent upon the division of labor in that group, and the efficiency in the various divisions of labor.

In other words, the farmer must produce more food than he needs for himself and his family before anyone else can be released to do something else, to take up other activities. The whole realization of this came to me when I was pondering the Pyramids in Egypt—something I had known before but had never realized. Then I remembered, as I had heard or had read, that some 6,000 years ago, a genius of a farmer had hitched his oxen to a hoe and invented the plow; the application of power for the first time to farming was accomplished. This made that farmer much more efficient in the production of food beyond his own needs, releasing other people for other tasks, which could then be done, beginning the division of labor in our civilization.

And in those days, wars were not so common, to make use of surplus manpower; and apparently the Pharaohs had some difficulty in finding work for these surplus unemployed. So, as I pondered the Pyramids, I suspected they were the first great W. P. A. projects.

The computation of how many people a land will support or absorb can be determined, first, on the available food supply. That food supply may be produced, first, by the land within the borders of the country. That is the safest condition of any country, as we well know in these times. There can also be food brought in, imported, from the outside, in exchange for manufactured products, and so on. So that the carrying capacity or absorption capacity of an area depends, then, upon how much food supply we can produce or import by the exchange of useful things.

We do not have time to go into all the methods of computation, but we find that in Palestine about 1,800,000, according to my computation in addition to the present population, can be fed from within, if this project we are going to speak of in a moment is carried out. But if we increase industry, which gives products for buying food from outsiders, for example, from Iraq which is nearby, there is practically no upper limit. It will depend upon the genius and the extent of development of industry within Palestine.

For example, we ask what is the absorption capacity of New York? It depends upon the means by which we can import food from the outside. So this absorption capacity is a dynamic thing, depending upon the resources and the genius of the people who make it up.

We find, when we examine the possibilities of land development in Palestine, that there is more land than we have water for. There is more land than we can irrigate. Such is the condition in California. We have more land in California than water to irrigate it. We are limited by water supply.

As for dry farming, we have more land than rainfall in Palestine. We find that our so-called dry farming, winter dry farming, is not successful with less than 8 inches of annual rainfall. So a great portion of southern Palestine and Trans-Jordan is left to grazing, to use entirely for grazing, and cannot be counted upon for farming, although the lands and soil are quite satisfactory for farming.

Now, water for irrigation is being developed from springs and wells and from cisterns, and also from the streams. But we won't say much more about that.

In closing I would like to lay before you the logic of geography, in the approach to this problem. I speak as a conservationist who likes to see the resources of the earth put to their highest use, in the interests of making them work. So I am going to suggest that there is a possibility of an irrigation and power project in Palestine that is unique in the world.

When I was flying over Palestine, I realized this narrow valley of the Jordan, with the Dead Sea 1,300 feet below sea level, was only a little way from the Mediterranean. Why not put a canal in from the Mediterranean and drop the water into the Dead Sea, and thereby produce power? But it would be necessary to take the sweet water of the Jordan out for irrigation. We propose that the waters of the Jordan River be developed for irrigation, so that most of them will be taken out of the Dead Sea. And then in their place put in a canal and tunnel and let in the Mediterranean water, into the Dead Sea, to produce hydroelectric power.

Mr. CHIPERFIELD. Pardon me. Who do you mean by "we"?

Dr. LOWDERMILK. This is just the proposal. Whatever organization may engage in it. I mean, it is the idea.

Chairman BLOOM. You mean a Lindbergh "we."

Dr. LOWDERMILK. Yes, sir. This would envisage what I have called a Jordan Valley Authority, on the order of the Tennessee Valley Authority, and it would include the entire drainage of the Jordan River, both Palestine and Trans-Jordan. It is the logic of geography in the development of this area.

By this we can develop power by the drop into the Dead Sea, as an evaporation pan. By raising the level about 75 feet increases the area 20 percent. By that means we would produce about 100,000 kilowatts, or about one-seventh of the power at Boulder Dam. By the connection of other power projects with it would give us a power of about one-fifth of that developed at Boulder Dam. So we have there the possibilities of power for industry on a big scale.

Then we have the possibilities of using sweet water for irrigation on a large scale. We have an intriguing potentiality for this region. And, to me as a conservationist, it would seem a shame if we fail to use it.

Now, the possibilities here involve power for industries of all sorts. We have in the Dead Sea one of the richest mineral deposits on earth, especially magnesium in great quantity, and bromine, and potassium. If industries develop, food may be supplied from Iraq, if that country is developed, to add to the production of food locally.

Raw materials may be brought in, because Palestine is at a strategic location at the cross-roads of three continents; waterways radiate out from Palestine, making it especially strategic from that point of view. Also, it is a logical place for the crossing of railroads between these three continents. Raw materials then would be available; transportation would be available—by steamship, by railroad, and by air. But how can this project be carried out without manpower? We need people to carry out a project of this sort.

Chairman BLOOM. You mean you need more people than are there now?

Dr. LOWDERMILK. Yes, sir; you cannot do it with the people who are there now.

Chairman BLOOM. Considering that there are between 550,000 and 600,000 Jews, we will say, there now, how many additional people do you think they would be able to absorb?

Dr. LOWDERMILK. Well, if in time we develop, I should say it is not too much to say 5,000,000 in addition to what there are now.

Mr. VORYS. I thought you said 1,800,000 if all of these things were done.

Dr. LOWDERMILK. I said 1,800,000 could be supported with food grown from the area locally. If we add industry to give the people buying power from outside there is hardly any upper limit to economic support of people.

Chairman BLOOM. Doctor, this is very interesting, and you said you wanted 2 minutes. I did not quite look close to see the time.

Dr. LOWDERMILK. I am afraid, Mr. Chairman, I did not either.

Chairman Bloom. I did not know whether you meant 2 hours. I know the committee is very anxious to ask you questions because Mrs. Rogers has just been anxiously waiting her time here, so if you do not mind, without objection, you will be permitted when you get your remarks back for correction to insert anything to elaborate upon your remarks that you think should be in the record.

Dr. Lowdermilk. Thank you, sir.

Chairman Bloom. Mr. Johnson.

Mr. Johnson. No questions.

Chairman Bloom. Mrs. Rogers.

Mrs. Rogers. You know, Dr. Lowdermilk, I am very much interested in having the Jewish people have this homeland.

Dr. Lowdermilk. Pardon me?

Mrs. Rogers. I have been very much interested in having the Jewish people have a homeland, and I gather from what you have said you feel Jewish persons could develop this land better than any other group because they have done so well thus far in this cooperative movement.

Dr. Lowdermilk. Yes, Mrs. Rogers, they have demonstrated their capacity.

Mrs. Rogers. That is what I understood.

Dr. Lowdermilk. Both in reclaiming and cultivating the land; that is what attracted me most because I found in lands misused, wasted, and spoiled a people restoring the land to a high state of production.

Mrs. Rogers. You feel it is the love of this land that has made them do so extremely well?

Dr. Lowdermilk. Yes, Mrs. Rogers.

Mrs. Rogers. How are they governed there? Is it by the rabbis, by the church?

Chairman Bloom. You could not get a Jew to be governed by a rabbi. [Laughter.] And he is not a Jew. Go ahead, Doctor.

Dr. Lowdermilk. The Palestine government was in charge when I was there.

Mrs. Rogers. And you are not going to explain what the Palestine government consisted of at the time?

Dr. Lowdermilk. It was the mandate government, of course, the British Mandate Government.

Mrs. Rogers. Do they have chambers of commerce there? I mean is it divided up into industrialists and labor and the labor is organized and the industrialists are organized, or do you have any division there?

Dr. Lowdermilk. I am not in a position to answer that.

Mrs. Rogers. Is it all cooperative?

Dr. Lowdermilk. Not all cooperative. People present who know these conditions can tell better than I about organizations. I was so busy working with farmers and agronomists and the people that I did not get acquainted with many other features of Palestine. I found there were many different groups but I did not get acquainted with all of them.

Mrs. Rogers. I was wondering; I noticed in that little book it said the labor movement was very highly organized there.

Dr. Lowdermilk. Yes; I believe it is.

Mr. Rogers. I was wondering why it was necessary to have them so highly organized, whether there was an industrial group there that interfered in any way with the labor movement?

Dr. Lowdermilk. I am not in a position to answer that I am afraid, Mrs. Rogers, because I am not well acquainted with it.

Mrs. Rogers. You said so much about the cooperative movement that is what made me think of it.

Dr. Lowdermilk. Yes.

Mrs. Rogers. Thank you very much, Mr. Chairman.

Chairman Bloom. If you will permit me, Dr. Lowdermilk, I would just like to ask a question which is in my mind. Have you found any other part of the world in all of your travels inspecting farms and so forth in which there is anything that is comparable to what the Jews have done in Palestine so far as the cultivation of the soil is concerned?

Dr. Lowdermilk. I have not found anything like it where people have taken old lands and reclaimed them.

Chairman Bloom. That is all, sir.

Dr. Lowdermilk. We did find in Lebanon what we believed were terraces that the Phoenicians had built some 4,000 years ago, and it was because they built rock walls and retained these terraces.

Chairman Bloom. The same as they have in Italy?

Dr. Lowdermilk. Yes; and they were still in use. But as nomads came in out of the desert they overran and broke down these terraces over most of the country. Measures of water and soil conservation had been worked out to high refinements so that 2,000 years ago this country must have been very beautifully taken care of, a lovely place and productive. These measures were allowed to fall into ruin and the soils washed away; the land deteriorated and declined.

Chairman Bloom. Thank you very much.

Mrs. Rogers. Did you go swimming in the Dead Sea?

Dr. Lowdermilk. Pardon me.

Mrs. Rogers. Did you go swimming in the Dead Sea? I did. [Laughter.]

Chairman Bloom. Mr. McMurray.

Mr. McMurray. Doctor Lowdermilk and Mr. Chairman, I would just like to ask one or two very short questions about the proposed development there. Did I understand you to say that the only source of fresh water for irrigation is the Jordan River; is that correct?

Dr. Lowdermilk. Yes, sir.

Mr. McMurray. You have to have fresh water for irrigation?

Dr. Lowdermilk. Oh, yes.

Mr. McMurray. You cannot use the other water?

Dr. Lowdermilk. Oh, no.

Mr. McMurray. And by using all of that water for irrigation you can then drain these waters from the Mediterranean into the Dead Sea to furnish the power there?

Dr. Lowdermilk. That is right.

Mr. McMurray. How much of the land there that needs irrigating in that valley can be furnished with water from the Jordan River; You said you would set up something like the Tennessee Valley Authority which would be an area already having land use, water power, and all of those things together. Have you any rough idea what is the reclaimable land in that valley, what percentage of it could be irrigated properly with the limited water supply that is there, that is, the water supply of the Jordan River?

Dr. LOWDERMILK. Well, the duty of the water is not entirely worked out, but about 800 to 1,000 cubic meters is the estimate at the present time. Since the quantity of water determines how much land can be irrigated, it works out something like 500,000 acres. But those figures are subject to detailed studies.

Mr. McMURRAY. Yes.

Dr. LOWDERMILK. I do not pretend to say they are exact. Surveys have not yet been made.

Mr. McMURRAY. But at least there is a significant amount of land there?

Dr. LOWDERMILK. Yes, sir.

Mr. McMURRAY. That would support an enormous amount of population compared to what it has been supporting in the past?

Dr. LOWDERMILK. Yes; it will support considerably more. As we said, roughly estimated, 1,800,000-and-some-odd thousand more people can be fed off the lands of this area. Now, that would be in addition to the present population.

Then, if these industries are developed——

Mr. McMURRAY. As the result of the power?

Dr. LOWDERMILK (continuing). As the result of the power the purchasing power of that area to exchange products for food is increased and still more people can be provided for.

Mr. McMURRAY. Thank you. That is all, Mr. Chairman.

Chairman BLOOM. Mr. Chiperfield.

Mr. CHIPERFIELD. No questions, thank you.

Chairman BLOOM. Mr. Wright.

Mr. WRIGHT. No questions.

Chairman BLOOM. Mr. Vorys.

Mr. VORYS. Doctor Lowdermilk, when I asked to look at this document from which you were reading I understood you said you were reading from an official report, and I find this is Palestine and the Jewish Future, published by the Jewish Socialist Labor Party, Poale, Zion, and in there I find the two quotations you read. One is marked on page 20 as coming from the Menorah Journal of New York of October 1, 1940, and the other quotation you read is on page 24, The Right to Land Use With Particular Reference to Palestine, by Walter C. Lowdermilk, the Menorah Journal, January 1, 1921. Are those official reports?

Dr. LOWDERMILK. No, sir; that was my official report which was copied. It was copied there.

Mr. VORYS. Was the official report published entitled "The Right to Land Use With Particular Reference to Palestine"?

Dr. LOWDERMILK. No, sir; I did not entitle it that.

Mr. VORYS. That is the title given to it on page 24 of this document. Did you write this official report for the Menorah Journal?

Dr. LOWDERMILK. No, sir.

Mr. VORYS. Who did you write the official report for?

Dr. LOWDERMILK. For our department.

Mr. VORYS. Was it on the subject "The Right to Land Use With Particular Reference to Palestine"?

Dr. LOWDERMILK. No, sir.

Mr. VORYS. Now, in this document the very first thing is a reference, and it starts off "Communist rabbi" and refers to a Moses Hess, and says on the first page here "To Hess Socialism and Zionism—that term was not created until over 20 years later—were not two separate ideas. He regarded socialism as the essence of Judaism and saw in the return to Zion the only way in which socialism could be realized in the life of the Jewish people." Did you in these collective farms and the activities you saw there see any carrying out of these ideas of the Communist rabbi referred to in the report?

Dr. LOWDERMILK. No, sir. I wanted a copy of this report to submit here, and I asked for those quotations and they were given to me, and I did not realize that was versed in that sort of thing.

Mr. VORYS. Did you ask the Department of Agriculture where the official report was? Who did you ask?

Dr. LOWDERMILK. I was asking Doctor Newman for them.

Mr. VORYS. When you referred repeatedly to what "we planned to do" and what "we had worked out" do you refer to the Department of Agriculture, or to the Jewish Socialist Labor Party or——

Dr. LOWDERMILK (interposing). No.

Mr. VORYS (continuing)—to the gentleman you just referred to? Who do you mean by "we" there?

Dr. LOWDERMILK. I have on my own account prepared a manuscript which will probably be published as a book on this problem, and it contains not that [indicating], but it contains this proposal for the development of the Jordan Valley Authority, and it has no reference to this matter.

Mr. VORYS. While the quotations here from this pamphlet that I have just described are in this document and the titles of the articles you can see are as I have given them to you yet you feel certain those words are not from your official report?

Dr. LOWDERMILK. Yes, sir. I can check that for you.

Mr. VORYS. I wish you would.

Dr. LOWDERMILK. Yes, sir.

Mr. VORYS. Now, as I understand it, if the Jordan Valley Authority project is worked out you would then have in Palestine a food population for 1,800,000 additional; is not that correct? That is where you brought in that figure?

Dr. LOWDERMILK. That is right.

Mr. VORYS. And of course there would from the industrial developments be a population capacity depending on how they could trade with other parts of the world?

Dr. LOWDERMILK. Yes, sir.

Mr. VORYS. Thank you. That is all.

Chairman BLOOM. May I see that book, please?

Mr. VORYS. Yes, Mr. Chairman.

Chairman BLOOM. Mr. Mundt.

Mr. MUNDT. I am not just clear in my mind yet as to the size of this area which is referred to in the bill as the land which is to "reconstitute Palestine" is the phrase that is used. Does that include Trans-Jordan or not?

Dr. LOWDERMILK. I am not sure what the resolution refers to in that regard. The Jordan Valley Authority which I proposed is independent of the resolution. It is simply a project which is indicated by the logic of the geography of the area.

Mr. MUNDT. How large is the area? We have got to know how large the area is before we can evaluate your theory for capacity. How large an area are you using?

Dr. LOWDERMILK. Palestine is about the size of Vermont, about 10,000 aquare miles.

Mr. MUNDT. Is that with or without Trans-Jordan?

Dr. LOWDERMILK. That is without Trans-Jordan. As to the Trans-Jordan I have forgotten the square miles of it, but it is considerably larger than Palestine.

Mr. MUNDT. Ten thousand square miles is the territory involved?

Dr. LOWDERMILK. Ten thousand square miles is the territory involved as it is now constituted; yes. But the Jordan Valley Authority includes considerably more area than that.

Mr. MUNDT. Mr. Chairman, is it just 10,000 square miles involved in this resolution or does it include the Trans-Jordan?

Chairman BLOOM. That is right, there are only 10,000 square miles involved in this resolution. The only thing this resolution calls for is 10,000 square miles. That is my understanding.

Mr. MUNDT. How many, if you have it accurately as you have made a scientific study of it, acres in this 10,000 square miles are subject to cultivation?

Dr. LOWDERMILK. There have been different estimates of 4,000,000 down to 2,000,000.

Mr. MUNDT. What would you estimate?

Mr. LOWDERMILK. I have taken an intermediate figure.

Mr. MUNDT. Three million?

Dr. LOWDERMILK. Three million in Palestine itself, then about 1,500,000 over in Trans-Jordan.

Mr. MUNDT. Now, do not get me confused. Is that on this one thing?

Dr. LOWDERMILK. Then it is Palestine itself?

Mr. MUNDT. Oh, yes.

Dr. LOWDERMILK. Of course, farming in that part of the world is not like farming over here. They have developed the slopes by terracing. It is possible to put in tree crops on slopes such as we do not do here. It is possible to plant trees on apparently rocky slopes because the country rock is limestone with porous crevices or pockets filled with soil.

Mr. MUNDT. Of the 3,000,000 acres how many would you say are suitable for the raising of food crops and so forth, and how many are suitable for grazing land?

Dr. LOWDERMILK. I would put about 2,000,000 estimate for crops. Of that about 750,000 acres can be irrigated, but we won't have quite enough water for all of that; about 2,000,000 for tree crops.

Mr. MUNDT. Fruit trees?

Dr. LOWDERMILK. Olive trees, vineyards, carab trees, and that type. And then about 2,000,000 for grazing and forests.

Mr. MUNDT. Now, you have totaled up more than 3,000,000 then?

Dr. LOWDERMILK. You said cultivation. The total area is something over 6,000,000 acres.

Mr. MUNDT. The total area is 6,000,000 acres?

Dr. LOWDERMILK. Yes; and 2,000,000 for the more intensive cultivation. It depends upon how steep you want to go upon these slopes.

Mr. MUNDT. I am a conservationist like you are. I want to go as far up as you can cultivate them?

Dr. LOWDERMILK. Safely.

Mr. MUNDT. Profitably.

The phrase "absorptive capacity" seems to occur in this testimony a great many times. Rabbi Silver used it. I find in reading the papers where I have heard that discussed before. So I was intrigued a little bit by your definition of that phrase. To me absorptive capacity is the capacity of a given area to sustain and feed the people who live in it. If we accept your amended definition of absorptive capacity it seems to me the phrase becomes meaningless.

If absorptive capacity is limited only by purchasing power of the people living in the area to move food into it then we could show the absorptive capacity of Manhattan Island is 30,000,000. It just depends on how high you build the apartment houses, how tall you build your hotels; it does not mean anything.

I wonder just what you as an agricultural scientist really would define absorptive capacity to be?

Dr. Lowdermilk. Well, what is absorptive capacity in Great Britain? Great Britain only produces in normal times two-thirds of her food supply. That is why it is necessary that the lanes for importation of foods be kept open.

Mr. Mundt. That is right.

Dr. Lowdermilk. So that the other one-third of the population be sure of their food.

If you are going to define the absorptive capacity of Great Britain as the capacity of the land to produce the food for the people the country is overpopulated now. There are too many people in Great Britain at the present time.

Mr. Mundt. If you use any other phrase it is meaningless because if great Britain gets additional purchasing power and accumulates assets of trade it will support twice as many?

Dr. Lowdermilk. That is right.

Mr. Mundt. Or four times?

Dr. Lowdermilk. That is right.

Mr. Mundt. Or eight times?

Dr. Lowdermilk. That is right.

Mr. Mundt. So absorptive capacity, if it means anything, means ability to support the people from the land. If it does not mean that it does not mean anything, because purchasing power can be derived from people and individuals and so forth, and I can see where the capacity of Manhattan Island could be 100,000,000 people; there is no limit.

Dr. Lowdermilk. But there is a limit to the absorptive capacity of the earth.

Mr. Mundt. That is correct.

Dr. Lowdermilk. But for any one corner which has the means of purchasing or has products that the rest of the world will exchange food for then they can support as many people as they can continue to buy food for.

Mr. Mundt. Precisely. Now, that is why I wonder what is the meaning of the term "absorptive capacity" in all of this discussion. It seems to me it does not mean anything unless it means the ability of the land to support the population. You say it does not mean that, or you said it does not mean that if you look at it from the standpoint of your amended definition.

Dr. Lowdermilk. I raised the question on the meaning of the phrase, "technical absorptive capacity," or I mean the economic absorptive capacity. That is the term that has been used to limit the immigration into Palestine. What does "economic absorptive capacity" mean?

Chairman BLOOM. I think we have so many witnesses here that time is important.

Mr. MUNDT. Of course, but I just wanted the comment.

Chairman BLOOM. We have a number of witnesses from out of town who want to get away. Mr. Compton wants to be heard.

Mr. MUNDT. I simply wanted to offer the comment as I interpret the witness' testimony, which I found to be interesting; it was all dedicated to showing the absorptive capacity of Palestine and all else was beside the point, and I was trying to clear it up. Either the testimony was useless, or it should be clarified. If you do not want me to ask any more questions I will cease.

Chairman BLOOM. Do not let me stop you.

Mr. MUNDT. No further questions.

Chairman BLOOM. No further questions? Mrs. Bolton.

Mrs. BOLTON. I have been very much interested in what I have heard of the witness' testimony because I think we are all thrilled over what has been done in Palestine. I think it is a most amazing thing. I did not honeymoon in Palestine, but I have been there. I have been very thrilled over the contacts I have had with those who have come out of Palestine and who have seen the fine things that have been done. Just where it leads to I am a little in Mr. Mundt's angle of it. I think the words need a little clarification, perhaps in our discussions later on, Mr. Chairman.

I won't hold the committee. But we are as interested, or I am as interested as anybody could be in whatever experimentation there is by way of making use particularly of the old lands all over the world. We have destroyed so much of our own country that we need to learn all we can wherever any such things take place.

I have no questions to ask, Mr. Chairman.

Chairman BLOOM. Mr. Mundt, the Chair would like to state the doctor is right here in Washington, and if the committee so desires we can call him back some day and talk this matter over in executive session.

You are right here, Doctor?

Dr. LOWDERMILK. Yes, sir.

Mr. MUNDT. I thought maybe we could enlighten some of you.

Chairman BLOOM. Mr. Wadsworth.

Mr. WADSWORTH. Dr. Lowdermilk, did you encounter any political repercussions during your visit to Palestine, and if so would you comment on them?

Dr. LOWDERMILK. I am sorry; I do not understand what you mean by "political."

Mr. WADSWORTH. You mentioned on several occasions there had been raids by terrorists?

Dr. LOWDERMILK. Yes, sir.

Mr. WADSWORTH. You were not quite familiar with the identity of the terrorists?

Dr. LOWDERMILK. No, sir.

Mr. WADSWORTH. Did you not gain some impression as to the reason for the underlying difference for the raids or political reasons?

Dr. LOWDERMILK. Of course, we heard a great deal about the terrorists from various sources. We were told the Mufti, who was still in Jerusalem at the time, was responsible for these terrorists.

Near where I lived at the time, the American School of Oriental Research was a school where the Mufti was in charge. We understood that the archaeologist—I have forgotten the name of the museum—had been shot by one of the Mufti's students. I was told that these students were pretty much anti-Jews and were carrying out raids locally.

Out in the country I was told by British officers that bands had been caught. One British officer—I have forgotten his name—said that they had found on one of the raiders that had been killed a check on the Bank of Rome. And I said, "What does that mean?" Then he said it looked as if these terrorists were being financed from outside. But one heard all sorts of theories and rumors about the terrorists.

Mr. WADSWORTH. You did not study the political situation?

Dr. LOWDERMILK. I did not study it. I had too much to do making my survey.

Mr. WADSWORTH. Because of course the political situation is highly important.

Dr. LOWDERMILK. Yes, sir.

Mr. WADSWORTH. That is all.

Chairman BLOOM. No more questions? Mr. Gerlach?

Mr. GERLACH. No questions.

Mrs. ROGERS. May I ask a question? Do you represent yourself here at the hearings or the Department of Agriculture?

Dr. LOWDERMILK. I represent myself.

Mrs. ROGERS. How long have you been with the Department of Agriculture?

Dr. LOWDERMILK. Nearly 30 years.

Mrs. ROGERS. Yes, I have known of your name.

Chairman BLOOM. Thank you very much. And you might hear from us again on that subject we want to know something about.

We will now hear from Dr. Henry Atkinson. He is president of the Christian Council on Palestine.

STATEMENT OF DR. HENRY ATKINSON, PRESIDENT OF THE CHRISTIAN COUNCIL ON PALESTINE

Mr. ATKINSON. Mr. Chairman, I want to thank you and the members of the committee for your courtesy in offering me the opportunity of appearing before you.

Our organization, the Christian Council on Palestine, of which I am president, was formed some 2 years ago for the purpose of bringing to the American people through Christian leadership and membership of the churches the conviction that in the post-war settlement Palestine should be made accessible to Jewish refugees from lands of persecution and that the ultimate destiny of the Jews depends upon the reaffirmation and fulfillment of the Balfour Declaration.

We have had our consciences hurt by the recognition that it is only in so-called Christian lands where things like that which happened in Germany could start. Outside of places where there are Christians the less Christian they are the more liberty there is for the Jewish people apparently, and we feel the time has come when we ought to face up to the responsibility and recognize that there is hardly a Jewish problem in the world but there is a very serious Christian problem that we have to face. This committee is made up of 1,100 Christian clergymen located in every part of our country. I have the list with many of the leading men of our country on it which is a cross section of the United States.

Chairman BLOOM. Where are you from, Doctor?

Mr. ATKINSON. New York; originally from California. I heard California being booted around a while ago.

This is the resolution adopted at our meeting the other day:

We strongly urge the adoption of House Resolution Nos. 418, 419 (Wright-Compton). We favor the establishment in Palestine of a national home for the Jewish people, and urge that the United States Government help provide appropriate measures to the end that the doors of Palestine be opened for further entry of homeless, stateless Jews of war-torn Europe. We urge that there be full opportunity for colonization in Palestine so that the Jewish people may reconstitute that country as a free and democratic Jewish commonwealth.

We are horrified by the indescribable brutality of Hitler and his Nazi oppressors and conscious of the tragic plight of millions of Jews in Europe today. We reaffirm our faith in the spirit as well as the letter of the Balfour declaration. We are convinced that the open door of a strongly established and recognized Jewish homeland in Palestine offers the only real hope for most of these suffering men, women, and children, who today linger in misery and ignominy under the heel of Hitler.

We join with a large majority of the British people in confidently following Winston Churchill who, in 1939, denounced the Chamberlain-MacDonald white paper on Palestine as "a breach and repudiation of the Balfour declaration."

We range ourselves also on the side of the Permanent Mandates Commission of the League of Nations under whose political authority Great Britain administers Palestine. This Commission condemned the white paper at the time of its promulgation as "an indefensible and flagrant breach of international good faith." Beyond all other considerations we call for the abrogation of the white paper on the grounds of justice and mercy and in the interests of our common humanity.

We believe that this problem is basically a Christian problem and thus we appeal on behalf of our members and the people in their churches.

That is signed by members of the committee, myself as chairman; Dr. Carl Hermann Voss, he is executive secretary; Dr. Howard B. Warren; Dr. John W. Bradbury; Prof. Reinhold Niebuhr; Prof. James Luther Adams; Rev. Richard E. Evans, who is here in the room; Dr. Daniel A. Poling; Prof. Paul Tillich; Prof. William F. Albright, a prominent pastor in Brooklyn; Rev. Karl M. Chworowsky; Prof. S. Ralph Harlow; Rev. Dr. John Haynes Holmes; Rev. Leslie T. Pennington, of Cambridge, Mass.; Rev. Dr. Harold Paul Sloan, and Mr. Pierre van Paassen.

I wish to add just a few words in support of this resolution, Mr. Chairman. First of all, I believe that from the standpoint of history the only relief for the sufferings of the Jewish people of the world is through the establishment of their homeland in Palestine. The history of Poland and Ireland through many centuries was that of people bereft of a national home and at the mercy of their enemies as well as their friends. From the eighteenth century on the Polish question was a topic of hot discussion in almost every international gathering, so much so that in France when a conversation or a discussion came to an end someone would pipe up, "Now, let's talk about the Polish question." After the World War when Poland was reconstituted the discussion of this question very largely disappeared. The same is true in regard to Ireland. The Irish movements within other countries was a constant source of misunderstanding, even among the Irish themselves. With the establishment of a free Ireland these divisive movements disappeared, and I have not heard of the Sein Fein since the last World War or any considerable movement or any force.

I conscientiously believe that the same will prove true in regard to the Jewish people when Palestine is established as our national Jewish homeland.

Secondly, no one expects that all the Jews of the world will move to Palestine. American and British citizens of Jewish descent live under good auspices. Certainly no large number of them would expect to go to Palestine any more than all the Irish in America would migrate to Ireland even if this is now a free state.

Chairman BLOOM. Or go on his honeymoon?

Mr. ATKINSON. Ninety-five percent of the Jewish of the world are hoping for this kind of a settlement.

Lastly, I firmly believe that Palestine is not only a means of salvation for the Jewish people, but in a larger sense is also a means of safeguarding our democracy. The attack on the Jews was the entering wedge by which the liberties of all the free people in all nations were attacked, and the Jew was attacked because he was the most vulnerable in Germany at that time.

I wish I had time to give you some of the experiences I had in Germany in 1933. I was there when Hitler came into power. I was there in 1934 and 1935. I saw an organization as strong in Germany as the Conference of Christians and Jews in this country. It was thoroughly organized by Prof. Rudolph Otto and Professor Stronheim, head of the Roman Catholic Church movement. It was a marvelous organization. When Hitler came into power he said he would do nothing about the Jews. Then overnight it became a state policy. Nobody could do anything.· I am terribly afraid if we fail in the peace settlements to do justice to the Jews of the world there is danger that on some periphery of this question there will be another Hitler who will precipitate another wholesale attack on the liberties and rights of all of us.

Therefore, Mr. Chairman, ladies and gentlemen of the committee, in the name of humanity and in the name of justice I strongly urge the passage of these resolutions in order that we may begin the establishment of a just and durable peace by affirming rather than denouncing and nullifying the Balfour Declaration, the best and most constructive single document that emerged from World War I.

I thank you.

Chairman BLOOM. Thank you very much, Doctor.

The Chair would like to state we have a couple of Members of Congress here, and we also have some people from out of town. One just left. I hope he is not angry with me. I am doing the best I can with the time available to us. I promised Rabbi Louis Wolsey, of Philadelphia, of the American Council on Judaism, to be heard next.

Mr. COMPTON. If it will save time I will be very glad to put my statement in the record.

STATEMENT OF HON. RANULF COMPTON, A REPRESENTATIVE IN CONGRESS FROM THE STATE OF CONNECTICUT

Mr. COMPTON. In order to save time, Mr. Chairman, I would like to leave this statement with you.

Unfortunately I was out of town on official business yesterday and was not able to be present, and I wanted to be present today to show my intense interest in this resolution and to let any that has any view to the contrary know that I was not here yesterday because it was impossible for me to be here.

I want to leave this statement and some 25 or 30 telegrams that I have received from all over the United States that I would like to make a part of the record.

Thank you for the privilege.

Chairman BLOOM. You wish to state for the record unfortunately you could not be here yesterday, and the record will so show that.

Mr. COMPTON. Thank you very much.

(The statement above referred to of Representative Ranulf Compton and the telegrams are as follows:)

I do not wish to take up too much of the committee's time, as I am fully aware that the dramatic and thrilling story of the Jews in Palestine can be better told by others. There are one or two factors which I should like to emphasize, however, and ask the committee to keep in mind.

First and foremost, of course, it should be remembered that action on the resolutions introduced by myself and my esteemed colleague from Pennsylvania, Mr. Wright, plus implementing action by the State Department, is the duty of the Government of the United States if we are to continue to respect our position in foreign relations. The convention of 1924 expressly sets forth that, and I quote "Nothing contained in the present convention shall be affected by any modification which may be made in the terms of the mandate, unless such modification shall have been assented to by the United States."

It seems to me that action by this Government is more than a privilege—it is a duty.

Next, I should like to remind you of the human aspects of the present situation. Too many of us permit our minds and our reasons to become clouded by extraneous issues. There should be only two issues here involved: Duty and love of mankind.

I have not come here for the purpose of heaping praise upon the Jews, even though their record is one of which they can well be proud. They know their virtues and they are practical enough to acknowledge their faults. I would prefer that my actions be the gage of my intent, that my tribute to their courage and ability be shown by my determination to lessen their suffering. Let us then be practical today.

It is the wish of most Americans and a great majority of the British public that the so-called white paper promulgated by the Chamberlin government in 1939 be abrogated. It may well be that the present British Government will be receptive to the type of pressure which the Government of the United States can exert toward abrogation of this document. We have the right to interfere and, more important, it is our sacred duty to mankind to interfere with the action of any nation which adversely affects a national policy in which we have a vital and human interest.

Adoption of our resolutions by this Congress will be notice to the British Government and to the world that the cooperative spirit we are anxious to extend toward the solution of international problems must be accorded equal importance in the solution of purely human, racial problems.

We are concerned here with a problem of human suffering. Much of this suffering can be alleviated by opening the doors of Palestine to the havenless Jew. But while we hesitate, the suffering continues on so fantastic a scale that it is impossible to contemplate in our everyday thoughts or explain in everyday language. It is like a childish nightmare that is impossible of description; a frightening dream that seems unreal. And because we cannot describe it, because our everyday thoughts cannot grasp the horror it has become commonplace; it passes lightly from our thoughts, or perhaps we speak appropriate words of regret for the condition or condemnation for those responsible.

Yet, if one out of the myriad of these horrible experiences occurred within our sight we would be sick at heart and aroused to immediate and positive action. The bird that strikes our windshield, the dog beaten or hurt in our presence, the story of a child burned in a building fire or crushed by a car, the news of a lost or wounded soldier being mistreated or mutilated by the enemy—each brings shock and personal pain and the will for action.

Why, then, should we pass off with platitudinous complacency the acts, abuses, and tortures multiplied a thousandfold against our fellow man, they who have joined us as brothers in arms, flesh and blood like our own, begat as we were begat, beholden to the same ideals of humanity, bedamned by the same intolerance that has swept the earth with the greatest scourge of all time.

We should not.

I come before you humbly and with a great feeling of futility, as I remember the great men who have espoused this cause. Without your support I am as helpless as the persecuted and tortured Jew. With your aid I, and more important the hopeless suffering Jews of Europe, have a weapon to defend their right to a free homeland, a weapon provided by an expression of strong public opinion from the greatest,[the strongest, the most humane, and the most tolerant nation on earth.

Some of us here today are Republicans, some are Democrats, and a few represent other political parties. Almost daily we unite, in whole or in part, for some fine purpose that raises us above our politics. So it is, and so it must be with the Jews, the Christians, and the representatives of any other faith. We may be divided in our belief, but we must be united in our aim for peace and good will on earth.

I do not want to clutter up the record, Mr. Chairman, but I have here a selected number of telegrams from States from coast to coast other than from Connecticut, the State I represent. Telegrams, letters, and post cards have come to my office by the hundreds. I have not had one in opposition to this resolution.

Chairman Bloom. Representative Francis J. Myers, of Pennsylvania.

STATEMENT OF HON. FRANCIS J. MYERS, A REPRESENTATIVE IN CONGRESS FROM THE STATE OF PENNSYLVANIA

Chairman Bloom. We will now hear Mr. Francis J. Myers, of Pennsylvania.

Mr. Myers. Mr. Chairman, ladies, and gentlemen of the committee, I appear before you in support of House Resolutions 418 and 419 and to urge that the committee report these resolutions favorably.

The United States should certainly use its good offices to the end that the doors of Palestine be kept open for the free entry of Jews into that country and that the immigration of Jews into Palestine scheduled to stop on March 31, 1944, might continue. The Balfour Declaration must not be nullified nor the provisions of the mandate disregarded. An opportunity for colonization in Palestine by the Jewish people must be continued, and they should be allowed to reconstitute Palestine as a free and democratic Jewish commonwealth. They should be helped to develop this homeland for we are all aware that millions of Jewish people in the conquered countries have been tortured and killed by the Nazis; indeed the extermination of a race is systematically going on at this very moment and if we are in earnest about this problem, and if we intend to do more than sympathize with these people who are suffering untold agonies, there is no better way to help them than by the adoption of these resolutions. It is therefore my hope that the resolutions be given the unanimous approval of this committee.

Chairman BLOOM. Thank you, Mr. Myers.

The Chair would also like to state that he has a letter to go into the record at this point from Representative Capozzoli, of New York.

(The letter referred to is as follows)

HOUSE OF REPRESENTATIVES,
Washington, D. C., February 9, 1944.

Hon. SOL BLOOM,
  Chairman, Foreign Affairs Committee, Washington, D. C.

MY DEAR COLLEAGUE: Due to a protracted meeting of the Merchant Marine and Fisheries Committee, of which I am a member, I am unable to appear in person before your committee to express my sentiments on the Wright-Compton resolution, which is now before you. I am taking this means of expressing my own ideas relative to this matter.

It is fitting and proper that the House of Representatives go on record as favoring the opening of the doors of Palestine for the free entry of Jews. They should have every opportunity for colonization, so that a free and democratic Jewish home may be ultimately established.

The adoption of this resolution will be in keeping with the policy of our country, which has long favored a Jewish national home. I most strongly urge your committee to report the resolution favorably.

With kindest regards, I remain,
  Cordially yours,

LOUIS J. CAPOZZOLI.

The CHAIRMAN. Dr. Louis Wolsey, you might give your full title?

STATEMENT OF DR. LOUIS WOLSEY, AMERICAN COUNCIL FOR JUDAISM

Mr. WOLSEY. My name is Rabbi Louis Wolsey, of the American Council for Judaism. Mr. Chairman, and members of the committee, I am very grateful to you for the opportunity to appear before this committee to register my views on the resolutions that you are considering. I came here as a rabbi, as one who for over 43 years has ministered to Jewish congregations in Little Rock, Ark., and Cleveland, Ohio. For the past 19 years I have been the rabbi of Congregation Rodeph Shalom, Philadelphia.

And, as a rabbi, I come to testify before you, and as one unschooled in politics; indeed, as one who is troubled by the intrusion of any political manifestation in an area of human expression that should be reserved for spiritual guidance to my coreligionists and brotherly service to all of my fellowmen. I come as an American passionately proud of the land of my birth and devoted to its sacred principles.

What brings me here is my concern, my agonized concern, for my surviving brethren in Europe. I thank God that the same compassionate motive inspires you, ladies and gentlemen, in these deliberations.

I am among those who believe Jews are a religious community. My nationality American. But, whatever my beliefs, I feel that in thinking about the harassed and persecuted and martyrized Jews of Europe, we must remember always that the problem is one not of political authority, not of possessions or claims to title sovereignty and authority, but of human beings, of sacred human lives already fearfully reduced in number and suffering beyond all imagination.

On your part I feel confident you want to help them, to assist their rescue, to help them reconstitute their lives, to help them embark on a more hopeful future. I know you do not want to offer them the empty cup of more pious sentiment. I know you do not want to raise false hopes involving American guaranties that may not be implemented. I know you do not propose to rest content with phrases and intimations—without responsibility. You want to do all—and only what is—consistent with the responsibility that this country can properly assume.

By these tests I earnestly pray you will examine the language of the resolutions that have been offered to you.

Here let me state that I am in complete accord with the views read to you yesterday by Mr. Lessing J. Rosenwald, the son of the distinguished Jewish philanthropist, Julius Rosenwald, who gave many millions to aid his fellow Jews, and whose bounty to his fellow Americans and his fellow men knew no distinction of race or creed. His son has worthily followed his father's noble philanthropic example.

I join with him because I believe the views he expressed come close to the real problem with which we must grapple.

What is that problem? From what does it derive?

History shows us the simple answer. The problem of Jews is linked inextricably with the problem of democratic equality. What is the solution of that problem? To extend and make democratic equality enduring, sincere, and real. There is no short cut.

As testimony, look to the happier condition of American citizens of the Jewish faith. Here, thank God, we are free and equal citizens of this great Republic in accordance with the principles of its founders and law givers. We ask for no more. We need no more. We could be content with no less. Here we worship our God in the ways of our ancient faith. Here, as equal citizens, we play our part in the affairs of our beloved country, and give it the utmost in service and love.

A similar life, a similar destiny, is what Europe's Jews most want for themselves. We think all European people should have it. There are imperfections even in democracy—we are not angels, but human beings—but give Jews equality of responsibility and opportunity, and they and their homelands of which they are citizens flourish like the green bay tree. Is it too much to ask that this goal be paramount with us, that its attainment be our moral priority? Is it too much to ask that as Americans we help advance a program whereby Jews shall enjoy equality as citizens of the countries from which they were forcibly driven by the Nazi conqueror, and enjoy equal rights to migrate wherever there is opportunity for migration and settlement? And yet the proposal to establish a Jewish commonwealth is premised upon the assumption that such equality can never be attained.

Nothing but equality will do for the enduring safety of the Jew—and the world. Not in Palestine, not in Europe, nowhere for anyone. The measure of that equality will also be the measure of democracy at the end of the war.

And this brings me to the resolutions. I earnestly commend the first part of the resolutions which extend freedom of opportunity in migration and settlement. I have grave doubts whether the rest of the resolutions will not achieve the very opposite effect of what in your benevolence you have in mind.

For this other part speaks of "a free and democratic Jewish commonwealth" created by the Jewish people. Shall Christians or

Moslems have no part? How can this be genuine democracy with such an unwise beginning? Indeed, how can the term democracy be applied to a proposal of one procedure when Jews are in a minority, and another procedure when Jews are a majority? This is not, and never can be, true democracy, true equality. Therefore, by my test, it cannot mean life for the Jews. It can only mean the transfer to another geographical area of conflict and hosility, of hatred and destruction.

Consider by the same test the effect of the second part of your resolutions upon the Jews who will remain in Europe. Unhappily, the most realistic expectations are that not many more than two million will survive the slaughter—outside of those in the Soviet Union. What shall we say to them? Shall we say—as those imply who speak so casually of two or more million Jews migrating into Palestine—shall we say to them, "Hitler has been defeated, but Hitlerism has triumphed. You must now think of clearing out of Europe to populate what we speak of as a Jewish commonwealth."

Shall we say to the Catholic Pole who fought side by side with the Polish Jew against the Nazi oppressor; to the Dutch clergyman who sheltered the Dutch Jews from the Gestapo at the risk of his life; to the French peasant who fed his Jewish fellow citizen in a secret hideout; to all those myriads of Europeans freed from the Nazi incubus; that the national home of their fellow Jews is elsewhere, that their will is not to rebuild in the land of their ancient domicile but to escape somewhere into a projected Jewish commonwealth?

Or, shall we say, "Hitler and all his evil works shall not endure. Europe can now create for all of its people, without regard to religion, a society of decency, democracy, and equality. And if some must seek homes elsewhere out of the eternal quest for greater opportunity, let it be done with no distinction on grounds of religion."

I beg you to study the resolutions with these reflections in mind and see whether their promise of a state or commonwealth in Palestine will do good or ill to those who have endured so much.

And what of other opportunities for migration, for colonization, for settlement? Who knows what prospects the future has in store in other countries? Who knows what new horizons are opening for human resourcefulness and ingenuity, and for the growth in populations that reflect them.

Will we not do a fearful injustice to the harassed Jews by implying, as unprecise language well may, that they may not look forward to those new vistas with the same freedom that their eager fellow citizens do; that instead their own aspirations must be channelized into something, called in their behalf and without inquiring as to their consent, their "national commonwealth." Is this an expansion of opportunity to which these driven souls are entitled, or is it a restriction of opportunity? It is a vague, subtle, but none the less real limitation upon their freedom of choice.

Will this not, the second part of this resolution, make more complex or even preclude any serious attempts to secure equal opportunities for immigration elsewhere, since this resolution implies preferential immigration for Jews into Palestine?

And then, if this is so, there is a realistic, humanitarian consideration involved. For by so inelastically linking Jewish rehabilitation to Palestine, rehabilitation, upon the basis of equality, becomes more difficult in Europe. It becomes also more difficult for them to escape elsewhere. The most optimistic figures suggest that Palestine cannot absorb more than 100,000 new immigrants a year. Forgetting any normal increase in the population of 2,000,000 Jews who may be left, that would require 20 years. During that time a substantial number of these people would be left in the untenable position of having their nationality a matter of debate in the countries in which they live.

I hope I have not spoken with too much emotion, although God knows this is a subject freighted with the deepest emotions. I say what I have said so that you may not in generosity of spirit produce the very opposite of the purposes you intend.

At the moment there is a great service that this Congress can render. As the result of an unfortunate twist in international history, Palestine is threatened with crystallizing a grievous discrimination everywhere against Jews as Jews in the form of the land and immigration restrictions of the white paper. To the extent that your voice can bring about a correction of those injustices, I pray that it will be heard. And I pray, too, that the simple justice with which you may make that appeal to the conscience of our noble ally, and instead of the civilized world, will not be diluted or confused by any elements enmeshed in far-reaching international complications, and in theoretical doctrines that involve complex interpretations of Jewish life and destiny.

I thank you.

Chairman BLOOM. Thank you, Rabbi Wolsey.

Mr. WRIGHT. Mr. Chairman, may we question the witness?

Chairman BLOOM. Rabbi, please do not go away. We are just beginning to like you.

Mr. Johnson.

Mr. JOHNSON. No questions, Mr. Chairman.

Chairman BLOOM. Mrs. Rogers.

Mrs. ROGERS. Rabbi, I am very much interested to know just what you think can be done to assist the Jewish persons. Is it your idea to have the bars let down somewhat in the immigration laws in the different countries in order to take them in?

Mr. WOLSEY. Quite definitely. And I believe in the abrogation of those principles of the white paper that close the doors of Palestine. I think there is no Jew in the United States who disagrees with that position.

Chairman BLOOM. May the Chair state that I do not think the rabbi got your question?

Mrs. ROGERS. I mean for the immigration laws to be changed in other countries, not in Palestine, in order to assist them. I think we are all interested in one thing, and it is just a way of working it out.

Mr. WOLSEY. There are two steps. The first step, I should say, is the reclamation of those nations of the world who have violated the principles of decency, equality, and thus to enable them to have their exiles restored to their nations. That is No. 1.

Now, No. 2: If the nations of the world commit themselves to those principles for the defense of which we and our allies are at war, it is quite possible that the benevolence of the nations of the world will be very glad to so revise their immigration laws that Jews might find hospitality in some areas of our world.

Mrs. ROGERS. You feel we should change our immigration laws somewhat so as to take in more of the persecuted persons? I do not mean just for the Jewish, but for all persecuted victims of the war?

Mr. Wolsey. You ask whether I recommend that?

Mrs. Rogers. Yes, Rabbi.

Mr. Wolsey. I am afraid I am not expert enough on our own immigration laws.

Chairman Bloom. No; I think the Chair will have to rule that question entirely out of order.

Mrs. Rogers. We want to help them; that is what I am trying to get at, Mr. Chairman.

Chairman Bloom. I am trying to help the rabbi.

Mrs. Rogers. I think the rabbi can take care of himself very well.

Mr. Wolsey. Thank you, Mrs. Rogers.

Chairman Bloom. Mr. McMurray.

Mr. McMurray. No questions.

Chairman Bloom. Mr. Chiperfield.

Mr. Chiperfield. Rabbi, do you have House Resolution 418 before you?

Mr. Wolsey. No, I have not. Now, I have 418.

Mr. Chiperfield. I just want to see if I understood you. You approve of this resolution down say to line 4 after the word "country"?

Mr. Wolsey. That is correct.

Mr. Chiperfield. And you would strike out the balance of the resolution?

Mr. Wolsey. Oh, yes.

Mr. Chiperfield. Yes; that is all.

Chairman Bloom. Mr. Wright.

Mr. Wright. I have several questions I would like to ask if you do not mind.

Chairman Bloom. Proceed, Mr. Wright.

Mr. Wright. I notice by reading the terms of the Balfour declaration it speaks there as the purpose of the declaration to be "the establishment in Palestine of a national home for the Jewish people." Those very words are echoed in the resolution of the Sixty-seventh Congress, in the convention between Great Britain and the United States, and also in the mandate. Do you disapprove of the purpose of the Balfour declaration, "the establishment in Palestine of a national home for the Jewish people"?

Mr. Wolsey. I definitely do not disapprove of it.

The only thing I disapprove is that your preamble in 418 retains the language of the Balfour declaration and very clearly, I should say, omits the third article——

Mr. Wright (interposing). That is a mistake.

Mr. Wolsey (continuing). Of the Balfour Declaration, and I do not understand why.

Chairman Bloom. It is a typographical error. Read the other one and you will find it in there.

Mr. Wright. They were both supposed to be in there.

Mr. Wolsey. But I may say to you, Congressman, that fourth article is very important.

Mr. Wright. It will be restored. Do not worry about it. If I may get on with my questioning, you say you do approve of the purpose of the Balfour Declaration to establish a national home in Palestine for the Jewish people. Do you feel that the national home should have the rights of self-government there eventually?

Mr. Wolsey. You mean Jewish self-government?

Mr. WRIGHT. Government for the national home or the Nation of Palestine.

Mr. WOLSEY. I am afraid that you do not answer my question. [Laughter.]

I believe on a democratic basis the country should be ruled by all the people who live in that country, and I do not believe in uniting church and State and simply reserve government to the power of the Jews. I do not believe that to be democratic.

Mr. WRIGHT. Let us get on just a moment from there. Under the present minority status of the Jews and the majority status of the Arabs with the record of terrorism which you have at the present time, do you feel if they did constitute a government there with the Arabs in the majority that the Jews would be permitted to migrate to Palestine?

Mr. WOLSEY. I believe if the situation is relieved of this commonwealth and state pressure that undoubtedly the British Government might be persuaded to open the doors of Palestine and that the Arabs would be conciliated.

Mr. WRIGHT. Yes, but I am talking about a government establishment.

Chairman BLOOM. Pardon me. The committee will kindly be in order and remain in order so the witness can hear the question and the committee can hear the answer.

Mr. WRIGHT. If you will pardon me, I think this is the crux of the differences between the two witnesses.

Chairman BLOOM. I want to get order for you, Mr. Wright.

Mr. WRIGHT. All right.

Do you feel if a government is established after the war with the Jewish population frozen, as it is now, and an Arab majority, do you think that the Arabs will permit further migration of Jews into Palestine?

Mr. WOLSEY. I do not know.

Mr. WRIGHT. Are you willing to take that chance? That seems to be the difference between your position and that of the other witnesses who have testified here. They feel it would be absolutely fatal to a commonwealth in Palestine if the Jews were not permitted to migrate there until they attain a majority, and then in the words of the Balfour declaration accord Arabs and Christians equal political status and rights. They feel the converse is true, and that if a government were established by the Arabs, a more or less medieval and feudal type of government, that the situation would be frozen and the Arabs would forbid any further migration to Palestine and defeat the purpose of the Balfour declaration. What do you have to say about that?

Mr. WOLSEY. You ask me to speak for the Arabs?

Mr. WRIGHT. Neither am I doing so. Do you not think what I said is likely to happen?

Mr. WOLSEY. I still adhere to the original answer that if you had a democratic organization it might definitely persuade the British Government to open the doors into Palestine. Then after the doors are open you have another answer as to the majority of Arabs.

Mr. WRIGHT. Rabbi, you spoke of an Arab majority. I am talking about taking away the authority of the British mandate and allowing the majority to govern, as we do here and in other democracies, but then do you not think the Arabs would not permit further migration of Jews and thus defeat the purpose of the Balfour Declaration?

Mr. WOLSEY. I do know in the days of the Sultan the Jews and the Arabs got along in Palestine very well together. It was only after the question of state or commonwealth was created that there was also created a counter-insistence upon Arab nationalism. If they once got along together, it is highly possible they could again. We know of a movement of Miss Henrietta Szold and Dr. Magnes in favor of trying to create peace between Jews and Arabs. Whether they succeed or not I cannot say, but I do know that has been proposed.

Mr. WRIGHT. Rabbi, if I follow you, you say under the Sultan the Jews and Arabs got along. Then, when the Balfour Declaration was made and this Palestine homeland was created, trouble started and perhaps it would have been better if the Balfour Declaration had never been passed?

Mr. WOLSEY. I have not said that.

Mr. WRIGHT. Which would be a fair inference?

Mr. WOLSEY. No, it would not in my judgment.

Mr. WRIGHT. I have several more questions. I do not want to hold up the committee, but I think this is important.

I do want to call your attention to the last provision of the Balfour Declaration:

His Majesty's Government view with favour the establishment in Palestine of a national home for the Jewish people, and will use their best endeavours to facilitate the achievement of this object, it being clearly understood that nothing shall be done which may prejudice the civil and religious rights of existing non-Jewish communities in Palestine, or the rights and political status enjoyed by the Jews in any other country.

Now, in America all people are considered equal regardless of religion. In America probably the national character of the Jewish people is not as prominent as it is in Europe, but in Europe where Jewish people have suffered persecutions from time to time do you not feel that those persecutions have banded them together not only religiously but also nationally? Do you not feel the love of a Jew for America might be one thing, the love of a Jew for Germany might be an entirely different thing, and that the aspirations of such a Jew might be to go to this homeland and this haven where they might be wanted, whereas it would be different with the American Jew and the British Jew?

Mr. WOLSEY. If you ask me the question on the basis of the third article of the Balfour declaration let me say my objection is that it quite definitely identifies the Jew as a member of a specific nation not alone in Palestine but all over the world.

I have tried to say I believe Jews represent a religious community, and their contribution to the world is a religious contribution. In other words, on the basis of nationalistic identity, I am looked upon as a member of a nation whose headquarters is in Palestine, and then I am subject to suspicion, alienism, and perhaps worse. Of course, I do not like to identify myself as a member of a Jewish nation because in my reading of Jewish history our nationality, if you call it that—I call it a theocracy which existed twice—during that time between the first and second commonwealth, the Jews were tributary to surrounding nations. Then the Jews never revolted and never insisted upon——

May I not finish my sentence?

Chairman BLOOM (interposing). The Chair would like to state we have gone on here for 2 days without any interruption, and the

witness is entitled to be heard and respected. Please do not do
that again. We do not allow any applause or demonstration of any
kind one way or the other, so the Chair hopes it will not happen
again.

Mr. WOLSEY. Congressman, what I tried to say was that from 536
B. C. E. to about 160 B. C. E., they did not revolt against those
nations because their religious liberty was protected. It was only in
165 that Syria interfered with their religious integrity and their religious prerogatives and the Jews definitely revolted against them.
In other words, religion was paramount in the consciousness of those
Jews, and not nationhood.

That is what I ask for now, that we shall have the right of our
religious identity and that we shall be distinguished purely by considerations of religion.

I do not believe in the Jewish nationality, or that the Jew as a Jew
is a member of that nation.

That represents my school of thought.

Mr. WRIGHT. May I just ask you one more question? Do you not
think when you speak about the Jew, if this resolution is passed, being
suspected as having a double nationality, that the American Jew will
still be an American and that the British Jew will be a Briton, and
that if any Jew goes to Palestine and becomes part of that commonwealth only then will he become a Palestine national? This "double
citizenship" status will therefore never be present.

Mr. WOLSEY. No.

Mr. WRIGHT. Do you not think the resolution is aimed at helping
people, not like the people in this country but people who have been
very cruelly treated, not only in past years but, as you know better
than myself, periodically during the history of the last hundred years?

Mr. WOLSEY. Yes; I would agree, but I prefer there be accentuated
the fact that what we need to do now is colonize Palestine and provide
a home for our persecuted brethren there. In other words, it is a
philanthropic situation we are confronted with. There is serious difficulty for Jews in various parts of the world. If Palestine can be a
refuge, I believe in encouraging it. But I do not believe in the question of nationality, or, of course, my position in America becomes
equivocal.

Mr. WRIGHT. I think it is a thing you are looking too closely at to
properly consider but I respect your point of view naturally.

May I ask if most Jews in America do not hold views different
to your own and views that have been more or less given here today
by Rabbi Silver and several other witnesses? Would you not say
the greater majority of the Jews in this country differ from you in
your ideas as to what should be done with this resolution?

Mr. WOLSEY. I have not taken the statistics of public Jewish
opinion and neither has anyone else. No one can answer that question
as to whether it is for or against.

Mr. WRIGHT. Neither have I. I am taking the conference figures
which recently met in New York representing 90 percent of the
Jewish societies. They represented the members of their congregations. I took that for granted.

Mr. WOLSEY. No one can say where the majority opinion lays.
I am the rabbi of a congregation in Philadelphia with something like
3,500 people, and I do not imagine there are 25 people in the entire
congregation who believe as you have suggested—not 20.

Mr. WRIGHT. I should not attempt to be the spokesman of the Jewish people. I am not a Jew myself, but I am merely stating what I have reason to believe which is that the overwhelming majority of the Jews do want a Jewish home and they want their own government so they can be assured of safety against terrorism.

Mr. WOLSEY. I am not so sure that is correct. That is a subjective opinion.

Mr. WRIGHT. Thank you very much.

Chairman BLOOM. Mr. Vorys.

Mr. VORYS. Rabbi, I wonder about this: You say that in Judaism the Jews are a religious community rather than a nation; is that correct?

Mr. WOLSEY. Yes.

Mr. VORYS. And I think you would agree with those who would say that the Jews are not a race, that is, the Arabs are of the same racial stock as the Jews; is not that correct?

Mr. WOLSEY. I have studied some of the statements of anthropologists and I cannot find anyone in the universities of the country who concede there is any such thing as a race in civilization, not one.

The word "race" is, in my judgment, purely a social term. It does not correspond to any biological reality at all. There is no such thing as race. At all times you have had interbreedings and intermarriages of the various stocks of the world regardless of the identity of the race. And the Jew, let me say to you, from the sources of our Jewish literature, never considered himself a member of a race until the nineteenth century when he borrowed the idea of race, and may I also say of nationalism, from his environment.

Mr. VORYS. We both agree then that the Jews are not a separate race, you and I, do we not?

Mr. WOLSEY. Definitely we do not agree that they are a race.

Mr. VORYS. You say there are not any races?

Mr. WOLSEY. No; there are no races.

Mr. VORYS. I read, for instance, that the Arabs and the Jews are Semitic people, whatever that means. So that there is no racial distinction involved in this Palestine question?

Mr. WOLSEY. I do not think there is.

Mr. VORYS. Now, therefore, it seems to be a religious matter, and what I wanted to ask you is whether Judaism is set up in such a way that there is a council of rabbis or a hierarchy of some kind that speaks for the Jews?

Mr. WOLSEY. You mean here in America?

Mr. VORYS. Yes; now among us here in America. Do I make myself clear?

Mr. WOLSEY. I do not quite understand; no. Are you asking whether there is such a thing as a hierarchy in the Jewish communion in America?

Mr. VORYS. Yes.

Mr. WOLSEY. Oh, definitely not.

Mr. VORYS. Definitely not?

Mr. WOLSEY. Definitely not.

Mr. VORYS. That is, you are of the so-called reform or orthodox?

Mr. WOLSEY. Correct. No; I belong to the Reform school.

Mr. VORYS. But among both the reformed and the orthodox group you feel sure there would be none who would say that there is a council or hierarchy that can interpret with authority what the religion means; is that correct?

Mr. Wolsey. No; they cannot interpret with the authority which becomes binding upon all Jews. Each man may think for himself and study for himself and give his conclusions. But those conclusions are not binding in our organizations. And there are three schools of Jewish thought and they are entirely advisory in character. They have no legislative ability of any kind whatsoever which is binding even upon themselves.

Mr. Vorys. The statement was made here yesterday by a distinguished rabbi that on such matters as whether the Jews were a race, nationality, or religion, rabbis should be consulted because they could speak with authority, and they interpreted the law, the Jewish law, to their people.

Mr. Wolsey. That is only because they happen to be specialists in a study of the religious traditions.

Mr. Vorys. So far as you know there is not in this communion or group or in the other groups anything in the Jewish faith that would require a Jew as part of his faith and his prayers to be for a Jewish commonwealth in Palestine?

Mr. Wolsey. There is no religious authority or any institution in Judaism that can require a Jew to believe in it or disbelieve in it. The Jew after all is an individualist upon the principles of freedom. Each Jew entertains the views which seem to him to be the true views. No one can dictate to him religiously.

Mr. Vorys. I think now that the connection between theology and the church and state is cleared up. I will yield.

Chairman Bloom. I would like to say to you, Rabbi, of the thousands of telegrams and letters that this committee has received through the chairman there have only been several opposed to the idea of this resolution.

Mr. Vorys. In view of that and the turn the discussion has taken I would like to ask the rabbi whether, discussing this thing on a democratic basis, the consideration of this committee should be what the greatest number of Jews want or what the greatest number of Americans of all faiths want, and what is the wise thing for our country? What would you say is the test we should be applying?

Mr. Wolsey. If you can find out their opinions of course I believe that would be valuable statistically. It has never been done.

My own experience has been, and this is entirely a personal opinion, that something like 2,500,000 to 3,000,000 Jews have not expressed themselves either one way or the other, and probably do not care to do it for reasons satisfactory to themselves.

Mr. Vorys. Have you any idea how many Jews there are in the United States?

Mr. Wolsey. I would say 5,000,000.

Mr. Vorys. Thank you.

Chairman Bloom. Mr. Mundt.

Mr. Mundt. I understand in your talk with Brother Vorys over here, because it has been a bit confusing to me to hear two equally persuasive and eloquent rabbis, one from Cleveland and one from Philadelphia——

Mr. Wolsey (interposing). Remember I came from Cleveland, too, in a day when most of the reform congregations there believed as I do.

Mr. MUNDT. They have fallen under the sway of another orator since that time?

Mr. WOLSEY. I am not unconscious of that.

Mr. MUNDT. So I was curious to learn in your answers to Mr. Vorys whether there is any higher authority than just a rabbi. I am a Methodist. We have the board of bishops who purport to speak for us. Sometimes they do not do a very good job. They put themselves in a room and out of the room comes very sagacious opinions. In the Catholics it is the college of cardinals and bishops. In your religion there is a board of rabbis or a higher group than the individual rabbi who could speak more or less for the organized Jewish?

Mr. WOLSEY. We have the Central Conference of American Rabbis, the Rabbinical Assembly, and the Orthodox Conference of Rabbis whose power is an advisory one. They cannot issue any orders, do not issue any, but they give advice born of their knowledge and study. But no individual Jew and no institution of Jews, particularly congregationals, are required to observe what they say. They have not that authority in either one of the three schools.

Mr. McMURRAY. Would the gentleman yield?

Mr. MUNDT. I yield.

Chairman BLOOM. Mr. McMurray.

Mr. McMURRAY. The three organizations of rabbis you mentioned are each one branches or schools of thought of the church. There is the reform group which you represent, I understand. There is the orthodox, and then there is a conservative, and each one of those has a separate organization?

Mr. WOLSEY. They have varying interpretations.

Mr. McMURRAY. I understand that. But each one of those has a separate and distinct organization of rabbis?

Mr. WOLSEY. Oh, yes.

Mr. McMURRAY. Whose voice is merely advisory to their groups?

Mr. WOLSEY. Yes; entirely.

Mr. McMURRAY. That is all the information I wanted.

Mr. WOLSEY. Entirely.

Mr. MUNDT. And I presume the policy of these boards of rabbis is to take a position primarily on matters of theology and proper practice rather than on public questions, is it not?

Mr. WOLSEY. I should like to say that is what I would like them to do.

Mr. MUNDT. I sometimes would like to say that for the Board of Methodist Churches. [Laughter.]

Just one more question. Mr. Wright in his questioning endeavored to impute to you a disbelief or disavowal of the Balfour Declaration. To me it is confusing. I am not quite clear whether the Balfour Declaration intended to include such an arrangement as is intended by the last part of this resolution, the reconstitution of Palestine as a democratic commonwealth, or whether it was simply set up in Palestine as a national home for the Jewish people to which they should have free and unrestricted access. The language is this very apt phrase you used, it is "unprecise" language because it says, "His Majesty's Government view with favour the establishment in Palestine of a national home for the Jewish people." It seems to me that does not necessarily include a phrase there "democratic Jewish commonwealth." You could have within Palestine a national home without creating a state?

Mr. WOLSEY. I think you are very visioning. I think you are completely correct. If I may express a point of view—I have no right to interpret—it seems to me lines 3, 4, 5, and 6 are definite supplements to the Balfour Declaration, and that they ask for more than the Balfour resolution provides.

Chairman BLOOM. I wish the audience would kindly refrain from demonstrations. It is not very respectful. Permit the rabbi to proceed in order. Proceed, please.

Mr. WOLSEY. The impression I get from these three lines of 418 which conclude it is this: That those who ask for congressional endorsement are not entirely satisfied with all the Balfour Declaration provides, and therefore, they ask for something more than what is in the Balfour Declaration. It is that "more" which is the nub of the disagreement between the two schools of thought. If they would surrender this I think there would be complete unity in Jewish life. That is my personal opinion.

Mr. MUNDT. So that, of course, enables you to support this resolution up to and including the word "country" and still be in complete support of the Balfour Declaration?

Mr. WOLSEY. That is right.

Chairman BLOOM. Mrs. Bolton.

Mrs. BOLTON. No questions.

Chairman BLOOM. Mr. Wadsworth.

Mr. WADSWORTH. None.

Chairman BLOOM. Mr. Gerlach.

Mr. GERLACH. None.

Mr. WRIGHT. Mr. Chairman, may I ask the witness one question?

Chairman BLOOM. Yes, Mr. Wright.

Mr. WRIGHT. Mr. Churchill, who happened to be in the Cabinet at the time of the Balfour Declaration, stated:

If, as may well happen, there should be created in our lifetime on the banks of the Jordan a Jewish state under the protection of the British Crown which might comprise three or four millions of Jews, an event will have occurred in the history of the world which would from every point of view be beneficial.

You are acquainted with that language of Mr. Churchill?

Mr. WOLSEY. Oh, yes.

Mr. WRIGHT. Then the report on page 89 of the pamphlet we have here, prepared by the chairman, states:

His Majesty's Government evidently realized that a Jewish state might in course of time be established.

That was the report of the Royal Commission which preceded the British White Paper. And there are several other declarations of statesmen——

Mr. WADSWORTH (interposing). Would the gentlemen mind reading the rest of the sentence, "but it was not in a position to say"?

Mr. WRIGHT. Yes; that was later on.

Mr. WADSWORTH. In the same sentence.

Mr. MUNDT. Mr. Chairman, I would like to correct the correction of mine which the gentleman from Pennsylvania made.

Mr. Churchill is a dreadfully loquacious fellow, and like most loquacious fellows he talks clear around the mulberry bush. On page 81 the same Winston Churchill said this:

I entirely accept the distinction between making a Jewish National Home in Palestine and making Palestine a Jewish National Home. I think I was one of the first to draw that distinction.

So that just sort of confounds the confusion so far as I am concerned.

Chairman BLOOM. Thank you very much, Rabbi, and it was very nice to have you here and get your views.

Dr. Heller.

STATEMENT OF RABBI JAMES G. HELLER, FORMER PRESIDENT, CENTRAL CONFERENCE OF AMERICAN RABBIS AND CHAIRMAN OF THE UNITED PALESTINE APPEAL

Mr. HELLER. Mr. Chairman and ladies and gentlemen of the committee, I am a little disturbed at the outset lest this committee may think this is a procession of rabbis and not of sufficient laymen. I happen to have the honor of being a rabbi, also.

First of all, may I have the privilege of saying, Mr. Chairman, that although an American citizen for many years, this is the first time in my life I have ever attended a hearing of the Committee on Foreign Affairs, and I have been tremendously interested in the conduct of the hearing—I hope this will be included in the record, Mr. Chairman—and greatly impressed with the conduct of the meeting and with the participation of the members of the committee in attempting to formulate their opinion in regard to what is a very difficult question.

I would like to do something, Mr. Chairman and ladies and gentlemen, which it is not usually my habit of doing. I think we all ought not to speak about ourselves, but the phrase has been used several times in this discussion that we are Americans of the Jewish faith, one which I fully accept for myself.

The impression has been gained that there is a distinction among American Jews toward this particular phrase and toward some of the concepts that underlie it.

Chairman BLOOM. Would you mind an interruption there? To what branch of the Jewish religion do you belong?

Mr. HELLER. I am going to express that in a moment.

Chairman BLOOM. All right; go ahead.

Mr. HELLER. I happen to be a Son of the American Revolution from two ancestors.

I am a rabbi of the Reform Jewish group. I was for 2 years, up until 8 months ago, the president of the Central Conference of American Rabbis, of which Rabbi Wolsey is a member, and of which he was president some years ago.

I served as a chaplain in the Army of the United States in France in the last war.

I happen also to be very actively identified with the Zionist movement for many years. As a matter of fact, I inherited that work from my father, one of the first rabbis in the United States, and one of the first graduates of the Hebrew Union College, to be so identified.

It must be very difficult, Mr. Chairman, for the members of the committee to formulate their own opinion when they discern differences in the opinions of those who approach them.

With entire courtesy to one who happens to be a very dear and almost lifelong friend of mine, Rabbi Wolsey, I would like to try to make clear the differences which obtain and also the extent to which this difference pervades the Jewish community.

The members of the committee will remember, I hope, that in the hearings in the Sixty-seventh Congress of 1922, when the resolution which has been referred to was passed, at least three rabbis appeared at those sessions and voiced their opposition to the Balfour Declaration and expressed it rather heatedly at the time. Nonetheless the committee voted unanimously for the resolution.

At that time there was a joint resolution, according to my recollection, which passed the Senate and the House.

I wish to God that we had complete unanimity among my people and my faith on this subject. Unfortunately we have not. We did not have in 1917 and 1918, nor have we now.

However, I think the committee ought to know much more clearly than has been said before it thus far, of the extent of the opposition to what is represented in the resolution that is before you. I believe I have some knowledge of this, Mr. Chairman. First of all, I served as president of the rabbinical group to which Mr. Wolsey belongs, and this subject was considered last November. They enacted two resolutions which I would like the privilege of reading in part.

As to the first, the relevant section reads as follows:

Of late, however, some of our members have renewed the assertion that Zionism is not compatible with Reform Judaism. The attempt has been ｜made to 'set in irreconcilable opposition "universalism" and "particularism." To the members of the conference, this appears unreal and misleading. Without impugning the right of members of the conference to be opposed to Zionism, for whatever reason they may choose, the conference declares that it discerns no essential incompatibility between Reform｜ Judaism and Zionism, no reason why those of its members who give allegiance to Zionism should not have the right to regard themselves as fully within the spirit and purpose of Reform Judaism.

That resolution was adopted by a viva voce vote with precisely two members recording their votes in the negative.

Then a second resolution was adopted. The relevant part reads as follows—this refers to the organization of which both these gentlemen are members. Mr. Rosenwald is president of the American Council of Judaism, and some of his articles of faith were read here, and Dr. Wolsey is one of its most prominent members—the resolution refers to them in this way:

While members of the C. C. A. R. are fully within their rights in espousing whatever philosophy of Jewish life they may accept; nevertheless, the American Council for Judaism, because of the special circumstances under which it came into being, has already endangered the unity of the Conference. Its continued existence would become a growing threat to our fellowship.

The American Council for Judaism was founded by members of the C. C. A. R. for the purpose of combating Zionism. The Zionist movement and masses of Jews everywhere, shocked by the rise of this organization at a time when Zionists and others are laboring hard to have the gates of Palestine reopened for the harassed Jews of Europe, could not avoid judging this event in the light of past controversies, or seeing in it an example of what they had come to consider the constant opposition of Reformed Judaism to Zionist aspirations. This impression does grave injustice to the many devoted Zionists in the C. C. A. R. and to the conference itself.

Therefore, without impugning the right of Zionists or non-Zionists to express and to disseminate their convictions within and without the conference, we, in the spirit of amity, urge our colleagues of the American Council for Judaism to terminate this organization.

The vote upon this resolution, which I recall vividly, was by 137 to 45 members.

You will recall, please, ladies and gentlemen, this is the one section in which opposition to Zionism has existed, which in all likelihood is about 5 percent of the Jewish population. It comprises a membership of 62,000, and if you multiply by four or five it would total 250,000. Even in this organization 3 to 1 of its spiritual leaders disagree.

In the second place, the American Council for Judaism, as Mr. Rosenwald reported, has a present membership of 2,500 people. The Zionists in this country have a membership of 314,000. Even this is not quite a correct figure, as we know who have been observing this for years.

And above all, Mr. Chairman, the American Jewish conference which was held last June seemed to us to be a complete demonstration of the point which we have made. It was not elected by direct vote, although the Zionist groups would have liked to have had it that. This was not done because it was felt that during the war it might create difficulty to have that machinery. Instead, an attempt was made to have all Jewish organizations in the United States in their respective communities select delegates and send them to a conference. And I need not tell you that every election held in this country reflected the opinion of the American Jewish communities. Five hundred delegates were elected. In the vote on the essential resolution, the Palestine resolution, as far as I could observe, by holding up cards, not by a roll call, there were probably only about five or six opposed. So this assembly which was selected upon a representative basis showed that probably a proportion of 85 to 90 percent at a minimum estimate of the representatives of the Jewish communities of this country were in favor of the resolution before you.

So I should like the committee to bear in mind that this point of view is that of a small minority of this country.

I note by some of the comments from the members of the committee that they appear to be confused by the constant emphasis upon a religious interpretation of the character of Jews in this country in contrast with that which has been spoken of as a nationalistic interpretation. The resolution which I have read from the Central Conference of American Rabbis says that is not true. They present no such antithesis as is implied in this. As a matter of fact a majority of the Jews in the orthodox, the conservative, and I think in the Reform group also are not accustomed to making this kind of separation. We are not accustomed to that. We regard ourselves as a strange amalgamation of historic continuity, possessing common ways of life and religion.

Among the Jews—I think this will be particularly interesting to Mr. Mundt—it is not like the religion in the Westminister Confession or in the Presbyterian Church and in various others. There has never been a credal test of the Jewish religion. Judaism is regarded as a way of life. Moreover, I should like to make the point that Jews regard this as a religious movement because to them in consonance with the tradition there is no religious duty that is more sacred than that of saving the sons of their people. For us to disassociate this from the religious idea in trying to find a haven would be destructive.

Our feeling is we are dealing not with ideologies but with facts. I hope the committee will also think so. That is an internal problem among Jews when they analyze themselves. What they are confronted with is a condition and not a theory. I hope you will not be diverted by this.

And similarly some of the things that have been said have pivoted around or seem to have been made upon the basis of the statement that has been made that we want a theocracy in Palestine.

The majority of the people who live in America are Christians. I wish they were better Christians, a great many of them. This is not a theocratic state merely because of this fact. And the Zionist program as stated in the Jewish conference says we are in favor of a separation of church and state in Palestine. Nor is it to be a racial state. There is no such intention in the Zionist movement.

I was rather distressed at the introduction of the King-Crane report. I am sure the gentleman who introduced it considered it a pertinent document.

I should like to introduce a note on the King-Crane report first, and, second, an analysis of it, so that those who may read the material submitted by Mr. Rosenwald may analyze it for themselves.

Chairman BLOOM. Without objection it is so ordered.

(The note referred to is as follows:)

AMERICAN ZIONIST EMERGENCY COUNCIL,
February 9, 1944.

NOTE ON THE KING-CRANE COMMISSION

The King-Crane Commission was appointed by President Wilson during the Peace Conference at Paris in 1919 to investigate conditions in the territories formerly belonging to the Ottoman Empire, with a view to helping decide a dispute between France and Great Britain—the Arabs being centrally involved—concerning the assignment of mandates. Originally, the Commission was planned to consist of representatives of all the Allies, but France, suspecting a political maneuver, withdrew, and Great Britain followed suit. The American section proceeded alone; they made a hasty tour of Syria and Palestine in an atmosphere which they admit was permeated with propaganda and intrigue. On the basis of oral interviews and of petitions whose value was dubious, they drew conclusions which coincided with the resolutions of the Syrian-Arab Congress held in Damascus during the investigation. There were three experts on the Commission. One joined Mr. Crane and Dr. King in their recommendations, but the two experts best acquainted with the area of Syria and Palestine presented separate reports differing radically from the suggestions of the Commission.

Before the Commission left, President Wilson had reassured Prof. Felix Frankfurter that he adhered to the Balfour Declaration. This was in May 1919, just 2 months after his famous declaration in favor of the Jewish commonwealth interpretation of the Balfour Declaration. The Commissioners, however, went out of their way to make a virulent attack against Zionism, strictly following the line of the extreme Arab nationalists; they recommended the radical limitation of Jewish immigration as well as the abandonment of the idea of a Jewish commonwealth. Incidentally, the King-Crane report shows that the Balfour Declaration was at that time interpreted both by its enemies as well as its friends as meaning the eventual establishment of a Jewish state or commonwealth.

The report of the Commission was delivered to the American delegation in Paris in August 1919. President Wilson had already left, and Mr. Crane cabled the contents of the recommendations to him. At the end of September, the full recommendations were submitted to the White House and filed with the State Department. Whether the document was considered by Wilson is not known but, at any rate, it had no effect on the subsequent action either of the United States or of the Allies.

Recently, the King-Crane recommendations have been unearthed by anti-Zionist forces, who have focused attention on the unfavorable opinion expressed in reference to Zionist aspirations in Palestine—without giving any indication of the fact that the method of investigation followed by the Commission was much open to question and that its conclusions, not only on Zionism but on the major problem it was appointed to investigate, were never seriously considered. The late George Antonius reproduced the recommendations of the commission in the Arab awakening. However, he gave only the recommendations, and not the full report as first published in 1922 in Editor and Publisher under date of December 2. The full report contains a section "For use of Americans only" which frankly tells the story of intrigue and propaganda which surrounded the work of the commission.

It is not clear what the official status of the report is. In any case, the major decisions on Palestine at San Remo in April 1920, and the approval of the mandate in July 1922, were taken after the report had been completed and filed, and the same is true of the official action by the United States in approval of the Balfour Declaration and the Mandate for Palestine.

(The analysis above referred to, entitled "The Abortive King-Crane Recommendations; Science or Propaganda, by I. B. Berkson," and published by the research department, American Zionist Emergency Council, January 1944, is as follows:)

THE ABORTIVE KING-CRANE RECOMMENDATIONS—SCIENCE OR PROPAGANDA?

By I. B. BERKSON*

The King-Crane report was prepared in 1919 for the Paris Peace Conference by an American commission appointed by President Wilson to investigate conditions in the Near East with the purpose of formulating an opinion concerning a proper division of the territories formerly belonging to the Ottoman Empire with due respect to the wishes of the peoples concerned. The original plan was to have an inter-Allied commission, but the British and the French who at first agreed to participate in the investigation withdrew, and the American section proceeded alone. The commission spent 6 weeks in Syria and Palestine; its report was delivered to the American delegation in Paris on April 28, 1919. By that time, Wilson had left for the United States; the contents of the report were cabled to him 2 days later and the full text was transmitted to the White House at the end of September. President Wilson was on his tour through the country defending his foreign policies, and he was stricken before he returned to Washington. The United States soon withdrew from active negotiations in the peace conference settlement, and the King-Crane recommendations were never acted upon; they were, however, as a matter of routine, filed in the archives of the State Department.

The recommendations of the commission were first published in 1922, in Editors and Publishers, a New York periodical, in the issue dated December 2, under the title, "The King-Crane Report on the Near East, A Suppressed Official Document of the United States Government."[1] It has, at times, been insinuated that French, British, and Zionist pressure combined to prevent publication, but of this there is no evidence whatsoever. The late George Antonius who made much of the report in his presentation of the Arab case, states that it was agreed in the first place that the document should be treated as confidential by everyone concerned and that when Wilson was approached in 1922 for permission to make its contents known, "he readily authorized publication."[2] In recent years anti-Zionists have unearthed the report and have focussed attention on the unfavorable opinion expressed in the recommendations with reference to Zionist aspirations in Palestine without giving any indication of the fact that the method of investigation followed by the commission as well as its conclusions are much open to question not only with reference to the Zionist problem, but with reference to the whole problem of the disposition of the Near East which it was instructed to investigate.

*This article is based on the Esco Foundation Palestine Study. For the major facts the writer leans heavily on the article by Harry N. Howard, An American Experiment in 'Peace-Making: The' King-Crane Commission, The Moslem World, April 1942, pp. 122–146. The responsibility for interpretation and evaluation—which differs in important respects from that made by Professor Howard—rests with the present writer.

1 It was reprinted in The New York Times.
2 George Antonius, The Arab Awakening, p. 296.

THE CIRCUMSTANCES SURROUNDING THE APPOINTMENT OF THE KING-CRANE COMMISSION

The 'appointment of the commission arose out of the dispute between Great Britain and France with reference to the methods of partitioning the Ottoman Empire, more particularly with reference to the territories in Syria and Iraq where the questions of boundaries and the degree of independence to be granted to the Arab population were greatly in dispute. As in other issues dealt with at the peace conference, there was a conflict between the secret agreements and understandings made among the allied governments for division of spheres of influence and control in case of a defeat of Turkey, on the one hand, and the idealistic public utterances made during the war, particularly on the part of President Wilson, concerning the rights of small nations and self-determination on the other. These pronouncements were seized upon by the subject peoples in the former Ottoman territory, Armenians, Greeks, and Arabs, as indicating their right to complete independence. However, even the most liberal of the statesmen at Paris recognized that the interests of the European powers could not be left out of account, not only for practical reasons, but because the countries in question were not regarded as ready for full independence. Moreover, a complete withdrawal from the Near East would have left the many racial and religious minorities unprotected. The mandate system suggested by Jan Christiaan Smuts and sponsored by Wilson as part of the League of Nations plan, was seized upon as a way out. The essence of the mandate idea was that the mandated territories would remain under the tutelage of a power which would govern the country from the point of view of the well-being and development of each people until they had reached a stage of development where their existence as independent nations could be recognized with international approval.

On January 30, 1919, a few days after the opening of the peace conference, the supreme council adopted a resolution calling for the partition of the Ottoman empire and the application to it of the mandate system. At the same time there was talk at the peace conference, particularly on the part of the Americans, it seems, of sending an expert commission to the Near East "to examine the problem on the spot." As early as February 1, 1 day after the resolution adopting the mandate system for the near eastern peoples, the American Commission to Negotiate Peace was giving consideration to sending Dr. James L. Barton, on the Near East relief, and Dr. Frederick C. Howe to investigate conditions, but this and similar projects suggested at that time were not acted upon. Apparently there was dispute as to the value of such a commission, and as usual in such cases, there were rivalries between persons and groups who hoped to be appointed as members or who wished to control the policy of the Commission.

The long train of negotiations—and possibly maneuvers—which led to the appointment of the King-Crane Commission began with a letter written to President Wilson on February 7, 1919, by Dr. Howard Bliss, president of the American University of Beirut.[3] Bliss, an American born in Syria, was in close touch with the Arab delegation in Paris. Dr. Bliss told the President that the people of Syria were relying on his ideals in their struggle for independence, and that the Arabs wanted "a fair opportunity to express their own political aspirations." He indicated his satisfaction with the reported intention to send an American Commission to the Near East. However, he suggested that it would be even more helpful if such a Commission were backed by the French and British authorities, and thus obtain the character of an international rather than a purely American, investigation. Moreover, Bliss seemed to be sure beforehand, what such a commission would find:[4]

"I believe that the report of any commission, made up of fair, wide-minded, and resourceful men, would show that the Syrians desire the erection of an independent state or states under the care, for the present, of a power, or of the "League of Nations." I believe the power designated by the people would be America, for the Syrians believe in American disinterestedness; or England, for the people trust her sense of justice and believe in her capacity. I believe that French guardianship would be rejected for three reasons: Serious-minded men in Syria fear that the people of Syria would imitate France's less desirable qualities; they do not consider the French to be good administrators; they believe that

---

[3] As is well known, the American University of Beirut—founded by American missionaries in 1866 as the Syrian Protestant College, has been one of the main forces in the development of Arab nationalism.
[4] Howard, p. 125.

France would exploit the country for her own material and political advantage. They do not trust her. If America should be indicated as the power desired I earnestly hope that she will not decline."

This view fitted well with the Arab political position, as we know from the testimony of Emir Feisal to the peace conference at about the same time. Feisal was acting as the representative of his father, King Hussein of the Hejaz—with whom the British had negotiated on Arab independence during the war—and he was recognized as the head of the Arab delegation in Paris. On February 6, just 1 day before Bliss' letter to President Wilson, Feisal appeared before the supreme council accompanied by T. E. Lawrence who had led the Arab revolt, and by three members of the Arab delegation. The Emir indicated that the Syrians wanted complete independence, if possible, but failing this would accept mandatory status in some loose association with the other Arab states. Wilson asked whether the Arabs would prefer a single mandatory or several. Feisal refused to assume responsibility for the answer, insisting that each people must be permitted to decide. Asked what his personal opinion was, he said that he said that he was opposed to a division of the territories under different powers and wishes to have a single mandatory over Syria and Iraq, the countries in question.[5] He suggested that the people of each region be allowed to indicate to the League of Nations the amount and nature of the foreign assistance they wished, and in case of disagreement, an international commission of inquiry should be appointed.

It is important in connection with our discussion to bear in mind what Feisal's attitude toward Palestine was at this time. There were two small areas which Feisal specifically excluded from the area of Arab rule in Syria, namely, the Lebanon and Palestine. In the case of the former which had a majority of Christians he indicated that he would be satisfied with an economic union with the surrounding countries and would not insist on political union. As to Palestine, David Hunter Miller, the American historian of the peace conference, reports in My Diary [6] that Feisal said, "Palestine for its universal character be left on one side for the mutual consideration of all parties interested." This was in accord with another statement he had made in a memorandum submitted on January 1, 1919, that while the majority of the people in Palestine were Arabs, the Jews were very close to the Arabs in blood and there was no conflict of character between the two races.[7] About the same time early in January 1919 Feisal had signed the famous accord with Weizmann in which the Emir agreed to act in harmony with the Zionists at the peace conference. In this agreement Feisal gave recognition to the Balfour Declaration, consented to a separation of Palestine from the projected Arab state, welcomed large scale Jewish immigration to Palestine and close settlement of the Jews on the land, and invited the collaboration of the Jews in the development of the Arab state and of Palestine.

About a week after he had sent his letter to Wilson, Dr. Bliss made a statement before the supreme council. This was on February 13, just 1 day before President Wilson left Paris for a month's stay in the United States. Dr. Bliss explained that in view of the Anglo-French military occupation of Syria it was impossible to obtain "an accurate statement of the Syrian point of view except by an examination on the spot by commissioners authorized by the peace conference." [8] He again urged the appointment of a commission on February 26, this time before the American delegation. He was informed that the project might be promoted if Great Britain agreed, but that as yet "no decision was imminent." It appears that Robert Lansing, the American Secretary of State, whose views on foreign policy differed in general from those of Wilson, was already very skeptical about the value of the Commission.[9]

---

[5] Paul L. Hanna, British Policy in Palestine, p. 49. It was common knowledge that he favored the British who were supporting him, and that he—as well as the Syrian nationalists—hated the French cordially as the French hated him.

[6] David Hunter Miller, My Diary at the Peace Conference, 1924, vol. II.

[7] Ibid., vol. IV, pp. 297–299. He goes on to say, "In principle we are absolutely at one. Nevertheless the Arabs cannot assume the responsibility of holding level the scales in the clash of the races and religions that have, in this one province, so often involved the world in difficulties. They would wish for the effective superposition of a great trustee, so long as a representative local administration commended itself by actively promoting the material properity of the country."

[8] As quoted by Howard, p. 125 from David Hunter Miller, My Diary, vol. XIV, p. 392.

[9] Howard, p. 125, n. 8.

The matter came to a head on March 20, 1919. Wilson had now returned from the United States. On that day there was a meeting of the British, French, Italian, and American heads of state. A violent dispute broke out between Stephen Pichon, the French Foreign Minister, and Lloyd George representing the British interests. Pichon announced that the French did not wish to control Palestine and were ready to yield it to the British, but would insist on receiving a mandate for the rest of Syria including the interior regions (up to the Mosul district) as well as the coastal region. This would have been in contradiction to the British understanding with Hussein as determined in the correspondence with McMahon. While the British had made reservations with reference to the coastal section in the light of French interests, they had agreed to support an Arab state— under British guidance—in the interior parts of Syria east of Damascus, Homs, Hamma, and Aleppo. Lloyd George insisted that the League of Nations could not be used to abrogate the Hussein-McMahon understanding.

It was at this point that President Wilson intervened. In view of the dispute between the British and French, he thought that the determining factor should be the wishes of the people concerned. He espoused the proposal made by Dr. Bliss and by Feisal for an international commission of inquiry. He suggested that, "The fittest men that could be obtained should be selected to form an inter-Allied Commission to go to Syria, extending their inquiries, if they led them beyond the confines of Syria." The Commission should be composed of an equal number of American, British, French, and Italian representatives. The object of the Commission should be "to elucidate the state of opinion and the soil to be worked on by any mandatory." The commissioners should be asked to come back and inform the conference of their findings. "He would send it with carte blanche to tell the facts as they found them." He said, "If we were to send a commission of men with no previous contacts with Syria, it would, at any rate, convince the world that the conference had tried to do all it could to find the most scientific basis possible for a settlement." [10]

Lloyd George at first agreed wholeheartedly: Clemenceau indicated that he agreed in principle, but the wily old "Tiger" added that the investigation should not be confined to Syria but should include Palestine, Mesopotamia, Armenia, and other parts of the Ottoman Empire. Lloyd George said that he had no objection, but his enthusiasm seemed to dampen with the mention of Mesopotamia, where the British were having their own troubles. Within the next few days Wilson drew up the terms of reference for the proposed Commission, and these were formally approved by the supreme council on March 25. The instructions to the Commission were: "To visit the Near East and to become as fully acquainted as possible with the state of public opinion and with the social, economic, and political conditions of the region, and to form an opinion concerning such a division of territory and assignment of mandates which would be 'most likely to promote the order, peace, and development of those peoples and countries'." [11]

THE CHANGE FROM AN INTERALLIED TO AN AMERICAN COMMISSION

However, when the experts on eastern questions were consulted, they expressed the view that "the presence of such a body in Syria would be a cause for intrigue and unrest." [12] The French soon placed difficulties in the way of constituting the Commission; they failed to appoint their members and indicated that they would not participate in an investigation, the main purpose of which, it now appeared, was to expose the anti-French feeling in Syria. The British were uncertain in their view. Sir Edmund Allenby, the commander in chief of the British forces in the east strongly urged British participation. He had appointed a very able group—as commissioners: Sir Henry McMahon, former High Commissioner in Egypt, and Commander David Hogarth, a distinguished authority on the Near and Middle East, associated with the Arab bureau in Cairo; and as secretary; Prof. Arnold J. Toynbee, the internationally renowned historian. T. E. Lawrence supported the idea for an international commission concerning which Feisal was enthusiastic, but he appears to have made sure first that the United States would not accept a mandate over the Arab territories in case the Arabs voted for this. [13] In the end, the British section of the Commission was

---

[10] Quotations in this paragraph are from Howard, p. 126, derived from Baker, Woodrow Wilson and the War Settlement, vol. III, document 1, pp. 16–19; David Lloyd George, Memoirs of the Peace Conference, vol. II, pp. 692–695.

[11] Howard, pp. 126–127.

[12] Hanna, p. 53, based on Miller, My Diary, vol. VII, pp. 169–170.

[13] In David Garnett, Editor, The Letters of T. E. Lawrence, see p. 275 (see p. 10). "Notes of a conversation between Colonel House and Emir Feisal." Since it was certain that Syria would not vote for a French mandate, the British had nothing to lose since even if they received second choice, the mandate would fall to them.

not sent, perhaps because His Majesty's Government did not wish to appear as partners in an anti-French move, or because if they had participated in the investigation they could hardly have avoided a visit of the Commission to Mesopotamia, for which they evidently were not anxious.

The Commission thus dwindled down to the American section, which had been quickly appointed. President Wilson chose Mr. Charles R. Crane and Dr. Henry C. King as the Commissioners responsible for the recommendations. Mr. Crane was a Chicago manufacturer [14] who had been a member of the American mission to Russia in 1917. Dr. King was president of Oberlin College and had directed the religious work at the Y. M. C. A. in France during the war. Besides, the Commission had three experts associated with it: Professor Albert H. Lybyer, a member of the Balkan section of the American delegation, whose work had recently terminated at Paris and who had applied as secretary to the American group; later he became the general technical adviser. On the recommendation of Prof. W. L. Westermann, chief of the Western Asia Division of the American Commission to Negotiate Peace, Dr. George L. Montgomery was appointed technical adviser for the northern regions of Turkey and Capt. William Yale as technical adviser for the southern regions of Turkey.[15] Lybyer, Montgomery and Yale were acquainted with the Near East through residence and study.

For months there was doubt whether the American section would go after all. In the middle of April when the Americans had planned to be off to Syria, a crisis was reached. At that time it was already clear that the French were opposing the Commission and that the British were doubtful. While Dr. King, Mr. Crane, and Professor Lybyer still believed that it would be desirable to send the American group even if the British and French would not participate, Professor Westermann now "held that a commission would do a great deal of harm, without achieving anything constructive or adding to the information already available in Paris itself." [16] When the American Commission to Negotiate Peace met on April 18, they agreed to abandon the idea of sending the investigating body to the Near East. Dr. King tried to see President Wilson, but failed and planned to return to America, while Crane intended to go to Constantinople with Lybyer as private secretary.

In the early part of May, matters looked brighter for the King-Crane Commission. On May 1, the Commission sent a memorandum signed by all five members to President Wilson regarding the dangers of permitting a "selfish exploitation of the Ottoman Empire." This memorandum, which may be regarded as the first report of the King-Crane Commission expressed the belief: "That the unity of Asia Minor at least and perhaps the entire Ottoman Empire should be preserved under some kind of mandatory system, though the rights of nationalities should be recognized and due weight should be given to the interests of Great Britain, France, and Italy." [17] Concretely, the following proposals were made: (1) British mandates in Mesopotamia and Palestine; (2) recognition of King Hussein as king of the Hejaz; (3) Great Britain's general supervision of Arabia, with maintenance of the "open door"; (4) possible acceptance of a "liberally interpreted" French mandate over Syria, though this was not based on the desires of the Syrians; (5) a general American mandate in the non-Arabic portions of the Ottoman Empire, with subsidiary special mandates for Armenia, Anatolia, and a Constantinopolitan state.

By the middle of May the prospects of the Commission again took a turn for the worse. While Admiral Mark Bristol, the American High Commissioner in Constantinople, strongly urged the sending of the Commission, President Caleb F. Gates, of Robert College, Constantinople, equally well informed, did not regard the investigation necessary and stressed the importance of keeping the Ottoman Empire intact under an American or British mandate. On May 6, Dr. King wrote to Colonel House, who was favorable to the Commission, insisting that pressure be brought to bear on the French to appoint their representatives. However, 2 days later, Prof. Felix Frankfurter, who was present in Paris with the Zionist delegation, wrote to Wilson expressing his apprehensions lest the appointment of the Interallied Commission would postpone the Near Eastern settlement beyond Wilson's stay in Paris, and that this would lead to disposition of the Palestine problem in a manner contradictory to the Balfour Declaration. Wilson replied a few days later reassuring Frankfurter on his adherence to the Balfour Declaration, but he said nothing about refraining from sending the Commission to Syria.

[14] He was a vice president of the Crane Co. of Chicago, manufacturers of valves and fittings.
[15] The Commission included two other members, Capt. Donald M. Brodie, who was chosen to act as secretary, and Laurence Moore, who was the business manager.
[16] Howard, p. 128.
[17] Ibid., p. 130; also footnote 21.

However, the May crisis also passed. On May 20 Colonel House received an urgent communication from the Hejaz delegation expressing determined opposition to any settlement of the Near Eastern problem without consulting the Arabs, and urged the sending of an investigating commission. Colonel House forwarded the letter to Wilson, adding that "it was something of a scandal that this Commission had not already gone to Syria as promised the Arabs." House furthermore informed Dr. King that he had suggested that the American group be sent immediately "regardless of the French and English." [18] Two days later Emir Feisal cabled Wilson stating that on his arrival in Syria he had "found everybody anxiously awaiting the arrival of the Commission." [19] On the same day, Dr. King, Mr. Crane, and Professor Westermann called on the President, and Wilson informed them of his conviction that the investigation should be made. The Commission left a few days later. Its official title was "American Section of the International Commission on Mandates in Turkey." [20] The American delegation at Paris generally referred to it as the Crane-King Commission. It is more often referred to as the King-Crane Commission.

THE WORK AND CONCLUSIONS OF THE KING-CRANE COMMISSION

Mr. Crane left for Constantinople on May 25 and was followed by other members of the Commission a few days later. Traveling by way of Constantinople where they stopped for a consultation with Admiral Bristol and other American officials, the King-Crane Commission proceeded almost immediately to Palestine, arriving there on June 10, 1919. They remained in Palestine and Syria until July 21. During these 6 weeks they visited some 40 towns and rural communities and interviewed a large number of delegations. Representatives from some 1,500 villages appeared before them and 1,863 petitions were received

On June 12, 2 days after their arrival, the Commissioners responsible for the report, Mr. Crane and Dr. King, sent an alarming telegram to President Wilson expressing doubt whether "any British or American official here believes it is possible to carry out the Zionist program except through the support of a large army." [21] On July 2, the Syrian National Congress was held at Damascus in which protest was made against the mandate system which the peace conference had prescribed for the near eastern countries, but expressing the view that failing complete independence the Syrians were willing to accept the guidance of America or Great Britain. This Congress voted for a unified Syria, including Lebanon and Palestine, and vehemently opposed "the Zionist pretentions to create a Jewish commonwealth in Palestine" which they considered the southern part of their country. The Congress also expressed itself against Jewish immigration to any part of Syria, including Palestine. As if vibrating in complete accord with the resolutions of the Syrian National Congress, the two Commissioners, now joined by Professor Lybyer, sent another cable to the President from Beirut describing the "unexpectedly strong expressions of national feeling" which they had met, involving firm opposition to French supervision and to the Zionist plans for a separate Palestine.

Neither Dr. Montgomery nor Captain Yale, the two experts best acquainted with the situation in the Near East, signed this telegram. Indeed, ever since the group had come to Palestine, these two experts had begun to disagree with the methods followed by King and Crane in their investigation and with the conclusions shaping themselves in the minds of the two lay members of the Commission and of Professor Lybyer. On July 26, therefore, Montgomery and Yale submitted separate memoranda stating their own conclusions. Montgomery recommended the following: (a) Palestine be separate from Syria and placed under a British mandate; (b) Mount Lebanon be made autonomous under a French mandate; (c) Syria proper be placed under a joint Anglo-French mandate with Feisal as prince. Captain Yale, who was particularly expert on these parts of the Ottoman Empire, doubted the genuine character of Arab or Syrian nationalism and suggested the following plan: (a) Palestine be separated from Syria under a British mandate and constituted as a Jewish national home; (b) Mount Lebanon should be made autonomous; (c) Damascus, Homs, Hama, Tripoli, and Latakia to be united under Feisal with either a British, French, or joint Anglo-French

---

[18] Howard, p. 131.
[19] Ibid.
[20] Antonius, p. 295.
[21] Howards, p. 133.

mandate.[22] Neither of the experts maintained that their plans were merely the product of the wishes of Palestine or Syria, but they offered them as practical working solutions, with due consideration of the various interests involved. Neither Yale nor Montgomery, moreover, considered that an American mandate was a practical proposal.

The official report of the Commission was drafted in Constantinople by Dr. King and Professor Lybyer. The plan which they formulated appears, however, to have been that of Mr. Crane, who was the most forceful member of the Commission.[23] The report,[24] which was completed by August 21, recommended a single mandate for a united Syria including the Lebanon and Palestine. This united Syria should be assigned, in accordance with the wishes of the majority of the people, to the United States, and failing American acceptance, to Great Britain, but in no circumstances should the mandate be given to France. A constitutional monarchy under the rule of Emir Feisal was recommended as the form "naturally adapted to the Arabs, with their long training under tribal traditions and with their traditional respect for their chiefs." The mandate should have a limited term, the time of expiration to be determined by the League of Nations. The mandatory should make itself responsible for the development of economic undertakings and educational institutions designed to promote the well-being and development of the Syrian people. One of the special functions of the mandatory administration would be education for citizenship in a democratic state and for the development of a sound national spirit. The report says: "This systematic cultivation of national spirit is particularly required in a country like Syria, which has only recently come to self-consciousness." [25]

The report gave much attention to the question of Zionism. The Commissioners reecho anti-Zionist allegations current at the time under the military administration, e. g., that the Jews intended to dispossess the non-Jewish inhabitants of Palestine by buying up the land; that to force Jewish immigration on a country where nine-tenths of its population were opposed, would be a gross violation of the principle of self-determination; that a military force of not less than 50,000 would be required to initiate the Zionist program.[26] In addition to these objections, the Commissioners added their own doubts which smack somewhat of anti-Semitism: It seemed to them a matter of doubt whether the "Jews could possibly seem to either Christians or Moslems proper guardians of the holy places, or custodians of the Holy Land as a whole. * * * The reason is this: The places which are most sacred to Christians—those having to do with Jesus—and which are also sacred to Moslems, are not only not sacred to Jews, but abhorrent to them. It is simply impossible under those circumstances, for Moslems and Christians to feel satisfied to have these places in Jewish hands, or under the custody of Jews." [27] They expressed extreme opposition not only to the idea of making Palestine a Jewish State, but advised that "Jewish immigration should be definitely limited."

The report of the Commission was filed with the American delegation in Paris on August 28. Mr. Crane cabled the gist of the official recommendations to Wilson 2 days later, and on September 27, Captain Brodie, the Secretary of the Commission, transmitted the full text so the White House. After the departure of Wilson from Paris, the American Commission to Negotiate Peace was left without authority to act on the King-Crane document or other reports that had been submitted to them. On November 26, the Commission turned to Washington with a request for guidance. They asked how far the American Government was prepared to adopt the recommendations of the Crane-King and Harbord reports; [28] whether the secret agreements made by the powers for the partition of

[22] Later in the year, during the month of October, Captain Yale submitted to the peace conference a revised version of this plan which, according to him, had the approval of T. E. Lawrence and of Nuri Said and Rastun Haidar who were members of the Arab delegation. The plan fell through because after President Wilson's departure no one had authority to make decisions or take action. David Garnett remarks: "It was remarkable position. All the parties to a deadlock were prepared to agree to a solution which had been formulated—provided it were imposed upon them from outside. But the Americans were not prepared to impose anything on any of them." (Letters of T. E. Lawrence, p. 288).

[23] Sir Ronald Storrs (Orientations, p. 417) remarks: "Few that had the privilege of meeting Dr. King and of knowing the surviving Commissioner will be disposed to doubt that, though the hands that signed their report were the hands of King-Crane, the voice was the voice of Crane."

[24] Only the recommendations on Syria, which the Commission visited, are here given. There were, also recommendations on Mesopotamia, Armenia, and on the Greek claims.

[25] Antonius, op. cit. pp. 443–444.

[26] As a matter of fact a smaller military force was required in Palestine than in Syria or Iraq. During the period from 1922, when the mandate was approved by the League of Nations, until 1929, when the Wailing Wall disturbances broke out, there was peace in Palestine, and the military forces were practically withdrawn. The Wailing Wall disturbances were instigated by the Mufti of Jerusalem through incitement on religious grounds.

[27] Antonius, p. 450. These remarks were not only insidious but gratuitous—in view of the fact that in none of the plans was there any idea of Jewish custody of the holy places.

[28] This was a report on Anatolia and Armenia.

Turkey would be recognized by the United States; whether the United States was prepared to provide money or troops necessary to prevent the territorial and political plans involved in the secret agreements from being carried out; whether the United States would be prepared to cooperate in the international control of those parts of Turkey which were not placed under mandate. There was no reply to these requests, unless the withdrawal of the last remnant of the American delegation from Paris in December 1919 is to be considered a reply. The King-Crane report had no affect whatsoever on the subsequent negotitations either with reference to Syria or any other parts of the Ottoman Empire.

COMMENTS AND EVALUATION

The publicized versions of the King-Crane recommendations [29] fail to mention the fact that the two experts on the Commission best acquainted with the situation in the Near East, disagreed with the methods of investigation as well as with the conclusions. Both Dr. Montgomery and Captain Yale believed that Palestine should be separated from Syria under a British mandate. Captain Yale who was assigned to the southern portions of the Turkish Empire, in which Palestine was included, made the explicit recommendation "that the Zionists should be permitted to carry out their plans." [30] Professor Lybyer who agreed with the lay heads of the Commission was, it appears better acquainted with the Balkans than with the Arab countries. It may not be irrelevant to point out, moreover, that he had originally applied for the position of Secretary in the American group directly, before W. L. Westermann, Chief of the Turkish Division, had secured the appointment of Montgomery and Yale. Technically, the responsibility for the report lay with the two Commissioners, and it was their privilege to accept or reject the advice of the experts. But failure to bring out the fact that there were dissenting views has served to create a false impression as to the nature of the King-Crane recommendations.

No doubt the King-Crane Commission's report reflected the majority view of organized political opinion in Syria. The main conclusion that the Syrian nationalists wanted a united Syria including the Lebanon and Palestine under Feisal and were opposed to French rule and Zionist aspirations was well known to everyone concerned and did not require an investigation. The Commissioners were no doubt sincere and well-meaning, but their investigation need not be regarded as a scientific and objective study. The character of the investigation has the earmarks of an organized piece of political propaganda in which the Commissioners may have been the unwitting collaborators. The conclusions of the Commission coincided with the view expressed by Dr. Howard Bliss when he proposed the appointment of the international commission. They were identical with the program of the extreme Syrian nationalists and with the views of the Christian-Moslem society in Palestine. The activities of the Commission, moreover, were remarkably well-timed with the Syrian Congress at Damascus.

The fact that Mr. Crane and Dr. King were prepared to send an extreme anti-Zionist telegram to Wilson 2 days after their arrival, repeating verbatim the well-known views of certain military officers in Palestine, hardly testifies to patience in investigation. The Commission visited a town a day; they did not know the language of the country; the delegations are said to have represented 1,500 villages. In the light of these facts it is hard to believe that the Commissioners could have formed any independent idea as to the prevalent views. The receipt of 1,863 petitions would hardly impress anyone who has lived in the Near East and knows that such petitions are obtained there even more easily than in countries more highly literate where they are not generally regarded as scientific evidence of the state of affairs. At Jerusalem 8 out of the 23 of the anti-Zionist petitions were practically identical in wording; in one case a printed form of the standard program for independence was handed in as a petition and the Commissioners say in their report, "doubtless other printed copies had been models for many of the petitions." The Commissioners also point out that the proportion of petitions from the different religious communities did not correspond with the numerical strength of the communities, particularly in the oral requests. The Christian delegations in Palestine outnumbered the Moslem delegations by three to one, although the Moslems were eight times as many in the population.

John de Vere Loder in commenting on the situation in the Middle East at this time says of the King-Crane Commission: "Attention was diverted for the moment from incitation to acts of mutual hostility to efforts to create a good

[29] For instance, see Antonius, The Arab Awakening.
[30] David Garnett, editor The Letters of T. E. Lawrence, p. 286.

impression, and the various sections of the community devoted themselves during the 4 months of the Commission's visit to a course of unlimited intrigue." [31] He continues as follows:

"It would have been difficult enough for the Commission to have achieved its object even had all concerned cooperated toward the discovery of a satisfactory solution. Under the conditions which existed it is not surprising that the Commission was somewhat baffled. The general conclusion of its report was that local opinion favoured independence without foreign control, but was prepared to accept a minimum of foreign assistance. Broadly speaking, the Christian communities in the Lebanon expressed themselves in favour of a French Mandate and the rest of the population in favour of an American or British Mandate, but it is not improbable tht considerations other than such as would have guided frank and free declarations influenced some of these decisions. The French and the Sherifians [32] openly accused each other of putting unfair pressure on those who did not agree with their respective contentions. The Damascus administration was alleged to have used the censorship to suppress friendly references to France and to have picketed the offices of the Commission for the purpose of intimidating the delegations of the Christian communities. On the other hand, the French were supposed to be using equally unjustifiable if less crude means of obtaining the same end in Beirout and the neighbourhood. On one point only does there appear to have been anything like unanimity, and that was in the demand for an integral Syria including Palestine, but not necessarily excluding special local administrations for certain areas."

To give due credit to the Commissioners, it should be stated that they admitted the shortcomings of their investigation. In a special supplement to their report, pointedly entitled "For the Use of Americans Only," they give instances of attempts at pressure on the part of the French, the British, and the Arabs to influence the witnesses. In the body of the report they said: "We were not blind to the fact that there was considerable propaganda; that often much pressure was put upon individuals and groups; that sometimes delegations were prevented from reaching the Commission; and that the representative authority of many petitions was questionable. But the Commission believes that these anomalous elements in the petitions tend to cancel one another when the whole country is taken into account, and that, as in the composite photograph, certain great, common emphases are unmistakable." [33] The Commission, however, does not give any inkling of what "these anomalous elements" were; in a question as complex as this it is obviously important to know the nature of divergent opinions as well as of the single majority view. The report also fails to express the reason for the difference between the opinion of the Syrian Congress and the compromise view expressed by Feisal in Paris when he agreed to autonomy for Christian Lebanon and recognized the validity of Zionist aspirations in Palestine.

With all this, the amazing thing is that the figures which are given in the full report of the Commission do not correspond wholly with recommendations made by the King-Crane Commission. According to the report, the impression is given that the great majority of the Arabs in Syria and Palestine voted for an American mandate, failing which they were ready to accept a British mandate. The truth is that on the question of a mandate the Americans received an insignificant number of votes. Of the total of 1,863 petitions, 271 indicated that they were ready to accept a Franch mandate (14.52 percent); 66 were for a British mandate (3.33 percent); 57 indicated an American mandate (3.05 percent). The Americans were first choice when a different question was asked, i. e., whose "assistance" would be preferred. In this case, 1,064 petitions (57 percent) indicated they were ready to accept American "assistance" as their first choice; 1,032 petitions (55.3 percent) indicated Great Britain as second choice, and only 70 petitions (3.75 percent) indicated that they wished to have French assistance. What the analysis of the petitions seems to indicate is the following: The petitioners did not wish to have any mandate; they were for an independent Syria. But if they had to take a mandate, a larger number wanted to have a French mandate than either a British or an American, although the total number voting for mandates was small. The preferred solution was an independent state with "assistance" from one of the European powers. In this the Arabs were pretty nearly equally

[31] John de Vere Loder, The Truth About Mesopotamia, Palestine, and Syria, London, 1923, p. 36.
[32] The term "Sherifians" refers to the supporters of Feisal, son of Hussein, Sherif of Mecca, the title by which he was generally known before he became King of the Hejaz.
[33] Quoted from Howard, p. 133.

divided between the British and the Americans, with the latter having somewhat the advantage.[34]

However, disregarding the petitions which are in any case worthless from the scientific point of view, and granting that the King-Crane recommendations truly reflected the opinion of the greater part of politically minded Syrians an'd Palestinians, and furthermore assuming that the general attitude of the large masses in Palestine, illiterate and inarticulate, was in harmony with the views of their self-appointed leaders, the question still remains whether in the circumstances in the Near East the wishes of the majority of the population could at the time be taken as the sole and determining factor. In all of the discussions at Paris, even in accordance with the view of President Wilson, the wishes of the peoples concerned were regarded as one factor, not the only factor. In their first memorandum to President Wilson in Paris the King-Crane Commission, then acting unanimously, recognized that there were other considerations, and it is clear that when Wilson agreed to send the commission, he assumed that the Balfour declaration would be honored.

The main fault of that part of the King-Crane report which deals with Palestine does not lie in its much criticized procedures, however inadequate these may have been. It is their whole approach ot the problem of Zionism that is open to question. Since the commission was acting as an international agency, an impartial and objective approach would have required their looking at Palestine in its international framework, giving consideration to the Jewish interest, along with the other claims. The Commissioners responsible for the report seemed to forget that the Allied Nations, whom they supposedly represented, had, after much discussion over a period of years, undertaken definite commitments with reference to the establishment of a Jewish national home in Palestine which could not in honor and in justice be evaded. The report was a partial report in the literal sense, that it gave due consideration to only one part of the issue.

Furthermore—and this is really the main point—The King-Crane Commission's proposals were unworkable and self-contradictory in the light of the practical situation at the time. The preferred solution was that the United States should undertake the mandate for Syria and Palestine. This was a fruitless recommendation since the United States was not ready to accept the mandate—as was fairly well established at the time that the Commission made its report. But even if the United States had been prepared to undertake the mandate, the problem of reconciling the Arab demand for complete self-determination with the promise of the Balfour Declaration would have stood with its difficulties. Only a few weeks prior to the appointment of the Commission, Wilson had made his famous statement saying, "I am persuaded that the Allied Nations, with the fullest concurrence of our Government and people, are agreed that in Palestine shall be laid the foundations of the Jewish Commonwealth." Indeed the American understanding of the Balfour Declaration at this time was, if anything, more favorable to the Zionist interpretation than that of cautious British opinion. The British on their part, who were the second choice, certainly could not accept the mandate without the Balfour Declaration, since it was the issuance of the Balfour Declaration which had given them a claim to the mandate for Palestine.

The recommendations of the King-Crane Commission were essentially irresponsible since they made recommendations that no one would, or could, carry out. The major effect was calculated to weaken the French position and to strengthen the hand of Great Britain, but could not lead to any constructive solution. This is well brought out in the comment made by Prof. William Earnest Hocking. He says: [35]

"But in Syria, the effect was not nil. Such an enquiry has a logic which works in spite of itself. If men are offered a choice of supervisors, it becomes evident that they are to have supervisors. They may express their preference for independence; and do so in dominant numbers. But they are prepared for something less. But again, if they are offered a choice of supervisors, it is certainly implied that they have a choice, that the possibilities set before them are not mythical. If it is already determined that France is to govern here, and Britain there,

[34] With reference to this advantage, Sir Ronald Storrs (Orientations, p. 417) says as follows: "When it is remembered that to the anticipating Eastern mind the nationality of the Commission (apart from the known wealth and rumored liberalism of America) predetermined that of the Mandatory, it will be understood that these findings were more favorable to Great Britain than would be gathered from a literal reading of their text."

[35] William Earnest Hocking, The Spirit of World Politics, The MacMillan Company, New York, 1932, p. 255. Professor Hocking's comment is all the more interesting in view of his sympathy with the Arab point of view.

it is misleading to ask people to choose between them, or between them and others. If it is not certain that the United States will accept a mandate in those regions, it is misleading to present the United States as one of the possible advisers. Unless there is some possibility that those choices shall count, the work of such an enquiry as that of the King-Crane Commission can hardly be other than mischievous.

"In the event, the work of the Commission, not discovering that France was the spontaneous choice of inner Syria, added materially to the difficulties of France in Syria. It was, so far, mischievous.

"Whether the blame must rest on Wilson for sending the bootless Commission, or on France for insisting on the obtaining which her professions had discountenanced, may remain open."

That the late George Antonius—outstanding Arab protagonist, whose book is affectionately dedicated to Mr. Crane, "aptly nicknamed Harun-al-Rashid"— should have characterized the report as a "wholly objective analysis" [36] is altogether understandable. It is, however, surprising in the light of the facts which he presents that Professor Howard should come to the conclusion that by appointing the King-Crane Commission "President Wilson made a genuinely challenging contribution to the technique of peace making," [37] which should serve as a precedent for the future. In support of his view as to the value of commissions which examine situations on the spot, Professor Howard points to the British commissions which had been sent out to various regions in the Empire.

It would appear, however, that the differences between the type of commission represented by the King-Crane investigation and the British commissions are more striking than are the similarities. When the British intended to appoint their section of the Inter-Allied Commission they chose as the responsible heads Sir Henry McMahon and Captain Hogarth who were not only experts in Near Eastern affairs, but who had been principals in previous negotiations with the Arabs. They were, moreover, officers responsible to the British Government. How different is this from Wilson's notion of sending "men with no previous contact with Syria." There is, of course, much to be said for the approach of the layman who may view the situation with a fresh outlook, but obviously where the opinion is not mingled with the knowledge of the expert, it is the more likely to be influenced by pressure groups and propaganda. Nor in other respects was there any resemblance between the methods of the King-Crane Commission and those usually followed in appointing British commissions. The British commissions are appointed by well worked out procedures under legal authority. The King-Crane Commission was a personal appointment by the President as a result of pressure from the Arab side—despite strong differences of opinion concerning the value of such a commission. The main point, however, is that no one regards the British commissions as being purely scientific investigations, even though they frequently develop a considerable amount of objective data. The commissions do not pretend to be concerned only or mainly with the welfare of native inhabitants; their purpose is to solve problems that have arisen and their main purpose is to enable His Majesty's Government to administer territories under their control with the least amount of friction. Their purpose is practical, and they do not indulge in recommendations which are obviously unworkable in the first instance.

A commission appointed to study the social, economic, and political conditions of the Near East could certainly make a contribution to the solution of the postwar problems, if it were conducted in a scientific spirit, under clear terms of political reference. It is obvious that whatever of science and expert knowledge the King-Crane Commission had at its disposal was made secondary to political wishful thinking. It cannot be seriously maintained that the hasty tour of the King-Crane Commission through Palestine during the summer of 1919 constituted an objective analysis of the situation which confronted the peace conference at the time, or that the procedure followed in its appointment and its method of investigation could possibly do anything but harm in the future consideration of the problem.

Mr. HELLER. The King-Crane Commission reported to Mr. Wilson, as I recall, in 1919. It was after the report was made that Mr. Wilson went to Paris and helped in the incorporation of the Balfour Federation into the policy of 52 nations. Therefore, the King-Crane report, was

[36] The Arab Awakening, p. 296.
[37] Op. cit., p. 146.

only one expression of people who had a special point of view and is in contrast to all the other material on this subject that is available. It is very difficult to find anything in which no factors have to be differentiated from the rest.

One of the things which I think troubles my friends is the establishment of a commonwealth in Palestine which will not somehow impair rights in this country. I think the assurance ought to be given to our friends, that no one proposes citizenship or political fealty on the part of any one else who lives anywhere else in the world.

There was an attempt in 1918 and 1919 to restore Czechoslovakia as a free state in which many sections participated in Chicago and other parts of the country.

There is simply a belief on the part of a great number of Jews that this will be for those who want a new free life. There is no political aspiration in it for themselves. They will have a share in its future attainment, but it does not signify their political position will be impaired.

Equally, Mr. Chairman and ladies and gentlemen, I feel to call this a philosophy of defeatism is an inversion of the facts. As I shall try to explain in a moment this is quite the contrary to the fact.

We favor this resolution because of the great human project which is behind it.

I would like to call once more to the attention of the committee what these gentlemen favor is not merely the limitation of the resolution which is now before this committee but also the cancelation of the promises that have been made to the Jewish people. The discussion by Mr. Wright here was straight to the point.

The Balfour Declaration, as interpreted by Mr. Lloyd George, by Mr. Churchill at the time before he became Foreign Secretary, and numerous other Great Britons like Lord Robert Cecil will prove it was intended to set up in Palestine a majority of Jews by the facilitation of immigration until a point when they could constitute a self-governing community. This is a reaffirmation of that hope. It does involve making explicit what was not before. Its original meaning seems to be quite clear as to national ambitions so that we should like to see whatever documents come out of this war much clearer in their significance in regard to Palestine.

I think one of the most important questions raised before this committee is the contention as to transporting Jews to Palestine that the gates be opened to them of that country, holding out the hope when the proper moment arrives they shall become self-governing as every other people on earth wish to become. Our friends contend that Jews in lands of persecution should stay where they are after the war. I should like to deal with that for a moment because I think that is important. First of all, if we accepted that principle as a generalization then there would be no United States of America. Our forefathers should have stayed where they were in England, Holland, or in France, and continued to fight for the time when there should have been full democratic principles there.

Every thoughtful person distinguishes between short-time and long-time objectives. Some day there will be complete democracy and equality all over the world. I regret to say that is not going to be in our time. I do not believe it is even going to be after the war, because, Mr. Chairman, we have before us the example of the last war, as I think has been said, when clauses were written into the treaties to achieve precisely the same objective. Unfortunately, it proved futile. In the case of some countries like Poland the ink was hardly dry before pogroms were in progress, taking out from under the Jewish community the very basis for its very precarious existence. We are afraid, and in fact we feel confident, this is a fear which cannot be overlooked with the long experience that is behind it.

There is going to be a tremendous pressure to insist that this problem has to be solved in these countries, which is fearfully inhuman, as it would have been to say to the Pilgrim Fathers: Stay in England rather than to seek a refuge on the rock-bound coast of New England.

We want the chance for a new life for these people. If we could have gotten them out in Palestine, if the gates had been wide open from 1922 to 1939 I think there would have been a million or two Jews there now who would be alive, whereas now they lie in graves into which they have been thrown from starvation, gas, and machinegun bullets.

I trust, therefore, ladies and gentlemen and Mr. Chairman, that the committee will face the facts, and that it will not let itself be confused by ideological discussions. It will bear in mind the overwhelming majority of Jews of this country I think, those who sympathize with their brothers abroad, feel that this is one thing that already stands upon the statutes of the world, and one which must be a part of any democratic charter that will come out of this.

Last of all, I have with me a book compiled from the addresses of Mr. Justice Louis D. Brandeis, who, I think it may be admitted, was one of the foremost Americans of our day, and who gave great service to his country and his people. Mr. Brandeis wrote repeatedly some of the very things to which you have been listening and spoke of the fear of some American Jews and the distinction made between Americanism and Jewish nationalism. If I may have the right, Mr. Chairman, I should like to put into the record also these addresses of Mr. Brandeis in the sections which I have marked.

Chairman BLOOM. How much is it?

Mr. HELLER. There are not more than about 10 paragraphs included in here.

Mrs. ROGERS. Mr. Chairman, may I ask a question at that point?

Chairman BLOOM. Without objection it is so ordered.

(The excerpts above referred to in the book entitled "Brandeis on Zionism, by Louis D. Brandeis," are as follows:)

(P. 24–25:) Zionism seeks to establish in Palestine, for such Jews as choose to go and remain there, and for their descendents, a legally secured home, where they may live together and lead a Jewish life, where they may expect ultimately to constitute a majority of the population, and may look forward to what we should call home rule. The Zionists seek to establish this home in Palestine because they are convinced that the undying longing of Jews for Palestine is a fact of deepest significance; that it is a manifestation in the struggle for existence by an ancient people which has established its right to live, a people whose 3,000 years of civilization has produced a faith, culture, and individuality which enable it to contribute largely in the future, as it has in the past, to the advance of civilization; and that it is a right not merely but a duty of the Jewish nationality to survive and develop. They believe that only in Palestine can Jewish life be fully protected from the forces of distintegration; that there alone can the Jewish spirit reach its full and natural development; and that by securing for those Jews who wish to settle there the opportunity to do so, not only those Jews, but all other Jews will be benefited, and that the long-perplexing Jewism problem will, at last, find solution.

(P. 28:) Let no American imagine that Zionism is inconsistent with patriotism. Multiple loyalties are objectionable only if they are inconsistent. A man is a better citizen of the United States for being also a loyal citizen of his State and of his city; for being loyal to his family, and to his profession or trade; for being loyal to his college or his lodge.   Every Irish American who contributed toward advancing home rule was a better American for the sacrifice he made.   Every American Jew who aids in advancing the Jewish settlement in Palestine, though he feels that neither he nor his descendants will ever live there, will likewise be a better man and a better American for doing so.

(P. 29:) Indeed, loyalty to America demands rather that each American Jew become a Zionist.   For only through the ennobling effect of its strivings can we develop the best that is in us and give to this country the full benefit of our great inheritance.   The Jewish spirit, so long preserved, the character developed by so many centuries of sacrifice, should be preserved and developed further, so that in America, as elsewhere, the sons of the race may in future live lives and do deeds worthy of their ancestors.

(P. 33–34:) Our fellow Americans are infused with a high and generous spirit, which insures approval of our struggle to ennoble, liberate, and otherwise improve the condition of an important part of the human race, and their innate manliness makes them sympathize particularly with our efforts at self-help.   America's detachment from the old world problem relieves us from suspicions and embarrassments frequently attending the activities of Jews of rival European countries.   And a conflict between American interests or ambitions and Jewish aims is not conceivable.   Our loyalty to America can never be questioned.

Chairman BLOOM. Go ahead, Mrs. Rogers.

Mrs. ROGERS. Did Mr. Justice Brandeis speak of a Jewish commonwealth?

Mr. HELLER. Yes, repeatedly.   He was strongly of the opinion that no project could succeed unless it moved toward this goal.

Chairman BLOOM. Continue, Rabbi.   Is that all?

Mr. HELLER. Mr. Chairman, only this: I just want to thank the committee for the splendid friendliness and open-mindedness which characterize them, and thank them for the opportunity of speaking what is in my heart, which is a part of my religion as a Jew and a part of my belief for that justice and that helpfulness which is part of the justice of America.

Chairman BLOOM. Mr. McMurray.

Mr. McMURRAY. No questions.   I would like to thank Rabbi Heller for giving us a very clear picture of this situation and clearing up in my mind a good many questions that have been raised.

That is all, Mr. Chairman.

Chairman BLOOM. Mrs. Rogers.

Mrs. ROGERS. Rabbi, I am very much interested in your very able statement.   At the Zionists' meetings you have taken up always the advisability of having this resolution passed at this time during the war?

Mr. HELLER. Yes.

Mrs. ROGERS. You analyzed that?

Mr. HELLER. Yes.

Mrs. ROGERS. And went into that very fully?

Mr. HELLER. This will be of very great value when the House and Senate come to consider the treaties to be made and when the policy of the United Nations comes to be made.   It will be quite a step toward the establishment of world peace.

Mrs. ROGERS. Did you work upon the provisions of your resolution in your conferences to be exact?

Mr. HELLER. The resolution as read is an expression in more concise form than many of the resolutions adopted by many groups.

Mrs. ROGERS. But you did not pass upon it?

Mr. HELLER. No.

Chairman BLOOM. This was not introduced until long after their conference.

Mrs. ROGERS. Yes, I recall how far you went on it.

Mr. HELLER. I do not want to leave the impression that it has been drawn up without plenty of discussion with Mr. Wright and Mr. Compton, who have submitted it to the Committee on Foreign Affairs as their presentation.

Mrs. ROGERS. Rabbi, I would like to know your opinion of a good Christian. You said you wished there were better Christians.

Chairman BLOOM. The Chair will rule that out because somebody may ask what a good Jew is.

Mr. Chiperfield.

Mr. CHIPERFIELD. I have no questions. Thank you.

Chairman BLOOM. Mr. Vorys.

Mr. VORYS. Not at this time.

Chairman BLOOM. Mr. Wright.

Mr. WRIGHT. I think it would be helpful, Rabbi, if you would compile from the speeches of those interested at the time in the Balfour Declaration, in the mandate, and also in the convention between the United States and Great Britain the expressions of opinion by those statesmen who explained the phrase "national home." I got a little bit snarled up in my quotation, as pointed out by my brother on the right, because I was not too well acquainted with those speeches.

Mr. HELLER. Is it permitted to ask for an interruption on the part of the witness?

Mr. WRIGHT. Surely.

Mr. HELLER. I would like to say to Mr. Wright and to the committee that at the American Jewish Conference a statement was read, which was made yesterday by Mr. Robert Szold, and it is part of the stenographic record, compiling a complete record in regard to using the term "national commonwealth." This will give you the very information you ask.

Mr. WRIGHT. May I ask a question of the chairman? If that is not too long, I ask that it be incorporated in the record because the question was raised that where a national homeland is stated that a Jewish commonwealth was meant. I think that is important.

Chairman BLOOM. Without objection, it will be inserted in the record.

(The statement referred to is as follows:)

(Must be secured from The American Jewish Conference, 41 East 42nd St., N. Y. City.)

Mr. WRIGHT. As to the time element you spoke about the fact that it would be a good idea to arrange for this before it gets too cold, and that is all immigration under the white paper must stop April 1 of this year?

Mr. HELLER. Thank you, Mr. Wright, for bringing that out. I should not have forgotten it.

Chairman BLOOM. The Chair would like to state that it is supposed to stop according to the white paper, but the time has been extended indefinitely if the quota has not been used up. There are 30,000 odd.

Mr. WRIGHT. Thirty thousand?

Chairman BLOOM. And that time was extended. And that legislation started at Bermuda and was passed by the British Parliament.

So that is indefinite. It may take a year and it may take 2 years, but whatever time is necessary to absorb the remainder of the 75,000 will be admitted to Palestine if they get there.

Mr. WRIGHT. But, as I understand it, there will be no new quotas after April 1 of this year under the white paper?

Chairman BLOOM. No; except the extension of time. The white paper is the extension of time.

Mr. Vorys.

Mr. VORYS. Mr. Heller, I regret I was called out of the room for part of your brilliant discourse because I realized from the portions I heard how good it was. I just wanted to ask you whether on the theological questions that I asked Rabbi Wolsey you would concur in general with his statement as to the authority of rabbis or a group of rabbis or any one to speak for the Jews?

Mr. HELLER. I am delighted that you asked that, Mr. Vorys, because I was simply aching at that time to say something. I think it is chiefly a difference in emphasis and moreover a clear distinction in Jewish history and in Jewish life among different groups.

In ancient Palestine the final authority rested in the Sanhedrin. The court was the highest court in Palestine. After the destruction of the temples the final authority rested in academies in Palestine. And questions were referred to higher authorities. With the codification of these laws questions were decided by submission to rabbis who gave answers to them which were accepted. And that is still the case in orthodox Jewish life. In orthodox Judaism rabbis still have the right to decide upon the questions based upon the law.

Chairman BLOOM. Supposing they do not?

Mr. HELLER. Supposing they do not what—resemble?

Chairman BLOOM. Supposing they do not carry out the instructions of the rabbi, there is no power to compel them?

And I would like to say though there may be differences of opinion there have been very few cases where the rabbi's decision was not adhered to. That is a human condition which may not be expressed in law, but it exists in fact.

Mr. VORYS. You spoke of law and you referred to ancient days when there was a Jewish theocratic state and the interpretation of those laws of that day in the light of modern life. I do not quite get it. Those laws are rules of conduct, are they not, affecting daily life and various things?

Mr. HELLER. Mr. Vorys, the laws of ancient Palestine were precisely like this country. There was the common law as decided by the courts. There was law of civil and criminal jurisdiction. No distinction was made in Jewish law then between sacred and secular. They were commonly administered by a common system of courts with the Sanhedrin at the time.

Mr. VORYS. Are those laws still in effect insofar as they have been enforced?

Mr. HELLER. In orthodox Judaism those which are applicable to the life of the Jews at present are still in force. We substitute one of individual preference based upon the Bible. That is a very inadequate explanation of a rather difficult subject.

Chairman BLOOM. In executive session I will take it up with you, Mr. Vorys.

Mr. Mundt, have you any questions?

Mr. MUNDT. Since Rabbi Bloom has offered to take up a lot of these matters in executive session I won't ask any further questions about the relationship of authority a rabbi can speak for the congregation, but what about the authority over the rabbis?

Mr. HELLER. There is nothing but a financial one.

Mr. MUNDT. I want to ask just a question about the purport of the resolution. At the bottom of the resolution it says, "*Resolved*, That the United States shall use its good offices and take appropriate measures to the end," and so forth. As Mr. Wright has pointed out, the resolution deals with a dual situation, one looking to the terms of the peace treaty, and I agree that now during the war is the time when we should be making our plans for terms in post-war peace, but the other, in more human aspects of it, is that which would provide some haven of rescue for Jews, which are being murdered, and unless something is done quickly they won't be around unless something is developed, so I wish you would enlighten the committee as to just what the recommendation includes. I understand all right how its good offices function and the spokesmen for this Government attempting to influence other governments, and presumably that has already been done, and if not it might well be done. What is the exact purport of the phrase "appropriate measures"? What do you favor the United States doing under that?

Mr. HELLER. I am delighted you asked that question because I had the feeling it was said with the best of intentions which might have seemed to go too far. It seems too much to urge during the war before anyone knows what system will emerge before the end of the war to define the international system, the methods for maintaining it, and for maintaining the peace that will come out of this war.

All this means, Mr. Chairman, in my opinion, is in the light of the future system as that will arise this country shall use its good offices which is persuasion and shall take the necessary measures through Congress which may influence international decision. That is all.

I do not think it means we have to send an army into Palestine to police it, or anything like that whatsoever.

Does that make it clear?

It seems to me those measures should be used and not an enforcement system if it exists.

Mr. MUNDT. If I correctly interpret your position had it been written the United States shall use its good offices to the end you would not have needed to include the other phrase?

Mr. HELLER. I think it is a redundancy, Congressman.

Mr. WRIGHT. As author of the resolution I agree with you.

Mr. HELLER. There is one other thing. The question was asked Should not the United States use its good offices to relieve? I happen to be president of the United Palestine Appeal. It is our hope it will move at once to put them whereover they can be placed in other lands. On the other hand, it is our opinion from a practical point of view that it will be discovered that the problem of taking Jews out of Europe also is concomitant with taking them in some other places. So that the two are linked as I think they are humanely in this resolution.

Chairman BLOOM. Thank you.

Mrs. Bolton.

Mrs. Bolton. I very much enjoyed your interpretation, Rabbi, and I wanted to ask if you would give us your definition of "Zionism."

Mr. Heller. To me Zionism is that movement which rests upon the religious hopes of countless generations of Jews for the restoration in Palestine of a Jewish commonwealth which hopes to achieve there for those of our people who can and will go to it the opportunity for a free life.

Mrs. Bolton. Thank you.

Chairman Bloom. Mr. Wadsworth.

Mr. Wadsworth. No questions.

Chairman Bloom. Is there anyone else? Thank you very much, Rabbi. Representative Weiss, I understand you want to talk for about a minute.

STATEMENT OF HON. SAMUEL A. WEISS, A REPRESENTATIVE IN CONGRESS FROM THE STATE OF PENNSYLVANIA

Mr. Weiss. I urge the committee favorably recommend the enactment of these resolutions

We all know by reason of history and tradition that Palestine has been considered the home of the Jews by international law following the Balfour Declaration, and the world considered it such until the recent white paper.

I say I am probably a biased witness because I am an ardent Zionist, but we should not follow a policy of appeasement. We should ask the abrogation of the White Paper and permit free immigration of all Jews into Palestine.

I hope the committee will see fit to promptly enact these resolutions.

Chairman Bloom. Thank you. The time of the gentleman has expired. Rabbi Gold.

STATEMENT OF RABBI WOLF GOLD, HONORARY PRESIDENT, MIZRACHI ORGANIZATION OF AMERICA, AND CHAIRMAN, NATIONAL ORTHODOX CONFERENCE

Mr. Gold. Mr. Chairman and members of the committee, I wish to thank you for the opportunity you give me at this late hour, and I notice the patience of the members of the committee as well as the chairman is overtaxed.

Mr. Mundt. Especially the chairman?

Mr. Gold. Possibly. I appreciate it under the circumstances and I know how I feel myself sitting here for 2 days almost, although it has been very interesting, but at the same time it is rather a very difficult thing to sit for 2 days on one particular subject.

However, I feel it is a necessity for me to read a few remarks because they represent the opinion of a group of Jews that even our colleagues of the Reform Movement in Judaism recognize that it is the majority of the Jewish people.

In speaking for the Mizrachi Organization of America, religious section of the Zionist movement, I wish to give particular expression to the profound sentiments of tradition-true, historic Jewry, which sees in the effort for the reconstitution of Palestine as a Jewish commonwealth, not only the righting of an historic wrong committed centuries ago against the people of Israel, but also the fulfillment of Divine prophecy, which gave assurance to wandering Israel of an ultimate renewal of his days of yore on the sacred soil of Palestine. It is also my privilege to speak for those to whom Judaism is not merely a profession of faith, but rather a mode of life, regulating their every day thoughts and acts, hopes, and deeds.

Mine is, simultaneously, the privilege and the honor to represent today the National Conference of Orthodox Jewry, which at a conclave held only a week ago in the city of New York, and participated in by 450 rabbis and many hundreds of delegates from the length and breadth of the country, spoke for approximately a million and a half of Orthodox Jews, and enthusiastically endorsed the entirety of the program for a Jewish commonwealth.

Religious Jewry is of the unshakable and firm conviction that Israel as a nation will never perish, as confirmed by the reassuring and unmistakable words of the prophet Jeremiah:

Thus saith the Lord, Who gives the sun for a light by day, and the ordinances of the moon and of the stars for a light by night, Who stirreth up the seas, that the waves thereof roar, if these ordinances depart from before Me, then the seed of Israel also shall cease from being a nation before Me forever.

In accordance with this ancient prophecy, it is inconceivable for any individual Jew or group of Jews to speak in the same breath of the inherent glory and need to strengthen the Jewish religion, while denying, simultaneously, the existence of the Jewish nation. It is similarly contradictory to accept the prophets, without absorbing to any extent their passionate devotion to the land of Israel as the eternal home for the people of Israel.

The same prophet Jeremiah, who experienced the misfortune of witnessing the destruction of the Holy Temple, also envisaged the devastation as a mere temporary interruption of Jewish national life and thus laid also the foundation of Jewish reconstruction of Palestine, as reflected in the following passage:

For thus saith the Lord of Hosts, the God of Israel: Houses and fields and vineyards shall yet again be brought in this land.

Ample voice has already been given at these hearings to our moral anguish in face of the unprecedented and unparalleled tragedy that has befallen the Jewish people. Hundreds of thousands of the more than 3,000,000 Jews that have perished as victims of the Nazi campaign of annihilation, it may be stated, are the kith and kin of the women and men in whose name the Zionist leaders have spoken. Effective measures must be taken and, thank God, have recently been taken to rescue as many survivors of the holocaust as may be possible.

We cannot, however, limit our concern to the immediate problem of rescue, urgent as that problem is. In the tasks of reconstruction, which the nations will face after the war, the solution of the age-old problem of Jewish homelessness will demand the attention not only of the Jews themselves, but also of the organized will and conscience of mankind. And here again we respectfully submit, that without Palestine as the dominant factor, any program for the solution of that problem is doomed to failure. The post-war world must, and, no doubt, will recognize the right of the uprooted and despoiled Jews of Europe to return to their former domiciles as equal citizens. It is certain, however, that many of them, perhaps most of them, will find it impossible to do so. The social atmosphere of Europe will have been poisoned against them by the vicious propaganda of the enemy. In addition, the memory of what they have recently suffered, as well as the recollection of the frustration of their hopes that followed the

First World War, will make them turn their footsteps to a land where they can rebuild their own lives, as well as the life of their people. For they are conscious that they belong to an ancient and noble people that is entitled to a dignified life and future of its own in the family of nations.

Let it also be said at this time that, not only the Jewish people but, alas, also Judaism, that great and ancient religion, has been a victim of the devastating wrath of nazi-ism. Ancient and well-entrenched centers of Jewish learning have been uprooted. Those fountain-heads of complete Jewish religious living, which I had occasion to observe during numerous visits in eastern Europe, are unfortunately a thing of the past. The broken and shattered body of the stricken Jew needs the good earth of Palestine in order to regain life and vigor. Surely, the Jewish soul needs the inspiring atmosphere of the land of prophecy and the word of God in order to recreate that spiritual life which our foe so utterly destroyed.

We hope and trust that the resolution, introduced under bipartisan auspices, will receive the unanimous approval of Congress, thus re-affirming the historic policy of our country with respect to the restoration of Palestine and Israel, a cause to which the vast majority of the Jews of America are profoundly attached. And as we invoke the blessing of the Almighty upon you, we pray that it may be among your shining deeds to have served greatly in the furtherance and attainment of this goal.

Chairman BLOOM. Thank you, Rabbi Gold.

The Chair wishes to state that he wants to thank all of the witnesses, and we feel very grateful to our guests for being so attentive, quiet, and helpful in every way possible.

We have a few witnesses left, but we must adjourn now. It is very unusual for the committee to sit as late as this, especially when the House is in session. I want you folks to understand that we have sat here all of this time when we should not have done so. We knew you came from out of town. We wanted to hear you.

There are several witnesses here and I would like to have them put their addresses or any letters, telegrams, or petitions they have in the record. If you do not have anything with you kindly write it out and send it to me, I will see it is inserted in the record.

I want to call upon Mr. David Wertheim, national secretary of the Poale Zion, a Labor Zionist Organization, to insert his statement in the record.

STATEMENT OF DAVID WERTHEIM, NATIONAL SECRETARY OF THE POALE ZION (LABOR ZIONIST ORGANIZATION)

Mr. WERTHEIM. Speaking for the thousands of members and many more sympathizers of the Labor Zionist Organization, Poale, Zion, we join with other Jewish bodies in expressing our support of the Palestine resolution which is now before the distinguished committee of the House of Representatives.

Ours is a movement of American Jewish workers organized nearly 40 years ago in order to help, morally and financially, the endeavors to reestablish the Jewish commonwealth in the ancestral home of the race along the lines of economic democracy. Many of our members who have migrated to this country from eastern Europe have per-sonally experienced the economic and social disabilities, the constant insecurity and degradation, which have been the immemorial lot of the Jewish masses in most European countries. They have felt that it was their duty to help their fellow Jews, particularly the under-privileged and economically dispossessed, to build through self-help and pioneering efforts a home for themselves and a haven of refuge for millions of Jews in search for economic and political security and spiritual regeneration.

In Palestine nearly 600,000 Jews, victims of economic discrimination, political persecution, refugees from savage massacres and the threat of annihilation have found a home. There they have succeeded in laying the firm foundations of a well-balanced economy, based on intensive agriculture and industry. Their children, trained in the spirit of sturdy independence and pride in their heritage, have been given the chance to grow up, upright and happy human beings. The achievements of Jewish pioneering in Palestine have been a source of infinite encouragement to the Jewish people throughout the world in its hour of darkest despair.

Outstanding authorities in agriculture and industry, economists, and farsighted statesmen are in agreement with the humble men and women who have made possible the miracle of a rejuvenated Palestine so that country can under favorable circumstances become the home of many more hundreds of thousands and millions. The hope that such favorable conditions be created in Palestine is the sole hold on life of those Jews who will survive the present catastrophe in ravaged Europe, Africa, and Asia.

The enormous sacrifices which our country, together with its allies, is now making will have been in vain, if a better world does not emerge after this war. Shall the Jews, the first victims of Nazi-Fascist madness, be forgotten when that happy day will arrive? Shall the survivors of Hitler's concentration camps and annihilation centers be driven back to their destroyed homes, to the insecure existence which is the cause of their present plight? Shall they not be given the opportunity to settle on the soil and establish for themselves a permanent home in the country of their ancient hopes?

The resolution now before your committee broadly outlines the elements of a just and humane solution of the Palestine problem. Giving expression to the sympathy of the American Congress to the establishment of a Jewish commonwealth in Palestine would, we are certain, serve as a powerful stimulus to the realization of one of the most constructive social undertakings in our time. It would be a welcome encouragement to those responsible and humanitarian elements in Great Britain who are anxious to see the fulfillment of the pledge which their people has given to world Jewry. It would be a decisive factor in the abrogation of the disastrous White Paper and encourage the only just and fair solution of a vexed problem.

As Jews and Americans we support the adoption of this resolution, which will not only bring encouragement and hope to millions of victims of our mortal enemy, but add greatly to the honor and glory of the United States.

Mr. Chairman, I will be able to submit later an answer to Mrs. Rogers about labor in Palestine.

Chairman BLOOM. Kindly send it to the clerk.

I want to thank you, and I hope you appreciate the position the committee is in.

The committee is adjourned subject to the call of the Chair.
(Thereupon the committee adjourned at 5:40 p. m., subject to the call of the Chair.)
(The following was submitted for the record:)

STATEMENT SUBMITTED BY PHILLIP MURRAY, PRESIDENT, CONGRESS OF INDUS-
TRIAL ORGANIZATIONS, ON BEHALF OF PALESTINE RESOLUTIONS NO. 418 AND
No. 419 BEFORE THE FOREIGN AFFAIRS COMMITTEE OF THE HOUSE OF REP-
RESENTATIVES

The Congress of Industrial Organizations, through its representative, is happy to appear before this committee to voice its endorsement of the resolutions now under consideration. The great labor organizations of the United States have watched with admiration the development of the Jewish National Home in Palestine, and the splendid progress made by the Jewish pioneers there in developing the agriculture and industry of the country. We are particularly proud of the outstanding achievements of Jewish labor in Palestine. We believe that the progress of the Jewish National Home should be permitted to continue unimpeded and unimpaired, particularly in view of the tragic plight of hundreds of thousands of Jews in Europe, and the necessity of providing for them a place of resettlement and rehabilitation after the war.

The half million who have settled in Palestine since the issuance of the Balfour Declaration have demonstrated their capacity for building in days to come a free and democratic Jewish commonwealth based upon the principles of equality and justice. We believe that one of the most important results which can come out of the present struggle being waged by the democratic forces of the world will be an expanded opportunity for the Jewish people to construct a healthy and normal natural life for itself in Palestine. The resolutions now pending before this committee will voice the overwhelming sentiment of America in favor of affording the Jewish people this opportunity. We urge their favorable consideration.

May we, in conclusion, call your attention to the following excerpts from the resolution which was adopted at the Sixth Constitutional Convention of the Congress of Industrial Organizations meeting at Philadelphia, in November 1943:

"All of civilized humanity is outraged by the Nazis' barbaric drive to exterminate the Jewish people. The annals of human history do not record any reign of terror more inhuman than this Fascist terror which has already murdered more than 4,000,000 Jewish men, women, and children in Nazi Germany and in Nazi-occupied countries.

"The Jewish people in the ghettos of Warsaw and in all the occupied countries have written epic pages of heroism in their refusal to submit to Nazi extermination.

"The great tradition of labor throughout the world and the great tradition of American labor is that there can be no division between race, color, or creed; that all working people must stand united if civilization is to continue. The Jewish people in America and throughout the world today as in the past join with all other people of the world as workers in the mines and mills and factories, as farmers and as soldiers on the battle fronts in joint contribution to the advancement of humanity and in the joint fight to defeat the forces of tyranny and barbarism.

"American workers are making an outstanding contribution in this great battle. They will oppose any Nazi attempt to arouse race against race and to use this division as a means to fully entrench themselves and put through their Fascist ideology of barbarism, destruction, and the wiping out of civilization.

"American workers are making an outstanding contribution in their great war of national liberation. American workers know that this war is a people's war and that the gains labor has made through its many years of struggle and sacrifice are at stake in this war.

"We look with great sorrow on what is taking place in Nazi-occupied Europe today. We join hands with our fellow workers in all the occupied countries; with the downtrodden, persecuted Jewish people in protest against the barbarous acts of the Fascists.

"We, organized labor in America, we of the Congress of Industrial Organizations, support the Jewish people in their fight for survival and freedom.

"We wholeheartedly support the program of the American Jewish Conference, representing more than 60 Jewish organizations, which calls on the United Nations to warn the Nazi gangsters that the atrocities against the Jewish people will be avenged.

*   *   *   *   *   *   *

"We note with great satisfaction that the Jewish communities in Palestine have already made noteworthy contributions to the winning of the war against fascism.

"We support the demands of Palestinian Jews for full opportunity for unrestricted participation on the battlefield and for the unrestricted opportunity to make an agricultural and industrial contribution to the war effort.

"We join in their demands for the abrogation of the so-called Chamberlain white paper which would close all Jewish immigration into Palestine by April 1944, as discriminatory, unfair, unjust, and a hindrance to the war effort."

STATEMENT BY DR. LOUIS M. LEVITSKY, PRESIDENT, RABBINICAL ASSEMBLY OF AMERICA, ON BEHALF OF THE RABBINICAL ASSEMBLY, ADDRESSED THE COMMITTEE ON FOREIGN AFFAIRS

As president of the Rabbinical Assembly of America, I have come here to present the views of the conservative rabbinate of America on the white paper. We rabbis call upon the Congress of the United States to use its good offices with Great Britain, in the name of justice and humanity, to fulfill the promise solemnly given to the Jewish people of the world to facilitate "the establishment in Palestine of a national home for the Jewish people * * * it being clearly understood that nothing shall be done which may prejudice the civil or religious rights of existing non-Jewish communities in Palestine, or the rights and political status enjoyed by Jews in any other country."

We demand the repeal of the white paper which proposes to put an end' to Jewish immigration into Palestine on April 1, 1944, and which restricts the right of Jews to purchase land in Palestine. We feel that the implementation of the white paper policy is a breach of contract with the Jewish people, which 'has spent blood and treasure in carrying out its obligations in the development of Palestine, and which, despite riots and massacres directed against Jews by non-Jews, has consistently respected the rights of the non-Jewish communities in Palestine and the holy places of non-Jewish religions.

To deny or restrict the right of Jews to settle in Palestine involves not only tragic suffering for multitudes of individual Jews who are subject to persecution, assault, or ignominy, it involves also the frustration of Jewish religious aspirations. For ever since the dispersion and the destruction of the Judean state, we have yearned and prayed for the restoration of Palestine. We have felt intuitively that, for Judaism to flourish, it must draw inspiration from a self-governing Jewish community living in the land hallowed by Jewish history. The difficulty in our day of maintaining Jewish religious and cultural institutions in countries in which Jews constitutue but a small minority of the population has made religious Jews keenly aware of the need of having a national home in which Judaism could inform every aspect of the social and cultural life of Jews. From the Jewish community in the land of Israel, if it is permitted to develop into a genuine national home for the Jewish people, Jews all over the world would derive encouragement, guidance, and inspiration for perpetuating their religious and ethical ideals and contributing to the spiritual and social welfare of the countries of their citizenship and political allegiance.

At a time when the Axis Powers are seeking to exterminate the Jewish people without mercy, and when the conditions of life everywhere expose Judaism to disintegrating environmental influences, we cannot waive the historic claim of our people to Palestine. We therefore appeal to the Congress of the United States to use its good offices with Great Britain to complete the act of historic justice begun with the issuing of the Balfour Declaration. We ask not only that the White Paper be abrogated, but that the right of the Jewish people to establish its national home in Palestine be expressly and explicitly reaffirmed and implemented. We deem it just to demand that the gates of Palestine be opened to all Jews who need or desire to make it their home; that every encouragement be given to Jews to become as quickly as possible a majority in Palestine; that, to this end, the Jewish Agency for Palestine be given exclusive authority to regulate immigration into the country, and that it be aided in its effort to increase Palestine's economic absorptive capacity by the development of its industry and agriculture; and that, finally, when a Jewish majority shall have been achieved and before, Palestine be given the status of a free and autonomous commonwealth under a democratic constitution which would guarantee equality of all rights to all citizens regardless of race, nationality, or religion.

HOUSE OF REPRESENTATIVES,
Washington, D. C., February 8, 1944.

RESOLUTIONS AND TELEGRAMS RECEIVED FROM SAN FRANCISCO IN CONNECTION
WITH THE ABROGATION OF THE CHAMBERLAIN WHITE PAPER AND URGING THE
ESTABLISHMENT OF A JEWISH HOMELAND IN PALESTINE, PURSUANT TO HOUSE
RESOLUTION 418 AND HOUSE RESOLUTION 419

Resolutions

San Francisco Lodge, No. 21, B'nai B'rith, 703 Market Street.
California Lodge, No. 163, B'nai B'rith, 1087 Market Street.
Pacific Hebrew Orphan Asylum and Home Society, 1600 Scott Street.
Jewish Educational Society, 745 Buchanan Street.
National Home for Jewish Children, San Francisco Chapter, 733 Thirty-first Avenue.
Zionist Organization of America, 369 Pine Street.
Temple Sherith Israel Men's Club, California and Webster Streets.
Beth Israel Sisterhood, 1839 Geary Street.
San Francisco Emergency Committee for the Abrogation of the White Paper, 110 Sutter Street.

Telegrams

Mrs. Louis Bloch; Mrs. Jessie Gans; Mrs. Henry Sahlein; Mrs. Carl Jacob; Mrs. Maurice Heppner, president, San Francisco Chapter of Hadassah; Prof. Sam Lepkowsky; Prof. Zev Hassid; Prof. Michael Goodman; Prof. Ben Bernstein; Prof. Jacob Traum; Mrs. Richard M. Neustadt; and Mrs. Henry Harris.

STATEMENT BY MAX ZARITSKY, GENERAL PRESIDENT, UNITED HATTERS CAP AND
MILLINERY WORKERS, INTERNATIONAL UNION, NEW YORK CITY

I appear on behalf of the United Hatters Cap and Millinery Workers International Union of which organization I am the general president, and which is an affiliate of the American Federation of Labor, in support of the pending resolutions Nos. 418 and 419, endorsing the establishment of a Jewish commonwealth in Palestine.

What is proposed by the resolutions represents a reaffirmation of the historic position our country has taken whenever and wherever oppressed and persecuted peoples have striven to secure their liberty and to establish their position in the family of nations.

So far as the struggle of the Jewish people for a homeland is concerned, it is a reaffirmation such as this that is more desperately needed today than it was needed in 1922 when our Congress endorsed the Balfour Declaration, promising that Palestine would be restored as the Jewish national homeland. It was wise, sound, and statesmanlike to make our position clear then. It is infinitely more so to make our position clear today.

I need not tell you that the position of the Jewish people in the lands across the seas in which they have lived for centuries is more precarious today than it ever was. Even the victory of the United Nations to which we can look forward today with greater confidence than we dared entertain 2 years ago, cannot bring tangible or immediately relief to the Jewish people in the countries devastated by the war.

They have been driven from their homes and lands that were once their own and were forced to seek refuge throughout the world. In some places they have been granted temporary havens, but the stipulation that when peace returns they will be obliged to leave.

But where shall they go? What shall be done with them? What shall be done with the hundreds of thousands of Jews who have been completely uprooted from their soil by the Nazi barbarians and their satellites and who have been rendered homeless and stateless—men without a country?

Shall they go to Germany?—to a Germany where hate, paganism, racialism, contempt for human dignity have been instilled in the minds of the people—to a Germany where the extinction of the Jews is the first commandant of the Nazi bible?

Shall they be told to strike roots in the soil of devastated Poland, which is saturated with the blood of millions of slaughtered civilian Jewish men and women—where the memories of horrible tortures and cruelty and murder will haunt them like nightmares for decades to come?

Shall the Christian conscience permit the perpetuation of the Jewish status of homeless refugees?

Their eyes turn to America, the America which is the conscience of democracy. We owe it to our traditional devotion to the cause of the persecuted and oppressed to adopt this resolution and to restate as emphatically as we can our country's position in favor of a Jewish homeland in Palestine.

Twenty-two years ago when Congress placed itself on record in favor of the Balfour Declaration, it was on the assumption that the land would be restored—that it would be made productive, and that it would provide a permanent home for those willing to go there.

The Jewish people in Palestine have kept their faith. They have built on the ruins of an ancient civilization a country capable of providing opportunities to all who wish to labor and earn their living by the sweat of their brow. Every visitor to Palestine has come back thrilled and inspired by the miraculous achievements of men and women who just wanted to live in peace and security—to build their homeland—a land in which there shall be no persecution nor oppression—no exploitation of men by men—where democratic institutions can flourish.

They did all this and more, not only for themselves, but the benefits of their pioneering labors have been of inestimable benefit to their Arab neighbors whose economic and social conditions improved, whose standard of living has been raised, and who now share with the Jews the benefits that have come from the initiative, self-sacrifice, and hard toil of the Jewish settlers.

Indeed, the Jewish people who were given encouragement by our Government almost a quarter of a century ago have kept their faith. Today as the remnants of a people whose extinction has been decreed and to a large extent carried out by the dark forces that would extinguish civilizations throughout the world, ask for an opportunity to go to this land of asylum, where they can live and work without the dreadful fear of torture and hate and threat of destruction.

There, in that far-off land they will create a citadel of democracy that will strengthen the hands of all democratic forces.

During these frightful months and years of war the Jews of Palestine have served in the armies of the United Nations. They are today contributing to the fullest extent to the cause of freedom and democracy. They are helping push back the forces of savagery and are hastening the day of final victory.

For all the battered and pitiful homeless human beings now scattered all over the world the thought of Palestime is a final hope. In their hour of tribulation it is that hope which sustains them.

I have not discussed the fundamental question itself, which is the right—the God-given right of the Jewish people to have a homeland which they can call their own—to share with all others in the family of nations—the rights, privileges, and prerogatives which other peoples enjoy.

I have not discussed it because I consider it elementary and self-evident. There is no reason why the Jewish people should continue forever to wander, or to be more accurate, to be driven from pillar to post—when their ancient homeland beckons—a homeland which by their toil, sweat, and blood they have rebuilt—where they can live in peace with their neighbors, and where they can contribute out of their culture to the advancement of civilization.

I do not have the authority to speak for the 12,000,000 of America's organized workers. However, I will state for the record that the American Federation of Labor has at its annual conventions year after year restated and reiterated its demand that the Jewish people be given every facility to establish Palestine as their homeland. Permit me to quote one short paragraph from the declaration unanimously adopted by the American Federation of Labor at its last convention held in Boston October last:

"Surely the least that the civilized world can do is to carry out the pledge so freely given by Great Britain in 1917, affirmed by the League of Nations when it accorded to that nation the mandate over Palestine in 1922, and approved by our own American Congress in the same year. The American Federation of Labor urges that the restriction on Jewish immigration and settlement contained in the British White Paper of 1939 be withdrawn and that the Balfour Declaration be so implemented that the hopes and aspirations of the Jewish people to build their own commonwealth in Palestine may be realized. Thus will this ancient people be enabled to take its rightful place among the democratic nations of the world and make its full contribution to that progressive world order which we all pray will emerge from the horrible sufferings of this global war."

The Congress of Industrial Organizations at its last convention held in Philadelphia also October last, adopted a similar declaration.

In short, American organized labor—12,000,000 strong—unreservedly and unequivocably supports the aspirations of the Jewish people for the establishment of their homeland in Palestine.

As a trade economist and as an American, I urge your committee to add the power of our Nation's voice—a voice that has always been lifted in behalf of the weak and the oppressed—to those who seek the realization of a dream which the Jewish people have dreamed from time immemorial, and in the realization of which mankind will be made better and happier.

STATEMENT BY THE REVEREND RICHARD E. EVANS, MEMBER OF THE EXECUTIVE COMMITTEE OF THE CHRISTIAN COUNCIL ON PALESTINE

May I at the very outset say how greatly I appreciate the privilege of appearing before this committee and saying a word in support of the splendid resolution now before Congress in behalf of abrogating the White Paper and implementing the Balfour Declaration. I desire to record my wholehearted approbation of the fine statement made by Dr. Henry A. Atkinson on behalf of the Christian Council on Palestine. I believe profoundly that our being here today represents a shining illustration of true American democracy. When Christian ministers like ourselves can join with our brethren of the rabbinate in speaking for the liberation of oppressed Jewry throughout the world—that is the way it should be —that is the spirit of America—where men of all faiths and creeds can come together on the common ground of good will and understanding and support each other in causes which are for the benefit of all mankind.

There are three principal reasons why I support heartily these resolutions and why I believe deeply in this Zionist movement. These reasons are represented by three simple fundamental American words. First, I support these resolutions because I believe in justice. I have said in many Christian pulpits throughout the country in these past weeks that if this war, as we feel it is, is a war of moral justice, then there will be no complete and final victory for justice unless that victory is shared by those who have suffered the worst cruelties and the most savage brutalities of this war. There will be no triumph for justice until the helpless, homeless, stricken victims of Nazi tyranny—the surviving members of European Jewry—are rescued from the slaughter pens and charnel houses of Hitler's Europe and are set free to live lives of decency and dignity in the Jewish Commonwealth to be reconstituted on the soil of their ancient and historic homeland of Palestine.

Over 26 years ago the Balfour Declaration was passed. Over 22 years ago the League of Nations mandate was ratified by 52 nations and endorsed unanimously by our own Houses of Congress. These historic documents ratified in man-made laws the ancient promise of the Book of Books written thousands of years ago declaring in all solemn and majestic truths this great concept. So, by all the laws of God and man the time has come when at long last this ancient wrong of the homelessness of the Jewish people must be righted, this age-old evil must be corrected, and the hosts of Israel who have escaped the dreadful fate of their brethren must be enabled to make their way and settle their lives and build their future in the land of their fathers. These resolutions which will express the voice of America in calling for the abrogation of the White Paper and the implementation of the Balfour Declaration will play a great part in bringing this ancient promise into reality. Not only do I support these resolutions because I believe in justice, but also because I believe in another great American word—freedom. That is the word over which this whole war is being fought. It is a struggle between freedom and slavery, between liberty and tyranny. Men are dying today all across the world in order that mankind, all mankind, might be liberated from the chains of despotism. It would be tragic mockery indeed if their deaths shall have been in vain and we fail to liberate the people and the land from which the old concept of freedom came. That is why I have little patience with the man who says, "Well, I am an American. I am not much interested in what happens to Palestine." To me he represents a pretty poor type of American. Because the America that I believe in and love, the America that I cherish and admire, is concerned with the fate of suffering needy humanity the world over. I believe in the America that stretches out its arms and opens up its heart for the salvation and rescue of dying despairing mankind in every part of the world.

We are fighting today for the right of every man to think his thoughts, to speak his mind, to live his life, and to worship his God according to the dictates of his conscience. Those are the things contained in our own great Bill of Rights. We cherish our Bill of Rights deeply and gratefully, but the time has come in the life of the world when we must all bear our share of responsibility in seeing to it that a Bill of Rights is established for all mankind. And the ideal of freedom will never fully come to pass in this world until in the ancient land of Palestine under the banner of the star of David the stricken and slaved Jewish people of Nazi-ridden lands are finally enabled to rebuild their torn and shattered lives in an order of decency and honor through the establishment of a Jewish Commonwealth.

And third, I support these resolutions because I believe in democracy. There again is what the world is fighting for today and it shall only be through the force and power of democracy that this great hope and dream of the centuries can be translated into a living fact. It is only as public opinion all over America speaks out through the channel of these resolutions that the voice of democracy can be heard, and the will of the people shall make its impact on the forces of government both here and in Britain to see that this thing shall come to pass.

No more gallant story is told in all the long history of a people than that magnificent story of what has taken place in this last generation in the land of Palestine. In the quarter of a century since the Balfour Declaration and the mandate opened the gates of Palestine, the record has been one of glorious progress and development. The economic, agricultural, and industrial achievements have been nothing short of miraculous. From arid desert wasteland of 25 years ago there have come accomplishments in agriculture, manufacturing, and other areas that stand as a living monument of the heroic efforts of the more than 600,000 colonists who have come to make this their home. It is altogether too little known that in the last few years Palestine Jewry has played a splendid part in the whole war effort, both through military and civilian manpower as well as through food, supplies, and industrial resources. Such gallant efforts for the cause of democracy must find their just and true reward in rallying of all the forces of democracy back of the hopes and aspirations of this people. All of us together, Christian and Jew alike, must strike a vigorous blow against the insidious kind of anti-Semitism and bigotry that will close the gates of Palestine, shatter the dream of these stricken, helpless victims of brutality, and seal the walls of doom over the heads of those who are left to face further brutality and extermination.

Some months ago on Bill of Rights Day in the city of Philadelphia, I stood before a great shrine of American life—the shrine of the Liberty Bell—and I read again the words that are on the top of that Bell; words which are in a sense the motto of America. The words are these: "Proclaim liberty throughout the land and on all the inhabitants thereof." Where do those words come from? They come from the book of Leviticus, the great sacred writing of the Jewish people. And what land do they come from? What part of the world gave them to us? Those words came from Palestine. It was in Palestine that they were born—the motto of America began in Palestine as did all the concepts of justice, freedom, and democracy that we cherish. Then if we as Americans possess the sense of gratitude and obligation that we should, we will not rest until we help give back to that land of Palestine the liberty and justice that they gave to us and to all mankind.

I speak today as a minister of Christ. Many years ago I made the decision to follow one great life as did doubtless other men in this room today, too. I am conscious of the fact that I have followed that life all too inadequately and all too imperfectly. But I recall vividly the moment that I made that decision, as every man here can recall the moment when he made his decision. For me, it was in the room of my little foster mother, when I was standing before a certain picture. It is the picture of a boy in the temple, both hearing the rabbis and asking them questions. He was a boy of the Jewish people. He came from the land of Palestine. It was in that land that He taught and preached and lived His great gospel of love for all mankind. And I believe with all my heart that it would be His will that His people be redeemed from their agony and their slavery and their horror, and that His land be made once more a land of the Book and the prophets, a land of hope and truth and beauty for all time to come. To that end we of the Christian world must raise our voices in support of these resolutions and in behalf of every cause and every movement that shall bring about the ultimate fulfillment of this great purpose, so help us God.

House of Representatives,
Washington, D. C., February 7, 1944.
Hon. Sol Bloom,
  Chairman, House Committee on Foreign Affairs,
      House Office Building, Washington, D. C.

Dear Sol: I have had the pleasure of examining House Resolutions 418 and 419 and I just want you to know that the objectives of these resolutions meet with my wholehearted approval.

A large number of my constituents are likewise interested in this matter, and we sincerely trust that your committee will take favorable action upon these resolutions.

With kindest personal regards, I am.
  Sincerely,

Hugh Peterson.

House of Representatives,
Washington, D. C., February 10, 1944.
Hon. Sol Bloom,
  Chairman, Committee on Foreign Affairs,
      House of Representatives, Washington, D. C.

Dear Mr. Bloom: I am writing to express my deep interest in House Resolution 418 and House Resolution 419.

I believe that the establishment of the Jewish Homeland is a worthy purpose and has the approval of the people of America and I hope that your committee can see its way clear to report this legislation so that the Congress may consider and pass it, at the earliest possible date.

With kind regards,
  Very sincerely,

Louis Ludlow.

House of Representatives,
Washington, D. C., February 11, 1944.
Hon. Sol Bloom,
  Chairman, House Foreign Affairs Committee,
      House of Representatives, Washington, D. C.

Dear Mr. Chairman: I wish to express my approval of House Resolutions 418 and 419. I am very much in favor of the abrogation of the White Paper and the reestablishment of Palestine as a Jewish homeland.

Sincerely yours,

Robert F. Rockwell.

House of Representatives,
Washington, D. C., February 14, 1944.
Hon. Sol Bloom,
  Chairman, Committee on Foreign Affairs,
      New House Office Building, Washington, D. C.

My Dear Chairman: Please record me in favor of House Resolution ¦419, submitted by Mr. Compton, of Connecticut, relative to the establishment in Palestine of a national home for the Jewish people.

It is my understanding that this resolution is a reaffirmation of the position of the position taken by Congress some years ago in the endorsement of the Balfour Declaration, setting aside Palestine as a national home for the Jewish people. I am given to understand that the Jewish people who have since inhabited Palestine have done a magnificent job in the development of the economic conditions of that area. I am further informed there still remains a much greater area undeveloped to which these people can address their talents.

I have no knowledge of the international implications involved during this war period, but undoubtedly the Secretary of State and the Chiefs of Staff will provide such information. The plight of the Jewish people in Europe demands the attention of the freedom-loving people of the world, particularly this country. Consistent with our war efforts, I believe we should lend a helping hand in every way possible.

Very truly yours,

George J. Bates.

THE JEWISH NATIONAL HOME IN PALESTINE

TUESDAY, FEBRUARY 15, 1944

House of Representatives,
Committee on Foreign Affairs,
Washington, D. C.

The committee met at 10 a. m., pursuant to call, Hon. Sol Bloom (chairman) presiding.

Chairman BLOOM. The committee will kindly come to order.

The committee has before it for further consideration House Resolution 418 and House Resolution 419 relative to the Jewish national home in Palestine.

We have several witnesses to be heard today and there will be no afternoon session. There has been some complaint because the last session lasted until half-past 5 which is a little too long for the committee to sit.

We will try to conclude with the witnesses today and we will kindly ask the witnesses to make their statements as brief as possible.

I would like to call the attention of the members to the fact that you have before you one of the best maps of Palestine and Syria and it is folded in such a way that you will be able to follow the witnesses as they make their explanations.

Just take the map the way it is. Our first witness is Dr. Philip K. Hitti, of Princeton University.

STATEMENT OF DR. PHILIP K. HITTI, PROFESSOR, PRINCETON UNIVERSITY

Chairman BLOOM. Would you give your full name?

Dr. HITTI. Philip K. Hitti.

Chairman BLOOM. From Princeton University?

Dr. HITTI. Yes, sir.

Chairman BLOOM. Who do you represent?

Dr. HITTI. No one but myself.

Chairman BLOOM. Will you kindly proceed? You may remain standing or be seated, just as you please.

Dr. HITTI. Perhaps if you do not mind, Mr. Chairman, I will remain standing.

Chairman BLOOM. It is perfectly all right.

Dr. HITTI. Mr. Chairman, ladies and gentlemen of the committee, To the Arabs, political Zionism is an exotic movement, internationally financed, artificially stimulated and holds no hope of ultimate or permanent success. Not only to the 50,000,000 Arabs, many of whom are descendants of the Canaanites who were in the land long before the Hebrews entered Palestine under Joshua, but to the entire Moslem society, of whom the Arabs form the spearhead, a sovereign Jewish

241

state in Palestine appears as an anachronism. These Moslems constitute a somewhat self-conscious society of about 275,000,000 who dominate a large portion of Africa and Asia. Even if the Zionist political program, supported by British and American diplomacy and bayonets, should some day become a reality, what chance of survival has such an alien state amidst a camp of a would-be hostile Arabic and unsympathetic Islamic world? There was a time in which a foreign state, a Latin one, was established in the Holy Land; but its memory lives today only in books on the crusades.

For, be it remembered, on no other issue did the Moslems in modern times seem to manifest such a unanimity. Even on the question of the restoration of the caliphate, after it was destroyed by Mustafa Kamal in 1924, there has been more friction and less solidarity, as evidenced by the proceedings of the Islamic congresses held in Cairo and Mecca. Verbal protests against the Zionist political program, which this resolution adopts, and cash to fight its provisions have poured in the last two decades from Morocco to Malay. In India a "Palestine day" was celebrated in 1936 and the All India Moslem League passed a resolution at its annual session on October 18, 1939, and another in its April meeting of 1943 warning the British against converting Palestine into a Jewish state. Jerusalem in Moslem eyes is the third haram, the third holy city after Mecca and Medina. It was the first qiblah, the first direction in which the early Moslems prayed before they began to turn in prayer toward Mecca. The land was given by Allah as a result of a jihad (holy war) and therefore for the Moslems to relinquish their claim on it constitutes a betrayal of their faith. It is even more sacred to the Christians, of whom there are today some one hundred and thirty thousand in Palestine.

This uncompromising, persistent opposition to political Zionism, whose cause the resolution espoused, does not spell anti-Semitism. Of all the major peoples of the world, the Arabs perhaps come nearest to being free from race prejudice. Besides, they, like the Jews, are Semites and they know it. They also know that their two religions are closest of kin, closer than either of them is to Christianity. Nowhere throughout medieval and modern times were Jews better treated than in Moslem-Arab lands. So welcome were American Jewish ambassadors to the Sublime Porte at Constantinople that our Government appointed three of them in a row: Straus, Elkus, and Morgenthau.

These Arabs and Moslems cannot understand why the Jewish problem, which is not of their making, should be solved at their expense. They deeply sympathize with the afflicted Jews but are not convinced that Palestine solves the Jewish problem; Palestine does not qualify as a country without a people ready to receive a people without a country. They fail to understand why the American legislators, so solicitous for the welfare of the European Jews, should not lift the bars of immigration and admit Jewish refugees, millions of whom could be settled on the unoccupied plains of Arizona or Texas. This certainly falls within their jurisdiction. The word "reconstitute" in the resolution would no doubt interest them and they would like to remake the map of Europe and put up their claim on Spain, which they occupied at a much later date and for a longer period of time. Some of them would raise the question how would the people of the United States react to a suggestion from, say, Russia, to reconstitute Oklahoma an Indian Territory. They realize they have no spokesmen in America, no high-pressure groups, no machinery for influencing American public opinion or legislation, but they are willing to rest their case upon its merits and upon America's sense of justice.

Some of them may have forgotten the Anglo-French declaration of November 8, 1918, promising the peoples so long oppressed by the Turks complete and definitive liberation and "the establishment of national governments and administrations drawing their authority from the initiative and free choice of the indigenous population"; or the words of Woodrow Wilson's twelfth point that the non-Turkish—

nationalities which are now under Turkish rule should be assured an undoubted security of life and an absolute opportunity of autonomous development—

or the corresponding provision in the Covenant of the League of Nations, article 22; but they certainly do remember the third article of the Atlantic Charter that Great Britain and the United States—

respect the right of all people to choose the form of government under which they will live.

No westerner, or Ifranji as called in Arabic, is more highly respected and more implicitly trusted by the Arab and Moslem people than the American. There is a reason for it. For years American teachers, preachers, physicians, archeologists, pilgrims, and philantropists have frequented the eastern shore of the Mediterranean with the intent of giving rather than taking and with no imperialistic designs. The American press at Beirut, the first well-equipped press in that region, celebrated its hundredth anniversary 8 years ago. The American University of Beirut celebrated its seventy-fifth anniversary 3 years ago. In this institution a large number of the leaders of thought and action throughout the Arab East was trained. In the First World War and the immediate period following, no less than $100,000,000 was raised by the American public to relieve suffering among the people of the Near East and to rehabilitate their land—an unparalleled figure in the history of private philanthropy. No wonder the word "American" has become associated in the minds of Arabs and Moslems with fair play, honorable dealing, and democratic conduct. All this reservoir of goodwill accumulated through generations of unselfish and hard working Americans will be threatened with destruction by the passage of the resolution now before this committee.

The United States is now engaged in a gigantic struggle with an unscrupulous, powerful, and far-from-being-beaten enemy. No drier and more explosive powder could we provide for his propaganda weapons. The Germans, we can be sure, will fully capitalize this resolution—as they did the Balfour Declaration, hold it out before Arab eyes as a sample of the kind of Anglo-American "democracy" and "freedom" for which this war is fought, and assure the Arabs that the Zionist control of Palestine is but the prelude to the Jewish control of Trans-Jordan, Syria, Lebanon, Arabia—the camel's head intruding into the tent about which they read in their Arabian Nights. This is no time to turn old friends into potential enemies.

Chairman BLOOM. Do you mind an interruption there?

Dr. HITTI. No, sir.

Chairman BLOOM. You do not mean that the Jews would control Syria.

Dr. HITTI. No; I said the Germans would make use of the resolution and say that. The radios of the Axis have already said that.

Chairman BLOOM. You do not believe everything you hear over the Nazi radio?

Dr. HITTI. No.

Chairman BLOOM. Why do you believe it?

Dr. HITTI. I do not believe it.

Chairman BLOOM. But why? You have made that statement.

Dr. HITTI. May I repeat what I just said.

Chairman BLOOM. Yes.

Dr. HITTI. The United States is now engaged in a gigantic struggle with an unscrupulous, powerful, and far-from-being-beaten enemy. No drier and more explosive powder could we provide for his propaganda weapons. The Germans, we can be sure, will fully capitalize this resolution—as they did the Balfour Declaration, hold it out before Arab eyes as a sample of the kind of Anglo-American "democracy" and "freedom" for which this war is fought, and assure the Arabs that the Zionist control of Palestine is but the prelude to the Jewish control of Trans-Jordan, Syria, Lebanon, Arabia—the camel's head intruding into the tent about which they read in their Arabian Nights. This is no time to turn old friends into potential enemies.

Chairman BLOOM. The Chair wishes to state the way I understood it, you secured this information over the Nazi radio. You have not mentioned that. You ought to state where you obtained that information and I would like to have the record show this is not your belief.

Dr. HITTI. The Germans would make use of that in such a way as to influence the Arabs.

Mr. JARMAN. Mr. Chairman, I understood it to be just the opposite. I understood from him that is what the Germans would do.

Chairman BLOOM. Through Nazi propaganda.

Mr. JARMAN. That is right.

Dr. HITTI. It is right here.

The United States is now engaged in a gigantic struggle with an unscrupulous, powerful, and far-from-being-beaten enemy. No drier and more explosive powder could we provide for his propaganda weapons. The Germans, we can be sure, will fully capitalize this resolution—as they did the Balfour Declaration, hold it out before Arab eyes as a sample of the kind of Anglo-American "democracy" and "freedom" for which this war is fought, and assure the Arabs that the Zionist control of Palestine is but the prelude to the Jewish control of Trans-Jordan, Syria, Lebanon, Arabia—the camel's head intruding into the tent about which they read in their Arabian Nights. This is no time to turn old friends into potential enemies.

The people of the United States are not only interested in winning the war but in contributing to the establishment of a post-war world order in which regional stability is somewhat secure and the chances of future conflicts are at least reduced. Nothing, in the judgment of the speaker, is more conducive to a state of perpetual unrest and conflict than the establishment of a Jewish commonwealth at the expense of the Arabs in Palestine. If such a commonwealth were established at the insistence of the United States, we then assume moral responsibility for its perservation. Will the people of the United States be willing to send their Navy to protect such a commonwealth if established?

The British never contemplated such an ambitious scheme as the conversion of Palestine into a Jewish commonwealth. Sandwiched in between conflicting promises to the Arabs—which made the once-promised land multi-promised—the Balfour Declaration, which was echoed in the United States Congress resolution of 1922, viewed with favor, "the establishment in Palestine of a national home for the Jewish people"—quite a different thing from converting Palestine into a Jewish state. And that was viewed with a big proviso: "It being understood that nothing shall be done which may prejudice the civil and religious rights of non-Jewish communities in Palestine." The Zionist representatives proposed to the then British Government this text "The reconstitution of Palestine as the national home of the Jewish people," which is practically the same as the resolution before us had it, but that was not the text adopted.

In its white paper of June 3, 1922, the British Government said:

Unauthorized statements have been made to the effect that the purpose in view is to create a wholly Jewish Palestine. Phrases have been used such as that Palestine is to become as Jewish as England is English. His Majesty's Government regard such expectation as unpracticable and have no such aim in view * * *. They would draw attention to the fact that the terms of the declaration referred to do not contemplate that Palestine as a whole be converted into a Jewish national home but that such a home should be founded in Palestine. When it is asked what is meant by the development of the Jewish national home in Palestine, it may be answered that it is not the imposition of a Jewish nationality upon the inhabitants of Palestine as a whole, but the further development of the existing Jewish community, with the assistance of Jews from other parts of the world, in order that it may become a center in which the Jewish people as a whole may take, on grounds of religion and race, an interest and a pride.

The author of this statement was Winston Churchill, then Colonial Secretary; and the Zoinist accepted it.

In its statement of policy of 1937 the British Government declare—

that their obligations to Arabs and Jews, respectively, were not incompatible, on the assumption that in the process of time the two races would so adjust their national aspirations as to render possible the establishment of a single commonwealth under a unitary government.

In the 1939 statement it was again made clear that Palestine shall be constituted a sovereign independent state, a Palestinian state in which all Palestinians—irrespective of race or origin—will be citizens enjoying equal political, civil and religious rights. In that statement the provision was made for limiting Jewish immigration for economic as well as political reasons.

Even then the British administration of Palestine has been confronted throughout its history with a series of strikes and disturbances beginning April 1920 and culminating in the serious revolution of 1936.

As early as August 1919 and before Arab nationalism attained the intensity that it has since assumed, the King-Crane Commission sent by President Wilson reported as follows:

A national home for the Jewish people is not equivalent to making Palestine into a Jewish state; nor can the erection of such a Jewish state be accomplished without the greatest trespass upon the civil and religious rights of existing non-Jewish communities in Palestine.

The report warned that the Zionist program could not be carried out except by force of arms.

The more enlightened and realistic among the Zionists themselves have begun to adopt the British Government point of view, concentrate on the cultural and spiritual aspects of their cause and cooperate with the Arabs. Dr. Judah L. Magnes, president of the Hebrew University of Jerusalem—a Zionist institution—declared in September 1941:

> As far as I am able to see, there is no chance whatsoever that this formula "establishment of Palestine as a Jewish commonwealth" instead of a national home in Palestine would be acceptable by any responsible Arab or Arab party or any part of Arabic public opinion.

The Union Association organized in September 1942 by Zionists in Jerusalem declared its conviction that the problem of Palestine was inseparable from that of the Near East, advocated a Jewish Arab state and held that the two people's equality was vital to the future of Palestine. Albert M. Hyamson, a British Zionist, in Palestine: A Policy (1942) interprets "national" as pertaining to nationality rather than nation. President Julian Morgenstern, of Hebrew Union College, Cincinnati, in his last contribution entitled "Nation, People, Religion: What Are We?" (1943) declares:

> Despite the oft-repeated, high-sounding asseverations of the beneficent role which a restored Jewish state or commonwealth may play or will play in setting a happy pattern of equitable social relations for all other nations to emulate, the most recent formulating of which is in the highly bombastic peroration of the so-called Palestine resolution of the American-Jewish Conference, the fact incontestably established by history still confronts us with brazen truth, that the true genius and destiny of Israel find expression only in its role as a religious people, the bearers of a spiritual heritage.

Chairman BLOOM. Are you finished now, Doctor?

Dr. HITTI. That is all, sir.

Chairman BLOOM. Judge Kee?

Mr. KEE. No questions.

Chairman BLOOM. Dr. Eaton?

Dr. EATON. I would like very much if the gentleman would locate himself a little more fully. I used to represent or misrepresent Princeton University.

Dr. HITTI. I was born at Mt. Lebanon. I am presently professor of Semitic literature at Princeton. I was educated in American high schools and the American University of Beirut. I went to Columbia and I have been connected with Princeton since 1926.

Dr. EATON. If it is not too personal, are you an Arab?

Dr. HITTI. The word Arab is very misleading. The word Arab is a linguistic, not ethnic word and means one whose mother tongue is Arabic, especially if a Moslem. I am a Christian. My people have been Christians from time immemorial. I claim I am a descendant of the ancient Canaanites or Phoenicians, who also occupied Palestine. Palestine was not empty when the Moslem Arabians went there. It had the Philistines on the east coast. There were people in Palestine before the Jews ever came. There were people in Palestine after the Jews left the country, and those are the people we call Arabs. They are descendants of old stock who have maintained themselves for ages there, remained; they are the forgotten men. Nobody should deprive people who have been on the soil in their country for centuries of their soil. Their fathers and mothers are buried there. We call them Arabs only because they speak the Arabic language, but they are descendants of the ancient Semitic people.

Chairman BLOOM. Thank you, Doctor.

Dr. HITTI. I wanted to take advantage of this situation because there is a great deal of confusion as to who the "Arabs" of Palestine are.

Dr. EATON. The professor will not forget the old testament is really the story of the Jewish people, whether in or out of Palestine, because they had quite a right in that land too.

Dr. HITTI. Absolutely.

Dr. EATON. That is all, Mr. Chairman.

Chairman BLOOM. Mr. Jarman.

Mr. JARMAN. Doctor, I would like to hear a little more about the riots I have heard repeatedly referred to.

Dr. HITTI. The people of Palestine never accepted the terms of the mandate. They were often in a state of revolt. There were strikes and bloodshed in April 1920, May 1921, August 1929, and October 1936. Undoubtedly you remember the 1936 riot in which there was a great deal of bloodshed from both the Arab and Jewish sides. I have a little document showing some of the destruction in 1936 and some of the homes destroyed, but unfortunately it is in Arabic and I do not think it will do much good here.

Mr. JARMAN. Do you mean the Arab and Jews were fighting each other?

Dr. HITTI. Yes; they were.

Mr. JARMAN. That is all.

Chairman BLOOM. Mrs. Rogers.

Mrs. ROGERS. Do you see any solution for the Jewish people. They have had a very difficult time and have been persecuted.

Dr. HITTI. I know you have a great deal of sympathy for them as I have. You may not believe it, but I am of the Semitic stock. We want to find a new home for the Jews. Every right-minded man, whether Jew or Christian, is in sympathy with them. In 1920 Palestine had forty or fifty thousand Jews. Since that time those Jews have been multiplied by practically 10. In other words, between 1919 and 1939 the Jewish population was multiplied by 10.

Now if anybody would expect a small country like Palestine to take over 10 times its Jewish population, he would expect too much. I am not going to foretell what would happen if we insist, but I think one of the witnesses who will come next, an American engineer who had something to do with the organization of the Arabian Mining Syndicate and has been into every nook and corner of Arabia, can tell you. Besides, the country has reached its absorptive capacity.

Mrs. ROGERS. Do you see any difference in giving them a homeland instead of a Jewish commonwealth?

Dr. HITTI. There is a great deal of difference. That is agreed to by the British Government, by liberal-minded Jews, and by many others.

Mrs. ROGERS. Have you discussed the matter with the State Department about bringing it up in wartime?

Dr. HITTI. I do not remember that I took this up during the war, but I recall correspondence prior to the present war.

Mrs. ROGERS. Thank you very much.

Chairman BLOOM. Mr. Burgin.

Mr. BURGIN. Are you in favor of the resolution to construct a Jewish state and make it?

Dr. HITTI. I cannot speak officially for Palestine; but the 1939 White Paper promised it a constitutional government which would speak for it. I was teaching in Beirut 1920–24. At that time many Armenians and Assyrians were coming there that had been persecuted by the Turks and were all received with open arms. There were Jews coming into Palestine and everyone was eyeing the Jews with suspicion. The Jews and the Arabs were getting along all right until the political Zionists of New York came in.

Mr. BURGIN. I yield to Mr. Jarman.

Chairman BLOOM. Mr. Jarman.

Mr. JARMAN. I want to get your distinction between a home and a Jewish commonwealth.

Dr. HITTI. The British Government promised a home and fulfilled its obligation. The British Government never said we want to constitute Palestine a Jewish commonwealth. It is the Zionists of New York who say that.

Mr. JARMAN. The 1922 resolution has an entirely different meaning from this.

Dr. HITTI. To my mind, yes.

Now, you want to go the British one better. You want to reconstitute Palestine into a Jewish commonwealth.

Mr. JARMAN. Your position is that there already is a Jewish national home in Palestine?

Dr. HITTI. Yes; and so far as I am concerned I would like to see more Jews in Lebanon and Syria, with the idea of cooperation with the natives, not controlling them.

Mr. JARMAN. When were you in Palestine last?

Dr. HITTI. I have not been there since 1924 or 1925.

Chairman BLOOM. The Chair wishes to call attention again to the map before you so you can see the location.

Mr. JARMAN. That was just before the mandate?

Dr. HITTI. No; it was in effect. In my contacts with the British officials I can say without hesitation I did not meet a single official or member of the British community who thought it would be possible to establish a Jewish commonwealth in Palestine. I may go further. I never met an American or an European, unless he had an ax to grind, who thought that the establishment of Palestine as a Jewish commonwealth was in the realm of possibility.

Mr. JARMAN. Why do they regard it as not within the realm of possibility?

Dr. HITTI. Because it is predicated upon two premises, first that Palestine is an unoccupied country ready to receive people from the outside, but Palestine is already occupied. It is partly barren. There is a place, the Dead Sea, which is 1,200 feet below sea level. It has a limited capacity. It is already populated.

Even in the mind of the author of Balfour Declaration this fact was not clear. Prof. John Garstang, of the University of Liverpool, reports that on the occasion of the opening of the Hebrew University in Jerusalem, Mr. Balfour at a private dinner party looked through the window and asked, "Who are these long-robed gentlemen one sees in the streets?" And when told that those were the native Arab sheiks, he remarked with surprise, "Arabs!—but I understood that when the Turks evacuated Palestine it was left desolate and without population."

The second premise is that there is a lack of national feeling. The fact is that there is a strong Arab national feeling aroused mainly by American influence. Arab nationalism draws its inspiration from American ideology. I was an American before I took my first papers in New York, because I attended in Lebanon, American schools. If you will permit me I refer you to the King-Crane report, which noted the rising national feeling and drew the distinction between a national home in Palestine and reconstitution of Palestine as a Commonwealth. You cannot establish anything against the will of the people You would have to support it with your bayonets. Are you willing to do that?

There are reasonable responsible Arabs who would like to see a modern reconstituted Palestine, but on the basis of equality and cooperation among citizens. Is that not fair? Is anything wrong with that?

We have 275,000,000 Moslems here. How are we to hold them down, and how can we? There is danger sir. I am very sorry to say I saw Zionist advertisements in the New York Times referring to civil war. A civil war in Palestine would endanger the lives of Jews throughout the Moslem world. There are 40,000 Jews in the heart of Arabia proper. Their lives will be in danger, and in Syria and Iraq, too.

Chairman BLOOM. Mr. Chiperfield.

Mr. CHIPERFIELD. Would you approve at this time passage by this committee of the resolution if it eliminated the words "Jewish commonwealth"?

Dr. HITTI. That was already passed in 1923; so what is the use of passing it again.

Mr. CHIPERFIELD. Is that your answer?

Dr. HITTI. Yes.

Chairman BLOOM. Any further questions?

Mr. CHIPERFIELD. No.

Chairman BLOOM. Mr. Gordon.

Mr. GORDON. No questions.

Chairman BLOOM. Mr. Stearns.

Mr. STEARNS. This resolution as I see it contains two distinct propositions, that Palestine should be open to free entry, and that a Jewish Commonwealth should be established there.

Dr. HITTI. Yes.

Mr. STEARNS. You object to establishing it as a free and democratic Jewish commonwealth?

Dr. HITTI. Yes.

Mr. STEARNS. I notice Mr. Churchill said in the House of Commons:

Not only did the War Cabinet of those days take the decision, but all cabinets of every party after the war, after examining it in the varying circumstances which have arisen, have endorsed a decision and taken the fullest responsibility for it.

I think I was one of the first to draw that conclusion. Do you object to the first part, the opening of the door?

Dr. HITTI. No, as far as I am personally concerned, if there is some power to accomplish this, but it is impossible at the present time. The Zionist propaganda has been so strong as to make us think it can be done. Do you see how we can do it? It is too late. I have no objection to the Jews, myself.

Mr. STEARNS. I understood you to say you would not be prepared to oppose the opening of the doors of Palestine for the entry of the Jews.

Dr. HITTI. Theoretically, no.

Mr. STEARNS. I am talking about what this committee may pass. Would you object?

Dr. HITTI. This is the question the gentleman before you raised, but we are already committed to that.

Chairman BLOOM. You have no objection to leaving the last part out?

Dr. HITTI. I have no personal objection, but I am telling you of the danger involved.

Mr. STEARNS. That is all.

Chairman BLOOM. Mr. Fulbright.

Mr. FULBRIGHT. Is this the language you would approve of, that it should be opened up for colonization and ultimately to be constituted a free and democratic commonwealth?

Dr. HITTI. That is the most objectionable part.

Mr. FULBRIGHT. That is to change the last phrase.

Dr. HITTI. Yes, sir.

Mr. FULBRIGHT. And the other shall be full opportunity for colonization and leave out the word "Jewish"? I was trying to get your idea how this might be acceptable.

Dr. HITTI. You want to introduce more colonization. Palestine is already overcolonized and it is promised a constitutional government by the 1939 white paper. What is the point in introducing more people if your object is to make it a free and democratic state? The relation between the first part——

Mr. FULBRIGHT. That would remove the principal objection to the resolution which you state you would not oppose.

Dr. HITTI. If you will stop there, rather than continue and say you want to establish a free and democratic Jewish commonwealth.

Mr. FULBRIGHT. I do not think it would change it much.

Dr. HITTI. I fail to see the connection between introducing new immigrants and converting Palestine into a commonwealth unless it is Jewish, but my personal views do not affect this situation. The people there in Palestine now have developed such hostile objections which to my mind would not justify the introduction of new immigrants. These people are going to come back and say, "We are a small country and a poor country, why don't you take them; you being so solicitous about the Jews, why don't you do something yourselves?"

Is that not the same thing anyone would ask?

Mr. FULBRIGHT. It might occur to me that since you are now an American citizen what is your idea?

Dr. HITTI. If I were a Member of Congress, I would introduce a bill to permit refugees into this country, Jew or not Jew.

Mr. FULBRIGHT. That is all.

Chairman BLOOM. Mr. Courtney.

Mr. COURTNEY. No questions.

Chairman BLOOM. Mr. Wright.

Mr. WRIGHT. To come back to the historical background prior to the last World War, Arabia generally was governed by Turkey.

Dr. HITTI. That is right.

Mr. WRIGHT. And the Arabian states were liberated by the Allies and constituted self-governing countries.

Dr. HITTI. With the cooperation of the Arabs.

Mr. WRIGHT. But General Allenby came into Arabia and finally defeated the Turkish Army.

Dr. HITTI. Yes.

Mr. WRIGHT. I am not going to quarrel with you on the question of cooperation. At the time of the writing of the peace treaty the Allies set up independent countries in Arabia.

Dr. HITTI. You are using Arabia in the sense of Arabic-speaking countries.

Mr. WRIGHT. That was the intention.

Dr. HITTI. Yes, sir.

Mr. WRIGHT. At the same time it was also the intention of the signatories to the League of Nations to set up a Jewish Home in Palestine.

Dr. HITTI. That is correct.

Mr. WRIGHT. Are you acquainted with the convention which was signed—it probably did not rise to the dignity of a convention, but it was signed by Prince Feisal.

Dr. HITTI. I am familiar with that.

Mr. WRIGHT. And I believe article 3 of that treaty stated as follows:

(Article 3 is as follows:)

Dr. HITTI. Yes.

Mr. WRIGHT. In other words, Prince Feisal did agree to the Balfour Declaration?

Dr. HITTI. Yes.

Mr. WRIGHT. And yet you state——

Dr. HITTI. May I ask you to read the last statement between——

Mr. WRIGHT (interposing). I do not know whether I have it.

Dr. HITTI. That Feisal Weizmann agreement was quoted several times, the last in Life magazine, minus the rider. I have it, may I read it, sir?

Chairman BLOOM. Yes.

Dr. HITTI. It reads as follows:

(The quotation is as follows:)

Provided the Arabs obtain their independence as demanded in my memorandum dated the 4th of January 1919, to the Foreign Office of the Government of Great Britain, I shall concur in the above articles. But if the slightest modification or departure were to be made [sc. in relation to the demands of the memorandum] I shall not then be bound by a single word of the present agreement which shall be deemed void and of no account or validity, and I shall not be answerable in any way whatsoever.

FAISAL IBN HUSAIN.
CHAIM WEIZMANN.

Mr. WRIGHT. You also said the Arabs later objected to the Balfour Declaration.

Dr. HITTI. They did, yes.

Mr. WRIGHT. In your testimony before the committee you stated that was the cause of the riots.

Dr. HITTI. That is one of the causes, yes.

Mr. WRIGHT. I want to bring out at the time Prince Feisal approved of the Balfour Declaration.

Dr. HITTI. Yes, subject to this provision which you did not have.

Mr. WRIGHT. As to the meaning of the Balfour Declaration, I believe it would probably be interesting to refer to the convention between the United States and Great Britain.

In Article 6 it states they shall encourage Jewish immigration, and if you did not do that you could not have——

Chairman BLOOM. Was that the convention? That was the mandate, was it not, which was embodied in the Convention?

Mr. WRIGHT. The mandate was included in the convention.

Chairman BLOOM. That is the convention signed by President Coolidge?

Mr. WRIGHT. Yes, sir. I believe that the convention between the United States and Great Britain included the terms of the mandate.

Chairman BLOOM. Oh, yes.

Mr. WRIGHT. Then at the time it was contemplated there would be Jewish immigration.

Dr. HITTI. Subject to this proviso, compliance with the memorandum submitted to the British Government. Even Feisal objected later.

Mr. WRIGHT. Then I suppose you were also acquainted with the speech of Lord Balfour not long after the Balfour Declaration.

I am quoting that to illustrate the purpose of the Balfour Declaration and I think that pretty generally states——

Chairman BLOOM. Did you put the date in there?

Mr. WRIGHT. July 20, 1920.

Chairman BLOOM. By Lord Balfour.

Mr. WRIGHT. By Lord Balfour. Are you acquainted with the statement made by Prince Feisal on December 12, 1918?

Now since that was the situation do you think there was any justification in shutting off immigration?

Dr. HITTI. It has been multiplied by 10.

Mr. WRIGHT. Was there any limitation at the time?

Dr. HITTI. The idea of a politically converted Palestine into a Jewish commonwealth did not then loom high, not even in Weizmann's mind.

Shall we talk frankly and freely?

Chairman BLOOM. I thought we were.

Mr. WRIGHT. I think we were all the time.

Dr. HITTI. Feisal wanted to get some cooperation from the Jews. Feisal was not a diplomat; he made this bargain. You give us the Arabian Empire, you give us——

Mr. WRIGHT (interposing). The 'Jews 'never opposed the concessions to the Arabs in Arabia.

Dr. HITTI. No.

Mr. WRIGHT. You agree the position of the Arabs is much better and if it had not been for General Allenby they would not have chased the Turks out.

Dr. HITTI. Except——

Mr. WRIGHT (interposing). I have no desire to minimize contributions by the Arabs.

Dr. HITTI. The point that we should never lose sight of is that Palestine has been occupied by people who are called Arabs. It is theirs by natural right. The people have the right of occupancy. They owned it before Christ.

Mr. WRIGHT. As a practical matter the Arabs did not govern Palestine since the seventh century, although there may be some merit in what you say, but do you not think this makes a different situation? You spoke a while ago about telling the United States to make a Jewish home in Arizona. The United States governs Arizona.

Dr. HITTI. I am taking exceptions, Mr. Chairman, to the statement the Arabs didn't rule Palestine. I wrote a history on the Arabs myself.

Chairman BLOOM. The committee will be very glad to have a copy.

Dr. HITTI. The Arabs were in control, but the point which I wish to bring out——

Mr. WRIGHT (interposing). May I just interject at that point?

Dr. HITTI. Yes.

Mr. WRIGHT. You said you are a descendant from an ancient line?

Dr. HITTI. I cannot prove it.

Mr. WRIGHT. Your own people were conquered by Arabs in the seventh century?

Dr. HITTI. Yes.

Mr. WRIGHT. Although you speak the Arabic tongue the people you speak for were subjected in the seventh century.

Dr. HITTI. Yes; so far as Lebanon is concerned. It was practically an independent state. Our people after 1860 never contributed soldiers, or paid taxes to the Ottoman government.

Chairman BLOOM. Pardon an interruption. The Chair would like to state that it would be well for you to get down to this resolution, because the gentleman has occupied an hour and a quarter.

Mr. WRIGHT. Probably I am contributing to the delay.

Chairman BLOOM. No; please continue with the resolution.

Dr. HITTI. This is my last point, this Balfour Declaration to which you attach so much importance is sandwiched in between other promises to the Arabs. In this legal tangle the Palestinan Arab is the forgotten man

Mr. WRIGHT. Did these promises ever mention Palestine?

Dr. HITTI. Never by name. At that time the British made several promises including a promise to themselves, so we have too many promises.

Mr. WRIGHT. The only public document we have which was agreed to is that which was agreed to by signatories to the League of Nations.

Dr. HITTI. How about the League of Nations covenant article 22?

Mr. WRIGHT. Since the mandate has been established the Arab population has increased from 600,000 to a million.

Dr. HITTI. Almost correct; yes.

Mr. WRIGHT. There can be no justification that the Jews are driving the Arabs out. You do not say that there can be any fear of the Jews.

Dr. HITTI. The fear is based on such Zionist statements as the advertisement in the New York Times and the book entitled "Middle East: The Cross Roads." They said definitely the proposition is to transfer two or three million Arabs.

Mr. WRIGHT. Is that an official statement by anyone responsible?

Chairman BLOOM. No.

Dr. HITTI. But that advertisement appeared.

Mr. WRIGHT. You are not responsible for everything anyone might say.

Dr. HITTI. No; but when I refer to the Arabs I find myself thinking——

Mr. WRIGHT (interposing). It is quite possible there may be various opinions but I think we should consider the practical opinion.

Dr. HITTI. There is an article in Foreign Affairs (January 1942) by Dr. Weizmann saying the transfer of the Arabs would be facilitated——

Mr. WRIGHT. There are a million there now.

Dr. HITTI. Correct.

Mr. WRIGHT. That is all.

Chairman BLOOM. Mrs. Bolton.

Mrs. BOLTON. No questions.

Chairman BLOOM. Doctor, you are acquainted with the convention, the treaty of 1925, which was signed by President Coolidge?

Dr. HITTI. No, sir.

Chairman BLOOM. Yes; in 1925 the convention between the United States and Great Britain.

Dr. HITTI. Yes.

Chairman BLOOM. You made the statement here the United States is so concerned about that thing that it seems to be just agitation. If we have a convention signed by the President of the United States, call it a treaty or whatever you want, they live up to the promises.

Dr. HITTI. Yes.

Chairman BLOOM. Do not articles 1, 2, and 7 specifically cover immigration?

Dr. HITTI. The convention was in 1925.

Chairman BLOOM. There has always been immigration.

On pages 18 and 19 it is the Covenant signed by President Coolidge and, I think, Chamberlain. You would not have any objection to the United States asking that all portions are carried out?

Dr. HITTI. Which particular articles have been violated?

Chairman BLOOM. I will have the clerk read articles 1, 2, and 7, from page 18.

(The clerk thereupon read articles 1, 2, and 7 from p. 18:)

ARTICLE 1

Subject to the provisions of the present convention the United States consents to the administration of Palestine by His Britannic Majesty, pursuant to the mandate recited above.

ARTICLE 2

The United States and its nationals shall have and enjoy all the rights and benefits secured under the terms of the mandate to members of the League of Nations and their nationals, notwithstanding the fact that the United States is not a member of the League of Nations.

ARTICLE 7

Nothing contained in the present convention shall be affected by any modification which may be made in the terms of the mandate, as recited above, unless such modification shall have been assented to by the United States.

Chairman BLOOM. Now if the British Government according to the convention and the mandate have done things which they should not have done without the consent of the United States, do you not think the Congress should ask the British Government to adhere to the mandate of the convention of 1925?

Dr. HITTI. Absolutely.

Chairman Bloom. Would you concede immigration and conditions and things that have been existing have nothing to do with this?

Dr. Hitti. So far as I now see there is nothing in the 1939 white paper to modify its terms.

Chairman Bloom. Doctor, if they restrict immigration, if you say there shall not be any immigration or limited immigration whatever, if it is contrary to the articles as contained in this convention of 1925 without the consent of the United States, would you say that is wrong and the United States has a right to make their objection?

Dr. Hitti. Your question implies that in the mandate there was a provision for an unlimited admission of Jews.

Chairman Bloom. I just took the word of the mandate and the convention.

Dr. Hitti. Yes.

Chairman Bloom. If there was any change in the mandate or convention without the consent of the United States, the United States Government has a right to protest. Is that all right?

Dr. Hitti. Absolutely.

Chairman Bloom. We have a right to protest in that regard and the Government of the United States has the right to suggest to the British Government the advisability of living up to the agreement.

Dr. Hitti. I am beginning to analyze this——

Chairman Bloom. We are not analyzing.

Dr. Hitti. It is a theoretical matter.

Chairman Bloom. What I am trying to make clear here is, Do we have the right to do that or not, if the British Government has done anything contrary to the convention of 1925 with reference to anything contained therein then the United States has the right to protest?

Dr. Hitti. I agree to that, in theory. The resolution——

Chairman Bloom. We are asking the British Government to reconstitute Palestine in a Jewish home—check me on the sections.

Mr. Wright. Sections 14 and 15 of the mandate.

Dr. Hitti. Will you read it?

Chairman Bloom. The Chair wishes to state that Mr. Wadsworth is next, but until he returns the Chair will recognize Dr. Pfeifer.

Dr. Pfeifer. Doctor, you are an American citizen?

Dr. Hitti. Yes.

Dr. Pfeifer. You believe in civilization?

Dr. Hitti. In civilization, I hope I do.

Dr. Pfeifer. Do you believe in the democratic way of life?

Dr. Hitti. Absolutely.

Dr. Pfeifer. You are happy over the fact of the Arabs being removed from the Turkish yoke?

Dr. Hitti. Absolutely.

Dr. Pfeifer. Before you made the statement about speaking frankly, the Arabs were allowed there and the fact that they were permitted to come into Palestine simply for one reason on account of what they got from the Jews.

Dr. Hitti. I did not say that.

Dr. Pfeifer. Did you not say the Arab rejection was the fact that immigration was permitted into Palestine by the Jews for one reason, simply to get what you could from the Jewish immigrants. Is that right?

Dr. Hitti. No.

Dr. PFEIFER. The population of Palestine, Doctor, as you stated, numbers about a million.   I mean as far as the Arabs are concerned.

Dr. HITTI. Correct.

Dr. PFEIFER. In the past 25 years it increased almost double.

Dr. HITTI. Yes, sir.

Dr. PFEIFER. And that increase was due to one thing—the immigrant Jew?

Dr. HITTI. No, sir.

Dr. PFEIFER. What made the Arabs inhabit Palestine to a greater extent?

Dr. HITTI. The regime was very good.   Obviously there were better public health conditions, not due to the Zionist activities but due to mandatory power.   Because of that fact the Arabs contributed much to the population of Palestine and to blame it entirely on the Zionists is unfair.

Dr. PFEIFER. Do you not think the greater degree of improvement was due to the Zionist immigrant?

Dr. HITTI. They did not produce much improvement except in their colonies.

Dr. PFEIFER. Did not the Arabs go to Palestine to get help?

Dr. HITTI. No, sir; because the Jewish economy is more or less of a closed shop.   Many of the Arabs were dispossessed by the purchase of their lands.

Chairman BLOOM. They sold it of their own free will.

Dr. PFEIFER. They did.

Dr. HITTI. They were dispossessed and did not know where to go. They were refused employment in the Jewish shops because they were not Jews.

Dr. PFEIFER. Do you not believe if the Jews did not immigrate to Palestine today Palestine would be sparsely settled?

Dr. HITTI. No; if you notice the increase in population in Lebanon, Iraq, Egypt, where there was no Jewish immigration.

Dr. PFEIFER. Doctor, we are interested solely in Palestine.

Is it not true the land itself showed a remarkable depreciation in value and of use while under the Arabian rule; did not the Arabs neglect their own land to such a degree it became uninhabitable?

Dr. HITTI. No, I beg to differ with you.   The comparison has often been made between Jewish and non-Jewish lands in Palestine. There were Jews in Palestine before the Zionists, and you will find there is very little difference between their lands and the Arabs' lands.

Dr. PFEIFER. This small area of Palestine measures about what, 10,000 square miles?

Dr. HITTI. Approximately.

Dr. PFEIFER. Today Palestine is an outstanding portion of territory.

Is it so outstanding, the fact that the Arabian regime made it so or because the Jewish immigrants through their hard labor converted it into a Holy Land?

Dr. HITTI. You mean outstanding in getting headlines in the paper?

Dr. PFEIFER. The land, the beautiful cities are now shining cities of the world.   Do you think that was due to the Arabs or the Jewish immigrants?

Dr. HITTI. I would not admit it except insofar as Jewish colonies. The Arabs say, "We would not barter our independence for the sake of money from the Jews. We have suffered more than under the Turkish regime." You ask me if I believe in democracy, the democratic way of life. Let us apply it to this situation.

Dr. PFEIFER. Do you not believe the improvements in Palestine, do you not believe they are benefited and the benefit is felt by them through the activities of the Jewish immigrants? Do you not think the Arabs have gained immensely?

Dr. HITTI. What do you have in mind? How did they benefit?

Dr. PFEIFER. By following the technique and methods of the Jewish immigrants. Jewish immigrants have undertaken not only to build their own homes and cities but attempted to instruct those that came to them for advice. They were liberal and to the extent of being liberal the Arabs want to kick them out of Palestine.

Dr. HITTI. No.

Dr. PFEIFER. What objection do you have?

Dr. HITTI. Conversion to a commonwealth, the resolution before you——

Dr. PFEIFER. Do you not believe the Jews are entitled to their own land?

Dr. HITTI. Just as much as the Arabs are entitled to theirs.

Dr. PFEIFER. Do the Arabs still say Palestine is theirs?

Dr. HITTI. Yes.

Dr. PFEIFER. Does this mandate approve the immigration of Arabs to Palestine?

Dr. HITTI. It did.

Dr. PFEIFER. Does it today?

Dr. HITTI. Yes.

Dr. PFEIFER. Doctor, you have made some statements you know already that are not right. If you do not know the facts please say so. I do not want this record filled up with a lot of explanations and fears. Let us get around to the facts. You have been on the stand an hour and a half.

Mr. WADSWORTH. I think it is a question that elicits the answer.

Chairman BLOOM. That is very true. Please go ahead now.

Dr. PFEIFER. Then you maintain there was a limitation of Arabian people into Palestine?

Dr. HITTI. There is. If it is not legal it is still being done.

Dr. PFEIFER. We are talking about law.

Dr. HITTI. The Jews have multiplied by 10 times.

Dr. PFEIFER. There is no limitation as far as immigration into Palestine is concerned.

Dr. HITTI. So far as the legal side.

Dr. PFEIFER. As the chairman mentioned to you about being an American citizen and believing in the democratic way of life, you believe in fulfilling contracts entered into. Is that right?

Dr. HITTI. Surely.

Dr. PFEIFER. We have entered into a contract. You believe in carrying out that mandate?

Dr. HITTI. Sure.

Dr. PFEIFER. Why is it now you object to it?

Dr. HITTI. I do not.

Dr. PFEIFER. You were confirming the white paper's action and not believing. That is just indirectly going against your belief in the white paper.

Dr. HITTI. I believe in what the white paper says. We have fulfilled our obligation.

Dr. PFEIFER. You intend to establish a national home for the Jews?

Dr. HITTI. In Palestine, yes.

Dr. PFEIFER. Not the Jews in Palestine. That was for the Jews all over.

Dr. HITTI. In Palestine there is a national home already.

Dr. PFEIFER. This interpretation depends upon your own interpretation.

Dr. HITTI. Not only mine but of the British and others; is that not true?

Dr. PFEIFER. You have got to permit immigration to go in Palestine if you agree the Balfour Declaration is the right thing.

Dr. HITTI. What do you want me to do?

Dr. PFEIFER. I want to live up to the Balfour Declaration.

Dr. HITTI. Where is the end of it?

Chairman BLOOM. The Chair will have to stop this now. It is 12 o'clock and we have 8 or 10 more witnesses.

Dr. PFEIFER. I am through Mr. Chairman.

Chairman BLOOM. Are there any further questions?

Mrs. ROGERS. May I ask a question?

Chairman BLOOM. Yes.

Mrs. ROGERS. You say you would favor allowing more Jewish people to come here.

Chairman BLOOM. The Chair rules the question out of order. That is a matter of immigration. I think the witness has contributed all he knows.

Mrs. ROGERS. I introduced a bill to permit Jewish refugees to enter the country.

Chairman BLOOM. Thank you very much, Doctor.

Is Mr. Emanuel Neumann here?

Mr. NEUMANN. Yes, sir.

STATEMENT OF EMANUEL NEUMANN, ATTORNEY, NEW YORK, N. Y.

Chairman BLOOM. Give your full name and address.

Mr. NEUMANN. New York, 749 West End Avenue.

Chairman BLOOM. That is in my district.

Mr. NEUMANN. I am fortunate it is.

Chairman BLOOM. Whom do you represent?

Mr. NEUMANN. I am here in my own capacity and I have been in the Zionist movement all my life. In 1932 and 1933 I served for the Zionist organization in Palestine, and saw 8 years' experience in Palestine.

Chairman BLOOM. Pardon me, we have Representative Lynch, of New York. Mr. Lynch.

STATEMENT OF HON. WALTER A. LYNCH, A REPRESENTATIVE IN CONGRESS FROM THE STATE OF NEW YORK

Mr. LYNCH. Mr. Chairman, I wish to thank you and the committee for giving me the opportunity to appear here at this time. I am thoroughly in favor of House Resolutions 417 and 418, which are before you for consideration this morning.

We Americans have little use for double talk—the language of international diplomacy. When the Sixty-seventh Congress of the United States on June 30, 1922, passed the resolution, later signed by President Harding, "that the United States of America favors the establishment in Palestine of a national home for the Jewish people" there was no equivocation. The ruthless persecution of the Jews in Europe had aroused the sympathies of the American people, and our Congress, by its resolution, sought to give expression to the deep-seated conviction of the people of the United States that all men are created equal and that freedom of religion is the inalienable right of every individual. The centuries have been the tortuous trek of the Jews through the countries of the world, and have witnessed the persecutions that have relentlessly pursued them. Through the years and despite the persecutions the Jewish heart clung with deep-seated affection to Palestine—the home of Jewry and the birthplace of Christendom.

The world has too long denied the Jews their Palestine. It is time their right to their homeland be recognized. The hour has come when justice be done, when appeasement cease and the doors of Palestine be opened as a haven to the millions of homeless Jews who are victims of persecution.

Neither in the resolution of the Sixty-seventh Congress nor in the Balfour Declaration is there any intimation that there was to be a limitation of the number of Jews for whom Palestine might be a haven. Indeed, under article 6 of the Convention between the United States and Great Britain, as proclaimed by President Calvin Coolidge on December 15, 1925, it specifically provides that the administration of Palestine—

shall facilitate Jewish immigration under suitable conditions and shall encourage, in cooperation with the Jewish agency referred to in article 4, close settlement of the Jews on the land, including State lands and waste lands not required for public purposes.

The only restriction that was placed on immigration prior to the British white paper—and the only one that could possibly have ever been intended—was that the volume of immigration should not be so great as to exceed the economic capacity of the country to absorb such immigration. The reason for this was to prevent the immigrants from becoming a burden upon the community. This was sound policy.

To my mind, restriction of immigration, based on political consid-erations, as outlined in the British white paper defeats the very pur-pose of the Balfour Declaration and the resolution of the Sixty-seventh Congress. While calling Palestine a haven for homeless Jews it shuts the doors of that home against all but a minimum of Jewish refugees. Instead of becoming a "center in which the Jewish people may take on ground of religion and race, an interest and price" Palestine, under the British white paper, becomes a community surrounded by a wall of politics, which bars the hopeless and unfortunate Jewish refugees who in their desperate need, seek succor amongst their coreligionists— and in vain.

STATEMENT OF HON. JAMES J. HEFFERNAN, A REPRESENTATIVE IN CONGRESS FROM THE FIFTH DISTRICT, STATE OF NEW YORK

Mr. HEFFERNAN. Gentlemen, I wish to record my support of the Palestine resolutions now being considered by this committee. The persecution of the Jewish people in Europe has demonstrated the need for a Jewish homeland and I believe that the United States should do everything it can to permit free entry of Jews into Palestine.

I hope that you gentlemen will recognize the need for a Jewish commonwealth and an open-door policy in Palestine at this time.

STATEMENT OF THE HONORABLE JOSEPH L. PFEIFER, A REPRESENTATIVE IN CONGRESS FROM THE THIRD DISTRICT, STATE OF NEW YORK

Mr. PFEIFER. Mr. Chairman, your fairness at all times has again been exemplified in these hearings on Resolutions 418 and 419. From what we have learned from the witnesses confirms my opinion of long ago, that drastic action should be taken immediately to give all aid possible to this group of suffering humanity. It is very evident the time is at hand when we cannot go any further without raising our voice in protest over the continued unwillingness of Great Britain to relax her stringent rule regarding the immigration of Jews to Palestine.

The humiliation and atrocities to which they have been subjected, particularly on the European Continent, surpasses anything that has come to the attention of the civilized world.

Their position is insecure. In the countries where they are not persecuted, they feel a gratitude tempered by fear lest this may not endure. This constant atmosphere of fear is no good for any individual or group of individuals in the free exercise and development of mind and body. Anti-Semitism is always lurking around the corner. A danger not only to the Jews but to the moral and mental balance of their Gentile neighbors.

What can we do to relieve this situation? We can either take them into our fold or help to secure for them a place where they may gather and develop into a nation and a country of their own. A national existence of their own seems to be the consensus of opinion. But where? Each nation seems to shirk the responsibility. Several areas have been mentioned but have proven to be a fiasco. Jewish tradition, religious and national, knows only one Promised Land, and that is Palestine. It is the rightful home of the Jewish people. This territory which has been assigned for the Jewish national home, through the Balfour Declaration to the Jews, on November 2, 1917, is only 10,000 miles square—a very small portion of the vast Arabian territory which is about 1,500,000 square miles.

This is the same Palestine which the Bible has described as a land flowing with milk and honey, and the historians tell us that it supported a population of 4,000,000 in the Roman and Grecian eras.

During the centuries that followed, misrule has been so evident that neglect of this holy place soon converted it into a desolated area. Sand dunes replaced vegetation and cities dwindled.

Now let us see what has been done to this Holy Land, which is about the size of Belgium or Sicily, since the Jews began their development in 1920. They have not only doubled its population, but through their determination to rebuild the ancient homeland of the Jewish people, they have converted this rapidly disintegrating area into a semi-industrial and agricultural country. They not only had to acquire land but had to reclaim it, drain it, reforest it, fertilize it, irrigate it, electrify it, and industrialize it with new industries which today number textile, chemical, electrical, building, and clothing—a credit to any nation. Its agricultural population of 800,000 will be trebled in the near future due to irrigation possibilities. Its cities now, which at one time were deserted, are well inhabited and electrified. Tel-Aviv is now a city of 200,000 where only 30 years ago were merely sand dunes, and Haifa rapidly growing into a city of 500,000.

This growth of the Jewish people's national home and its achievements in many fields command the admiration of the world and certainly a source of pride to the Jewish people.

Palestine in general has become a new world. The large increase of Jewish population, which is about 1,500,000 today, has not displaced any of the native population. In fact, we are informed that it has caused an increase in the Arab population. This has been confirmed by Mr. Malcolm MacDonald, Secretary for the Colonies in the Chamberlain government, when he stated in the House of Commons, on November 24, 1938:

The Arabs cannot say that the Jews are driving them out of their country. If not a single Jew had come to Palestine after 1918, I believe that the Arab population of Palestine today would still have been around the 600,000 figure, instead of over 1,000,000 as at present, at which it had been stable under the Turkish rule. It is because the Jews who have come to Palestine bring modern health services and other advantages, that the Arab men and women who would have been dead are alive today, that Arab children who would never have drawn breath have been born and grow strong.

The assurance by the English Government of a Jewish national home in Palestine, initiated over a quarter of a century ago, was mainly responsible for the country's mighty advance. The persecutions of the minorities during the First World War was the seed for the development of this home, with the hope that such atrocities would never again occur. But before and during the present World War, the atrocities became more and more brutal. Millions of Jews were slaughtered. Every attempt was made to stop these atrocities, but to no avail. His Holiness, Pope Pius XI, cognizant of these brutalities, interceded on several occasions and offered his services to guarantee safe passage, whenever possible, for the transportation of the oppressed minorities to their homeland in Palestine. But unfortunately this did not materialize. His pleas and the increased atrocities has stirred the entire civilized world to act with greater urgency toward making it a reality. Palestine for the Jews. A homeland of their own. But what have we accomplished, and how does the situation stand today?

At a time when millions of European Jews have been massacred by the Nazis, we face a possibility of closure of the only door of escape for the 2,000,000 Jews who still survive the tortures and who are imploring the civilized world to provide them with means of escape from the Nazi murderers, through the white paper of May 17, 1939, issued by the British Government, which closes Palestine to all Jewish immigration on March 31, 1944, and to which I protested, at the time of issuance of this white paper, and asked President Franklin D. Roosevelt to do all in his power to have Great Britain rescind that order, and to remind His Britannic Majesty of the "Mandate for Palestine" adopted by the Council of the League of Nations on July 24, 1922. This treaty specifically stated that any changes must be with our assent.

Mr. Winston Churchill informs us that—

His Majesty's Government have no intentions of repudiating the obligations into which they have entered toward the Jewish people—

and also stated:

The position is that His Majesty's Government are bound by a pledge which is antecedent to the Covenant of the League of Nations * * * and regrets very much that the pledge of the Balfour Declaration, endorsed as it has been by successive governments, and the conditions under which we obtained the mandate, have both been violated by the governments' proposals. There is much in this white paper which is alien to the spirit of the Balfour Declaration.

Is it fair then for the democratic world to be standing idly by and permit this white paper to go into effect? I, for one, do not believe so. This pledge of a home for refuge should not be closed to the still wandering persecuted scattered Jews throughout Europe, numbering about 2,000,000, whose eyes are focused on Palestine.

Should the doors of Palestine be closed to them through the action of the white paper, we ought then bow our heads in shame, for through this act of closure, we would encourage the Nasis regime to continue their brutalities and exterminate the remaining Jews. It would be a signal for Hitler to continue his atrocities until his aim has been accomplished.

We, as a democratic people, cannot and will not tolerate such brutalities. The Congress of the United States should and undoubtedly will approve unanimously any resolution that offers protection of the persecuted minorities.

You all recall the statement of Prime Minister Neville Chamberlain, 20 years ago, when he said:

A great responsibility will rest upon the Zionists, who, before long, will be proceeding, with joy in their hearts, to the ancient seat of their people. Theirs will be the task to build up a new prosperity and a new civilization in old Palestine, so long neglected and misruled.

Now, let us look over the record of the Jewish people since occupying Palestine. What do we find? We find that the Jewish people have lived up to their responsibility and have made Palestine what it is today. I agree with Prime Minister Churchill, referring to the Chamberlain statement, when he said:

Well, they have answered his call. They have fulfilled his hopes. How can he find it in his heart to strike them this mortal blow?

The Jewish people of Palestine have not only shown interest in their homeland but have done much to aid the Allied cause. The Jewish troops now number over 30,000 volunteers and have contributed much toward winning the war. Many of the Jewish youth of Palestine have already paid the supreme sacrifice in the line of battle and their loved ones at home aid our Allied armies by operating war plants and in the transportation of vital implements of war.

The Jewish troops are not only fighting to save their Jewish brethren of Europe but are fighting to help save the lives of our boys as well. They are a part of our integrate forces. They are fighting to help save the democratic way of life to which they have already contributed much.

Mr. Churchill, the dynamic force that he is, respected by all, even by the Axis Nations though they care not to admit, has the opportunity now to enforce his words by concrete action. He should persuade His Britannic Majesty to abrogate this white paper, and together with the Allied Nations, particularly with the United States through its War Refugee Board, create now a haven for these Jews. Get them out of the Nazi-controlled countries. Give them temporary shelter with the hope that Palestine will keep its doors open forever to welcome them.

STATEMENT OF DR. EMANUEL NEUMANN, ATTORNEY, 749 WEST END AVENUE, NEW YORK

Mr. NEUMANN. Mr. Chairman, ladies, and gentlemen, may I, in the first place, express my appreciation of the courtesy extended to me and also of the manner in which these hearings are conducted.

I am an American of Jewish descent and have been interested in the Zionist movement since my youth. In 1932–33 I served as a member of the executive of the Jewish Agency for Palestine and resided there for several years thereafter in a private capacity. Those 7 or 8 years spent on the spot have helped me, I believe, to a better understanding of the problem.

In order to deal with the question under consideration within a short space of time, it is necessary, I think, to strip it so far as possible of nonessentials and cut through to the heart and core of the matter. The issue, whatever its complexities, can be reduced to its essential elementary terms.

The case as between the Jews and the Arabs is in the nature of an international dispute submitted to the bar of public opinion. Actually it was adjudicated many years ago, and the resolution we are considering is essentially a reaffirmation of a judgment rendered in the past. The case may be considered under two heads: (1) Zionism and the Arab world, and (2) the position of the Palestinian Arabs. While the two aspects are related they are nevertheless distinct.

So far as the Arab world is concerned—and by that I mean for the moment the Arabs of southwestern Asia—Arabia, Iraq, Syria, and so forth—their case regarding Palestine is easily stated. They claim Palestine as part of the Arab domain, which Arabs are entitled to rule, and they assert that Palestine should have been included in the Arab domain and should never have been promised to the Jews in any form. They rest this claim chiefly on rights of possession, the record of the Arab revolt in the First World War, and the promises allegedly made to them at the time.

From the point of view of international law the record is by this time pretty clear, having been minutely studied and dealt with by many competent authorities. I will attempt to summarize it briefly. Historically, the Arabs had lost their sovereignty over nearly all of these lands many centuries ago—in fact, during the Middle Ages. They had been overrun by successive invasions and finally conquered by the Turks, and the countries in question were incorporated in the Ottoman Empire and governed as such since the year 1517. The Arabs were subjected to the autocratic rule of the Turkish sultans. They were steeped in poverty and misery. Their physical as well as moral fiber was affected. Their hopes for freedom and a brighter future depended upon the ultimate collapse of Turkish power and the dismemberment of the Ottoman Empire. But there was little prospect of this being brought about through the efforts of the Arabs themselves. They were too weak, too dispirited, disunited, lacking in leadership and resources.

Their chance came with the outbreak of the First World War, when Turkey took her plunge on the side of Germany, which brought her into conflict with Great Britain, France, and Russia. For the Arabs it was an historic opportunity. Even so it required a great effort on the part of the British and all their skill and diplomacy, as well as the expenditure of large sums of money, to induce the Arabs of the Hejaz in the interior of Arabia to revolt under Hussein and Feisal. And it took continued British effort, British leadership, and British money—more than $50,000,000 of it—to keep the revolt from collapsing after it was started. This revolt was confined to only a part of the tribes in the Arabian peninsula and some of the Transjordanians; while other sections of Arabia as well as the Arabs of Mesopotamia, Syria, and Palestine did not participate in it, but remained largely passive. On the other hand, many of them served with the Turkish armies fighting against the British. Authorities differ as to the military value of the revolt. Certainly it has often been exaggerated beyond all proportion. Whatever assistance was given by the tribesmen, by harrying the Turkish flank, unquestionably it was British troops and British Empire forces who fought the major campaigns, defeated the Turkish armies, and liberated all these regions. The cost in British life and treasure was heavy, particularly in Mesopotamia.

What would have happened in an earlier age under these circumstances? Either the annexation of these countries, their incorporation in the British Empire, or the establishment of protectorates on the old model. But there was a new spirit abroad, and new ideas, which found expression in Wilson's Fourteen Points. The principle of national self-determination had been enunciated primarily to hasten the disintrgration of the Austro-Hungarian Empire, but there was a disposition to apply these principles reasonably and to the extent possible in the case of the less developed countries of the Near East, which were not considered quite ripe for self-government. In that spirit, negotiations went forward between the representatives of the British and the leaders of the Arab revolt. These negotiations were complicated by parallel negotiations which were going on simultaneously among the Allied Powers themselves regarding their respective spheres of influence. But the British and Arabs did reach a certain understanding.

What was that understanding? In a nutshell it was this: The Arabs were to get independence in Arabia proper, that is, in the Arabian peninsula, and they were to get semi-independence in what is now Iraq and the interior of Syria. Two small areas were definitely excluded under the terms of this understanding, two small countries which were reserved because of special circumstances and considerations. The first was Lebanon, with its important Christian population, who had been oriented toward France as their traditional protector. The other was Palestine, which was to be set aside for Jewish resettlement and the reconstitution of the Jewish national home.

This, in substance, was the Anglo-Arab understanding, the plan which they hoped to put through at the peace conference. The Arabs were there and represented by a delegation headed by Feisal, who agreed with these plans which gave them 95 percent of what they claimed. Hussein was already recognized as King of the Hejaz in Arabia, while his son, Feisal, was to reign in Damascus, capital of Syria, and Abdullah was slated to become King of Iraq. Under the contemplated arrangement the Arabs had the prospect of independence and semi-independence in all these areas, aggregating over 1,000,000 square miles of territory. Moreover, they had the prospect of ultimate unity or confederation through the circumstance that these countries would be ruled by members of the same family, the new dynasty of Hussein. It was from their point of view an excellent bargain. Under the circumstances they considered it reasonable and prudent not to press their claims with respect to Lebanon and Palestine, in view of British commitments there. As the matter was put by the Royal Commission:

If King Hussein and the Emir Feisal secured their big Arab State they would concede little Palestine to the Jews.

Before and during the peace conference Feisal had numerous conferences with Dr. Weizmann and other Zionist leaders and repeatedly placed himself on record in support of Zionist aspirations. Indeed the Arabs and Zionists presented a united front at the peace conference, and they supported one another reciprocally, as had been agreed between them. In the sight of the world, by word and deed, the Arab spokesmen recognized the validity of Jewish aspirations with regard to Palestine.

Had the Anglo-Arab understanding been fully carried out at the time the subsequent history of Arab-Jewish relations might have been different. The Arab-Jewish alliance established by Emir Feisal and Dr. Weizmann might have continued indefinitely. It was unfortunate from the point of view of Arab-Jewish relations that, as it turned out, the Anglo-Arab understanding was not implemented at one stroke, but only in stages in successive years after much agitation in Syria and Iraq, which had its repercussion also in Palestine. Step by step, however, the Arabs achieved almost all that had been promised to them, and in some respects even more.

In April 1920 the Supreme Council met at San Remo to decide 'on the disposition of the Ottoman Empire and the terms of the Turkish peace treaty. It awarded to France the mandate over Syria and Lebanon and to Britain mandates over Iraq and Palestine. The Arabs protested this arrangement, chiefly with respect to Syria, and Feisel had himself proclaimed King in Damascus, only to be driven out by the French. Thereupon the British, in the following year, placed Feisal upon the throne of Iraq, while his brother Abdullah, who had turned up in Trans-Jordan, was recognized as the ruling prince in that country. So far as Palestine was concerned, the terms of the Balfour Declaration were incorporated in the Treaty of Sevres negotiated between Turkey and the Allied Powers. As is well known, the Balfour Declaration, as subsequently incorporated in the mandate for Palestine, was recognized and accepted by all the Allied Powers and indeed by 52 nations, by the community of nations. It had become part of the fabric of international law.

The British mandate for Iraq was terminated in 1932 and replaced by a treaty of alliance between Great Britain and the independent kingdom of Iraq. Four years later a similar development seemed imminent in Syria, where the French Government in 1936 negotiated with the Syrian Arabs for the termination of the French mandate and the recognition of independent states in Syria and Lebanon, with treaties of alliance between them and France. This arrangement failed of ratification by the French Chamber of Deputies at the time. Recently, however, during the present war, official declarations were made, both on behalf of the French and the British, declarations which were approved by the Government of the United States, promising the independence of those countries in the near future.

In the net result, the democracies have finally recognized virtually all the original claims of Arab nationalism to Arab independence with respect to Arabia, Iraq, Syria, and Trans-Jordan—an area covering about 1,200,000 square miles of territory and equivalent to the combined areas of England, France, Germany, Italy, and Spain—embracing all so-called Arab lands in Asia, and including some non-Arab districts, with the single exception of western Palestine, with its 10,000 square miles, constituting less than 1 percent of the total area. Even that ardent champion of the Arab cause, the famous Lawrence of Arabia, declared years ago that the promises made to the Arabs had been fulfilled and "we have come out of the Arab affair with clean hands."

So far then as the Arab world is concerned, it has, substantially speaking, achieved 99 percent of its goal and had given up no more than 1 percent of its total claim, namely, Palestine. And though it took years to achieve, the deal has been on the whole a highly satisfactory and profitable one from their point of view.

All in all, the Arabs were perhaps the greatest beneficiaries of Allied victory in the First World War, considering their very modest contribution toward that victory. Perhaps no other nation had gained so much in territory and independence for so little as the Arabs had contributed toward their own liberation. If today they come forward and renew their claim to the inclusion of Palestine in their vast domain, that claim is unwarranted from every point of view. Not only have other rights and interests intervened, not only has Palestine advanced a long way in its evolution as the Jewish National Home, not only is there today a more pressing need than ever for maintaining that National Home, but what is also pertinent and relevant, there is no pressing need which should actuate the Arab states to demand this additional strip of land. Their present domain is not only vast but greatly underpopulated.

The combined population of all the Arab territories I have mentioned does not exceed 15,000,000. All of them could be comfortably accommodated in Iraq alone if fully developed and there would still be room for many more millions in the future. Actually, the sparseness of population in the Arab countries is one of their greatest problems, their greatest weakness, and the greatest source of danger for their future security. The Arabs have not too little land, but too much land, and lack the means and the manpower to develop what they have and to defend it.

In a paper presented to the Royal Asia Society in England in 1926, Jafar Pasha al-Askari, the Prime Minister of Iraq, stated:

The size of the country is 150,000 square miles, about three times that of England and Wales, while the population is only 3,000,000. * * * What Iraq wants above everything else is more population.

A similar situation obtains in Syria, where only a fraction of the cultivable land is being cultivated. For the Arab world, thus richly endowed, to reach out its hand today to strike at the international commitments solemnly made with respect to Palestine, with a view to its annexation and its incorporation in the Arab domain, is not only a breach of international law but a case of incipient Arab imperialism.

I come now to the second part of our discussion—the position of the Palestinian Arabs. Here the position taken by their spokesmen is simple to the point of oversimplification. They are there; they have been there for centuries; they therefore have the right of ownership, as it were, of sovereignty, of domination. They contend that whatever Feisal and the other Arab delegates to the peace conference might have said or done by way of waiving Arab claims to Palestine in favor of the Jews, they, the Arabs of Palestine, had not given their consent and were entitled to be masters of the land.

But the question is not so simple. Considered as a group, the people who inhabited what is now Palestine at the time of the World War were not a nation, had never been recognizeed as such, and had never exercised national sovereignty over that territory. In fact, there was no such thing as Palestine, in the political sense. It was merely a geographical concept. What is now Palestine is made up of certain parts of the Turkish Vilayet or Province, of Beirut, the Sanjak of Jerusalem and other administrative units. The inhabitants were largely Arab-speaking but of diversified and mixed origins. The majority were Moslems, with important Christian and Jewish minorities. They had no sense of nationality as Palestinians, and such of them as were Arab nationalists insisted that Palestine was and should remain southern Syria. There was no Palestinian nation.

Nor had the Arabs of Palestine helped the Allies to liberate the country as did Palestinian Jews, who enlisted in the famous Jewish battalions. They either fought with the Turks against the British or deserted in large numbers to become prisoners of war, fed and sheltered by the British Army.

The Palestine we know today was the creation of the peace conference and the mandate. Palestine was constituted as a distinct country in its present frontiers, precisely because the Allied Powers, representing the democratic world, did not intend to constitute it as another Arab state. If that had been the intention, there was no need or justification for carving out this territory and separating it from the surrounding country. On the contrary, the Allied Nations clearly recognized that this small country held a unique position, unique in many respects. It was the birthplace of three great religions; it was held in veneration by half the world; it was the ancestral home of the Jewish people, whose continued historical association with the land was known and widely recognized throughout Christendom. On these grounds and because of the determination of the civilized world to facilitate the establishment of the Jewish National Home, Palestine was excluded from what was to be the Arab domain, and was placed under a special mandate which recognized. the peculiar character of the land and the special purposes to which it was to be dedicated. That mandate, an international instrument validated by 52 nations, expressly recognizes the historical connection of the Jewish people with Palestine and the grounds for reconstituting there their national home. In this connection, the prefix "re" is of decisive importance. What was clearly intended was not the creation of something new, vague and without precedent, but essentially the reconstitution of something which had existed in the past. By the force of this word "reconstitute" the national home was identified with the Jewish Commonwealth which had existed in Palestine in the Biblical period and in post-Biblical times.

The argument now offered is that this determination does not square with the principle of national self-determination, as a part of the Palestinian Arabs would interpret that principle. The discovery that there is at present a majority of Arab-speaking people in Palestine is not a new discovery. It was vividly present to the minds of Lloyd George and Balfour, of Woodrow Wilson and Prime Minister Smuts, and of all the allied statesmen when they rendered their verdict in favor of the Jewish National Home. The principle of self-determination did not emanate from Arabia, but from the minds and hearts of the most enlightened and progressive statesmen in Christendom. They, if anyone, were entitled to interpret the principle and give it proper application. If they made this determination in the case of Palestine, they did so after weighing all the equities and balancing the needs and claims both of the Arabs and the Jews, the claims of both races to life, liberty, and happiness. They decided that the Jews were likewise entitled to national self-determination in the sense that they should be given the opportunity to reestablish a national existence on the one tiny spot of the entire globe to which they had a moral and historical claim. They squared it fully with their conscience on the ground that this disposition was necessitated and sanctioned by the dictates of humanity and justice on the highest plane. In their view the national interests of the Arab peoples and their national aspirations were being recognized in the vast Arab domain. So far as the Arab-speaking population of Palestine was concerned, who numbered at the time between 500,000 and 600,000 souls, their rights were to be safeguarded in Palestine not only as individuals but also as a religious and cultural community. All of these rights have been scrupulously safeguarded hitherto and must be scrupulously safeguarded in the future. No one who has spent time in Palestine can fail to be impressed with the extraordinary extent to which the Arabs of that country, the common people, have prospered under the mandate and benefited by Jewish immigration and economic development. They are undoubtedly in that regard the most fortunate group of Arabs in the world.

There is one further consideration. It must be borne in mind that whatever was the position in 1919 or 1922, and whatever were the contentions of the Arabs a quarter of a century ago, the situation has changed materially during the years which have intervened. The Palestine we know today is not the country we knew then. In a very real sense it is a new country, a new Palestine. The land has been transformed. In reliance upon the solemn pledges made to the Jewish people then, in reliance upon solemn international covenants, a half million Jews have entered and settled in the country. They have poured into it their energy, their love and devotion, and some $600,000,000 in cold cash. They have drained its swamps, reforested its naked hills, built cities, established industries, planted great stretches of orange groves, harnessed the waterpower of the Jordan and electrified the countryside, developed the mineral resources of the Dead Sea. In short, they took a neglected and derelict country, the mere carcass of a land, as someone has described it, and transmuted it by their labor, sweat, and blood into something new—a thriving, modern, progressive, semi-industrial country. The new Palestine is almost as different from the old as southern California is different from the desert which we took over about a century ago. And it is this new Palestine, this oasis of civilization on the rim of the desert, which Arab nationalism would now have the democratic world place under Arab national control.

And why? What new claim has Pan-Arab nationalism upon the consideration of the democratic world? What contribution have the Arabs made to the democratic cause during this, its greatest crisis? Where did they stand when Rommel stood at the gates of Alexandria? What Arab banner was carried to the field of battle to defend, not only the cause of democracy but their own countries, the freedom and independence which had been so dearly won for them with the lives of Britons and Frenchmen and Americans, during the First World War? For now it may be told. Now that the dire threat to the Near East which was so imminent 2 and 3 years ago has been definitely removed, the truth may be spoken. During those dark and anxious days, the whole Near East was a veritable quagmire of intrigue and treachery. Would-be Quislings, the leaders of fifth columns, were active everywhere. Axis-minded, Fascist-ridden Arab oligarchies attempted to seize power and stab the democratic nations in the back. In Egypt the Prime Minister himself, Ali Maher Pasha, had to be removed from power and kept in isolation in a country villa. The Egyptian Chief of Staff, al-Masri, had to be arrested under suspicious circumstances. In Iraq, Rashid Bey al-Gailani, struck at the British prematurely before help could reach him from his Nazi allies. The leader of the Arab extremists in Palestine, the notorious Mufti, was commuting between Rome and Berlin doing the Fuehrer's work. Nowhere in this entire region did the democratic cause, hard pressed as it was, find firm and active allies save in Palestine, which had become an outpost and bulwark on our far-flung front—Palestine, with its Jewish National Home.

Ladies and gentlemen, the resolution you are considering is a reaffirmation of an American policy and a word of cheer and of hope to the harassed multitudes of the Jewish people in Europe and their brave vanguard in Palestine. Why this reaffirmation and why the express reference to the goal of a free and democratic Jewish commonwealth? The answer is obvious. The Balfour Declaration was unquestionably meant to help, in the words of President Wilson, "to lay the foundations of a Jewish commonwealth." The policy was so understood, quite definitely, by our own Government at the time. There is clear documentary evidence of that fact. But in the course of these years, under pressure of Arab intransigeance and a campaign of terror carried on with the help of the Axis, the original contract was gradually whittled down, interpreted and reinterpreted beyond recognition, a process which culminated in the White Paper. It is therefore, not enough to repudiate the White Paper, but to avoid recurrence, in the future. It is therefore necessary to go over the old contract now and cross the t's and dot the i's. That can best be done by a clear and unmistakable reference to the underlying purpose of the Balfour Declaration and the goal it contemplated—a free and democratic Jewish Commonwealth.

I am through, Mr. Chairman. I would only like to offer this American document as evidence. There was only passing reference made to it the other day. It is quoted in the diary of David Hunter Miller in connection with the peace conference. It is a memorandum prepared by the Intelligence Section in accordance with instructions for the President (Wilson) and the plenipotentiaries, January 21, 1919.

I would like to read it. This document drawn up more than a year after the Balfour Declaration sheds a remarkably clear light upon the manner in which the United States understood and interpreted that Declaration. It proves incontestably that our Government then contemplated the establishment of Palestine as a Jewish State. It says so in language of classic simplicity and with characteristically American directness.

Chairman BLOOM. Very well, proceed.

Mr. NEUMANN (reading):

THE SECTIONS ON PALESTINE IN THE "OUTLINE OF TENTATIVE REPORT AND RECOMMENDATIONS PREPARED BY THE INTELLIGENCE SECTION IN ACCORDANCE WITH INSTRUCTIONS FOR THE PRESIDENT (WILSON) AND THE PLENIPOTENTIARIES, JANUARY 21, 1919"

It is recommended:
(1) That there be established a separate state of Palestine.
(2) That this state be placed under Great Britain as a mandatory of the League of Nations.
(3) That the Jews be invited to return to Palestine aɛd settle there, being assured by the conference of all proper assistance in so doing that may be consistent with the protection of the personal (especially the religious) and the property rights of the non-Jewish population, and being further assured that it will be the policy of the League of Nations to recognize Palestine as a Jewish state as soon as it is a Jewish state in fact.
(4) That the holy places and religious rights of all creeds in Palestine be placed under the protection of the League of Nations and its mandatory.

DISCUSSION

(1) It is recommended that there be established a separate state of Palestine.
The separation of the Palestinian area from Syria finds justification in the religious experience of mankind. The Jewish and Christian churches were born in Palestine, and Jerusalem was for long years at different periods, the capital of each. And while the relation of the Mohammedans to Palestine is not so intimate, from the beginning they have regarded Jerusalem as a holy place. Only by establishing Palestine as a separate state can justice be done to these great facts.
As drawn upon the map, the new state would control its own source of water power and irrigation, on Mount Hermon in the east to the Jordan; a feature of great importance since the success of the new state would depend upon the possibilities of agricultural development.
(2) It is recommended that this state be placed under Great Britain as a mandatory of the League of Nations.
Palestine would obviously need wise and firm guidance. Its population is without political experience, is racially composite, and could easily become distracted by fanaticism and bitter religious differences.
The success of Great Britain in dealing with similar situations, her relations to Egypt, and her administrative achievements, since General Allenby freed Palestine from the Turk, all indicate her as the logical mandatory.

(3) It is recommended that the Jews be invited to return to Palestine and settle there, being assured by the conference of all proper assistance in so doing that may be consistent with the protection of the personal (especially the religious) and the property rights of the non-Jewish population and being further assured that it will be the policy of the League of Nations to recognize Palestine as a Jewish state as soon as it is a Jewish state in fact.

"It is right that Palestine should become a Jewish state, if the Jews, being given the full opportunity, make it such. It was the cradle and home of their vital race, which has made large spiritual contributions to mankind, and is the only land in which they can hope to find a home of their own; they being in this last respect unique among significant peoples."

At present, however, the Jews form barely a sixth of the total population of 700,000 in Palestine, and whether they are to form a majority, or even a plurality, of the population in the future state remains uncertain. Palestine, in short, is far from being a Jewish country now. England, as mandatory, can be relied on to give the Jews the privileged position they should have without sacrificing the rights of non-Jews.

(4) It is recommended that the holy places and religious rights of all creeds in Palestine be placed under the protection of the League of Nations and its mandatory.

The basis for this recommendation is self-evident.

Chairman BLOOM. Thank you very much. Are there any questions? (No response.)

The Chair wishes to state that Rabbi Stephen Wise has come from California, and if you will be patient we will hear Rabbi Wise, and then there is one short witness after that and then we will recess until tomorrow morning.

STATEMENT OF RABBI STEPHEN S. WISE, REPRESENTING THE ZIONIST ORGANIZATIONS OF AMERICA

Rabbi WISE. I do happen to represent the Zionist organizations of America, of which I was the founder 46 years ago, and I am one of two cochairmen, together with Dr. Silver, of Cleveland, of the American Emergency Zionist Council.

Mr. Chairman, ladies and gentlemen, some of the things that Dr. Hitti said today might be considered valid if we had come to you and in a resolution proposed that Pan Arabia, the Arab Empire be converted or transmuted into a Jewish state. It happens though Dr. Hitti has made no reference thereto, but if you examine your map, Palestine constitutes about 1 percent, its 10,000 square miles of what is commonly known as Arab complex.

So, we are not dealing in any action with reference to the utility of Arabia or the Arabian Empire of the many Arab cantonments. We are dealing only with Palestine, reconstituting only 1 percent. Dr. Hitti told you today of the statement of Professor Gostein, whom I happen to know, a distinguished English archeologist. Dr. Hitti got it third or fourth hand, quoting Mrs. Gostein, who quoted Professor Gostein, quoting Lord Balfour, the statement that he was aghast over his discovery that there were Arabs in Palestine.

I had the privilege and the honor of meeting him through President Wilson of a long talk over the tea cups with Mr. Balfour, then Secretary for Foreign Affairs. Mr. Balfour's words were these:

Rabbi Wise, I think the question as to a home for the Jews who may now or in the future wish to live in Palestine, is in Palestine.

That was Mr. Balfour's statement and he made it not to me personally alone, for personal testimony is always more or less of dubious value, but he made the parallel statement in most emphatic and un-mistakable terms on a number of occasions.

The term was heard "pressure group," and Professor Hitti of Princeton does not represent any pressure group. I represent, too, the members of which are in tragic need, the Jewish survivors of the thrice-damned Hitler regime, those surviving victims among the Jewish people who still dwell in those blighted lands. Well, that is a pressure group. I represent my people's prayers, prayers which have been uttered since the year 70 A. D. of the Christian era when Titus expelled Jews for the most part from Palestine.

We were told today that England, the United Nations, or the Allies, as they were known in 1917 and 1918, looked upon the Arabs as potential friends. They may have been potential friends but they have not borne themelves as friends and I venture with an amount of the knowledge of history to say to you the Arabs had a most insignificant part in the liberation of Palestine. General Allenby had virtually no help from the Arab, except from a handful, but the Arabs have done next to nothing for the United Nations in the present crisis.

Dr. Neumann has told you the story of Iraq going over to the coast, and Egypt and Arabia, what they have done. On the other hand, Mr. Chairman, if you happen to recall it, we had to keep down the figures of our enrollment in order that we should not outnumber them. In the British Army we had to reduce our figures to the lowest, and while 30,000 Jews enlisted under the British command and have ren-dered important service, most important service. If I were Dr. Hitti I would not say that the Arabs never accepted the Balfour Decla-ration. They have rioted, rioted, rioted continuosly for 20 years against the Balfour Declaration which after all was not the personal declaration of Mr. Balfour but represented the considered judgment, for reasons of which I shall speak, of the Allied Nations, England, America, France, with no inconsiderable amount from His Holiness at Rome.

A highfalutin term "revolution" was used. There have been assassinations and crimes led by and instigated by Hitler's personal representative, Mufti, who unhappily for civilization was pardoned by a Jew.

May I say a word about the Jewish population and the Arab? There are about 600,000 Jews in Palestine. There are somewhat over a million Arabs in Palestine. The Arabs have that vast territorial place of a million square miles in which to dwell. What have we done against the Arabs? I know Palestine and I have been in Palestine often. In 1880 the wage rate was 80 centimes. Today it runs to an increase of 500 percent, but more than that because of Jews in Pales-tine has not only lifted up the standards of the Arabs, but the Arabs today are free people because England intervened on their behalf. You say the Arabs control. I have seen Arabs bastinadoed by the Turks, treated with scorn and contempt. The Arabs have no part in the government, either in Palestine or any other part. They were merely condemned subjects out of whom the maximum of taxes were squeezed. I cannot understand it. I had the honor of meeting King Feisal, who was every inch a king. He was a great statesman. King Feisal was wise enough to know that lest an arrangement that was proposed to him would be of equal benefit to the Arabs and Jews it would not be worth while, but I have heard the term. I wish I were a lawyer and understood it. I heard a term I never heard before. Professor Hitti used the term the Arabs were dispossessed by purchase. I would like to sell a house of mine in New York. I am overtaxed. Suppose I find some fellow tomorrow to purchase it and he can have it for next to nothing. In fact I am prepared to make a gift to you, Mr. Chairman, of that house for any purpose you may designate.

Chairman BLOOM. I am prepared to accept it.

Rabbi WISE. I wish you would. Purchase is a legal thing and Professor Hitti neglected to say the Arabs in Palestine could only buy little tracts of land. Our whole land possession is a little more than a quarter of a million acres. One is as large as the King Ranch in Texas.

We paid 50 times as much as they would have gotten if they had sold the land to one another.

Not only have they been enriched by our purchases, we have benefited the Arabs in every way.

I am here as a personal witness of the processing of the Balfour resolution. Three men were the authors of the Balfour Declaration. Their names were Woodrow Wilson, President of the United States, speaking not for himself, not for the Presbyterian Church, of which his father was a renowned pastor. Mr. Balfour spoke for England that trusted and followed him. Mr. Balfour, who knew of the historic interest and concern of the English people for centuries and centuries with everything related to Palestine. And for the Jews there was Dr. Weizmann, a great chemist and statesman, and Mr. Justice Brandeis, whom the Jews trusted and followed. I think it was the early spring when Mr. Balfour came to America. What was it that was in the heart of Mr. Balfour and Mr. Wilson representing America? He brought us proof he was one who understood the heart of America. He said he felt the world owed something to the Jews for 1917 and 1918. What would he say they owed now? The next place they felt the war of 1914–18 was a war for self determination.

That declaration was issued. My own eyes were the last to see it in America before it went back to Mr. Balfour. I am proud to say, Mr. Balfour, the President, Colonel House, and Secretary Lansing entrusted me with the privilege of returning the declaration to England.

Under the Balfour Declaration the 50,000 Jews of Palestine grew to more than a half a million, transformed the arid waste of Palestine into one of the most lovely, beautiful countries with a modern university, with hundreds of schools and developed a civilization which had never been possible but for some European Jews and American Jews. Things grew and grew, and then in 1939 there came the white paper. I was present when that unhappy document was drawn up. I venture to say while it bore the seal of the House of Commons it represents the appeasement policy of the spring of 1938 and the spring of 1939. We protested and protested and I may say to you we are amazed to think that the present eminent representative of his great country here in Washington, Lord Halifax came to the pitiful necessity of presiding over that proceeding out of which grew the white paper, an attempt to appease Hitler and his adjutant, Mufti.

There is nothing new in the term we use, the democratic Jewish commonwealth. The only thing that is new is the white paper.

I may quote Mr. Churchill. He was not the Prime Minister in 1939, but he made one of his greatest utterances in the history of the country speaking of the white paper as a betrayal of the Balfour Declaration. Mr. Churchill as early as 1922 stated the Jews are in Palestine of right and not on sufferance.

One thing more, the Jewish national home. You know, Mr. Chairman, the Jewish national home has welcomed about a quarter of a million from Hitler-dominated Europe.

Now what is it that we ask for, that all refugees may enter. No, there will not be a million. Professor Hitti may not have any fear because half of the Jewish citizens will be in Europe. I do not believe that more than one million and a half Jews in Europe today have the strength, have the will, have the power, and have the opportunity to go to Palestine. It is not a matter of millions. There may be several thousand from the United States and several thousand from the Soviet Union, the two countries of the world with the greatest Jewish populations. Those refugees that go to Palestine, some will return. They will not choose to repatriate themselves from lands of torture. Some may go to Latin America, but they are homeless. They have always understood and looked upon Palestine not as their Biblical home but traditionally as their home. They want to go to a home but they do not want to go to the lands of torture under the domination of Hitler.

I think I will say one last word and I am done. We had an American-Jewish Conference in August and September 1943, and I think it is fair to say they represent 3,000,000 of the 5,000,000 Jews. I happened to be the chairman of the session for which Dr. Silver made a most brilliant presentation of the commonwealth. We took a vote. There were some who abstained from voting but the vote was 498 to 4 in favor of the adoption of the resolution which finds its counterpart in the resolution proposed by the Members of Congress. If there could be a referendum of 5,000,000 American Jews I venture to say, and I cannot work for 50 years as a rabbi without knowing something about the Jewish people, if an honest vote could be taken 90 to 95 percent of the Jews of America would support this resolution.

Chairman BLOOM. Would you mind an interruption, Rabbi?

Rabbi WISE. No.

Chairman BLOOM. On the center of the table there are thousands and thousands of telegrams and letters from all over, every State in the Union. There are only, I think, 10 letters and telegrams of disapproval of the resolution. The letters and telegrams represent organizations of many thousands.

Rabbi WISE. Tens of thousands.

Chairman BLOOM. But that will bear out your statement.

Rabbi WISE. Ninety to ninety-five percent if they could vote would say "yes, we favor the resolution." It is not merely the Jews. I know my country. I was a citizen of Oregon for a number of years and was in danger of being elected to Congress and I might have had your place much 'to the loss of our country if I had accepted political office. Congressmen come and Congressmen go, but I go on forever. I visited President Wilson and he said, "Wise, what can I do for you"?, and I replied "nothing." He said, "Wise, you are the first man that has come to me who does not want something."

I think I have a right to say I know my country and its people, and if a plebiscite could be taken of the American people I think the American feeling in the depth of the Christian faith in the light of its understanding of the plight of my tragic people would vote on a parity with the Jews. If the Jews wanted to have a democratic commonwealth in the land which was their homeland, I venture to say that some of my fellow Jews may follow them, but I repeat I know America and I know American integrity and I respect it and I know my people, and I assure you, Mr. Chairman, it is worth the while of my Christian fellow Americans to take into account the unutterable suffering of my people, almost their destruction, and tell you every day my people will watch with breathless attention what your country and what the Congress will do. It begs your help, but we are not beggars. We are self-revering people. We need a free and democratic Jewish commonwealth.

And as my last word I want my people to have the chance side by side with the Arabs to translate the teachings of the Bible into practice and into the manners and morale and spiritual achievement day by day of the Jewish commonwealth, free and democratic which with your help may yet come to pass.

Chairman Bloom. Rabbi Wise, thank you very much, and in 1922 you appeared before this committee. You appeared here at that time.

Rabbi Wise. Yes.

Chairman Bloom. And at that time there was inserted in the record a letter from Woodrow Wilson, then President of the United States. Would you desire that letter read?

Rabbi Wise. If the Chairman wishes it.

(The letter referred to was thereupon read by the clerk of the committee and is as follows:)

THE WHITE HOUSE,
Washington, D. C., August 31, 1918.

Dr..Stephen S. Wise,
Chairman, Provisional Executive Committee for General Zionist Affairs,
New York.

My Dear Rabbi Wise: I have watched with deep and sincere interest the reconstructive work which the Weizmann Commission has done in Palestine at the instance of the British Government, and I welcome an opportunity to express the satisfaction I have felt in the progress of the Zionist movement in the United States and in the Allied countries since the declaration of Mr. Balfour, on behalf of the British Government, of Great Britain's approval of the establishment in Palestine of a national home for the Jewish people, and his promise that the British Government would use its best endeavors to facilitate the achievement of that object, with the understanding that nothing would be done to prejudice the civil and religious rights of non-Jewish people in Palestine or the rights and political status enjoyed by Jews in other countries.

I think that all Americans will be deeply moved by the report that even in this time of stress the Weizmann Commission has been able to lay the foundation of the Hebrew University at Jerusalem with the promise that that bears of spiritual rebirth.

Cordially and sincerely yours,

WOODROW WILSON.

Chairman Bloom. I thought you would like to be reminded of this and of the days gone by.

Rabbi Wise. I am glad to remember it, Mr. Chairman.

Chairman Bloom. I remember a lot of others.

The Chair wishes to state that the opposition has used an hour and three-quarters and the proponents of these resolutions have used an hour and a half. We have several witnesses yet for and against and we would like to hear them all, but it is half past one now and the committee cannot sit all day as we did before. We have one witness who wishes to place a statement in the record.

STATEMENT OF JOHN SLAWSON, EXECUTIVE VICE PRESIDENT, AMERICAN JEWISH COMMITTEE, NEW YORK CITY

Mr. SLAWSON. I do not wish to make any verbal statement, Mr. Chairman; merely to file this memorandum for your record.

Chairman BLOOM. Without objection that will be done.

(The memorandum referred to is as follows:)

MEMORANDUM ON THE WRIGHT-COMPTON RESOLUTION BY THE AMERICAN JEWISH COMMITTEE, NEW YORK, N. Y.

(Submitted to House Committee on Foreign Affairs, February 15, 1944)

The American Jewish Committee respectfully submits to the House Committee on Foreign Affairs the following memorandum on the Wright-Compton resolution:

1. Concerned with the welfare of Jews everywhere, the American Jewish Committee which was established in 1906 has been deeply and actively interested in the development of the Jewish settlement in Palestine. Entirely apart from the political status of Palestine, we have given consistent and uninterrupted encouragement and support to all measures that have been taken to build there a large and prosperous Jewish community, which would dwell in the Holy Land "as of right and not on sufferance."

2. With respect to so much of the resolution as deals with the subject of Jewish immigration into Palestine and with opportunity for colonization therein, the American Jewish Committee records itself as in full accord with the purposes of the resolution and strongly urges the adoption of this portion of the resolution.

In respect to the opening of the doors of Palestine, the American Jewish Committee pledged its "most diligent efforts to bring about the abrogation of the White Paper." In conformity with that pledge, the committee prepared a memorandum on the White Paper in which it urged "that the British Government reexamine the 1939 White Paper, considering such reexamination to be of the utmost urgency in the light of the present needs of European Jewry." In this memorandum, the committee pleaded for the abrogation of the White Paper which among other things "discriminates against Jews as such" and for the liberal immigration policy embodied in the Balfour Declaration and the Palestine mandate. This memorandum was submitted on January 17, 1944, by representatives of the American Jewish Committee to Viscount Halifax, Ambassador of Great Britain to the United States. A copy of this memorandum is submitted for the information of the committee.

3. With respect to so much of the resolution that declares the purpose ultimately to reconstitute Palestine as "a free and democratic Jewish commonwealth," the American Jewish Committee, for the reasons stated below, earnestly urges that the final determination of this controversial question be deferred and that the resolution be amended accordingly.

A. The American Jewish Committee, as a preliminary to the discussion of this question, is glad to record its belief that all sections of American Jewry are in accord with the position heretofore taken by this committee and stated as follows: "Since we hold that in the United States, as in all other countries, Jews, like all other citizens, are nationals of those nations and of no other, there can be no political identification of Jews outside of Palestine with whatever government may there be instituted."

B. The committee at its thirty-sixth annual meeting, held on January 31, 1943, adopted a specific position with respect to the future government of Palestine, on which we believe all persons interested in the welfare of the Jews in Palestine can unite.

The factors upon which the position of the American Jewish Committee is based are as follows:

(a) We recognize that there are more than a half million Jews in Palestine who have built up a sound and flourishing economic life and a satisfying spiritual and cultural life and that they comprise approximately one-third of the populat

But, while Palestine immigration has been a blessed amelioration in the condition of this large number of Jews, settlement in Palestine, though an important factor, cannot alone furnish and should not be expected to furnish the sole solution of the problem of post-war Jewish rehabilitation.

(b) We recognize wide divergence of opinion with respect to the ultimate government that should obtain in Palestine. It is a fact that there are many thousands of Jews in America and Europe today who do not favor the creation ultimately of a Palestinian Jewish state, and there are many thousands who do. The sharpness of this division is clearly indicated by the heated controversy which developed in the hearings before your congressional committee.

(c) Any predetermination of this question at this time must necessarily be affected by war conditions and problems. Many Zionists, proponents of a Jewish state, have themselves taken the view that the settlement of these problems must precede the determination of the ultimate form of government in Palestine. In the post-war world, many of these issues, it is earnestly believed, will fade in their sharpness as a result of the development of events, and we profoundly believe that a cool, dispassionate, and humane solution of this problem of the ultimate government of Palestine can much better be effected after the lapse of some years.

The position of the American Jewish Committee (based on the creation of an international trusteeship for Palestine which must in any event be an interim necessity) is as follows:

"We approve for Palestine an international trusteeship responsible to the United Nations for the following purposes:

"(1) To safeguard the Jewish settlement in and Jewish immigration into Palestine and to guarantee adequate scope for future growth and development to the full extent of the economic absorptive capacity of the country.

"(2) To safeguard and protect the fundamental rights of all inhabitants.

"(3) To safeguard and protect the holy places of all faiths.

"(4) To prepare the country to become, within a reasonable period of years, a self-governing commonwealth under a constitution and a bill of rights that will safeguard and protect these purposes and basic rights for all."

4. The House Committee on Foreign Affairs will thus see that the American Jewish Committee takes into full consideration the immediate needs of the suffering Jews but does not prejudge the ultimate world order into the framework of which the determination of the political status of Palestine will be obliged to fit.

5. We accordingly ask that there be substituted in the resolution for the clause reading "so that the Jewish people may ultimately reconstitute Palestine as a free and democratic Jewish Commonwealth" a provision approving an international trusteeship as set forth in this memorandum.

We believe that the proposed amendment to the resolution, if adopted, will advance the basic purpose which is to help many thousands of persecuted Jews to hospitable refuge in Palestine.

We believe that such action by the Committee on Foreign Affairs would be a long step forward toward reaching an ultimately just, fair, and beneficent solution of the Palestinian problem.

Respectfully submitted.

> AMERICAN JEWISH COMMITTEE,
> JOSEPH M. PROSKAUER,
> President,
> ALAN M. STROOCK,
> Chairman, Administrative Committee.
> JACOB BLAUSTEIN,
> Chairman, Executive Committee.
> JOHN SLAWSON,
> Executive Vice President.

Chairman BLOOM. I regret very much to have to ask the witnesses to come back tomorrow, but as I say, the first witness took up an hour and three-quarters and Dr. Neumann and Rabbi Wise took up an hour and a half. I do not want the thought to go out that we are not fair in dividing the time for the witnesses.

So, without objection the committee will stand in recess until 10 o'clock tomorrow morning.

(Whereupon, at 1:35 p. m., the committee adjourned until 10 a. m. Wednesday, February 16, 1944.)

THE JEWISH NATIONAL HOME IN PALESTINE

WEDNESDAY, FEBRUARY 16, 1944

House of Representatives,
Committee on Foreign Affairs,
Washington, D. C.

The committee met at 10 a. m., pursuant to adjournment, Hon. Sol Bloom (chairman) presiding.

Chairman BLOOM. The committee will kindly come to order.

The committee has under consideration House Resolutions 418 and 419 relative to the Jewish national home in Palestine.

The Chair would like to state that we have seven witnesses that want to appear today. We would like to close these hearings. Yesterday we sat for 3 hours and a half, which is rather unusual, which is twice as long as committees generally sit for hearings of this kind.

The Chair would like to suggest with the approval of the committee that we hold the witnesses down to 20 minutes each, 10 minutes to make their statement and 10 minutes for questioning; and if there is no objection to that we will proceed in that order, and the committee will kindly limit their questions to things pertinent to the resolution itself.

So, without objection, the suggestion of the Chair will be approved. The first witness we have this morning is Mr. Twitchell.

STATEMENT OF K. S. TWITCHELL, CONSULTING ENGINEER, SAUDI ARABIA MINING SYNDICATE, AND FORMER CHIEF OF UNITED STATES AGRICULTURAL MISSION TO SAUDI ARABIA, MAMARONECK, N. Y.

The CHAIRMAN. Mr. Twitchell, will you kindly take a seat, and would you kindly for the record state just who you are and who you represent; and the Chair will notify you when your 10 minutes are up.

Mr. TWITCHELL. Thank you. Mr. Chairman and gentlemen, I am simply a free-born American citizen and I represent nobody but myself.

I have been in that part of the world a great deal, and my last trip was last year, I returned last year. It was a trip to Saudi Arabia. That is not part of Palestine, but it is part of that section. I visited Palestine for a short period last year.

In the hope that my experience in Yemen and Saudi Arabia, and so forth, may be of benefit in considering the matter of Palestine, I have come here. Everyone agrees upon two aspects:

(1) That it is a most complex matter.

(2) That Americans have the greatest sympathy for the persecuted Jewish and other minorities.

279

As I have spent a number of years in the Near East, 1915–19 and 1926 to date, it is possible that I realize the dangers and ramifications better than many people. We desire to help solve this question in a way that will not involve bloodshed and injustice. First, I want to point out the dangerous possibilities, as I see them and I may be wrong; and secondly, I wish to make suggestions for your consideration.

At the outset, I wish to emphasize that it is not only the 1,000,000 or less Arabs which are concerned in Palestine, but that 300,000,000 Moslems throughout the Near East and India are vitally interested in this matter.

DANGERS OF IMPLEMENTING THE PROPOSED RESOLUTION

Supposing the recommendation I have seen advertised in one of the great newspapers were adopted for the removal of Arabs from Palestine to Iraq? Who would finance such a removal and the development of new farms and homes? Would not the average American taxpayer resent any such thought and consequently become perhaps anti-Semetic? I am afraid there would be the following results:

First. Recent history indicates there would be a great deal of resistance and bloodshed in Palestine itself as it is well known that both Arabs and Jews have considerable amounts of arms;

Second. The Moslems in Yemen, Arabia, might annihilate the 40,000 Jews now there. I wonder if they might not be viewed as hostages and in a similar manner the 100,000 Jews now in Iraq and who have lived there peacefully for over 1,300 years.

Third. In Egypt there might be great riots and anti-non-Moslem reactions which could result in the greatly handicapping of the large non-Moslem interest in education, the American University, and so forth, and in businesses.

Fourth. In Turkey the non-Moslems might be treated in a manner similar to the Arabs from Palestine and be deported—in this case, Jews (70,000) and Christian Armenians would, perhaps, suffer most.

Fifth. In India the 90,000,000 Moslems who have upheld the British Government when the Hindu Indian Congress was making passive resistance, would very probably voice great opposition to a removal of Arab Moslems and might cause great disturbance and trouble which would interfere with our war against Japan in that sphere.

Sixth. There are many Moslems in Java, China, and the Philippines to whom this matter would undoubtedly be broadcast by the Japs and Germans so might cause a great antagonism toward the Allies as these people might fear similar removals after the war.

Seventh. Along the African routes of our air transport, most of the countries traversed are Moslem inhabited; could not there be many acts of sabotage by angry Moslems all along both the north African and central African routes?

Eighth. If the proposed pipe line for bringing American-controlled oil from the Persian Gulf eventuates, an unfriendly Arab people along this line would be a constant menace and might involve American troops.

Do you believe the American public would wish their sons to be sent to the many points in Molsem countries on police duty and possibly lose their lives in a matter entirely aside from our fight for the four freedoms? Might this not cause anti-Semitic feeling? Troubles in Boston suggest this possibility.

The British Government can tell you what it has cost in lives and money to keep their Palestine Mandate. Does the American Government wish to assume such liabilities?

Would it not be wise to leave such a many sided question to be worked out cooperatively with the British after victory is won?

Now for the other side. The United States Department of Agriculture can confirm, or not, my statement that Palestine has now been developed to nearly its maximum productivity under present conditions. The Palestine Government Partition Report to the British Government, 1938, Command 5854, tends to confirm this statement. Only if the irrigation project to bring water from Syria to Palestine eventuates, can any very considerable additional acreage be cultivated. But in Palestine there are great areas which are steep limestone mountains with very thin soil and able only to support grazing— and not much of that during the hottest parts of the summer seasons. My first trip from Jerusalem to Jerico was in July 1929. The progress made to date in agriculture is a very great achievement and a credit to the energy of the present population and Jewish financing.

To add greatly to the present population would not seem to be sound economy and would not attain the aims of those of Jewish faith for the above reasons.

There are four places which I suggest be seriously investigated for the benefit of those who wish new homes. Other locations like the Dominican Republic and Benguela in Angola, Portuguese West Africa have already been suggested and considered, I believe.

Chairman BLOOM. Your time is up. You can put your statement in the record.

(Discussion off the record.)

Chairman BLOOM. Proceed, Mr. Twitchell. We will see how far we can get along. Confine yourself to the resolution we have under consideration and state your views with respect to that.

Mr. TWITCHELL. Mr. Chairman, my thought was this resolution might raise these different troubles which I point out.

Chairman BLOOM. That is your personal opinion?

Mr. TWITCHELL. Yes. Our Government is made up of personal opinions.

Mr. JARMAN. You are appearing here personally?

Mr. TWITCHELL. Yes, sir.

Chairman BLOOM. Proceed, please.

Mr. TWITCHELL. We wish to help out minorities. Now, do you wish to hear these suggestions or not? I am entirely at your service.

Mrs. BOLTON. I wonder if it would help matters if Mr. Twitchell were permitted to insert the balance of this in the record.

Chairman BLOOM. Proceed, Mr. Twitchell.

Mr. TWITCHELL. Shall I read the suggestions? I will go as fast as I can.

Chairman BLOOM. Proceed, please.

Mr. TWITCHELL. Cirenaica, north Africa: This is of cultural and historical interest, as well as agricultural. The Italians have established a very fine foundation on which much could be developed. Our Government can furnish details.

Gojam, Abyssinia: There have been people of Jewish faith in this province for a great many centuries. I have seen the country to the south of here which is said to be similar. It has a fertile, deep soil, good rainfall and invigorating climate, and is largely a plateau region of approximately 5,000 feet elevation. The Italians have made this country much more accessible than formerly by building good roads to connect with the seaport of Masowa via Asmara, or via Addis Ababa to the seaport of Jibouti. Our Government and Army have full details of this whole country. I was in Abyssinia in 1926–27.

Brazil: The district about Barreiras in the Province of Minas Geraes is reported to be very sparsely populated and to be a fine flat brush country with an average elevation of 2,500 to 3,000 feet. The area is roughly 5° to 15° south latitude and 45° west longitude. The Brazilian Government could give complete information.

British Guiana: Roraima and vicinity, latitude 5° south, longitude 60° west. The great plateaus are 4,000 to 7,000 feet above sea level with broad, flat, fertile brush-covered river valleys at elevations of 1,700 feet and more. A road of 100 to 150 miles could be built from the neighborhood of Georgetown to give access to a huge area where only a few hundreds of people now live. There might be profits from mining diamonds and gold in this vicinity as well as from agricultural developments.

I am very much afraid that the Jewish interests in America as well as in the Near East will suffer if the proposed resolution is passed, especially during this present time of stress when we should be cooperating to the fullest with our allies and not raising controversial questions and resolutions.

I shall be glad to try to answer any questions to which I am competent to reply.

Dr. EATON. Mr. Twitchell, I would like to call attention to the fact that the object of this resolution is to permit the Jewish people to return to their ancestral homes in Palestine.

Mr. TWITCHELL. That is just it. From what I have seen there it is not a country that can support many other people, and I am afraid if they go there they will push some already there out and there may be bloodshed.

Dr. EATON. What we are anxious about is how to find out the actual conditions that will confront us in Palestine and how they can be solved best for everybody.

Mr. TWITCHELL. That is why I was calling attention to these other places where there is room.

I am an American. I am not of any one faith or the other. I want to see the whole thing done for the good of America and I foresee a good many ramifications that perhaps some people do not see.

Chairman BLOOM. Proceed.

Mr. TWITCHELL. That is all.

Chairman BLOOM. Judge Kee?

Mr. KEE. Mr. Twitchell, you seem to fear that the passage of this resolution would cause trouble to Jews in other sections of the world, many other places, and I think you mentioned 100,000 in Iraq.

Mr. TWITCHELL. Yes.

Mr. KEE. Do you think the Jews can be given any more trouble than they are already in?

Mr. TWITCHELL. Yes, indeed, in Yemen and Iraq, they have been there for centuries and centuries and they are well treated, but if there were a strong anti-Jewish movement, I fear the treatment would not be so good.

Mr. KEE. You would have us avoid passing a resolution to avoid trouble for a few Jews in other countries. Is that your idea?

Mr. TWITCHELL. It would seem to me that would be true. It would be better that you do not make that resolution now.

Mr. KEE. Do you not think the question of finding other places throughout the world to settle the Jews has already been gone into?

Mr. TWITCHELL. Yes, but I have not heard of these four places mentioned. I imagine a great deal has been done, but having had a little different knowledge I offer my suggestions for what they are worth. It is my desire to help, not to add to the controversy. That is my only thought.

Mr. KEE. You have no information whatever as to whether the Jewish people would be welcome to any of these countries?

Mr. TWITCHELL. I think it is pretty well indicated with our own people there would be no trouble about people coming in, the same as we settled our western plains.

Mr. KEE. You know so far as the history of the movement shows that the doors have been closed to them in practically all the countries?

Mr. TWITCHELL. Not these places I have mentioned.

Mr. KEE. You mean down in the jungles of Brazil?

Mr. TWITCHELL. Yes; I think they could do well there, but also Cirenaica is a place that has just been released from the Italians. I do not know details. These are constructive suggestions.

Mr. KEE. Yes; I recognize that fact.

Chairman BLOOM. Mr. Chiperfield?

Mr. CHIPERFIELD. Do you not think this committee should also secure the views of the War Department and State Department on this resolution and to a considerable extent be guided by those views?

Mr. TWITCHELL. That is why I put in the very last part. Would it not be better to give more time for a correct solution that would be equitable to everybody, as you say, from the State Department and War Department, certainly all of this has a bearing. A very great deal of care should be taken, especially during time of war.

Mr. CHIPERFIELD. That is all.

Chairman BLOOM. Mr. Jarman?

Mr. JARMAN. No questions.

Chairman BLOOM. Mr. Jonkman?

Mr. JONKMAN. No questions.

Chairman BLOOM. Mr. Burgin?

Mr. BURGIN. No questions.

Chairman BLOOM. Mrs. Bolton?

Mrs. BOLTON. No questions.

Chairman BLOOM. Mr. Rogers?

Mr. ROGERS. No questions.

Chairman BLOOM. Mr. Wadsworth?

Mr. WADSWORTH. No questions.

Chairman BLOOM. Mr. Wright?

Mr. WRIGHT. No questions.

Chairman BLOOM. Thank you very much, Mr. Twitchell.

Mr. TWITCHELL. Thank you, Mr. Chairman, ladies and gentlemen.

STATEMENT OF FARIS S. MALOUF, PRESIDENT, SYRIAN AND LEBANESE AMERICAN FEDERATION OF THE EASTERN STATES, BOSTON, MASS.

Chairman Bloom. Please state your name, address, and connections for the record.

Mr. Malouf. My name is Faris S. Malouf, attorney, from Boston, president of and represent the Syrian and Lebanese American Federation of the Eastern States composed of 65 clubs of American citizens of Syrian and Lebanese extraction.

Mr. Chairman, I think I can save time if I could now be told about how much time I will be given. I have taken much time and pains to prepare a presentation in 17 typewritten pages and have limited myself to the issues presented by this resolution. I think it fair that this committee should hear all that I have to say.

Chairman Bloom. Go ahead please.

Mr. Malouf. I do not understand that this committee is sitting as a court to judge the merits and demerits of the conflicting Jewish-Arabic claims. Therefore, I shall not enter into controversial details and much discussion of ancient as well as modern historical facts which may have very remote bearing on the resolution. I think your committee has been very patient. The chairman probably was sometimes oversolicitous and patient.

The only question before your committee is whether or not the Congress shall adopt this resolution and whether or not the United States can properly use its good offices with the Government of Great Britain to abrogate the white paper of 1939 and advocate the establishment of a Jewish commonwealth in Palestine.

I, as a citizen of the United States, question the advisability of the adoption of this resolution and very much question the right of the United States to interfere in this matter.

I also think that the rank and file of American citizens will not want to have anything to do with the Palestine controversy although they will very much like to help solve the Jewish problem and protect them against persecution.

Rabbi Wise stated yesterday that he thinks an overwhelming majority of the American people, if given an opportunity to vote whether or not this resolution should be adopted, will vote for it.

I say to you, Mr. Chairman, and members of this committee, the Zionist organization is very powerful in this country and they are located in every State in the Union. I don't know of any reason why they can't carry some such policy as raised by this resolution to the voters of the individual States or at least some of them and thus test the will of the people. I am positive that the American people will not want to impose on a free people an artificial religious foreign state.

There was a long period of time, the last part of which is in the memory of us here when there was no claim by anybody in the world to Palestine contrary to the rights of the people living in Palestine, for centuries, long before the advent of the Jews, and ever since they were banished from the land, something happened which gave birth to this dispute.

Some speakers for the resolution have stated that the Arabs did not seek independence prior to the First World War or even during the present war. I think it is only fair that I should make a very brief statement regarding this point.

Speaking about the efforts of the Arabs for independence, the Royal Commission, under the chairmanship of Earl Peel, reported as follows:

For many years before the war the Arab Provinces of the Turkish Empire were restive under the Sultan at Constantinople, and the Turkish Army had often been engaged in repressing the outbreaks of the free spirited Arabs. No less dangerous to Ottoman ascendancy was the growth of a nationalistic movement among the young intelligentsia of Syria. Its origin may be traced to the awakening, about 1860, of the new interest in Arab history and culture * * *. Among them were the ideas of self-government and nationalism.

Therefore no just, peaceful or lasting disposition can be made of Palestine which does not take into consideration the righteous claims of Syria and the entire Arabic world.

It is a well-known fact that hundreds of Syrians, Lebanese, and Palestinians died on the gallows as martyrs for the cause of the Allies because they carried out organized efforts to hamper the German-Turkish armies and to facilitate the conquest by General Allenby of the Arab land. One-third of the population of Lebanon and many thousands of other parts of Syria and Palestine were starved to death by Jamal Pasha. At the same time Arab recruits were dying on the battlefields under the leadership of Emir Faisal and Colonel Lawrence.

At a time when Great Britain was fighting with its back to the wall, as then described by Lloyd George, shrewd Zionist leaders drove a bargain with His Majesty's Government and in an unfortunate moment for the three parties, the Jews, the Arabs, and the English, the Balfour Declaration—a secret document secrely arrived at, so far as the Arabs were concerned—was born, and with it began the Palestine controversy. The Zionists then began their efforts for a national home which has since then developed through their ambitions into a Jewish commonwealth. For the following reasons the claims of the Zionists cannot be maintained:

1. The most important element in this whole controversy which is being lost sight of is that Palestine has been an integral part of Syria for 25 centuries. The fact that international chicanery and Zionist-British schemes separated it from her motherland does not make it a separate country. Syria is determined that the Balfour Declaration and Congressional resolutions based upon it shall not be the final chapter in the history of Palestine or binding on either Syria or Palestine.

2. At the time Lord Balfour made this declaration, November 2, 1917, Palestine was not a part of the British Empire, nor was it in possession of the Jews, whose population of Palestine was only 55,000 as against 800,000 Arabs, and England had no right to make any promises in respect thereto.

3. At the time Balfour made his declaration, Britain had through Sir Henry MacMahon already entered into a solemn agreement with King Husein in behalf of the Arabs, October 25, 1915, that England would recognize and assist in the establishment of an independent Arab state, including Palestine. The Arabs were then in complete possession of Palestine and were about to declare their independence and revolt against the Turkish Empire. In consideration of this agreement on the part of England the Arabs revolted against Turkey and shed their blood for 3 years with the armies of the Allies against the combined forces of the Central Powers and Turkey.

4. Lord Balfour's declaration was made secretly to a private English gentleman, Lord Rothschild, and it was more than a year later that the Arabs learned of it. One cannot help asking what right has England to give somebody else's country to a people who were disunited, unorganized, and scattered among the nations of the world, without consulting the people who are immediately concerned and who have occupied that land as its natives from time immemorial and certainly owned it and inhabited it exclusively for the last 13 centuries?

5. In view of the clear binding agreement between England and King Husein, the Balfour declaration, secretly issued and intentionally concealed from the Arabs, was dishonest, insincere, ambiguous and impossible of enforcement.

It was dishonest because the Arabs who were the primary party in interest were not consulted; it was insincere because it does not purport to give the Jews any definite or specific rights, for careful study and consideration of the wording of the declaration will show that the establishment of a Jewish homeland in Palestine is subordinated to and conditioned upon a statement which reveals conscious guilt on the part of England. That statement is found in the second half of the declaration as follows:

It being clearly understood that nothing shall be done which may prejudice the civil or religious rights of existing non-Jewish communities in Palestine.

One wonders what does the phrase "A home for the Jewish people in Palestine" mean.

Does it mean independent Jewish state?

Does it mean the superimposition of a Jewish majority upon the Arab people in Palestine?

Does it mean unrestricted Jewish immigration into Palestine?

And if it does not mean any one of these three propositions, what else can it mean?

And if it means any one of these three propositions, how could that be obtained without "prejudicing the civil or religious rights of existing non-Jewish communities in Palestine."

With the Balfour Declaration and the efforts of the Zionists to establish their Jewish national home in Palestine in disregard of the Arabs' wishes, a revolution was begun. Concerning this revolution the Royal Commission reported the following findings of facts:

It is, indeed, one of the most unhappy aspects of the present situation—this opening of a breach between the Jewry and the Arab world. We believe that in ordinary circumstances the Arabs would be ready enough to permit a measure of Jewish immigration under their own conditions and control, but the creation of a national home has been neither conditioned nor controlled by the Arabs of Palestine. It has been established directly against their will. * * * The reasons of this breach are:

First. The establishment of a national home involved at the outset a blank negation of the right implied in the principle of national self-government;

Second. It soon proved to be not merely an obstacle to the development of national self-government, but apparently the only serious obstacle;

Third. As the home has grown, the fear has grown with it, that if and when self-government is conceded, it may not be national in the Arab sense, but government by a Jewish majority.

I should make this distinction. I should say to the Zionists: Your resolution is based upon the Balfour Declaration and if the Balfour Declaration is weak and invalid in any respect—I feel as a free American citizen I am entitled, rather it is my duty to say that it ill behooves the United States to support that declaration. I would rather see our Government take an initial step in saving my cousins, the Jews, and not simply blindly follow the Balfour Declaration, which does not mean anything at all and which is without authority.

Chairman BLOOM. Pardon me. Did I understand you to say your cousins, the Jews?

Mr. MALOUF. Yes. I am proud of it. As a matter of fact, I am happy to see so many of them here. If the room was not so small, I would have brought some of my division of the cousins here, but I hardly think it is a matter for a crowd or mob psychology.

I would rather my country put out a policy of its own.

Chairman BLOOM. Would you mind an interruption there?

Mr. MALOUF. No.

Chairman BLOOM. Has not the United States already established a policy in the convention signed by President Coolidge?

Mr. MALOUF. I am happy you brought that up. I will be happy to discuss it after I finish the reading of my prepared presentation.

Chairman BLOOM. Proceed in your own way.

Mr. MALOUF. I would be very happy to discuss it later on.

My friends, if you would present this conspiracy of the Balfour Declaration and this resolution to any court and jury in the land an indictment would be issued. The value of any citizen lies in the fact he can speak freely.

Let us see why you cannot establish a commonwealth or home in Palestine without prejudicing the rights of the people already there.

I know what freedom and opportunity mean. I arrived here 37 years ago, penniless, and trudged the dusty roads of Alabama and Georgia peddling. There were some of my Jewish cousins peddling too. So I have learned the true American spirit and the American way of life the hard way. I also know the great pressure being exerted on this committee to pass this resolution.

The resolution before your honorable committee is based on the Balfour Declaration and follows a similar resolution adopted by the Congress June 30, 1922, which is better known as the Lodge-Fish resolution, except that the present resolution goes much farther than the Lodge-Fish resolution.

The Balfour Declaration goes as far as "viewing with favor the establishment in Palestine of a national home for the Jewish people" and pledges His Majesty's Government to "use their best endeavors to facilitate the achievement of this objective." The Lodge-Fish resolution does not go any farther than that "the United States of America favors the establishment in Palestine of a national home for the Jewish people."

The present resolution advocates the establishment of a Jewish commonwealth in Palestine.

Now, there are countless reasons and I shall deal with only a few of those reasons why this resolution should not pass.

There are countless reasons why this resolution ought not to pass. I shall deal with only a few of these reasons.

1. All the three documents, the Balfour Declaration, the Lodge-Fish resolution and the present resolution, are full of inconsistencies. If these inconsistencies could be removed or someone could reconcile them perhaps it would go a long way toward solving the problem, for each one of them provides that nothing shall be done to prejudice the

rights of the people in Palestine. Here the reference is to the people who were in Palestine prior to the Balfour Declaration. Then the language of these documents goes on to provide for a national home and now a Jewish commonwealth. How can anyone establish a political state composed of people who are recently gathered and more of them are to be gathered from the four corners of the globe and put them in Palestine and wait until such a time as they become the majority before self-government can be established? This certainly prejudices the rights of the Arabs in Palestine.

The next inconsistency is the establishment of a Jewish commonwealth which is a religious state. How can you establish a Jewish state after the Jews have become the majority in Palestine and still call it a democratic state as against the people who profess different religions? Our understanding of democracy is a complete separation of the state and the church.

2. It took Great Britain 22 years, from November 1917 to the spring of 1939, to discover its grave mistake at the cost of several uprisings in Palestine which culminated in the Arabs' war for independence from 1936 to 1939, resulting in the destruction of thousands of Arab homes and the shedding of much Arab, Jewish, and English blood, and also after endangering the relations of Great Britain with the Arab and Moslem world.

"In 1939, England sought to rectify the wrong by issuing the white paper, after long conferences with representatives of the Arabs and Jews and after recommendations of several royal commissions appointed by His Majesty's Government to study the situation. Therefore the white paper is not an appeasement measure. Rather, it is a solemn pledge and a binding 'open covenant openly arrived at' after exhaustive study and consultations by the British Government with both the Arabs and the Zionists. Now, after all of this, we find the Zionist influence at work in these United States to get Congress to adopt this resolution as if the lesson learned by Great Britain after a quarter of a century of struggle and bloodshed has been of no value to the Zionists in the United States who would advocate a Jewish commonwealth in Palestine at the expense of the Arabs. Great Britain is now seeking to recify this wrong. Shall we go on to aggravate it? Do we want Great Britain to break a promise?

3. Passage of this resolution makes imperative the continuation of the British mandate over Palestine until such a time as the Jews shall become the majority there, and not even then, but until both the Jews and Arabs have been forced by the sword to live together in peace. Is there anything in your experience or in history to show that such a thing is possible if the Arabs are forced to remember forever that they were denied their independence and self-government for the sole purpose of imposing upon them a Jewish state in which they shall become the minority?

4. In order to make the mandate of this resolution effective, force must be used. If Great Britain rejects our good offices does the Congress want the United States Government to war upon our friends, the Arabs? Will the American people sanction the use of force upon the Arabs so that they may give way to the establishment of a Jewish commonwealth in Palestine? If this is not contemplated by this resolution, is it then our purpose simply to give the Jews lip service without any genuine conviction behind it? Or is it simply a nice

expression of sympathy which might be all right to please the Zionists among us, but which will gain for us the suspicions and the lack of confidence on the part of the Arabs.

If you entertain the possibility of subduing and silencing the Arabs of Palestine by some magic and because they are not a strong nation, what about the 50,000,000 Arabs in the Near and Middle East? What about the 300,000,000 more Mohammedans in Asia and Africa? Great Britain has heard from them and saw the justice of their cause.

5. The passage of this resolution strikes at the foundation and the principles for which our men and women are dying on every battle field and on every continent today. Its passage will strike at the confidence the United States enjoys throughout the world. It will nullify the Atlantic Charter which guarantees self-government and sovereignty for all nations.

Here I want to beg your indulgence to mention statements made to this committee by the House leaders of both the majority and minority parties who appeared before you the other day and pleaded for approval of this resolution. My purpose in mentioning what these two gentlemen had to say to you is not in the spirit of condemning persons whom I respect, but for the sole purpose of touching upon the noble motives which constrain some of our governmental and civil leaders to support the establishment of a Jewish homeland in Palestine, and to show that these noble motives, to say the least, are misplaced, misguided, and wrongly applied. I deeply regret to say that such an attitude on the part of public officials and legislators as displayed by my two good Massachusetts neighbors and representatives, marks them as men who have not familiarized themselves with the truth or that they willfully disregarded the truth out of respect for organized pressure groups. This is especially so when such an attitude seeks to influence legislation which affects international relations and world peace. Such an attitude will in the long run corrupt and weaken the confidence of the American people and threaten our institutions.

My neighbor from south Boston is reported by the United Press to have said: "The least the House of Representatives can do is to go on record showing it thinks along humane lines."

Is it humane to drive the Arabs out of their homes and country in order to give them to others who by all the legal and moral codes have lost any claim to them for more than 2,000 years?

Is it humane to reduce the Arabs to a minority in their land which the Royal Peel Commission described in its report to the British Government in July 1937 as follows: "Palestine or, more strictly speaking, Syria, of which Palestine had been a part since the days of Nebuchadnezzar (605–562 B. C.), was to the Arabs their country, their home, the land in which their people for centuries past had lived and left their graves."

The speaker before you last week further said, "We could not close our eyes to the plight of 2,000,000 homeless Jews in Europe. This is a challenge of all kinds of justice, particularly Christian justice." O Lord! How many iniquities have been committed in Thy name? Will it not be more within the right and privilege of the majority leader to offer part of his own country to the Zionists than to be so humane, Christian and generous at someone else's expense?

The other gentleman, also from Massachusetts, said he had been in sympathy with the attitude of the resolution for 20 years and believed the guaranty of Palestine as a Jewish homeland offered "solution to a world problem." This gentleman, leader of the minority, failed to take into consideration the sacred rights of the people of Palestine who have been its rightful owners and whose soil is made of their blood and of the remains of their forebears long before the Jews came into Palestine. This gentleman has utterly failed to visualize the bloodshed which will be necessary in order to oust the Arabs out of their homes.

6. The passage of this resolution will strike at the principles for which we are fighting this war as declared in the Atlantic Charter, because it tends to withhold self-government from the Arabs of Palestine until such a time as the Jews have become the majority when they and not the Arabs will be in control.

7. The passage of this resolution broadcasts to the willing ears of our enemies as well as to India, the Balkans, eastern Europe, and all of the countries whose future will need to be influenced either by their confidence in us and our way of life or to be influenced by some other theories and alinements if their confidence in us is undermined. So if this resolution is passed it will weaken their confidence and make us just another nation whose pronounced fundamental theories of what is politically true and right are not controlling in the face of organized racial, religious, and sectional pressures.

Chairman BLOOM. Mr. Witness, you have occupied an hour and a half and we have not gone on with the questions.

Mr. MALOUF. I have almost finished, Mr. Chairman.

Chairman BLOOM. Go ahead.

Mr. MALOUF. 8. The passage of this resolution will be contrary to the spirit expressed by a Jewish leader, Chancelor Magnes:

> The Joshua method is not the way for us of entering the Promised Land. The retention of bayonets against the will of the majority of the population is repugnant to men of good will, and the Eternal People should rather continue its long wait than attempt to establish a home in the Holy Land except on terms of understanding and peace.

9. It is very important for the molding of the United States policy toward the Near East to take into consideration the fact that Palestine is the southern part of Syria and has been a part of Syria for 25 centuries, that Syria and Lebanon inspired, I believe, by the United States and Great Britain have just attained their full independence and Syria has never relinquished her right to Palestine as its natural southern part, nor do the people of Palestine wish to be separated from Syria.

10. The passage of this resolution is an interference with the affairs of Great Britain. We have just witnessed the indignation of a great allied nation when one of our prominent citizens unofficially expressed an opinion concerning Poland. Let us not do too much interference.

11. The passage of this resolution will be the greatest disservice to innocent Jews everywhere. Those who have succeeded in getting into Palestine in the last 20 years and who number 500,000 may, if further immigration is stopped and the establishment of a political Jewish state is given up, live in Palestine in peace and participate in its affairs on equal footing with the Arabs. If this resolution is passed and if our Government and the Government of Great Britain undertake to

enforce its provisions, you will have endangered not only the interest but the very lives of the Jews in Palestine and consequently placed them in an unenviable position throughout the world.

Proposals for solution of the Jewish problem:

I wish to say with the most sincere conviction that history cannot justly attribute to any distinct element of mankind greater, continuous, or more lasting contributions to civilization, than those made and being made by the Jews. Those of us who are opposing this resolution do condemn and abhor their persecution as repulsive to human conscience and we do not attempt to ignore the existence of a Jewish problem or the urgency for its just solution. The solution, however, requires frankness and courage to face the truth.

If the Jews are really seeking a refuge and a homeland where they can live in peace and develop their distinct abilities, Palestine can never become that refuge and it can never solve their problem, certainly not through political Zionism. Palestine, however, will welcome the establishment within its gates of spiritual and cultural Zionism which will revive for the benefit of the entire world the idealism which marked the ancient Hebrews and Jews as a distinct people.

This can be accomplished by a restricted and moderate immigration into Palestine of the type of Jewish people who desire to revive for themselves and the world a spiritual and cultural Zionism in the same manner as that of the American missionaries and educational groups who have gone to work in the Near East and in other parts of the world.

It is not for me and it is doubtful whether it is for anybody else but the Jews themselves to determine their future course. I will, however, say that if the great and able leaders of thought among the Jews insist that they should have a political state, then it would seem to be the sacred duty and the happy privilege of the United States and Great Britain to offer out of their vast, and practically vacant territories, a suitable place for the establishment of a Jewish state, where they can enjoy self-government without losing the sentimental and religious values which they entertain for Palestine, and let Palestine be their missionary home.

A Jewish state can be an economic as well as social blessing to the British Empire or the United States if it could be established in some territory where the present population is so thin that racial adjustments could be made without inflicting injustice as it is in the case of Palestine.

I cannot conceive of any Jewish state with a greater population than anywhere from 1,000,000 to 5,000,000 for many generations to come, and certainly that number compared to the vast territories in question cannot constitute inconvenience to any part of the British Empire or the United States. Any statesman or organization of leaders who can reason this proposition to the acceptance of the Jews and the English speaking people will have rendered the greatest service to the world which history may record.

Insofar as the present Jewish population in Palestine is concerned, the Arabs intend, provided immigration is stopped and a proportionate representative government is created, to afford them protection with all the privileges of the land which are enjoyed by the Arabs themselves, and to guaranty their minority rights by constitutional provisions and proper international obligations. This the Arabs will consider their sacred obligation for a world trust.

Finally, as the Jewish problem calls for a just solution, it ill behooves the Jews who are rightly clamoring for their minority rights, and who are protesting against Hitler's methods, to disregard the rights of the great majority in Palestine, and to urge and advocate a policy which requires the use of force against the Arabs.

It certainly ill behooves the Jews that while arousing the sympathy of the American people against their persecutors to at the same time bring pressure upon our politicians, statesmen, clergymen, Government, and people generally to use their influence with the British Government for the purpose of having it force upon the Arabs of Palestine an alien Jewish majority for the establishment there of a Jewish homeland. The building of such a national home by force of arms is neither a fulfillment of Biblical prophesies nor a task worthy of the chosen people. Indeed, Orthodox Jews have repeatedly expressed their disapproval of the ungodly methods employed by political Zionists.

While the Arabs acclaim the efforts of America and England against the German atrocities, there can be but little justification and a great deal of inconsistency in finding these good people urging greater atrocities by Great Britain and political Zionism against the Arabs.

Finally, I can close my effort here in no better words than to say in the spirit of the immortal emancipator, Abraham Lincoln, that "The world will little note nor long remember what we say here" but will never forget what you do here. So, Mr. Chairman and members of this honorable committee, the world will to a great extent judge our sincerity and our future dealings as a great democracy by what we do in this matter.

Mr. Chairman, I have a statement by Mahatma Gandhi which I shall not take the time to read but would like to include in the record.

Chairman BLOOM. You may put that in the record, without objection.

Mr. MALOUF. All right.

(The statement referred to is as follows:)

[Reprinted from the Christian Science Monitor, March 3, 1939, by the Arab National League, Boston Chapter, room 315, 60 State Street, Boston, Mass.]

GANDHI'S MESSAGE TO JEWRY—PALESTINE BELONGS TO THE ARABS

By a staff correspondent of the Christian Science Monitor

LONDON, March 3.—Mohandas K. Gandhi who, according to Bombay dispatches, today stated a hunger strike to induce the native ruler of the State of Rajkot, in the northwest corner of India, to give his people "a voice in the government," has expressed his views on the Arab-Jew question in Palestine.

At the moment when the London Conference with Arabs and Jews is almost deadlocked over the British proposal for an Arab state, his name is in a Church of England newspaper which said: "My sympathies are all with the Jews."

"I have known them intimately in South Africa," he went on. "But my sympathy does not blind me to the requirements of justice. The cry for a national home for the Jews does not make much of an appeal to me. The sanction for it is sought in the Bible and the tenacity with which the Jews have hankered after Palestine. Why should they not, like other peoples of the earth, make that country their home where they are born and where they earn their livelihood?"

"PALESTINE BELONGS TO THE ARABS

"Palestine belongs to the Arabs in the same sense that England belongs to the English or France to the French. It is wrong and inhuman to impose the Jews on the Arabs. What is going on in Palestine today cannot be justified by any moral code of conduct. The mandates have no sanction but that of the last war. Surely it would be a crime against humanity to reduce the proud Arabs so that Palestine can be restored to the Jews, partly or wholly as their national home.

"The nobler course would be to insist on a just treatment of the Jews wherever they are born and bred.

"This cry for the national home affords a colorable justification for the German expulsion of the Jews.

"But the German persecution of the Jews seems to have no parallel in history. If there could be a justifiable war in the name of and for humanity; a war against Germany to prevent the wantom persecution of a whole race would be completely justified. But I do not believe in any war. A discussion of the pros and cons of such a war is therefore outside my province or horizon.

NO ALLIANCE WITH GERMANY

"But if there can be no war against Germany, even for such a crime as is being committed against the Jews, surely there can be no alliance with Germany. How can there be alliance between a nation which claims to stand for justice and democracy and one which is the declared enemy of both? Or is England drifting toward armed dictatorship and all it means?

"Can the Jews resist this organized and shameless persecution? Is there a way to preserve their self-respect and not feel helpless, neglected, and forlorn? I submit that there is.

"I am convinced that if someone with courage and vision can arise among them to lead them in nonviolent action, the winter of their despair can in the twinkling of an eye be turned into the summer of hope. And what has today become a degrading man hunt can be turned into a calm and determined stand offered by unarmed men and women possessing the strength of suffering, given them by Jehovah. It will then be a truly religious resistance offered against the Godless fury of dehumanized man.

PALESTINE IN THE HEART

"And now a word to the Jews in Palestine. I have no doubt that they are going about it the wrong way. The Palestine of the Biblical conception is not a geographical tract. It is in their hearts. But if they must look to the Palestine of geography as their national home, it is wrong to enter it under the shadow of the British gun.

"A religious act cannot be performed with the aid of the bayonet or the bomb. They can settle in Palestine only by the goodness of the Arabs.

"They should seek to convert the Arab heart. The same God rules the Arab heart who rules the Jewish heart.

"I am not defending the Arab excesses. I wish they had chosen the way of nonviolence in resisting what they rightly regard as an unwarrantable encroachment upon their country. But, according to the accepted canons of right and wrong, nothing can be said against the Arab resistance in the face of overwhelming odds.

"Let the Jews who claim to be the chosen race prove their title by choosing the way of nonviolence for vindicating their position on earth. Every country is their home, including Palestine, not by aggression but by loving service."

Chairman BLOOM. In your last statement you claim in your opinion it would be a disservice to the Jews to adopt this resolution. Now, do you not think the Jews are best able to decide for themselves what is best for them?

Mr. MALOUF. I would love to see the Jews decide for themselves, but I am not sure the Zionists represent the Jews.

Chairman BLOOM. Do you not think the Jews should say who represents them?

Mr. MALOUF. Right.

Chairman BLOOM. I want to get these things right because there are so many things in your statement as to the Jews I object to. I do object to your opening remarks when you referred to those people who took part in the mandate. You called them shrewd Zionist leaders. I think Dr. Weizmann and all of those people did not do anything improper, and they were working for something the Jews have been praying for for thousands of years, and I think it is wrong to put in the record that these people were shrewd.

Mr. MALOUF. I thank you for calling it to my attention. I did not intend to carry any insult by any means. I mean by shrewd, men who are on the job and who are looking out for themselves. If it meant otherwise I certainly apologize.

Chairman BLOOM. Thank you. You have not discussed the convention.

Mr. MALOUF. No; but I shall do that.

Chairman BLOOM. Very well. Mr. Johnson?

Mr. JOHNSON. No questions.

Chairman BLOOM. Dr. Eaton?

Dr. EATON. No questions.

Chairman BLOOM. Mr. Kee?

Mr. KEE. No questions.

Chairman BLOOM. Mrs. Rogers?

Mrs. ROGERS. I think you said your home was in Concord?

Mr. MALOUF. No, in Boston.

Mrs. ROGERS. Mr. Chairman, I was very much interested in his solution, and if he will put that in the record I will ask no questions.

Chairman BLOOM. Mr. Jarman?

Mr. JARMAN. You referred to your cousins because you are both Semetic?

Mr. MALOUF. Yes; and we issue out of the same spiritual depths. We came from that spot of land there. I hope nobody else will get between us and make us enemies.

Mr. JARMAN. I think you spoke of roads in Alabama and Georgia, did you not?

Mr. MALOUF. Yes, sir.

Mr. JARMAN. I am glad to say those roads in Alabama are not nearly so dusty now.

Mr. MALOUF. I know, because I passed by last winter.

Chairman BLOOM. Mr. Chiperfield?

Mr. CHIPERFIELD. You stated there was great pressure on this committee?

Mr. MALOUF. Yes, sir.

Mr. CHIPERFIELD. I want to say for myself there has been no pressure on me. Strange as it may seem I have not received one single letter from my district either for or against and I hope your statement will not be construed as an invitation to write.

Chairman BLOOM. Mr. Burgin?

Mr. BURGIN. No questions.

Chairman BLOOM. Mr. Jonkman?

Mr. JONKMAN. No questions.

Chairman BLOOM. Mr. Rogers?

Mr. ROGERS. Yes; I have a few questions.

Is most of your opposition to this resolution because it seeks the establishment of a commonwealth?

Mr. MALOUF. No; that is not so.

Mr. ROGERS. Would you be opposed to this question of immigration?

Mr. MALOUF. Yes; and if you want my reasons I will state them.

Mr. ROGERS. Yes.

Mr. MALOUF. I think it is a fundamental principle throughout the civilized world that the immigration into a nation is a matter of right inherent in the people of that nation. We had that question in California. Probably you were not born then. Personally, if I were a legislator in Palestine elected by the people of Palestine, I would want my say about it.

Chairman BLOOM. What was that in California?

Mr. MALOUF. I am referring to the Chinese and Japanese exclusion.

Chairman BLOOM. It was cured by the Congress.

Mr. MALOUF. Probably, but the Congress did not give up the right to legislate. I am in hearty sympathy with that cure.

Mr. ROGERS. It is the governments of the various countries which have the right to raise or lower the immigration quotas.

Mr. MALOUF. If the government is a government of the people, by the people, and for the people.

Mr. ROGERS. It has not always been.

Mr. MALOUF. I wish you would keep that in mind on this resolution.

Mr. ROGERS. You are opposed to Jewish immigration?

Mr. MALOUF. I am opposed to anything that does not come from the heart and soul of the people of Palestine themselves as a self-governing people.

Mr. ROGERS. I have understood there are several different types of Arabs and that in the main the opposition has come from the wealthy ones.

I think you called this the Arab war for independence. I understood a good part of that was stirred up by Nazi and Fascist groups who were spreading anti-Semetic propaganda all over the world and had particularly good success with it in Palestine. So much so that some of the Arab leaders found themselves in Berlin.

Mr. MALOUF. I would like to say it is not true. First, the Arab resistence is not the result of any propaganda by the Nazi or Fascist. It dates back to the Zionist-Balfour Declaration long before the advent of Hitler or Mussolini. Secondly, it is the right of the people to determine what system they want to live under. It is not a matter for us to dictate to the Arabs unless we are willing to declare war. What you say is absolutely impertinent to the question.

Mr. JOHNSON. Mr. Chairman, I want to make a point of order. I think the witness should be a little more respectful in his answers to the committee and instead of arguing he should attempt to answer.

Mr. MALOUF. I accept the correction and I have no intention of being discourteous. I have great faith in the committee.

Chairman BLOOM. Any other questions, Mr. Rogers?

Mr. ROGERS. No.

Chairman BLOOM. Mrs. Bolton?

Mrs. BOLTON. No questions.

Chairman BLOOM. Mr. Wadsworth?

Mr. WADSWORTH. No questions.

Chairman BLOOM. Mr. Wright?

Mr. WRIGHT. Yes, Mr. Chairman.

In the first part of your testimony you said we were sitting as a court, to judge the merits of the controversy, I believe?

Mr. MALOUF. Will you permit me to make a statement? I did not state that you are sitting as a court. I said you are not sitting as a court.

Mr. WRIGHT. I refer you again to the convention, and we thought it was to our national interest to agree to the mandate and require that Britain make no changes in the terms of the mandate without our consent.

As to your point that the shrewd Zionist leaders high-pressured the British when their backs were against the wall, I wish to say it was consented to by this country and the Allies and the League of Nations, and as a consequence it was an expression of settled policy, not only by Britain in time of stress, but all nations after mature deliberation.

Mr. MALOUF. Let me say on this point that Great Britain had issued what to every fair-minded student or judge, a paper which has no legal standing, which was not binding on the other parties; the ratification of it or approval of it by anybody else does not give it that which it lacked at its inception.

Mr. WRIGHT. All right.

Mr. MALOUF. And further if that declaration was in every respect according to the standard I would still say it cannot blind us to the elementary principle no matter how many nations combined to give somebody's home to somebody else, as——

Mr. WRIGHT (interposing). I would like to go to the point where you say the declaration had no binding effect.

Mr. MALOUF. Yes.

Mr. WRIGHT. I think you will agree an agreement of all nations at least had force.

Mr. MALOUF. United States was never a party to that mandate.

Mr. WRIGHT. By later convention it affirmed the mandate.

Mr. MALOUF. It never did.

Chairman BLOOM. It certainly did. You are mistaken.

Mr. MALOUF. No; you are mistaken. I know what you have in mind.

Chairman BLOOM. I say you are mistaken.

Mr. WRIGHT. You stated that the Arabs were in possession of Palestine. I believe it was true until General Allenby, with some help of the Arabs, freed the entire peninsula and although they were on the land were subjects of the Turks.

Mr. MALOUF. That was historically true.

Mr. WRIGHT. Also I might refer you to the statement and even the agreement signed by Feisal, who was the accredited representative of the Arab delegation to the Peace Conference at Versailles, agreeing to the establishment of a national home and sympathizing with the Jew.

Mr. MALOUF. You do not have it complete yet. I am referring to the Life magazine article.

Mr. WRIGHT. You state further we should have our own policy rather than follow the policy of an old man in Britain.

Mr. MALOUF. Yes.

Mr. WRIGHT. I believe our policy was stated in the convention between the United States and Great Britain, and rather than being a mere pronouncement of an individual Britain, that the settled policy of the United States at that time was that the mandate should be enforced in accordance with the terms.

Mr. MALOUF. If any one has the convention I would like to have it. Chairman BLOOM. It begins on page 10 of this pamphlet. That is the convention, and it is agreed to between the United States Government and signed by President Coolidge and by Mr. Chamberlain.

Mr. KEE. Will the gentleman yield just a moment?

Mr. WRIGHT. Yes, sir.

Mr. KEE. In the first three lines on page 18 you will find it. It states:

Whereas the Government of the United States and the Government of His Britannic Majesty desire to reach a definite understanding with respect to the rights of the two Governments and their respective nationals in Palestine;

The President of the United States of America and His Britannic Majesty have decided to conclude a convention to this effect.

Mr. MALOUF. All right, what is the question about it?

Chairman BLOOM. I do not think there should be any question about it.

Mr. MALOUF. I do not think there ought to be.

Chairman BLOOM. Mr. Wright, the witness has been on for nearly an hour.

Mr. BURGIN. Mr. Wright is asking questions.

Chairman BLOOM. We would like to get through in a couple of minutes.

Mr. MALOUF. That evidently was for the only purpose of protecting interest of American nationals in Palestine, because we were not parties to the Treaty of Versailles. There was a change of situation in Palestine. We entered into a convention with Great Britain together with seven other nations. The 1924–25 convention addresses itself to the rights of American nationals and their institutions in Palestine.

This explanation was given word for word in a letter from President Roosevelt to the mayor of Hartford, and after a great deal of discussion, Secretary Hull stated——

Chairman BLOOM. We have everything here.

Mr. WRIGHT. I do not like to delay the proceedings but I have several further questions.

Chairman BLOOM. If you can get the answers it will be all right.

Mr. WRIGHT. Now, you further stated the White Paper was an open covenant openly arrived at unlike the Balfour Declaration, and I think we agree the mandate was; but the white paper was unilateral and consequently it is not a covenant at all.

Mr. MALOUF. It is in this respect.

Mr. WRIGHT. You are a lawyer.

Mr. MALOUF. The mandate which Great Britain agreed to assume charged Great Britain with the duty not to use it as it pleases but to assist the people of Palestine in their efforts for self-government as soon as possible and to consult them along in that direction and Great Britain has a perfect right to change the mandate for that purpose.

Mr. WRIGHT (interposing). Are you aware of the letter which Mr. Ramsay MacDonald, then Prime Minister, sent to Secretary Lansing, and also the resolutions of the Permanent Mandates Commission?

Mr. MALOUF. Yes.

Mr. WRIGHT. You further state that the Arabs are being forced to leave Palestine by the immigration of the Jew. You probably know the Arab population of Palestine has increased from 600,000 to a million since the mandate was established.

Mr. MALOUF. They do not have birth control in Palestine.

Mr. WRIGHT. You seem to be opposed to Jewish immigration, and do you think your attitude is the attitude of the Arab people in Palestine.

Mr. MALOUF. Yes.

Mr. WRIGHT. Would it not follow if the Arab majority were allowed to control the government there would not be any more Jewish immigration?

Mr. MALOUF. No; that does not follow.

Mr. WRIGHT. If your ideas are the ideas of the Arabs——

Mr. MALOUF. The Arabs do not want anything imposed on them by other than their own wishes.

Mr. WRIGHT. You stated that the Arabs resented coming of the Jews into their land. You further said they are not going to give up their lands without a fight.

Mr. MALOUF. That is right.

Mr. WRIGHT. At the time of the Balfour Declaration and the mandate at least Feisel was satisfied with the Jews coming in, and was very happy because the Arabs were being liberated by the British, and this opposition to the Jew started afterward.

Mr. MALOUF. You put the Balfour Declaration and the mandate as coming at one time and of course that is not true. Feisel was faced with the Balfour Declaration, great pressure from a great empire which in effect was "either take this or don't take anything." He was confronted with a demand of a great empire "take this or nothing."

Mr. WRIGHT. He agreed to the Jewish Home and to national independence. He was the accredited representative and made that agreement.

Do you not think that should be binding?

Mr. MALOUF. This is a term which means a person elects another person as his representative, but Feisel came there as a military leader who represented himself and could by no stretch of the imagination be considered as an accredited representative.

Mr. WRIGHT. If he did not speak for the Arabs, who did? I understand they do not have any democratic processes.

Mr. VORYS. I would like to have in the record the letter or letters the Government referred to.

Chairman BLOOM. The Chair is going to state we will get copies.

Mr. MALOUF. I have the President's letter of October 21, 1938.

Chairman BLOOM. How long is it?

Mr. MALOUF. One paragraph.

Chairman BLOOM. Read it.

Mr. MALOUF. It will take a moment to find it.

The President's letter to Mr. Thomas J. Spellman, dated October 21, 1938:

I understand, however, that under the terms of our convention with Great Britain regarding the Palestine mandate we are unable to prevent modification of the mandate. The most we can do is to decline to accept as applicable to American interest any modification affecting such interests unless we have given our consent to them.

Chairman BLOOM. Who is that signed by?

Mr. MALOUF. President Roosevelt. If you want to have Secretary Hull's letter, I will read it.

Chairman Bloom. Is it long?

Mr. Malouf. No.

Chairman Bloom. Give us the date and we will get a copy.

Mr. Malouf. A statement made publicly by the New York Times.

Chairman Bloom. It is a public statement by Cordell Hull?

Mr. Malouf. It is a public statement by Cordell Hull.

Chairman Bloom. What is the date? The Chair would like to ask this question, did that letter from the President contain other matter besides what you read?

Mr. Malouf. No I am not sure. To the best of my memory that is all that appeared in the New York Times.

Chairman Bloom. Does the letter contain other paragraphs?

Mr. Malouf. I am not sure.

Chairman Bloom. You have not the letter?

Mr. Malouf. Of course not.

Chairman Bloom. Mr. Schiffler?

Mr. Schiffler. Mr. Witness, are you acquainted with the provisions of the original resolution passed by the Congress of the United States in 1922 and signed by President Harding?

Mr. Malouf. Yes, sir.

Mr. Schiffler. Are you also familiar with the peace treaty, particularly the renunciation by Turkey of jurisdiction over any part of Palestine?

Mr. Malouf. Yes, sir.

Mr. Schiffler. Are you familiar with the provisions of the mandate, especially articles 2 and 6?

Mr. Malouf. In a general manner.

Mr. Schiffler. And its final approval and the signing of it by the Secretary of the State and President Coolidge?

Mr. Malouf. Yes, sir.

Mr. Schiffler. Suppose this committee took action today or any time, do you not think that action is belated in view of the action taken by Britain in 1939, and that action should have been taken at the time of the issuance of the white paper and may wipe out the white paper or protest its issuance by our action here?

Mr. Malouf. I think we would not be justified in doing so.

Mr. Schiffler. Assuming this resolution was in accordance with articles 2 and 6, then we would be treating it purely realistically irrespective of the rights of the Arabs or anybody else, who insisted that conditions be complied with, by wiping out the white paper. Would we be justified in taking action?

Mr. Malouf. No; there is no connection between the articles you referred to and the pending resolution. The articles are a part of the mandate binding only on Great Britain and which we simply recognized.

Mr. Schiffler. Please do not evade my question. I say if we had a resolution insisting the provisions in accordance with articles 2 and 6 be carried out, which is in existence and which——

Mr. Malouf (interposing). We had no right to.

Mr. Schiffler. We are party signatory to it.

Mr. Malouf. We are not signatory to the mandate or any of its articles. I know what you are driving at. The convention does not make us a party to the mandate. The convention simply recognizes the mandate.

Mr. SCHIFFLER. We were not a party to the League of Nations and did not join in the original.

Mr. MALOUF. No.

Mr. SCHIFFLER. But we did by this agreement executed in complete form and consented to by our Congress in joint resolution in 1922 and in 1925 and proclaimed under President Coolidge and Secretary Kellogg. Is there anything we can think of doing 5 years later?

Mr. MALOUF. No, We only recognize the mandate and that recognition gave us no right to interfere now.

Mr. SCHIFFLER. Unfortunately, you and I disagree.

Chairman BLOOM. The Chair would like to ask unanimous consent that that part of the President's letter the witness read be deleted from the record at this time, and the entire record be inserted.

Mr. VORYS. I think the witness' testimony can stand.

Chairman BLOOM. It is unfair to the President to have part of the letter. The question was asked the witness and he said it was only one paragraph. I think it is unfair to the President and of course if we are going to have part of it we should have it all.

Mr. MALOUF. I think that was all of that letter, but I am not sure.

Chairman BLOOM. If that is all, that is all right, but if it is not I want the complete letter.

Mr. MALOUF. I think unless the full letter and the statement of the Secretary of State goes in, we should let it stand, one paragraph.

Mr. VORYS. These two statements, one the witness has not read and one he has read I want to have them in, and the President's letter in there.

Chairman BLOOM. I ask unanimous consent the entire letter be put in and not a misstatement.

Mr. JONKMAN. I think this statement should go in, but I do not think we should testify in place of the witness.

Chairman BLOOM. The Chair wishes to state the answer of the witness to the Chair, is that the letter is one paragraph. If it is only one paragraph let it stay. Otherwise, I would have objected. I think it is wrong to place only a portion of the President's letter in.

Mr. VORYS. His testimony fully explains it is only part.

Mr. WADSWORTH. It is a part of this record. The stenographer has been taking down this very discussion. We all understand that is possibly not the entire letter.

Chairman BLOOM. Thank you. That is all right then.

(Further statement submitted by Faris S. Malouf:)

The international obligations and rights of the United States with reference to Palestine were definitely determined by a treaty between the United States and Great Britain signed on December 3, 1924, and ratified in due course. This treaty was entitled "A Convention between the United Kingdom and the United States of America Respecting the Rights of the Governments of the Two Countries and Their Respective Nationals in Palestine."

After reciting the full text of the Palestine mandate including the preamble, the complete text of the convention is as follows:

"Whereas the mandate in the above terms came into force on the 29th September, 1923; and

Whereas the United States of America, by participating in the war against Germany, contributed to her defeat and the defeat of her Allies, and to the renunciation of the rights and titles of her Allies in the territory transferred by them but has not ratified the Covenant of the League of Nations embodied in the Treaty of Versailles; and

Whereas the Government of the United States and the Government of His Britannic Majesty desire to reach a definite understanding with respect to the rights of the two Governments and their respective nationals in Palestine;

The President of the United States of America and His Britannic Majesty have decided to conclude a convention to this effect, and have named as their plenipotentiaries:—
The President of the United States of America.
His Excellency the Honourable Frank B. Kellogg, Ambassador Extraordinary and Plenipotentiary of the United States at London.
His Majesty the King of the United Kingdom of Great Britain and Ireland and of the British Dominions beyond the Seas, Emperor of India.
The Right Honourable Joseph Austen Chamberlain, M. P., His Majesty's Principal Secretary of State for Foreign Affairs.

who, after having communicated to each other their respective full powers, found in good and due form, have agreed as follows:

ARTICLE I

Subject to the provisions of the present convention the United States consents to the administration of Palestine by His Britannic Majesty, pursuant to the Mandate recited above.

ARTICLE II

The United States and its nationals shall have and enjoy all the rights and benefits secured under the terms of the mandate to members of the League of Nations and their nationals, notwithstanding the fact that the United States is not a member of the League of Nations.

ARTICLE III

Vested American property rights in the mandated territory shall be respected and in no way impaired.

ARTICLE IV

A duplicate of the annual report to be made by the Mandatory under article 24 of the mandate shall be furnished to the United States.

ARTICLE V

Subject to the provisions of any local laws for the maintenance of public order and public morals, the nationals of the United States will be permitted freely to establish and maintain education, philanthropic and religious institutions in the mandated territory, to receive voluntary applicants and to teach in the English language.

ARTICLE VI

The extradition treaties and conventions which are, or may be, in force between the United States and Great Britain, and the provisions of any treaties which are, or may be, in force between the two countries which relate to extradition or consular rights shall apply to the mandated territory.

ARTICLE VII

Nothing contained in the present convention shall be affected by any modification which may be made in the terms of the mandate, as recited above, unless such modification shall have been assented to by the United States.

ARTICLE VIII

The present convention shall be ratified in accordance with the respective constitutional methods of the High Contracting Parties. The ratifications shall be exchanged in London as soon as practicable. The present convention shall take effect on the date of the exchange of ratifications.
In witness whereof, the undersigned have signed the present convention, and have thereunto affixed their seals.
Done in duplicate at London, this 3rd day of December, 1924.
[SEAL]   FRANK B. KELLOGG.
[SEAL]   AUSTEN CHAMBERLAIN.

It could be readily seen that the eight articles of the convention are concerned with rights of American nationals, property and institutions in Palestine. Article I simply recognizes the Mandate and the authority of the British Government to administer the affairs of Palestine accordingly.

Article II provides a guarantee that American nationals shall enjoy on equal footing with nationals of Members of the League of Nations all the rights and benefits secured under the Mandate.

Article III provides for protection of vested American interests in the mandated territory.

Article IV places an obligation on the mandatory power to furnish a copy of its annual report concerning its mandate to the United States.

Article V provides for the protection of and continuation of the educational, philanthropic, and religious institutions in the mandated territory.

Article VI concerns itself solely with extradition proceedings and consular rights.

Article VII provides that the rights guaranteed by the previous articles shall not be affected by any modifications in the terms of the Mandate unless such modifications shall have been assented to by the United States.

Article VIII concerns itself solely with the manner of the ratification of the convention and has no bearing on the questions raised by Resolutions 418 and 419.

The proponents of the Resolutions seem to rely to a great extent on this convention, especially on Article VII thereof. A few members of the Committee seem to be impressed by the emphasis laid by the proponents on this article.

A careful analysis of the whole convention, especially Article VII will show clearly that all that was intended by the convention and this article was that the rights of American nationals shall not be affected by any change in the Mandate unless the United States had previously agreed to the change. By no stretch of the imagination can this convention be interpreted as placing an obligation on the United States or giving it any right to take steps for the establishment of a Jewish Commonwealth in Palestine, nor does it give the United States the right to object to any change in the Mandate unless such a change jeopardizes the rights of American citizens in Palestine. It must be emphasized again that this convention does not make us a party to the Mandate, and that the White Paper of 1939 was simply a step in the right direction, and within the spirit of the Covenant of the League of Nations, especially Article 22 thereof which places a sacred responsibility upon the Mandatory power to lead the mandated country into final independence and self-government.

The first paragraph of Article 22 of the convention of the League of Nations states that the purpose of the Mandate was that "There should be applied the principle that the well-being and development of such peoples (inhabitants of the mandated territories) form a sacred trust of civilization and that securities for the performance of this trust should be embodied in this Covenant." Article 22 of the convention also includes this provision that the wishes of the people of the mandated territory should be the principal consideration of the Mandate.

Article VII of the convention is substantially identical with corresponding articles included in eight other existing agreements concluded by this Government with respect to these mandated territories of Syria and Lebanon, former German islands in the North Pacific; French Cameroons, French Togoland, Belgium East Africa, British Cameroons, British Togoland.

The articles of the convention in question are executed the same as the articles in the other eight existing treaties concerning the above-mentioned Mandated countries and none of these articles empower the Government of the United States to prevent the modification of the terms of any of the Mandates. Under the provisions of these articles, however, the Government of the United States can decline to recognize the validity of the application to American interests of any modification of the Mandate unless such modifications were assented to by the Government of the United States.

The above is the exact interpretation placed on these conventions by both the President of the United States and our Secretary of State, Cordell Hull. In a letter written by President Roosevelt to Mayor Thomas J. Spellacy of Hartford, Conn., who had appealed to the President to intervene in behalf of a Jewish Homeland in Palestine, the full text of the President's letter dated October 21, 1938, as it appeared in the New York Times of October 22, 1938, was as follows:

"My Dear Mayor Spellacy: I fully appreciate the concern expressed by you in your telegram of October 13, 1938, regarding the Palestine situation. I have on numerous occasions, as you know, expressed my sympathy in the establishment of a national home for the Jews in Palestine and despite the setbacks caused by disorders there during the last few years, I have been heartened by the progress which has been made and by the remarkable accomplishments of the Jewish settlers in that country.

"We have kept constantly before the British Government through our Ambassador in London, the interest which the American people have in Palestine and that that Government is fully cognizant of public opinion on the matter in this country.

"We were assured, in the discussions that took place in London a little more than a year ago, that the British Government would keep us fully informed of any proposals which it might make to the council of the League of Nations for the modification of the Palestine mandate. We expect, therefore, to have the opportunity afforded us of communicating to the British Government our views with respect to any changes in the mandate which may be proposed as a result of the forthcoming report of the Palestine Partition Commission.

"I understand, however, that, under the terms of our convention with Great Britain regarding the Palestine mandate, we are unable to prevent modifications in the mandate. The most we can do is to decline to accept as applicable to American interests any modifications affecting such interests unless we have given our assent to them.

"You may be sure that we shall continue to follow the situation with the closest attention.

"Sincerely yours,

"FRANKLIN D. ROOSEVELT."

Bearing on the rights of the United States under the convention with Great Britain, Secretary Hull, under pressure of frantic petitions and telegrams received during the middle of October 1938, made to him by the Zionists and their friends who appealed to the United States for intervention, issued the following statement on October 14, 1938.

"On several occasions this Government has brought its views regarding the rights of the United States and its nationals in Palestine to the attentions of the British Government. As recently as 1937 a formal exchange of correspondence took place and the following self-explanatory paragraph is quoted from the concluding note dated August 4, 1937, communicated by the American Ambassador in London to the British Foreign Office.

"In expressing satisfaction and appreciation for the assurances furnished that His Majesty's Government intends to keep the United States Government fully informed of any proposals which may be made to the council of the League of Nations for the modification of the Palestine Mandate. I am instructed to request that these proposals may be communicated to my Government in ample time to enable it to determine what, if any, observations it may desire to make with a view to the preservation of American rights in Palestine.

"It is expected, therefore, that this Government will have an opportunity to submit its views to the British Government with respect to any change affecting American rights which may be proposed in the Palestine Mandate. These rights which are defined by the American-British Mandate Convention or Treaty of December 3, 1924, comprise nondiscriminating treatment in matters of commerce, nonimpairment of vested American property rights, permission for American nationals to establish and maintain educational, philanthropic, and religious institutions in Palestine, safeguard with respect to the judiciary and in general, equality of treatment with other foreign nationals."

The Chair wishes to state at this time one of our witnesses had to leave, Judge Leventhal, and the Chair wishes also to state the last witness consumed an hour and a quarter.

Mr. VORYS. Can we not hear from Representative Dingell?

Chairman BLOOM. Certainly.

STATEMENT OF HON. JOHN D. DINGELL, A REPRESENTATIVE IN CONGRESS FROM THE STATE OF MICHIGAN

Mr. DINGELL. Mr. Chairman, I want to enter an appearance here and insert in the record my remarks which were made before a congregation of my constituents at Shaarey Zedek Synagogue, on May 21, 1939, under the auspices of the Detroit Zionist Emergency Committee, consisting of all Zionist organizations in cooperation with the Jewish Community Council.

It served the purpose at that time, I thought, and I think it is appropriate to have it in the record now and I merely offer it, and realizing the pressure of business on the committee, I do not desire to consume any more time.

Chairman BLOOM. Without objection, it will be inserted.

The Chair hears none.

(The address referred to is as follows:)

ADDRESS OF HON. JOHN D. DINGELL, MAY 21, 1939, AT SHAAREY ZEDEK SYNAGOGUE, DETROIT, MICH., UNDER THE AUSPICES OF THE DETROIT ZIONIST EMERGENCY COMMITTEE, CONSISTING OF ALL ZIONIST ORGANIZATIONS IN COOPERATION WITH THE JEWISH COMMUNITY COUNCIL

Mr. Chairman and fellow citizens, I have come here today not alone for the purpose of discussing a grave problem, but also as concrete evidence of my sympathy for you and your cause, and if I can, to help you in the solution of your problem. Moreover, my appearance here today as a member of a Christian faith is intended by me at least to indicate the interest and the concern of my fellow coreligionists toward you in your hour of trial.

Recent pronouncements by the British Government with regard to the proposed political change in the status of Palestine as enunciated by Mr. Chamberlain have not only shocked the world in general but have caused certain elements within it to recoil because of the violation of a solemn pledge. I, for one, cannot accept Mr. Chamberlain's expressions as indicative of the attitude of the English people any more than I could accept the acts of madness on the part of Hitler and Mussolini as being the reflections of the German and Italian peoples. From my earliest childhood I have always been taught to believe that Palestine was the ancestral, the historic, and the God-given land of the Jews; and I was taught, moreover, that it was ordained by God that some day the Jews of the world would return to their homeland. Biblical prophets and sincere and saintly men throughout the ages have prophesied the great homecoming of the Jews back to what in my mind will always be the Holy Land, there to enjoy the peace, happiness, and contentment which for centuries have been denied them by other countries of the world.

Christians and non-Christians, men of fairness throughout the world, rejoiced with you and your oppressed brethren when the great Woodrow Wilson expressed himself in your behalf. The world was thrilled when the Palestinian mandate was drawn. The Balfour Declaration clarified and gave additional substance to a practical, though not a new idea. The expression of the Congress of the United States convinced the world of our American interest in this belated reestablishment of the Jewish homeland.

Great Britian voluntarily—yes, eagerly—assumed a responsibility in the Near East. Great Britain consulted with the Government of the United States along with other Governments, and we have given our approval, our official assent to the course proposed by His Majesty's Government.

Peaceful settlement and development of the ancient land of the Jews began almost immediately, and as persecutions flared throughout Europe, migrations to the Holy Land were increased, under stress of necessity were speeded up, and that portion of Palestine which was peopled by the incoming immigrant Jew was reclaimed from desolation of the desert and became a productive paradise. Men and women became prosperous in their newly found freedom. Industries, hospitals, libraries, and homes were built. Agricultural development advanced at an almost unbelievable rate, both as to quality of the products and increased productivity. Palestine was absorbing more and more of the oppressed, of the persecuted, and of brokenhearted Jews who gathered the remnants of their homes, fortunes, and families, and treked back to the promised land to their historic home.

The advancement of the Jews in the family of nations seemed to be a certainty. Suddenly, however, the world began to hear of brawls, riots, skirmishes with the inevitable and final British military interference; all of this commotion in the peaceful land inhabited by an unusually peace-loving people. This sudden change was not spontaneous; it was incited. As a matter of fact, we know that it was created by the anti-Semitic dictators in Germany and Italy as retaliation against Britain, and was calculated to embarrass the British Government. A prolonged reign of terror followed in the wake of propaganda, eventually giving Britain no alternative but to interfere with military force. Only recently the whole civilized world was shocked by disclosures which indicate clearly the duplicity of British diplomacy. The world learned that certain promises distinctly contradictory were made on the one hand to the Jews and on the other hand to the Moslem Arabs. Britain toyed with the destiny of the unfortunate Jew. Britain viewed the entire matter as one of expediency and of self-gain, and as time went on this double dealing of Great Britain was brought to light; and at this juncture Mr. Chamberlain authorized the issuance of the so-called white paper, which has for its purpose the nullification and destruction of sacred promises voluntarily given to the Jews and accepted by the world as having been given in good faith and subject to being fulfilled.

The aims, the aspirations for the development of Palestine brought about by substantial migrations of the Jews were now placed in complete jeopardy. The moderate quotas permitted to enter Palestine well within the ability of the land to absorb and sustain them, are now to be reduced to a negligible minimum. These quotas intended to save the face of the British Government, condemn the Jews to a permanent status of the minority subject to violent hatreds and oppressions by the Arabs who are to be by agreement and understanding masters of your people who sought respite from persecution, who sought the opportunity in the homeland to start life anew, to rehabilitate themselves.

As Dr. Goldman stated recently, Britain condoned and encouraged—yes, became a party to—the proposed establishment of a territorial ghetto in the Near East, in the traditional home of the Jews which would be far more confining and oppressive than any heretofore established on the European Continent.

After a stipulated period of years, England insists that Palestine shall become dominated by the Moslem Arab, that the culture, the development, and the peaceful settlement of the homeland shall be stifled by Arabian influence and control, and this with the full approval of His Majesty's Government. It is not too late for England to recalculate the possibilities of the future, reconsider and make such corrections as would permit the peaceful adjustment of the differences between the Jews and the Arabs. I am confident that if the Government of Great Britain in consultation with other interested nations should call together the parties involved, that a permanent solution is not only possible but absolutely certain. The subjection of the Jews in Palestine can never be a lasting solution of the Jewish-Arab difficulties. The Jews throughout the world will not and should not bow down to it. The nations of the world will not accept it. Bloodshed and the continued reign of terror with the attendant cost of human lives and misery will continue. Britain holds within her hand the possibilities of a just and equitable solution, if she will but deal openly, honestly, and fairly with the Jews and the Arabs.

The people of America interested in a permanent and peaceful solution, being a party to the establishment of Palestine under the mandate, look to Britain, as we have a right, to extend her energies to the utmost in reestablishing tranquillity in the Holy Land. England cannot afford, under any circumstances, to make of the Jews a pawn in order to gain a temporary military advantage. As a matter of fact, England should know that her own best move for security and the maintenance of peace in the Near East should be predicated upon the establishment and maintenance of an inviolate Jewish Palestine. The loyalty, the devotion, and the gratitude of the Jews will repay England a thousand-fold for her steadfastness and moral courage. England has lost her sense of equilibrium. England has been goaded into an action that is against her own best interests. A strong and consistently expanding Jewish Palestine should become the keystone of safety in the arch of the British Empire. I feel that millions of people throughout the world, and particularly in the Western Hemisphere, will sustain that opinion. It is not my purpose today, my friends, to extend myself in an unduly lengthy discourse, but I do want to say before closing that I believe England can be made to, and will, capitulate. It is not too late for her to redeem her solemn pledges.

It is incumbent upon us, however, to assume a militant and aggressive attitude in this matter. It is mandatory that we make known our demands, that we insist upon the scrupulous carrying out of the provisions of the mandate and of the Balfour Declaration.

We, who are privileged to live in this glorious land of freedom, should be the first to offer encouragement to the Jews of Palestine and we should remain steadfast and devoted to the one and only outline which holds promise of permanency and of peace, not only for the Jews but the rest of the world as well. Let us then, Jew and gentile alike, pledge ourselves in accordance with the ancient Jewish psalmist, "If I forget thee, O Jerusalem, may my right hand forget its cunning."

Let me add for the benefit of those who do not understand my position, or my viewpoint, and I hope that there are not many who do not, that I feel strongly on the point that inasmuch as America has been a party to the reestablishment of Palestine, that the Government of the United States must of necessity be consulted in any change, modification, or alteration of the original mandate. We have accepted the mandate and the Balfour declaration as sincere and sound. It is my belief that the fairness of the American people toward the Jews will insist that there can be no change without American assent.

I have dispatched a letter of protest to the [Honorable Cordell Hull, Secretary of State, which clearly indicates the position which I have assumed in this matter. For your information, although not at this juncture for publication, I shall read separately the letter in its entirety. I feel that until the Secretary has had an opportunity to reply, that I should in fairness, defer giving publicity to this communication, for it is well known that the American State Department guards jealously its prerogative in matters bearing upon our foreign policy.

HOUSE OF REPRESENTATIVES,
Washington, D. C., May 20, 1939.

Hon. CORDELL HULL,
    Secretary of State, Washington, D. C.

MY DEAR MR. SECRETARY: Recent unfavorable developments pertaining to the future of Palestine have aroused great concern generally among the people of the world and in particular have aroused the citizens of the United States.

The issuance of the so-called white paper by the British Government indicates clearly the abandonment of pledges of permanency given the Jews and accepted by the world as guaranties for the maintenance of Palestine as the historic homeland of these unfortunate and persecuted people. This change in attitude is in direct contravention of the mandate and the subsequent Balfour Declaration.

I hasten to register my most emphatic protest against any modification or alteration of the mandate to which the Government of the United States has given assent and support. I urge therefore to make formal representation to His Majesty's Government demanding at the same time the carrying out of the provisions in accordance with the stipulations contained in the document.

There can be no arbitrary emasculation or change without consultation and agreement among the interested nations. Unilateral action on the part of Great Britain in violation of the rights of the Jews should be denounced and proclaimed as invalid.

Being mindful of the fact that you are charged with the responsibility of our foreign policy I, nevertheless, make these suggestions in the hope that you will use your good offices and bring about the fulfillment of the mandate.

I subscribe myself
    Very respectfully yours.

*   *   *   *   *   *   *

Chairman BLOOM. Now, Dr. Neumann.

FURTHER STATEMENT OF DR. EMANUEL NEUMANN, ATTORNEY, NEW YORK CITY

Dr. NEUMANN. If there are no questions following my statement I would like to make a few observations.

Chairman BLOOM. Are there any questions?

Mrs. BOLTON. Is this a secondary deposition?

Chairman BLOOM. No, the Chair stated the judge was supposed to be here and was called away, and it was requested Dr. Neumann should take his place and answer whatever questions might be propounded.

Dr. Neumann is taking the place of Judge Levinthal who was one of the seven to be called. The judge could not stay. Then again, Dr. Neumann was not questioned yesterday because we did not have the time, so if there are any questions any members would like to ask on his statement made yesterday, the Doctor would like to answer them. If not, he would like to make the statement Judge Levinthal would have made if he could have remained here.

Mrs. BOLTON. The witness' statement was somewhat different. He stated he wanted to speak in reference to some of the statements made. Yet, with Judge Levinthal not being here there would be a difference.

Chairman BLOOM. I do not think so.

Mrs. BOLTON. The Judge probably would say the things that have been said.

Dr. NEUMANN. I do not want to impose on the committee.

Mrs. BOLTON. Not at all.

Chairman BLOOM. Proceed, Doctor.

Dr. NEUMANN. I listened very attentively to what has been said today, and I am very happy this discussion took place because I think it has contributed to a clearer understanding.

Mr. MALOUF. Mr. Chairman, I may be out of order and if so I will take my seat, but may I have a chance to rebut Dr. Neumann's testimony because he evidently intends to rebut mine.

Chairman BLOOM. We sit here and hear argumentative testimony and rebuttal, and surrebuttal. I think you have been given every consideration. You have been given over an hour and a quarter. We have been nearly 2 hours on this and the judge could not wait, and I think it perfectly proper for Dr. Neumann to be able to answer you in lieu of the judge.

Mr. JARMAN. Was the judge here?

Mr. MALOUF. I think I should be given an opportunity.

Chairman BLOOM. You had every opportunity. If there is no objection we will hear further from Dr. Neumann.

Dr. NEUMANN. Judge Levinthal and I are members of the same Zionist committee. He was here yesterday. I know precisely what was in his mind and I think I am well qualified to represent his point of view at his request this morning and I am willing to do that.

Chairman BLOOM. Is there objection? The Chair hears none. Proceed, Doctor.

Dr. NEUMANN. Mr. Chairman, throughout the hearings a great deal has been said on the subject of the possible consequences of the adoption of this resolution by the House and pictures have been painted, lurid pictures have been painted of repercussions not only in Palestine and not only in the neighboring countries but throughout the Arab world, in North Africa, India, even in Malay and Java. The premise on which this inference is made to rest is entirely without foundation.

It is based on the premise that these resolutions imply the removal of the Arabs from Palestine elsewhere.

I would like to make the statement for the record that at no time in the long history of the Zionist movement in its many conventions and congresses and public declarations and pronouncements by its official spokesmen, at no time in its long history has the Zionist movement ever demanded the removal of the Arabs from Palestine.

The head of the Zionist Organization has opposed it and repeatedly taken the position that the population in Palestine, Arab and otherwise, have every right to be there; and therefore, I would like the members of the committee to dismiss from their minds once and for all any such notion which is not, so far as I can see, part of the resolution either expressly or by implication.

We insist there is room in Palestine for those already there and many that will come. In proof of that we point to the fact that whereas Palestine's population at the end of the last war was about half a million, it is now a million and a half. It has increased three-fold. That does not look like pushing anybody out.

I have lived in Palestine 8 years, and can testify that because of the growing attractiveness of Palestine, because of its economic progress and rise in social conditions it has been attracting people from surrounding countries.

It has been sucking them in.

I want to point to one neighboring country, namely, Trans-Jordan, which is about three times as large as Palestine and a population only one-fifth as large. It is almost an empty country. From the Arab nationalist point of view there is an ideal situation: No Jewish National Home, no Jewish immigration, but an Arab state under Arab rule.

What has happened? Trans-Jordan has remained almost in the condition it was before the World War, except for some improvements which were brought about by the Mandatory Power; but there has been no radical change, no growth, no prosperity, but stagnation. Therefore, Trans-Jordanians come to Palestine. Jews are prohibited from going into Trans-Jordan but there is no prohibition against Trans-Jordanians crossing over into Palestine—that is, Western Palestine.

The condition of that country is lamentable.

When I was serving as a member of the Executive of the Jewish Agency for Palestine in 1932 and 1933 there was a regular invasion of shieks from Trans-Jordan to Palestine. They came to see the Jews, urging us to come forward and buy a part of their empty land and help develop their neglected country.

I have here in my possession a photograph of a luncheon at the King David Hotel in Jerusalem where we had a meeting with some of these Trans-Jordan shieks.

Mr. WRIGHT. Mr. Chairman, may I interrupt to ask a question just at that point?

Chairman BLOOM. Mr. Wright.

Mr. WRIGHT. How widespread is the Arab opposition to Jewish immigration? Is it general throughout the entire peninsula?

Dr. NEUMANN. There is a great deal of misunderstanding about Arab life. Arab society is not modeled along the lines of the American which makes it easy here to determine what the people think. The Arabs live under an authoritarian society. They are led by the headmen, shieks, and feudal landlords. There is an almost total absence of the democratic process as we understand it.

Chairman BLOOM. When you say headmen you mean leaders?

Dr. NEUMANN. Yes, sir. Therefore, when you ask what is the position of the Arabs it is hard to answer. You have someone who says he represents the Arabs and somebody else says he does. Along comes a third and claims he is the spokesman.

Trans-Jordanians wanted us to come to not only Palestine, but also to Trans-Jordan. They said they wanted some of the "milk" in Trans-Jordan and that is why they wanted Jewish immigration and all the benefits which accrued from Jewish settlement.

I will go further, and this is the first time I have said it in public. Among those who came forward and desired the Jews to acquire land in Trans-Jordan was his Highness Emir Abdullah himself. We had long conferences with him and finally agreed, and he signed in my presence an option agreement covering 70,000 dunams of land under his control. This agreement expressly provided for Jewish settlement in Trans-Jordan under the Emir's protection.

Mr. Chairman, anyone who has lived there, knows that these rumors that have been circulated, these stories, are greatly exaggerated.

Mr. WRIGHT. I would like to get your idea of the poorer Arabs, what is their attitude?

Dr. NEUMANN. That varies. Normally the relations are quite satisfactory, people buying and selling, people meeting around the table. I was a member of the board of directors of a mixed company having Jews and Arabs on the board. This kind of thing has gone on all over the country. In the citrus industry the Arabs and Jews act together frequently.

There is a mixed municipality in Haifa, with an Arab mayor and a Jewish vice mayor. Everything has gone on beautifully.

Mr. WRIGHT. When you have these terrors would it be the poor who would be involved.

Dr. NEUMANN. The instigators and leaders of the bands were men of the "upper class" of the feudal aristocracy. The Arab masses by and large wanted to be let alone and resisted the demands and exactions of the terrorists. So when you read the record you find that the terror, considered quantitatively, was not merely anti-Jewish but largely an internal Arab terror. Violence was employed by the extremists against moderate and peaceful Arabs to compel them to join in.

Mr. WRIGHT. Join in what?

Dr. NEUMANN. To join in the campaign of arson and assassination directed chiefly against the Jewish population. I don't know whether you know what was going on. The campaign of Arab terror has been dignified here by such terms as "a revolution" and a "war of independence" and an attempt is made to compare these bandits with the heroes of Lexington and Concord. A revolution is a rising of the people against the armed might of a government or a foreign oppressor. It is quite another matter to attack unarmed and inoffensive men, women, and children from ambush, to shoot at taxies and busses from behind rocks, to explode bombs in a crowded theater, to kill nurses on their way to the hospital, to murder a Jewish doctor while visiting his Arab patients in an Arab village, to murder whole families, to burn down groves and orchards, to pillage houses. That is what went on.

Mr. JARMAN. Will the gentleman yield?

Mr. WRIGHT. Yes.

Chairman BLOOM. Mr. Jarman.

Mr. JARMAN. The casualties, were there more Arab or Jewish?

Dr. NEUMANN. In the end Arab casualties exceeded the Jewish. Both because of the internal Arab terror and because the terrorist bands were finally engaged by the British military and suppressed. The Jewish settlements managed to defend themselves well on the whole and not a single Jewish settlement was overwhelmed. The attacks were made chiefly on the roads. I used to travel back and forth between Jerusalem and Tel Aviv and was frequently exposed to shots from ambush. One day I stopped alongside a truck at which a bomb had been thrown. There were two Yemenite Jews; one had his hand cut off and was bleeding to death; the other had his eye gouged out. They were taken to the hospital and died the next day.

Mr. JARMAN. I understood you to say awhile ago the Arabs attacked Arabs.

Dr. NEUMAN. They did, because the mass of Arabs could not be induced to join the terror or to make contributions in money or in kind, except by coercion. The total number who participated in the terror never exceeded 1,500 to 2,000, including those who were attracted from Syria by the prospect of excitement and loot. Even 2,000 out of an Arab population of more than 1,000,000 is not a high proportion. The great majority was unwilling to be drawn in. But the leader of the violent minority, murderous Mufti, was a Nazi and used Nazi strong arm methods against fellow Arabs. They would go to a village and levy a "quota" of so many "volunteers" to join the terror and so much money or food. Resistance was punished by murder. Political opponents, moderate Arab leaders, were freely assassinated.

Of course, the mandatory power which took the matter too lightly in the beginning finally adopted energetic measures and wiped out the bands. As a result, while the Jews suffered casualties—nearly 1,000—total Arab casualties were higher.

Here I have the photo to which I referred, of Arab chiefs from Trans-Jordan with Dr. Weizman and myself and other members of the Executive of the Jewish Agency for Palestine. I will pass it around.

Chairman BLOOM. What year was that?

Dr. NEUMANN. The spring of 1933. Mr. Twitchell has spoken of the possibility of creating a Jewish settlement or settlements all over the world.

Mr. JOHNSON. Mr. Chairman.

Chairman BLOOM. Mr. Johnson.

Mr. JOHNSON. I want to ask the witness a question, whether Trans-Jordan is recognized. As I understand under the treaty the limits of Palestine were confined to 10,000 square miles. Does this Trans-Jordan country where these Arabs come from, is that considered by the Jewish people and the Zionist movement as part of Palestine?

Dr. NEUMANN. Historically it is; and in many other ways. Both are covered by the same mandate, but a distinction has been made. The Jewish National Home clauses of the mandate are not operative in Trans-Jordan. The area of the Jewish National Home was thereby reduced by 75 percent and confined to 10,000 square miles.

Mr. JOHNSON. Do the Jewish people follow the geographical or historical line with reference to Trans-Jordan?

Dr. NEUMANN. The discussion as I understand refers to western Palestine.

Mr. JOHNSON. I do not know whether the Jewish people would be inclined to accept that as part of the Holy Land.

Dr. NEUMANN. The Jewish people would very much like to. From the point of view of history and sentiment Trans-Jordan has always been and will always be part of the Holy Land. We would certainly wish to help in its development and restoration. But a political decision was made by Great Britain cutting it off from western Palestine, a decision we were powerless to affect.

Mr. JOHNSON. In response to this invitation from Trans-Jordan did any Jews acquire land in Trans-Jordan?

Dr. Neumann. No; because of the firm opposition of the mandatory government. Nothing of a practical nature resulted except to demonstrate to the world that the universal opposition of the Arabs was largely mythical and artificial and that many people in Trans-Jordan were anxious to have Jewish colonization and development take place there.

Mr. Kee. Dr. Neumann, I would like you to pursue the subject on which you were talking before you were interrupted with reference to attempts that had been made by a certain portion of your people to find places elsewhere.

Dr. Neumann. I will be glad to speak about that.

Mr. Kee. As briefly as possible.

Dr. Neumann. There was a Jewish territorialist organization formed 40 years ago headed by the late Israel Zangwill, noted author of the Children of the Ghetto and the Melting Pot. This organization sent out competent expeditions to discover a suitable territory. Curiously the first territory investigated about 40 years ago was the one Mr. Twitchell had first on his list this morning—Cyrenaica, which is part of Libya. Anyone interested can find a voluminous and detailed report on it in the New York Public Library and probably also in the Library of Congress. For 40 years such efforts to find a substitute for Palestine have been going on without success. All sorts of exotic places have been suggested—places that are either too hot or too cold, in the equatorial deserts, in inaccessible jungles. The fair and habitable portions of the globe are all either inhabited or occupied and possessed by nations who have no inclination to give them up or to permit large-scale Jewish colonization. Brazil was mentioned this morning. Does the gentleman know the attitude of the Brazilian Government? We have had some experience with some of the South American countries. We would bring in a limited number of refugees, then there would be a reaction; no more refugees. The opposition, for that matter, is not limited to Jewish refugees. Dr. Hitti went further than Mr. Twitchell and asked why not Arizona? Indeed, why not Arizona? It is all very well for learned and well-intentioned gentlemen to sit and discuss geography while millions are being slaughtered. The Jewish people have been studying geography for 2,000 years. We have become experts in geography, not theoretically, but by wandering over the face of the earth for centuries down to the present day. The situation in recent years has been summed up by Dr. Weizmann who said that the countries of the world are divided roughly in two categories: countries which force Jews to leave and countries which refuse to admit them.

In Palestine we have spent 60 to 70 years in preparation. We have experimented widely. We have laid the foundations for the Jewish National Home. As a result that small country is ready to absorb large numbers. But try to do it in some strange exotic country with which the Jews have no ties and to which they have no legal or historical claim and the practical results will be nil.

Mr. Wright. May I pursue my question a little?

Chairman Bloom. Mr. Wright.

Mr. Wright. You were discussing the Arabs of Palestine and also the surrounding countries. Do you think there would be any widespread resentment among the inhabitants of India and various places like that if the provisions of the Balfour Declaration were enforced?

Mr. Neumann. In my humble opinion, Mr. Wright, the inhabitants of all these oriental countries have other things to think about. They have serious problems and worries of their own. There is no doubt whatever that if the Palestine question exists at all in their minds it is on the fringe or periphery of their consciousness—unless someone deliberately sets out to incite them. Ignorant, illiterate, and fanatical people can, of course, be incited—particularly if the authorities are lax. For example, the riots of 1929 in Palestine were started by spreading a wild rumor that the Jews had bombed a mosque in Jerusalem.

Chairman BLOOM. Have they done it?

Dr. NEUMANN. They have other things to do.

Chairman BLOOM. I know the answer.

Dr. NEUMANN. I am sure you all know it.

Chairman BLOOM. But you had better have the record show.

Dr. NEUMANN. The Jews never bombed any mosque. Of course, it's absurd.

I would like to add a word about the Balfour Declaration and the so-called McMahon correspondence which embodied the original British promises to the Arabs. The attempt has been made to describe the McMahon correspondence as a public commitment and the Balfour Declaration as a secret treaty. Mr. Chairman, the reverse happens to be true. The McMahon letters were secret and kept secret for more than 20 years and never made public until 1939. They were published then in order to prove British contentions that Palestine had never been promised to the Arabs.

As to the Balfour Declaration I will say there was never a policy more carefully considered and weighed after the fullest exchange of views. It was not issued until the views of the American Government and those of the French and Russian Governments had been canvassed. Likewise Italy and the Holy See. It was anything but a secret document. Immediately upon its signature by Mr. Balfour, then Foreign Minister, it was published to the world. It touched off a large number of celebrations and great public meetings addressed by leading British statesmen. It was an "open covenant," if there ever was one.

Much has been said here about democracy and self-determination. No attempt is make to apply these ideas in the case of Palestine in the sense that the Arabs of Palestine have a right to exclude the Jews and perhaps even the right to evacuate Jews who are already there. One would suppose from the tenor of these remarks that the right of national self-determination attached to all the peoples of the world everywhere with apparently one single exception—the Jews. They alone are apparently to be denied the right to build up a free national existence anywhere.

But, as I pointed out yesterday, the statesmen who issued the Balfour Declaration and the statesmen who approved it took all of these questions fully into account and found it right and just that in one spot the Jewish people shall also exercise national self-determination. They therefore created mandated Palestine.

The White Paper of 1939 far from being a treaty with anyone was nothing more than a unilateral repudiation of the Balfour Declaration at a difficult moment in world affairs, a surrender to terror and Axis intrigue. The same had happened to Czechoslovakia. Both were sacrificed, thrown to the wolves. The White Paper was the Munich of the Near East.

We are told America may be militarily involved. No one suggests an American expeditionary force to maintain order in Palestine. There is a mandatory government which assumed definite responsibilities. Moreover, there are enough peace-loving people in Palestine who could and would shoulder the responsibility of policing the country and maintaining order if called upon to do so.

The problem of external defense is quite another problem which Palestine faces in common with all other small countries everywhere. Our own Government seems to approve the setting up of the Lebanon as an autonomous republic. It is much smaller than Palestine in area and has a much smaller population, only 800,000. How will it be able to stand up? Obviously only under some kind of international protection in a world-wide system of security which will provide for the safety of small nations.

Certainly America is assuming no military obligations by these resolutions. No American lives are involved. What is involved is American good will and moral as well as diplomatic support of a traditional American policy.

Reference has been made to Emir Feisal and some doubt cast upon the validity of his commitments in favor of Zionism. I have here a copy of a letter from Emir Feisal, head of the Arab delegation to the peace conference, written in Paris, March 3, 1919 to Prof. Felix Frankfurter.

Mr. JOHNSON. What is the date of the letter?

Dr. NEUMANN. March 3, 1919.

Mr. JOHNSON. The writer of the letter was who?

Dr. NEUMANN. Emir Feisal, subsequently King of Iraq.

Mr. VORYS. Was the recipient of the letter our present Justice Frankfurter?

Dr. NEUMANN. Yes. Feisal's letter reads as follows:

I want to take this opportunity of my first contact with American Zionists to tell you what I have often been able to say to Dr. Weizmann in Arabia and Europe.

We feel that the Arabs and Jews are cousins in race, have suffered similar oppression at the hands of powers stronger than themselves, and by a happy coincidence have been able to take the first step toward the attainment of their national ideals together.

We Arabs, especially the educated among us, look with the deepest sympathy on the Zionist movement. Our deputation here in Paris is fully acquainted with the proposals submitted yesterday by the Zionist organization to the peace conference, and we regard them as moderate and proper. We will do our best, insofar as we are concerned, to help them through; we will wish the Jews a most hearty welcome home.

With the chiefs of your movement, especially with Dr. Weizmann, we have had, and continue to have, the closest relations. He has been a great helper of our cause, and I hope the Arabs may soon be in a position to make the Jews some return for their kindness. We are working together for a reformed and revived Near East, and our two movements complete one another. The Jewish movement is national and not imperialist. Our movement is national and not imperialist, and there is room in Syria for us both. Indeed I think that neither can be a real success without the other.

People less informed and less responsible than our leaders and yours, ignoring the need for cooperation of the Arabs and Zionists, have been trying to exploit the official difficulties that must necessarily arise in Palestine in the early stages of our movements. Some of them have, I am afraid, misrepresented your aims to the Arab peasantry, and our aims to the Jewish peasantry, with the result that interested parties have been able to make capital out of what they call our differences.

I wish to give you my firm conviction that these differences are not on questions of principle, but on matters of detail such as must inevitably occur in every contact of neighboring peoples, and as are easily adjusted by mutual good will. Indeed, nearly all of them will disappear with fuller knowledge.

I look forward, and my people with me look forward to a future in which we will help you and you will help us, so that the countries in which we are mutually interested may once again take their place in the community of civilized people of the world.

Believe me,
　　Yours sincerely,

FEISAL.

There are similar statements by Feisal and other Arabs.

Chairman BLOOM. Just insert them.

Dr. NEUMANN. Gladly. If I may revert for a moment to the question of a transfer of Arabs. I want to state that the first time this idea was ever mentioned by any responsible group was in the report of the royal commission headed by Lord Peel in connection with their proposal to partition Palestine and set up an Arab state and a Jewish state in that territory. They proposed an exchange of populations, the transfer of Arabs to the Arab state and of Jews from the Arab part of the country to the Jewish state. These proposals came as a surprise to Jews and Arabs alike. This was in 1937. Since then the idea of solving the Palestine problem by means of an exchange or transfer of population, first suggested by the royal commission, has been put forward on occasion by various persons, but never by the Zionist organization. Englishmen as well as Arabs have thought of resettling some of the poor peasants of Palestine in the wide open spaces of Iraq or at least of encouraging the more enterprising among them to migrate there and settle on irrigated land. May I insert certain documents in the record?

Chairman BLOOM. Without objection, it is so ordered. Mr. Jonson.

Mr. JONSON. No questions.

Chairman BLOOM. Mr. Vorys.

Mr. VORYS. You have given us your opinions, which I suppose are considered opinions on diplomatic and military phases. I wonder before this committee acts whether we should have the opinion of the responsible branches of our Government, particularly the military and diplomatic.

Dr. NEUMANN. I wonder whether it would be proper for me to advise the committee on its procedure. I suppose the committee has its own procedure and knows what it will do under given circumstances. I believe the legislative branch has on occasion adopted resolutions which seemed to carry international implications. To what extent they have taken into consideration the views of the executive branch I do not know. There may have been divergence of views, but I do not feel qualified to advise on this.

Mr. VORYS. That is all.

Chairman BLOOM. Judge Kee.

Mr. KEE. No questions.

Chairman BLOOM. Mr. Chiperfield.

Mr. CHIPERFIELD. No questions.

Chairman BLOOM. Mr. Jarman.

Mr. JARMAN. No questions.

Chairman BLOOM. Mr. Jonkman.

Mr. JONKMAN. No questions.

Chairman BLOOM. Mrs. Rogers.

Mrs. ROGERS. When the White Paper went into effect in 1939 were any representations made to the British Government by this Government?

Dr. NEUMANN. I was not in the United States at the time. So far as I know no effective action was taken by our Government, if any. Perhaps something was said about it privately, but so far as I know there is nothing on record by way of a protest.

Chairman BLOOM. You know this committee signed a petition at that time.

Dr. NEUMANN. Yes, sir.

Chairman BLOOM. Mrs. Bolton.

Mrs. BOLTON. No questions.

Chairman BLOOM. Mr. Wright.

Mr. WRIGHT. No questions.

Chairman BLOOM. Mr. Wadsworth.

Mr. WADSWORTH. When you say or use the phrase Jewish commonwealth, what do you envisage politically and economically?

Dr. NEUMANN. I am very glad to answer the question. I am on record regarding my views on the subject of the Jewish commonwealth in an address I delivered in Cleveland, Ohio, on November 27, 1943, before the national convention of Junior Hadassah—the young women's Zionist organization. I would like to read the following excerpts from that address:

By a Jewish commonwealth we certainly do not mean a state which is exclusively Jewish. We do not mean to drive the existing Arab population into the desert or cast it into the sea. On the contrary, those who choose to do so are to remain. Moreover, their civic and personal rights shall be inviolate. There shall be a full and complete equality before the law. Not only that, but the Arabs shall have every right and possibility to preserve and develop their cultural and religious heritage. Their language shall be recognized and their traditions respected. And in addition they shall share fully in the economic advantages and opportunities and the prosperity which will come with the modernization of the country and the development of its resources.

Indeed, this has already been the case in a substantial measure. If, then, we are asked what do we mean by the adjective "Jewish" as applied to the future commonwealth my answer is that it is a short and abbreviated way of saying that through the repatriation of large numbers of European and other Jews, the Jewish people will attain a numerical majority in Palestine and thereby permanently guarantee the open door for others who may follow; so that Palestine shall never cease to serve as a sanctuary and homeland for any and all Jews from whatever part of the world who may choose to go there in the future. It will also be a Jewish commonwealth in the vital sense that in that country, in that little corner of the world, the Jewish people, no longer living under minority conditions but as a majority, will be free to apply their talent, their industry, their genius and leave the intangible impress of their civilization upon their ancestral land as in the days of the kings and the prophets.

But the development of this Jewish commonwealth shall take place under democratic institutions and in a democratic spirit. The Jews will preponderate and lead in the development of the country without dominating or oppressing the minority. Jew and Arab devoted to their respective cultures and traditions shall cooperate as free and equal citizens and jointly contribute to the prosperity and welfare of a common single unitary state. The Arab citizens of the Jewish commonwealth will be as favorably situated as are the French-speaking citizens of the British Dominion of Canada. It will be a free and democratic Jewish state composed of Jews, Moslems, Christians and, if there are any, Buddhists, as well—compatriots, all. All shall be eligible to public office, even the highest.

Mr. WADSWORTH. No further questions.

Mr. CHIPERFIELD. May I ask a question?

Chairman BLOOM. Yes, sir.

Mr. CHIPERFIELD. I think this is a very timely statement. But how can you guarantee that will be accomplished and that will result?

Dr. NEUMANN. What particular point?

Mr. CHIPERFIELD. The whole conception.

Dr. Neumann. I am glad the question is put. I want to say first on bahalf of the Jews that there is probably no group of people on earth who have suffered more as a minority than the Jews. Is it not reasonable to suppose that when at last they are given national status as a majority in Palestine they will scrupulously avoid oppressing any minority, but will rather try to set an example? At least that is our ideal.

Moreover, I would like to point out that a preponderantly Jewish Palestine will still be surrounded by a large aggregation of Arabs in the neighboring Arab states. They will regard the Arabs of Palestine as the special object of their solicitude. All we do there will be done under their watchful eyes and the glare of the public opinion of the world. And, as has been said, there are Jewish minorities living under Arab rule, hostages in a sense. Is it conceivable that under all these circumstances the Jews would oppress the Arabs in Palestine?

On the other hand if you freeze the Jewish population of Palestine into permanent minority, there is no ground for optimism as to their ultimate fate and future. The present position of Jewish and other minorities in independent Arab states is none too happy or secure. There are some 40,000 Jews in Yemen—in southern Arabia—hardworking, pious, industrious people. They have lived there for centuries; but thier condition is lamentable and they are immigrating to Palestine in a steady stream.

Let me cite one or two striking illustrations of the problem of minorities in Moslem-Arab lands. There are such ethnic and religious minorities in Syria and Iraq. There is a large Christian community in the Lebanon. Back in 1800, while under Turkish rule, they were attacked by their immediate neighbors and massacred by the tens of thousands. The Christian powers intervened, special provisions were made whereby Lebanon achieved a measure of autonomy and France became its traditional protector.

Dr. Neumann. Recently, in 1932, Britain sought the consent of the League of Nations for terminating her mandate over Iraq and granting that country independence. The Mandates Commission of the League was apprehensive over the fate of the minorities in Iraq once the mandate was terminated. It questioned the representatives of the British Government closely on this subject and withdrew its objections only after the British assumed moral responsibility for the safety of the minorities. Iraq was accordingly emancipated from the mandate. Scarcely a year passed when the world was shocked and horrified by the massacre of the Assyrians, an ancient Christian group who had settled in a corner of Iraq—precisely what the Mandates Commission had feared. Through international action part of the Assyrians were then helped to resettle elsewhere.

All things considered, which is the more hazardous in the case of Palestine, to have an Arab minority in the midst of an enlightened Jewish majority or the Jews as a minority under Arab rule? In the light of my personal observation and experience I would say that if the latter is to happen, if a wave of militant Arab nationalism is to close in on the 600,000 Jews of Palestine, the time will come when congressional committees or other committees will be pondering a new problem: what to do about a new and unique kind of refugees— Jewish refugees driven from the Jewish National Home.

No such danger will exist in the case of an Arab minority in a democratic Jewish commonwealth. In many ways they will be among the most fortunately placed of all the children of Arabia. In any case it is to be hoped that as part of the post-war world there will be set up some international agency to concern itself with the position of ethnic and religious minorities everywhere. If that happens we would certainly agree that the Jewish commonwealth shall be subject to the same degree of scrutiny and supervision on the part of such an international agency or commission as will be applied to other countries. That would be my answer.

Chairman BLOOM. Mr. Fulbright.

Mr. ·FULBRIGHT. If you care to make any comment along the line of Mr. Vory's question, has any official action been taken with regard to the view of King Ibn Saud, of Saudi Arabia?

Dr. NEUMANN. I know very little about that. I suppose you are referring to what was stated in the article in Life magazine. The future of Palestine and the Jewish ‚National Home is a matter of interest to the whole civilized world; it cannot depend or be made to appear to depend upon the views of this or that Arab ruler. From the standpoint of international law, they have no more to say about the future of Palestine than we here about the future of Saudi Arabia, and as a practical matter, infinitely less. We don't even know how permanent is the present regime in the Arabia Peninsula. All in all it's only 20 years old. Before King Ibn Saud there was King Hussein and the Kingdom of the Hejaz. The two princes were rivals, each backed and financed by a different branch of the British Imperial administration. Such kingdoms come and go. Lawrence of Arabia referred to the present regime as a tyranny built on sand and cemented with blood, which will pass like so many others that preceded it. "Nothing static," he said, "will arise in the desert."

Chairman BLOOM. Any further questions, Mr. Fulbright?

Mr. FULBRIGHT. No, sir.

Chairman BLOOM. Mr. Gerlach?

Mr. GERLACH. No questions.

Chairman BLOOM. Mr. Schiffler?

Mr. SCHIFFLER. No questions.

Chairman BLOOM. The Chair would like to state we have a couple of witnesses here from out of town. If you will bear with us for a while we will hear them.

THE HUSSEIN-McMAHON UNDERSTANDING

(Supplementary documented note submitted by Dr. Emanuel Neumann)

The Arabs have contended that, in accordance with the Hussein-McMahon understanding, Palestine was included in the area in which the British promised to help them obtain independence. The British Government and all of the British officials connected with the negotiations have repeatedly and consistently held that it was their intention to exclude Palestine from any commitments made. Sir Henry McMahon has put himself on record on two occasions (March 12, 1922; July 23, 1937), in letters to *The Times* to the effect that he definitely intended to exclude Palestine from the arrangements made and had reason to believe that Hussein understood this at the time.

The British Government did not publish the complete text of the correspondence between McMahon and Hussein until recently. His Majesty's Government always maintained that the delay in publication had nothing to do with Palestine but was in the interests of other aspects of British policy. But the suppression of parts of the correspondence lent color to the Arab contentions. In 1939, however, in connection with the Round Table Conferences held in London before the issuance of the White Paper, a Committee was set up to examine the letters. The British were, at the time, anxious to find as much basis for Arab claims as they could. Nevertheless, the committee decided that "on a proper construction of the correspondence, Palestine was in fact excluded." [1] This view was confirmed by the Lord Chancellor who held that "the correspondence as a whole, and particularly the reservation in respect of French interests in Sir Henry McMahon's letter of the 24th of October, 1915, not only did exclude Palestine but should have been understood to do so * * *." [2]

The British contention is that Palestine was excluded along with the northern parts of the Syrian coast. Palestine was not mentioned by name, but the explanation of this is very simple since Palestine did not exist at the time as a political entity. The district of Beirut, which is specifically excluded, extends through what is now the larger part of Northern Palestine. The Southern part known in those days as the Sanjak of Jerusalem was autonomous in Turkish times. The reasons given by McMahon for excluding the Northern part of the coast apply with greater force to the Southern part of Syria contained in the Sanjak of Jerusalem. Moreover, Feisal, the emissary of Hussein at the Peace Conference in 1919, definitely stated that he agreed to the exclusion of Palestine from the areas for which the Arab requested independence.

The clear and definite denials made by the British officials and statesmen of high standing receive additional support—if this were needed—from the fact that Hussein did not at the time claim that Palestine was included in the British promise, although later he made vague and equivocal statements which led others to believe that he did understand Palestine to be included in the British statement. The credibility of Hussein may be judged from the following thumbnail sketch made of him by John Van Ess in his recent book, *Meet the Arab:*

"For a few years Hussein, in his new position as sherif and controller of the pilgrimage, made hay vigorously—for himself, for he had his hand in pretty well everything that was lucrative. He sold the scant water supply to pilgrims at exorbitant prices, he controlled the sheep market where sacrifices were bought, he cornered the food supply and sold it again on his own terms, he forebore to punish looters, and gossip had it that he even shared the loot; in short he had his hand on everything save the air the people breathed and that, to be sure, was foul enough through lack of the most primitive sanitation."

STATEMENTS BY BRITISH REPRESENTATIVES ON THE NEGOTIATIONS

1. Sir Henry McMahon's Letter to the Times, July 23, 1937:

"Many references have been made in the Palestine Royal Commission Report and in the course of the recent debates in both Houses of Parliament to the 'McMahon Pledge,' especially to that portion of the pledge which concerns Palestine and of which one interpretation has been claimed by the Jews and another by the Arabs.

"It has been suggested to me that continued silence on the part of the giver of the pledge may itself be misunderstood.

"I feel, therefore, called upon to make some statement on the subject, but I will confine myself in doing so to the point now at issue—i. e., whether that portion of Syria now known as Palestine was or was not intended to be included in the territories in which the independence of the Arabs was guaranteed in my pledge.

"I feel it my duty to state, and I do so definitely and emphatically, that it was not intended by me in giving this pledge to King Hussein to include Palestine in the area in which Arab independence was promised.

"I also had every reason to believe at the time that the fact that Palestine was not included in my pledge was well understood by King Hussein."

2. Colonel C. E. Vickery, who was a master of Arabic, was sent from Cairo in 1920 on an official mission to inspect the original Arabic text as actually received by the Sherif. In a letter published in the Times on the 21st of February, 1939, referring to this visit, he wrote:

"I read the letter through very slowly. * * * It was quite evident that Palestine was not included in the proposals to the King. * * * I can say most definitely that the whole of the King's demands were centered around Syria, and only around Syria. Time after time he referred to that vineyard, to the exclusion of any other claim or interest. He stated most emphatically that he did not concern himself at all with Palestine and had no desire to have suzerainty over it for himself or his successors."

1 Royal Institute of International Affairs, Great Britain and Palestine 1915–39, p. 6.
2 Great Britain, Statement of the Lord Chancellor, Cmd 5974, 1939, p. 46.

3. Sir Gilbert Clayton was closely associated with Sir Henry McMahon in the negotiations with the Sherif. On the 12th April, 1923, when he was Chief Secretary to the Government of Palestine, he gave Lord Samuel, then High Commissioner, the following note in reply to an enquiry as to the scope of the McMahon pledge:

"I was in daily touch with Sir Henry McMahon throughout the negotiations with King Hussein, and made the preliminary drafts of all the letters. I can bear out the statement that it was never the intention that Palestine should be included in the general pledge given to the Sherif. The introductory words of Sir Henry's letter were thought at the time, perhaps erroneously, clearly to cover the point. It was, I think, obvious that the peculiar interests involved in Palestine precluded any definite pledges in regard to its future at so early a stage."

OFFICIAL STATEMENTS BY THE BRITISH GOVERNMENT

1. Statement of British Policy in Palestine, June 3rd, 1922 (Churchill White Paper), Cmd. 1700, p. 20:

"That letter [October 24th, 1915, from McMahon to Hussein] is quoted as conveying the promise to the Sherif of Mecca to recognize and support the independence of the Arabs within the territories proposed by him. But this promise was given subject to a reservation made in the same letter, which excluded from its scope, among other territories, the portions of Syria lying to the west of the district of Damascus. This reservation has always been regarded by His Majesty's Government as covering the vilayet of Beirut and the independent Sanjak of Jerusalem. The whole of Palestine west of the Jordan was thus excluded from Sir H. McMahon's pledge."

2. The Secretary of State for the Colonies (The Duke of Devonshire), House of Lords Official Report, March 1st, 1923, col. 233:

"Whether they [the promises] were expressed in the best terms or not, it is perhaps not for me to say, but undoubtedly there never was any intention, when the pledge was given, to recognize the independence of the Arabs so as to include Palestine. I think that is perfectly clear, and in my own mind I am certain of it. Although the terms may not have been expressed language, I think it was the intention of both Sir H. McMahon and the Government at the time, when those pledges were given, that Palestine should not be included."

3. Secretary of State for the Colonies (Mr. Ormsby-Gore), House of Commons, July 21st, 1937, House of Commons Official Report, July 21, 1937, col. 2249/50:

"I served in 1916 in the Arab Bureau in Cairo on Sir Henry McMahon's staff, and I wish myself to testify to the fact that it never was in the mind of anyone on that staff that Palestine west of the Jordan was in the area within which the British Government then undertook to further the cause of Arab independence. * * * I want it clearly and finally understood that His Majesty's Government, neither then nor now, can or will admit that Palestine west of the Jordan was included in the pledge given to the Sherif, and that they have always in mind that special considerations must obtain in regard to the future government of the Holy Land. The unique character of Palestine was recognized by the Arab Delegates to the Peace Conference. It is recognized all over the world."

THE WAR SERVICES OF THE ARABS

(Supplementary documented note submitted by Dr. Emanuel Neumann)

The Arab leaders have placed a great deal of emphasis on war services rendered to the Allies in the defeat of the Turks during the First World War. Arab tribesmen from the Hejaz and some from Transjordan were admittedly of help to the British although authorities differ as to how substantial this help was. But the Syrian and Palestinian Arabs who have been talking so much about their great contribution to the Allied war effort had nothing whatsoever to do with the matter. For the most part they remained passive, or worse, at times treacherously aided the Turks. While the Zionists do not stress the Jewish war services, nevertheless the fact is that they responded enthusiastically to whatever opportunities were offered them to fight with the British and to serve in special Jewish battalions. In Palestine alone about 1,200 Jews were recruited against 150 Arabs, although the Arab population was ten times that of the Jews.

In accordance with the understanding between McMahon and Hussein the Syrian nationalists were to have raised the standard of revolt along with Hussein, but several of their leaders were executed by the Turks after the discovery of incriminating documents, the nationalists lost courage, and the uprising of the Syrians never came off. Hussein, the Sherif of Mecca, waited to make sure that he was "backing the right horse." [1] In fact he did not move until the Turks, accompanied by a German military mission ostensibly on its way to Southern Arabia, approached his territory. Besides the promises of help in their struggle for independence from the Turks, the British subsidized Hussein very heavily. Sir Ronald Storrs, who acted the principal role in making the early arrangements with Hussein, estimates that the Arab revolt cost the British taxpayers the sum of £11,000,000, of which almost one million went to Hussein in the way of a monthly subsidy.[2]

The tribes from the Hejaz and Transjordan who took part in the revolt consisted of undisciplined tribesmen. The campaign was organized by British officers aided by Feisal and a few Syrian officers from the Turkish Army who had deserted. The general view of British military officers is that the contribution of the Arab forces was mainly confined to wrecking and looting operations in which there was little risk of loss of life. Although some of the writings of T. E. Lawrence, who played the chief part in organizing the Arab revolt, convey a more romantic impression, careful reading of *The Seven Pillars of Wisdom*, which is the full account, confirms this view.

SERVICES OF THE SYRIAN AND PALESTINE ARABS

1. Sir Philip Graves, *The Land of Three Faiths*, London, 1923, pp. 112–113:
"Most annoying, to anyone who has served with the British and the Sherifian Arab forces in the Palestine campaign and knows something of the history of that campaign, are the pretensions of the Arabs of Palestine to have rendered important military services to the Allies in the Great War.

"Many of the Transjordanians and the Hejazis, whom, for all their talk of Arab union, the Palestine Arabs dislike and fear as rude and hardy men, played their part right well under the inspiring leadership of Emir Feisal and Colonel T. E. Lawrence; but the Palestinians confined themselves to deserting in large numbers to the British, who fed and clothed and paid for the maintenance of many thousand such prisoners of war, few indeed of whom could be induced to obtain their liberty by serving in the Sherifian Army."

2. A. Biscoe Moore, *The Mounted Riflemen in Syria and Palestine*, pp. 64, 107, 156, 169:
"They (the Arabs) were on many occasions suspected of carrying information to the Turks of British movements. They will do anything for material gain, a little loot or 'backsheesh,' and on more than one occasion were responsible for the deaths of New Zealanders.

"Treacherous as the Bedouins are known to be, it was very necessary to keep well clear of their camps, as none of them would be above trying for a little 'backsheesh' from the Turks if they thought it could be obtained by giving warning of our approach.

"Our men had suffered from the treachery of the natives throughout the campaign * * * and the feeling against them was to come to a head with tragic results."

3. C. S. Jarvis (late Governor of Sinai) *Three Deserts*, p. 302:
"The Syrians as a people did nothing whatsoever towards assisting the Arabs cause except for the isolated action of some Bedouins in the very last stages of the campaign and the services of a few Syrian officers who deserted from the Turkish Army. The great mass of the Syrians did absolutely nothing beyond hold secret meetings and talk. The inhabitants of Palestine did rather less than this."

---

[1] John de Vere Loder, *The Truth About Mesopotamia, Palestine, and Syria*, London, 1923, p. 18.
[2] Ronald Storrs, *Orientations*, note, p. 177.

FIGHTING QUALITIES OF THE TRIBESMEN FROM THE HEJAZ AND TRANSJORDAN

1. T. E. Lawrence, *Seven Pillars of Wisdom*, pp. 103–104:
"Blood feuds were nominally healed. * * * All the same, the members of one tribe were shy of those of another, and within the tribe no man would quite trust his neighbour. Each might be, usually was, whole-hearted against the Turk, but perhaps not quite to the point of failing to work off a family grudge upon a family enemy in the field. Consequently they could not attack. One company of Turks firmly entrenched in open country could have defied the entire army of them; and a pitched defeat, with its casualties, would have ended the war by sheer horror.

"I concluded that the tribesmen were good for defence only. Their acquisitive recklessness made them keen on booty, and whetted them to tear up railway, plunder caravans, and steal camels; but they were too free-minded to endure command, or to fight in team."

2. Major C. S. Jarvis, *Three Deserts*, p. 299–303, who spent eighteen years living and working with the Arabs describes the situation in even more realistic terms:
"The truth of the matter is that the national desire for independence was confined solely to the few educated Arabs in the cause, such as Feisal, and that among the fighting men and the sheikhs of the tribes who led them this feeling was conspicuous by its absence. * * * The only method of keeping these patriots in the field was by payment in gold, and when the Arab sees gold his natural avarice causes him to lose all control of himself, so that squabbles as to the respective donations to various tribes were of daily occurrence.

"In action they were entirely without discipline, and the first hint of loot meant that the greater part of the attacking force broke off the engagement before it was completed, to rifle the enemy's captured baggage. After a successful raid when the Arabs were loaded with looted corn and rations nothing would keep them in the field, and they trickled back to their tents and womenfolk so that a striking force on which their commander was relying for another attack on the railway would scatter into the desert in a night."

3. Lieutenant Colonel Vickery, "Journal of the Central Asian Society," 1923, pt. 1, p. 57.
"One Arab [says Vickery] had attracted my notice—one Saleh, and he was asked to act as chief of staff. He replied that he could only answer for his own men—thirty in all. On trying to form up the remainder, three hundred at once sat down on the beach, saying they were tired, and they had come ashore for a little rest and a sleep. They started to light fires, and were obviously not going to fight. I turned to the remainder, two hundred of whom at once announced that they were not fighting men; they had come to loot. Off they went along the seashore, saying that they would wait outside the town till I had captured it, an operation they hoped that I should execute with great promptitude, as they were in a hurry. The remainder condescended to follow us at the moment when the first gun of the S. N. O.'s flagship opened on the town. A seaplane which went up was received with a brisk fire by the Turkish garrison, and the observer was unfortunately killed. Shortly afterwards we ran into a Turkish patrol. We were lucky enough to shoot first, and dropped three of them, but it was enough for some 250 of the Arabs."

SERVICES OF PALESTINIAN JEWS

1. Handbook of the Foreign Office, No. 60, 1920, pp. 62–63:
"The most important event which has taken place so far as the Jewish community in Palestine is concerned, since our occupation, has been the recruiting of Palestine Jews, whatever their national status, into the British Army; and practically the whole available Jewish youth of the colonies, and many of the townsmen of military age came forward for voluntary enlistment in the Jewish battalions, took the oath to King George V, and were clad in British uniforms. The initiative in favour of the recruiting movement took place as the result of the demand of the Jewish population itself, rather than from any desire or even encouragement from the British authorities. The campaign in Palestine is regarded by the Jews as a campaign for the liberation of the country from the thraldom of Turkish misrule, and the return of even Turkish suzerainty would be regarded by them as a betrayal."

2. Mr. James de Rothschild, House of Commons, November 17, 1930: "During the War, in 1918, I was detailed by Lord Allenby to recruit the Jewish Battalion in Palestine. There were then, in that part of Palestine which had been conquered by the British Army, about 18,000 to 20,000 Jews. They were mostly in Jerusalem, and a few of them in the surrounding colonies, but the greater number had already been deported to the north,ᵗto Syria, Damascus, and Konia, by the Turks. In just over a fortnight, out of this population of 20,000, a great number over age, and a great number tired out by the fatigues and the hardships of a long famine during the War, a thousand men came forward, solid good soldiers, who were enrolled in the 40th Battalion of the Royal Fusiliers."

ARAB SELF-GOVERNMENT AND TREATMENT OF MINORITIES

(Supplementary documented note submitted by Dr. Emanuel Neumann)

Whatever may have been the attitude of Moslem Powers toward minorities under the Ottoman Regime—a complex question which requires analysis—Arab nationalism since the last war has assumed an extreme character. In countries where the Moslems are the majority, there is definite evidence of intolerance toward minorities, both in case of religious and national minorities. Arab nationalism became increasingly truculent after the rise of the Nazis to power in Europe. The Royal Institute of International Affairs states in its Survey for 1936: "In the Arab world, a triplex blend of fascism—anti-French, anti-British and anti-Jewish—was running like wildfire across North Africa, South West Asia, from Morocco and Algeria and Tunisia through Egypt and Palestine and Syria to Iraq." [1]

Iraq which was the first of the mandated Arab countries to receive independence under a treaty with Britain (1932) has a black record as far as the treatment of minorities is concerned. The Permanent Mandates Commission expressed serious doubts as to whether Iraq had advanced far enough for self-government, and acquiesced in the granting of independence to Iraq only because Great Britain urged this and took the moral responsibility. As a result of the pressure of the League of Nations, the declaration made by the Kingdom of Iraq on the occasion of the termination of the mandatory regime included special articles designed to safeguard the equality and rights of all religious groups and of the minority nationalities. But these provisions were not honored by the Iraqi Government.

Despite the fact that Christians and Jews had long occupied an important place in the business life and in the government service at Bagdad under the Ottoman Regime, as early as 1921 when the Iraqi Kingdom was established, opposition developed against the employment of any but Iraqis professing Islam in the Government, and this tendency grew stronger as time went on. In 1930, even before the admission of Iraq to the League of Nations, the Shiite (Moslem) community of Bagdad by threatening a disturbance of the public peace prevailed over King Feisal to issue an order evicting the Bahi Church from houses which they had occupied and used for religious purposes for a number of generations. Despite efforts of the British Government and the intercession of the Permanent Mandates Commission the property was never restored to the Bahais. A more serious problem presented itself in the case of the Kurds to whom autonomous minority rights had been granted by the Permanent Mandates Commission. The Iraqi Government did nothing to implement the minority provisions until the Kurds grew restive, rebelled and defeated the Iraqi army in an engagement. A column of the Iraqi army was saved from annihilation only when the British airplanes bombed the Kurdish tribesmen. After this revolt the British forced the Iraqi Government to implement the measures granting autonomy.

The worst case was the tragedy of the Assyrian Christian minority, the remnants of an old community of Nestorian Christians. The Royal Institute of International Affairs makes the following comment: "The newly fledged Iraqi-Arab nation applied * * * the Western principles of *Gleichschaltung* by Middle Eastern methods of barbarism." [2] An exchange of shots had taken place

---

ʼ 1936 Survey of International Affairs, p. 24.
Royal Institute of International Affairs, 1934 Survey, p. 97.

between Assyrians and the Iraqi army: the latter took matters into their own hands and carried out a methodical massacre of all men and boys whom they could find in nearby Assyrian villages. The Royal Institute of International Affairs says: "The blackness of this crime was deepened by the fact that the Assyrian population of the district had taken refuge at Simel from the villages round about in order to be under the protection of the local Iraqi police post."

According to the testimony of Bayard Dodge, President of the University of Beirut, later a member of the Assyrian Resettlement Board, no less than 600 persons were brutally slain.[3] In a report subsequently submitted to the League of Nations[4] by Mar Shimun, the patriarch of the Assyrian Christian community, it was stated that 62 villages, out of a total of 95, had been looted.

At Geneva, the Iraqi Delegation condemned the massacre as the irresponsible act of the military who had gotten out of hand. At home, the officers concerned were praised and promoted: there was a feeling of satisfaction that "the Assyrians were 'settled.' "[5] General Sidqi Baqir, who led the Iraqi forces in the massacre of the Assyrians, won great popularity. In 1936, he carried out a *coup d'etat* which resulted in a military dictatorship. King Feisal, who had attempted to restrain the extreme nationalists, was very much distressed by the Assyrian massacres, and it is thought that he intended to abdicate.[6] He was ill and soon died in Switzerland.

Due to the work of American educators in Syria, many leading Christian Arabs have been imbued with the idea that their future depends on the development of Arab nationalism. As a result of a more modern type of education received in missionary schools, Arab Christians predominate in Government offices in Syria and Palestine, and many of them, no doubt, believe that the best course for them is to work along with the Moslem majority. Nevertheless, there are indications that the Christian Arabs are fearful that political power in the hands of the Moslem majority may lead to anti-Christian terrorism. Professor W. F. Albright (Head of the Oriental Seminary at Johns Hopkins University), who has lived in Palestine for many years and who has had intimate contact with many Christian Arabs, writes: "The Christians of Syria have no more confidence in their eventual future as a minority in a Moslem State than the Nestorians of Iraq or the Copts of Egypt, both of whom are hated and despised (quite unjustly) by the Moslems."[7]

ILLUSTRATIONS

1. *The Problem of Minorities.*—Comment of the Royal Institute of International Affairs (1934 Survey, p. 114) on the hesitation of the Permanent Mandates Commission in granting self-government to Iraq.

"The defence of a minority's rights against an aggressive majority's Nationalism, and not the defence of a subject nationality against an aggressive foreign Imperialism, was thus the cause which the Mandates Commission found itself called upon to champion; and this was a sign of the times in an age when, throughout a Westernized world, the totalitarian national state was taking the place of the multinational empire as the standard form of parochial political organ zation. The Assyrians in Iraq were the victims of the same turn of the political wheel as the Germans in Poland or the Jews in Germany; and from the humanitarian standpoint the change was not for the better; for the subject nationalities of the old regime had not been faced with that prospect of the total suppression of their national individuality which was the prospective doom, under the new regime, of the alien minorities. This particular change for the worse was world-wide; but it was aggravated, in non-Western countries like Iraq, by the fact that here Nationalism itself was not a native disease but an exotic infection whose ravages were the greater inasmuch as the patients had not been inoculated against the germ."

2. *The Treatment of the Bahai Community.*—Comment of the Royal Institute of International Affairs (1934 Survey, p. 122):

[3] Bayard Dodge, "The Resettlement of the Assyrians on the Khabbur", Journal of the Central Asian Scy, 1940, p. 306.
[4] League of Nations Document, C. 625, 1933, I.
[5] Royal Institute of International Affairs, 1934 Survey, p. 165.
[6] Margret Boveri, Minaret and Pipeline, Oxford University Press, 1939, p.|365.
[7] W. F. Albright, "Japhet in the Tents of Shem" in Asia, December 1942.

"This affair was particularly deplorable in as much as the Bahais were a small and weak community which could not under any circumstances have menaced the security of the Iraqi state, even if its members had not been bound by their religious tenets to be good citizens. If the Bahais were the victims of so flagrant an injustice before Iraq was emancipated from British mandatory control, it seemed unlikely that the Chaldaeans, Armenians, Jews, and other weak minorities could depend upon either the moral courage or even the good will of a completely sovereign and independent Iraqui Government in the event of their becoming targets for the animus of one or another of the dominant communities in the country. In the case of the Bahais, the pressure of the Shiite Arab community in Iraq had prevailed upon the highest executive and judicial authorities in the kingdom to fly in the face of the British Government and of the League of Nations in persisting in a course of action which they must have known to be morally indefensible from first to last."

3. *Christian-Arab Fear of Moslems.*—W. F. Albright (Johns Hopkins University), "Japheth in the Tents of Shem," Asia and the Americas, December 1942: "I have had many experiences illustrating this state of tension which always exists between Christian and Moslem Arabs. A number of years ago I was a frequent visitor at the home of a certain Christian Arab editor (since deceased). At the time of an anti-Jewish outbreak he called his little boy of five into the room and told him what he must do to a Jewish boy if he should get a chance. He even put cruel words into the little chap's mouth: 'I will take a knife and stab him; I will take a pistol and shoot him!' Not long afterwards there was a rumor that an Arab state was about to be set up by the British. Calling on the same editor, I found him pale as death. He said to me, 'If the Moslems get control one of their first acts will be to massacre the Christians' * * * (p. 694).

"* * * There are many young idealists among both Christians and Moslems, particularly among graduates of the American University of Beirut, who are firmly convinced that the days when Moslem hated Christian and Christian plotted against Moslem with representatives of European powers, are over for good. Only one who has come into contact mainly with educated people in the cities can take so naive a view; one whose knowledge of the Arabs includes the peasants of southern Palestine and eastern Syria, or the Bedouins of Trans-jordan and the Syrian Desert, sees realities. * * * Those who have seen the 'teetotal' peasants become intoxicated with blood lust at Nebi Musa and on other occasions, know how little is required to start an orgy of brutal murder almost anywhere in Syria or Palestine" (p. 694).

CONDITIONS IN THE NEAR EAST AND THE PROBLEM OF SELF-GOVERNMENT

(Supplementary documented note submitted by Dr. Emanuel Neumann)

The Arab peoples are by all accounts potentially as capable and as intelligent as any Western nation; but at the present time they are living in a transitional period. Modern democratic ideas and technical innovations introduced from the West have thus far had only a superficial effect on the life of the Near East. American students and writers agree that before Western ideas can take any root there must be more popular education, more public health, and the reduction of the widespread poverty of the masses. The Near East countries are characterized by the existence of a very small wealthy upper class of land owners and a very large class of illiterate peasants and tenant farmers living in an impoverished condition under a terrible burden of debt to the upper class. There is only a small middle class and this class is largely associated with the upper class. It is the conclusion of Western observers that unless the basic economic and social conditions are improved and a substantial middle class created, the slogans of self-government may be exploited by reactionary forces aiming for dictatorship.

ILLUSTRATIONS

1. John Van Ess, *Meet the Arab*, John Day 1943. John Van Ess, an American missionary, has lived for forty years among the Arabs in Iraq, has a high opinion of their intelligence and abilities, and is sympathetic to their aspirations. Nevertheless, he has the following to say about the present situation in Iraq:

"A third weakness was the introduction of the electoral system in a country where even now less than twenty percent of the men and four percent of the women are literate. In a municipal election in Basrah a few years ago, each candidate received more votes than the total number of votes registered" (p. 175).

"A fourth, and to my mind most fatal defect, was the setting up of a vast machinery of government, court, parliament, army, and air force and an educational system which trained only for government jobs, all that before the country had become at all economically independent" (p. 175).

"Education in all the Arab states has been superficial, laying entire stress on learning facts, colored to be sure by passing ideologies, but not at all inculcating the dignity of manual labor. * * * The boy has, therefore, found his home atmosphere uncongenial and has sought expansion in the cafes and clubs where he learned and practiced the patter of chauvinism. Indeed, such training seemed to be the surest guarantee of a government job, while, after all, all other doors, chiefly economic, were closed to him anyway" (p. 208).

"* * * You see, in Iraq we had a technique all our own. When a cabinet had become unpopular either on account of what it had or had not done, or generally because it had had its feet in the trough too long, we didn't bother with elections. We short circuited the process and shot up the opposition. Those who didn't get shot hopped a plane for Egypt or India. It saved a lot of time and got results of a kind" (pp. 176, 177).

"Rashid Ali, together with a group of four cronies called the Golden Square, had seized power. By the time the British General Staff had had their bath and tea, so to speak, they began to realize that the Iraqis weren't going to play cricket. Had it not been for the fact that Hitler was slowed up six weeks in Greece and Crete, the British would have been caught flat-footed both in Iraq and Iran. The British, after a month' of hard fighting and severe losses, occupied Baghdad. * * * But the near disaster to the British forces in the rebellion of 1941 was the direct result of trying to play cricket with a crowd who were heavily bribed by the Axis and who cared not a whit for the good of their own country" (pp. 176, 177).

2. Philip Willard Ireland, *Iraq, A Study in Political Development*, Macmillan 1938. Ireland, of the Department of Government of Harvard University, is a noted authority on the Near East and has made a particularly thorough study of the Government of Iraq. Although well disposed toward Arab self-government, but sees its dark aspects and dangers. The following paragraphs from his concluding chapter gives an idea of the situation.

"It is a fact that although Iraqis universally proclaimed their familiarity with democratic institutions from the time of the Ottoman regime, and boldly asserted their competence to run them, conditions in Iraq were far from ideal for the introduction of such institutions. No adequate class existed from which responsible and public-spirited officials could be drawn, nor was there a substantial body of literate and informed citizens with which to work the democratic institutions as provided in the Constitution" (p. 424).

"An even greater obstacle was the lack of social consciousness embracing the State. Not yet had a sense of loyalty and duty to the nation arisen to surmount the differences between tribesmen and townsmen, between Sunni and Shiite, and between Muslims and minority communities or to replace personal opportunism. Patriotism still denoted independence without obligations to the State" (p. 425).

"Examination of the statute books of Iraq, not only from 1925 to 1932 but also to the present date, seems to suggest that the deputies have not failed to make free use of their position. Many of the financial measures granting remission of arrears in revenue and of other financial legislation, while passed by the Chamber for the benefit of Iraq as a whole, particularly after the agricultural crisis of 1931, have especially favoured the land-owning class which has been predominant in Parliament. Other evidence seems to point to the exercise by the deputies of their influence outside of Parliament, either to secure preferential treatment from revenue officials or to obtain appointments for their proteges" (pp. 432, 433).

3. Wendell L. Willkie, *One World*, Simon and Schuster 1943. The above quotations deal with Iraq which was the first of the mandated territories to receive independence. Mr. Willkie found similar social and economic problems throughout the Near East as a whole. A few characteristic passages follow.

"Modern air lines, oil pipe lines, macadam streets, or even plumbing constitute a thin veneer on the surface [of a life which in essence is as simple and as hard as it was before there was any West * * *" (p. 14).

"But the major reason (for the general social backwardness) seemed to be the complete absence of a middle class. Throughout the Middle East there is a small percentage of wealthy landowners whose property is largely hereditary. I met a number of them and found them largely disinterested in any political movement, except as it affected the perpetuation of their own status. The great mass of the people, outside of the roaming tribes, are impoverished, own no property, are hideously ruled by the practices of ancient priestcraft, and are living in conditions of squalor * * *" (p. 15).

"Yet, strange as it may seem, one senses a ferment in these lands, a groping of the long-inert masses, a growing disregard of restrictive religious rites and practices. * * * Likewise I found in this part of the world, as * * * everywhere, a growing spirit of fervid nationalism, a disturbing thing to one who believes that the only hope of the world lies in the opposite trend. I found much the same discontent, hunger, and impatience in Iraq, in the Lebanon, in Iran, and much the same time lag in official recognition of the problem, though the Prime and Foreign Ministers of those countries are knowing and able men." (p. 15).

_____

STATEMENT OF JUDGE LOUIS E. LEVINTHAL

(Submitted by Dr. Emanuel Neumann)

Judge Louis E. Levinthal, of Philadelphia, Pa., President of the Zionist Organization of America from 1941 to 1943, attended the hearing before the House Committee on Foreign Affairs held Tuesday, February 15, 1944, prepared to testify in support of House Resolutions 418 and 419. His judicial duties necessitated his return to Philadelphia, and he respectfully requests of the Chairman and the members of the Committee the privilege to have this statement read into the record of the proceedings:

I respectfully urge the adoption of House Resolutions 418 and 419—

(1) because they are in accord with the well-established policy of the United States (as expressed in the Joint Resolution of Congress of 1922 and in the Convention between the United States and Great Britain of 1924);

(2) because of the remarkable record of Jewish colonization and achievements in Palestine since the Mandate was promulgated;

(3) because the rights of the non-Jewish inhabitants of Palestine have not been, and will not be, prejudiced by Jewish immigration and colonization and by the reconstitution of a Jewish commonwealth, which is to be free and democratic;

(4) because the reaffirmation and clarification of the rights of the Jewish people with respect to Palestine will tend to improve Arab-Jewish relations and give hope and courage to the tragically afflicted Jewish victims of Hitler who look to Palestine as their sole refuge.

There seems to be no serious objection to the provisions of the Resolutions relating to the free entry of Jews into Palestine and for full opportunity for colonization, but some persons oppose the reference to the Jewish people reconstituting Palestine as a free and democratic Jewish commonwealth. It is respectfully submitted that the last mentioned provision is an essential and indispensable part of the Resolutions.

It is obvious that Palestine will in the future either have a majority of Jews and thus constitute a Jewish commonwealth, or it will have a majority of Arabs and thus constitute an Arab state. The Arabs already have numerous lands in which they constitute the majority, indeed almost the totality, of the population. The Jews, on the other hand constitute a minority of the population everywhere. Is it not fair and just that the Jews be given the opportunity to become the majority of one small country on the face of the earth—in that land made immortal by their ancestors—in the Land of Israel?

It was contended by one of the witnesses, who testified in opposition to the Resolution, that there is serious danger of violence on the part of the Arabs in the Near East if these Resolutions be approved by Congress. It is respectfully submitted that the Arab riots in the past have not only been instigated by the Axis powers but have also been the result of successive acts of capitulation by the Mandatory Power which constantly whittled down the provisions of the Mandate. It is my profound conviction that when an end will be put to the policy of appeasement, and when the nations of the world will make explicit what was implicit in the Balfour Declaration and in the Mandate, there will be a greater liklihood of a genuine Arab-Jewish rapprochement. It has been my experience as a practicing attorney for more than twenty years, and as a Judge for more than seven years, that animosity and acrimony persist between litigants who quibble about the interpretation of the provisions of a contract to which they are parties, just so long as the litigation, and the uncertainty as to the ultimate construction of the agreement, continues. Once a final decision by a competent tribunal is handed down interpreting the contract, invariably the parties accept the situation, and the bitterness and hostility come to an end. So, also, when the Arabs shall learn that

America intends to see that the Balfour Declaration and the Mandate shall be fulfilled in accordance with their real intent, and when that intent is unmistakably expressed, I firmly believe that peace and harmony between the two Semitic peoples—the Arabs and the Jews—will happily be restored.

It was stated by one of the witnesses that the Arabs have been injured by the Jewish development of Palestine. May I be permitted to call your attention to a significant statement of the Secretary of State for the Colonies, Mr. Malcolm Mac Donald, in the House of Commons on November 24, 1938, which reads as follows:

"The Arabs cannot say that the Jews are driving them out of their country. If not a single Jew had come to Palestine after 1918, I believe that the Arab population of Palestine today would still have been round about the 600,000 figure (instead of over 1,000,000, as at present), at which it had been stable under the Turkish rule. It is because the Jews who have come to Palestine bring modern health services and other advantages that Arab men and women who would have been dead are alive today, that Arab children who would never have drawn breath have been born and grow strong" (Great Britain: Parliamentary Debates, House of Commons, Nov. 24, 1938; Vol. 341, No. 13; p. 1994).

Finally, may I be permitted to conclude by quoting from a memorable address by Dr. Chaim Weizmann delivered in Philadelphia on May 2, 1943.

"I believe that if I were to utter that which stirs in the depths of the conscience of the United Nations, I would speak thus to the Arabs:

"'You are a people recognized by the world. Palestine is one—and it is among the smallest—of the many countries which you inhabit, but none of which you fill to the extent of one half, one quarter, or one tenth of their capacity. You have territories which could harbor seventy or eighty millions, occupied by a handful of people.'

"And I would say: 'If the chance is given you to develop in freedom and peace, if you call your lands your own, remember that this is due to the efforts of the democracies in the last war, and of the United Nations in this war. What you will get out of this war you will owe to the sacrifices of the peoples of America, of England, who have poured out their blood on a score of battlefields for the freedom of the world.'

"And I would say: 'You owe it also in a measure to the Jewish people, to the very soldiers which Jewish Palestine has furnished—the flower of its manhood—without compulsion, to swell the armies of the United Nations in the Near East. We think it right and proper that this Jewish people should be restored at last to that small niche which it has cherished through thousands of years of homelessness, that niche in which were born the principles of the civilization for which we fight. We think that in such a restoration you Arabs will not come to any harm. Your legitimate rights, your religion, your language, your culture, your property will suffer no diminution; not a hair of your heads shall be touched. We think that if you and Jews will cooperate, you will build up, for your mutual benefit, and for the benefit of the world, those tremendous areas which today are a desert and a reproach to humanity. Such an upbuilding, indeed, is a life and death necessity for you. An empty country, a political and geographical vacuum invites aggression, it invites predatory nations. You and the Jews can make this part of the world safe for yourselves and for us; for all three of us have a strake in this part of the world.'"

The adoption of the Resolutions how being considered by the House Committee on Foreign Affairs will, in my opinion, be heartily approved by the conscience of America and the conscience of all civilized mankind.

STATEMENT OF RABBI MORRIS LAZARON, BALTIMORE, MD.

Dr. LAZARON. Mr. Chairman and ladies and gentlemen, I appreciate the privilege of appearing here, and I need hardly state that I am grateful too for the sympathy and desire to help my brother Jews that are implied in this proposed resolution.

As a teacher in Israel and as a Jew it is not a very pleasant thing to realize that the greatest power on earth has organized its resources to destroy your coreligionists.

I should like to point out, however, that while it is true that there is more hate against the Jew than ever before, it is also true today, that we have more understanding friends.

It is not an easy thing for a Jewish teacher to oppose a resolution of this sort. I do so with hesitation because of those deep instinctive feelings which go out to my brethern. I believe that the resolution should not be passed in its present form.

I yield to no one in appreciation of the great work that has been done in Palestine, in pride in it and the sacrificial devotion that has been expended there. I am cognizant of the opportunity that Palestine offers as a haven to our brethern, the economy that has been built by blood and sweat and tears. I am familiar with the great contribution that Palestine has made to the effort of the war. I believe that the Jewish position in Palestine should be maintained and should be extended.

I believe that there is complete unanimity among Jews that some move must be made that will mitigate the harsh terms of the White Paper. To keep out only Jews is serious and unwarranted discrimination. I believe that the door of Palestine should be kept, open as wide as possible to receive as many stricken and driven as in the present conditions can be admitted.

Let me say to you, ladies and gentlemen, that neither side in this disputed question has a monopoly of feeling or of Jewish loyalty.

Your desire to help prompts the introduction of the resolution. The resolution, however, is based on the presumption that masses of Jews will go and are waiting to go. There is no assurance as to the number of Jews who desire to go to Palestine. God knows how many Jews will be left in the lands occupied by Nazi Germany. Furthermore, those who are left may desire to remain in their homelands. There are no authentic data available on this subject.

May I refer you to an article in the current number of the Menorah Journal by William Zuckerman, a very keen observer. He says:

There is a new spirit abroad in Europe. * * *
This spirit is reflected particularly in the new attitude toward the Jews. * * *
No other Nazi measures in Europe are more sabotaged than are the anti-Jewish laws. * * *
Well-meaning American Jews who have set out thus to save the European Jews may have some very unpleasant surprises in store for themselves when the war is over. They may find that when the machinery for the big Jewish evacuation from Europe is ready the "evacuees" will refuse to be "saved."

Furthermore, machinery for help has been set up through the U. N. R. R. A. and the President's War Refugee Board, a representative of which is already in the Near East.

This resolution would commit our country to the establishment of a Jewish state.

The attempt has been made to interpret the Balfour Declaration as intended to establish "a Jewish state." It is claimed that our convention with England on the terms of her mandatory commits us to support the establishment of a Jewish commonwealth—that that is a disputed question. How the Balfour Declaration which "looked with favor upon the establishment in Palestine of a national home for the Jewish people" and which explicitly reserved the rights of the existing non-Jewish population of Palestine as well as Jews outside Palestine—could be interpreted as identical with the terms of the proposed resolution is difficult to see.

It is true that in 1922 the Congress passed a concurrent resolution associating itself with the Balfour Declaration. I was the only Reform rabbi at that time who stood with my Zionist brethren.

There are faces here that will remember it. But I made it perfectly clear at that time before the Committee on Foreign Affairs, as then composed, that I was not interested in the political aspect of the program. I was interested in opening up Palestine as a haven and as a cultural center. I am still profoundly interested in such goals. I would like to point out that that concurrent resolution was not passed until 1922. The Balfour Declaration was passed in 1917. The war was over in 1922. Four years had passed. The victory had been won. It was at that time that this Government saw fit to pass that resolution. You are asking the Government now to commit itself to this proposed Jewish state while the war is still on.

Has any suggestion been made as to how to deal with Arabian intransigency? I have an article here in the Menorah Journal, written by Oscar I. Janowsky, himself a confessed and leading Zionist. He writes with reference to Arab nationalism:

> To ignore the Arabs would be neither statesmanlike nor helpful. They constitute a national community and form today the numerical majority of the population of Palestine. The national consciousness of the servile and illiterate masses may be dim; their leaders may be self-seeking, corrupt, and unscrupulous; they may be stirred by religious fanaticism and motivated by a desire for loot. But to dismiss Arab nationalism in Palestine as the concoction of a handful of rapacious landlords and reactionary priests is to indulge in self-delusion. For two decades scores of thousands of Arab youth have been indoctrinated with nationalist sentiments in the schools; today many of them occupy posts in the central and local administrations and educational establishments, or exert influence as members of the liberal professions. These intellectuals and the Arab middle class, which the economic development of the country has nurtured, are the twin pillars of Arab nationalism. That their influence will wane, or that the Arab masses will remain lethargic, are assumptions not borne out by similar developments in other countries.

All reports from Palestine confirm Professor Janowsky's contention. The situation is already tense.

Will anyone deny that the passage of this resolution will be noted in Palestine? Will anyone deny that the passage of this resolution will have some effect in Palestine? I have quotations here from the press of the Near East into which I have not time to go. Will the Jewish nationalists take the responsibility for any trouble that might happen in Palestine? Is our Government to take that responsibility? This resolution is designed to help. But I say to you as an American citizen and as a Jewish teacher: Can anyone guarantee that it will not endanger what has already been built up and will not create an even more difficult situation?

Should some consideration, ladies and gentlemen, not be given to the fact that we are at war? Great problems of military strategy are involved. Complex political, economic, racial, and religious factors confuse the situation in the Near East. Can our Government commit itself while we are at war to a policy deeply involving our ally Great Britain; to one side in a controversy which raises the bitterest feelings and holds the possibility of disaffection behind our own lines?

Dr. LAZARON. I suggest that the most earnest consideration be given to the fact that Jews are divided on the Jewish state issue. None of us wants to keep a single Jew out of Palestine. I have worked in the Zionist cause in the years when I was a Zionist. I say to you as a Jewish teacher that passage of this resolution—now, hear my words—will give a nationalist and secular direction to Jewish life for centuries, not only in Palestine but here and everywhere else.

It will inject certain emphases and certain biases into Jewish life that are potentially dangerous.

Have you thought of the effect of the establishment of a Jewish state on the millions of Jews who must perforce live outside of Palestine?

Prof. Morris Jastrow, a friend of Palestine, in a book called Zionism and the Future of Zionism, said:

> While Zionism as a doctrine of faith is intelligible, and Zionism as an economic scheme to promote agricultural colonies in Palestine is timely and should be encouraged by all interested in the welfare of such Jews as wish to settle in Palestine, Zionism as a political measure is an anachronism. It is an anachronism because the combination of politics with religion is no longer tolerable.
>
> It is an anachronism because the true modern answer to nationalistic persecution is not a claim to separate nationality, but a demand for equality within each nationality; it is an anachronism because it destroys the religious unity of the House of Israel. * * * But political Zionism is above all an anachronism because on the one hand it fails to take account of the emancipation of the great masses of the Jews who must perforce live outside Palestine and, on the other hand, neglects to consider the changes within Palestine which have made it impossible for that country to be constituted into a Jewish state.

Has even this august body sufficient reason to take sides in an intra-Jewish matter? I ask you very earnestly to consider that point of view.

It was asserted here between 90 and 95 percent of the Jews are in favor of a Jewish state. I very earnestly question that statement. The American-Jewish Conference, which it was hoped would be representative of all shades of Jewish opinion and would reach conclusions upon which all Jews could agree, was dominated by political Zionists and eventually committed itself to Jewish nationalism, to unlimited immigration into Palestine under Jewish control, and to a Jewish state. At this conference a large labor group abstained from associating themselves with political implications and objectives of the Conference. Similarly, the Union of American Hebrew Congregations with half a million constituency took a neutral position, and the powerful American Jewish Committee withdrew.

As a matter of fact the registered Zionists as reported in the American Jewish Year Book for 1943–44, the last issue, numbered only 59,000, with affiliated and constituent organizations bringing the number to only 207,000. (There are over 5,000,000 Jews in the United States.) It should also be pointed out that in the 207,000 there is much duplication of membership, and women in Hadassah, the women's Zionist organization, joined Hadassah because of the splendid philanthropic work Hadassah is doing.

One has to understand the situation, the processes of concern, of deep feeling, the threat of destruction of loved ones, friends, fellow Jews—Jews are frantic to help.

The political implications in Zionism are muted or not understood, and many Jews and non-Jews moved only by a desire to help unwittingly lend their support to these political objectives. I am sure that many Gentile friends who lend support do so because of genuine sympathy for Jewish suffering. But they have little idea of the profound issues that are involved.

Under the terms of this resolution the future political form of Palestine is fixed, determined; and our Government commits itself to the establishment of a Jewish state now. Is this democratic procedure? Again, in the words of Professor Jastrow:

It would be nothing short of sacrilegious to miss the present opportunity to reorganize Palestine on the broadest possible basis, the basis suggested by its eventful history and by its present position as a genuine gathering place of the nations, because of the sacred associations with which the land is filled. I plead for a Palestine reorganized as this country is, as are England, France, and other European lands—on the broad platform of democracy.

I appreciate, I say, the desire to help and the sympathy expressed. I believe that anything that can be done to remove the restrictions of the White Paper should be done on the ground that they are discriminatory against one particular group that may care to go to Palestine. But this is not the way, ladies and gentlemen.

I suggest at this particular time public resolutions, advertisements, and broadsides in the newspapers are not the way. Our part will not be envied by what at times are even crude promises that kept neither the black tragedy nor the dire need of my brethren nor the dignity of Jews the world over. Greater and more effective influence with our ally can be effected quietly and through more appropriate means.

After all it was England who first issued the Balfour Declaration. It was England under whose aegis the Jewish population of Palestine has grown from a mere 50,000 to nearly 600,000.

To sum up then I suggest the Congress move most cautiously before passing especially the last paragraph of this resolution, because (1) it involves an idea on which Jews are divided; (2) it intimately involves one of our partners in the war; (3) because the resolution is political in its nature, whose implications might affect the strategic and military balance; (4) because the resolution is a resolution concerning a religious group, and Congress might well consider the propriety of entering into this situation; (5) it is a resolution whose passage might do more harm than good and make the tense Palestine situation even worse; and (6) it is a resolution whose commitments for our own country cannot now be foreseen.

Finally, I believe that the reconstruction of the Holy Land can be promoted only through the cooperation of the racial, national, and religious groups that live there, and I believe that the passage of this resolution will not create the conditions for such cooperation.

I am grateful to you.

Chairman BLOOM. Just a second. We will have time for questions. Mr. Vorys, any questions?

Mr. VORYS. No.

Dr. LAZARON. Mr. Chairman, may I, by the way, in the record include two pamphlets of mine that deal with this issue? They are "Homeland or State" and "Is this the Way," which was an attempt to find a medium position.

And I also want to offer a chapter in my book "Common Ground," entitled "Palestine and Jewish Nationalism" (pp. 61-131).

Chairman BLOOM. They are not very long, are they, Rabbi?

Dr. LAZARON. The chapter is about 70 pages.

Chairman BLOOM. How long are the pamphlets?

Dr. LAZARON. The pamphlets are about 20 pages each.

Mr. VORYS. It may be boiled down and summarized.

Chairman BLOOM. Without objection, we will put as much as we can in, Rabbi.

(The pamphlets above referred to are as follows:)

HOMELAND OR STATE—THE REAL ISSUE

(By Morris S. Lazaron)

Palestine is in the news—that little strip of land at the eastern end of the Mediterranean where so much of the holiest memories and the highest hopes of western civilization have their origin. Across its awe-inspiring terrain of magnificent contrasts, men in armor have marched, as well as prophets and psalmists. Again and again in history it has drawn the eye of men with an insistence and a power far beyond its size. Ha-Levi's description of it as "the heart of the world" seems prophecy as well as poetry.

Strange murmurings come from the Near East today: Rumors of armies taking position, movements of fleets and troops and air forces, the hush of expectancy and unpredictable things to come. It is believed in many quarters that the fighting may move to the Near East and the little land that has ever been the bridge of empire may once again be called upon to play its fateful role in the dramatic unfolding of history. Amid the insidious maneuvers of the world's ambitious madmen, the crash of nations and the wreck of peoples, a steady tide of immigration into Palestine has increased its Jewish population from 78,000 in 1917 to nearly 500,000 today. Last year alone, 35,000 victims of the German terror found haven there.

The visits of many European political-Zionist leaders to this country now and in the coming months, their insistence upon the primacy of Palestine, their determination, together with certain American Jewish leaders to organize the Jews of the world for political ends centering in Palestine, make it pertinent to inquire just what is to be the position of American Jews in these regards.

For all Jews the name Palestine touches profound depths of sentiment. This is understandable and, for religious reasons, it is shared to considerable degree, by non-Jews as well. There is no difference of opinion among Jews on the question of promoting Jewish immigration into the Holy Land. American Jewry has contributed in generous measure toward Palestine reconstruction and is prepared to contribute further to this end and to bring as many refugees there as possible. Today when the Jewish communities of Europe are threatened with destruction and the need to find homes for the stricken wanderers is immediate and pressing, the age-old land has offered hospice and healing, opportunity and hope. It is natural with so many doors closed that Jews should seek homes in the land which cradled their forebears. It is also natural for them to view with keen disappointment any policy which would bar entrance to Palestine at this time.

All Jews share these feelings. Sharp differences of opinion, however, appear as to the place of Palestine in Jewish thinking and the methods and program for meeting and solving the difficult situation in which the Jews of the world find themselves.

In general, there are two groups among us. One group, with gradations and variations of emphasis, looks to the establishment in Palestine of an independent Jewish state. Jews in this group would like to organize the Jews of the world to make representations to this end at whatever conferences after the war will settle the terms of peace. They believe the Jews to be a people like any other people, entitled for its own dignity to free political existence and that the establishment of such a Jewish state will be the most effective instrumentality in stabilizing the position of the Jew in the world. They believe that Jews throughout the world should organize and act politically on an international basis. United political action for world Jewry is their technique and program, through which only will come surcease and salvation for the Jew.

This group is compact, organized, has a press, writers of its own, knows what it wants, and is effectively vocal in presenting its ideas and claims. It derives seeming support from many who are deeply moved by the current Jewish tragedy and desire to do something about it; who are stirred by the romance of Palestine restored; who yield to a program which appears to offer something immediate, definite, plausible, and practical—a share in a great constructive, romantic adventure.

The second group is at a disadvantage. Its emphasis upon the practical factors of the Jewish situation seems to make its position arid, devoid of emotional appeal. Its ringing challenge to a return to traditional culturo-religious values is hard to hear above the cries of renascent nationalism. It has no press. It has no militant, compact constituency. Several well-established national organizations might well be expected to represent and speak for it, but a natural nostalgia for Jewish unity as well as other factors apparently paralyze action, thus, unfortunately, leaving the field to the more voluble. Its actual constituency is certainly as large as the first group. Its potential constituency is limited only by the millions of American Jews who wait for an organization and a leadership which represent and express the American Jewish point of view.

These Jews refuse to make united political action the basis of their hope. They fear such a program as a departure from the Jewish culturo-religious tradition. They appreciate and would conserve the sense of brotherhood among the Jews of the world but they do not look with favor upon having that brotherhood take the form of secular nationalism. They are pro-Palestine but anti political Zionist. They believe that a Jewish homeland in Palestine can serve its purpose as a center of Jewish life without the accompaniment of political considerations, which they deem not only unnecessary but dangerous.

Meanwhile, a strenuous effort of education and propaganda is apparently being undertaken among American Jews by the first group to capture American Jewish opinion for its point of view.

The London Jewish Chronicle, the leading organ of British Jewry, Zionist in its sympathies, has an illuminating article in its edition of December 1, 1939, titled "Zionism Goes West: Hope Centered on the Americas." After referring to the tragic destruction of Polish Jewry and the necessity to find new areas for "Zionist mobilization," the article declares:

"There are today over 6,000,000 Jews in North and South America. It is therefore only natural that the attention of the movement should now be directed toward the western hemisphere. The 'colonization' of America by leading Zionists, propagandists, and cultural workers is now being planned by the leading circles of the Zionist organization."

The article continues:

"Zionists have entirely failed to make the Jewish people in the States understand that Zionism is a great progressive and practically idealistic political— [italics ours]—movement, a political movement which as such is the intimate concern of every Jew. An attempt is now being made in New York to rectify the mistakes of the past, with the active assistance and help of Zionists from abroad, many of whom have been now released by circumstances from their usual activities at home. Delegations are being organized and plans drafted for intensive activities in the Americas. In addition to the Zionist Executive, almost every Zionist party and institution is planning the dispatch of delegations * * * "

This is illuminating indeed. A grand offensive has been launched against the alleged passivity and disinterestedness of American Jewry to the present and proposed post-war political efforts of the Zionist-Congress group. The offensive has already started, as is witnessed by the number of visitors here from organizations abroad, the number of meetings and rallies that are being held throughout the country. The American Jewish community should appraise the situation in the light of the facts. It is tragic business to lift the hopes of men and women to a point where all reality has fled. Disappointment will be all the more keen. Can Palestine solve the physical homelessness of the Jew? Are an independent Jewish state and international political action among Jews feasible or practical or desirable? Does American Jewry desire to commit itself to this philosophy and program?

Mr. Neville Laski, K. C., erstwhile president of the board of deputies of British Jews, discussed Anglo-Jewry and a Jewish national home in a book, Jewish Rights and Jewish Wrongs, published in the summer of 1939. He declared that the concept of the Jewish national home by its very name "might be supposed to make some claim on the allegiance of all Jews wherever domiciled, and this claim might conceivably come into conflict with the claims of the countries of which they are citizens." Therefore, the idea of a Jewish national home, whether in Palestine or elsewhere, repelled many English Jews who fought shy of the movement, seeing in it danger to their own enjoyment of civil rights.

The leaders of Anglo-Jewry feared the prospect of a Jewish state because it might compromise the position of Jews who enjoyed civil rights in other countries by raising awkward questions of a dual allegiance. In their view, such a State could not be established without involving injustice and hardship to the native Arab population. "Anxious as they were to remove disabilities unjustly imposed upon Jewish minorities in Eastern Europe, they were doubly anxious not themselves to impose wrongs on others."

The Balfour Declaration was issued in November 1917. It said nothing about the creation of a Jewish State: "It simply promised that opportunity should be given for 'the establishment in Palestine of a national home for the Jewish people' and that such establishment should be facilitated * * *. The British Jews found themselves able to accept this formula, but they emphasized that it should not connote the creation of a Jewish political state or impose any test of religious or racial disability on anyone." The policy of the mandatory power was formulated by the Churchill memorandum (1922) along the above lines. Mr. Laski declares: "The effect of the memorandum was practically to deprive the expression 'Jewish national home' of any political connotation, giving it rather a cultural and economic significance." This was satisfactory to responsible American as well as British Jewish leadership.

Since that time the controversy has continued. It rises more sharply today because of the alleged threat to implement the last British white paper, which would temporarily stop Jewish immigration to Palestine. The Zionists claim that Britain has foresworn its obligations. The Arabs accuse the British of violating their rights. Under the pressure to find homes for Jewish refugees, it is serious indeed to shut the door through which thousands found freedom last year and the gate of hope to thousands of others. Moreover, the Zionists fear that their dreams of a Jewish State will be forever lost.

But responsible American Jewish leadership agrees today with Mr. Laski when he says "the idea of a Jewish state is no less distasteful now than it was 20 years ago." And, it might be added, will continue to be after the war. And such leadership will oppose any attempt to organize Jews on an international basis for international political action.

Registered American Zionists number under 50,000. There are between four and a half and five million Jews in the United States. The claims of the Zionist-Congress group are constantly projected into the thinking of the Jewish and general community. It may be considered, therefore, that this group speaks the mind of American Jews and does indeed represent the philosophy, aspirations and program of American Jews. It thus becomes necessary to state the position of American Jews friendly to Palestine, earnestly desirous of bringing surcease to their coreligionists and of finding homes for them in Palestine and elsewhere, but who do not wish by their silence to be misrepresented before their fellow-Americans.

We understand the position of European Jewry with its long memories of cruel oppression. We understand how from these memories as well as from the European scene itself there could logically come the desire for political nationalism centering in a Jewish state in Palestine as the way out. Many of us, however, are not disposed to import to these shores the concepts of European Jewry born out of heartache and oppression, out of the "pale" and the ghetto. The American background is different. American Jews will think for themselves and in terms of our American experience. We insist there is an American Jewish approach, instinct with the free spirit of America. We believe in the culturo-religious unity of the Jewish people and that here and elsewhere Israel has survived and will survive as a religious community. We would avoid introducing into American Jewish life influences we believe would delay the processes of integration. We believe that a Jewish state or Jewish international political action will not solve the problem of anti-Semitism but will aggravate it by building barriers between ourselves and our fellow citizens and by giving ammunition to the anti-Semite. We recognize that the Zionists may be and are good Americans. We do not charge them with lack of patriotism. We declare only that the political way is not for us. We see clearly that Palestine can absorb only a limited number of Jews; that the vast millions must live throughout the world. We are unwilling to take the chance to prejudice the status of those millions nor submit the most powerful Jewish community in the world, the American Jewish community, to the possible charge of divided loyalty. We believe that Jewish life here can be rich and creative. We believe that greater effort than ever before should be exerted to promote among Jews here a knowledge of Jewish history, literature and tradition and to deepen the religious life of the American Jew. We profoundly desire to help our stricken brethren. At the same time, we bear other things in mind.

Our Government is attempting the difficult task of keeping out of the involvements of the war. That effort receives, as it should, the unqualified support of all our citizens regardless of party affiliations. In that effort the Government has followed a program which not only relinquishes for the moment rights for which the Nation has previously gone to war but which calls for personal and financial sacrifice from large groups of our citizens. It is the duty of all of us to avoid any hazard to the delicate poise of our State Department's relations with any belligerent power.

The American national scene is admittedly difficult. There are forces at work which will capitalize any opportunity to turn against the Jews. This is a Presidential year. Feelings and prejudices run high. Want and need are still in the land. A scapegoat might be useful to certain groups. It is obvious that the projection of Palestine as the primary hope of the Jew and the exercise of pressure by American Jews in diplomatic quarters at this time might be useful weapons in the hands of unscrupulous anti-Semites.

No influence that any American Jews might possibly bring to bear on the British Government will make any change in the situation in Palestine. Britain is fighting mortal enemies who aim to destroy her. Palestine and the Near East are key positions in the line of Empire. Jews who have enjoyed in the British Empire the completest realization of their free citizenship—economic, political, religious, and social—should be the last people in the world to embarrass England now. British Zionists have pledged and are giving allegiance to Britain and the World Zionist Organization has expressed identity of interest with the cause of the democracies. Should they not make good that pledge in fact as well as in theory by refraining from putting forward their specific claims now? Their hands are tied by the war and they—naturally enough, perhaps—try to shift the burden of pressure on Britain in regard to Palestine to the shoulders of American Jewry. That is serious. It has many implications. It would be most unwise for us to lend ourselves to any such program now or at the end of the war.

The political-Zionist group is ambitious. It is therefore all the more important that American Jewry should be clear in its thinking and statesmanlike in its action. One immediate need would seem to be that we make plain our position on Palestine. The political Zionist group charges all of us who do not accept their program with Jewish disloyalty and labels us antagonists of Palestine. Some go so far as to read us out of Jewish life. It would be unfortunate if we permit these charges to go by default. American Jews who are not secularists or political nationalists will not let themselves be jockeyed into this position. They will not permit themselves to become involved in political maneuverings under the guise of philanthropy or friendship for Palestine, not even for the much desired goal of Jewish unity. These are not the issues. The issue is the political program, methods and goal of the Zionist-Congress group in Amerca and in the international field.

American Jews should make some things very clear:

1. We have contributed substantial sums to Palestine work.

2. We desire to maintain what has been established in Palestine and extend it, and we have expressed that desire by word and deed. We would bring as many Jewish refugees into Palestine as conditions permit.

3. We will resist pressure to commit ourselves to a philosophy or program which recognizes secular nationalism as the basis of Jewish unity and an independent Jewish State in Palestine either as the primary concern of Jewish life or its means of redemption.

A paragraph in the leading editorial in The New Palestine of December 29, Welcome Dr. Weizmann, is of unusual interest:

"Dr. Weizmann comes to us to submit for consideration an invitation to American Jewry to take the lead in the reconciliation of what has for too long been regarded as two parallel lines of action destined never to meet but which, in reality, must be construed as lines to be bound together in one conception, in one plan, into which the resources of all Jews are to be poured."

If this means the willingness of the Zionist-Congress group to disavow all claims to impose its position on American Jewry; it means the desire to] give as well as to take; if it means the abandonment of political pressures; if it means discontinuing insistence on majority rights in Palestine and concentration on the work of maintaining and extending what has been done there within the absorptive capacity of the land; if it means forgetting the Jewish state and choosing the homeland; if it means economics and not politics there, religion and not politics here; if it really means an earnest attempt to arrive at a common platform on which all groups of Jews can unite, there could be great hope for united effort.

But no statement to that effect from Zionist-Congress leadership has as yet been forthcoming.

If there is to be concerted action on Jewish affairs, it should surely be on some platform on which all Jews can agree. Unity on any other basis would be spurious. If others want more perhaps they should continue to agitate separately for that more. It is the insistence upon international Jewish political action and a Jewish state that disturbs the Arabs, that projects the Jewish communities of the world into the international political game and that may possibly involve us in every land where we live. It is the insistence upon nationalism as a philosophy of Jewish life which forges weapons for the anti-Semite and builds psychic barriers between ourselves and our fellow citizens. These are tragic delusions. They give a false sense of escape from our problems. The constant projection of these ideas into Jewish communities here is a persistent source of irritation, upsetting whatever harmony we have thus far won in American Jewish communal life.

This is the profound division among American Jews. One group—let us call them The Polit-Zis.—offers the program of Jewish international, political organization, centering in a Jewish state in Palestine. It asks American Jews and the Jews of the world to support this program now and to demand its fulfillment at the conferences which will define peace terms after the war. The other group opposes this philosophy and program as erroneous and disastrous.

It is not enough to be silently indifferent. Many well-meaning and devoted people subscribe to this position. If, however, we believe it to be a departure from Jewish tradition, the implications of which will harm not help, will wound not heal, we must offer an alternate program. Such a program will recognize the realities of the international situation and the Jews' place in it. It must be calculated to promote the general welfare of Jews the world over. It must be in keeping with the spirit of traditional Jewish values. It must preserve as its dynamic the sense of Jewish brotherhood and purpose in a cause—the cause of universal freedom, justice, and humanity.

Stripped of all extraneous detail yet in an effort to find a platform which will embody the above ideas and on which American Jews can unite, I suggest the following as a basis for discussion:

1. The right of Jews to full citizenship wherever they may live, so long as they obey the laws of the land. These full rights to be not only civil and political and religious but economic as well. These rights to be guaranteed.

2. In those lands where culturo-religious autonomy is recognized, the right of the Jewish community to such autonomy should be recognized and guaranteed.

3. We regret the necessity to restrict immigration to Palestine but we understand the causes in the international scene which move the mandatory power at this time. We continue to urge the moral obligations undertaken by the mandatory power and the League under the terms of the Balfour Declaration and interpreted in the Churchill memorandum of 1922.

4. We earnestly desire to see the cooperation of Palestine Jewry, the Arabs, and the British Government to establish conditions which will permit the maximum immigration to Palestine on the basis of the capacity and ability of the country to absorb it. We believe it necessary, however, to free such immigration from political implications and to allay the fears of the Arabs that derive therefrom. To this end it may be wise to look ahead only 10, 15, or 20 years and to work out a program of economic reconstruction for this period on the above lines, meanwhile making unremitting effort in practical, constructive ways to win the confidence, friendship, and cooperation of the Arabs.

5. We hope that the ultimate constitution will establish a Palestine state in which Palestine Jews will individually possess the full rights of citizenship and at the same time have full communal, cultural and religious autonomy; that this position will be permanently guaranteed by the British Government and by whatever League of Nations may in the future be established.

Despite the immeasurable calamity of today, the future is not black nor hopeless. I see great advance in understanding of the Jew and Judaism, in sympathy with us, in appreciation of us. I see the willingness to defend us by forces more powerful than any we could organize in our own defense. If Jews throughout the world act reasonably and wisely now, happier and freer days will dawn for far larger numbers of Jews than ever before in Jewish history when this holocaust has spent itself. I believe this not only as a student of men and events. I believe this because as a Jew I believe that God moves with irresistible power through history toward goals whose glory and grandeur man falteringly senses as the highest purpose of life.

This is the time to set the Jewish problem in the matrix of the world situation; to see it as a part of the world picture. The spiritual and ethical life of humanity is involved, the future of mankind. Out of the primal muck evil and malignant forces have thrust themselves up to destroy the hard-won victories of the spirit which the sacrifices of generations have bequeathed to us. Never was hate so widespread. It is hate which eats the soul of men and peoples like a cancer. The good in them withers, the humane dies. They rage like beasts and tear each other apart like wild animals in the jungle.

Are there none in all this madness who will rise above their own presumed self-interest, rise above the battle and bear witness by their lives, as they have in their deaths, to universal, eternal, moral, and religious values?

We have been oppressed. We have suffered. We, too, long for friendship and for freedom and for peace. We are like other men. Others have been oppressed and have suffered. But others are strong. They can organize and demand and fight and take. They are strong.

We are weak. We have not even the symbol of physical strength and political power. That is our strength. Would to God we could see it and, understanding, act upon it. We have no hidden ax to grind. We seek no sovereign power. We ask only those inalienable rights to which all men are entitled.

Our hurt shall not make us hate. Our heartache shall not cause us to make demands. We feel the misery of the world. We are its symbol. The grief burden of the peoples we share. This is a moment of destiny. This is the opportunity for the world Jewish religious community to play its role.

Let us fling our challenge into the hate chaos of today.

Freedom and friendship for all. Freedom and friendship for German and Russian and Italian and Pole and Arab; even for those who oppress us. A peace of justice and compassion for all.

These are the golden threads in the age-old pattern of the Jewish dream for humanity.

The modern despots will go the way of the tyrants of old. Our strength and our purpose are today as they have always been in the past—not in the weapons which men and nations forge but in bearing silent yet terrible witness to the eternal truths of justice and human brotherhood which derive from God Himself.

MORRIS S. LAZARON.

IS THIS THE WAY?

We are the greatest Jewish community in the world. We came here from all lands, conditions, circumstances. The fathers of some of us settled here over 200 years ago when America was young. Others came in great numbers in the middle of the last century to escape the oppressions of Europe. And still others came as a vast tidal wave by the millions, seeking freedom from the tyranny of Czarist Russia. We labored, we sweated, we sacrificed. We built great institutions of philanthropy, set standards of social giving. We built synagogs and temples as symbols of Israel's faith. We enriched the life of our country by our work, by our intelligence, by the creative and artistic genius of the Jewish spirit.

But we have not forgotten the roots whence we sprang. We have not held aloof from Jewish suffering, even as we have not held aloof from human suffering anywhere. Our Jewish heart throbbed in sympathy with the anguish of our brethren in foreign lands. We have stretched forth our hands across the sea. We have fed and clothed and sheltered the stricken and the needy. We have found new homes for the orphaned and the driven wanderer. We have shared in the reconstruction of Jewish life in all the miserable ghettoes of eastern Europe. We have helped to bring our sons and daughters to Palestine and we have, through them, plowed its soil, fertilized its land, dotted its countryside with villages. We have found homes for others in more hospitable lands. Out of the depths of gratitude that our lives have fallen in pleasant places, we, the American Jewish community, have been brothers of our people in all the ends of the earth.

We have done this under supreme difficulties and at great sacrifices, in times of war and in times of peace, nobly and generously. That which we have done is no mean service in the long anabasis of the Jew.

Yet, with all this, we have indeed not done all that we could or should. Too many of us are smug, indifferent, and ignorant, selfish and materialistic. Too many of us are spiritually dead, living and feeling without the disciplines and refinements of our Judaism, seeking in secular concerns, even if worthy, the warmth which comes from religious thinking and feeling. We exhaust ourselves in efforts for defense—necessary, of course—but we too often overlook the strong bulwarks of our heritage, the ramparts of Israel's faith which have never been breached.

We would save our brother Jews from the physical and mental torture of the tyrant. And our very sympathies often mislead us to follow threadbare nationalistic shibboleths which the world is rejecting. It is hard for some to see that the contemporary travail will give birth to a different world in which the concepts of nation and culture will take on more profound meaning, meaning implicit in our Jewish tradition about ourselves. Can we not understand that that which gives worth and dignity to the Jewish people is the Jewish spirit and the

Jewish people are worth redemption as a people only as that spirit lives in us? "We are a people only by reason of our Torah, our teaching."

And, which is of supreme practical importance, at this time when more than ever in our long history unity among us is necessary, we have thus far failed to achieve it. Is it a hapless and hopeless task to seek some common ground on which all Jews may agree?

We Jews are a people of sentiment. We are quick to feel because we are well acquainted with sorrow. And yet we are intelligent. If suffering has mellowed our hearts, it has also disciplined our minds. We are an old people too, and we should be a wiser people. We must not weaken our own ability to help our fellow Jews. At the end of the war, when the world will be reorganized, the future of millions of our fellow Jews will be determined. Certainly no voice will be more powerful in those deliberations than the voice of America. If we can unite now on some common platform, if we exercise restraint and statesmanship now, at that time we shall be able to achieve more. Let us take care not to irritate but to build friends. We should not, through misguided feeling or misdirected activity now or then, tear down that which has been builded here, in Palestine or anywhere else in the world. We should not jeopardize the future.

Many and grave are the problems that beset us: We must maintain our institutions of religion, of Jewish education, our agencies of philanthropy, and all our communal activities here; we must measurably meet the cries for relief from abroad; we must lay the foundations for rebuilding Jewish life everywhere So grave are these problems that if it is possible for us to act together we can accomplish so much more—we shall be able to ride the storm, to serve our Jewish brethren everywhere, to serve our country, the embattled cause of freedom the world over, and fulfill our historic destiny in the spirit of our religious heritage. Before these tasks which require all our material, intellectual, and spiritual resources, surely we should act together.

I say act together, for it is not possible for all of us to think alike. There have always been differences of opinion among Jews. There is a passage in the Talmud which refers to a hammer which breaks a rock in pieces. So say the rabbis: It is possible to expound a single verse in the Bible in many different ways. There were always parties and sects among us—Pharisees, Sadducees, Essenes, Karaites, Chassidim, Mithnaggedim—even as there are today. Diversity of thinking, variance of opinion is written in the record of Jewish history. "Some may forbid and some allow," say the rabbis, "yet both are the words of the living God," if only these words proceed from the sincere and earnest spirit.

It should be possible even in the midst of the marked differences to reach basic propositions upon which all of us can agree. There is no single philosophy or program that will be valid for all Jewish communities everywhere. What is true or wise in one place may not be wise or practicable in another. Why, then, should any group presume to speak for all or seek to impose its will on all?

What is it that we Jews want from the war?

Nothing more or less than that which our fellow citizens want. We want the victory of the Allied Nations because in that victory are bound up the freedom of man and the future of civilization. We desire opportunities for all peoples. We wish no punitive peace based on hate, because we know such a peace will not endure. We have no wish to enslave the German, Italian, or Japanese peoples but rather to redeem them from the tyrant who destroys their spirit and uses their bodies for cannon fodder. We shall work for the security, the stability of all men. We deeply pray as we fight for a peace based on righteousness, for we are taught that only the work of righteousness is peace.

For ourselves, we Jews desire the right to live as citizens anywhere in the world so long as we obey the laws of the land where we live. We desire to create in the post-war world such conditions as shall make impossible another eruption of the universal barbarism which parades as anti-Semitism. We desire homes for wandering Jews. We desire to help build a religio-cultural homeland in Palestine, even as we pray that such a center may send forth its beneficent and inspiring influences to enrich the life of the world. We realize that Jewish homelessness is but a part of the vast migration of other uprooted and driven peoples, and we will share the burden of rebuilding their lives in happier lands as well as the lives of our co-religionists, for "we are our brother's keeper."

It is around the question of Palestine and the place of Palestine in Jewish life that discussion centers.

Every Jewish community in the country has been torn by dissentions on this issue. A semblance of unity, it is true, has been preserved in fund-raising activities in order to insure the support of existing Jewish social agencies but, if we are frank with ourselves, we know that under the surface of every Jewish community there are tensions so sharp that only great forbearance on the part of community leadership has been able to keep it within bounds. We know also that the vast majority of Jews in America want unity. Many of us are asking, however, what is the price we shall have to pay for unity. Take the issue of the Jewish Army, for instance. A strong case can be made out for an army of Palestinian Jews. Why shouldn't Jews who have poured not only their money but their blood and their lives into Palestine be given opportunity to defend themselves against the threat of Nazi invasion? It appeals to sentiments grounded deep in many Jewish hearts. Jews in Palestine have appealed for the right to form a separate Jewish Army under a Jewish flag. This community, built up by the toil and sacrifice of decades is now in mortal danger and, as freemen everywhere, have not only the right but the duty and responsibility to defend their homes and their homeland. That demand has thus far been denied. Nevertheless, thousands of Palestinian Jews have enlisted in the British forces in the Near East. They have fought valiantly in the campaigns in Greece, Syria and Africa and have received the distinction of special commendation in official war reports.

The wisdom or unwisdom of the British in denying to Palestine Jews the right to form a Jewish Army is a matter involving British Imperial policy in its relation to the whole strategy of war. To establish a Jewish Army in Palestine under its own flag at this time might well upset the balance in this strategic area. A Jewish army and a Jewish flag would be the symbols of Jewish sovereignty. This is, of course, just what certain extremists wish. But a different result than the one they foresee might well ensue. Is the distrust with which certain Jewish quarters view British policy in Palestine, and which indeed has justification, sufficient to press the issue? Are the proponents of the idea willing to risk the loss of all that has been gained in Palestine merely to establish the symbol of statehood? Is it not rather the role of statesmanship for Zionist leaders to urge Palestinian Jews to continue to fight as they are now fighting—as Palestinians? The Jewish agency several days ago urged able-bodied Jews to enlist in the British forces. It would then be feasible to urge the British to arm all Palestinians loyal to the United Nations' cause.

Indeed, one of the leading Zionists of England, Lt. Col. Norman Bentwich, broadcast an appeal some weeks ago from London that the agitation for a Jewish army cease. Yet it has gone on. Many feel that this is no time to bring particularistic pressures on our State Department or in England for specific Jewish demands. Many of us feel this is no time to inject into the American scene such divisive issues, that Jews should be the last to do anything that will hinder the war effort. Everything is secondary to the primary objective—winning the war. But the problem affects us as American citizens. And this is what so many well-meaning Jews, in their anxiety to help their stricken brethren, do not see. The United States is a partner in the war. It is deeply concerned with the general war strategy in which the Near East is an important link. Matériel, munitions, planes, personnel have been and are being sent there steadily week by week. Is it unreasonable to question the wisdom of citizens of this country, belonging to a religious group, pursuing specific aims of a political-military character in that area at this time? If the purpose of a Jewish Army is to create the symbol of sovereignty—and that, indeed, is the goal—it must be obvious to thoughtful Jews that they cannot share in such agitation without laying themselves open to the charge of divided loyalty. Such Jews are no less loyal to the Jewish tradition. But we take the position that the unity which binds Jews together is their common religio-cultural inheritance. It has nothing to do with politics. If Britain did something to offend American citizens, American citizens who are Jews would take offense at British Jews as well as British gentiles. The unity between British and American Jews has thus no other basis than a spiritual one. To adopt any other course, to accept any other philosophy will jeopardize the citizenship rights of Jews in all the free countries of the world. But agitation for a Jewish army and the philosophy of Jewish political nationalism imply just this. On these basic issues a despairing heart must be disciplined by a wise head.

Many of us feel, too, that from the specific Jewish angle, it is unwise to press such questions now—that more good can in the long run be accomplished by not putting forward irritating issues when British and American leadership must center its attention upon the vast problems of strategy and offense. And after all this, question of a Jewish army is one for the strategist to decide. Even though to the Jewish nationalist it is a political question, in the light of the war it is a military problem and should be decided on that basis.

Often friends are lost for a cause by untimely activity. I have been told by not unimportant people here and abroad, "Why do they do this now?" Many who are sympathetic with Jewish activity in Palestine are annoyed and often irritated at persistent sniping. Such criticisms from friendly sources should not be summarily dismissed.

The question of a Jewish army in Palestine, is not simple, But certainly no good can come from agitation which divides Jews, distresses our friends and strengthens our enemies.

The important issue is this: We all wish to share in building a culturo-religious center in the Holy Land. What are the best possible, most practical steps to take to achieve that end?

Let us look at the picture. There are certain irreducible facts which cannot be argued away.

Jewish need is a fact. One has only to read any day's cable dispatches of the Jewish Telegraphic Agency to understand the heartbreaking poignancy of Jewish need.

Arab nationalism is a fact. It cannot lightly be dismissed by the remark, "The Arabs have vast territories and we want only this small land, around which centers so much of Jewish sentiment." The Arabs have been living in Palestine in uninterrupted residence for 1,300 years. Jews who understand Jewish nationalism should certainly be the first to understand Arab nationalism. Arab nationalism is a fact.

British necessity to regard the millions of Mohammedans in the Near and Far East and in northern Africa from Egypt to Morrocco is a fact.

The peculiar importance of the Near East and Palestine in the grand strategy of the war is a fact.

The profoundest sentiment among Jews about Palestine is a fact.

The will to create a Jewish state is, among some Jews, a fact.

Diaspora nationalism, unfortunately, in certain Jewish quarters, is a fact. Opposition to diaspora nationalism is also a fact. The disincilnation of many Jews to have anything to do with a Jewish political international program centering in Palestine or anywhere else is much more widely accepted than is currently recognized.

Finally, the wish to rebuild Palestine as a culturo-religious center is found among practically all Jews. It is a fact of Jewish life.

What is the statesmanlike procedure in the midst of all these differing and often conflicting interests? What will best serve the larger Jewish interest? What course will best promote victory of our country and the United Nations—the supreme objective? What practical steps are possible? Is there a Palestinian program upon which all Jews can agree? These are immediate questions with which American Jews should concern themselves.

Let us set forth certain principles.

First, there is one thing on which all Jews are united: That is, the right of all men to live as citizens everywhere. Any post-war settlement should not only assert but, so far as possible, guarantee this right. Indeed, it is inherent in the Atlantic Charter.

Second: Any approach to the reconstruction of Jewish life must be made in the light of the general setting of the war and the complex situation after the war. It must be integrated into the world picture. Not only Jews but millions of other peoples in central, eastern, and southeastern Europe and Asia have been uprooted and driven out.

Third: Any plan to be effective must appeal to the unbiased and objective as wise and practical. It is so easy to raise hopes which may be impossible of realization. Any plan to be measurably successful must be based upon the realities of the international picture, not on what some would like those realities to be. The facts of international life cannot be ignored and they often and necessarily limit the scope of possible action.

Fourth: Any plan for the reconstruction of Jewish life must, above all, emphasize the spiritual purpose and mission of Israel as the priest people, the servant of the living God.

What sort of program for Palestine would seem to meet these conditions and offer a possible basis for unity?

A. Behind all the differences and conflicting philosophies, programs, and methods is the desire to utilize Palestine as an outlet for Jewish immigration to the fullest possible extent. Practically all Jews can unite on a program for the economic development of the land.

B. The Jewish agency was originally designed as the instrument through which the British Government would act jointly with the Jews of the world to fulfill the terms of the Balfour Declaration. It was to include both Zionists and non-Zionists. The Zionists have, however, secured control of the agency and it is therefore no longer representative, except of one group.

C. For many reasons the situation in Palestine has become more complicated and difficult. No one is satisfied—not the Arabs, not the Jews, and not the British Government.

D. It is suggested that a new start be made:

1. Let the British Government reaffirm the Balfour Declaration and indicate its desire to promote a homeland for Jews in Palestine, in fulfillment of the moral obligation undertaken by the mandatory power.

2. The agency might be reconstituted as an economic agency, working on a definite though flexible economic, fiscal, and immigration program over a period of years. We earnestly desire to see the cooperation of the Arabs, Palestine Jewry, and the British Government to establish conditions which will permit the maximum immigration to Palestine, on the basic proposition already enunciated: the economic absorptive capacity of the land. We desire to see this immigration extended as generously as conditions permit.

We believe it necessary, however, to free such immigration from political implications and to allay the fears of the Arabs that derive therefrom. To this end, it may be wise to look ahead only 5, 10, or 20 years and to work out a program of economic reconstruction along the above lines, meanwhile making unremitting effort in practical, constructive ways to win the confidence, the friendship and cooperation of the Arabs.

3. The future political status of the Jewish community in Palestine cannot in the very nature of things be determined now, nor is it a matter to be decided by Jews who live outside Palestine. It is for Palestine Jewry to decide. The political status of the Jewish community in Palestine is to be determined by the Jewish community there, the mandatory power or powers controlling at the end of the war and in consultation with the Arabs. It should be a normal evolution out of conditions and events. Under any circumstances, the cultural autonomy of Palestine Jews should be guaranteed.

I suggest, that the above approach to this complex problem is, in the circumstances, the most practical, the wisest, and the best designed in the long run to serve the larger welfare of Jews both in Palestine and in the world.

But this implies flexibility, give-and-take on both sides. It does not ask more than under the circumstances can be gotten. Extremists on both sides may be dissatisfied. To some it will be too little; to others it may be too much.

This means too that certain groups will relinquish their secular and diaspora nationalism. It means that certain groups will disconitnue their attempt to speak for all American Jews. It means that they will cease agitations within the American Jewish communities which disrupt and divide. It means, as Lord Samuel suggested several years ago, relinquishing the insistence on majority rights now in Palestine.

This also means the support of Palestine reconstruction by all groups of Jews. It means that all will submit to the discipline of the community and set their hands to the task within the limits of the program adopted. It means concentration on the work of maintaining and extending what has been done there. It means forgetting the Jewish state and choosing the Jewish homeland. It means economics and politics there, religion and not politics here.

Let us be clear. The issue is not Palestine reconstruction. The issue is the secular philosophy, the political program, methods and goal of the Zionist-Congress group in America and in the international field.

Most Jews feel keenly the tie that binds them to the community of Israel. We want to share in the rebuilding of Jewish life in Palestine. Ours is not a negative but a positive and affirmative attitude. But we cannot accept secular nationalism for the Jew. We see grave dangers resulting from it for the vast millions who must live outside Palestine. We dare not let our feelings for our oppressed brethren blind us to those dangers. It is the insistence upon international, political Jewish action and a Jewish state that disturbs the Arabs, that projects the Jewish communities of the world into the international political game and that may possibly involve us in every land where we live. It is the insistence upon nationalism as a philosophy of Jewish life which forges weapons for the anti-Semites and builds psychic barriers between ourselves and our fellow citizens.

In the period of reconstruction that will follow the fighting there will be desperate need for cooperation of all groups in all nations. This united cooperation will be vitally necessary here in our own country. The period of transition after the war is obviously fraught with difficulties and dangers. For no group of American citizens will it be so hazardous as for Jews. The anti-Semite is even now, while we are at war, whispering, printing, spreading, proclaiming his lies and hatred of us. War weariness and the disappointments, delays, and perhaps the dire need of many of our fellow citizens may be fruitful soil for the anti-Semitic agitator.

Why should we, by ill-advised Jewish agitation, feed ammunition to the enemy? Why should we propagate philosophies that present the Jew as an alien, utterly different, unassimilable, interested in a future somewhere else than in America? Why should we consciously by our silence connive at, or suffer to continue without opposition, influences that may endanger the last great Jewish community in the world and possibly disarm ourselves of the power to help our brethren in less favored lands, when that help is and will be so desperately needed?

The things that are at stake in this world are the things for which our fathers died generation after generation. The mighty battle to free the human spirit was fought silently in the ghettoes of Europe by brave men and women. The struggle has now moved out on the stage of the world.

Our Christian and gentile friends did not at first sense the significance of the forces that are loose in the world. They do now. Everything to which we Jews have borne witness throughout the dreary centuries is threatened. The brute has risen to drag us down.

At this season we read in the Seder Haggadah: "Not one tyrant alone rose to destroy us but many tyrants in many different lands and ages rose up to destroy us. But the Holy One, blessed be He, redeemed and saved. Let us take heart at this season of our freedom."

The rejection of reason and the elevation of a romantic cult of blood and brutality; an extreme nationalism which rides to power upon the back of millions of the enslaved; the denial of human dignity and the rejection of God; the battering down of the foundations of human brotherhood, so arduously built on the bodies of the martyrs that our bodies and spirits might be free; the prophetic vision of peace among the nations, founded on righteousness—all these are gifts of the Jewish genius incorporated in the thinking and feeling of the daughter religion. What is at stake in this struggle are these universal insights of our Torah, of our teaching. Indeed, they are the pillars on which the great Judaeo—Christian tradition is built. It is this Torah, this teaching, which has preserved Israel in all the lands of his wandering. This is the reason for our existence. To these truths we still cling, in the deathless hope: kimizion tetse Torah ud'var Adonoi mirushalaim.

We know. We have felt. We have said: O, God, we are tired. We are weary. Our strength is failing. It is too much. Our enemies rise up to destroy us!

But we may not weary now—now, when the embattled hosts of free men have risen—white and black and brown and yellow; Moslem and Christian and Jew. The road is hard. It may be long, but victory lies ahead.

We may keep our differences, but let us unite where we can unite: on a practical and statesmanlike program. Let us have done with parties and politics which becloud the universal issues at stake. There is no reason why American Jews should not be pro-Palestine, but America not Palestine should be the focal point of our interest. Judaism, not Zionism; God, not Palestine should have primacy in our thinking. This has been. It should be. Our world needs the Jewish message. Now is our opportunity to serve it in greater measure than ever before. Let us not underestimate the glorious witness of our past nor the present witness of millions of stricken, driven Jews whose heroism today lends dignity and glory to Jewish life and the deathless truths of Judaism.

To your tents, then, O Israel!

TO MY FELLOW JEWS

Before the grave problems which confront us we should unite. We cannot all think alike—we Jews never did, but we should try to come together on certain basic propositions.

The question of Palestine is the center around which most controversy rages. Yet all Jews would like to share in rebuilding the ancient land.

This paper represents an effort to reach a practical working basis for Jewish united effort in Palestine. While it is written by one whose opposition to Jewish political nationalism is well known, it is pro-Palestine. It is the affirmative and constructive position of one who loves Palestine and, rejoicing in what has been accomplished there, would like to see Jewish settlement there not only maintained but extended.

It will serve also to enlighten those whose only knowledge of the author is based upon current and widespread misrepresentation of his position. It was delivered in the Madison Avenue Temple on the first day of Pesach and is sent forth to a larger audience with the earnest prayer that it may help to bring about that harmony among us which our hearts and the times demand.

MORRIS S. LAZARON.

Chairman BLOOM. Mr. Jarman?

Mr. JARMAN. No questions.

Mr. VORYS. I wondered at the name of the author of the first article that the Rabbi referred to.

Dr. LAZARON. William Zuckerman, an observor, a European correspondent.

Chairman BLOOM. Mr. Chiperfield?

Mr. CHIPERFIELD. No questions.

Chairman BLOOM. Mr. Rogers.

Mr. ROGERS. I should like to take issue on just one thing. You say this is an inter-Jewish matter and we should not take sides. I disagree with you. I think this is a matter for the American Congress. It is a matter for the country. It is a matter for all people.

It has been made a matter of concern to the whole world by reason of the Nazi persecution. The fact that there are Jews who are divided should not influence our decision one way or the other. Nor should we be influenced if all groups belonged to the Zionists or if none belonged to the Zionists. This is a political matter, a military matter, and it has become a grave matter to the future of democracy and the preservation of democracy. As such this Congress should be interested. This is not an inter-Jewish question in any way at all. It is far more important than that in my opinion.

Dr. LAZARON. May I take this opportunity to express thanks to you for your undoubted help in this tragic situation, while reserving the right as a rabbi to differ from you.

Mr. ROGERS. That is all I have.

Chairman BLOOM. Mr. Rogers, have you finished?

Mr. ROGERS. Yes.

Chairman BLOOM. Mr. Jonkman?

Mr. JONKMAN. No.

Chairman BLOOM. Mr. Wright?

Mr. WRIGHT. No.

Chairman BLOOM. Mrs. Bolton?

Mrs. BOLTON. No.

Chairman BLOOM. Mr. Wadsworth?

Mr. WADSWORTH. No.

Chairman BLOOM. Thank you very much, Rabbi. What is the pleasure of the committee?

We shall return at 2:30 this afternoon and the witnesses that were called this morning will return at that time.

(Thereupon, at 1:30 p. m., a recess was taken until 2:30 p. m., of the same day.)

The committee reconvened at 2:30 p. m., pursuant to the taking of a recess.

Chairman BLOOM. The committee will come to order for further consideration of House Resolutions 418–419.

We have before the committee at the present time Representative Bates, of Massachusetts, who desires to make a statement. Proceed, Mr. Bates.

STATEMENT OF HON. GEORGE J. BATES, A REPRESENTATIVE IN CONGRESS FROM THE STATE OF MASSACHUSETTS

Mr. BATES. Mr. Chairman, as to this resolution before the committee at least its language is not new to me. For a period of over 20 years the question of the establishment of a Jewish homeland in Palestine has been continually before the legislative bodies of which I have been a member.

I well recall back in 1919 as a member of the General Court of Massachusetts when we had a resolution presented to us relative to the establishment of a Jewish homeland in Palestine and the protection of Jewish rights and liberties in the settlement of the European war. That resolution was overwhelmingly adopted in February of that year.

I submit that resolution to the committee so it can be made a matter of record.

(The resolution above referred to is as follows:)

THE COMMONWEALTH OF MASSACHUSETTS, IN THE YEAR ONE THOUSAND NINE HUNDRED AND NINETEEN

RESOLUTIONS

Relative to the establishment of a Jewish homeland in Palestine and the protection of Jewish rights and liberties in the settlement of the European war.

Whereas the future prosperity and peace of the world depend upon a just settlement of the European war whereby every nationality, however small, shall be granted the right to determine its own destiny and the opportunity of living its own life; and

Whereas the Government of the United States is recognized as an ardent exponent of the rights of the small nations; therefore, be it

Resolved, That, in the opinion of the House of Representatives of the Commonwealth of Massachusetts, the national aspirations and historic claims of the Jewish people with regard to Palestine should be recognized at the peace conference, and that, in accordance with the British Government's declaration of November 2, 1917, there should be established such political, administrative, and economic conditions in Palestine as will assure the development of Palestine into a Jewish commonwealth, and that the American representatives at the peace conference should use their best endeavors to accomplish this object; and be it further

Resolved, That, in the opinion of the House of Representatives of Massachusetts, express provision should be made at the peace conference for granting to the Jewish people in every land the complete enjoyment of life and liberty, and the opportunities for national development, to the end that justice may be done to that people which, in the long course of history, has suffered more than any other on earth; and be it further

Resolved, That a copy of these resolutions be transmitted by the Secretary of Commonwealth to the President of the United States.

In House of Representatives, adopted, February 13, 1919.

A true copy. Attest:

ALBERT P. LANGTRY,
Secretary of the Commonwealth.

Mr. Bates. Subsequent to that time in 1922 while still a member of the legislature of that State other similar resolutions approving the Balfour Declaration were approved by the general court. Also there was a resolution adopted by the general court in May 1939.

Mr. Johnson. Mr. Chairman, I did not get what it was, a general what?

Mr. Bates. A General Court of Massachusetts which is the legislature.

Mr. Johnson. The legislature you call a general court?

Mr. Bates. It is called a general court in Massachusetts.

Mr. Johnson. Oh, I see.

Mr. Bates. And on May 11, 1939, another resolution memorializing relative to the Jewish national home in Palestine was adopted by the General Court of Massachusetts in that year.

I offer that resolution for the record.

Chairman Bloom. Without objection the resolutions referred to by Mr. Bates will be made a part of the record.

(The resolution above referred to is as follows:)

The Commonwealth of Massachusetts in the Year One Thousand Nine Hundred and Thirty-Nine

RESOLUTIONS MEMORIALIZING CONGRESS RELATIVE TO THE JEWISH NATIONAL HOME IN PALESTINE

Whereas recognition has been given by the nations of the world to the historical connection of the Jewish people with Palestine and to the grounds for reconstituting their national home in that country; and

Whereas the United States of America has given its approval to the reestabl shment of the Jewish national home in Palestine as embodied in a resolution adopted by the Congress of the United States known as the Lodge resolution; and

Whereas, the General Court of Massachusetts deplores the persecution of peoples in any land based upon racial bigotry and religious intolerance and has on previous occasions expressed its sympathetic interest in the Jewish national aspirations; therefore be it

Resolved, That the General Court of Massachusetts expresses its concern in the welfare of the Jewish national home and its admiration of the progress made in Palestine by the efforts of the Jewish pioneers;

That it is inspiring to behold an ancient people return to the land of its origin for the purpose of being able to live its own life, to develop their own culture and civilization and to mold its national destiny; and

That it views with favor the achievements of the Jewish pioneers in Palestine where opportunities were created for tens of thousands of Jews to return to the land of their fathers as of right and not on sufferance; and be it further

Resolved, That the United States of America be and is respectfully solicited to use its good offices for the purpose of safeguarding the integrity of the Balfour Declaration and the interest of the Jewish national home, in accordance with the terms of the Palestine mandate, and to the end that the doors of Palestine may be opened for the purpose of admitting the homeless Jewish victims of racial bigotry and religious intolerance, where they may find the opportunity of rebuilding their broken lives; and be it further

Resolved, That copies of these resolutions be forwarded by the secretary of the Commonwealth, to the President of the United States, to the Vice President of the United States, to the Speaker of the House of Representatives, and to the Representatives in Congress from this Commonwealth.

In Senate, adopted, May 1, 1939.

Irving N. Hayden, Clerk.

In House of Representatives, adopted, in concurrence, May 12, 1939.

Lawrence R. Grove, Clerk.

[STATE SEAL]

A true copy] Attest:

F. W. Cook,
Secretary of the Commonwealth.

Mr. Bates. This thing, as I say, down through many years, has been a pretty live question with some of us who have been continually in public life during that period of time, and the hope and the aspirations of the Jewish people throughout the world have been uppermost in the minds of all people who believe in human rights and the right to live, and of course we are entirely in sympathy with the Jewish people and the plight they find themselves in throughout the world today.

And from those thoughts I have been able to pursue and gain some idea showing the results of the migration of Jews to Palestine down through the past 15 or 20 years, and apparently they have done a remarkable job throughout that era.

Generally, I am in sympathy, and I believe the feeling of every Member of Congress is, with the aspirations of the Jews in this respect.

I want to simply be recorded in favor of the reaffirmation of the acts of the Congress in 1922 as enunciated in the Fish-Lodge resolution that everything be done that can possibly be done to see to it that the Jews be given the right to go to Palestine and to continue their migration to build up that area and live in peace.

That is my position in the matter, Mr. Chairman.

Chairman Bloom. We will now hear from Representative Thomas D'Alesandro, Jr.

STATEMENT OF HON. THOMAS D'ALESANDRO, Jr., A REPRESENTATIVE IN CONGRESS FROM THE STATE OF MARYLAND

Mr. D'Alesandro. Mr. Chairman, I favor the Wright-Compton resolution as I have always objected to persecution of any kind, and I feel that our country must take the leadership in this matter and that Palestine must be kept open as a haven to the Jewish people.

In 1922 we passed the Balfour Declaration. Great Britain was given the mandate by the League of Nations. It promised the Jewish people a national homeland. Some fifty-odd nations constituted the League. This promise must be kept. The covenant must be respected.

The bleeding children of Israel have no place to lay their heads. How can we in America stand by without sounding a mighty protest that will be heard around the world, should the doors of Palestine be closed next April. Several years ago I cabled Neville Chamberlain that England must keep its sacred covenant.

The Wright-Compton resolution must be passed, and I urge favorable action by your committee so that the stricken, bleeding, homeless refugees may be saved. There is one country which was designated by the nations of the world after the last World War as the national home for the Jewish people—that country is Palestine, the land of their forefathers.

Chairman Bloom. Rabbi William H. Fineshriber.

STATEMENT OF RABBI WILLIAM H. FINESHRIBER, D. D., PHILADELPHIA, PA.

Chairman Bloom. Rabbi, you are from Philadelphia, are you not?
Dr. Fineshriber. I am, sir.
Chairman Bloom. You may be seated if you would prefer it.
Dr. Fineshriber. Thank you.

Chairman BLOOM. Will you kindly give a little more detail about yourself and who you represent and the synagogue you represent?

Dr. FINESHRIBER. I am a rabbi of the Reform Congregation of the Temple Keneseth Israel of Philadelphia, Pa.

I do not speak for any organization though I am connected with a number of organizations.

I come here because I feel very keenly the gravity of the situation, and I want to contribute what I have in order that it may help to at least a partial solution of one of the most difficult problems we have had to face in many years.

Chairman BLOOM. Rabbi, kindly keep your voice up.

Dr. FINESHRIBER. I come to you as a spiritual leader of my people, to lay before you my views in regard to the resolutions that are here being deliberated. I come, in particular, to protest, as earnestly as is in my power, against that section of your resolution which speaks of the "Jewish people" constituting a so-called Jewish commonwealth.

I confess that I may not quite understand what that means, so alien is it to my thinking as a teacher of Judaism, so bizarre is it to a preacher of God's truth. Palestine, a "Jewish commonwealth." Does this mean that all of the citizens of the "commonwealth" will become Jews, just as we are Americans by virtue of being citizens of the United States of America? Does it mean that Jews outside of that so-called "Jewish commonwealth" shall, thereafter, cease to be Jews just as those not native or citizens of this country are not Americans? Or does it mean some confused mixed pattern, unlike anything else in the world political order, a bewildering intermixture tending to make Jews an abnormal group, a riddle to the rest of the world?

What strange experiment is here being considered, when the simple, the humane, the urgent task is to help rescue people, to help extend freedom of opportunity?

What is this puzzling attempt to "reconstitute a Jewish commonwealth", if it does not mean setting back the clock 2,000 years? For there was such a commonwealth up to about 2,000 years ago, a state like other states, only smaller and perhaps more helpless.

That nation had its own language, its own authorities, its own political development. And it went the way of all nations. It had its beginning, it had its flowering, it had its decline. During its history it went through all of the vicissitudes, normal to man's political structures. It conquered. It was in turn conquered more than once. It laid tribute upon others; it, in turn, paid tribute to other countries. It fought wars, it had internal strife, civil war, dissensions, political upheavals, until finally the enmity of its neighbors swept over it and the Jewish nation was obliterated.

One thing only survived; one thing that being greater than a nation ever is, could hope to endure through the millenia that followed. For from among the people living in that land of Palestine a vision emerged that gradually took form as a great religion. From this land came the vision of the oneness of God and, consonant with that, the eternal brotherhood of man. Out of those people came, first, the Ten Commandments as a guide to conduct, and later the exhortations of prophets and rabbis. And those prophets gave voice to eternal truths. In our own literature, later to be known as the Bible, there was the admonition, "Thy shall love thy neighbor as thyself" (Leviticus 19: 18) of which Rabbi Akiba said: "This is a fundamental principle of religion." The prophets of that Bible spoke of a vision of peace when "the lion shall lie down with the lamb." The great Rabbi Hillel said: "Whatever is hateful unto thee, do it not unto thy fellow. This is the whole law, the rest is but commentary." And the great prophet Micah gave the essence of our faith when he said: "What doth the Lord require of thee? Only to do justly, and to love mercy, and to walk humbly with thy God."

It is, of course, true that much of the Jewish religion, going back to its ancient cradle in Zion, has local characteristics. But as the years proceeded those local qualities were transmuted and given a wider spiritual interpretation. They have become symbolic, as religion must be, of man's eternal quest for the true and the good and the holy.

From these deep spiritual wells there gushed forth a great religion, a world-wide, a universal religion. It gave birth to a daughter religion, Christianity, which has since enriched the Western World. It profoundly influenced still another manifestation of the divine in the religion of the Moslems.

The religion of the Jews, Judaism, has survived and has sustained its adherents through centuries of religious conflict and hostility, through trial and agony, through persecution and exile. It is a faith by which men have known how to die; it is a faith by which men have lived and can hope to live the good life. It is today the touchstone of those who call themselves Jews. There is no other.

Will you now take it upon yourself to turn the block back to divert that ancient and universal faith into secular channels, into the channels of nationalism?

All this is premised on the proposition that the Jews are a nation or a nationality.

What are the elements that make for nationality or nationhood? A common language, common folkways, customs, laws, social traditions, and a land on which the nationals have lived continuously for generations. We Jews possess few of these characteristics. We have no common language. Hebrew is spoken as a living tongue only by Jews in Palestine, and that only within recent years. Five million Jews in America speak English; French Jews speak French. When there were Jews in Germany they spoke German. Millions speak Russian, Polish, Yiddish, Spanish, Portuguese, Italian, Turkish, Arabic, and so forth. Hebrew is the language of prayer.

We have no folkways and customs common to all Jews. Since the destruction of the second commonwealth we have been nationals of various countries and have adopted the customs and manners of the land in which we lived, even when we were immured in ghettos. The folkways of Jews in northern Africa differ widely from those in Poland or India or Russia. There is no such thing as a Jewish culture or Jewish civilization. There are Jewish cultures if by culture we mean the complex of ways of life.

There is no such thing as Jewish sculpture or painting, and I have had no convincing proof that there is a specific Jewish music.

(Discussion off the record, after which the following occurred.) And there has been no Jewish land for 2,000 years. How then can we speak of a Jewish nation?

What is the link that binds us? The answer is on every page of our history. Religion is this tie that binds us. We have a common religious tradition, a common origin and common suffering.

The Friends or Quakers have had a similar experience. Can we speak of a Quaker nation? Our enemies speak of us as a nation, hoping thereby to insinuate the idea of alienism, and it seems to me stark tragedy that Jews under the impact of fear and panic should adopt the language of anti-Semitism.

What do you think was the force that kept Israel alive during all the 2,000 years of torment and suffering? Was it the passionate attachment to a land they have never seen or lived in? Do you think that Jewish Americans, Jewish Russians, Jewish Britains, Jewish Frenchmen, Jewish Hollanders in the muck of the South Seas are dying or fighting for Palestine? They are fighting for their homelands in which they and their ancestors were born, lands in which they have lived for centuries animated by faith in a God of justice and mercy who had been revealed to them by their religion.

When Jews prayed and today pray for restoration to Jerusalem, mark you, Jerusalem, not Palestine, they pray not because of an impelling Jewish national consciousness desirous of fulfillment in a Jewish State, but because Jerusalem and Zion are symbols of our faith. It is a devout religious aspiration, a simple yearning for communion with the source of our spiritual strength. For from Zion shall go forth the Law and the Word of God from Jerusalem. The Law and the Word of God are synonymous.

I know that in a period of great strain and stress and emotional confusion, under the pressure of tragedy, there is always the inclination to raise a hue and cry for false gods. But do not for a moment suppose that in the quiet of our hearts we have anything to hold us together but our ancient faith. The very messages you have received supporting this resolution, out of the compassionate concern for our fellow Jews, no doubt speak to you in the name of "Americans of Jewish faith." Ask your Jewish fellow citizen in this room, or anywhere in the wide expanse of our beloved country, ask him what his religion is. His answer will be: "I am of the Jewish faith." Ask him what his nationality is. And he will speak with justified pride in the world's greatest title: "I am an American."

This being so, I pray that no act of yours, no act of the American people whom you represent, will entangle this crystal-clear concept of a religion with secular, political complexities of a state or commonwealth.

And just as I turn to you with a profound appeal not to let this wrong be done, so I turn to you with equal fervor to plead that you give expression to the purpose of the first part of the resolution.

The doors of Palestine threaten to be shut to Jews as Jews. Our great ally has, alas, under the pressure of darker circumstances, permitted discrimination against Jews who seek to enter Palestine and acquire land there. Your voice may well have a determining influence. Your clear expression against discrimination may make all the difference.

The Jews of Europe, and indeed all the world over, are going through a nightmare. It will not fully be lifted until the powers of tyranny and brutality will have been utterly laid low. God alone knows how many will survive the systematic extermination which has been planned for them. Those who have survived must not be further shamed by the spectacle of a great democracy raising barriers against them as Jews and of its great ally, the United States, standing by without protest.

I am no prophet, nor son of a prophet. I do not know the shape of things to come. It is my hope and prayer that after the war the free world for which we are fighting will be a freer world than we have yet had, and that the remaining Jews of Europe may find equality in the homes from which the invading scourge shall have finally been driven; equality, their one quest, their basic quest.

The first part of your resolution is consistent with the spirit of the statement by that great American, our Secretary of State, the Honorable Cordell Hull, who said that we must have a world in which Jews, like all others, "are free to abide in peace and in honor."

By that worthy standard I appeal to you in behalf of the purpose of the first part of the resolution.

I am not in sympathy with the attitude of the Arab world. Palestine must be kept open to free immigration to Jews who have no other place to come. There they will have a home which will be adequate for them, a home which has been prepared for them, and I am glad to pay my tribute of intense admiration to the Zionist organization which has made possible the preparation of that home, and to those Jews not Zionists who have quietly and with humility also contributed to make it possible for them.

But as a teacher of an ancient faith I ask you not to blur the shining luster of that appeal for equality by injecting secular and deeply controversial elements such as are found in the second part of your Resolution.

I thank you.

(Discussion off the record, after which the following occurred:)

Chairman BLOOM. Do I understand, Rabbi, that you would say then that you believe that the mandate and the Convention entered into between the United States and Great Britain should be adhered to to the letter? Is that your contention?

Dr. FINESHRIBER. Mr. Chairman, I do not pose as an expert on international law, nor upon the legality or validity of the Balfour Declaration or of the mandate. I think this question has been sufficiently ventilated by the previous speakers who have been here. I speak only as a rabbi, as a teacher of the Jewish faith.

Chairman BLOOM. I am a little bit out of order. I should ask the other members if they wish to ask questions, but I would like to get this thought clear. You said the first part of the resolution you agreed to?

Dr. FINESHRIBER. Correct.

Chairman BLOOM. That is considered part of the mandate and also of the Convention entered into between the United States and Great Britain?

Dr. FINESHRIBER. Correct.

Chairman BLOOM. Now, would you not say if we had a convention or a treaty, or whatever you want to call it, all of it should be adhered to?

Dr. FINESHRIBER. No, sir; I do not think so.

Chairman BLOOM. You do not?

Dr. FINESHRIBER. I think the second part has very little relation to the first part of this resolution.

Chairman BLOOM. No, I am talking about the Convention between the United States and Great Britain, the Convention signed by President Coolidge in 1925. Would you not say that that, Rabbi, in its entirety should be lived up to by the signatories of that convention?

Dr. FINESHRIBER. I do not so interpret it, if you compel me to answer that question.

Chairman BLOOM. I do not compel you.

Dr. FINESHRIBER. I do not interpret the Balfour Declaration as being the equivalent of a Jewish State in Palestine.

Chairman BLOOM. Whatever is in there, irrespective of that interpretation, we have a mandate and we have a convention, and that mandate is part of that convention. And the two countries agreed to adhere to that because Coolidge signed it as President of the United States for the United States in 1925, and Chamberlain signed it for Great Britain. That was in 1925. Would you not say whatever is in that mandate should be lived up to by the two countries?

Dr. FINESHRIBER. Does not that depend on the last interpretation of the mandate?

Chairman BLOOM. I am not asking you to interpret it. Whatever the two Governments should agree, do you not think the entire paper should be lived up to? I am through if you answer that.

Dr. FINESHRIBER. I think I have answered it.

Chairman BLOOM. And your answer is?

Dr. FINESHRIBER. My answer is it depends upon the many interpretations of the Balfour Declaration and the mandate. Which of those interpretations do you want me to discuss?

Chairman BLOOM. None at all. I take your answer as you gave it. Mr. Johnson?

Mr. JOHNSON. No questions.

Chairman BLOOM. Dr. Eaton?

Dr. EATON. First of all, as a member of this committee I want to express my gratitude to the rabbi for the instruction he has given our chairman on Jewish music. He evidently needed it very badly.

Dr. FINESHRIBER. I am glad to have been helpful to the chairman.

Dr. EATON. And I have a suspicion a good deal of his music would not go in a synagogue.

Secondly—I am not going to question you—I want to express my feeling, and I am sure it is agreeable to every member of our committee including our chairman, of pleasure and satisfaction over the very fine spirit which the rabbi has exhibited here.

I have had something to do in days gone by with the word of God, and I was greatly impressed with your speech. I am afraid if I lived in your neighborhood I would be seduced to come and hear you preach occasionally.

Dr. FINESHRIBER. I am very grateful to you.

(Discussion off the record, after which the following occurred:)

Chairman BLOOM. Mr. Jarman?

Mr. JARMAN. No questions, Mr. Chairman.

Chairman BLOOM. Mr. Chiperfield?

Mr. CHIPERFIELD. No questions.

Chairman BLOOM. Mr. Burgin?

Mr. BURGIN. No questions.

Chairman BLOOM. Mr. Vorys?

Mr. VORYS. No questions.

Chairman BLOOM. Mr. Rogers?

Mr. Rogers. Well, sir, I came in a little late. Was your disagreement with this resolution the word "commonwealth"? If it happened to have been the word "homeland" would you similarly have felt it should not be passed?

Dr. Fineshriber. No, I object to the words "Jewish commonwealth." I have no objections to the Palestine commonwealth being formed, but I object to the words "Jewish commonwealth."

Mr. Rogers. How would you feel about the words "Jewish homeland"?

Dr. Fineshriber. It is a very ambiguous term.

Mr. Rogers. Yes; I know.

Dr. Fineshriber. That is the difficulty about it.

For example, you speak of a Jewish homeland. Is not America a Jewish homeland for a great many Jews?

Mr. Rogers. I understood the words "Jewish homeland" had a religious connotations and had been used in previous documents and that it might be a satisfactory solution to getting the groups together.

Dr. Fineshriber. I do not know of any document prior to the document of the Balfour Declaration in which the phrase "Jewish homeland" was used. My own feeling about the matter was that was an ambiguous term consciously devised.

Mr. Rogers. Then you would have the same opposition even if it included the words "Jewish homeland" instead of the word "commonwealth"?

Dr. Fineshriber. Even greater oppostion. I prefer the words "Palestine commonwealth" to either "Jewish homeland" or "Jewish commonwealth."

Mr. Rogers. No more questions.

Chairman Bloom. Mr. Stearns?

Mr. Stearns. No questions.

Chairman Bloom. Mr. Wright?

Mr. Wright. No questions.

Chairman Bloom. Mrs. Bolton?

Mrs. Bolton. No questions.

Chairman Bloom. Mr. Wadsworth? I did not see you, Mr. Jonkman.

Mr. Jonkman. That is all right. I have no questions.

Mr. Wadsworth. Rabbi, you have undoubtedly studied the Balfour Declaration, the Mandate, the convention and the background and history of this whole movement?

Dr. Fineshriber. Yes.

Mr. Wadsworth. Can you identify or point out, rather, the use of the term "Jewish commonwealth" has ever been in any of the official documents up to this point?

Dr. Fineshriber. I do not think so.

The word "commonwealth" was introduced into the famous Biltmore organization meeting of the Zionists organization of America in the Biltmore Hotel in New York, and they used the word "commonwealth" because they were a little afraid of using the word "State" at that time. There had been a good deal of opposition on the part of the Zionists themselves to the use of the words "Jewish State," and they decided to use the word "commonwealth."

Mr. Wadsworth. I was going to ask the difference.

Dr. Fineshriber. Personally, I have never seen any difference.

Mr. WADSWORTH. You referred to its first use at a conference held at the Hotel Biltmore. I meant has it been used in any of the official communications, treaties or declarations?

Dr. FINESHRIBER. Not to my knowledge.

Mr. WADSWORTH. Up to this point?

Dr. FINESHRIBER. Not to my knowledge.

Mr. WADSWORTH. Am I far wrong in saying if it was included in this resolution it is the first time used by a governmental body?

Dr. FINESHRIBER. The phrase "Jewish commonwealth"?

Mr. WADSWORTH. That is right.

Dr. FINESHRIBER. I think so.

Mr. WRIGHT. Mr. Wadsworth, the phrase was used by Lloyd George in his testimony before the Royal Commission. Of course, that is not an official declaration.

Mr. WADSWORTH. Of course, I would like to see the context as to that.

Mr. WRIGHT. Here it is. You might want to read it.

Dr. FINESHRIBER. To my mind they are synonymous.

Mr. WADSWORTH. Mr. Lloyd George, giving evidence before the Royal Commission, said:

The idea was, and this was * * * that a Jewish state was not to be set up immediately by the peace treaty, without reference to the wishes of the majority of the inhabitants. On the other hand, it was contemplated that, when the time arrived for according representative institutions to Palestine, if the Jews had meanwhile responded to the opportunity afforded them by the idea of a national home and had become a definite majority of the inhabitants, then Palestine would thus become a Jewish commonwealth.

Mr. WRIGHT. May I also refer on page 89 to what President Wilson stated on March 3, 1919? I have it underlined.

Mr. WADSWORTH. With that suggestion of Mr. Lloyd George you are not in agreement?

Dr. FINESHRIBER. As to what?

Mr. WADSWORTH. I mean what I have just read to you?

Dr. FINESHRIBER. What was the particular point? I do not remember.

Mr. WADSWORTH. On the other hand, it was contemplated—

I suppose he is referring to the Balfour Declaration—

that, when the time arrived for according representative institutions to'Palestine, if the Jews had meanwhile responded to the opportunity afforded them by the idea of a national home and had become a definite majority of the inhabitants, then Palestine would thus become a Jewish commonwealth.

Dr. FINESHRIBER. I am not in agreement with that point of view.

Mr. WADSWORTH. Why?

Dr. FINESHRIBER. I am not in favor of a Jewish commonwealth at any time. I am in favor, however, if I may express msyelf, Mr. Chairman, ladies and gentlemen——

Chairman BLOOM (interposing). Yes, please do. The floor is yours.

Dr. FINESHRIBER. May I? I am in favor of free immigration of Jews into Palestine. I, personally, am not concerned as to whether they have a majority or not. And the reason I think so is because I have a rather radical suggestion to make in reference to the solution of this problem.

May I be permitted to state it?

Chairman Bloom. Please do.

Dr. Fineshriber. I am convinced that the position of the Zionists of the world will not change. I am equally convinced that the position of the Arabs in opposition to a Jewish state or commonwealth will not change. One of the reasons why I agree also the reconstitution of the Jewish commonwealth is not wise is because I fear the effect upon the Jewish people in Palestine to say nothing of the repercussion against the rest of the Jews in the rest of the world. I anticipate bloodshed and destruction of much of the things worth while that have been achieved. They, I think, are in inevitable conflict, and so I have been thinking for sometime as to how we can manage to get away from this dilemma.

My suggestion, as I say, is radical and it may be thoroughly impractical. Why not constitute all of Palestine into a Holy Land which neither the Jews nor the Arabs shall dominate politically? After all Palestine is a Holy Land to Jews, Christians, and Moslems. It is one of the great historic places of the world. We have set aside historic places of that kind not dominated by any particular group, religious or political. The District of Columbia is a place set aside in which inhabitants have no vote. It is controlled politically by, I believe, a commission of Congress.

The Vatican is another place set aside by Italy with, I believe, the tacit accord of the rest of the world into a holy place. Why cannot we do that with Palestine and thereby avoid the horrible destruction and pain and suffering I am afraid will come inevitably if we allow either of those groups to dominate? Then as many Jews as possible may come into the land to develop it. Then the Jews will develop their talents to the greatest possible extent. After all a political domination will be of no avail to them and they may emphasize their religious and spiritual powers.

In my interpretation of Jewish history I find Jews have been great in that and in that alone. We have had men of great talent who have made amazing contributions to all forms of civilized life, but it has never been unique. In the realm of philosophy we have had a great number of philosophers, but it cannot be said we are a people that develop philosophies. There are many non-Jewish philosophers greater than we have produced. We have a great many Jewish scientists that have done much for the world. It cannot be said our greatest scientists are Jews. Our talents are spiritual things. That is what we have done.

Take the literature of Judaism throughout the ages and there are thousands upon thousands of volumes written by Jews, not only the Bible, but the great Talmud, and the Babylonian Talmud is the one they follow, and not the Palestinian as to their great code of laws. The tremendous bulk of Jewish literature has been religious. That leads me to the conclusion that our talents are in this specific channel.

I say to you even if we constitute a Jewish state there it will be a little state. Do you think that will save the Jews of Palestine and of the world from pain and suffering simply because there is a little state there? Zionists say by that means we create dignity and give the Jews self-respect.

If by any mischance—God forbid—there should be a kind of pogrom in America or anywhere in the world do you think that the appeal or protest of the Jewish ambassador is going to make the slightest difference? Do you think the chancelors of Europe will tremble when the little Jewish state in Palestine will threaten?

And that is why I say, ladies and gentlemen, it would be wise if we can devise a plan whereby this terrible threat of political domination could be removed from the scene. And that is why I suggest, which may be fantastic, let the land of Israel be Holy Land to all the world. Let refugees of all kinds and faiths go there and let political matters be vested in the United Nations of the world.

And let us not forget in our great emphasis upon Palestine even at its best or its highest it can contain only a few Jews. Dr. Weizmann prays for 2,000,000 to occupy Palestine. There are still 14,000,000 left. Should we not give some consideration to the possible chance for the Jews' status elsewhere in the world? I wish it were possible to have a united Jewish world. It might have been possible a little while ago, but some men decided against it. To me that is tragedy.

Chairman BLOOM. Thank you very much.

Mr. CHIPERFIELD. What do you mean by that last statement?

Dr. FINESHRIBER. I mean this: There was called into being an organization called the American Jewish Conference. It should have been a real representative gathering of all kinds of Jews no matter what their political views or their religious views may be. It did not so eventuate. The Zionist Organization of America, which is a very powerful organization, dominated the scene, and among them some men had the power to insist upon the adoption of that one platform; namely, to reconstitute a Jewish state in Palestine. If that would have been omitted all the Jews in America would have been united. There would have been no opposition whatever. We missed that opportunity. I consider that one of the great tragedies of history.

Chairman BLOOM. Are there any further questions?

Is it the wish of the committee to go down and answer the roll call and then come back?

(Discussion off the record, after which the following occurred:)

Chairman BLOOM. We will recess for 10 or 15 minutes.

Thank you very much, Rabbi.

Dr. FINESHRIBER. I appreciate the courtesy, Mr. Chairman.

(The committee then recessed because of a vote on the floor of the House.)

AFTER RECESS

Chairman BLOOM. The committee will resume its discussion of H. R. 418 and 419.

Before calling the next witness, we have Members of Congress here who would like to be heard.

Mr. Marcantonio, Representative from New York, the floor is yours, sir.

STATEMENT OF THE HONORABLE VITO MARCANTONIO, A REPRESENTATIVE FROM THE STATE OF NEW YORK

Mr. MARCANTONIO. Mr. Chairman and members of the committee, I would like to state for the record that I wholeheartedly recommend the adoption of this resolution and do hope that the committee will act on it speedily. I deem that this is a most realistic approach to this whole problem. There is no question of imperialism involved; there is no question of trampling upon the rights of any other people at all. The problem can be worked out amicably between existing people in that territory if the leading nations of the world take a hand in it, cooperate in it, support it.

I am confident there will be the minimum of friction if the leading nations of the world go into this thing with a full desire to bring about the solution as set forth in the House Resolutions 418 and 419, and I hope the committee will act upon them as speedily as possible.

Chairman BLOOM. Mr. Klein, do you wish to make a statement?

Mr. ARTHUR G. KLEIN (Member of Congress from New York). No. I have made my position clear.

Chairman BLOOM. Are there any other Members of the House here, who wish to be heard? (None.)

For the record, in case we adjourn before he gets here, I would like to mention the fact that Representative Sabath, of Illinois, wishes to be recorded as in favor of the resolution also.

Mr. Herman Schulman is next. Mr. Schulman, would you kindly give your name, address, and whom you represent?

STATEMENT OF HERMAN SHULMAN, MEMBER, EXECUTIVE COMMITTEE, AMERICAN ZIONIST EMERGENCY COUNCIL, STAMFORD, CONN.

Mr. SHULMAN. My full name is Herman Shulman. I am from Stamford, Conn. I am a member of the executive committee of the American Zionist Emergency Council; also a member of the interim and administrative committees of the American Jewish Conference.

I come here on my own behalf to present some views concerning the proposed resolutions and to speak in support of House Resolutions 418 and 419. I had intended, Mr. Chairman, to devote the few minutes allotted to me to a brief discussion of two aspects of the resolution before the committee; (1) what is meant by a "free and democratic Jewish commonwealth," and (2) why the two parts of the resolution are inseparable, each part being definitely dependent upon the other.

As a result of the pertinent question asked by Representative Wadsworth, Mr. Neumann did answer the first question; namely, What do we mean by a "free and democratic Jewish commonwealth"? I therefore shall not take up your time to discuss that issue, except to say that I identify myself completely with the definition which he has already given you.

Now with respect to the second question, the resolution asks that the doors of Palestine shall be open for free entry of Jews into that country, and that there shall be full opportunity for colonization, so that the Jewish people may ultimately reconstitute Palestine as a free and democratic Jewish commonwealth.

Now, ladies and gentlemen of the committee, what in my humble judgment is asked for is a reaffirmation of an established policy. What is asked for is the full and speedy implementation of the underlying intent and purpose of the Balfour Declaration and the mandate. What was the original intent and purpose of the Balfour Declaration at the time when it was issued?

Fortunately I have before me the report of the Palestine Royal Commission of July 1937, the commission which was headed by the late Lord Peel. That question was examined into by the royal commission. They took testimony on that subject and made certain findings, which I should like to read to you.

Mr. JOHNSON of Texas. May I ask the date of the instrument you are going to read?

Mr. SHULMAN. July, 1937.

I am reading now from paragraph 20 on page 24 of that report. "We must now consider what the Balfour Declaration meant." They then proceeded to give the answer. Mr. Lloyd George, who was Prime Minister at the time, informed us in evidence that:

The idea was, and this was the interpretation put upon it at the time—

("it" meaning, of course, the Balfour Declaration)—

that a Jewish state was not to be set up immediately by the peace treaty without reference to the wishes of the majority of the inhabitants. On the other hand, it was contemplated that when the time arrived for according representative institutions to Palestine, if the Jews had meanwhile responded to the opportunity afforded them by the idea of a national home, and had become a definite majority of the inhabitants, then Palestine would thus become a Jewish commonwealth.

The Royal Commission then reached the following conclusion:

Thus His Majesty's Government evidently realized that a Jewish state might, in the course of time, be established, but it was not in a position to say that that would happen, still less to bring it about of its own motion. The Zionist leaders, for their part, recognized that an ultimate Jewish state was not precluded by the terms of the declaration, and so it was understood elsewhere.

"I am persuaded," said President Wilson, on the 3d of March 1919, "that the Allied Nations with the fullest concurrence of our own Government and people are agreed that in Palestine shall be laid the foundation of a Jewish commonwealth."

General Smuts, who had been a member of the Imperial War Cabinet when the Declaration was published, speaking at Johannesburg on the 3d of November 1919, foretold an increasing stream of Jewish immigration into Palestine and "in generations to come a great Jewish state arising there once more."

Lord Robert Cecil, in 1917, Sir Herbert Samuel, in 1919, and Mr. Winston Churchill, in 1920, spoke or wrote in terms that could only mean that they contemplated the eventual establishment of a Jewish state.

These were the findings made by the Royal Commission after reviewing the testimony before it on the meaning and intent of the Balfour Declaration. The report then goes on to say:

The leading British newspapers were equally explicit in their comments on the Declaration.

Mr. Wadsworth asked one of the witnesses whether he knew of any official document in which the term "Jewish commonwealth" was used. Answering that question, I should like to say that, in addition to the documents I have already referred to, Chief Justice Hughes, then Secretary of State Hughes, also used the term "Jewish commonwealth" in his correspondence with the British Government concerning the 1925 convention.

Chairman BLOOM. Would you mind an interruption? Could you go on to something else and wait until Mr. Wadsworth returns? You can then give him the benefit of that.

We will return to that when Mr. Wadsworth returns.

Mr. SHULMAN. I shall be glad to do that, but at this point I should like to refer to another finding of the Royal Commission which has a bearing on a statement made by Mr. Mundt on either the first or second day of these hearings. Mr. Mundt at that time intimated that statements made by Mr. Churchill in 1922 contradicted certain prior statements made by him concerning the meaning and intent of the Balfour Declaration. The Royal Commission also dealt with Mr. Churchill's statements as contained in his 1922 Declaration of Policy. Mr. Churchill testified before the Royal Commission on the subject. After hearing his testimony the Royal Commission concluded that nothing which Mr. Churchill said in 1922 was intended to preclude the establishment of a Jewish commonwealth in accordance with the original intent and purpose of the Balfour Declaration. In this connection the Royal Commission said (par. 39, p. 33 of its report):

> This definition of the National Home (the definition contained in the 1922 Declaration of Policy) has sometimes been taken to preclude the establishment of a Jewish state. But, though the phraseology was clearly intended to conciliate, as far as might be, Arab antagonism to the National Home, there is nothing in it to prohibit the ultimate establishment of a Jewish state and Mr. Churchill himself has told us in evidence that no such prohibition was intended.

I say, therefore, Mr. Chairman and ladies and gentlemen of the committee, what we are asking for is a reaffirmation of what was promised the Jewish people 25 years ago and it is entirely just and proper that we should ask it at this particular time. The Jewish people were the beneficiaries of the promise made by 52 nations of the world. We today are in a sense the trustees of that promise. It is our task to see to it that that promise is fully implemented and to do everything in our power to aid in its speedy fulfillment. It is just and proper, therefore, that we should at this time, when the terms of the peace are in the making, when many groups are presenting their just claims, when conferences and discussions are going on continuously concerning the formation of an Arab federation, that we ask the nations of the world to fulfill the promise made to the Jewish people in accordance with its underlying intent and purpose.

When we ask you, as we do, to pass this resolution, we are asking you again to do no more than you have done heretofore. It has been the traditional American policy to favor the full implementation of the Balfour Declaration. It has already been pointed out that every successive administration since the adoption of the 1922 joint resolution has favored that policy, and I might at this point bring to your attention a declaration which was issued November 2, 1942, on the occasion of the twenty-fifth anniversary of the Balfour Declaration. It was a statement called "A Traditional American Policy Reaffirmed." This statement was signed by 68 Members of the Senate and 194 Members of the House of Representatives of the Seventy-seventh Congress. Among those who signed the statement were 18 members of the Foreign Relations Committee of the Senate. I am also happy to say that many members of this committee, including Representative Bolton, Representative Jonkman, Representative Mundt, Representative Pfeifer, Representative Rogers, Representative Vorys, Representative Wright, and Representative Wadsworth also signed this declaration.

That statement, after reviewing the 1922 joint resolution, declares:

> The Balfour Declaration was justly hailed throughout the world as an act of historic reparation and as a charter of freedom for the Jewish people. It was designed to open the gates of Palestine to homeless and harassed multitudes and to pave the way for the establishment of a Jewish commonwealth.

It then proceeds to speak of the tragic plight of the Jewish people, and indicates clearly that the need for the reestablishment of that commonwealth is a thousandfold greater today, and concludes with the statement—

Our Government may be assured that in continuing the traditional American policy in favor of so just a cause, it can rely upon our individual support and the approbation of the American people.

I think, Mr. Chairman, it might be helpful if I file this statement, because I cannot begin to tell you what hope and what courage the issuance of that statement brought to the Jews of this country and to Jews everywhere.

Chairman Bloom. There were no riots after that statement?

Mr. Shulman. There were no riots after that statement, and it was widely publicized throughout the Near East. Despite all the predictions that if the Crimean laws were reinstated there would be riots and revolts, there were also no riots after these laws were reinstated.

The fact of the matter is, Mr. Chairman, that the military situation in the Near East has improved so considerably, that what the Arabs are concerned with today is to press their own claims, and a day hardly passes without some reference in some newspaper to some proposal for an Arab federation.

Is it just and proper that at this time, when the terms of the peace are in the making, that we ask this Government again to reaffirm its traditional American policy? And may I remind you that the Balfour Declaration itself was issued during the midst of World War I. The statesmen then did not wait then until after the war to issue that declaration, and it was issued, as Mr. Neumann has already pointed out, only after open consultation with our Government and with other governments.

Now, Mr. Chairman, I say that this resolution must be adopted as a whole, because whatever rights we have to the free entry of Jews into Palestine and to the full opportunity for colonization in that country rest upon the fact that as a result of the decision made some 25 years ago the Jews of the world were given a special right, a privileged position with respect to that particular part of the world. Our rights there rest not, as some of the witnesses have said, because there should be no discrimination against Jews because of their religion. Of course it is unthinkable that Jews will be denied the right to enter their own national home because of their religion. But the right of the Jews to go to Palestine rests upon the fact that 25 years ago it was determined, after weighing all the equities of the case, that the Jews as a people were entitled to settle in Palestine and to reconstitute their national home there. By virtue of that decision they were given the right to enter Palestine freely and the right to insist that that opportunity be continued.

Once you remove the basis for that right, namely, the decision which was made at that time to permit the Jews to reestablish their national home there, then the whole structure falls.

Chairman Bloom. Mr. Shulman, I see that Mr. Wadsworth is here.

Mr. Wadsworth, Mr. Shulman was answering the question you asked the previous witness, so it was requested that he withhold his answer until you returned, so that you could hear his answer.

Mr. WADSWORTH. I shall not interrupt his testimony. I can read it afterward.

Chairman BLOOM. He has not stated it yet. He is going to state it now.

Mr. SHULMAN. Mr. Wadsworth, I shall not go over that again. I shall merely point out that I was reading from the findings made by the Royal Commission in 1937, after examining into the question what was the original intent and purpose of the Balfour Declaration. I indicated to the committee that Mr. Lloyd George, the then Prime Minister, Mr. Winston Churchill, and other important witnesses testified before the Royal Commission on that question, and the conclusion of the Royal Commission was that the original intent and purpose was to afford the Jews an opportunity to create a Jewish state there if, in fact, they become a majority in that country.

I was about to say that the statement of policy of Mr. Winston Churchill of 1922 was also reviewed at that time, and after hearing Mr. Churchill the committee said that "the definition of the national home has sometimes been taken to preclude the establishment of a Jewish state, but though the phraseology was clearly intended to conciliate so far as possible Arab antagonism to the national home, there is nothing in it to prohibit the ultimate establishment of a Jewish state, and Mr. Churchill himself has told us in evidence that no such prohibition was intended."

I might add that the findings of that commission in the main were adopted by the British Government.

I was also about to say, in response to the question which you raised, namely whether there is any official document which speaks of the Jewish commonwealth, that the former Chief Justice, the then Secretary of State of the United States, Charles Evans Hughes, in his correspondence with Great Britain dealing with the 1925 convention, referred to the Jewish commonwealth.

I also quoted before you arrived, Mr. Wadsworth, statements of President Wilson, General Smuts, Lord Robert Cecil, Sir Herbert Samuel, and Mr. Winston Churchill. That will all be found in this report which I shall introduce as evidence, Mr. Chairman.

Mr. Smuts said, on the 3d of November 1919, there will be "in generations to come a great Jewish state arising there once more."

Now, Mr. Chairman, there were a number of witnesses who indicated that they do not oppose the first part of the resolution, but that they object to the second part of the resolution. The last witness said it did not matter to him whether the Jews became a majority or whether the Arabs constituted a majority in Palestine.

It seems to me that they fail to appreciate what was the opportunity afforded to the Jewish people by the issuance of the Balfour Declaration, and they fail to appreciate that our right to come to this committee and to our Government, and to ask that the Jews be given the right to enter Palestine freely, and a full opportunity for colonization in that country, springs from the fact that the Balfour Declaration gave us a privileged position, a special interest, in that part of the world. Unless we are entitled to establish a Jewish majority in accordance with the original intent and purpose of the Balfour Declaration and to reconstitute our national home in Palestine, it seems to me, sir, that we have no greater right to ask for the free entry of Jews into Palestine than we have a right to ask for the free entry of Jews into this country.

These gentlemen, whether they realize it or not, fail to appreciate that what the Balfour Declaration gave us, was not the same right to emigrate into Palestine as we have to emigrate into any other country, but a special right to reconstitute there our national home. The emphasis is not on the right of the individual Jew, but the right of the Jewish people to reconstitute their national home in Palestine. And when the last witness told you that it mattered not to him whether the Jews were a majority or a minority, or whether or not a self-governing commonwealth was established there with a guaranteed Jewish majority, he does not appreciate what would happen to Jewish immigration into Palestine should an Arab state be established in Palestine.

The Mufti also testified before the Royal Commission, and it might be of interest to you if I read a few questions and answers from his testimony. In the course of his testimony before the Royal Commission the Mufti was questioned as to what the position of the Jews would be in case Arab independence were granted in Palestine, and testified as follows:

Question. If the Arabs had this treaty, they would be pleased to welcome the Jews already in the country?

The MUFTI. That will be left to 'the discretion of the government which will be set up under the treaty, and will be decided by the government on conditions most favorable and most beneficial to the country.

Question. Does His Eminence think that the country can assimilate and digest the 400,000 Jews now in the country?

The MUFTI. No.

Question. What would happen?

The MUFTI. Some of them would have to be removed by a process kindly or painful, as the case may be. We must leave this to the future.

It is also important, Mr. Chairman, to call to your attention the testimony given before the Royal Commission of Auni Bey, the leader of the Arab Independence Party. He testified as follows. His attitude is revealed by the following remarks:

In Germany, 70,000,000 Germans who are cultured and civilized, and have all the necessary means of government, cannot bear 600,000 Jews.

The implication is clear. Palestine cannot bear 400,000 Jews. He then said further:

Frankly speaking, we object to the existence of 400,000 Jews in the country.

The CHAIRMAN. They are not to be driven out, and yet there are too many of them. What happens, then?

AUNI BEY. A large number of them are not Palestinians.

In other words, those who are not Palestinians should be sent out of the country.

The CHAIRMAN. Auni Bey says that he does not want to drive them out, but he says that there are too many, and I want to know how he would reduce them.

AUNI BEY. That is not a question that can be decided here.

Now, Mr. Chairman, those of us who deal in the field of business or in our professions or in the field of government must view this problem from a practical point of view. We surely realize that if there is created a self-government in Palestine, with a guaranteed Arab majority, the national home of the Jewish people would, for all practical purposes, be liquidated. And what is overlooked by these gentlemen who object to the white paper is that it deals not only with stoppage of immigration, with restrictions against the purchase of land, but that there is a third part to that white paper, the constitutional provisions by

the terms of which Great Britain promises to establish a self-government in Palestine with a guaranteed Arab majority in 10 years, in complete violation of the underlying intent and purpose of the Balfour
Declaration.

Now, when we oppose the white paper we must oppose the white
paper in its entirety and all of its provisions, and those provisions
include not only the complete stoppage of immigration by the end of
March, the prohibitions against the purchase of land, but also the
crystallization of the Jewish population in Palestine into a permanent
minority; in other words, to fix their status there as their status is now
fixed in all other parts of the world.

Therefore I say to you that if you really oppose the white paper as
being a clear breach and repudiation of the Balfour Declaration, of
the Palestine mandate, of the 1922 joint resolution unanimously passed
by the Sixty-seventh Congress of the United States, and signed by
the President of the United States, as well as the terms of the 1925
convention between Great Britain and America, then you must oppose
each and every part of the white paper. That means the restrictions
against immigration, the restrictions against the purchase of land by
Jews, and the constitutional provisions, and there must be a continuation of the opportunity afforded to the Jewish people to constitute a
majority there and to reconstitute their commonwealth in their
ancestral home.

Either the decision made at the time of the issuance of the Balfour
Declaration stands or it is repudiated. And surely today there is
every reason why the promise made then should be fully and speedily
performed. The conditions which made imperative the reestablishment of the Jewish homeland over 25 years ago have been intensified
beyond the darkest forbodings. The last hope of millions of homeless
Jews is threatened with extinction. The Jews of Palestine have
demonstrated a constructive capacity which, as Dr. Lowdermilk has
pointed out to you, has converted a derelict area into a progressive
and thriving agricultural and industrial country. Palestine can
absorb most of the homeless and tortured Jews of central and eastern
Europe who may survive the present struggle. Surely every consideration of justice requires that the promise made to the Jewish
people over a quarter of a century ago be fulfilled now as speedily
as possible.

Mr. Chairman, I say, therefore, that the resolution stands as a
whole. Each part is dependent upon the other, and it must be
adopted as a whole. And in adopting this resolution you are doing
no more and no less than to give effect to the original intent and
purpose of the Balfour Declaration at the time when it was issued.

One more word with respect to the testimony of the last two
witnesses. You have heard the last two speakers, Mr. Chairman,
draw a distinction between the Jewish religion and Zionism, which
recognizes that there is a Jewish people, that there exists a historical
connection between the Jewish people and Palestine, and that the
Jewish people are entitled to reconstitute their national home in
Palestine. These witnesses apparently find some inconsistence between their Jewish religion and Zionism.

I should like, Mr. Chairman, to take a minute of your time to read
from an article two paragraphs which have a bearing upon that
subject:

Take my case, and you will pardon, please, the personal reference. I use it only to illustrate and strengthen my point. I was not always a Zionist. I remember to my regret an occasion shortly after I came to Baltimore when I, too, took the position that to be a Jewish nationalist meant to lay one's self open to the charge of dual loyalty. I made the eagle scream one night when Stephen Wise was explaining the meaning of Jewish nationalism.

I trust whatever little service I may have rendered to the Jewish national cause since then has more than made right that wrong.

I became a Zionist when I made contact with the Jewish masses, when I knew intimately the spirit of my people, when I studied more earnestly the needs of my people; above all, when I had achieved the ability to feel emotionally and intellectually with my people. I do not believe I am any less a good citizen. Jewish nationalism does not set itself up as opposed to the Jewish religion, nor the state where the Jew makes his home, but by inculcating definitely, positively, loyalty to Israel, love of Israel, it deepens the Jewish love of Israel's religion and makes him a better citizen.

This quotation, Mr. Chairman and ladies and gentlemen of the committee, is from an article entitled "Reformed Judaism and Jewish Nationalism," by Rabbi Morris S. Lazaron, who has just testified here today. It was printed in the Jewish Times of Baltimore on January 2, 1931.

Mr. Chairman, I say most respectfully that it seems that the learned rabbi thinks in cycles. First he was a non-Zionist. Then he became a Zionist. Now apparently he is an anti-Zionist. We do not know what he may be tomorrow. But I humbly submit that the tragic plight of the Jewish people, their need for a homeland, their imperative need to be among their own people in Palestine, who are prepared to share their bread with them, their homes with them, and to make them welcome at a time when they so desperately need that welcome—that crying need cannot wait, Mr. Chairman, until Rabbi Lazaron completes another cycle in his thinking.

And I submit that no more should be asked of us than would be asked of any other group of American citizens. There is no more reason for all Jews in this country to agree upon Zionism or to favor the establishment of a free and democratic Jewish commonwealth in Palestine than there is for all Americans to agree upon any other issue concerning which some Government action is urged. The important fact is that the overwhelming majority of the Jews in this country supported the Palestine resolution which was adopted at the American Jewish Conference and favor the passage of this resolution. It is true, as Rabbi Fineschriber stated, that at the American Jewish Conference we did not achieve complete unity. What he failed to point out was that such complete unity was not achieved because the 500-odd delegates at that conference, in line with the American tradition, felt that the obligation which rested upon them was to express the will of the overwhelming majority and not to barter away their right and obligation to do so in order to satisfy a small and insignificant minority and for the sake of getting a unanimous verdict.

And may I call your attention to the fact—it has already been stated by Rabbi Heller—it needs to be restated—that all of the gentlemen who have spoken to you, that is, Rabbi Woolsey, Rabbi Fineschriber, and Rabbi Lazaron represent only a minority view in only the reform rabbinate. Even in their own rabbinate they clearly represent a minority view. Rabbi Heller has given you the figures; I do not need to repeat them. In the conservative rabbinate there is no difference of opinion, and in the orthodox rabbinate there surely is no difference of opinion.

We can only ask you, with respect to their testimony, to consider the fact that theirs is a minority opinion, and it must be considered as such. In fact, in speaking to you of the opinion of the over- whelming majority of the Jewish people on this issue, as I believe Congressman Rogers correctly stated, what we are doing is merely to bring to your attention one pertinent fact, namely, that the Jewish citizens of this country are overwhelmingly in favor of this resolution because they feel that a sacred trust has been placed in their hands to continue to do their part to see to it that the Jewish national home is reestablished in Palestine. And I might add in that connection that only recently on the occasion of the last convention of the Zionist Organization of America, the President of the United States said:

> I am confident that the helpful contributions made by American citizens toward the establishment of a national home for the Jewish people in Palestine will be continued.

We shall continue to make these contributions.

Chairman BLOOM. The date of that?

Mr. SHULMAN. September 11, 1943.

Mr. CHIPERFIELD. Is that the President of the United States?

Mr. SHULMAN. Signed, "Franklin D. Roosevelt."

Mr. CHIPERFIELD. Would you repeat it? I did not quite get it.

Mr. SHULMAN (reading):

> I am confident that the helpful contributions made by American citizens toward the establishment of a national home for the Jewish people in Palestine will be continued—

And may I remind you, sir, that up to the present time there has been invested in Palestine some $600,000,000; and that 550,000 Jews have settled there. There is in public law, as in private law, a doctrine of estoppel. In reliance upon the promise made to the Jewish people by the issuance of the Balfour Declaration we went forward and made this contribution and this investment, to the great benefit of our fellow Jews. And I say to you, sir, that this is not the time when we should be asked to liquidate that national home. On the contrary, there is every reason why, quite apart from the considerations of justice and equity the law of estoppel requires that the nations of the world carry out their promise to the Jewish people.

Thank you, sir.

Chairman BLOOM. Thank you very much.

Judge Kee?

Mr. KEE. No questions.

Chairman BLOOM. Dr. Eaton?

Mr. EATON. No questions.

Chairman BLOOM. Mr. Jarman?

Mr. JARMAN. No questions.

Chairman BLOOM. Mr. Chiperfield?

Mr. CHIPERFIELD. If the executive branch of our Government favors the passage of this resolution at this time, do you not think they should come down before our committee in open and public hearings and say that they favor it or are against it, and give the reasons why?

Mr. SHULMAN. Well, Mr. Chairman, I cannot say what is proper for the executive branch of the Government to do. I have been under the impression that on many occasions Congress has taken action without the consent or approval of the executive branch of the Government. I certainly do not want, however, to have my answer misunderstood, because I have no reason to believe that the executive branch of the Government does not intend to carry out its clear obligation in this respect.

Mr. CHIPERFIELD. May I call attention to this: The President, in a message very recently, did not hesitate to give his views on a certain current issue, and asked us to stand up and be counted. All I am doing is asking for the same thing now.

Mr. SHULMAN. I do not question your right; sir, to ask it. I merely say that I believe that the legislative branch of the Government has the right to make the laws of the land, and you have a right to reaffirm the position which you took by unanimous action in 1922.

Mr. CHIPERFIELD. I will agree with that statement. I have no more questions.

Chairman BLOOM. Mr. Rogers?

Mr. ROGERS. No questions.

Chairman BLOOM. Mr. Vorys?

Mr. VORYS. You spoke about the Congress having the duty and the right to make laws. In your judgment does this resolution have any effect as a law?

Mr. SHULMAN. No; I think, unlike the 1922 resolution, this is not a joint resolution, and therefore will not require the signature of the President or joint passage by both Houses of Congress. Therefore it is, as I understand it, a restatement of the traditional American policy, and it is in effect a recommendation to the executive branch—an expression of the will of this honorable body.

Mr. VORYS. It is not a restatement. It goes further than any statement that has ever been made by the Congress before, in that it does not merely restate either the Balfour Declaration or the resolution of the Congress back in 1922, but adds some further expressions which are considered of importance. There is no use to sit here and say it is a restatement when it is something more than a restatement? Now, what else is it, in your judgment?

Mr. SHULMAN. No. I would like to differ with you, that it is more than a restatement. What it does is to make clear what might have been ambiguous, and it is necessary that it be made clear at this time because, as I pointed out, the white paper not only prohibits immigration and the purchase of the land; it also would constitute Palestine as an Arab state and crystallize the Jewish population there into a permanent minority, thus forever depriving the Jews of an opportunity to continue to enter Palestine freely until they become a majority, and then to reconstitute the Jewish Commonwealth. And, as I pointed out, while it was premature to speak of the Jewish Commonwealth in 1922, it certainly is not unrealistic to do so today, because in the first place there are 550,000 Jews there, and there will be this compelling necessity to transfer to Palestine many hundreds of thousands, if not millions, as soon as the occupied countries are liberated.

Therefore, Mr. Chairman and Representative Vorys, it seems to me that you are doing no more than to carry out the original intent and purpose of the Balfour Declaration, but what you are doing is to indicate in clear and unequivocal language, what was that intent, and it seems to me that it is just and proper for those of us who urge the

passage of this resolution to come to you and tell you what we conceive
to be the original intent and purpose of the Balfour Declaration,
and to point out to you as we have our conception of that intent and
purpose as well as the understanding of the persons who were most
prominent in framing the declaration and the findings of the Royal
Commission.

Mr. VORYS. Of course, it is quite proper for you to come here and
tell us your views. I am trying to get your views on just what force
this resolution has, or would have. You mentioned, in answer to an
earlier question by my colleague, that it is the duty and the right of
the Congress to make laws.

Mr. SHULMAN. Right.

Mr. VORYS. I want to get from you what the legal significance in
your judgment is of this resolution now before us.

Mr. SHULMAN. Clearly, unless it is a joint resolution which in turn
is signed by the President of the United States, it is my understanding
it would not become the law of the land. Therefore it is an expression
of good will and support, and a reaffirmation of a policy which we hope
will be favorably considered by the executive branch of the Government, by those who are in charge of dealing with the matter; and I, for
one, am confident it will greatly strengthen the hands of those friends
in Great Britain—and there are many, including Mr. Winston
Churchill and other members of the Cabinet—who want to see the
promise fulfilled and the 1939 white paper repudiated.

Mr. VORYS. But even if we passed this resolution, any action
would be taken by the executive, is that not correct, in our country—
any action to use the good offices of the United States, or to take
appropriate measures, would be taken by the executive? Is that not
true?

Mr. SHULMAN. Well, that is true, is it not, of all situations where
our Government seeks to have its policy implemented or enforced?

Mr. VORYS. Yes.

Mr. SHULMAN. This being a matter of foreign policy, the Government would necessarily act through the Secretary of State, so therefore
I assume that whatever actions are to be taken will be taken through
the proper executive branch of the Government.

Mr. VORYS. And since this adds no legal sanction or authority to
their present authority, the President and the Secretary of State are in
as good a position to act now as they would be after this would pass,
so far as any legal authority or power to act, is that not true?

Mr. SHULMAN. Well, Mr. Vorys, may I just answer that this way,
if I may.

Mr. VORYS. I just wish you would answer it.

Chairman BLOOM. Answer it, if you please. We would like to get
on here, because we have another witness and we are late.

Mr. SHULMAN. This Congress acted in 1922. In 1939 the white
paper clearly violates the 1925 convention between Great Britain and
this country; it definitely violates the act of this Congress of 1922.
Do you not feel that a responsibility rests upon you to take action
to see to it that that act is not violated or repudiated or whittled down
so that it is absolutely meaningless, to see to it that the national home
is not liquidated, quite apart from whatever action is taken by the
executive branch of the Government?

Mr. VORYS. The gentleman has not answered my question, but I
will yield to Mr. Rogers and not ask any further questions.

Chairman Bloom. Mr. Rogers.

Mr. Rogers. I just wanted to say I thought the point Mr. Shulman was making here was a very good one, about the Commonwealth and the reason why this whole resolution hangs together. I agree with Mr. Vorys; this is not a restatement. It is a clarification and it is a much needed clarification, because the word "homeland" has now been distorted out of all previous meaning by the white paper, and it is needed at this time because the white paper has distorted this past definition of the homeland. That is why I feel that it all hangs together and that it is essential that it be passed or not passed as a unit.

Chairman Bloom. Is that all, Mr. Rogers?

Mr. Rogers. I would like to have one more word.

It would strengthen the hands and hopes of many good people in England who are disturbed over the present British policy in Palestine. I know that, because I was there and spoke with many members of the House of Commons, and I do know that if we should make such an expression, purely unofficially but just an expression, it would bring great heart and hope to them.

Chairman Bloom. Mr. Jonkman?

Mr. Jonkman. No questions.

Chairman Bloom. Mr. Wright?

Mr. Wright. No questions.

Chairman Bloom. Mrs. Bolton?

Mrs. Bolton. No questions.

Chairman Bloom. Mr. Wadsworth?

Mr. Wadsworth. Are you of the opinion that the passage of this resolution would have its principal effect in England?

Mr. Shulman. Well, I think that since we are dealing with the mandatory power, it would definitely have its principal effect there.

Mr. Wadsworth. Then it is directed more to the British than it is to our President?

Mr. Shulman. Well, I think it would definitely have an effect on the British policy. I think it may also have an effect, and in all probably will have the effect, of indicating to the President where the House of Representatives stands on the question. My own feeling is that it would serve a useful purpose, both in this country and in Great Britain.

Mr. Wadsworth. That is all.

Chairman Bloom. Mr. Mansfield?

Mr. Mansfield. No questions.

Chairman Bloom. Mr. Schiffler?

Mr. Shiffler. I have one question. Have these questions ever been presented to the International Court of Justice, so far as you know, since the issuance of the white paper?

Mr. Shulman. The 1939 white paper was submitted to the Mandates Commission of the League of Nations and I think, as has been testified to, it was considered by the Mandates Commission as clearly in violation of the terms of the mandate. We will put in evidence the decision of the Mandate Commission to that effect.

Chairman Bloom. You mean you will put in evidence?

Mr. Shulman. Yes, sir.

Chairman Bloom. Without objection it is so ordered.

Thank you very much, Mr. Shulman.

(Notes submitted for the record, by Mr. Herman Shulman: (1) Testimony submitted to Royal Commission by Arab leaders. (2) On the observations of the Permanent Mandates Commission relative to the 1939 White Paper:)

TESTIMONY SUBMITTED TO ROYAL COMMISSION BY ARAB LEADERS

EVIDENCE OF HAJ AMIN AL-HUSSEIN, MUFTI OF JERUSALEM

Question. If the Arabs had this treaty (proposed treaty between Palestine Arab State and Britain) they would be prepared to welcome the Jews already in the country?

MUFTI. That will be left to the discretion of the Government which will be set up under the treaty and will be decided by the Government on considerations most equitable and most beneficial to the country.

Question. Does His Eminence think that this country can assimilate and digest the 400,000 Jews now in the country?

MUFTI. No.

Question. Some of them would have to be removed, by a process kindly or painful, as the case may be?

MUFTI. We must leave all this to the future.

EVIDENCE OF AUNI BEY ABDUL-HADI, LEADER OF THE ARAB INDEPENDENCE PARTY (ISTIQLAL)

ABDUL-HADI. Frankly speaking, we object to the existence of 400,000 Jews in the country.

Question. They are not to be driven out and yet there are too many of them. What happens then?

ABDUL-HADI. A large number of them are not Palestinians.

Question. Auni Bey says that he does not want to drive them out, but he says there are too many and I want to know how he would reduce them.

ABDUL-HADI. That is not a question which can be decided here.

(Palestine Royal Commission, Minutes of Evidence Heard at Public Sessions, London 1939, Col. No. 134, p. 298 and p. 314.)

SUPPLEMENTARY NOTE ON THE OBSERVATIONS OF THE PERMANENT MANDATES COMMISSION ON THE 1939 WHITE PAPER

In its Report to the Council of the League of Nations, the Permanent Mandates Commission at the Thirty-Sixth Session held at Geneva, June 1939, unanimously declared: "The policy set out in the White Paper was not in accordance with the interpretation which, in agreement with the Mandatory Power and the Council, the Commission had placed upon the Palestine Mandate."

(Permanent Mandates Commission, Minutes of the Thirty-Sixth Session, Geneva 1939, p. 206.)

THE COMMON PURPOSE OF CIVILIZED MANKIND

A Declaration by 68 Members of the Senate and 194 Members of the House of Representatives of the Seventy-seventh Congress on the Occasion of the Twenty-fifth Anniversary of the Balfour Declaration, November 2d, 1942

A TRADITIONAL AMERICAN POLICY REAFFIRMED

(American Palestine Committee, New York)

THE BALFOUR DECLARATION

Issued by the British War Cabinet November 2, 1917, and signed by Arthur James (later Lord) Balfour, Secretary of State for Foreign Affairs

His Majesty's Government view with favour the establishment in Palestine of a national home for the Jewish people, and will use their best endeavors to facilitate the achievement of this object, it being clearly understood that nothing shall be done which may prejudice the civil and religious rights of existing non-Jewish communities in Palestine, or the rights and political status enjoyed by Jews in any other country.

Twenty-five years ago the British Government issued the Balfour Declaration pledging itself to facilitate the establishment of a National Home for the Jewish people in Palestine. The Declaration was published to the world with the approval of the other Powers allied with Great Britain in the World War, and with the encouragement and support of the Government of the United States. It was written into the Peace Treaty with the aid and approval of President Wilson who publicly expressed his confidence that the purposes of the Declaration would be fulfilled. A few years later, the House of Representatives and the Senate of the United States, by unanimous vote, adopted a joint resolution favoring the establishing of the Jewish National Home, and on September 21, 1922, the resolution was duly signed by President Harding. Since then, this policy has been reaffirmed by every succeeding Administration, including the present. It has thus become the declared and traditional policy of the United States to favor the restoration of the Jewish National Home.

The Balfour Declaration was justly hailed throughout the world as an act of historic reparation and as a charter of freedom for the Jewish people. It was designed to open the gates of Palestine to homeless and harassed multitudes and to pave the way for the establishment of a Jewish Commonwealth.

The reasons which, twenty-five years ago, led the American people and the Government of the United States to favor the cause of Jewish national restoration in Palestine are still valid today. In fact, the case for a Jewish Homeland is overwhelmingly stronger and the need more urgent now than ever before. In Palestine the resettlement has advanced from the status of a hopeful experiment to that of a heartening reality, while in Europe the position of the Jews has deteriorated to an appalling degree. Millions of uprooted and homeless Jews will strive to reconstruct their lives anew in their ancestral home when the hour of deliverance will come.

We, therefore, take this occasion, the twenty-fifth anniversary of the issuance of the Balfour Declaration, to record our continued interest in and support of the purposes and principles which it embodies. We wish to send a message of hope and cheer to those in Palestine who are confronting the common enemy with courage and fortitude and are contributing unstintingly of their manpower and effort to the democratic cause.

Faced as we are by the fact that the Nazi government, in its Jewish policy, is attempting to exterminate a whole people, we declare that, when the war is over, it shall be the common purpose of civilized mankind to right this cruel wrong insofar as may lie in our power, and, above all, to enable large numbers of the survivors to reconstruct their lives in Palestine where the Jewish people may once more assume a position of dignity and equality among the peoples of the earth.

Our Government may be assured that in continuing the traditional American policy in favor of so just a cause, it can rely upon our individual support and the approbation of the American people.

The Signatories

The subjoined list of signatories includes Senator Alben W. Barkley, of Kentucky, Majority Leader of the Senate, Senator Charles L. McNary, of Oregon, Minority Leader of the Senate, John W. McCormack, of Massachusetts, Majority Leader of the House of Representatives, and Joseph W. Martin, Jr., of Massachusetts, Minority Leader of the House of Representatives.

The list contains also 18 members of the Foreign Relations Committee of the Senate, including Senator Tom Connally of Texas, Chairman of the Committee.

MEMBERS OF THE UNITED STATES SENATE

Joseph H. Ball of Minnesota.
John H. Bankhead, 2d of Alabama.
W. Warren Barbour of New Jersey.
Alben W. Barkley of Kentucky.
Theodore G. Bilbo of Mississippi.
Ralph O. Brewster of Maine.
Styles Bridges of New Hampshire.
Prentiss M. Brown of Michigan.
Harold H. Burton of Ohio.
Hugh A. Butler of Nebraska.
Harry Flood Byrd of Virginia.
Arthur Capper of Kansas.
Albert B. Chandler of Kentucky.
D. Worth Clark of Idaho.
Tom Connally of Texas.
James J. Davis of Pennsylvania.
Sheridan Downey of California.
Walter F. George of Georgia.
Guy M. Gillette of Iowa.
Carter Glass of Virginia.
Theodore Francis Green of Rhode Island.
Joseph F. Guffey of Pennsylvania.
Chan Gurney of South Dakota.
Carl A. Hatch of New Mexico.
Carl Hayden of Arizona.
Clyde L. Herring of Iowa.
Lister Hill of Alabama.
Rufus C. Holman of Oregon.
James H. Hughes of Delaware.
Edwin C. Johnson of Colorado.
Harley M. Kilgore of West Virginia.
William Langer of North Dakota.
Josh Lee of Oklahoma.
Henry Cabot Lodge, Jr. of Massachusetts.

Kenneth McKellar of Tennessee.
Charles L. McNary of Oregon.
Francis Maloney of Connecticut.
Burnet R. Maybank of South Carolina.
James M. Mead of New York.
Abe Murdock of Utah.
James E. Murray of Montana.
Arthur E. Nelson of Minnesota.
George W. Norris of Nebraska.
Gerald P. Nye of North Dakota.
W. Lee O'Daniel of Texas
Joseph C. O'Mahoney of Wyoming.
John H. Overton of Louisiana.
Claude Pepper of Florida.
George L. Radcliffe of Maryland.
Robert R. Reynolds of North Carolina.
Joseph Rosier of West Virginia.
Richard B. Russell of Georgia.
H. H. Schwartz of Wyoming.
William H. Smathers of New Jersey.
Tom Stewart of Tennessee.
Robert A. Taft of Ohio.
Elbert D. Thomas of Utah.
Elmer Thomas of Oklahoma.
Charles W. Tobey of New Hampshire.
Harry S. Truman of Missouri.
James M. Tunnell of Delaware.
Millard E. Tydings of Maryland.
Arthur H. Vandenberg of Michigan.
Frederick Van Nuys of Indiana.
Robert F. Wagner of New York.
David I. Walsh of Massachusetts.
Alexander Wiley of Wisconsin.
Raymond E. Willis of Indiana.

MEMBERS OF THE HOUSE OF REPRESENTATIVES

Leo E. Allen of Illinois.
John Z. Anderson of California.
August H. Andresen of Minnesota.
Walter G. Andrews of New York.
Homer D. Angell of Oregon.
Joseph Clark Baldwin of New York.
William B. Barry of New York.
Alfred F. Beiter of New York.
George H. Bender of Ohio.
Philip A. Bennett of Missouri.
Hale Boggs of Louisiana.
Frances P. Bolton of Ohio.
Frank W. Boykin of Alabama.
Fred Bradley of Michigan.
Michael J. Bradley of Pennsylvania.
Charles A. Buckley of New York.
Alfred L. Bulwinkle of North Carolina.
Thomas G. Burch of Virginia.
Usher L. Burdick of North Dakota.
William T. Byrne of New York.
Gordon Canfield of New Jersey.
Clarence Cannon of Missouri.
Pat Cannon of Florida.
Louis J. Capozzoli of New York.
Francis Case of South Dakota.
Joseph E. Casey of Massachusetts.
Emanuel Celler of New York.

Virgil Chapman of Kentucky.
J. Edgar Chenoweth of Colorado.
Charles R. Clason of Massachusetts.
John M. Coffee of Washington.
John M. Costello of California.
Francis D. Culkin of New York.
Thomas H. Cullen of New York.
Paul Cunningham of Iowa.
Thomas D'Alesandro, Jr. of Maryland.
Clifford Davis of Tennessee.
John J. Delaney of New York.
Charles S. Dewey of Illinois.
Samuel Dickstein of New York.
John D. Dingell of Michigan.
Everett M. Dirksen of Illinois.
James Domengeaux of Louisiana.
Fred J. Douglas of New York.
Le Roy D. Downs of Connecticut.
Carl T. Durham of North Carolina.
Herman P. Eberharter of Pennsylvania.
Clyde T. Ellis of Arkansas.
Charles H. Elston of Ohio.
Albert J. Engel of Michigan.
Charles I. Faddis of Pennsylvania.
Frank Fellows of Maine.
Ivor D. Fenton of Pennsylvania.
William J. Fitzgerald of Connecticut.

James M. Fitzpatrick of New York.
Thomas A. Flaherty of Massachusetts.
John H. Folger of North Carolina.
Aime J. Forand of Rhode Island.
Leland M. Ford of California.
Thomas F. Ford of California.
Richard P. Gale of Minnesota.
Ralph A. Gamble of New York.
E. C. Gathings of Arkansas.
Joseph A. Gavagan of New York.
Bertrand W. Gearhart of California.
Charles L. Gerlach of Pennsylvania.
Charles L. Gifford of Massachusetts.
Wilson D. Gillette of Pennsylvania.
George W. Gillie of Indiana.
George M. Grant of Alabama.
Robert A. Grant of Indiana.
Lex Green of Florida.
Leonard W. Hall of New York.
Charles A. Halleck of Indiana.
Oren Harris of Arkansas.
Winder R. Harris of Virginia.
Edward J. Hart of New Jersey.
Dow W. Harter of Ohio.
Fred A. Hartley, Jr., of New Jersey.
Joe Hendricks of Florida.
Elmer J. Holland of Pennsylvania.
Pehr G. Holmes of Massachusetts.
Frank E. Hook of Michigan.
John M. Houston of Kansas.
Evan Howell of Illinois.
Ed. V. Izac of California.
Joshua L. Johns of Wisconsin.
Anton J. Johnson of Illinois.
Lyndon B. Johnson of Texas.
Noble J. Johnson of Indiana.
Bartel J. Jonkman of Michigan.
Robert W. Kean of New Jersey.
John Kee of West Virginia.
Frank B. Keefe of Wisconsin.
Estes Kefauver of Tennessee.
Augustine B. Kelley of Pennsylvania.
Edward A. Kelly of Illinois.
John H. Kerr of North Carolina.
Clarence E. Kilburn of New York.
Cecil R. King of California.
Arthur G. Klein of New York.
Harold Knutson of Minnesota.
Herman P. Kopplemann of Connecticut.
Charles Kramer of California.
John C. Kunkel of Pennsylvania.
Thomas Lane of Massachusetts.
Clarence F. Lea of California.
Karl M. LeCompte of Iowa.
Louis Ludlow of Indiana.
Walter A. Lynch of New York.
John W. McCormack of Massachusetts.
Raymond S. McKeough of Illinois.
Donald H. McLean of New Jersey.
Melvin J. Maas of Minnesota.
Anton F. Maciejewski of Illinois.
Lucien J. Maciora of Connecticut.
Joseph W. Martin, Jr., of Massachusetts.
Noah M. Mason of Illinois.
Matthew J. Merritt of New York.

John A. Meyer of Maryland.
Thomas B. Miller of Pennsylvania.
Wilbur D. Mills of Arkansas.
Arthur W. Mitchell of Illinois.
Karl E. Mundt of South Dakota.
Francis J. Myers of Pennsylvania.
Mary T. Norton of New Jersey.
Joseph J. O'Brien of New York.
Caroline O'Day of New York.
Joseph P. O'Hara of Minnesota.
Emmet O'Neal of Kentucky.
Donald L. O'Toole of New York.
Nat Patton of Texas.
Joseph L. Pfeifer of New York.
William T. Pheiffer of New York.
Walter C. Ploeser of Missouri.
Charles A. Plumley of Vermont.
D. Lane Powers of New Jersey.
J. Percy Priest of Tennessee.
Robert Ramspeck of Georgia.
Chauncey W. Reed of Illinois.
Robert F. Rich of Pennsylvania.
A. Willis Robertson of Virginia.
Charles R. Robertson of North Dakota.
Lewis K. Rockefeller of New York.
Robert F. Rockwell of Colorado.
Robert L. Rodgers of Pennsylvania.
Edith Nourse Rogers of Massachusetts,
Thomas Rolph of California.
Sam M. Russell of Texas.
Adolph J. Sabath of Illinois.
Leon Sacks of Pennsylvania.
Lansdale G. Sasscer of Maryland.
Dave E. Satterfield, Jr., of Virginia.
Harry Sauthoff of Wisconsin.
Thomas E. Scanlon of Pennsylvania,
Leonard W. Schuetz of Illinois.
Hugh D. Scott, Jr., of Pennsylvania.
James A. Shanley of Connecticut.
Harry R. Sheppard of California.
John Edward Sheridan of Pennsylvania.
Robert L. F. Sikes of Florida.
Francis R. Smith of Pennsylvania.
Joe L. Smith of West Virginia.
Lawrence H. Smith of Wisconsin.
Margaret Chase Smith of Maine.
Martin F. Smith of Washington.
John J. Sparkman of Alabama.
Brent Spence of Kentucky.
William H. Stevenson of Wisconsin.
William H. Sutphin of New Jersey.
Joseph E. Talbot of Connecticut.
Henry O. Talle of Iowa.
Rudolph G. Tenerowicz of Michigan.
Lewis D. Thill of Wisconsin.
William R. Thom of Ohio.
Harve Tibbott of Pennsylvania.
John H. Tolan of California.
Philip A. Traynor of Delaware.
James E. Van Zandt of Pennsylvania.
Jerry Voorhis of California.
John M. Vorys of Ohio.
James W. Wadsworth of New York.
Zebulon Weaver of North Carolina.
Samuel A. Weiss of Pennsylvania.

Richard J. Welch of California.
Compton I. White of Idaho.
William M. Whittington of Mississippi.
Earl Wilson of Indiana.
Charles A. Wolverton of New Jersey.

Roy O. Woodruff of Michigan.
James A. Wright of Pennsylvania.
Stephen M. Young of Ohio.
Oscar Youngdahl of Minnesota.

STATEMENT BY SENATOR ROBERT F. WAGNER OF NEW YORK, CHAIRMAN OF THE
AMERICAN PALESTINE COMMITTEE

This declaration, signed by Sixty-eight members of the United States Senate and 194 members of the House of Representatives, is an action of world significance. It is expressive of a deep-seated sentiment in favor of the Jewish Homeland in Palestine which is widespread among the American people, and represents also a striking reaffirmation of a traditional American Policy. I am gratified that the initiative in this matter has come from the American Palestine Committee which Senator McNary and I have the honor to head, and by the further fact that more than two-thirds of the Senate has expressed itself in such clear terms. It will be noted that the 'support which it records is nonpartisan. The list of signatories is headed by Majority Leader Barkley and Minority Leader McNary in the Senate and by Majority Leader McCormack and Minority Leader Martin in the House of Representatives. It includes eighteen members of the Senate Committee on Foreign Relations.

We have been impelled to reiterate our position at this time by the horrifying reports which have been pouring in concerning the mass slaughter of European Jews—acts of brutality which have shocked decent humanity everywhere. These terrible facts not only call for universal condemnation of the Nazis and sympathy for their victims, but also demand of us a statesmanlike, constructive policy which will provide a more secure and dignified future for the Jewish people in the democratic world of tomorrow. The statement which we are releasing today is in a sense an answer to the Nazis; but it is, above all, the public declaration of such a constructive policy aiming at the solution of the problem through the reestablishing of a Jewish Commonwealth in Palestine.

In behalf of the signatories, I have today submitted the statement to President Roosevelt and to Secretary of State Hull.

I just would like to state for the information of the committee that we have one more witness. Time is getting on. Mr. Louis Lipsky, our remaining witness, appeared before this committee in 1922 on a similar resolution. Mr. Lipsky, will you kindly give your name, business, and place of residence to the reporter?

STATEMENT OF LOUIS LIPSKY, REPRESENTING THE ZIONIST ORGANI-
ZATION OF AMERICA AND THE AMERICAN JEWISH CONFERENCE

Mr. LIPSKY. Louis Lipsky, 386 Fourth Avenue, New York. I am representing the Zionist Organization of America and the American Jewish Conference.

Chairman BLOOM. And your position there is what, Mr. Lipsky?

Mr. LIPSKY. I am the American member of the Jewish Agency for Palestine.

Chairman BLOOM. That is the official agency under the mandate?

Mr. LIPSKY. Yes. I am also a member of the Zionist Emergency Commission and of the interim committee of the American Jewish Conference.

Mr. ROGERS. Are you the American member of the Jewish Agency?

Mr. LIPSKY. Yes.

Chairman BLOOM. Proceed, Mr. Lipsky.

Mr. LIPSKY. I may also add that, as the chairman has indicated, I am one of the survivors of the hearing of 1922 before this House committee.

Chairman BLOOM. At this very table.

Mr. LIPSKY. It was at this very table, and we went through a similar interesting experience with similar excitement, satisfactions, and disappointments. But in the end the resolution which we submitted at that time was adopted unanimously. It was then a smaller committee, as I recall.

Chairman BLOOM. Twenty-one members.

Mr. LIPSKY. It seemed to me smaller.

Chairman BLOOM. And there are no members of the committee today that were members at that time.

Mr. LIPSKY. Except Ham Fish.

Chairman BLOOM. He is no longer a member of the committee.

Mr. LIPSKY. But the hearing was animated by the same courtesy and tact and sympathy as has permeated the sessions of the committee before whom I am now privileged to appear. In fact, the members were even more active in their inquisitions. Some of the members became so interested in their probings that they greatly lightened the burden of the Zionist representatives.

I still remember the historic knowledge and penetrating wisdom of Bourke Cockran, one of the great Democratic orators of his day, who at that time harassed with unusual pertinacity the anti-Zionist counterpart of Rabbi Lazaron, who at that time was Dr. David Philipson of Cincinnati. Dr. Philipson, in his old age, in spite of the revolution that has taken place in the world, in spite of the disastrous conditions that now confront the Jewish people, still remains an opponent of the national home of his people, and still regards himself as a teacher in Israel, although all of Israel refuses to follow his teaching.

It may not be proper for me to observe—it may not be tactful, but I think it is accurate to say—that the Syrian Arab representatives, who come from Lebanon—not from Palestine—are far abler and more adroit and more generally complicated than those who spoke at that time against the joint resolution. The only difficulty we had then was to convince Stephen Porter, of Pittsburgh, who was the chairman of the committee.

Chairman BLOOM. Tom Connally was on the committee.

Mr. LIPSKY. And Judge Cooper.

Chairman BLOOM. And Judge Sabath. We had a good committee then.

Mr. LIPSKY. And Representative Burton.

Chairman BLOOM. Representative Porter was chairman.

Mr. LIPSKY. However, Mr. Porter, after the acrimonious debates that took place, joined in voting for the resolution, which was unanimously adopted.

Chairman BLOOM. I may state, if you will permit an interruption there, that Mr. Rogers, the husband of Mrs. Rogers, who is now a member of the committee, was the ranking Republican member of the committee at that time.

Mr. LIPSKY. Not all of them are clear in my mind, but I remember vividly Mr. Cochran, Judge Cooper, Mr. Burton, Mr. Linthicum, and others.

Life was much more simple then than it is today from a foreign political point of view. The joint resolution was a joint resolution; it had to be signed by the President. It was simple, clear. It was a formula that everybody could understand. At that time the resolution represented the affirmation on the part of the people of the United

States of an ancient hope of the Jewish people which was to be fulfilled by an agreement between all nations. Specifically, it reaffirmed and endorsed the Balfour Declaration.

The fact that Henry Cabot Lodge, one of the leading Republicans in opposition to President Wilson's peace proposals, was the prime mover, the most eloquent advocate of the Zionist resolution, was an indication of the fact that the resolution was most generally regarded as a subject that transcended parties. It touched a sentiment which reflected a manifest American tradition. Mr. Lodge approached the subject not only as any American but, as I know and as Mr. E. D. Stone, who sits here, remembers through personal conversations with him, as a Christian of the old school.

He had certain ideas about Palestine and the presence of the Turks controlling the land. His public address after the resolution had been adopted—he did not speak in the Senate because there was no discussion in the Senate—reflected the sentiment that Palestine and the Jewish people are historically bound together, and that the Holy Land, the birthplace of the Christian and the Jewish religions, could with justice be given back to the people from whose travail a great religious impulse incorporated in two great religions had radiated throughout the world for thousands of years.

He believed that that people could be entrusted with the task of protecting the sanctity of the holy places and that they would find there freedom and security in the promised land for their own benefit and for the good of mankind in general.

I would like to put into the record the speech that Mr. Lodge made at that time.

Chairman BLOOM. Without objection, it is so ordered.

(Address of Senator Henry Cabot Lodge is as follows:)

In 1917 I gave public expression to my approval of the Balfour Declaration, dated November 2nd of that year, which, as you all know, set forth the policy of the British Government in regard to Palestine. This declaration was issued just before General Allenby took possession of Jerusalem on December 11, 1917. Since that date, Great Britain has held possession of Palestine, and will no doubt continue to do so in any event, although it is probable that she will soon receive a mandate from the League for that purpose. This means that Great Britain will be in control of Palestine and that the laws will be administered there by British courts. It is under this declaration of Mr. Balfour in behalf of the British Government, and the further agreement of San Remo, that the question has arisen about the establishment of a national home by the Jewish people in Palestine. It is this propostion which is favored by the resolution which I had the pleasure of presenting to the Senate, by which it was passed unanimously.

It seemed to me that it was entirely becoming and commendable that the Jewish people in all portions of the world should desire to have a national home for such members of their race as wished to return to the country which was the cradle of their race, and where they lived and labored for several thousand years, running back to days just apparent in the dim dawn of recorded history. What could be more praiseworthy or more appealing than such a desire? Why should it not be gratified? Surely the days of religious intolerance have gone by among all the most highly civilized nations of the western world. Religious freedom is one of the cornerstones of the constitutional government of the United States.

Complete religious tolerance is an American doctrine, and I think all Americans would deplore, and ought to deplore, any attempt to bring race or religion in any manner into our political life. It seems to me that religious freedom as we understand it in the United States must always be one of our most cherished principles.

For this reason, I was glad to propose the resolution to the Senate which favored allowing the Jewish people to have a national home in Palestine. There seem to be many mistaken ideas abroad in regard to this national home for the Jews in the land from which they sprang. Some people seem to think that it is a project to have all the Jews in the world go to Palestine. I cannot conceive that anyone who gives it a moment's thought should not see the utter impracticability of any such plan. There are twelve to fourteen million Jews, I suppose, in the world, according to the best statistics, and it would be physically impossible for them to go to Palestine and live there.

It is a small country, not suited for a great industrial population. It has a population now of seven hundred thousand, and the prospect of development, which must be chiefly along agricultural lines, is necessarily limited. The Jewish people in the world generally have a very deep sentiment in regard to it, and it would be astonishing indeed if they did not have it; but, as I understand it, the idea is that this national home should be created and protected, and those of the Jewish people who desire to go there will then be able to go, find employment, and establish themselves upon their ancestral soil. The great mass of the Jewish people will remain necessarily where they now are taking an active and important part in the life of the countries in which they live, but they would be something more or less than human if they did not cherish and reverence this sentiment for the representation of their people in the ancient land from which they come.

I am unable to see any possible objection to it, and, on the other hand, there ought to be great sympathy in the gratification of such a sentiment, at once so powerful and honorable, among the people who hold it. The United States has no direct interest in Palestine of a material kind, but its people have as Christians the profoundest feeling of veneration for the country which enshrines the holy places, the very holy of holies of all Christendom. This resolution of sympathy with the desires of the Jewish people neither threatens nor invades any rights of any other people. It says, to quote the words of the Senate Resolution: "That the United States of America favors the establishment in Palestine of a national home for the Jewish people, it being clearly understood that nothing shall be done which may prejudice the civil and religious rights of non-Jewish communities in Palestine, and that the holy places and religious buildings and sites in Palestine shall be adequately protected."

That protection will, of course, be afforded by Great Britain, a great Christian nation, thoroughly devoted to the principles of religious freedom and toleration, and all the rights and all the religious feelings of Christians and Jews alike, to whom the land is sacred, will be guarded as never before. The President of the United States has also recently given public utterance to the cordial sympathy which he feels for the wishes of the Jewish people to have in Palestine a national home. But, strongly as I believe in religious freedom and religious tolerance, I never could accept in patience the thought that Jerusalem and Palestine should be under the control of the Mohammedans, as they have been since 1244 with only a brief interval.

You may smile when I tell you that, although as a child I read my Bible, both the Old and New Testaments, I got my first idea of the present condition of Palestine and of the Mohammedan possession from two of Scott's novels, which absorbed my thoughts when, as a boy of nine, I read with most passionate interest Sir Walter Scott's stories of The Talisman and Ivanhoe. I had, of course, intense synpathy with the Crusaders, and it seemed to me a great wrong that Jerusalem should be beneath the Moslem rule. You will also recall that in those two stories the Jewish characters were touched by the great writer with a sympathetic hand, and I am sure all of you remember that beautiful character, Rebecca, the daughter of Isaac of York, in Ivanhoe, the real heroine of the story, and you must, I think, know by heart Rebecca's hymn of devotion, uttered in the darkest hour alike of her own life and of her race, which begins:

> When Israel, of the Lord beloved,
>   Out of the land of bondage came,
> Her father's God before her moved,
>   An awful guide, in smoke and flame.
> By day, along the astonish'd lands
>   The cloudy pillar glided slow;
> By night, Arabia's crimson'd sands
>   Return'd the fiery column's glow.

and ending:

> Our harps we left by Babel's streams,
>   The tyrant's jest, the Gentile's scorn;
> No censer round our altar beams,
>   And mute our timbrel, trump, and horn.
> But THOU hast said, "The blood of goat,
>   The flesh of rams, I will not prize;
> A contrite heart, and humble thought,
>   Are Mine accepted sacrifice."

But the dominant impression of the boyish mind was hostility to the Mohammedan and an intense admiration for Richard of the Lion-Heart. As I grew older, I learned that the followers of Saladin—great warriors, great artists, great architects, great men of learning—no longer held Jerusalem, but that in 1517 it passed into the hands of the Turks, where it has remained ever since. The Turks were very different from the Saracens or the Moors, as they were later known in Northern Africa and Spain. The latter were Semitic. The Turks were of a race generally regarded as related to the Mongols, who had come down from Asia and invaded the Empire of Byzantium. If they ever did anything of value to mankind, history does not disclose it. They were brave soldiers— that has never been questioned—they could fight and oppress weaker peoples, and there their ability stopped. The prosperous towns and cities which had grown up in the region we now call the Balkans, after the fall of the Roman Empire, and which enjoyed great commercial prosperity and high civilization for that period, withered away into wretched villages. Wherever the Turk set his foot, poverty, ignorance, and degeneration followed. He could conquer, but he could not govern, and his rule has been a curse to every land it touched. That Jerusalem and Palestine, sacred to the Jews, who had fought through centuries to hold their city and their temple, a land profoundly holy to all the great Christian nations of the West, should remain permanently in the hands of the Turks has seemed to me for many years one of the great blots on the face of civilization, which ought to be erassed.

The rescue of Palestine by Great Britain and the Allies removed this stigma from the western nations, and never again must the Holy Land, as all Christians call it, pass into Turkish possession. This great result, I am sure, has been not only a joy to all those who think of the Holy Land with devout reverence, but will be a service to all mankind. If its government be properly administered, it must carry with it an extension to hate oppression and persecution born of religious differences. Thus will be spread farther than ever before among the people of the earth the belief which all Americans cherish so deeply—that no man's liberty of conscience must be questioned so long as he does not question that of his neighbor, and that men of varying faiths may live together in harmony and good will.

Mr. LIPSKY. The joint resolution did reflect the sentiments of the American people and when under consideration in the House, it was given generous support in the editorial columns of the American press. The views of a large number of Senators and Representatives favorable to the resolution were given wide circulation. They can all be found, if the committee desires to read them, in a little book— not a little book; quite a big book—entitled "The War Congress and Zionism." I do not know who of the membership of the House is not represented in this book—that is, the membership of the House at that time. It seemed to be practically a roll call of the House, because there was none opposed to the proposal.

The adoption of the joint resolution was not a chance register of a resolution, as often happens, but the expression of a conclusion thoroughly discussed and quite well understood throughout the country. The position taken by Woodrow Wilson was based upon his deep knowledge of American traditions as well as by his Christian attitude. The same thoughts were expressed in the endorsement of the Zionist position by succeeding American Presidents; they were reflected in the views of our State Department. The joint resolution was immediately signed by President Harding and within less than 2 years, after a great deal of discussion between the State Department and the British Foreign Office, a convention was entered into in 1924 or 1925——

Chairman BLOOM. December 1925.

Mr. LIPSKY. At the suggestion of Lord Curzon, the British Secretary for Foreign Affairs, the convention included the text of the preamble

of the mandate in which the following relevant paragraphs appear—
that is, in the American convention:

Whereas the principal Allied Powers have also agreed that the mandatory should
be responsible for putting into effect the declaration originally made on the 2d
November 1917 by the Government of His Britannic Majesty, and adopted by
the said powers, in favor of the establishment in Palestine of a national home for
the Jewish people, it being clearly understood that nothing should be done which
might prejudice the civil and religious rights of existing non-Jewish communities
in Palestine, or the rights and political status enjoyed by Jews in any other country;
and

Whereas recognition has thereby been given to the historical connection of the
Jewish people with Palestine and to the grounds for reconstituting their national
home in that country;   *   *   *

In the hearing before the House committee, a discussion on practically the same lines as we have had here took place.   In spite of the
fact that surrounding the hearing there was manifested in press and
in pulpit an overwhelming popular support of the resolution, the same
categories of opponents appeared.   Their names are different; but the
same arguments were presented, with the same fervor and the same
eloquence and the same piety on the part of some rabbis.

I am very reluctant to enter the dispute raised by the opposing
Jewish representatives as to the distinction between race and religion
in Jewish life.   It is better to leave it to rabbis.   This is a matter
that has gone on among Jews for 40 years, and the matter has become
very clear, and there is no serious difference between Jews except as
between the vast overwhelming majority of the Jews and a few dissenting minority groups who take positions that are wholly at variance
with what is regarded by all Jews as their fundamental, vital interest.

In my opinion this discussion is irrevelant to the question in issue.
The definitions given as to race and religion and people and proposals
for a new regime in Palestine, all have to have some relation to the
realities they attempt to describe.   You cannot come into a committee
meeting and propose things that have no relation to the political
thinking of the world, that have nothing to do with things that have
been under consideration for decades, and assume that an operation
that emanates out of a solution of a practical problem can be taken up
de novo and made the subject of discussion in a House committee,
which is called upon to act in a practical, political situation.

The House is not in a position to enter into these devious discussions
as to proposals as to what could be done in the ultimate with Palestine
or with any other country, if, in connection with these countries,
certain positions have been taken and certain relations have been
established, as have been established in the case of Palestine.

There is no doubt whatsoever, it is a matter of continuous recording
by the Jews themselves, of how they regarded themselves in world
relations and their relations to one another.   No one will question the
constant and uninterrupted and unequivocal hope of the Jewish people
throughout the ages up to this very day, which is imbedded in their
religious ideals, principles, in their customs, in their legends, in their
laws, in the constant trickle of Jews into Palestine; that there is
evident on the part of the Jewish people a clear expression of the
aspirations of an enduring people, who express themselves through their
deomocratic forms, but who never are able to reach unanimity.

It is a peculiar characteristic of the Jews, as it may be regarded a
peculiar characteristic of other peoples, that they never agree unanimously.   And the farther away you go from the United States, you

will probably find that these differences prevail much more frequently among other peoples than among the Jews themselves.

Always there has been a small contingent of secessionists who have reasons of their own that condition their thinking, that motivate their action. Always there has been a fringe of Jewish life, due to pressure, eager to disappear into the anonymity they might be able to find in alien circles, or in establishing contacts with these other circles, and they have always tried to impress Jewish life with their opinions. They have never prevailed; they have never made any impression, and either they have come back to the fold or they have disappeared into nothingness. That historic fact is recorded in Jewish history over hundreds of years.

The strange situation is that Jewish advocates have appeared here who are not content with merely expressing their opinions or their convictions in Jewish circles, and living their own lives in their own way and preaching the Judaism that they believe in; but they have appeared as active crusaders, determined to frustrate the hopes of their people. Because they are not frank, their position is equivocal and inconsistent.

We are talking of the life and the destiny of Jews throughout the world. We are talking of a people who are fundamentally religious, but who have other qualities in addition. We are talking of this people which is now suffering persecution and humiliations. We are talking of a people whose life is spread out upon the map of Europe in blood which still continues to flow. You cannot approach a situation like this and preach an abstract idea of Jewish life and confine it within a shell they call Jewish religion.

The most peculiar thing about the preachers of this form of Judaism is that among Jews they are regarded as being as far away from Jewish religion as anybody could possibly be without becoming a Unitarian or a Universalist. Among Jews they are not regarded as being representatives of Jewish religion; they have so reformed Jewish religion that it has become almost unrecognizable as Jewish. And so Jews regard them.

It may be said, "Well, they have a perfect right under a democratic form of government to do as they please." But they are engaged in an active campaign to disprove what has been established by the Jews themselves. We have established a registered point of view of the Jewish people. At that time, in 1919, we had an American Jewish Congress. If you will read the record which I have here of the hearing in 1922, you will see that Dr. Philipson appeared and presented the record to show that the Jews are not in favor of the Jewish National Home, and he cited figures. At that time the Central Congress of American Rabbis, which is the Reform Jewish body, was officially, by a majority vote, against the Jewish National Home. But the joint resolution was adopted by the House committee and by the House and Senate and signed by the President of the United States. But at that time the Reform Jews were not in favor of it.

Today an overwhelming majority of the members of the Central Conference of American Rabbis is on record in favor of this resolution, in favor of our position. At that time the Union of American Hebrew Congregations was wholly against us. The House committee adopted it unanimously nevertheless. Today the Union of American Hebrew Congregations is a member of the American Jewish Conference.

At that time the B'nai Brith was neutral; today it is a member of the American Jewish Conference which adopted the Palestine resolution. Today the same group, represented by Dr. Philipson in 1922, is an emaciated group, a group that has lost its standing among Jews, that is, fumbling around for some formula that will keep them within the fold of Jewish life and at the same time enable them to establish their isolation from the ancient hope of the Jewish people.

I was an official of the American Jewish Conference that conducted the elections. We devised a system of democratic representation of proportional group representation within the conference. We organized a conference which gave an opportunity to every group to express its opinion. We represented, according to our calculations—there being 1 delegate for every 50 Jews that came to the conference—we had a representation there of two and a half million Jews, of all the national organizations with the exception of two. It was the most impressive ceremonial act on the part of the Jewish people when they voted on the Palestine resolution. And the vote on the Palestine resolution was taken after there had been 2 days' deliberation in a subcommittee in which some of these men, who subsequently did not vote, participated in the debate. They participated on the floor by making statements and declarations. And at the end of the proceedings every Jew in the United States was convinced that this represented the opinion of the Jews of this country.

Now, how can the impression be avoided that there are some who do not agree? Mr. Rosenwald testified here that he represented, after an effort, after an expenditure of quite a good deal of money, the achievement of 2,500 Jews who had registered with the Council for American Judaism—2,500 Jews as against the two and a half million who were in the American Jewish Conference, as against the active elements of Jewish life which control and direct the Zionist movement, which is a permeating influence in every field of Jewish life, in the religious, in the social, in the philanthropic features of Jewish life. Yet the impression that is made by well-meaning gentlemen with erudition and piety is that this represents dissension.

If that is dissension, then the United States is a seething maelstrom of dissension. If that is dissension, England today, in the midst of the war, is a turbulent revolutionary country. In any well-ordered democracy that would be regarded as disorderliness, not dissension, as the refusal on the part of eccentric persons to abide by majority rule.

I said that the position, because of the uncertainties and the two-faced attitude they take with regard to Jewish life—one looking to life on the outside; the other looking to the Jews—produces equivocation and inconsistency. They say they favor all the practical aspects of the building of a Jewish community in the promised land. They say they favor free Jewish immigration. They say they favor a cultural and social center for the Jewish people in Palestine. They seem to be sympathetic to the creation of a Jewish economic life in Palestine, and a social and spiritual center that might be the reflection of that life in Palestine, but for reasons that are incomprehensible, they are averse to the establishment of the necessary political armaments that may be required to maintain the life thus created, whether it be religious or social or economic.

There must be some protection for that life. All the Jews may be religious, and of the school of Rabbi Fineshriber, or all the Jews may be religious of the school of Rabbi Gold, but it must be recognized that they have common interests that are human and mundane, and these interests have to be protected by the forms of political institutions. But they refuse to accept the possibilities of the Jews becoming the majority. They are willing to abandon the idea of majority rule in Palestine as soon as the Jews become the majority. And for what reason? Is there anything offensive to good taste in the Jewish people having a majority in a land which they built up themselves with their own labor and sacrifice? Is there anything that is offensive to justice? Is there anything offensive to democracy if the Jews come to Palestine under the mandate and establish a majority?

On the contrary, is it not very proper for them to establish a majority and to maintain that majority and to give certain agreements, if necessary, as to the fundamental rights that are to be guaranteed to all citizens, regardless of race or creed.

Does anybody sitting around this table believe for one second that the Jews will go back to Palestine, after their experience of hundreds of years of persecution, and start their state with an attempt to oppress people, with an attempt to get the best of people, who are, as has been said here, their cousins, and with whom they would get along very well if there were no political implications involved? Does anybody believe for 1 minute that the Jews will not endeavor to the best of their ability to establish for their own interests a state in which every man will be free and equal, regardless of race or color or religion? Does anybody doubt that? Do the Arabs need to be protected against the Jews, or the Jews against the Arabs?

What is happening today is the best proof of what Jews are capable of doing. Without any compulsion, without any control of the state, the Jewish people have moved into the building of Palestine with the utmost consideration for every individual living in the land. They have not conquered the land by force; they have bought land in a free market. They have overpaid for the land. They have walked in peace and with justice as their guide. They have given every consideration to Arab citizens there, regardless of the attitude taken by the irregulars among the Arabs. And that can be expected also in the future.

It seems to me—it may not be fair for me to say this—that our rabbinical friends who are opposing the resolution cling to these inconsistencies in spite of their obviousness because of their fear that the words that are being used contradict their self-chosen definitions, and that they may inconvenience them or embarrass them in the preaching of the doctrine that they have adopted 40 or 50 years ago, before Hitler, and which they still maintain, regardless of what life has done to the Jewish people. Even if the Jewish people are a religious group, the essence of a political situation still remains and it has to be applied, whether we are a race or a religion.

I say that this situation here has been greatly complicated unnecessarily. We are not dealing with a new problem nor with a new issue, with a new conflict. So far as the United States is concerned, what the policy with regard to Palestine was to be was determined and registered in 1922, and through Executive action in 1925. What we are called upon to do relates to an unwarranted, an unsanctioned, an illegal departure from a policy which was agreed to in 1917, which was confirmed in 1922 by the Chief Executive of the American Government, which was incorporated in 1922 in the joint resolution unanimously adopted by the Congress and by the convention with England adopted in 1925.

That policy is now being threatened. It is not a secret matter; it has been published all over the world since 1939. The intention of the British Government is to change that policy without consulting either with the United States or any of the nations signatory to the mandate. That policy is threatened through the abandonment of the Balfour Declaration by the mandatory government in its declared policy incorporated in the MacDonald White Paper of 1939. That policy blots out the judgment of 52 nations, including the United States. It renders null and void the basic promise of the British Government and disregards the enforcement of those promises by the League of Nations and by the Government of the United States. It abandons the idea of the Jewish National Home completely in favor of the idea of a determined, guaranteed majority Arab state in Palestine. That is a violation of everything contained in the papers you have been questioning witnesses about.

The great promises of Balfour and Lloyd George and Churchill, as well as the promises of Woodrow Wilson and General Smuts and others, were abandoned by the British Government almost simultaneously with the abandonment of the policy of appeasement of Hitler. England took up arms in defense of civilization. At the same time, almost within a few months, on its own motion, without consulting its friends, without ascertaining their views, without consulting the endorsers of the promise, it undertook, in the course of 5 years, to eliminate its promise to the Jewish people, disregarding utterly the fate of five or six hundred thousand Jews who had come into Palestine and built up their lives under the British promise and undertook to transfer the sovereignty of Palestine, not to the Jews, not to take it itself, but to transfer it to the Arabs of Palestine, who at that time were engaged in a campaign of terror and murder under the instigation and with the support of the Nazis and the Fascists. That was not a revolution or a revolt. It was a conspiracy, the cost of which was paid for in money by Germany and Italy and in blood by Jews and Arabs and English soldiers. For that statement, we have the authority of Mr. Churchill himself as to what were the underlying causes of this reign of terror.

What does the resolution under discussion involve? As was indicated in the questions raised by Mr. Voorhis, it merely reaffirms the sentiment of the Congress of 1922. It tenders its views with regard to a great humanitarian movement to the executive department of our Government for its guidance. It undertakes to convey to the executive department what it regards as the prevailing American sentiment on a matter with which the executive department is now dealing.

It is very important that the executive department should be informed, and that the executive department should inform this committee with regard to the situation. The peace of the world is being made piecemeal from day to day, and the conditions that are to prevail in the Near East are being determined from day to day by individual acts of Government representatives. What will be the future of Palestine is being determined right now, just as the future of the Arab states in the vicinity is being agreed to.

These relations are being fixed. They are being determined by the discussion which is being held in the capital of the United States at the present time with regard to the oil of Arabia. Do you suppose that the question of the oil of Arabia, when determined, is not going to affect Jewish rights in Palestine in one form or another? Is it not important that this committee at this time give the executive department the information that it represents through its representative capacity, so that the Government of the United States may know what is public opinion with regard to this matter? Does public opinion stand by 1922, or is it also involved in the mixture called the oil of Arabia, and in the mixture called secret sessions at Cairo; in different propositions that are being made about an Arab federation, which may pop up some morning as an established federation, which will reflect itself in what Palestine is to become? Is it not important that this committee advise the executive department with regard to this matter?

This resolution reaffirms a position which was taken in 1922 and which remains valid so far as the American people are concerned also in 1944.

In the light of the developments of the past 22 years, the resolution submitted is clear and less equivocal. The equivocations of the mandate have become so confusing that not even the English Government and its officials are in a position to understand exactly where they are going, and it is important that we express a view with regard to that situation through the advices that may be given from the House to the executive department.

When this resolution is adopted, it will reflect the compassion of the vast majority of American citizens and of their elected representatives for the millions of Jews, victims of Hitler's barbarism. It will indicate American sympathy with the just claims of the Jewish people for the fulfillment of promises made and internationally accepted in 1917.

At the end of the First World War, the grand mood of justice and peace and democracy captured the spirit of the Allied states. They sought to materialize the hopes of many peoples in Europe. They did the best that they could under the circumstances. The hopes and aspirations of the Jewish people were given form and substance in the Balfour Declaration. They were given practical significance in the decisions that established the mandate. An ancient wrong was to be righted, a sanctuary was to be created. The homelessness of the Jewish people was to come to an end. They were not thinking then of Zionism as lawyers; but as men imbued with an ideal of justice. They were not afraid to speak of reconstituting the Jewish Commonwealth, of the return of the Jewish people to Zion.

But the mood passed in stages from one retreat to another. The field of operations was restricted, becoming smaller from year to year. The retreat came to its climax in 1939, when the MacDonald White Paper cut away the foundations upon which the covenant for the Jewish National Home rested.

I was in London at that time, at the so-called Arab-Jewish Conference, which was not an Arab-Jewish Conference at all. The Arabs met in one corner one day and we met in another corner the next day, and the intermediary between us was Malcolm MacDonald, who finally, in desperation, gave up his attempts and said he would do it himself, and he drew up the MacDonald White Paper at a time when England was in the greatest confusion. England was at that time considering how to protect iteslf by concession and appeasement, for it was not in a position to defend its imperial interests. They were considering, "How can we preserve some parts of our empire?" And in desperation they forced this White Paper through Parliament.

There was a tremendous number of Members of the House who were opposed to the policy. Mr. Churchill delivered an address that touched the conscience of every Member of Parliament, because he personally was responsible for the Balfour Declaration, and he had something to do with the making of the mandate, and he was a party to everything that related to the building of the Jewish National Home. He thought the White Paper represented moral bankruptcy.

They passed it through. And they attempted to implement it. They attempted to implement this policy at a time when the Jewish people were scurrying to all corners of Europe seeking a haven of refuge, and finding few. And they implemented the White Paper strictly as to immigration, as to land purchase, and they were considering how to build up the Arab state right in the midst of the confusion of the war. And they are doing so to this day, in spite of the fact that Mr. Churchill represents an opinion which is quite contrary to the opinion of the Palestine administration.

It therefore becomes necessary for the American Congress, functioning in a time of war, when it is important that the executive branch of the Government should be informed as to what the state of public opinion may be, when we are fighting together with England, to express its views on this important matter. This is not a time of peace. England is our ally. We are fighting together with them, and our interests are common, and we are not approaching strangers with strange requests. It has comething to do with a matter in which the American Government, in the time of the first war, joined with England in a common cause.

We have a right to intervene at this time, when we are fighting especially together with England for the preservation of the principles of democracy and for the integrity of international law and international covenants.

It is important that this resolution be adopted as an indication that the just principles adopted in 1922 remain valid in 1944.

Thank you.

Chairman Bloom. Is that all?

Mr. Lipsky. That is all.

Chairman Bloom. Judge Kee.

Mr. Kee. I have no questions.

Chairman Bloom. Dr. Eaton.

Mr. Eaton. No questions.

Chairman Bloom. Mr. Jarman.

Mr. Jarman. Not at this hour.

Chairman Bloom. Mr. Chiperfield.

Mr. Chiperfield. No.

Chairman Bloom. Mr. Rogers.

Mr. ROGERS. Just to say that it was a brilliant explanation of some of the points which have been brought out.

I have no questions.

Chairman BLOOM. Mr. Jonkman?

Mr. JONKMAN. No questions.

Chairman BLOOM. Mr. Wright.

Mr. WRIGHT. No questions.

Chairman BLOOM. Mrs. Bolton.

Mrs. BOLTON. No questions.

Chairman BLOOM. Mr. Wadsworth.

Mr. WADSWORTH. No questions.

Chairman BLOOM. Mr. Lipsky, we appreciate your coming back after so many years.

Mr. LIPSKY. I am glad I am still here.

Chairman BLOOM. I want to say for the benefit of the members, if you would like to read the proceedings of 1922, the clerk has the hearings here of that time. They are here for you to read.

Mr. Lipsky, we thank you very, very much. We thank all witnesses who appeared here today for being so patient and waiting until this hour. The Chair wishes to state that up to the present time, the time today has been divided, 2¾ hours for the proponents, and 3 hours and 10 minutes for the opponents, and in making that statement just wants to have it as a matter of record that the committee has been very patient to hear both sides of this question, and has tried to give everyone a fair hearing.

Thank you very, very much.

The committee stands adjourned to the call of the chairman.

(Whereupon, at 5:20 p. m., the hearing was adjourned, to reconvene upon the call of the chairman.)

(The following letters and statements were submitted for the information of the committee:)

HOUSE OF REPRESENTATIVES,
Washington, D. C., February 22, 1944.

Hon. SOL BLOOM,
Chairman, and Members of the Foreign Affairs Committee of the House of Representatives:

As Representative At Large from the State of New York, and also as a member of the American Committee For Palestine, I wish to urge the members of the House Foreign Affairs Committee to report favorably Resolution 418, introduced by Representative Compton, of Connecticut, and Resolution 419, introduced by Representative Wright, of Pennsylvania. At a time when millions are being persecuted and slaughtered because of their religious, racial, or nationality background, all Americans are interested in doing everything possible to prevent such persecution and slaughter.

The Balfour Declaration of 1917, which had the effect of establishing Palestine as a Jewish homeland, and under the terms of which Jewish immigration was not limited, was, as a matter of record, endorsed by the 67th Congress in 1922. As a matter of simple justice and much-needed humanitarianism it would seem that the so-called British White Paper of 1939 should be repealed. To close Palestine so far as Jewish immigration subsequent to March 31, 1944, is concerned, would be to refuse a place of refuge to many persecuted Jews.

It is part of our priceless heritage as Americans to oppose any and all discrimination or persecution based on race, religion, or nationality. By reporting favorably as to Resolutions No. 418 and No. 419, the distinguished Foreign Affairs Committee of the House of Representatives will, in my opinion, express the vehement sentiment of the many patriotic American Jews who reside in the Empire State, and who have written hundreds of letters urging such action.

WINIFRED C. STANLEY, M. C.

House of Representatives,
Washington, D. C., February 24, 1944.
Hon. Sol Bloom,
House Office Building, Washington, D. C.

My Dear Representative Bloom: I am writing to say that I am favorable to the passage of Resolution 418 or 419, as I understand they are practically identical.
Respectfully yours,

E. G. Rohrbough.

_____

House of Representatives,
Washington, D. C., February 25, 1944.
Hon. Sol Bloom, M. C.,
Foreign Affairs Committee.

My Dear Mr. Chairman: I am very strong for H. R. 418 and 419. When it is reported to the House I shall do everything I can for its adoption.
Very sincerely yours,

Clifford Davis.

_____

House of Representatives,
Washington, D. C., February 25, 1944.
Hon. Sol Bloom,
Chairman, House Foreign Affairs Committee,
House of Representatives, Washington, D. C.

Dear Mr. Bloom: I strongly urge that your great Committee report favorably a resolution containing the purpose and intent of H. R. 418 and 419.

I believe that the cause of Democracy throughout the world will be greatly benefited by the reopening of Palestine to immigration and land settlement of the Jewish people, as provided for in the Balfour Declaration issued on November 2, 1917, and the Mandate for Palestine accorded to Great Britain in 1922 with the consent of the 51 member nations of the League of Nations and with the unanimous approval of the Congress of the United States.

As the fulfillment of the Balfour Declaration and the Mandate for Palestine have been nullified by the Palestine White Paper of May 1939, issued by the British Government, I believe the prestige of our own great Democracy should be utilized to call to the attention of the present British Government that we consider the said British White Paper a "breach and a repudiation of the Balfour Declaration" as declared by their own Prime Minister, Winston Churchill.

Unless the purpose and intent of the Balfour Declaration is reestablished very soon, it will in effect sentence thousands of Jewish people who are refugees to annihilation. In the name of humanity, we should do all in our power to see that the gates of Palestine are opened to these unfortunate people.
Sincerely yours,

Chet Holifield,
Member of Congress, Nineteenth District, California.

_____

House of Representatives,
Washington, D. C., February 29, 1944.
Hon. Sol Bloom,
Chairman, Committee on Foreign Affairs,
House of Representatives, Washington, D. C.

Dear Mr. Chairman: In further reference to my letter of February 10, and your reply of February 12, I am herewith submitting a statement on House Resolution 418 and House Resolution 419, which I would appreciate very much having incorporated at the proper point in the printed hearings on these Resolutions. Please be kind enough to advise me as to whether or not this consistently can be done.
Cordially yours,

Winder R. Harris.

STATEMENT SUBMITTED BY REPRESENTATIVE WINDER R. HARRIS, OF VIRGINIA, FOR THE HEARINGS ON HOUSE RESOLUTION 418 AND HOUSE RESOLUTION 419, "RELATIVE TO THE JEWISH NATIONAL HOME IN PALESTINE"

Mr. Chairman, I bespeak an opportunity to record my strong views in support of pending proposal relative to the Jewish National Home in Palestine. This is a noble cause in which all persons concerned with human rights and plain, four-square justice should take an active interest. The expression of interest by the United States in the creation of the Jewish National Home in Palestine, as provided in the resolutions before this committee, is made urgently necessary by the fact that the MacDonald White Paper of May 17, 1939, is approaching its effective date, which would mean that after this month, Jewish immigration into Palestine would have to stop, unless Arab consent were obtained, and that the Jewish population in this refuge from the tyrannies of unconscionable dictators and inflamed nationalist majorities would be forced into a permanently restricted minority state.

That would be a far cry from the Commonwealth definitely promised in the Balfour Declaration and of which the Jewish people had a right to expect fulfillment.

It may not be possible to attain the full goal—the establishment of the Commonwealth—at this time, but it certainly should be possible to keep open the doors of Palestine to those who need so urgently to find there surcease from persecution and succor. It may be good policy, in the light of the practicalities of international politics, to leave the question of a Commonwealth for determination after victory in the War of Liberty is won. But with all the tortures and suffering the Jewish people are undergoing in Europe today, in view of all the talk the United Nations leaders are indulging in about self-determination, fairness, and justice to all peoples—about minorities and even the citizens of defeated lands—to say, in the midst of the present struggle for freedom, we are going to deny to the homeless Jews the right already given to them to establish a national home—and going still farther and say they cannot even migrate to the refuge which has been set up for them.

The Four Freedoms about which we prate so much would become a hollow mockery and a sham, were we in the United States to take such a stand.

There are a million and a half nationless Jews, according to statistics which I have seen. Where are they going to be absorbed, if not in Palestine? Immigration barriers and economic conditions combine to make it certain that only a few of these pitiable people are going to be taken into other countries. Yet, they cannot possibly remain with any degree of safety in the countries which have shown hearty approval of a policy of extermination.

We hear much about establishing freedom from fear. The homeless Jews never could be free from fear for a single moment, if they were forced to go back and take up their homes among the people who have been taught to hate them. Reinstatement of these refugees on a basis of equality is impossible, under existing deplorable conditions.

Palestine is a demonstrated success as a colonization project. It is the rightful place for the nationless Jews to go. We must not let the doors be shut against them.

There is no question about the fact that the White Paper had its birth in that shameful period of appeasement which merely fed the warlike appetites of ruthless aggressors. It was promulgated in the same spirit of timidity that produced the destruction of Czechoslovakia. The Arab uprising undoubtedly was fomented by Germany and Italy. We then could see that the Near East was going to be an important area in the war. Great Britain might have had on its hands more than it could handle if the Arab terrorists were not appeased and succeeded in stirring up anti-British sentiment, and attempted to throw the country into the hands of the Axis powers.

But the situation is entirely different now. The Arab terrorists can do the Allies no harm militarily. They never have joined in the war, even though Egypt actually was invaded.

In sharp and glorious contrast, little Palestine has contributed generously of its manpower and resources.

The United Nations are amply able to say to the Arabs: "There will be no appeasement this time; justice and right are going to prevail. There is plenty of available and sparsely settled territory for you. An amicable adjustment can and must be worked out that will make possible the establishment of a National Jewish Homeland in Palestine."

When the freedom-loving, victorious Allied Nations foregather about the peace table, the Palestine mandate should be reviewed. There is serious question as to whether it has not been actually misused. The White Paper itself has been declared by many authorities to be illegal.

The United States has a definite obligation in this matter. The Balfour Declaration was issued after consultation with the United States. Congress added its sanction in a joint resolution which said:

"The United States of America favors the establishment in Palestine of a National Home for the Jewish people."

A special treaty with Great Britain, after rejection of the Versailles Treaty and the League of Nations Covenant, incorporated the text of the Palestine Mandate, which included the Balfour Declaration.

Moreover, every President from Woodrow Wilson down to Franklin D. Roosevelt has given favorable expression to the Palestine project.

It is highly important, too, to keep in mind that in giving sympathy and support to the present movement to prevent the White Paper from being made effective after this month, there can be no question of offering offense to the present British Government, for the very plain and simple reason that the leaders of the present British Government condemned the White Paper in the strongest terms when it was issued. Mr. Winston Churchill himself said in Parliamentary debate on May 23, 1939:

"There is much in this White Paper which is alien to the spirit of the Balfour Declaration, but I will not trouble about that. I select the one point upon which there is plainly a breach and repudiation of the Balfour Declaration—the provision that Jewish immigration can be stopped in five years' time by the decision of the Arab majority."

Mr. Churchill should make good on that statement. The United States should do what it consistently can to bring him to that action.

The day of liberation is close at hand for the victims of Axis conquest on the Continent of Europe—and in the Far East. This same day of liberation should make freemen of the Jews of Europe who have escaped torture and death, and who have fought to survive until victory comes.

Let there be no hypocritical peace, with freedom for only a part of the people of the world.

The Atlantic Charter solemnly promises that all men in all lands shall be allowed to live out their lives in freedom.

The doors of Palestine must be reopened—and kept open.

NEW YORK, N. Y., *February 16, 1944.*

Hon. SOL BLOOM,
    Chairman, Committee on Foreign Affairs,
        House of Representatives, Washington, D. C.

SIR: As a delegate of the American Federation of Jews from Central Europe I was present at the hearings on February 7th and 8th. Following your suggestion, made at the conclusion of the hearings, I beg to submit to you the following statement:

On various occasions and also in the course of the hearings the return of the Jews to Central Europe after the war has been advocated as a proper way for, at least, a partial solution of the Jewish problem. Those in favor of such a return forget that many parents depend on their children who, on their part, will refuse to live in countries which to them hold out no prospects of liberty, dignity, and happiness.

They lose sight of the fact that German education for more than 10 years has been most thorough. For those subjected to that sort of education it will be easier to cross continents and oceans than to overcome the distance to people which they have learned to despise and to murder. The same difficulty exists for the Jews with regard to their persecutors.

Again, the same small amount of energy, left in a Nazi victim that will enable him to carry on in the stimulating atmosphere of Palestine, will not be sufficient to have him resume his life in Germany and to have him fight against the background of ghastly memories, unredeemed souls and of a slowly, if at all, receding flood of bias and hatred.

Therefore, the majority of those who will survive the dreadful camps as well as those who have found only temporary refuge in various parts of the world will know that going back is not identical with coming home. They will want to stay away from the land of their persecutors.

I should like to call your attention to another point. There are thousands of Jewish orphans—a strange sort of orphans indeed—for they have become so while their parents were still alive and dragged away from them into no man's land. Their arrival in Palestine, as experience has shown, means to them reunion with their greater family before their reunion with their own family—if such a reunion will ever take place.

The adults among the immigrants from Central Europe who have made numerous and genuine contributions to industry and agriculture of Palestine, their strong and healthy children together with the whole Jewish population in Palestine— they have all the tools for complete self-government. They wait for the right to use them and they wait for their brothers to come.

May I state. my dear Mr. Bloom, that those whom I represent, are the natural supporters of the resolution now pending in both Houses.

Very truly yours,

MAX GRUENEWALD.

APPENDIX

THE JEWISH NATIONAL HOME IN PALESTINE

COMMITTEE ON FOREIGN AFFAIRS
HOUSE OF REPRESENTATIVES
SEVENTY-EIGHTH CONGRESS
SECOND SESSION

H. Res. 418 and H. Res. 419

THE JEWISH NATIONAL HOME IN PALESTINE

House Resolution 418 and House Resolution 419, relative to the Jewish National Home in Palestine, were introduced and referred to the Committee on Foreign Affairs on January 27, 1944. Much of the basic source material relating to this question has not heretofore been collated. In order that it may have at hand such data, and in an effort to provide the Committee on Foreign Affairs with full information regarding the issues involved, the chairman has assembled copies of the following original documents: The texts of the Mandate on Palestine; the joint resolution of the Sixty-seventh Congress, signed by President Harding, favoring the establishment in Palestine of a National Home for the Jews; the British White Paper on Palestine of May 1939; the Convention of 1924 between the United States and Great Britain relative to Palestine; and other data on this subject contained in official documents of the State Department, the British House of Lords and House of Commons, and also of the Jewish Agency in Palestine.

ACTION INITIATED AT BERMUDA CONFERENCE, APRIL 1943, INDEFINITELY POSTPONING BRITISH WHITE PAPER BAN ON IMIGRATION

Under provisions of the British White Paper of 1939, further Jewish immigration into Palestine was limited to 75,000 immigrants and refugees and all Jewish immigration was to cease on March 31, 1944. By 1943 only a little more than half of the 75,000 Jews permitted to enter under terms of the White Paper had been able to reach Palestine. As the result of action initiated at the Bermuda Conference of April 1943, the expiration date of March 31, 1944, was indefinitely postponed by the British Parliament to enable the authorized remainder, approximately 30,000 Jews in number, to enter Palestine whenever they should succeed in reaching that haven.

The resolutions now pending before the Committee on Foreign Affairs provide:

That the United States shall use its good offices and take appropriate measures to the end that the doors of Palestine shall be opened for free entry of Jews into that country, and that there shall be full opportunity for colonization, so that the Jewish people may ultimately reconstitute Palestine as a free and democratic Jewish commonwealth.

SOL BLOOM,
Chairman, Committee on Foreign Affairs.

[H. Res. 418, 78th Cong., 2d sess.]

JANUARY 27, 1944

Mr. WRIGHT submitted the following resolution; which was referred to the Committee on Foreign Affairs

RESOLUTION

Relative to the Jewish National Home in Palestine

Whereas the Sixty-seventh Congress of the United States on June 30, 1922, unanimously resolved "that the United States of America favors the establishment in Palestine of a national home for the Jewish people, it being clearly understood that nothing shall be done which may prejudice the civil and religious rights of Christian and all other non-Jewish communities in Palestine shall be adequately protected"; and

Whereas the ruthless persecution of the Jewish people in Europe has clearly demonstrated the need for a Jewish homeland as a haven for the large numbers who have become homeless as a result of this persecution: Therefore be it

Resolved, That the United States shall use its good offices and take appropriate measures to the end that the doors of Palestine shall be opened for free entry of Jews into that country, and that there shall be full opportunity for colonization, so that the Jewish people may ultimately reconstitute Palestine as a free and democratic Jewish commonwealth.

(NOTE.—House Resolution 419, introduced by Mr. Compton of Connecticut is an identical measure.)

392

EXCERPTS FROM STATE DEPARTMENT PUBLICATION NO. 153

Near Eastern Series, No. 1

MANDATE FOR PALESTINE

I. INTRODUCTION

1. EXPLANATION OF THE TERM "PALESTINE"

The World War and subsequent international agreements have given to the term "Palestine" a new meaning. Formerly hardly more than a geographic name conventionally used in referring to that portion of the Ottoman Empire which included the ancient lands of the Hebrews and the coastal plain of Philistia, it now connotes an area which, but for an incompletely delimited eastern boundary, is of definite extent and is administered by Great Britain under a mandate from the League of Nations which entered into effect on September 29, 1923.

Even now, however, an explanation of the term "Palestine" is necessary, for, as used in the "Mandate for Palestine" and related documents, it connotes two territories, Palestine proper and Trans-Jordan. Though both are included in the single mandated territory and controlled by Great Britain through a single British High Commissioner for Palestine, they are administered in radically different fashion and present radically different problems of a racial, social, and administrative nature. Palestine proper and Trans-Jordan were in September, 1922, divided by "a line drawn from a point two miles west of the town of Akaba on the Gulf of that name up the centre of the Wady Araba, Dead Sea and River Jordan to its junction of the River Yarmuk; thence up the centre of that river to the Syrian Frontier." To the west of this line the terms of the mandate for Palestine apply *in toto;* to the east, only such terms of the mandate apply as do not relate to the establishment in Palestine of a Jewish national home.[1]

2. PALESTINE UNDER THE TURKS

In 1517 Palestine was, by right of conquest, added to the possessions of the Ottoman Sultans. During the first three centuries of Ottoman dominion, however, but little direct control was exercised by the Sublime Porte over the numerous Pashas and Beys under whose immediate overlordship the population lived in a state closely resembling that which existed in Europe under the feudal system; and it was only during the early years of the nineteenth century, during the reign of Sultan Mahmud, sometimes called "The Re-

---

[1] See Sec. I (8), *post*, pp. 23–24.

former," that the beginnings of a centralized administration were established. The power of the local feudal chieftains was largely broken during the period of the occupation (1831–1840) of Moham-med Ali, the semi-independent Pasha of Egypt; and the highly cen-tralized rule of Abd-ul-Hamid II (1876–1909), although marked by numerous oppressive measures, resulted in the definite establishment of an organized local administration under the direct control of a governor appointed and controlled by the Sublime Porte.

In 1914 the territory which is now Palestine supported an esti-mated population of 700,000, including something over 500,000 Mo-hammedans, some 80,000 to 90,000 Jews, and an approximately equal number of native Christians. Foreign enterprise was prominent in commerce and foreign capital in a limited number of public works and investments of a commercial character, as well as in the exten-sive establishments maintained by foreign missions. But in the eyes of the world it was then, as it is to-day, primarily known as the land in which Judaism and Christianity had their source and which had played an important rôle in the development of Mohammedanism, the last of the three great Semitic religions.[2]

3. PALESTINE DURING THE WORLD WAR

Following the Allies' declaration of war against the Ottoman Em-pire on November 5, 1914, Allied warships blockaded the coast of Syria and Palestine, while by the Turks Palestine was used as a base for operations against Egypt (declared a British protectorate on December 18, 1914). Unsuccessful Turkish attacks were launched against the Suez Canal in January, 1915, and July, 1916.

During the latter half of 1916, following the second of these at-tacks, the British forces in Egypt began preparations for the inva-sion of Palestine. A railway and a pipe line for water were pushed rapidly forward across the intervening desert. In December, 1916, the Turkish forces were obliged to evacuate El Arish, the northern border post on the Siani-Palestine frontier, and by October, 1917 General Allenby was in a position to launch the first of his main attacks against the Turkish forces in Palestine.

Meanwhile, as a result of an exchange of correspondence during 1915 between the British High Commissioner in Egypt and Sherif Hussein of Mecca [3] and the activities of British intelligence agents in the Hedjaz, a considerable portion of the Arab tribes of northwestern Arabia had been brought to a point where they were prepared to proclaim their independence of Turkish rule. In June, 1916, the Arab revolutionaries under the leadership of Sherif Hussein cap-tured the Turkish garrisons at Mecca and Jedda; and during the ensuing British campaign in western Palestine, flying columns of Arab levies harassed the left flank of the Turkish forces.

The main British advance began in October, 1917, Gaza falling on November 7 after a series of severe engagements. Jerusalem sur-rendered on December 9, and by February, 1918, the whole of south-ern Palestine west of the Dead Sea was brought under British control.

---

[2] An excellent recapitulation of the economic situation in Palestine following the World War may be found in Special Consular Report No. 83, entitled *Palestine: Its Commercial Resources with Particular Refer-ence to American Trade*, by Minister Resident and Consul General (then Consul) Addison E. Southard, published by the Department of Commerce, Washington, in 1922.

[3] See *infra.*, 4 (a).

Northern Palestine and Syria were occupied in September and October of the same year. In this final offensive, the Arab forces, under the guidance of British officers and with the help of British technical units, played an important role in eastern Palestine and Syria.

4. POLITICAL SITUATION AT THE END OF THE WAR

Before passing to a discussion of the situation in Palestine as it developed after the Turkish defeat and the armistice signed between the Allies and Turkey at Mudros on October 30, 1918, it is well to consider the principal political factors affecting that situation. These may be grouped under three heads: (a) The so-called British pledges to the Arabs; (b) Zionism and the Balfour Declaration; and (c) the secret agreements relating to the Near East entered into during the war by certain of the Allied powers. A brief discussion of each of these factors follows.

(a) British pledges to the Arabs

As indicated in the foregoing section, negotiations were entered into during 1915 between the British High Commissioner in Egypt, on behalf of the British Government, and Sherif Hussein of Mecca. From the Allied standpoint these negotiations had as their object the crystallization of Arab dissatisfaction with Turkish rule and the utilization of the resulting Arab movement as a weapon to counter Turkish efforts to incite the Mohammedan world to a Djihad, or Holy War, against the Allies. Hussein, on his part, when he had become convinced of the ultimate victory of the Allies, had as his object the obtaining of British support in Arab efforts to throw off the Turkish yoke and the recognition by the Allies of the right of the Arabs, once such independence should have been gained, to establish an independent empire which would embrace all the Arab lands, excepting Aden, from the southern mountains of Asia Minor to the Arabian Ocean. A request for the recognition of an Arab caliphate was also advanced; and it is not to be doubted that, even in these early years of the war, Hussein was inspired by dreams of future imperial rank and caliphal dignity.

During the course of the discussions which followed, the British position with reference to these Arab aspirations was stated as follows in a communication addressed to Hussein by the British High Commission at Cairo under date of October 24, 1915:

The districts of Mersina and Alexandretta and the portions of Syria lying to the west of the districts of Damascus, Hama, Homs, and Aleppo cannot be said to be purely Arab, and should be excluded from the proposed limits and boundaries. With the above modification, and without prejudice to our existing treaties with Arab chiefs, we accept these limits and boundaries, and in regard to those portions of the territories therein in which Great Britain is free to act without detriment to the interest of her ally, France, I am empowered in the name of the Government of Great Britain to give the following assurance and make the following reply to your letter:

Subject to the above modifications, Great Britain is prepared to recognize and support the independence of the Arabs within the territories included in the limits and boundaries proposed by the Sheriff of Mecca.

Great Britain will guarantee the Holy Places against all external aggression and will recognize their individuality.

When the situation admits, Great Britain will give to the Arabs her advice and will assist them to establish what may appear to be the most suitable forms of government in these various territories.

On the other hand, it is understood that the Arabs have decided to seek the advice and guidance of Great Britain only, and that such European advisers and officials as may be required for the formation of a sound form of administration will be British.

With regard to the vilayets of Baghdad and Basra, the Arabs will recognize that the established position and interests of Great Britain necessitate special measures of administrative control, in order to secure these territories from foreign aggression, to promote the welfare of the local populations, and to safeguard our mutual economic interests.[4]

Hussein, however, would not agree to these proposed "modifications" of the territorial and other claims advanced by him on behalf of the Arabs. He objected particularly to those parts of the British proposals pointing to the establishment of French control in Syria and British ascendency in Mesopotamia. The matter appears to have rested on a general assurance given by the British Government that "Great Britain has no intention of concluding any peace on terms of which the freedom of the Arab peoples from German and Turkish domination does not form an essential condition." [5]

It should be noted, also, that the independence of the Hedjaz was recognized formally by Great Britain, France, and Russia on December 10, 1916. A brief recapitulation of the circumstances surrounding this recognition is given in 'the following *aide mémoire* furnished the American Diplomatic Agency at Cairo by the Arab bureau of the British Residency under date of October 24, 1917:

The Sherif of Mecca revolted against the Turks on June 5, 1916.

On October 29, 1916, the British Agent at Jeddah received a telegram from the Under Secretary of State for Foreign Affairs at Mecca asking him to notify H. M. Government that the Sherif had been recognized by the Assembly of Ulema at Mecca as King of the Arab Nation. The same announcement was communicated by telegram from Mecca to Cairo, London, Paris, and Petrograd. The formal ceremony took place in Mecca on 6 November, 1916. No representative of any foreign power attended.

After some discussion the Governments of Great Britain, France and Russia agreed to recognize the Sherif as lawful independent ruler of the Hedjaz and to use the title of "King of the Hedjaz" when addressing him, and a note to this effect was handed to him on December 10, 1916.

(b) Zionism and the Balfour Declaration

Zionism is a movement of return; in particular it is the movement of an organized body of modern Jewry for the establishment in Palestine of a national home for the Jews. In its broader aspect it dates from the final destruction (135 A. D.) of the Jewish Kingdom and the resulting edict of Rome which denied to the Jews further access to Palestine; for, scattered throughout the world, the Jewish people have ever held tenaciously to the ideal of reestablishment in their ancient homeland. In its modern sense, Zionism may be said to date from the beginning of Jewish recolonization in Palestine in 1880 following persecutions in eastern European countries, and from

[4] Loder's *Truth about Mesopotamia, Syria & Palestine*, p. 21. This text of the statement of how far the British Government was prepared to go in meeting Arab aspirations is believed to be official, as extensive quotations therefrom appear in official sources: e. g., on March 20, 1919, during the course of the Peace Conference at Paris, Mr. Lloyd George quoted the first two paragraphs of this communication and stated that "the whole of the agreement of 1916 (Sykes-Picot)" was based thereon. See *Woodrow Wilson and World Settlement*, by R. S. Baker.
[5] Loder, *ibid*, p. 23.

[NOTE.—See, however, statement of policy (British White Paper on Palestine) presented by the Secretary of State for the Colonies to Parliament May 1939, p. 20.]

the summoning in 1897 at Basle of a Congress of Jews which defined the meaning of Zionism as the effort to win "a legally secured, publicly recognized Home for the Jewish People in Palestine."

The original program of the Zionist organization was to obtain, with the approval of the powers, a charter from the Ottoman Government authorizing the realization of its aim. Failing in this, its leaders concentrated their efforts on colonization projects and on fostering in the minds of Jews throughout the world the idea of the creation in Palestine of what was termed "a home for the Jewish spirit." With the advent of the World War, however, a new opportunity was offered to the Zionist leaders to press for the recognition and support of their original program. Their overtures finally met with success in London, where on November 2, 1917, Mr. Balfour, then His Majesty's Principal Secretary of State for Foreign Affairs, issued what has since come to be known as "the Balfour Declaration," reading as follows:

BALFOUR DECLARATION

His Majesty's Government view with favour the establishment in Palestine of a national home for the Jewish people, and will use their best endeavours to facilitate the achievement of this object, it being clearly understood that nothing shall be done which may prejudice the civil and religious rights of existing non-Jewish communities in Palestine, or the rights and political status enjoyed by the Jews in any other country.

This declaration was endorsed by the principal Allied powers, and the statement of principle embodied therein played an important part in the definition of the terms of the mandate for Palestine and the resulting administration in that territory. In 1922 it received recognition in the United States through joint resolution [6] reading as follows:

JOINT RESOLUTION OF THE CONGRESS OF THE UNITED STATES FAVORING THE ESTABLISHMENT IN PALESTINE OF A NATIONAL HOME FOR THE JEWISH PEOPLE

Resolved by the Senate and House of Representatives of the United States of America in Congress assembled, That the United States of America favors the establishment in Palestine of a national home for the Jewish people, it being clearly understood that nothing shall be done which may prejudice the civil and religious rights of Christian and all other non-Jewish communities in Palestine, and that the holy places and religious buildings and sites in Palestine shall be adequately protected.

(c) Secret agreements between certain of the Allies

Of the various secret agreements entered into during the war by certain of the Allied powers, four related directly to the Near East. These were:

First: The Constantinople agreement of 1915 between Great Britain, France, and Russia regarding the future of Constantinople, the Straits, other parts of the Ottoman Empire, and Persia. A memorandum embodying the understanding of the Russian Government with respect to these matters was handed to the British and French Ambassadors at Petrograd on March 4, 1915, by the Russian Minister for Foreign Affairs. One of the clauses of this memorandum recognized British and French rights in Asiatic Turkey and provided that these rights should

---

[6] Public No. 73, 67th Congress, signed by the President Harding on September 21, 1922.

be defined by a special agreement between Great Britain, France, and Russia. The Sykes-Picot agreement, referred to below, was reached in pursuance of the provisions of this clause.

Secondly: The Pact of London, signed by the representatives of Great Britain, France, Russia, and Italy on April 26, 1915, setting forth the bases on which Italy agreed to participate in the war on the side of the Allied powers.

Article 9 of this agreement, referring to the British and French claims in Asiatic Turkey mentioned above, recognized Italy's interest in "the maintenance of the balance of power in the Mediterranean"; and in Article 12 "Italy declares that she associates herself in the declaration made by France, Great Britain, and Russia to the effect that Arabia and the Moslem Holy Places in Arabia shall be left under the authority of an independent Moslem power."

Thirdly: The Sykes-Picot agreement effected by an exchange of notes between the French and British Governments, dated, respectively, May 9 and 16, 1916, defining their respective interests and claims in the Asiatic provinces of the Ottoman Empire.

Article 3 of this agreement provided for the establishment in that part of Palestine lying to the west of the Jordan River and exclusive of a small district including the ports of Haifa and Acre, of "an international administration of which the form shall be determined after consultation with Russia, and later in agreement with the other Allies and with representatives of the Sherif of Mecca." In general the agreement recognized French claims to Syria (as far east as the anti-Lebanon), Cilicia, a portion of Asia Minor, and a sphere of influence in eastern Syria; and British claims to Mesopotamia, a small district on the Mediterranean including the ports of Haifa and Acre, and a sphere of influence in the intervening territory between Mesopotamia and Palestine. In their respective spheres of influence the eventual establishment of Arab sovereignty was envisaged, and Article 11 provided that "the negotiations with the Arabs in regard to the frontiers of the Arab state or confederation of states shall proceed in the same way as before, in the name of the two powers."

Fourthly: The St. Jean de Maurienne agreement reached between representatives of France, Great Britain, and Italy and communicated by the Italian Ambassador in Paris to the Quai d'Orsay in a memorandum dated April 20, 1917.

The general object of this agreement was to define, "subject to the assent of the Russian Government," the territorial and economic gains in Asiatic Turkey which should accrue to Italy under the pertinent provisions of the Pact of London. With regard to Palestine it was set forth in Article 3 that "the form of international administration . . . will be decided upon in agreement with Italy"; and, with certain other similar reservations, Italy expressed her adherence to the Sykes-Picot agreement. Although Russian assent to this agreement was never given, its influence survived in subsequent discussions between the Allies and in their negotiations with Turkey and with the Arabs regarding the final disposition of the territories in question.

JEWISH NATIONAL HOME IN PALESTINE

5. BRITISH MILITARY ADMINISTRATION, 1917–1920

Following the occupation of southern Palestine in the fall of 1917 and spring of the following year,[7] a military administration was established under which the occupied territory was divided into five administrative districts. The principles on which this administration was founded were set forth by General Allenby in the following proclamation which, on December 11, 1917, the date of his official entry into the city of Jerusalem, he caused to be read to the people in English, French, Italian, Arabic, and Hebrew:

To the inhabitants of Jerusalem the Blessed and the people dwelling in the vicinity.

The defeat inflicted upon the Turks by the troops under my command has resulted in the occupation of your city by my forces. I, therefore, here and now proclaim it to be under martial law, under which form of administration it will remain so long as military considerations make necessary. However, lest any of you should be alarmed by reason of your experience at the hands of the enemy who has retired, I hereby inform you that it is my desire that every person should pursue his lawful business without fear of interruption.

Furthermore, since your city is regarded with affection by the adherents of three of the great religions of mankind, and its soil has been consecrated by the prayers and pilgrimages of multitudes of devout people of these three religions for many centuries, therefore do I make known to you that every sacred building, monument, holy spot, shrine, traditional site, endowment, pious bequest, or customary place of prayer, of whatsoever form of the three religions, will be maintained and protected according to the existing customs and beliefs of those to whose faiths they are sacred.

With the occupation of northern Palestine and Syria, following the brilliant advance of September, 1918, a first endeavor was made to meet the various political claims discussed in the preceding section of this report. Under the supreme command of General Allenby as commander in chief, France assumed administrative responsibility in Syria from the coast to the anti-Lebanon, an Arab administration was set up in Damascus and the hinterland, and British control was extended over all of Palestine west of the Jordan. This tentative division of control was confirmed in the Franco-British military convention of September 15, 1919, which, at the same time, abolished the office of the commander in chief.

The final status of Palestine, complicated as it was by Arab pretensions, Zionist aspirations, and Allied agreements pointing to an eventual international control, became a subject of Allied discussions at the Peace Conference which had met in Paris in December, 1918. There the theory of the mandatory system was evolved, and it was believed that, in the application of this theory to the Arab provinces of the Ottoman Empire, a solution of the problem would be found.

Meanwhile in Palestine, under British military administration, considerable progress was made towards the creation of a stable form of government and the rehabilitation of the economic life of the country.

6. THE GRANTING OF THE MANDATE

The mandate theory, as discussed and understood by the Allied peace delegations at Paris, was given definite form in the drafting of Article 22 of the Covenant of the League of Nations. As finally adopted this article read as follows:

---

[7] See *ante*, p. 5.

To those colonies and territories which as a consequence of the late war have ceased to be under the sovereignty of the States which formerly governed them and which are inhabited by peoples not yet able to stand by themselves under the strenuous conditions of the modern world, there should be applied the principle that the well-being and development of such peoples form a sacred trust of civilisation and that securities for the performance of this trust should be embodied in this Covenant.

The best method of giving practical effect to this principle is that the tutelage of such peoples should be entrusted to advanced nations who by reason of their resources, their experience or their geographical position can best undertake this responsibility, and who are willing to accept it, and that this tutelage should be exercised by them as Mandatories on behalf of the League.

The character of the mandate must differ according to the stage of the development of the people, the geographical situation of the territory, its economic conditions and other similar circumstances.

Certain communities formerly belonging to the Turkish Empire have reached a stage of development where their existence as independent nations can be provisionally recognised subject to the rendering of administrative advice and assistance by a Mandatory until such time as they are able to stand alone. The wishes of these communities must be a principal consideration in the selection of the Mandatory.

Other peoples, especially those of Central Africa, are at such a stage that the Mandatory must be responsible for the administration of the territory under conditions which will guarantee freedom of conscience and religion, subject only to the maintenance of public order and morals, the prohibition of abuses such as the slave trade, the arms traffic and the liquor traffic, and the prevention of the establishment of fortifications or military and naval bases and of military training of the natives for other than police purposes and the defence of territory, and will also secure equal opportunities for the trade and commerce of other Members of the League.

There are territories, such as South-West Africa and certain of the South Pacific Islands, which, owing to the sparseness of their population, or their small size, or their remoteness from the centres of civilisation, or their geographical contiguity to the territory of the Mandatory, and other circumstances, can be best administered under the laws of the Mandatory as integral portions of its territory, subject to the safeguards above mentioned in the interests of the indigenous population.

In every case of mandate, the Mandatory shall render to the Council an annual report in reference to the territory committed to its charge.

᛭ The degree of authority, control, or administration to be exercised by the Mandatory shall, if not previously agreed upon by the Members of the League, be explicitly defined in each case by the Council.

A permanent Commission shall be constituted to receive and examine the annual reports of the Mandatories and to advise the Council on all matters relating to the observance of the mandates.

The League Covenant entered into effect on January 10, 1920, the date of the *procès-verbal* drawn up by the French Government setting forth the deposit of ratifications of the treaty of Versailles by Germany and by three of the principal Allied powers. On this date, therefore, the League of Nations came into being and the Allied powers proceeded to deal with the "colonies and territories" referred to in Article 22 which were to be placed under the "tutelage" of "advanced nations," "exercised by them as Mandatories on behalf of the League." In the case of the territories formerly a part of the Ottoman Empire (known as "A" mandates, in contradistinction to the "B" and "C" mandates exercised over the less advanced communities of the overseas possessions lost to Germany in Africa and the Pacific Islands), although no treaty with Turkey whereby that state renounced sovereignty to such territories had come into effect, the Allies were in effective occupation; and on April 25, 1920, at the Allied Conference of San Remo, the allocation of the "A" mandates was made, Great Britain receiving the mandate for Palestine.

As early as June, 1919, the Supreme Council in Paris had entrusted the drafting of the projected mandates to a commission under Lord Milner. Although in the absence of a treaty of peace with Turkey, this commission abandoned its work on "A" mandate drafts, an exchange of views with reference to such drafts continued between the interested governments, a discussion in which the United States Government participated; and on December 6, 1920, Mr. Balfour addressed the following letter to the League:

In accordance with instructions received from my Government, I have the honour to transmit herewith copies of the texts of the Mandates for Mesopotamia and Palestine as drawn up by His Majesty's Government, and to request that you will be so good as to lay them before the Council of the League of Nations.

His Majesty's Government have prepared the terms of these Mandates in conformity with the spirit of Article 22 of the Covenant of the League of Nations, and have throughout been in consultation with the the French Government with whom they are in complete agreement on the subject.

His Majesty's Government venture to hope that an examination of these documents will satisfy the Council that they are in compliance with Article 22 of the Pact, and that the Council will be prepared to approve them.

I should add that, in the interests of the native inhabitants of Mesopotamia and Palestine and with the object of conferring upon them with the least possible delay the benefits of a system based on the stipulations of the Pact, His Majesty's Government desire to draw the attention of the Council to the advisability of bringing to an early close the temporary arrangements at present in force.

[Treaty Series, No. 728]

CONVENTION BETWEEN THE UNITED STATES AND GREAT BRITAIN

RIGHTS IN PALESTINE

Signed at London December 3, 1924
Ratification Advised by the Senate, February 20, 1925
Ratified by the President, March 2, 1925
Ratified by Great Britain, March 18, 1925
Ratifications Exchanged at London, December 3, 1925
Proclaimed, December 5, 1925

BY THE PRESIDENT OF THE UNITED STATES OF AMERICA

A PROCLAMATION

WHEREAS a Convention between the United States of America and His Britannic Majesty with respect to the rights of the two Governments and their nationals in Palestine was concluded and signed by their respective Plenipotentiaries at London on the third day of December, one thousand nine hundred and twenty-four, the original of which Convention is word for word as follows:

WHEREAS by the Treaty of Peace concluded with the Allied Powers, Turkey renounces all her rights and titles over Palestine; and

Whereas article 22 of the Covenant of the League of Nations in the Treaty of Versailles provides that in the case of certain territories which, as a consequence of the late war, ceased to be under the sovereignty of the States which formerly governed them, mandates should be issued, and that the terms of the mandate should be explicitly defined in each case by the Council of the League; and

Whereas the Principal Allied Powers have agreed to entrust the mandate for Palestine to His Britannic Majesty; and

Whereas the terms of the said mandate have been defined by the Council of the League of Nations, as follows:—

"The Council of the League of Nations:

"Whereas the Principal Allied Powers have agreed, for the purpose of giving effect to the provisions of article 22 of the Covenant of the League of Nations, to entrust to a Mandatory selected by the said Powers the administration of the territory of Palestine, which formerly belonged to the Turkish Empire, within such boundaries as may be fixed by them; and

"Whereas the Principal Allied Powers have also agreed that the Mandatory should be responsible for putting into effect the declaration originally made on the 2nd November, 1917, by the Government of His Britannic Majesty, and adopted by the said Powers, in favour of the establishment in Palestine of a national

402

home for the Jewish people, it being clearly understood that nothing should be done which might prejudice the civil and religious rights of existing non-Jewish communities in Palestine, or the rights and political status enjoyed by Jews in any other country; and

"Whereas recognition has thereby been given to the historical connection of the Jewish people with Palestine and to the grounds for reconstituting their national home in that country; and

"Whereas the Principal Allied Powers have selected His Britannic Majesty as the Mandatory for Palestine; and

"Whereas the mandate in respect of Palestine has been formulated in the following terms and submitted to the Council of the League for approval; and

"Whereas His Britannic Majesty has accepted the mandate in respect of Palestine and undertaken to exercise it on behalf of the League of Nations in conformity with the following provisions; and

"Whereas by the aforementioned article 22 (paragraph 8), it is provided that the degree of authority, control or administration to be exercised by the Mandatory, not having been previously agreed upon by the members of the League, shall be explicitly defined by the Council of the League of Nations;

"Confirming the said mandate, defines its terms as follows:—

"ARTICLE 1

"The Mandatory shall have full powers of legislation and of administration, save as they may be limited by the terms of this mandate.

"ARTICLE 2

"The Mandatory shall be responsible for placing the country under such political, administrative and economic conditions as will secure the establishment of the Jewish national home, as laid down in the preamble, and the development of self-governing institutions, and also for safeguarding the civil and religious rights of all the inhabitants of Palestine, irrespective of race and religion.

"ARTICLE 3

"The Mandatory shall, so far as circumstances permit, encourage local autonomy.

"ARTICLE 4

"An appropriate Jewish agency shall be recognised as a public body for the purpose of advising and co-operating with the Administration of Palestine in such economic, social and other matters as may affect the establishment of the Jewish national home and the interests of the Jewish population in Palestine, and, subject always to the control of the Administration, to assist and take part in the development of the country.

"The Zionist organisation, so long as its organisation and constitution are in the opinion of the Mandatory appropriate, shall be recognised as such agency. It shall take steps in consultation with His Britannic Majesty's Government to secure the co-operation of all Jews who are willing to assist in the establishment of the Jewish national home.

"ARTICLE 5

"The Mandatory shall be responsible for seeing that no Palestine territory shall be ceded or leased to, or in any way placed under the control of, the Government of any foreign Power.

"ARTICLE 6

"The Administration of Palestine, while ensuring that the rights and position of other sections of the population are not prejudiced, shall facilitate Jewish immigration under suitable conditions and shall encourage, in co-operation with the Jewish agency referred to in article 4, close settlement by Jews on the land, including State lands and waste lands not required for public purposes.

"ARTICLE 7

"The Administration of Palestine shall be responsible for enacting a nationality law. There shall be included in this law provisions framed so as to facilitate the acquisition of Palestinian citizenship by Jews who take up their permanent residence in Palestine.

"ARTICLE 8

"The privileges and immunities of foreigners, including the benefits of consular jurisdiction and protection as formerly enjoyed by Capitulation or usage in the Ottoman Empire, shall not be applicable in Palestine.

"Unless the Powers whose nationals enjoyed the aforementioned privileges and immunities on the 1st August, 1914, shall have previously renounced the right to their re-establishment, or shall have agreed to their non-application for a specified period, these privileges and immunities shall, at the expiration of the mandate, be immediately re-established in their entirety or with such modifications as may have been agreed upon between the Powers concerned.

"ARTICLE 9

"The Mandatory shall be responsible for seeing that the judicial system established in Palestine shall assure to foreigners, as well as to natives, a complete guarantee of their rights.

"Respect for the personal status of the various peoples and communities and for their religious interests shall be fully guaranteed. In particular, the control and administration of Wakfs shall be exercised in accordance with religious law and the dispositions of the founders.

"ARTICLE 10

"Pending the making of special extradition agreements relating to Palestine, the extradition treaties in force between the Mandatory and other foreign Powers shall apply to Palestine.

"Article 11

"The Administration of Palestine shall take all necessary measures to safeguard the interests of the community in connection with the development of the country, and, subject to any international obligations accepted by the Mandatory, shall have full power to provide for public ownership or control of any of the natural resources of the country or of the public works, services and utilities established or to be established therein. It shall introduce a land system appropriate to the needs of the country, having regard, among other things, to the desirability of promoting the close settlement and intensive cultivation of the land.

"The Administration may arrange with the Jewish agency mentioned in article 4 to construct or operate, upon fair and equitable terms, any public works, services and utilities, and to develop any of the natural resources of the country, in so far as these matters are not directly undertaken by the Administration. Any such arrangements shall provide that no profits distributed by such agency, directly or indirectly, shall exceed a reasonable rate of interest on the capital, and any further profits shall be utilised by it for the benefit of the country in a manner approved by the Administration.

"Article 12

"The Mandatory shall be entrusted with the control of the foreign relations of Palestine and the right to issue exequaturs to consuls appointed by foreign Powers. He shall also be entitled to afford diplomatic and consular protection to citizens of Palestine when outside its territorial limits.

"Article 13

"All responsibility in connection with the Holy Places and religious buildings or sites in Palestine, including that of preserving existing rights and of securing free access to the Holy Places, religious buildings and sites and the free exercise of worship, while ensuring the requirements of public order and decorum, is assumed by the Mandatory, who shall be responsible solely to the League of Nations in all matters connected herewith, provided that nothing in this article shall prevent the Mandatory from entering into such arrangements as he may deem reasonable with the Administration for the purpose of carrying the provisions of this article into effect; and provided also that nothing in this mandate shall be construed as conferring upon the Mandatory authority to interfere with the fabric or the management of purely Moslem sacred shrines, the immunities of which are guaranteed.

"Article 14

"A special Commission shall be appointed by the Mandatory to study, define and determine the rights and claims in connection with the Holy Places and the rights and claims relating to the different religious communities in Palestine. The method of nomination, the composition and the functions of this Commission shall be submitted to the Council of the League for its approval, and the Commission shall not be appointed or enter upon its functions without the approval of the Council.

"ARTICLE 15

"The Mandatory shall see that complete freedom of conscience and the free exercise of all forms of worship, subject only to the maintenance of public order and morals, are ensured to all. No discrimination of any kind shall be made between the inhabitants of Palestine on the ground of race, religion or language. No person shall be excluded from Palestine on the sole ground of his religious belief.

"The right of each community to maintain its own schools for the education of its own members in its own language, while conforming to such educational requirements of a general nature as the Administration may impose, shall not be denied or impaired.

"ARTICLE 16

"The Mandatory shall be responsible for exercising such supervision over religious or eleemosynary bodies of all faiths in Palestine as may be required for the maintenance of public order and good government. Subject to such supervision, no measures shall be taken in Palestine to obstruct or interfere with the enterprise of such bodies or to discriminate against any representative or member of them on the ground of his religion or nationality.

"ARTICLE 17

"The Administration of Palestine may organise on a voluntary basis the forces necessary for the preservation of peace and order, and also for the defence of the country, subject, however, to the supervision of the Mandatory, but shall not use them for purposes other than those above specified save with the consent of the Mandatory. Except for such purposes, no military, naval or air forces shall be raised or maintained by the Administration of Palestine.

"Nothing in this article shall preclude the Administration of Palestine from contributing to the cost of the maintenance of the forces of the Mandatory in Palestine.

"The Mandatory shall be entitled at all times to use the roads, railways and ports of Palestine for the movement of armed forces and the carriage of fuel and supplies.

"ARTICLE 18

"The Mandatory shall see that there is no discrimination in Palestine against the nationals of any State member of the League of Nations (including companies incorporated under its laws) as compared with those of the Mandatory or of any foreign State in matters concerning taxation, commerce or navigation, the exercise of industries or professions, or in the treatment of merchant vessels or civil aircraft. Similarly, there shall be no discrimination in Palestine against goods originating in or destined for any of the said States, and there shall be freedom of transit under equitable conditions across the mandated area.

"Subject as aforesaid and to the other provisions of this mandate, the Administration of Palestine may, on the advice of the Mandatory, impose such taxes and customs duties as it may consider necessary, and take such steps as it may think best to promote the development of the natural resources of the country and to safeguard the interests of the population. It may also, on the advice of the Mandatory, conclude a special customs agreement with any State the territory of which in 1914 was wholly included in Asiatic Turkey or Arabia.

"ARTICLE 19

"The Mandatory shall adhere on behalf of the Administration of Palestine to any general international conventions already existing, or which may be concluded hereafter with the approval of the League of Nations, respecting the slave traffic, the traffic in arms and ammunition, or the traffic in drugs, or relating to commercial equality, freedom of transit and navigation, aerial navigation and postal, telegraphic and wireless communication or literary, artistic or industrial property.

"ARTICLE 20

"The Mandatory shall co-operate on behalf of the Administration of Palestine, so far as religious, social and other conditions may permit, in the execution of any common policy adopted by the League of Nations for preventing and combating disease, including diseases of plants and animals.

"ARTICLE 21

"The Mandatory shall secure the enactment within twelve months from this date, and shall ensure the execution of a Law of Antiquities based on the following rules. This law shall ensure equality of treatment in the matter of excavations and archæological research to the nationals of all States members of the League of Nations.

"(1)

"'Antiquity' means any construction or any product of human activity earlier than the year A. D. 1700.

"(2)

"The law for the protection of antiquities shall proceed by encouragement rather than by threat.

"Any person who, having discovered an antiquity without being furnished with the authorisation referred to in paragraph 5, reports the same to an official of the competent Department, shall be rewarded according to the value of the discovery.

"(3)

"No antiquity may be disposed of except to the competent Department, unless this Department renounces the acquisition of any such antiquity.

"No antiquity may leave the country without an export licence from the said Department.

"(4)

"Any person who maliciously or negligently destroys or damages an antiquity shall be liable to a penalty to be fixed.

"(5)

"No clearing of ground or digging with the object of finding antiquities shall be permitted, under penalty of fine, except to persons authorised by the competent Department.

"(6)

"Equitable terms shall be fixed for expropriation, temporary or permanent, of lands which might be of historical or archæological interest.

"(7)

"Authorisation to excavate shall only be granted to persons who show sufficient guarantees of archæological experience. The Administration of Palestine shall not, in granting these authorisations, act in such a way as to exclude scholars of any nation without good grounds.

"(8)

"The proceeds of excavations may be divided between the excavator and the competent Department in a proportion fixed by that Department. If division seems impossible for scientific reasons, the excavator shall receive a fair indemnity in lieu of a part of the find.

"Article 22

"English, Arabic and Hebrew shall be the official languages of Palestine. Any statement or inscription in Arabic on stamps or money in Palestine shall be repeated in Hebrew, and any statement or inscription in Hebrew shall be repeated in Arabic.

"Article 23

"The Administration of Palestine shall recognise the holy days of the respective communities in Palestine as legal days of rest for the members of such communities.

"Article 24

"The Mandatory shall make to the Council of the League of Nations an annual report to the satisfaction of the Council as to the measures taken during the year to carry out the provisions of the mandate. Copies of all laws and regulations promulgated or issued during the year shall be communicated with the report.

"ARTICLE 25

"In the territories lying between the Jordan and the eastern boundary of Palestine as ultimately determined, the Mandatory shall be entitled, with the consent of the Council of the League of Nations, to postpone or withhold application of such provisions of this mandate as he may consider inapplicable to the existing local conditions, and to make such provision for the administration of the territories as he may consider suitable to those conditions, provided that no action shall be taken which is inconsistent with the provisions of articles 15, 16 and 18.

"ARTICLE 26

"The Mandatory agrees that if any dispute whatever should arise between the Mandatory and another member of the League of Nations relating to the interpretation or the application of the provisions of the mandate, such dispute, if it cannot be settled by negotiation, shall be submitted to the Permanent Court of International Justice provided for by article 14 of the Covenant of the League of Nations.

"ARTICLE 27

"The consent of the Council of the League of Nations is required for any modification of the terms of this mandate.

"ARTICLE 28

"In the event of the termination of the mandate hereby conferred upon the Mandatory, the Council of the League of Nations shall make such arrangements as may be deemed necessary for safeguarding in perpetuity, under guarantee of the League, the rights secured by articles 13 and 14, and shall use its influence for securing, under the guarantee of the League, that the Government of Palestine will fully honour the financial obligations legitimately incurred by the Administration of Palestine during the period of the mandate, including the rights of public servants to pensions or gratuities.

"The present instrument shall be deposited in original in the archives of the League of Nations, and certified copies shall be forwarded by the Secretary-General of the League of Nations to all members of the League.

"Done at London, the 24th day of July, 1922;" and

Whereas the mandate in the above terms came into force on the 29th September, 1923; and

Whereas the United States of America, by participating in the war against Germany, contributed to her defeat and the defeat of her Allies, and to the renunciation of the rights and titles of her Allies in the territory transferred by them but has not ratified the Covenant of the League of Nations embodied in the Treaty of Versailles; and

Whereas the Government of the United States and the Government of His Britannic Majesty desire to reach a definite understanding with respect to the rights of the two Governments and their respective nationals in Palestine;

The President of the United States of America and His Britannic Majesty have decided to conclude a convention to this effect, and have named as their plenipotentaries:—

The President of the United States of America:

His Excellency the Honourable Frank B. Kellogg, Ambassador Extraordinary and Plenipotentiary of the United States at London:

His Majesty the King of the United Kingdom of Great Britain and Ireland and of the British Dominions beyond the Seas, Emperor of India:

The Right Honourable Joseph Austen Chamberlain, M.P., His Majesty's Principal Secretary of State for Foreign Affairs:

who, after having communicated to each other their respective full powers, found in good and due form, have agreed as follows:—

ARTICLE 1

Subject to the provisions of the present convention the United States consents to the administration of Palestine by His Britannic Majesty, pursuant to the mandate recited above.

ARTICLE 2

The United States and its nationals shall have and enjoy all the rights and benefits secured under the terms of the mandate to members of the League of Nations and their nationals, notwithstanding the fact that the United States is not a member of the League of Nations.

ARTICLE 3

Vested American property rights in the mandated territory shall be respected and in no way impaired.

ARTICLE 4

A duplicate of the annual report to be made by the Mandatory under article 24 of the mandate shall be furnished to the United States.

ARTICLE 5

Subject to the provisions of any local laws for the maintenance of public order and public morals, the nationals of the United States will be permitted freely to establish and maintain educational, philanthropic and religious institutions in the mandated territory, to receive voluntary applicants and to teach in the English language.

ARTICLE 6

The extradition treaties and conventions which are, or may be, in force between the United States and Great Britain, and the provisions of any treaties which are, or may be, in force between the two countries which relate to extradition or consular rights shall apply to the mandated territory.

ARTICLE 7

Nothing contained in the present convention shall be affected by any modification which may be made in the terms of the mandate, as recited above, unless such modification shall have been assented to by the United States.

ARTICLE 8

The present convention shall be ratified in accordance with the respective constitutional methods of the High Contracting Parties. The ratifications shall be exchanged in London as soon as practicable. The present convention shall take effect on the date of the exchange of ratifications.

In witness whereof, the undersigned have signed the present convention, and have thereunto affixed their seals.

Done in duplicate at London, this 3rd day of December, 1924.

[SEAL]   FRANK B. KELLOGG
[SEAL]   AUSTEN CHAMBERLAIN

AND WHEREAS the said Convention has been duly ratified on both parts, and the ratifications of the two Governments were exchanged in the city of London on the third day of December, one thousand nine hundred and twenty-five;

NOW, THEREFORE, be it known that I, Calvin Coolidge, President of the United States of America, have caused the said Convention to be made public, to the end that the same and every article and clause thereof may be observed and fulfilled with good faith by the United States and the citizens thereof.

IN TESTIMONY WHEREOF, I have hereunto set my hand and caused the seal of the United States to be affixed.

DONE at the city of Washington, this fifth day of December, in the year of our Lord one thousand nine hundred and [SEAL] twenty-five, and of the Independence of the United States of America the one hundred and fiftieth.

CALVIN COOLIDGE

By the President:
FRANK B. KELLOGG
Secretary of State

BRITISH WHITE PAPER ON PALESTINE

PALESTINE

STATEMENT OF POLICY

Presented by the Secretary of State for the Colonies to Parliament by Command
of His Majesty, May 1939

In the Statement on Palestine, issued on 9th November, 1938,[1]
His Majesty's Government announced their intention to invite representatives of the Arabs of Palestine, of certain neighbouring countries
and of the Jewish Agency to confer with them in London regarding
future policy. It was their sincere hope that, as a result of full,
free and frank discussion, some understanding might be reached.
Conferences recently took place with Arab and Jewish delegations,
lasting for a period of several weeks, and served the purpose of a
complete exchange of views between British Ministers and the Arab
and Jewish representatives. In the light of the discussions as well
as of the situation in Palestine and of the Reports of the Royal Commission [2] and the Partition Commission,[3] certain proposals were
formulated by His Majesty's Government and were laid before the
Arab and Jewish delegations as the basis of an agreed settlement.
Neither the Arab nor the Jewish delegations felt able to accept these
proposals, and the conferences therefore did not result in an agreement. Accordingly His Majesty's Government are free to formulate
their own policy, and after careful consideration they have decided
to adhere generally to the proposals which were finally submitted
to, and discussed with, the Arab and Jewish delegations.

2. The Mandate for Palestine, the terms of which were confirmed
by the Council of the League of Nations in 1922, has governed the
policy of successive British Governments for nearly 20 years. It
embodies the Balfour Declaration and imposes on the Mandatory
four main obligations. These obligations are set out in Articles 2, 6
and 13 of the Mandate. There is no dispute regarding the interpretation of one of these obligations, that touching the protection of and
access to the Holy Places and religious buildings or sites. The other
three main obligations are generally as follows:—

(i) To place the country under such political, administrative
and economic conditions as will secure the establishment in
Palestine of a national home for the Jewish people, to facilitate
Jewish immigration under suitable conditions, and to encourage,
in co-operation with the Jewish Agency, close settlement by
Jews on the land.

[1] Cmd. 5893.
[2] Cmd. 5479.
[3] Cmd. 5854.

412

(ii) To safeguard the civil and religious rights of all the inhabitants of Palestine irrespective of race and religion, and, whilst facilitating Jewish immigration and settlement, to ensure that the rights and position of other sections of the population are not prejudiced.

(iii) To place the country under such political, administrative and economic conditions as will secure the development of self-governing institutions.

3. The Royal Commission and previous Commissions of Enquiry have drawn attention to the ambiguity of certain expressions in the Mandate, such as the expression "a national home for the Jewish people", and they have found in this ambiguity and the resulting uncertainty as to the objectives of policy a fundamental cause of unrest and hostility between Arabs and Jews. His Majesty's Government are convinced that in the interests of the peace and well-being of the whole people of Palestine a clear definition of policy and objectives is essential. The proposal of partition recommended by the Royal Commission would have afforded such clarity, but the establishment of self-supporting independent Arab and Jewish States within Palestine has been found to be impracticable. It has therefore been necessary for His Majesty's Government to devise an alternative policy which will, consistently with their obligations to Arabs and Jews, meet the needs of the situation in Palestine. Their views and proposals are set forth below under the three heads, (I) The Constitution, (II) Immigration, and (III) Land.

I. THE CONSTITUTION

4. It has been urged that the expression "a national home for the Jewish people" offered a prospect that Palestine might in due course become a Jewish State or Commonwealth. His Majesty's Government do not wish to contest the view, which was expressed by the Royal Commission, that the Zionist leaders at the time of the issue of the Balfour Declaration recognised that an ultimate Jewish State was not precluded by the terms of the Declaration. But, with the Royal Commission, His Majesty's Government believe that the framers of the Mandate in which the Balfour Declaration was embodied could not have intended that Palestine should be converted into a Jewish State against the will of the Arab population of the country. That Palestine was not to be converted into a Jewish State might be held to be implied in the passage from the Command Paper of 1922 [4] which reads as follows:—

"Unauthorised statements have been made to the effect that the purpose in view is to create a wholly Jewish Palestine. Phrases have been used such as that 'Palestine is to become as Jewish as England is English.' His Majesty's Government regard any such expectation as impracticable and have no such aim in view. Nor have they at any time contemplated . . . the disappearance or the subordination of the Arabic population, language or culture in Palestine. They would draw attention to the fact that the terms of the (Balfour) Declaration referred to do not contemplate that Palestine as a whole should be con-

[4] Cmd. 1700.

verted into a Jewish National Home, but that such a Home should be founded *in Palestine*".

But this statement has not removed doubts, and His Majesty's Government therefore now declare unequivocally that it is not part of their policy that Palestine should become a Jewish State. They would indeed regard it as contrary to their obligations to the Arabs under the Mandate, as well as to the assurances which have been given to the Arab people in the past, that the Arab population of Palestine should be made the subjects of a Jewish State against their will.

5. The nature of the Jewish National Home in Palestine was further described in the Command Paper of 1922 as follows:

"During the last two or three generations the Jews have recreated in Palestine a community, now numbering 80,000, of whom about one-fourth are farmers or workers upon the land. This community has its own political organs; an elected assembly for the direction of its domestic concerns; elected councils in the towns; and an organisation for the control of its schools. It has its elected Chief Rabbinate and Rabbinical Council for the direction of its religious affairs. Its business is conducted in Hebrew as a vernacular language, and a Hebrew press serves its needs. It has its distinctive intellectual life and displays considerable economic activity. This community, then, with its town and country population, its political, religious and social organisations, its own language, its own customs, its own life, has in fact 'national' characteristics. When it is asked what is meant by the development of the Jewish National Home in Palestine, it may be answered that it is not the imposition of a Jewish nationality upon the inhabitants of Palestine as a whole, but the further development of the existing Jewish community, with the assistance of Jews in other parts of the world, in order that it may become a centre in which the Jewish people as a whole may take, on grounds of religion and race, an interest and a pride. But in order that this community should have the best prospect of free development and provide a full opportunity for the Jewish people to display its capacities, it is essential that it should know that it is in Palestine as of right and not on sufferance. That is the reason why it is necessary that the existence of a Jewish National Home in Palestine should be internationally guaranteed, and that it should be formally recognised to rest upon ancient historic connection".

6. His Majesty's Government adhere to this interpretation of the Declaration of 1917 and regard it as an authoritative and comprehensive description of the character of the Jewish National Home in Palestine. It envisaged the further development of the existing Jewish community with the assistance of Jews in other parts of the world. Evidence that His Majesty's Government have been carrying out their obligation in this respect is to be found in the facts that, since the statement of 1922 was published, more than 300,000 Jews have immigrated to Palestine, and that the population of the National Home has risen to some 450,000, or approaching a third of the entire population of the country. Nor has the Jewish community failed to

take full advantage of the opportunities given to it. The growth of the Jewish National Home and its achievements in many fields are a remarkable constructive effort which must command the admiration of the world and must be, in particular, a source of pride to the Jewish people.

7. In the recent discussions the Arab delegations have repeated the contention that Palestine was included within the area in which Sir Henry McMahon, on behalf of the British Government, in October, 1915, undertook to recognise and support Arab independence. The validity of this claim, based on the terms of the correspondence which passed between Sir Henry McMahon and the Sharif of Mecca, was thoroughly and carefully investigated by British and Arab representatives during the recent conferences in London. Their Report, which has been published,[5] states that both the Arab and the British representatives endeavoured to understand the point of view of the other party but that they were unable to reach agreement upon an interpretation of the correspondence. There is no need to summarise here the arguments presented by each side. His Majesty's Government regret the misunderstandings which have arisen as regards some of the phrases used. For their part they can only adhere, for the reasons given by their representatives in the Report, to the view that the whole of Palestine west of Jordan was excluded from Sir Henry McMahon's pledge, and they therefore cannot agree that the McMahon correspondence forms a just basis for the claim that Palestine should be converted into an Arab State.

8. His Majesty's Government are charged as the Mandatory authority "to secure the development of self-governing institutions" in Palestine. Apart from this specific obligation, they would regard it as contrary to the whole spirit of the Mandate system that the population of Palestine should remain for ever under Mandatory tutelage. It is proper that the people of the country should as early as possible enjoy the rights of self-government which are exercised by the people of neighbouring countries. His Majesty's Government are unable at present to foresee the exact constitutional forms which government in Palestine will eventually take, but their objective is self-government, and they desire to see established ultimately an independent Palestine State. It should be a State in which the two peoples in Palestine, Arabs and Jews, share authority in government in such a way that the essential interests of each are secured.

9. The establishment of an independent State and the complete relinquishment of Mandatory control in Palestine would require such relations between the Arabs and the Jews as would make good government possible. Moreover, the growth of self-governing institutions in Palestine, as in other countries, must be an evolutionary process. A transitional period will be required before independence is achieved, throughout which ultimate responsibility for the Government of the country will be retained by His Majesty's Government as the Mandatory authority, while the people of the country are taking an increasing share in the Government, and understanding and co-operation amongst them are growing. It will be the constant endeavour of His Majesty's Government to promote good relations between the Arabs and the Jews.

---

[5] Cmd. 5974.

10. In the light of these considerations His Majesty's Government make the following declaration of their intentions regarding the future government of Palestine:—

(1) The objective of His Majesty's Government is the establishment within ten years of an independent Palestine State in such treaty relations with the United Kingdom as will provide satisfactorily for the commercial and strategic requirements of both countries in the future. This proposal for the establishment of the independent State would involve consultation with the Council of the League of Nations with a view to the termination of the Mandate.

(2) The independent State should be one in which Arabs and Jews share in government in such a way as to ensure that the essential interests of each community are safeguarded.

(3) The establishment of the independent State will be preceded by a transitional period throughout which His Majesty's Government will retain responsibility for the government of the country. During the transitional period the people of Palestine will be given an increasing part in the government of their country. Both sections of the population will have an opportunity to participate in the machinery of government, and the process will be carried on whether or not they both avail themselves of it.

(4) As soon as peace and order have been sufficiently restored in Palestine steps will be taken to carry out this policy of giving the people of Palestine an increasing part in the government of their country, the objective being to place Palestinians in charge of all the Departments of Government, with the assistance of British advisers and subject to the control of the High Commissioner. With this object in view His Majesty's Government will be prepared immediately to arrange that Palestinians shall be placed in charge of certain Departments, with British advisers. The Palestinian heads of Departments will sit on the Executive. Council, which advises the High Commissioner. Arab and Jewish representatives will be invited to serve as heads of Departments approximately in proportion to their respective populations. The number of Palestinians in charge of Departments will be increased as circumstances permit until all heads of Departments are Palestinians, exercising the administrative and advisory functions which are at present performed by British officials. When that stage is reached consideration will be given to the question of converting the Executive Council into a Council of Ministers with a consequential change in the status and functions of the Palestinian heads of Departments.

(5) His Majesty's Government make no proposals at this stage regarding the establishment of an elective legislature. Nevertheless they would regard this as an appropriate constitutional development, and, should public opinion in Palestine hereafter show itself in favour of such a development, they will be prepared, provided that local conditions permit, to establish the necessary machinery.

(6) At the end of five years from the restoration of peace and order, an appropriate body representative of the people of Palestine and of His Majesty's Government will be set up to review

the working of the constitutional arrangements during the transitional period and to consider and make recommendations regarding the constitution of the independent Palestine State.

(7) His Majesty's Government will require to be satisfied that in the treaty contemplated by sub-paragraph (1) or in the constitution contemplated by sub-paragraph (6) adequate provision has been made for:—

(a) the security of, and freedom of access to, the Holy Places, and the protection of the interests and property of the various religious bodies.

(b) the protection of the different communities in Palestine in accordance with the obligations of His Majesty's Government to both Arabs and Jews and for the special position in Palestine of the Jewish National Home.

(c) such requirements to meet the strategic situation as may be regarded as necessary by His Majesty's Government in the light of the circumstances then existing.

His Majesty's Government will also require to be satisfied that the interests of certain foreign countries in Palestine, for the preservation of which they are at present responsible, are adequately safeguarded.

(8) His Majesty's Government will do everything in their power to create conditions which will enable the independent Palestine State to come into being within ten years. If, at the end of ten years, it appears to His Majesty's Government that, contrary to their hope, circumstances require the postponement of the establishment of the independent State, they will consult with representatives of the people of Palestine, the Council of the League of Nations and the neighbouring Arab States before deciding on such a postponement. If His Majesty's Government come to the conclusion that postponement is unavoidable, they will invite the co-operation of these parties in framing plans for the future with a view to achieving the desired objective at the earliest possible date.

11. During the transitional period steps will be taken to increase the powers and responsibilities of municipal corporations and local councils.

II. IMMIGRATION

12. Under Article 6 of the Mandate, the Administration of Palestine, "while ensuring that the rights and position of other sections of the population are not prejudiced", is required to "facilitate Jewish immigration under suitable conditions". Beyond this, the extent to which Jewish immigration into Palestine is to be permitted is nowhere defined in the Mandate. But in the Command Paper of 1922 it was laid down that for the fulfilment of the policy of establishing a Jewish National Home.

"it is necessary that the Jewish community in Palestine should be able to increase its numbers by immigration. This immigration cannot be so great in volume as to exceed whatever may be the economic capacity of the country at the time to absorb new arrivals. It is essential to ensure that the immigrants should not be a burden upon the people of

Palestine as a whole, and that they should not deprive any section of the present population of their employment."

In practice, from that date onwards until recent times, the economic absorptive capacity of the country has been treated as the sole limiting factor, and in the letter which Mr. Ramsay MacDonald, as Prime Minister, sent to Dr. Weizmann in February 1931 [6] it was laid down as a matter of policy that economic absorptive capacity was the sole criterion. This interpretation has been supported by resolutions of the Permanent Mandates Commission. But His Majesty's Government do not read either the Statement of Policy of 1922 or the letter of 1931 as implying that the Mandate requires them, for all time and in all circumstances, to facilitate the immigration of Jews into Palestine subject only to consideration of the country's economic absorptive capacity. Nor do they find anything in the Mandate or in subsequent Statements of Policy to support the view that the establishment of a Jewish National Home in Palestine cannot be effected unless immigration is allowed to continue indefinitely. If immigration has an adverse effect on the economic position in the country, it should clearly be restricted; and equally if it has a seriously damaging effect on the political position in the country, that is a factor that should not be ignored. Although it is not difficult to contend that the large number of Jewish immigrants who have been admitted so far have been absorbed economically, the fear of the Arabs that this influx will continue indefinitely until the Jewish population is in a position to dominate them has produced consequences which are extremely grave for Jews and Arabs alike and for the peace and prosperity of Palestine. The lamentable disturbances of the past three years are only the latest and most sustained manifestation of this intense Arab apprehension. The methods employed by Arab terrorists against fellow-Arabs and Jews alike must receive unqualified condemnation. But it cannot be denied that fear of indefinite Jewish immigration is widespread amongst the Arab population and that this fear has made possible disturbances which have given a serious setback to economic progress, depleted the Palestine exchequer, rendered life and property insecure, and produced a bitterness between the Arab and Jewish populations which is deplorable between citizens of the same country. If in these circumstances immigration is continued up to the economic absorptive capacity of the country, regardless of all other considerations, a fatal enmity between the two peoples will be perpetuated, and the situation in Palestine may become a permanent source of friction amongst all peoples in the Near and Middle East. His Majesty's Government cannot take the view that either their obligations under the Mandate, or considerations of common sense and justice, require that they should ignore these circumstances in framing immigration policy.

13. In the view of the Royal Commission, the association of the policy of the Balfour Declaration with the Mandate system implied the belief that Arab hostility to the former would sooner or later be overcome. It has been the hope of British Governments ever since the Balfour Declaration was issued that in time the Arab population, recognizing the advantages to be derived from Jewish settlement and

⁶ Hansard, Vol. 248, 13/2/31, Cols. 751–7

development in Palestine, would become reconciled to the further growth of the Jewish National Home. This hope has not been fulfilled. The alternatives before His Majesty's Government are either (i) to seek to expand the Jewish National Home indefinitely by immigration, against the strongly expressed will of the Arab people of the country; or (ii) to permit further expansion of the Jewish National Home by immigration only if the Arabs are prepared to acquiesce in it. The former policy means rule by force. Apart from other considerations, such a policy seems to His Majesty's Government to be contrary to the whole spirit of Article 22 of the Covenant of the League of Nations, as well as to their specific obligations to the Arabs in the Palestine Mandate. Moreover, the relations between the Arabs and the Jews in Palestine must be based sooner or later on mutual tolerance and goodwill; the peace, security and progress of the Jewish National Home itself require this. Therefore His Majesty's Government, after earnest consideration, and taking into account the extent to which the growth of the Jewish National Home has been facilitated over the last twenty years, have decided that the time has come to adopt in principle the second of the alternatives referred to above.

14. It has been urged that all further Jewish immigration into Palestine should be stopped forthwith. His Majesty's Government cannot accept such a proposal. It would damage the whole of the financial and economic system of Palestine and thus affect adversely the interests of Arabs and Jews alike. Moreover, in the view of His Majesty's Government, abruptly to stop further immigration would be unjust to the Jewish National Home. But, above all, His Majesty's Government are conscious of the present unhappy plight of large numbers of Jews who seek a refuge from certain European countries, and they believe that Palestine can and should make a further contribution to the solution of this pressing world problem. In all these circumstances, they believe that they will be acting consistently with their Mandatory obligations to both Arabs and Jews, and in the manner best calculated to serve the interests of the whole people of Palestine, by adopting the following proposals regarding immigration:—

(1) Jewish immigration during the next five years will be at a rate which, if economic absorptive capacity permits, will bring the Jewish population up to approximately one-third of the total population of the country. Taking into account the expected natural increase of the Arab and Jewish populations, and the number of illegal Jewish immigrants now in the country, this would allow of the admission, as from the beginning of April this year, of some 75,000 immigrants over the next five years. These immigrants would, subject to the criterion of economic absorptive capacity, be admitted as follows:

(a) For each of the next five years a quota of 10,000 Jewish immigrants will be allowed, on the understanding that a shortage in any one year may be added to the quotas for subsequent years, within the five-year period, if economic absorptive capacity permits.

(b) In addition, as a contribution towards the solution of the Jewish refugee problem, 25,000 refugees will be admitted as soon as the High Commissioner is satisfied that adequate provision for their maintenance is ensured, special consideration being given to refugee children and dependants.

(2) The existing machinery for ascertaining economic absorptive capacity will be retained, and the High Commissioner will have the ultimate responsibility for deciding the limits of economic capacity. Before each periodic decision is taken, Jewish and Arab representatives will be consulted.

(3) After the period of five years no further Jewish immigration will be permitted unless the Arabs of Palestine are prepared to acquiesce in it.

(4) His Majesty's Government are determined to check illegal immigration, and further preventive measures are being adopted. The numbers of any Jewish illegal immigrants who, despite these measures, may succeed in coming into the country and cannot be deported will be deducted from the yearly quotas.

15. His Majesty's Government are satisfied that, when the immigration over five years which is now contemplated has taken place, they will not be justified in facilitating, nor will they be under any obligation to facilitate, the further development of the Jewish National Home by immigration regardless of the wishes of the Arab population.

III. Land

16. The Administration of Palestine is required, under Article 6 of the Mandate, "while ensuring that the rights and position of other sections of the population are not prejudiced", to encourage "close settlement by Jews on the land", and no restriction has been imposed hitherto on the transfer of land from Arabs to Jews. The Reports of several expert Commissions have indicated that, owing to the natural growth of the Arab population and the steady sale in recent years of Arab land to Jews, there is now in certain areas no room for further transfers of Arab land, whilst in some other areas such transfers of land must be restricted if Arab cultivators are to maintain their existing standard of life and a considerable landless Arab population is not soon to be created. In these circumstances, the High Commissioner will be given general powers to prohibit and regulate transfers of land. These powers will date from the publication of this statement of policy and the High Commissioner will retain them throughout the transitional period.

17. The policy of the Government will be directed towards the development of the land and the improvement, where possible, of methods of cultivation. In the light of such development it will be open to the High Commissioner, should he be satisfied that the "rights and position" of the Arab population will be duly preserved, to review and modify any orders passed relating to the prohibition or restriction of the transfer of land.

18. In framing these proposals His Majesty's Government have sincerely endeavoured to act in strict accordance with their obligations under the Mandate to both the Arabs and the Jews. The vagueness of the phrases employed in some instances to describe these obligations has led to controversy and has made the task of interpretation difficult.

His Majesty's Government cannot hope to satisfy the partisans of one party or the other in such controversy as the Mandate has aroused. Their purpose is to be just as between the two peoples in Palestine whose destinies in that country have been affected by the great events of recent years, and who, since they live side by side, must learn to practise mutual tolerance, goodwill and co-operation. In looking to the future, His Majesty's Government are not blind to the fact that some events of the past make the task of creating these relations difficult; but they are encouraged by the knowledge that at many times and in many places in Palestine during recent years the Arab and Jewish inhabitants have lived in friendship together. Each community has much to contribute to the welfare of their common land, and each must earnestly desire peace in which to assist in increasing the well-being of the whole people of the country. The responsibility which falls on them, no less than upon His Majesty's Government, to co-operate together to ensure peace is all the more solemn because their country is revered by many millions of Moslems, Jews and Christians throughout the world who pray for peace in Palestine and for the happiness of her people.

REMARKS OF BRITISH STATESMEN
IN OPPOSITION TO
THE WHITE PAPER ON PALESTINE

HOUSE OF LORDS

Rt. Hon. Lord Snell
Most Rev. Cosmo Gordon Lang, Archbishop of Canterbury
The Rt. Hon. Earl of Lytton

HOUSE OF COMMONS

Tom Williams, M. P.
Rt. Hon. Josiah Clement Wedgwood
Rt. Hon. Leopold Stennett Amery
Philip J. Noel-Baker, M. P.
Rt. Hon. Herbert Stanley Morrison
Rt. Hon. Sir Archibald Sinclair
Rt. Hon. Winston Churchill

RT. HON. LORD SNELL
HOUSE OF LORDS, MAY 23, 1939

My Lords, in moving the Amendment which stands in my name on the Paper I hope your Lordships will allow me to say at the outset that such criticisms of the policy of His Majesty's Government as I may offer are not against the presentation of it by the noble Marquess who has just sat down. He has, in my belief, a case to argue that could not have been made impressive by anyone at His Majesty's Government's disposal, and he did his task with clarity and with appreciated efficiency. The noble Marquess first of all assured us that the policy of His Majesty's Government was not a panic policy, that they had come to the conclusion that quiet, calm deliberation disentangles every knot, although we know that over a series of years the Government have varied between one policy and another, first swallowing partition without examining it and then repudiating it without giving any reasons for such repudiation. However, we appear now to have arrived at a crisis in this tragic, momentous, and, as I believe, continuously mismanaged question, and Parliament has once more to decide whether it will accept a policy of expediency put forward in this White Paper or whether it will get back to fundamentals and ask whether it has really and truly honoured its obligations to the great body that entrusted it with this responsibility.

I would remind your Lordships that Parliament has previously refused to accept policies which were commended by the same argu-

422

ments and with the same urgency. In 1930, for example, when the Government of Mr. Ramsay MacDonald appeared to be whittling down the conditions of the Mandate, and again when the Peel Commission presented their Report, Parliament withheld its approval, although this policy was liberal in comparison with the policy which is now presented to us. In the long run we are driven back here to consider the moral issues which confront us. It is, as was stated by the Secretary of State in another place yesterday, the honour of our nation that is engaged. "The good name," he said, "of Great Britain is involved," and debts of honour "cannot be paid in counterfeit coinage." I personally knowing the right honourable gentleman the Colonial Secretary very well, and having a deep regard for him, cannot believe that he is either the author or the proud defender of the policy which your Lordships are asked to accept.

The Mandate, as I understand it, was the most important international obligation ever entrusted to a single nation. If we had made a success of it it would have established for ever our prestige in history. If we make a failure of it—and our record up to now has been one of complete and unrelieved failure—that will count to us for incompetence or something worse. We accepted this Mandate knowing perfectly well what it involved. The Mandate is but an elaborated interpretation of the Balfour Declaration and in the Balfour Declaration the purpose of it was made perfectly clear, a declaration of sympathy with Zionist aspirations. Now the Jews, under the Balfour Declaration, were promised specific assistance in the establishment of their National Home, and other inhabitants were granted their civil and religious rights. In the policy which your Lordships are to-day asked to accept the scales are precisely reversed—that is to say, the Arabs are to have the veto. The noble Marquess has denied that a veto is involved, but sub-paragraph (3) of paragraph 14, on page 11 of the White Paper, says that—

"no further Jewish immigration will be permitted unless the Arabs of Palestine are prepared to acquiesce in it."

If that is not veto it comes to something perilously near to it. And in regard to land, again the Jews can only get more land with the consent of a political majority who, it is well known, will never concede an extra dunam.

The question for us my Lords, is: Is the Mandate a legal document, or is it not? If it is not, then those of us who are laymen have been grievously misled. Various Governments have sheltered themselves behind its provisions on the ground that they were bound, their hands were tied and they could not move at their own will. In the House of Commons, as long ago as April 3, 1930, Mr. Ramsay MacDonald, then Prime Minister, said it was an international obligation from which there could be no question of receding. Later the White Paper of that year was issued. Your Lordships may not remember the circumstances as acutely as I do, because I happen, together with my noble friend Lord Rushcliffe, to have been a member of a Parliamentary Commission to Palestine and I have had to examine this matter with some closeness. Directly this policy was proclaimed, there was outcry from every Tory newspaper in the land, and two very distinguished lawyers who were members of His Majesty's Government—one is still and one was until recently, Sir John Simon and Viscount Hailsham—issued a statement that the proposal of that White Paper (the Passfield White Paper, as it was called) which restricted immigration, was a betrayal of the Mandate. Then it was the Mandate, the whole Mandate and nothing but the Mandate. But at that time there was a purebred Labour Government in office. That made, of course, some difference. Now that we have this mongrel infliction at the present time, what we dare not do—it was betrayal in those days—becomes righteous realism in these days of a National Government.

Well, what does the Mandate mean? The Peel Commission sustained the view that its main purpose was the establishment of the Jewish National Home. The Shaw Commission, to which I have referred, agreed that it governed the entire situation. It has never been previously in doubt that it was to enable the Jewish people to obtain one place on earth where they might be as of right, and not on sufferance, and on the soil that was made glorious by their ancestors. The language of the Mandate appears to my mind to be clear. The preamble says

"* * * the Mandatory should be responsible for putting into effect the Declaration originally made on November 2, 1917, by the Government of His Britannic Majesty, and adopted by the said Powers, in favour of the establishment in Palestine of a National Home for the Jewish people."

Later it says:

"Whereas His Britannic Majesty has accepted the Mandate in respect of Palestine and undertaken to exercise it on behalf of the League of Nations in conformity with the following provisions"—

—and then the provisions are given.

"Now, it seems to me that that conferred upon our country an almost sacred obligation. Whatever the letter of the Mandate may be interpreted to mean, the spirit of it, beyond all doubt, was the establishment of a National Home for the Jewish people. It is perfectly true that the Mandate does not define what the National Home means. It is, in my judgment, the worst drafted document that was ever issued or accepted by a responsible Government. The noble Marquess spoke about "the Mandate and the people who drew up the Mandate"—to quote his own words—but the people who drew up the Mandate were ourselves. It was not forced upon us. The terms upon which it was drawn by ourselves were accepted.

*   *   *   *   *   *   *

If we do not know that the Mandate means there are statesmen still living who know what it meant to them at the time the Mandate was formulated. Mr. Lloyd George, giving evidence before the Royal Commission, said:

"The idea was that the Jewish State was not to be set up immediately by the Peace Treaty without reference to the wishes of the majority of the inhabitants. On the other hand it was contemplated that when the time arrived for according representative institutions to Palestine, if the Jews had meanwhile responded to the opportunity afforded to them and had become a definite majority of the inhabitants, then Palestine would thus become a Jewish commonwealth."

So that the whole thing depended on whether the Jewish people responded. That they did respond history will prove, and that they have created miracles of redemption in a somewhat desolate land is known to all who have had the privilege to see their work. What does a National Home mean? What does it mean in the language of homely, wayfaring men? Does it mean when a people are petrified, as a minority amid a majority of hostile people? Is it a home when you are an unwelcome lodger in the house of somebody else who hates and tries to injure you? If so, then the Jews already have their national home in several places: in Germany, Poland, Russia and elsewhere. "National Home" can only mean one thing: that is what a home means to the individual, a place where he may be by right and not on sufferance, a place where he can erect his own altars, a place that is indeed his home. That is what the word "home" always has meant, and it cannot mean anything else. It was the main purpose of the Mandate; all the rest was auxiliary and precautionary. Yet the Jews, for whose benefit it was established, are to be condemned to a perpetual minority. Immigration is to cease after five years. A State is to be created in which the Arabs, by a majority of two to one, will control the situation, control the sale of land, control immigration, and indeed control the life of the Jewish people. I venture to say that that was not the original purpose of the Mandate.

* * * * * * *

Now I must hasten to my close. In trying to be as short as possible one has to speak without shades and qualifications, and to put things in rather a bald way. If the noble Marquess asks me to excuse him because his language was vigorous, he will perhaps return the compliment and understand the difficulty that I am in. I would say only this about the future. The Jewish people, in my belief, have been heroically restrained. They have suffered one indignity after another. The Government have never fulfilled their elementary duty of keeping order and preserving life. The Jews have given no trouble; they have been patient, creative and orderly. I cannot tell what the reactions to this policy which you are asked to thrust through will be, but it will be very deeply resented, rightly or wrongly. It does not matter whether the thing is true or not for the moment; the Jewish people feel deeply wounded in their soul. I cannot help reflecting that before our time a deeply wounded Jewish Samson pulled the pillars of the house about his ears. We have missed a great opportunity. We might have had in the Eastern Mediterranean a great defensive bastion manned by a people passionately devoted to the soil of their fatherland. We have turned that people's mind to a sullen and resentful passivity. I believe that this is a wrong policy, and the Amendment which I have proposed suggests that it is inconsistent with the letter and the spirit of the Mandate, that it will not promote the peace desired, and that Parliament ought not to commit itself before the Mandates Commission has had an opportunity of considering it. I ask the support of your Lordships on this matter, not only because it is right but in order to preserve the honour of our nation. * * *

MOST REV. COSMO GORDON LANG
ARCHBISHOP OF CANTERBURY,
HOUSE OF LORDS, MAY 23, 1939

My Lords, I very greatly regret that, as I was in duty bound to preside over the Convocation of Canterbury this afternoon, I was prevented from hearing the speech of the noble Marquess who moved this Motion, and also the speech of the noble Lord opposite who moved this Amendment. I have no doubt that what I have to say would have been modified and improved if I had had that privilege. In any case I must speak with the greatest possible diffidence, because I imagine that we all agree that this Palestinian problem is one of the most difficult, complicated and intractable that any company of statesmen ever had to face. At the same time, I have taken such a long, deep and close interest in Palestine that I cannot be altogether silent.

We all agree that it is useless at this stage to review all the events that have occurred in the long and unhappy story which lies behind these Motions. It is quite useless to discuss the wisdom or the unwisdom of the famous Balfour Declaration. How little could any have foreseen the entanglements to which it would reach! It is useless to consider the ambiguities in both the meaning of the term "National Home" and in the meaning of the promises given to the Arabs, and the McMahon letters, into which the whole matter was allowed to drift. It is useless to consider whether any other terms that could have been used would have produced any other situation, and it is still more useless to grieve over the lamentable events of the last two or three years in Palestine. Also I suppose we are agreed that it is hopeless now to discuss the question of partition, although I am bold enough still to say—in spite of the noble Viscount opposite, who has so much more reason to speak than I have—and I am still impenitent enough to think, that if that policy had been adopted at once by the Government and had been immediately pursued with courage, it might have proved better than these other suggestions as a solution of the problem.

But it is otiose to consider these matters now. We have to face the situation with which at the present time we are confronted. I think the Government have made a most gallant effort to face that situation. They have held their Conference. It was right, and I only wish, as I have already said in this House, that it had been held earlier, before passions had become as embittered as they are. I must also pay my tribute of admiration to the patience and pertinacity of the Secretary of State in his conduct of these long and difficult negotiations. But when I come to the actual Government policy as outlined in this White Paper, then I am bound in honesty to say that I have very grave misgivings. I cannot feel that it holds out a prospect of reasonable justice to the Jews. Consider their position—as indeed it

426

was put before your Lordships by the noble Viscount opposite. In 1914 they were 80,000; they are now more than 450,000. They have been encouraged to enter the country; they have been encouraged to invest great sums of money in industrial and other enterprises. They have erected very noble buildings, and, apart from the industrial and agricultural improvements which they have wrought, they have set a seal upon the genuineness of their belief in a Jewish culture of their own by their noble University in Jerusalem.

As far as concerns the results of their presence in the part of Palestine in which they chiefly dwell, those of us who have seen those Jewish settlements must feel that they are a fulfilment of the old prophesy that "the desert shall blossom as the rose." All the while that they have carried out a plan about which the noble Viscount rightly quoted what was said, that it ought to excite the admiration of the world, they have been buoyed up by the thought that in some special way this territory which they have so wonderfully improved would justify the title of a National Home. Hitherto the immigration of the Jews has been governed by the limits of what has been called "economic absorptive capacity." I am told that if immigration for the next five years is confined to the limits of the White Paper, it will only reach about one-half of the possible economic absorptive capacity of the country, and then it is to cease altogether when the numbers reach one-third of the total population, unless the Arabs are prepared to acquiesce in an extension. If the Arabs were willing to allow an extension over that one-third of the population, another of the wonders of the world would have occurred! The position is, therefore, that the Jews are reduced to the status of a permanent minority in a preponderatingly Arab State. After all their hopes, they shall return in their National Home to that minority status which has been their lot through long centuries in every part of the world!

I venture to think that it was precisely from this permanent minority status that they had hoped to escape. They had hoped that in one place on this earth this people of something like sixteen and a half millions might have a sphere of their own, where they could show what was in them, where they could be masters of their own destiny and affairs, and where there could be a centre of Jewish life, culture, and influence throughout the world. If they have, for obvious reasons, thrown very special emphasis upon numbers, I believe that in their hearts what Zionists have desired more than anything is that they should get their freedom from this minority status. Now, I have to repeat, they are given the prospect that the minority status will be permanent, and whatever a National Home may have meant—we all know how many interpretations are put upon it—it surely cannot have meant that. It surely must have meant that somewhere in Palestine there would be a place where the Jews would be able to fulfil their aspirations, in some territory in which they had some autonomous control.

I have always had the greatest possible sympathy with the Arabs. I am bound to say that those who have been in Palestine cannot but have that sympathy. It is very widely felt in this country. I recognise the force of their claims upon it, and of their fears, but I feel bound to quote to your Lordships some words spoken in this House in 1923 by Lord Milner, at the very time when he professed himself in favour of a pro-Arab policy. I quote them as showing that it is not possible to regard the Arabs as those to whom a predominating influence in the future of Palestine should be entrusted. Lord Milner said:

> "Palestine can never be regarded as a country on the same footing as the other Arab countries. You cannot ignore the fact that this is the cradle of two of the great religions of the world. It is a sacred land to the Arabs, but it is also a sacred land to the Jew and the Christian, and the future of Palestine cannot possibly be left to be determined by the temporary impressions and feelings of the Arab majority in the country of the present day."

Then, I submit, it is still less reasonable that it should be determined by a permanent Arab majority in a single future Palestinian State.

I am well aware of other reasons, of another kind, which lie apparently behind these proposals, and which have led the Government to be particularly careful lest they should offend Arab susceptibilities. I recognise the force of those reasons. I think they may be exaggerated, but at least I cannot think they are sufficient to justify what seems like very scant justice to the Jews. I could not myself use the language which comes very bitterly from the lips of that most remarkable man Dr. Weizmann that this White Paper is a breach of faith. I am quite certain His Majesty's Government themselves have no kind of consciousness that this is the fact, and I am sure it certainly was not in their minds, but can we be surprised that Dr. Weizmann and his comrades regard it almost as taking back all that had been promised? Certainly they feel it so strongly that it is useless to dismiss from our minds that resistance to these proposals on the part of the Jewish community in Palestine will be obstinate and bitter.

   *   *   *   *   ⁑   *

I suggest that this of all times is not one in which we in this country can afford even the appearance of treating lightly promises on which we have led others to trust. It is for that reason that even at the last minute I make this appeal, though I know how natural it is for your Lordships to say: "Well, in this long affair the Government has made up their mind, let us stand by it and regard it at last as bringing finality." Admittedly it does not mean finality, and possibly along the lines which I have only roughly suggested a better solution may be found. I close by saying that I share with you all a longing, which no words can express, that at long last we might see this Palestine, with all its hallowed memories, a place of good will, and not of ceaseless strife.

My Lords, like the most reverend Primate, I wish it were possible for me to give support to the Motion which has been moved by the noble Marquess. I wish it, because I know how much time and careful thought the Secretary of State for the Colonies has given to it, and how sincerely he has tried to do justice to all parties. But, like the most reverend Primate, I feel I cannot support the Motion for reasons which I will endeavour to express to your Lordships. * * *

* * * * * * *

The reasons are these. In my opinion this policy will not bring peace to Palestine. It is inconsistent with pledges and promises, solemnly made and often repeated to the Jews, and it will not secure either the respect or the friendship of those Arabs who are at present hostile to the existing *regime*. And, lastly, I feel it will lower the prestige of this country, and seriously impair our relations with the United States of America. It is obvious that no one who thinks that the policy recommended to us this afternoon will have those consequences could possibly defend it. Let me therefore take these points in order, and give to your Lordships the reasons for the opinion I hold.

First, it will not bring peace to Palestine. I say that because, although I am convinced that it is untrue to say that Jews and Arabs cannot live in peace in Palestine, I am equally convinced that there is one condition essential to that harmony being achieved, and that condition is that neither should fear the domination of the other. That is not merely expression of opinion. What I say is based upon personal experience. I have had close contact with Palestine for the last eight years. In the company of which I am Chairman we employ 800 Jews and Arabs in almost exactly equal numbers, and there has never been the slightest friction between them. They have worked for a common purpose in perfect harmony and sympathy with each other. And why? Because in the first instance politics was eliminated from the business on which they were engaged, and secondly, because we were able to afford them complete physical protection. And I would ask your Lordships to remember, when we speak about Arab hostility, and this opinion and that opinion of Arabs, that it is not true to say that all the Arabs of Palestine feel in this way. In fact, there have been, I think, even more Arab victims of the recent terrorist crimes than Jewish victims.

Our workmen, just because they were not concerned with politics and refused to go out on strike during the Arab strike, were threatened with their lives, and they came to us and said: "What are we to do, can you protect us?" We said: "Certainly we can protect you."

And the whole of the property of our company is surrounded by an electrified wire entanglement, which affords complete security for those who live and work inside, and because that security is afforded to them we did not lose a single man. The relations between our Arab and Jewish workmen were as harmonious during those troubled times as they have always been. I am convinced that if it were possible to afford an equal security to the Arab population in the whole of Palestine against the mere handful of terrorists who are responsible for these outrages and disorders you would find an equal harmony was possible. I am convinced that the attitude of our Arab workers is also the attitude of the majority of the Arab population of Palestine, and that the opinions of a small number of terrorists no more represent the opinions of the Arabs of Palestine than any represent the opinions of Indians in India.

Though I refer to the operations of these people as terrorism, I do not deny for a moment that, however large or small their numbers may be, the Arabs who are opposed to the political regime in Palestine are very sincere in their attitude. Their opposition is based upon a fear—the fear that if Jewish immigration into that country continues unchecked, it is merely a question of time before they must find themselves in a minority, and the fear that all their political interests will be dominated by a majority of Jews. The White Paper does not remove that fear; it merely transfers it from one to the other. The fact that under this scheme the Jews will be placed in exactly the same position, with the certainty that they must for all time be a minority in Palestine, as everywhere else in the world, is a feature which will defeat the object of the White Paper. This policy means the creation of an Arab State to which the Jews will no longer have any access as of right. That is a policy which, as other speakers have said, I am certain the Jews will never accept. I am confident that all their resources—and they are great—will be used to resist it, and for that reason I say this policy will not bring peace to Palestine.

Secondly, I say it is inconsistent with the promises made in the past to the Jews. Let me remind your Lordships what these promises are. There was, first, the Balfour Declaration which promised, not just to the Jews in Palestine, but to Jews scattered throughout the world, that they might come to Palestine and make a National Home in that country. Secondly, there are the terms of the Mandate under which we administer the country, and which embodied that promise and placed upon the Mandatory Government an obligation to facilitate it in every possible way. Thirdly, there is the White Paper of 1922, which assured the Jews that they were in Palestine as of right and not on sufferance, and went on to explain that their numbers would be regulated only by the absorptive capacity of the country. The noble Marquess says that this formula, "the absorptive capacity of the country," has no sacred character for His Majesty's Government. I would ask him has also this assurance of the British Secretary of State, that the Jews are in Palestine as of right and not on sufferance, no sacred character for His Majesty's Government, because that statement was contained in the same document? Lastly, we have the letter of Mr. Ramsay MacDonald, who was then Prime Minister, to Dr. Weizmann in 1931, which added this further assurance that considerations relative to absorptive capacity were purely economic. The

Jewish National Home in Palestine rests on these four promises made on the authority of British statesmen and accepted with faith in their honourable intentions. They will all be broken if this policy is adopted.

I know it is argued—the noble Marquess argued it to-day—that all the promises to which I have referred have, in fact, been fulfilled. They base that on the ground that there are already some 400,000 Jews in Palestine to whom they say in effect:

"We promised you a National Home, and you have got it. We never promised you Palestine, and all we are doing now is to provide for a Constitution for that country in which your National Home is situated."

This argument entirely ignores the nature of the promise given. There has been, as usual, much discussion in the debate this afternoon about the meaning of the words "a National Home in Palestine." Whatever that somewhat novel phrase may mean or may not mean, it quite clearly meant this, that the Jews were promised in Palestine something which was not to be found anywhere else in the world; otherwise what was the meaning of the promise if merely some half million Jews may live in that country? That offers to them no conditions of life different from those which they enjoy to-day. As the noble Lord who spoke from the Front Opposition Bench reminded us, there are more Jews in Poland, in Germany, and in this country than there are in Palestine; but will any of your Lordships contend that because of their numbers they have a National Home in Poland, in Germany, or even in Great Britain? If not, what is the difference between the Jews in Palestine and the Jews in any other part of the world?

What security are you going to offer them that when the Mandatory Administration is withdrawn, and you have set up this independent State, even those who have come into the country will be allowed to remain there? I remember when I was being shown over the Mosque at Hebron by an Arab official, I was shown an opening in the wall which those of you who have visited the Mosque will well remember, and he said to me in these words: "Until the time of the expulsion of the Jews, the Jews were allowed to come to this hole and put their petitions through it and drop them down into the cave of Macpelah, the tomb of their ancestor Abraham, but since the expulsion they have not been allowed to do so." I asked, "What historical date are you referring to?" He said, "The expulsion of the Jews in 1920!" If the Arabs think that after the Mandatory Administration is withdrawn it is undesirable that the Jews should remain, there will be another expulsion of the Jews, not from Hebron merely, but from the whole of Palestine. Although the Secretary of State for the Colonies gave assurances in his speech in another place yesterday that the continuance of the National Home would be safeguarded, I can find nothing in this White Paper to indicate the way in which it will be secured. It is impossible to maintain that the policy indicated in this Paper is consistent with the various pledges to which I have referred or with the terms of the Mandate under which we administer the country.

I come to my third point. This policy will not secure the respect or friendship of those Arabs who are at present discontented. I am

sure you can never win the friendship of anyone at the price of breaking with faith somebody else, because it will always be known that
what has been done once can be done again.   Those whose friendship
you invite on the strength of a broken promise will always know that
the promise you are making to them is worthless because, as you have
broken one, you may break another.   I am certain that both the
Jews and the Arabs will remember the means by which His Majesty's
Government were forced to change their policy and break their promises.   My last point, therefore, is that this will not add to the prestige
of this country anywhere in the world.   On the contrary, political
unrest will be encouraged everywhere, and that in turn, I fear, will
impair our friendly relations with the United States of America which
it was one of the objects of the original Balfour Declaration to secure.
For these reasons I am unable to accept the Resolution submitted to
us by the noble Marquess this afternoon.

*   *   *   *   *   *   *

TOM WILLIAMS, M. P.
HOUSE OF COMMONS, MAY 22ND, 1939

The most intensely criticised Secretary of State for the Colonies for many years. He has this consolation, if my reading of the White Paper is correct, that he has been able in one year and two days to destroy what it took a great War and many years' efforts of Allied statesmen to build up. I repeat that, if my reading of the White Paper is correct, the right hon. Gentleman has destroyed the very basis of the Balfour Declaration. In all previous Debates on this question I have been careful to explain that, whatever else hon. and right hon. Members on these benches think about Palestine, they have never been anti-Arab or pro-Jew as such; they have been pro-Palestine all the time; if they have any partial affections, their partial affections are for the workers of both races. I did not hear the right hon. Gentleman make reference to the workers, either Arab or Jew, during the whole of his long speech. He talked about the Nationalist movement, but I did not hear him make a single observation with regard to the Arab workers.

I will concede this to the right hon. Gentleman, that the Prime Minister landed him with one of the most complex problems that has ever confronted this or any Government. We have always recognised that any set of proposals would be criticised from some quarters. To satisfy the Arab Nationalists would obviously dissatisfy the Jews, and to satisfy the Jews would obviously dissatisfy the Arab Nationalists. To that extent some sympathy is due from us to the right hon. Gentleman. But, having said that, we also recognise that we cannot readily and easily get rid of our solemn pledges. We are living in an age when far too many pledges have been broken, when far too many treaties and gentlemen's agreements have been broken, and the whole world in general, and this country in particular, is now suffering as a result of those broken pledges. In any case, we in this House ought to be very jealous of the reputation of this country where pledges or treaties or gentlemen's agreements are being undertaken. This is our approach to this problem, and I hope we shall not deviate from that point of view.

What is our reading of the White Paper? The right hon. Gentleman not only explained very carefully the pledges given to one side and the other, but he talked sufficiently long to be able to satisfy some members of the House that in fact our pledges were not pledges at all, or that our pledges were so mutual as to cancel each other out, and we were left at the end of his speech without having made a pledge at all. It is my confirmed opinion that this White Paper and all that it implies is directly contrary both to the spirit and to the letter of the Balfour Declaration, and is in effect tantamount almost to its abrogation. Even on the most generous interpretation of the right hon. Gentleman's proposals, they must conflict violently with the opinions expressed by those who devised the Balfour Declaration and by every statesman, be he British, Empire or American who has expressed opinions on the Balfour Declaration since. If our view is correct, this House certainly ought not to commit itself to that set of proposals. Perhaps, if we start at the very beginning and see exactly what our pledges were, we shall be better able to understand whether these proposals fulfill or whether they fail to redeem the pledges we made. The Balfour Declaration started with the Letter sent by Mr. Arthur James Balfour to Lord Rothschild. It commenced as follows:

"I have much pleasure in conveying to you, on behalf of His Majesty's Government, the following declaration of sympathy with Jewish Zionist aspirations which has been submitted to, and approved by, the Cabinet."

Then follow the contents of the letter which was to be sent to the Zionist Federation. I want to draw the special attention of the right hon. Gentleman to these words, because to me they are definitely fundamental:

"The following declaration of sympathy with Jewish Zionist aspirations which has been   *   *   *   approved by the Cabinet."

What, in essence, are the Jewish Zionist aspirations? If they mean anything at all, clearly they mean that the Zionist movement is in existence to get away from that inferiority, born of being of minority status, which the Jews suffer in every country in the world. If that is the true interpretation of what the Cabinet approved, then the proposals in this White Paper are an abrogation of the very essence of the Balfour Declaration. If we abandon this, then the whole object and purpose of the Balfour Declaration has gone. Under Article 6 of the Mandate our obligations are more concrete and precise. Our obligations are defined as facilitating immigration and encouraging close settlement on the land. My reading of the White Paper is that it cancels both those obligations, as I shall try to show later. The facilitation of immigration and the encouragement of close settlement on the land will be no more at the end of five years from the acceptance of these proposals. Lest there should be any doubt about our statesmen's interpretation of the Balfour Declaration, one or two questions may not be out of place. Take Lord Balfour himself:

"As to the meaning of the words 'National Home,' to which the Zionists attach so much importance, he understood it to mean some form of British, American or other protectorate, under which full facilities would be given to the Jews to work out their own salvation and to build up, by means of education, agriculture and industry a real centre of national culture and focus of national life. It did not necessarily involve the early establishment of an independent Jewish State which was a matter for gradual development in accordance with the ordinary laws of political evolution."

No Government can guarantee that a Jewish State shall be set up in Palestine. Quite obviously, economic development will determine the progress of immigration and the date, should there be a date, when a Jewish State can be set up. But it is clear that Lord Balfour did visualise the possibility of a Jewish State. That seems to me to be very clear. Then the right hon. Gentleman the Member for Epping (Mr. Churchill), in one of his rare bursts of optimism, when he was Secretary of State for War, said:

> "If, as may well happen, there should be created in our lifetime on the banks of the Jordan a Jewish State under the protection of the British Crown which might comprise three or four millions of Jews, an event will have occurred in the history of the world which would from every point of view be beneficial."

The White Paper visualises the stoppage of immigration after five years, and it argues that the Government see no reason why they should be called upon permanently to facilitate immigration. At least the right hon. Gentleman the Member for Epping, who was a member of the Government when the Balfour Declaration became known, at some time in 1920, when he made that statement, did visualise a Jewish national home of far greater size than the one the Government now contemplate. It is true that the right hon. Gentleman could not have foreseen the possibility of a National Government, but he did see the possibility of 3,000,000 or 4,000,000 people going to Palestine, which at that time, of course, would include Transjordan. Then Lord Milner made this statement relating to Palestine and the Arab and Jewish question:

> "If the Arabs go to the length of claiming Palestine, as one of their countries in the same sense as Mesopotamia or Arabia proper is an Arab country, then I think they are flying in the face of all facts, of all history, of all tradition and all associations of the most important character, I had almost said, the most sacred character. The future of Palestine cannot possibly be left to be determined by the temporary impressions and feelings of the Arab majority in the country at the present day."

*   *   *   *   *   *   *

There is one other quotation that I should like to make. It concerns America, and America, after all, is not altogether disinterested in this problem. President Wilson, stating the case for America, said:

> "I am persuaded that the Allied nations, with the fullest concurrence of our Government and our people, are agreed that in Palestine shall be laid the foundations of a Jewish Commonwealth."

It may be that any one, two, three, four or five of those statesmen were wrong, but surely they could not all have been wrong. If only some were right, two or three things were perfectly clear but the Government admit, on page 3 of the White Paper, that a Jewish State

> "was not precluded by the terms of the declaration."

If it was ever intended by those who produced the Balfour Declaration that the Jews should remain a permanent minority in Palestine, why were those very careful safeguards provided for the non-Jewish population? It must have been clear to those who produced those safeguards that the possibility of a Jewish majority was there; to that extent, a Jewish majority, a Jewish State, or Commonwealth were, rightly or wrongly, all visualised at that time. It might take 40, 50 or 100 years for that majority to be created, but as long as it was a question of economic absorptive capacity and as long as safeguards were applied, the Arabs need never be in fear of the domination of the Jews. The White Paper definitely cancels all those possibilities. On page 9, the Government deny that the Mandate required them to facilitate immigration for all time; but on page 4 are recorded these words from the Command Paper of 1922:

> "But in order that this community should have the best prospect of free development and provide a full opportunity for the Jewish people to display its capacities, it is essential that it should know it is in Palestine as of right and not on sufferance."

If the Jews can go to Palestine "as of right and not on sufferance," how can the right hon. Gentleman suggest that the Government have no further obligation to facilitate immigration? Moreover, if the Jews are going to Palestine as of right, quite clearly the Government are under almost a permanent obligation, as long as their mandatory authority continues, to facilitate immigration in accordance with the economic absorptive capacity, and I suggest that either that part of the White Paper is special pleading or the Government have misread their obligations.   The White Paper states:

> "Nor do they find anything in the Mandate * * * to support the view that the establishment of a Jewish National Home cannot be effected unless immigration is allowed to continue indefinitely."

The right hon. Gentleman repeated those words this afternoon.   It all depends on the kind of home one has in mind.   If one thinks in terms of the home envisaged by Lord Balfour, obviously immigration must continue.   If one thinks on the lines of the right hon. Gentleman the Member for Epping, of some 3,000,000 or 4,000,000 Jews making their home there, immigration will have to go on for a long time indeed. If one thinks in terms of a home where a happy, free and contented people are working out their destiny, that would be one kind of a home; but the White Paper seems to think in terms of a ramshackle council house—what has been described as a "territorial ghetto"—and which is not theirs to occupy, but where they are to be, like a lodger, in a position to be turned out at any moment.   If the White Paper is correct, the same sort of reasonable immigration could have stopped five or 15 years ago, and the same sort of justification could have been given for it as has been given to-day.   The right hon. Gentleman can find no more justification in the White Paper for establishing an Arab State and placing the Jews in a permanent minority than he can for doing the opposite.   He is going to turn those Jews who have gone to Palestine into persons who have gone there not as of right, but only on sufferance, which is directly contrary to the words of the Command paper.

The Government, on page 3 of the White Paper, categorically declare that the Arabs should not be made subjects of a Jewish State.   It may be that the Government are correct: that the Arabs ought not to be subjects of a Jewish State; but they go on to turn the Mandate completely upside down, and to turn the Jews into subjects of an Arab State.

They are to remain a minority in perpetuity, and when an independent State is set up, the Jews are to become subjects of an Arab State, particularly if the Arabs have the power to prevent any immigration after the first five years.

*   *   *   *   *   *   *

The right hon. Gentleman said that certain safeguards may be made when the new constitution is set up; but, in the meantime, those safeguards are not available for the Jewish minority. After the Assyrian experience, I should have thought that the right hon. Gentleman at least would have ensured, if he insisted upon a policy of this description, that there were doubly adequate safeguards to avoid a repetition of what happened in Assyria. In any case, are the Jews to be dependent upon the benevolence and generosity of the ex-Mufti's gangsters? There is no safeguard against those who have gone to Palestine being ultimately turned out. Does the right hon. Gentleman think this is going to encourage peaceful, prosperous development?

I know that he calls for co-operation from the Arabs and from the Jews. He admits that so far there has been no co-operation; and he knows very well that the moment the Jewish minority start to co-operate with the Arab majority, he will be able to state that "the relationships are so good that now we can start developing self-governing institutions." At that moment will the Jews seal their own fate in Palestine? If the Jews do co-operate, they will expedite the independent Arab State. They may get a few more immigrants for a time, but what is to be their position immediately the independent Arab State is set up? I want the right hon. Gentleman to say whether he thinks that in existing circumstances this is going to encourage the continuation of the very great constructive effort which the Jews have made in Palestine, where we have seen the greatest colonisation scheme on earth? Does this White Paper not visualise five years of slow progress; five years of stagnation, and perpetual uncertainty thereafter? It seems to be a real victory for the swamp, in which the mosquito and the terrorist alike will share.

*   *   *   *   *   *   *

On page 9 of the White Paper the right hon. Gentleman talks about intense Arab apprehension and widespread fear of immigration. If there is this apprehension and this widespread fear of immigration, how is it that the population has increased during the past few years from 600,000 to over 1,000,000? How is it that none of these terrified Arabs have gone to Iraq and Transjordan, if it is true that they are all in fear and trembling? How is it, if these Arabs are terrified, they have not raced across the border to Transjordan and Iraq? Why do these terrified Arabs want to remain in this Jewish chamber of horrors? It simply is not true, and the fear referred to by the right hon. Gentleman does not exist. The only persons that the Arabs need fear—the Arabs for whom I have any thought—are the Arab terrorists encouraged by the ex-Mufti, who have been responsible for killing about 3,000 of them during the last year or two. It is ridiculous to talk about the fear of Jewish domination, with Arab States all around Palestine where not only could come to the aid of their fellow Arabs,

but where no body of Jews would dare to dispose of the safeguards
that have been provided for them. This fear argument is a mere
excuse. It is another victory for Hitler and Mussolini and those who
think as they think, and those who have been guiding the terrorists
activities during the past three years.

We have watched the rise and fall of this Palestine problem. In
1917 Jewish hopes were raised in all parts of the world. It was
thought that at long last here was the Jewish Magna Charta. By
1921 Transjordan was lopped off; in 1922 free immigration became
immigration on the basis of economic absorptive capacity and very
properly; in 1933 land sales were restricted; in 1937 partition was accepted by the Government; in 1938 partition was rejected by the
Government; and in 1939 we see the funeral of the Mandate. That
is not a very proud record either for this, or for any other Government
that has gone before. I hope that the hon. Member for Stretford
(Mr. Crossley), when he makes his statement, will not forget the fact
that, while we have dealt with the Jewish problem in a very delicate
and half-hearted manner, we were not nearly so delicate or half-
hearted when dealing with the Arabs. Since the War they have
established independent States in Iraq, Saudi Arabia, Yemen, Syria
and Transjordan, an area as big as Great Britain, France, Germany,
Italy and Spain combined. Whereas the latter countries have 300,-
000,000, in the Arab State they have a mere 12,000,000 or 13,000,000.
To talk about these landless Arabs is not only special pleading, but
has no relation to the facts at all.

The right hon. Gentleman talks glibly about this vast nationalist
movement. I ask him, or the Under-Secretary of State for Foreign
Affairs, who may be replying to-night, why he thinks in terms of an
independent Arab State? Is it any form of government or type of
government whose object would be to promote economic prosperity
in Palestine, to improve the conditions of the workers, to establish
democratic institutions, trade unions, co-operative societies and the
rest? Can he visualise the possibility of that independent government rising above the Jewish tide of economic prosperity, or is there
a possibility that they may descend to the economic swamps of Iraq,
Transjordan and other Arab States? The right hon. Gentleman is
not only responsible for the rich landlord Arab or the High Church-
man Arab, but for the hundreds of thousands of Arab workers who
stand to gain most if economic prosperity is developed in that country.
We have had 20 years' experience of Palestine, and I agree that some
modification of our original desires and intentions may be necessary.
It is a crime always to promise more than one can fulfil, but as far as
this scheme is concerned, it seems to have no moral foundation and
is wholly inconsistent with the Mandate, and sacrifices moderate
Arab—I emphasize the word "moderate"—and Jew to administrative
expediency. It is a turning back of the wheels of history, and this
House ought not to commit itself to these terms until it knows more
about Government intentions.

I want to commend these words to every hon. Member sitting on
the benches opposite, and I am sure that they will not fall loose on
hon. Members sitting on these benches. A certain speech was made
which will be instantly recognised by hon. Members in this House.
Part of that speech contains these sentences:

"The terms which I was able to secure at Munich were not those that I myself would have desired, but as I explained then I had to deal with no new problem.

This was something which had existed ever since the Treaty of Versailles, a problem which ought to have been solved long ago if only the statesmen of the last 20 years had taken broader and more enlightened views of their duties.

It has become a disease that has been long neglected and a surgical operation was necessary to save the life of the patient."

The operation was performed, but the patient died none the less. To-day the Government are asking us to perform another surgical operation. The patient is not yet dead, but he is lingering in a painful attitude, and if the right hon. Gentleman the Prime Minister performs some more operations of this kind he will not only be struck off the surgical register, but he will be struck off the political register, too. In that same speech the right hon. Gentleman went on to say:

"Every man and woman in this country who remembers the fate of the Jews and political prisoners in Austria must be filled to-day with distrust and foreboding.

And who can fail to feel his heart go out in sympathy to a proud and brave people who have so suddenly been subjected to these inflictions, whose liberties are curtailed, whose national independence has gone?"

I repeat that question, which was submitted by the Prime Minister in his Birmingham speech. "who can fail to feel his heart go out in sympathy * * * to those who have so suddenly been subjected to these inflictions, whose liberties are curtailed to-day, whose national independence have gone?" I plead with this House not only not to accept the right hon. Gentleman's reading of Parliament's obligations, but to accept the instruction of the Government, who, after all, appear to be the only persons ready and willing to sell their friends for known and potential enemies, who are failing to redeem honourable pledges and doing this country an ill-deed by once more forfeiting the confidence of the people in this country, in all parts of the Empire, and in fact, in all parts of the United States, too.

RT. HON. JOSIAH CLEMENT WEDGWOOD
HOUSE OF COMMONS, MAY 22ND, 1939

We have had the views of the Arabs stated as well, possibly, as they could be by the hon. and gallant Member for Taunton (Lieut.-Colonel Wickham) and the hon. Member for Stretford (Mr. Crossley). We have had the views of the Jews stated admirably and cogently by my hon. Friend the Member for the Isle of Ely (Mr. de Rothschild). We have had the views of the Labour party stated equally eloquently. We have had the Government's views as to how to obscure the issue and to avoid any definition admirably stated by the right hon. Gentleman the Secretary of State. May I be permitted to put forward the point of view of Great Britain? May I say how pleased I am, for the honour of my country, that the right hon. Gentleman did not say anything about Guiana? I had a feeling that he was keeping Guiana as a sort of *bonne bouche*. I regard Guiana as the British concentration camp for Jews, and I am confident that it will not be a great success, even if it is run cheaply at the expense of the Jews themselves. I am also glad that we have had efforts made by the right hon. Gentleman to prove that we have not broken our word to the Jews. The most important thing in our public life, in a world where pledges are being broken with enthusiasm right and left, is that we in this country should make the attempt to keep our word to those people who cannot enforce it but who are dependent on the pledges we have given.

We must realise in this House that the White Paper proposal which we have had put before us to-day is a belated example of the policy of appeasement. The country and the Government have dropped the policy of appeasement as regards the Axis, appreciating at last that continual retreat merely invites further kicks. But here we have brought forward still another example of the policy of appeasing those people who have been sufficiently violent to make things uncomfortable. This is just another surrender to force. Therefore, it is extremely bad for our general reputation throughout the world. The right hon. Gentleman will have noticed that directly we put our foot down in foreign affairs and said, "Thus far and no farther," the danger of war has vanished and our position and the position of all peace-loving nations has become infinitely stronger. The right hon. Gentleman and the House must recognise, too, that this surrender will not be the last surrender. It is merely the latest of a long series of surrenders to violence which can be indefinitely continued. The Arabs are not satisfied even with this, and I warn the House and I warn the Jews of the world that the next step will be a demand for the disarmament of the Jews in Palestine so that they may be handed over, bound hand and foot, to this new Arab State.

440

We have to consider before we permit this crime—for it will be recognised as a crime—the effect it will have on our relations with other powers. We must realise the effect this policy has had upon America. We have certainly destroyed any faith which the Jews in Palestine or elsewhere may have had in the Government, but the effect on America is far more serious. Many hon. Members will have had cables from the United States. I have had over a dozen, four of them from Texas—From Galveston, Houston, San Antonio and Dallas. It will be remembered that 100 years ago the Americans in Texas were faced with almost the same position as that with which the Jews are faced in Palestine to-day. They were then under Mexican rule. The Mexican Government stopped immigration and attempted to disarm the Americans. The Americans were not "taking any" and in three years Texas, the lone star state, was one of the States of America, free for all time. That is an illustration, because it is as well that we should realise the past history of America as well as our own history.

This Debate is the culmination, I am afraid the final one, of a struggle which has been going on for 20 years between this House and officialdom, as represented principally by the administration in Palestine and by the Permanent officials in the Colonial Office. The last two Secretary's of State for the Colonies have gone to that office fervent supporters of Zionism and of justice in Palestine. The administration has been too strong even for them. It smashed both of them. They both brought forward proposals something like this, which meant retreat in obedience to official views. I have taken part in every Debate on this subject during the last 20 years, and I am certain that the reason for this struggle is that in this House there has always been a majority in favour of a scheme which has produced wonderful results without injuring anybody. In our history we have colonised all over the world, but this is the first case in which we have colonised without injuring the native population. In America, Australia, Africa, particularly South Africa, and even in Ireland our colonisation has been at the expense of the people who occupied the country that we were colonising. The record of that colonisation is a black one. It has been black right down to the present time.

We see in the Jewish colonisation of Palestine something quite different, something of which everyone in the House can approve. It is the first case in which the native population have not been exploited or exterminated, have not had their land stolen from them, and have been able to benefit by the civilisation which the settlers brought. One has only to go to-day to the neighbouring countries of Syria, or Egypt to see the condition of the fellahin, of the Arab workers of those two countries, and compare it with their position in Palestine, to see how enormously the natives of Palestine have benefited by the immigration of the Jews. It has been that superb example, something which none of us ever hoped to see, which has all along made this House take what I might call the Liberal view that it was right to banish prejudice and to encourage the settlement of Jews in Palestine and to take a certain reflective pride in the success of their colonisation. All along in every Debate the permanent officials, those in Palestine in particular, have complained that the House did not see the Arab point of view, and that this House, persuaded by the Jews, controlled by Jewish influence, was continually taking a view hostile to the Arabs and causing trouble. It was nothing of the sort.

Throughout we have been taking the side of civilisation and of the improvement of the native inhabitants of Palestine. Every time the officials have said that Debate in the House of Commons has been responsible for insurrection and for all the trouble; our refusal to allow the setting up of a representative responsible government under the Mufti has caused the trouble.

Everything has been put down to this House trying to check, and check successfully, in spite of the Government on various occasions, the illiberal point of view, in the interests of the population of Palestine, neglecting the interest of the landowners, the capitalists, the exploiters and, above all, that Arab intelligentsia, which sees in this agitation the chance of getting good Government jobs. The hon. Member for Stretford, who spoke for the Arabs, has rightly said that the officials in Palestine are to a man pro-Arab. I am glad to have that from the friend of the Arabs, because it is a statement which I have often made, but perhaps without having the same kind of authority for making it. I am perfectly certain it is true; and not only the officials but, I am afraid, the bulk of the officers in the Army are pro-Arab. I do not think I need argue it. Why are they pro-Arab and anti-Semite? Unless we can realise what is wrong with the administration there, or why they think like the hon. Member for Stretford, we shall not be able to improve matters.

I should say that those officials have never liked, and have never been willing, to carry out the Balfour Declaration. They are pro-Arab for reasons which really do appeal to many of us. In the first place the whole official class in this country, and, indeed, throughout the world, has a certain latent sympathy with Nazi Germany. The authoritarian ideal appeals particularly to officials. The totalitarian state also appeals instinctively to officials. Therefore, we have in the Civil Service, in the Army, in the Navy, and in the Air Force, among a good many of the people on top—I am not talking of the rank and file, but of the officers—a great deal of sympathy with the authoritarian view which is predominant in Germany and in Italy. We have changed all that here, but we have changed it very recently. It is the experience of the last six months which has changed the sympathy with Nazi Germany which prevailed among the governing class in this country.

Of course, changes like that take place more slowly in the outlying parts of the Empire, and one can quite well expect that point of view to drag on in Palestine. It is illustrated in the Palestine administration in various ways. For instance, "Mein Kampf" was allowed to be sold freely in Palestine, whereas a reply to it was not allowed to be published or issued in that country. Representation on the Legislative Council was desired for the German colony in Jerusalem—by nomination. Propaganda which has gone on from Germany, and which is recognised now, has been repeatedly denied from the officials as not existing. In all these ways we have seen the German attitude of mind; and, of course, with that there is the German attitude towards the Jews.

* * * * * * *

Now that this last scheme has been brought forward I hope and believe that we have seen a change. Dr. Weizmann, during the Conference discussions, would never go quite as far as I should have liked. He did say, "We will not accept this solution"; he did say, "We will resist," but he did not say how the Jews were going to resist, and that is the key. If they will resist now—and with their backs to the wall they must resist unless they are to lie down for ever—they will realise that the sympathy and the respect of the entire Anglo-Saxon world goes out to those who stand up for justice, stand up for equal treatment, and who will not continue indefinitely petitioning for justice and whining for mercy. Humanity! What has that got to do with the present world?

So to-day we seal the defeat of Parliament, as well as the eclipse of honour, friendship, humanity and common sense. So far as we are concerned this is the end—unless by some miracle some Members on the other side dare to vote against the Whips. But it is not the end so far as the Jewish people are concerned. They can yet secure liberty and gain the respect of all men. I do not think people realise how much of what we enjoy to-day is owing to the self-sacrifice of our forerunners. We are speaking here freely in Parliament because people have broken laws, because men have dared even to go the stake rather than obey the law. Because Prynne's ears were gouged out in Parliament Square, because Hampden died in the field and Sydney on the scaffold, because the seven bishops were thrown into the Tower rather than obey the law, because of the martyrs memorial on Carlton Hill, we have achieved a measure of freedom in this country. Because the American Colonies dared to break with England, dared to fight, America, that great Republic on which we rely so much to-day, came into being. Everything the Ango-Saxon race has achieved has been achieved by breaking laws, laws which have had the sanction of man but against which we have put the sanction of our own conscience. When you place people in the position of having to choose whether to obey man or to obey God, then you will find a determination to obey God first, and man second—and to face prison if need be. That has always been the only thing that has moved us forward in the past.

How can we instil that lesson, which no other nation in world has ever learned or known, into the Jews? We know that they have said they will not go into the new Government in Palestine. Officially they are going to boycott it. Officially they are going, apparently, to refuse to pay taxes. Unofficially I hear all sorts of excellent ideas about blowing up the pipe-line, blowing up bridges, bombing, and doing all that the I. R. A. are doing. But that is not good enough. Your self-sacrifice must be for something that you believe in more than that, and there are three things which the right hon. Gentleman will have to realise. In the first place, the Jew has a human right of access to his home. Whatever the law may be about keeping out immigrants, every Jew will feel justified in doing everything he can to break that law. And, of course, it is easy to break. As long as there is unity nothing can withstand them. An immigrant ship can land immigrants at Tel Aviv as long as there are 150,000 Jews in Tel Aviv who want it.

We must realise that laws made to prevent people from doing something which they have a God-given right to do, to live somewhere, particularly in their home, cannot be insisted upon. The law which has been passed is not only to punish people who land illegally but to punish those who harbour them. An exactly similar law was proposed in the French Convention in 1790. It was a law to make it a capital crime to emigrate and punishing all those who harboured the emigrants. Mirabeau, then nearly at the end of his life, rose in the Convention and said, "You may pass this law, but I swear that

I will never obey it." And the French Convention, being a very emotional assembly—quite unlike this House—were so moved by Mirabeau's speech that they rejected the law. Now here, in the twentieth century, we are inflicting precisely the same penalties upon people who have nowhere else to go, who have had the promise of Palestine not as their home but as "a" home, and we are asking 450,000 intelligent liberal minded Jews to co-operate with Government in enforcing that unjust law. The Government will never get it; I hope they will not get it. I shall certainly do my best to prevent it, and I hope everybody else here will do so.

*   *   *   *   *   *   *

The second law which to my mind is contrary to the law of nature and humanity and to the law of God is that you say that the Jews who go to Palestine shall not be allowed to use land whereon to live. All production and all life begin with access to land. If you make a law to say that Arabs may have land but that the Jews may not have land, that is the most invidious form of discrimination that can possibly be drawn. If the Jews of Palestine say, as I hope they will, that the law is inhuman and that they consider it their duty to break the law, I hope they will all unite to do so. The other day they started a colony somewhere out north of Huleh and Dr. Weizmann wrote to the Commander-in-Chief saying that they intended to plant their colonies on that land. If there was any opposition to it Dr. Weizmann intended to lead the march himself. Of course there was no opposition and they did start their colony there. They planted something else, because as a matter of fact one of the features of the plantation of this Jewish colony was that the Arabs of the neighbouring villages entertained them when they go there, so fictitious is the agitation. In future, when they buy land and the transfer is not authorised by the State, I hope the Jews will do exactly as they have done in respect of this colony.

*   *   *   *   *   *   *

I would point out a third unjust law. The Government of Jerusalem is manifestly unjust at the present time because there is a Jewish majority in Jerusalem and the Government insists upon the mayoralty and administration being in the hands of the Arabs. That is something which nobody can justify. There, too, the Jews will have the right and the duty to break down that form of Government. They have already refused to take any part in it. Much the best way to smash that local administration is to refuse taxes and to see that taxes are not paid. In that way you can break down any Government. Let us realise too that in this House we are yielding to force, and so compelling resistance; that the only way which the Jews in Palestine and in the world have of securing justice is by using those forces which we have blamed in other people although we have always exercised them ourselves.

We are now saying "good-bye" to control by this House and to constitutional methods. We are saying good-bye also to our dreams of seeing Palestine a happy colony within the Biritish Empire. It is now joining Iraq. The intelligent civilised and educated people of that country must look after themselves. The constitution is at an end. I inform the right hon. Gentleman that in spite of his policy, men are preparing to sacrifice their lives as our ancestors did, and in the long run to win that same freedom that we ourselves achieved.

RT. HON. LEOPOLD STENNETT AMERY
HOUSE OF COMMONS, MAY 22ND, 1939

*　　*　　*　　*　　*　　*　　*

My right hon. Friend, the Secretary of State for the Colonies, began with an account of the origins of our policy in Palestine. I confess that that account did not tally altogether with my own recollections. I had the privilege of being, as a Secretary to the War Cabinet very closely associated with the discussions, the long discussions, which preceded the Balfour Declaration. My right hon. Friend referred to that policy as having been born in the tumult of war, and he suggested that there was some lack of full consideration about it. He hinted to-day, indeed he told us more definitely last November, that the authors of the Balfour Declaration were not aware of the existence of a population of 600,000 Arabs in Palestine. Believe me, that is entirely remote from the situation as I remember it. That memorable document was not issued in haste or lightheartedly. It was not a sudden happy thought, a piece of war propaganda, meant to win the support of the American or Russian Jewry; still less was it issued in ignorance of the facts of the case.

On the contrary, all the relevant facts, all the difficulties that might arise, and were indeed bound to arise, from the natural reaction of a primitive population in contract with a new element, separated from it even more by centuries of development than by race and religion— all those aspects were canvassed for many months and were fully understood. But the statesmen of that day viewed their problems from a wider perspective. They saw in the approaching dissolution of the Ottoman Empire a unique opportunity, which could never recur, for contributing to the solution of that baffling and tragic problem, the fate of a people which is yet not a people, which is a minority everywhere, with no home to call its own, whether as actual refuge from oppression or merely as a focus for their pride and affection. They knew that that problem might become acute again at any moment, though they never dreamed of the insane orgy of persecution, of extirpation, which has since swept over Europe. In that respect, at any rate, they builded better than they knew. If foresight is the measure of statesmanship, then surely, we should be proud to-day that it was British statesmanship which, by bold, constructive prevision, planned the framework of a Home, a City of Refuge, which might, if it were allowed, be at this moment affording immeasurable relief, spiritual as well as material to the agony of the Jews. I should have thought that we might have been heartened and encouraged to-day to carry on a policy, so far-seeingly initiated and already so fruitfully advanced, with fresh confidence and with a keener determination to overcome all obstacles. Instead, we have this White Paper,

which, from beginning to end, is a confession of failure, a direct negation of the principles on which our administration in Palestine has been
based, and, in my view at any rate, a repudiation of the pledges on
the strength of which the government of Palestine was entrusted to
our hands.

There was another aspect of the question which appealed more particularly to some of the younger men like myself and the late Sir Mark
Sykes—too soon lost to this House—who travelled in the Near East
and who had taken a keen and sympathetic interest in the affairs of
the Moslem world long before either of us had ever come in contact
with Zionism. We believed that it was Britain's mission to restore
prosperity and civilisation to those ancient lands that had once been
the very centre of the civilised and prosperous life of the world and of
its creative thought. We knew that, while we might give the indispensable frame-work from some more intimate and directly quickening
influence. It seemed to us that the Jews alone could bring Western
civilisation to the East with an instinctive understanding of its outlook.
Above all, they would come, not as transient administrators, not even
as colonists looking back to a motherland elsewhere, but as a people
coming back to their own homeland, prepared unreservedly and wholeheartedly to identify themselves with its fortunes. That was a view
which appealed, not only to the Zionist leaders, but to the best among
the Arab leaders at that time. Some day, I dare say, it may appeal
to them again, but that will require a very different approach, a very
different attitude on our part from that revealed in the White Paper.

There was, lastly, a more narrowly British view—and I, at any rate,
have never been ashamed of regarding these issues primarily from the
point of view of their effect on British interests. It was based on the
fact that Palestine occupies a position of unique strategical importance,
in relation both to the Suez Canal and to the junction of the air routes
between the three Continents of the Old World. In our view it was a
vital British interest that Palestine should be a prosperous, progressive
State, bound to us by ties of good will and gratitude, able in the hour
of need to furnish resources both of personnel and of material which
only a densely populated, developed modern community could furnish.
Had we known of the dangers which face us to-day, how much more
eagerly should we have pushed on the policy in which we then believed!
Now, with the terrible dangers which confront us, it is tragic to think
of the use we might be making to-day of the manpower, the ability,
the enterprise, the loyalty and trust—for till now the loyalty and
trust were still there—of the Jews in Palestine.

Those were the reasons which justified the policy of the Balfour
Declaration, and for those reasons the statesmen of that day had no
hesitation in demanding of the Arabs, whom they were liberating over
the whole of the vast Arab world, that to this one small corner of it,
containing at that moment perhaps one-fifteenth of its population,
the Jews should be admitted on the basis of equal rights of citizenship
with the older population. My hon. Friend the Member for Stretford (Mr. Crossley) objected. He took the view that the population
of any given area, whatever its size or character, is entitled entirely
to dispose of its own destiny, regardless of all circumstances, domestic
or international. I would ask him, if he were here, whether the view
he has taken about the indefeasible and unlimited right of the 600,000
Arabs of Palestine to control their destiny would apply equally to the

unlimited right of the 450,000 Germans of Danzig to dispose of their destiny without any regard to the wider issues at stake? In any event that demand was admitted, and readily admitted, by the one person most entitled to speak for the Arabs, by King Feisal and by his Arab colleagues at the Peace Conference. Whether that admission involved or did not involve some limitation or qualification of what the Arabs thought was implied, either in the McMahon correspondence or in Dr. Hogarth's statement, is surely completely irrelevant to-day. Of course it is equally irrelevant for the Jews to go back to any expectations which they may have been encouraged to entertain before their position was definitely laid down by the Mandate and by the White Paper issued in 1922 by my right hon. Friend the Member for Epping (Mr. Churchill). For the Arabs the Peace Negotiations, and for the Jews the Mandate and the White Paper, must mark the limit of their claims;

Of that final settlement of 1922, I would only say that it marked a drastic scaling down of Jewish hopes. It began by taking out of Palestine the larger and better half, the half more suitable to large-scale colonisation, namely, Trans-jordan. That was the first partition. It also made it clear to the Jews that there was no question of Palestine ever becoming a Jewish State or a Jewish country in the sense in which England is English. It made it clear that not only the individual, civil and religious rights of the Arabs, which the Balfour Declaration affirmed, but the existence of the Arab community as such, with its culture and its language, had to be recognized. We took the view then, and I should have wished to see it maintained to-day—the White Paper does not maintain it—that Palestine, like Canada or South Africa, must always be a State in which two different elements had to recognise each other's rights. The essential fact was laid that they were equal rights. The Jews were to be in Palestine as of right, and not on sufferance, and no other consideration was to be allowed to prevent their free entry and free settlement as long as that entry and that settlement did not inflict direct injury upon the existing community, Jew or Arab. That was the meaning, the only possible meaning, of the test of economic absorptive capacity. To the principal of that test every British Government since has been pledged. My right hon. Friend has said that it is not in the Mandate. That is quite true, but the Permanent Mandates Commission and the League of Nations accepted it as a legitimate limitation of wider demands which the Jews might otherwise have been encouraged to advance. They never accepted it as a mere maximum which might be whittled down at the convenience of the administration at any moment.

* * * * * * *

In November my right hon. Friend told us that he had adopted from my right hon. Friend the Member for Epping the watchword "not partition, but perseverance." What is the watchword now? Partition has faded into the background; perseverance has oozed away. The watchword is, "appease the Arabs," appease the Mufti. Appease them at all costs. Appease them by abandoning the declared policy of every Government for 20 years past. Appease them at the cost of sacrificing all the prestige which we might have gained from either Jews or Arabs by consistency, by firmness, by justice to both sides. After all, stripped of all verbiage, what does the White Paper mean? It means, to begin with, that the Arab contention that Palestine is an Arab country in which Arab point of view must prevail over all other considerations, is accepted without qualification. No, with one very important qualification—delay. The Jews are to be a permanent minority. After an interval their entry is to be on sufferance, and no longer as of right. After that they are to be— subject to indefinite safeguards under a guarantee, which, we imagine, will be pretty worthless—as a National Home carried on under the rule of the Mufti. In every pledge that we have given—and I need not delay the House by repeating all the pledges that have been given right through to the Debate last November; and it was repeated to a deputation by the Prime Minister only a few weeks ago—the Jews were not to be placed in a position of permanent minority under the Arabs.

Why has this policy been adopted? The House is entitled to ask why there should have been this sudden and complete reversal of policy at this moment. Arab resistance in Palestine has been largely overcome. As far as Palestine is concerned, it may to-day prove easier to override the Arabs than the Jews. Is it the fear that Arab States will suddenly espouse the cause of the Axis Powers? They know better than that. If ever they should attempt to desert us, it will not be for anything we may do in Palestine, but because they have lost confidence in our power to defend them. These are not the reasons, even if they may be the excuse. The real reasons that have been brought us to the present position are not the inherent difficulties of the situation. They are not the difficulties either of the internal or external situation. They are lack of purpose, lack of that belief in one mission both to Jews and Arabs which underlay the policy of the Mandate, lack of faith in ourselves, sheer inability to govern. The state of Palestine is deplorable to-day, and is likely to be even more deplorable before long, as the result of what Burke once called "the irresistible operation of feeble councils."

Looking at the matter from the point of view of one who has had to administer Palestine, I ask myself, how is the new policy going to work out on the spot? The Arabs have had all their claims acknowledged. The actual settlement of these claims is relegated to the future. Jewish immigration will not be stopped for five years, self-government is to come, perhaps in 10 years. Knowing that what they have secured has been secured by violence, they will draw the obvious conclusion that, unless His Majesty's Government are kept on the run, by more intransigence, more violence, more pressure from neighbouring States, the hopes that are now raised may possibly never be fulfilled. The White Paper is a direct invitation to Arabs to continue to make trouble. As for the Jews, they are now told that all the hopes that they have been encouraged to hold for 20 years are to be dashed to the ground, all their amazing effort wasted—in so far as it was an effort to create a National Home—all the pledges and promises that have been given to them, broken. That is to be their reward for loyalty, for patience, for almost unbelievable self-restraint. Let us not forget of whom we are asking this. These are not like the Jews in Germany, a helpless, hopeless minority. They are a formidable body of people. They are composed largely of younger men who have undergone military training and are quite capable of defending themselves, of holding their own, if only we allowed them. They are people who have felt the breath of freedom and who mean to remain free. They are people who believe the land in which they are living is their own, not merely by old sentimental associations, or even international sanction, but because, such as it is to-day, they have created it. Does my right hon. Friend believe that these people will be contented to be relegated to the position of a statutory minority, to be denied all hope of giving refuge and relief to their tortured kinsfolk in other countries; that they will wait passively until, in due course, they and the land they created are to be handed over to the Mufti? That is not only my view, but the view of the Royal Commission, whose language I could give if I did not hesitate to keep the House much longer.

I wonder how the Government envisage the actual administration of Palestine under their new policy. New heads of departments are to be appointed immediately. They are to be "Palestinians," a blessed world, like Mesopotamia, under cover of which, the white paper shirks all the difficulties of the position. No Jew will accept office. No Arab dare do so, without the Mufti's express permission, without his visa. The Government still keep up the pretence of treating the Mufti as a criminal and an outlaw. But they made no attempt to exclude his nominees from the conference. I assume that they will make no effort to exclude them from these quasi-ministerial appointments. My right hon. Friend says that in the last resort they will be subject to the High Commissioner. If a man has to choose between two masters, one of whom can dismiss him, but who may find it very embarrassing to do so, and another who would have no hesitation in ordering his assassination, which master is he the more likely to obey? If any man is to be pitied in this world under the new project it is His Majesty's High Commissioner in Palestine. I wonder if Sir Harold McMichael was ever consulted about it. I wonder if General Haining was ever consulted, and I wonder if Sir Charles Teggart, who has worked so valiantly to restore order, was ever consulted. The whole of this policy is stillborn. If it is not swept away by the greater storm that may break upon us at any moment, it is bound to peter out in bitterness and confusion.

Meanwhile, this panic scheme is to be pushed in panic haste through Parliament. Why? The whole matter is to come up before the Mandates Commission in a few weeks. Would it not be wiser for the Government to make sure that the Mandates Commission are prepared to endorse so complete a departure from the conditions of the Mandate? Why should this House make itself look foolish by approving a scheme in advance which is more than likely to be rejected as a breach of our mandatory obligations? That was the view taken by this House even on so minor a question as partition two years ago. Again, two years ago this House insisted upon having something more definite than the Royal Commission's proposals. Those proposals were precision itself compared with the scheme which my right hon. Friend has asked us this afternoon to approve. With the exception of the one definite figure of Jewish immigration, the whole of it is vague and absolutely undefined. There is to be this scheme of new heads of Departments, which Departments? Is the Mufti to appoint his nominee to the department of Justice? Is his nominee to control immigration or land? We ought to know. Land, we are told is to be under the absolute discretion, to sanction or veto transfer, of the High Commissioner, through his head of Department. On what principle? Within what area? We ought to know. What about the holy places? We were assured by my right hon. Friend in general terms that something is to be arranged about them. The Royal Commission made very definite provision in respect of the holy places. It said they should be permanently under British administrattion.

Lastly, we are told that when the independent State is set up Arabs and Jews are to share in the government in such a way that the essential interests of each are safeguarded. What on earth does that mean? Does it mean some equal voting power by which the Jews can veto legislation prejudicial to them? Is it a vague hint at some sort of quasi federation? If so, why are we not told? Why it is not made clear that no federal scheme is possible consistent with any fulfilment of the Mandate which does not give the Jews control of immigration and land settlement or does it just mean nothing at all? It is preposterous to ask the house to shut its eyes, open its mouth and swallow this half-baked project.

I hope even now the Government may accept the Amendment standing in the name of the hon. and gallant Member for Chippenham (Captain Cazalet), and secure the agreement of the House upon it. If not then we must each vote for or against the Government as our conscience may direct. For my part I feel that I cannot divest myself of a definite personal responsibility in this matter. For nearly seven years I was directly concerned in the administration not only of Palestine, but of Transjordania, Iraq and other Arab countries. I worked wholeheartedly for what I believed to be the interests of all the peoples of those countries, of every race. I believe that I enjoyed the good will and the respect of both Jews and Arabs. I could never hold up my head again to either Jew or Arab if I voted tomorrow for what, in good faith, I repeatedly told both Jews and Arabs was inconceivable, namely, that any British Government would ever go back upon the pledge given not only to Jews but the whole civilised world when it assumed the Mandate. In the absence of any alternative accepted by the whole House, I shall most certainly give my vote for the Opposition Amendment to-morrow. I should be ashamed to take any other course.

PHILIP J. NOEL-BAKER, M. P.
HOUSE OF COMMONS, MAY 22ND, 1939

My hon. Friend the Member for Don Valley (Mr. T. Williams) said this afternoon that we are against the policy which the Secretary of State for the Colonies explained. We are against it, not because we are anti-Arab or pro-Jew, but because we are pro-Mandate. We believe in the Mandate; we believe that we ought to carry out the trust we undertook; we believe that it is only by the policy of the Mandate that the problem of Palestine can be solved and that the real interests of the Jews and the Arabs can be served.

I saw the Mandate being made in Paris and Geneva 20 years ago. Day by day I talked about it with those, on the Arab side, on the Jewish side and in the British Foreign Office who worked it out. Perhaps it is because of that experience that I have never been able to understand why some people think that the Mandate does injustice to the Arabs. I have never been able to understand how the Secretary of State could tell the House last November that if he were an Arab he would be afraid of the coming of the Jew. I thought it the more extraordinary that he should have made that statement last November because, in the very same speech, he told us that, thanks to the Mandate, thanks to the Jews, there were 400,000 more Arabs alive and prosperous to-day than there would otherwise have been. No one has forgotten the generous tribute he made last November, and which he repeated in a lesser measure this afternoon, to the work which the Jews have done, and to the way in which they have expanded the soil of Palestine and have enlarged the common patrimony of the country for both Arabs and Jews.

It was because I remembered what he said then that I was utterly mystified by what he said about the Hogarth Message this afternoon. He relied very much upon that Message. I leave aside the point that he put it upon almost equal footing as a pledge with the Balfour Declaration and the Mandate—a procedure which by any test is utterly grotesque. I leave aside also the point that a year after the Hogarth Declaration the Emir Feisal and the Arab delegation in Paris accepted the Mandate and the Jewish National Home—

Mr. MacDonald. On conditions.

Mr. Noel-Baker. Yes, on conditions, which have been fulfilled, that the other Arab countries should be made independent; they have been made independent, except Syria and Transjordan, which are very nearly so. In 1919 the Emir Feisal wrote to the Jewish agency to say that Arabs looked forward to collaboration with the Jews, that he understood their plans, and that the Arabs would welcome them back to their Home. I leave aside those points, and I come simply to the text of the Hogarth Message itself.

451

The Secretary of State read a little section of that message; I will read the whole of the last paragraph on which he principally relied It said:

"Since the Jewish opinion of the world is in favour of the return of the Jews to Palestine, and inasmuch as this opinion must remain a constant factor, and further, as His Majesty's Government view with favour the realisation of this aspiration, His Majesty's Government are determined that, in so far as is compatible with the freedom of existing populations both economic and political, no obstacle should be put in the way of the realisation of this ideal."

After what the Secretary of State told us last November of the economic work of the Jews and of the 400,000 Arabs alive and prosperous to-day who would not have been so but for that work, he cannot say to-day that the coming of the Jews imperilled the economic freedom of the Arabs.

So there remains their political freedom. How can the right hon. Gentleman interpret the Hogarth message as he did this afternoon unless he is ready to say that political freedom means that the Arabs must always be in a majority, in Palestine? That is what he does say. By all his talk about the fears of the Arabs of Jewish domination, the Secretary of State has got himself into a very strange position. He said to-day that it would be repugnant to our own national spirit and traditions, repugnant to the spirit of the Mandate and, if I understood him aright, repugnant even to the letter of the Mandate itself, to convert Palestine into a Jewish State against the will of the Arab population. So he arrives at this extraordinary result: That the will of the Arab population, or what the Mufti and his followers choose to call the will of the Arab population, must be decisive, and that, after a period of adjustment, the Jews must not exceed the number to which the Arabs will agree. Thus under the Mandate and the Balfour Declaration, the Arabs are to be in the majority for ever.

If the speech of the Secretary of State and the White Paper do not mean that, they do not mean anything at all. An ingenuous leader writer in the "Times" put the matter very plainly the other day in his comment upon the White Paper. He said:

"The unrestricted increase of Jewish immigration must in time contradict the terms of the Mandate by converting the Arab population into a minority and thereby varying or subverting their existing political rights."

That is the doctrine of the White Paper, writ plain and large. I challenge the right hon. Gentleman to deny, that in the light of the Balfour Declaration and the Mandate, that doctrine is utterly grotesque. The Balfour Declaration provided for the establishment of the Jewish Home; and went on to say that nothing should be done which "prejudice the civil and religious rights" of existing non-Jewish sections of the population. Why "non-Jewish," if the Arabs were to be in the majority? In that case, it would plainly have been necessary to protect the Jews.

But look a little closer at the Balfour Declaration. The White Paper says that the Government did not contest the view of the Royal Commission that "the Zionist leaders at the time of the Balfour

Declaration, recognised that an ultimate Jewish State was not precluded by the terms of the Declaration." That is a very disingenuous version of what the Royal Commission actually said:

> "The Jews understood that if the experiment succeeded the National Home would develop in course of time into a Jewish State."

Why did the Jews understand that to be the case? Because from 1918 to 1920 they were told so by the rulers of the world. They were told so by President Wilson, by Lord Balfour and by the right hon. Gentleman the Member for Carnarvon Boroughs (Mr. Lloyd George). Not one leader ever hinted that there would not be a Jewish Commonwealth in Palestine in time to come. The right hon. Gentleman the Member for Carnarvon Boroughs has said that the notion that Jewish immigration would be restricted never entered into anybody's mind because it would have been regarded "as unjust and as a fraud on the people to whom we were pledged." I know that is true, because I talked to the men day by day who made the Mandate. The Secretary of State reminded us to-day that the White Paper of 1922 tells us that we did not intend to make a wholly Jewish State. It went on to say something which is very important, that we "did not intend to stamp out or subordinate the Arab population, language or culture." Of course not; no one ever suggested such a thing. That White Paper may have repudiated the suggestion that Palestine was to be made as Jewish as England is English; but did anybody doubt that it was the intention that Palestine should be as Jewish as Canada is British?

The analogy is exact. The Secretary of State said this afternoon that we would not in any part of the world force immigrants on unwilling populations in countries that we rule. What did we do in Canada? We had a violent conflict with the French, and they were in a majority. We conquered Canada, and we sent immigrants there for centuries; and to-day the people live in harmony together, as some day the Jews and Arabs will in Palestine. In 1922, as in 1919, we meant to create a Commonwealth in Palestine in which Jews and Arabs would have common democratic rights and freedom, but in which the Jews would predominate in numbers. But for that, the experiment of a National Home would never have been attempted. As late as 1927, both the Royal Commission and the Government themselves in their White Paper said that the primary objective of Zionism, and, therefore, of the Mandate, was "escape from minority life." And, in this regard the present White Paper and the policy of the Secretary of State are in flagrant violation of the Balfour Declaration of the Mandate, and, indeed, of the whole policy which the British Government as Mandatory has hitherto pursued. The Royal Commission declared in 1937 that

> "The primary purpose of the Mandate as expressed in its preamble and its articles, is to promote the establishment of a Jewish National Home,"

and the Government, in the famous letter written in 1931 by Mr. Ramsay MacDonald, which has already been quoted this afternoon, recognised that that was an undertaking, not only to the Jews in

Palestine, but to Jews throughout the world. All these solemn pledges, these international obligations—for such they are—the Secretary of State puts aside. For him, the primary purpose of the Mandate is no longer the establishments of a Jewish National Home, but the protection of Arab rights; and not the rights of the Balfour Declaration—political freedom and civil justice in a free State—but a new right which he has invented, the right that the Arabs shall be in a majority for ever. So he condemns the Jews for ever to minority status; minority status among Arabs—not minority status among the European peoples, or among the American people, whose countries they have left to go to Palestine; Minority Status, from which the whole purpose of the Mandate was that, after 15 centuries of dispersion and persecution, they should at last escape.

This afternoon the Secretary of State tried to comfort us by talking of constitutional safeguards for the Jews. I ask him, what safeguards? I hope the Under-Secretary will tell us. He spoke of federation. In the Jewish unit of the federation, will there be freedom of immigration? I ask him to tell me. I wish he would tell me now. If he uses a word like "federation," he ought to have clear ideas on a fundamental point like that. I ask him, if constitutional safeguards will protect the Jews, why will they not protect the Arabs, especially with the great Arab hinterland behind? I ask him why, if the Arabs are afraid of Jewish domination, he never mentioned the Jewish offer of political parity which they have made, and have always stood by, from the very start? He cannot give us an answer to these questions, for there is none. By inventing this new Arab right to be in a majority, he has utterly destroyed the purpose and the meaning of the Mandate, and has violated its spirit in every possible way.

But in his White Paper and in his speech he not only violates the spirit and purpose of the Mandate, but he violates the letter of its articles as well. Article 2, which deals with immigration, lays it down that we as Mandatory shall—not *may* or *should* but *shall*—facilitate Jewish immigration, and encourage close Jewish settlement on the land. As the right hon. Gentleman the Member for Carnarvon Boroughs has said no one at the time ever dreamt that there would be a restriction on that right of immigration; they doubted, rather, whether the Jews would really want to go. But a restriction was in fact instituted. As the Secretary of State said in 1922 the right hon. Gentleman the Member for Epping (Mr. Churchill) brought in the principle of economic absorptive capacity. It was a restriction on Jewish rights, on their right to go to Palestine; but it was accepted, however reluctantly, by the Jews. The Secretary of State said to-day that that principle does not mean that we must allow the Jews to go up to the limit of economic absorptive capacity; he challenged that interpretation completely. Has he forgotten that, when the White Paper of 1922 was issued, the Jews wrote a letter in which they gave exactly that interpretation to the new principle, namely, that they should be allowed to go to the limit of economic absorptive capacity? Has he forgotten that the British Government of the day sent that letter, together with the White Paper and their draft of the Mandate, to the League of Nations, without any dissenting note of any kind, and that it was on those three documents together that the Mandate was approved? Not only that, but the Government have gone on asserting almost ever since that the principle of economic absorptive capacity means precisely what the Jews claimed that it should.   I could quote a score of Government declarations; I will quote only one. Lord Swinton, who was then Secretary of State for the Colonies, said in 1933:

"It has always been the policy followed by the Mandatory Power—and no other policy could possibly be pursued in Palestine in carrying out the idea of a National Home—that the economic conditions of the country must govern the number of immigrants."

Time after time, in 1933, 1934, 1935, and 1936, Government spokesmen have used the word "govern" or "determine" in that same sense. To-day, the Secretary of State challenges that principle; he says that political factors must also be considered—that if the Arabs are against continued immigration, it must stop.   And so he substitutes for economic absorptive capacity what my right hon. Friend the Member for South Hackney last November called the principle of political absorptive capacity, with the consent of the Mufti and his colleagues as the test of the application of this new principle.   I again without hesitation that that new principle is in open conflict with the Mandate and with the White Paper of 1922, and I am certain that, if the right hon. Gentleman who wrote that White Paper were here, he would agree.   I cannot believe that the Mandates Commission of the League will approve of this new principle, or that this House should approve of it until it knows what that Commission is going to do.

This is not the first time that the Secretary of State's argument about political considerations has been put forward, and he, if anyone, ought to remember that fact.   It was put forward in the famous and ill-fated White Paper of 1930, which was the Government's response, as this White Paper is, to Arab violence.   It proposed, as the Secretary of State now proposes, to throw over the principle of economic absorptive capacity, and drastically to reduce Jewish immigration on political grounds.   What happened?   British opinion was so incensed that the Government were obliged virtually to withdraw the White Paper, abandon their restrictions on immigration and reassert the principle of economic absorptive capacity as the decisive and the *only* test.   The restrictions proposed in that White Paper of 1930 were challenged at the time as a violation of the Mandate.   They were challenged by Lord Baldwin, the late Sir Austin Chamberlain and the right hon. Member for Sparkbrook (Mr. Amery), who together said that it would have been contrary to the intention of the Mandate if the Jewish National Home had "crystallised at its present stage of development."   They were challenged also on legal grounds by two of the greatest legal luminaries in the country, the Chancellor of the Exchequer and Lord Hailsham, who together wrote a letter to the "Times" in which they analysed the White Paper, recited its restrictions on immigration, and then said:

"In all these respects the White Paper appears to us to involve a departure from the obligations of the Mandate.   This country cannot afford to allow any suspicion to rest on its faith or on its determination to carry out to the full its international obligations.   If, therefore, the terms of the White Paper are the deliberate and considered announcement of Government policy, we would suggest that immediate steps be taken to induce the

Council of the League of Nations to obtain from the Hague Court an advisory opinion on the questions involved, and that the British Government should not enforce these paragraphs unless and until the Court has pronounced in their favour."

Such persuasion from such quarters brought Lord Passfield—with the help, if I remember rightly, of the present Secretary of State himself—to his knees. Mr. Ramsay MacDonald wrote the letter to which I have already referred, in which he laid down "that no political factor should affect the right to immigrate, and it should be based on purely economic considerations." And in another passage of that letter, the then Prime Minister said:

"The obligation to facilitate Jewish immigration * * * can be fulfilled without prejudice to the rights and position"—

the phrase that the Secretary of State quoted this afternoon, and on which he considerably relied—

"The rights and position of other sections of the population of Palestine."

That sentence of Mr. Ramsay MacDonald's letter demolishes, at a single blow, the whole case put up by the Secretary of State this afternoon. Nor is that the end. The point arose again in 1936. We then restricted immigration because of the troubles which began the year before. The Mandates Commission raised the question, and our Foreign Secretary was compelled to tell the Assembly of the League that it was a purely temporary expedient to meet a temporary situation. Will the Secretary of State accept the plan which the Chancellor of the Exchequer proposed in 1931? Will he send the matter to the Hague Court. Will he let the Mandates Commission draft the question which is put? Will he accept the verdict given?

I do not believe that, in his heart of hearts, the Secretary of State greatly differs from much that I have said. He knows that he is proposing a change in the meaning and purpose of the Mandate. He justifies it because he says that to continue Jewish immigration means Government by force. None of us wants government by force; but in the present situation the Secretary of State's proposition is a euphemism for giving way to lawless force. It is a polite way of saying that we will surrender to the Mufti and his gang that, in the hope of getting peace, we must do another Munich on the Jews. When you contemplate a Munich the first question to ask is, "Shall we really get peace or shall we not?" What is the terrorism to which the Secretary of State is now surrendering? When did the present disturbances begin, and by whom were they organised? They began in 1935, at the time of the Abyssinian affair, when we were imposing our feeble economic sanctions on Mussolini. They were organised by the Mufti, who for nearly 20 years has worked against the Mandate, and who threatened to the Royal Commission that the Jews would be expelled when the Arab State had been set up. It was paid for and assisted by the aggressive Powers who have kept Europe in a ferment, and against whom to-day we are compelled to prepare for war. Money, arms, officers, organisers, everything came from Italy and Germany. Already in 1935—I am quoting the editor of the "Quarterly Review"—50 German agents were sent to Africa and the Near East. Their destinations, among others, were Haifa and Jaffa.

They were given instructions to carry on the most intensive propaganda efforts among the natives. In 1936—I am quoting the "Daily Telegraph"—the Jerusalem police intercepted documents proving that the Arab raiders received £ 50,000 from Germany and £ 20,000 from Italy for the purpose of strengthening their resistance. We know that British officers in Palestine talk freely of the German and Italian arms and money that the terrorists have received. We know that the land mines by which British soldiers have been murdered could not be made and could not be operated by the Arabs. We know that on one occasion the bloodhounds followed the trail from a land mine to a blacksmith's shop in the German colony of Waldenheim. We know that Dr. Goebbels has established a propaganda school for Arabs in Berlin.

Is this terror really the work of the Arab population of Palestine? Have they done the fighting? If so, why have cut-throats and gangsters come in from all over the Middle East? Lord Lytton goes to Palestine every year. He knows the country well. He told me last week that in his belief the real followers of the Mufti do not number more than about 1,000 men. All through the trouble far more Arabs have been killed by Arabs than have Jews. All through the troubles the Arab fellahin, in many places, and in many ways, have been trying, in spite of terrorism, to show their friendship for the Jews. Two weeks ago 1,500 Jews went to occupy a new settlement in the Gallilean Hills. The Arabs of the region came to bid them welcome. They stayed three days, and helped them to make the road. They said that they thanked God that they had come because they would now be free of the Mufti's armed bands and their incursions. That is not an isolated example. There is not an isolated example. There is a settlement at Hanita on the Lebanon frontier, where for 18 months Jews have lived without being molested in any way. All over the country there are such settlements, including out of the way and most difficult parts.

As the right hon. Gentleman the Member for Sparkbrook said tonight that the British Empire has dealt with many more serious revolts than this. Indeed, although it sounds like a paradox, it may well be that at the present moment there is a better chance of securing real Arab-Jewish co-operation than ever before. Before this White Paper was produced, the Mufti was utterly discredited, and his gangsters had been scattered or destroyed. The vast majority of the Arab people were known to be longing for the end of terror and for peace; they knew that the Jewish immigration had brought not only Jewish prosperity, but Arab prosperity as well. It is at this moment, when the foreign-fomented terrorism has been almost ended, when order has been very largely restored, when the Jews are suffering a persecution such as they have not known in their long history, and such as was not dreamed of in 1919 when the National Home was first conceived, when the National Home has proved that, spiritually, financially, and economically, to be a practical success; it is at this moment, when very many of the doubts of 1919 have been resolved, that the Government throw aside the policy of the Balfour Declaration of the National Home. It is not that policy which has failed; it is the Government who have failed because they have never really tried to make the policy work.

If one thing is more certain than another it is that this new policy will be a failure. The Jews will not have it. The British will not have it. They will not have it because it is cowardly and wrong. Last Friday I sat by chance in the train beside a German Jewish girl. She had left the Rhineland the day before. She told me of her life at home, how the Nazis had attacked her father's house a score of times, smashed their windows, their furniture, and their cups and saucers, torn up and scattered their mattresses and feather beds. Her aged mother had to sleep on the floor. Her brother had just come home from Dachau where he had been for nine months. He had not been tortured, only beaten and kicked every day. But he was so broken that if the door bell rang he rushed to hide himself away. We forget it, but this is what is happening every day in Germany under Dr. Goebbels' devilish decrees—no homes, no work, no hope, brutality and starvation for half a million Jews. And when these Jews try to escape and go to Palestine, they are what the Government call "illegal immigrants."

Three weeks ago a Greek ship arrived with 500 "illegal immigrants" from Germany. I have here the facts, typed out by the hand of Michael Clarke, whom the Mufti murdered last week on the road to Tel Aviv. In this ship of 750 tons there were 500 passengers. They paid fares of £20 each. The captain raised by blackmail £2,000 more. They travelled the Mediterranean from port to port for 48 days, almost without food, often without water, always without soap or sanitation. Men from Dachau said the ship was worse. At last, one dark night, they made their landing. They waded up to their shoulders through the sea. Three hundred of the younger and more active managed to escape to Jewish colonies and homes, but the rest, too beaten, too exhausted to do more, fell on the beach and kissed the holy ground. There British soldiers found them and took them into camp, clothed them, fed them and gave them tea.

If the Secretary of State's policy is now adopted, the illegal immigration of these tortured people from Germany and elsewhere will enormously increase. The Jews of Palestine will go by the tens of thousands down to the beach to welcome them and to cover and protect their landings. The only way to stop them is to tell those kindly British soldiers to shoot them down. Does the Secretary of State believe that he could give that order? He knows that he could not. For that, if for no other reason, this policy is bound to fail. It will fail because in the most tragic hour of Jewish history the British people will not deny them their Promised Land.

RT. HON. HERBERT STANLEY MORRISON
HOUSE OF COMMONS, MAY 23RD, 1939

I must first apologise, in the absence of the Secretary of State for the Colonies, that it was impossible for me to be present in order to hear personally his speech in opening the Debate yesterday, but I have taken pains to read his speech, and, having apologised for my absence, I will now tell the right hon. Gentleman what I think of his speech. The right hon. Gentleman took as his text two promises that appear to have been made by representatives of His Majesty's Government during the progress of the Great War. If I were asked to select the text of the speech of Secretary of State these are the words that I would select. The right hon. Gentleman said:

> "there were two people who were interested from the point of view of settlement in Palestine—the Arabs and the Jews—and largely on the strength of promises made to them by His Majesty's Government, promises touching Palestine, each of them played a certain part in the War and each of them took certain risks for the Allied cause. This question then is a matter of honour. The good name of Great Britain is involved. The obligations which we contracted towards the Jews and Arabs during the War are debts of honour, which cannot be paid in counterfeit coinage." (Official Report, 22nd May, 1939; col. 1948, Vol. 347.)

It seems to me that the right hon. Gentleman took the view that we had made contradictory promises, that there was a moral and honourable obligation on our country to respect both of those promises, and that then he went on to face the problem that came to him. I am bound to say that, having read with great care the speech which he made, I cannot accept the view that His Majesty's Government is doing anything other than counterfeiting this business, or that it is doing anything other than breaking its promises and acting dishonourably before the whole of the civilised world. The right hon. Gentleman, having referred to the two promises and to British honour, it seems to me, devoted the rest of an hour's speech to an endeavour to twist the Balfour Declaration and the Mandate into some sort of harmony with the White Paper, notwithstanding the fact, as was proved by hon. and right hon. Gentlemen yesterday, that the White Paper is not in harmony with either the Balfour Declaration or the Mandate, is not in harmony with their wording, is not in harmony with their spirit. The policy which the Government have embodied in the White Paper, in my judgment—I do not think there can be serious argument about it—is in direct conflict with Ministerial declarations, including the declarations of right hon. Gentlemen who are now Members of the Government. They seem, first, to twist the Balfour Declaration and the Mandate to fit in with the policy of the White

Paper, and then to prove that the White Paper was not out of harmony with the Declaration or the Mandate. I think the subsequent Debate showed that the right hon. Gentleman failed in that endeavour.

The right hon. Gentleman's second purpose seemed to me to be to flatter the Jews for the purpose of reconciling them to becoming another permanent minority problem in the world. The Jews, already victims of other races as a minority in certain countries, are now to be made a permanent minority in the country that has been promised to them as the Jewish National Home in Palestine. I am afraid that the flattering of the Jews by the right hon. Gentleman will not reconcile them to becoming the victims of another permanent minority problem. Thirdly, the right hon. Gentleman referred to, but he avoided the slightest clarity as to the future protection of the Jewish minority. Having decided that the Jewish people were to be in Palestine a permanent minority, not exceeding one-third of the population, having said that His Majesty's Government would at the time provide means for the protection of that minority, the right hon. Gentleman was utterly unwilling or utterly unable, or both, to give any indication as to how that protection would be afforded.

*   *   *   *   *   *   *

His Majesty's Government, looking around the world, witnessing the persecution of Jewish minorities all over the world, deliberately planned a policy whereby in their own National Home the Jews are to be a permanent 33⅓ per cent. minority, and no more, in that country. Knowing the problems of Jewish minorities, knowing of the persecution that is proceeding, the Government decides deliberately to make permanent that minority. When the right hon. Gentleman is asked, "what are you going to do to protect them; what steps are you going to take to prevent their being persecuted and oppressed by a 66⅔ per cent. majority, possibly possessing all the supreme powers of the State?" he says, "I do not know; I have not thought about it; I have not considered it; I am not going to consider it until that imminent point is reached." I say that the right hon. Gentleman has shamefully neglected his responsibilities and his duties; I say that he has no right deliberately to create this Jewish minority and then, in answer to the right hon. Gentleman the Member for Caithness, to be lightly indifferent as to how protection for the Jewish minority is to be achieved. All that he did in his speech was to talk of honour, to talk of counterfeiting, then to twist the Balfour Declaration and the Mandate all over the place in order to fit in with this precious White Paper, then to flatter the Jews in the hope that they would be reconciled to becoming another permanent minority problem, and, finally, deliberately to avoid any clarity as to how the Jewish minority is to be protected in due course.

I do not wish to be violent in my language towards the right hon. Gentleman, but I am bound to say that on reading his speech the impression I formed was that the longer he spoke the more he quibbled, the more evasive and inconclusive he became. I should have had more respect for his speech if he had frankly admitted that the Jews were to be sacrificed to the incompetence of the Government in the matter, to be sacrificed to its inability to govern, to be sacrificed to its apparent fear of, if not, indeed, its sympathy with, violence and these methods of murder and assassination—that the Jews must be sacrificed to the Government's preoccupation with exclusively Imperialist rather than human considerations. Probably the right hon. Gentleman's speech was the best he could do with the case he had to present, but it is not a speech which is going to reflect much to the credit of British honour standing on the printed records of the House of Commons.

*   *   *   *   *   *   *

This White Paper contains a lot of wishful thinking which is in conflict with the hard facts of the situation. It is useless continually wishing and hoping that the Arabs and the Jews will live together in friendly harmony. Wishing for things does not make those things happen. Hoping for change does not make the change occur. If change is to be brought about, if improvement is to be achieved, things have to be done, Ministers have to act, Administrations have to make changes in their administration in order that things may be done. I am weary of listening to the right hon. Gentleman the Secretary of State, and still more weary of listening to the Under-Secretary of State for Foreign Affairs, saying to the Arabs and the Jews, "Be friends, live together in harmony," just as they said it to the Franco people and the Republicans in Spain. At least, I would not mind making these moral urgings if they would do something about it and make some contribution to a new situation. It is not enough merely to wish that things may get better. Statesmanship must create social, economic, and political conditions that make that possible. Government must be just, but it must also repress disorder, or Government must abdicate, and His Majesty's Government, faced with this disorder, have not consistently faced the implications of the disorder. They have run away, and they have neither repressed disorder effectively and permanently, nor have they abdicated from their functions.

Knowing that most of the trouble in Palestine has been created, not by the masses of the Arab people at all, but through a minority of certain classes of Arabs, probably mostly by agents of Herr Hitler and Signor Mussolini, knowing that that was so—and it began in the days when the Prime Minister had a particular friendship with Herr Hitler and Signor Mussolini—knowing that this trouble was largely the creation of foreign intervention and the activities of foreign agents, the Government nevertheless ran away in the earlier days of these difficulties. They plucked up some courage, and the Army was sent out. The disorders were largely stopped, order was largely restored, and now the Government propose to run away again. Properly handled, the Government need not send any material British force to Palestine at all to keep order. Properly handled, the Government could have had, and can still have, the active cooperation of the Jews and of a large proportion of the Arabs in maintaining order in Palestine; and I do not see why the Government should not at any rate in part, solve this problem on that line. There are people willing to train themselves to fight for the defence, order and security of their own country, and I suggest that, subject to proper safeguards and answerable to the High Commissioner, they should be able to co-operate with the British Government in preserving order in their own country.

But instead of taking such a line, the Palestinian Government have been weak and uncreative, and so leave the home Government, with their consistent inconsistencies of policy and with their constant vacillations, and the unfortunate consequence is that a widespread impression has been created that the way to make the British lion run is to make disorder, to murder, to ambush, and to assassinate. I venture to say that it is really a most unfortunate state of affairs when the impression has been created that the way to get things out of the British Government, the way to impress them, the way to modify their policy, is not to be reasonable, not to argue, not to persuade, but to resort to force and violence. As the present Paymaster-General said in the House of Commons on 29th April, 1920:

> "It would be intolerable, if the legitimate hopes of the Zionists were in any way affected by serious disturbances in that country."—(Official Report, 29th April, 1920; col. 1514; Vol. 128.)

That is exactly what is happening today, and it is almost admitted in the words of the White Paper itself, to which I now come. This White Paper can be shortly summarised. It proposes to see to it that there shall be a minority in Palestine. That is definitely laid down, but it was said in the 1922 Declaration, for which right hon. Member for Epping (Mr. Churchill) was responsible:

> "But in order that this (that is to say, the Jewish) community should have the best prospect of free development and provide a full opportunity for the Jewish people to display its capacities, it is essential that it should know that it is in Palestine as of right and not on sufferance." If they are going to be there in a permanent minority and in due course under a Government in which they are a permanent minority, they will obviously be there, not, "as of right," but "on sufferance."

*   *   *   *   *   *   *

We regard this White Paper and the policy in it as a cynical breach of pledges given to the Jews and the world, including America. This policy will do us no good in the United States, where we need to be done good, and where we need the good will of the great American people. It comes at a time of tragedy and apprehension for the Jewish race throughout the world, and it ought not to be approved by the House to-day. The Mandates Commission of the League of Nations ought to have an opportunity of discussing it. If there is dispute about the quasi-legal arguments, they ought to be referred for decision to an appropriate international legal tribunal. I beg of the House not to approve this White Paper, at the very least to insist that the Government shall engage the appropriate international consultations before the House is asked to make a decision on a matter which is not only a British matter but one for the international conscience of the world, and a matter in which all other countries of the world are by implication involved.

If we do this thing to-day we shall have done a thing which is dishonourable to our good name, which is discreditable to our capacity to govern and which is dangerous to British security, to peace and to the economic interest of the world in general and of our own country. Moreover, it will not work. The Jews and the Arabs have both said they will not have this solution. Therefore, illegal disorders will probably go on and the friction will continue. This does not solve the problem. It is not even an effective surrender that brings peace to a country that so badly needs peace. Remember, that if the troubles continue scope will be given to the agents of Herr Hitler and Signor Mussolini who in various places seem to have the habit of lodging bombs in canvas suit-cases; it happened in Jerusalem and I gather that it is happening in London, and I am apprehensive that if things go on as they are there will be a shortage of canvas suit-cases in Germany and Italy in a short time to come.

Remember that ten years hence there is to be, if all goes well, responsible self-government in the country, subject to certain reservations in the interest of Imperial strategy. We are told that there is to be responsible self-government. There will be at least a two-thirds Arab majority. It is known in all parts of the House, it is known to Ministers, that a number of the leaders of the Arab disturbances in Palestine have been acting by the encouragment of German and Italian agents. It is known that part of those disturbances, a large part, can be traced to German and Italian activities in that country. Suppose Herr Hitler is in power in ten years and suppose Mussolini is in power, what is to stop them then still sending their agents to Palestine and working upon the Arab people in the way they have been doing—working for the persecution of the Jewish race, working for the disarmament of the Jewish race by the new Government, working for the exclusion and persecution of the Jewish race in Palestine? What is to prevent them from doing that? As far as I can see, nothing, and about that possibility the right hon. Gentleman thinks nothing at all.

I do not know what Government will be in power in ten years time, and it would certainly be wrong for me to indicate that such a Government would do in circumstances that we cannot foresee and cannot know, but I think it ought to be known by the House that this breach of faith, which we regret, this breach of British honour, with its policy, with which we have no sympathy, is such that the least that can be said is that the Government must not expect that this is going to be automatically binding upon their successors. They must not expect that. I will go no further than that, but they must understand that this document will not be automatically binding upon their successors in office, whatever the circumstances of the time may be.

We cannot prevent this evil thing being done. We cannot prevent this White Paper being approved. Hon. Members opposite alone can stop this thing happening, and I appeal to them. I ask them to remember the sufferings of these Jewish people all over the world. I ask them to remember that Palestine, of all the places in the world, was certainly the place where they had some right to expect not to suffer or to have restrictions imposed upon them. Look at the extent of the country—this little patch of territory. Transjordan has been taken away, and the rest of the Arabian countries released from Turkish rule as a result of the War have also been taken away. This tiny patch, Palestine, about the size of Wales, is left, and we are to stop these people from going there. I appeal to hon. Members opposite to take their courage in both hands, to put the honour of their country before the narrow claims of party, and to bring to bear all the pressure they can, all the influence they can, to prevent His Majesty's Government doing this thing that they ought not to do.

RT. HON. SIR ARCHIBALD SINCLAIR
HOUSE OF COMMONS, MAY 23RD, 1939

I am under no temptation to fail to follow the hon. Member for
Abingdon (Sir R. Glyn), who has spoken with such good humour and
breadth of view.   I have no Jewish blood and no Jewish constituents,
so I am able to speak, as he has done, with impartiality.   But the
hon. Member has told us, with great eloquence, what his idea of a
Jewish National Home would be—a sort of Vatican City, a centre of
Jewish art and culture.   It is that now.   It has a great university
and a great school of medicine.   While that may be the hon. Member's idea of a Jewish National Home, while it may have been his idea
from the beginning, it was certainly not the kind of National Home
that was in fact promised to the Jews on behalf of His Majesty's
Government and the British people.   I will not delay the House with
quotations, though I could do so, but I will refer the hon. Member to
innumerable speeches which have been made by great leaders of the
British people, like Lord Balfour, the right hon. Gentleman the Member for Carnarvon Boroughs (Mr. Lloyd George), the present Prime
Minister, Mr. Ramsay MacDonald, and many others, who held out
to the Jewish people the hope of returning to that land which they
loved so much, but which the hon. Member for Abingdon seems to
think a matter of such very little importance.   I do not happen to
be a Jew, but I am a Scotsman; and the people of my country really
do love the land with an instinctive feeling which the Englishman,
I think, does not quite understand.   So we understand the Jewish
love of the soil of Palestine.   It is that feeling which has held together
the 16,000,000 Jews throughout the world through the centuries of
their dispersion, the love of their own homeland to which they always
hope and believe they are destined to return.   That was the conception of the Jewish National Home which the leaders of British public
opinion have since the War constantly encouraged the Jews to hold.
While the hon. and gallant Gentleman may have a different conception, that will not shield the Government, and Parliament, if it endorses this policy, from the accusation of betrayal which will be
levelled against them by the Jews of the world and by their innumerable sympathisers who are not of the Jewish race.
   The hon. Gentleman said that we really ought to help the Arabs to
develop their share in the life of Palestine, and certainly there would
be no opposition from anybody in any part of this House to any
well-judged measures which the Government might devise for that
purpose.   Indeed many of us have for many years been urging the
Government and the local administration in Palestine to be more
active in the development of the country along these lines.   If they
had been more active, some of the more unhappy developments of
recent years might have been avoided, but at the same time I feel

bound to say this is the name of that impartiality which the hon. Member enjoined upon us, that the Jews have devoted themselves with energy, brains, sacrifice, money to the development of that country, and such development as has been carried out in Palestine by the Government has been with the fruits of Jewish labour.   It is not true, as the hon. Gentleman thinks, that the British taxpayer has been subscribing substantial sums of money to Palestine.   I assure him that it is quite untrue. If he looks at the facts, he will find that, apart from the cost of the Army in Palestine and apart from Transjordan, no money at all has been spent from British funds in Palestine since 1920.   The Jews have spent this money and energy and have made these sacrifices for the development of the country.   Why do not the Arabs do the same?   It is not true to say that there are no Arabs that have the capital.   We have met these wealthy Arabs.   We know them, and if they can find money for arms and equipment for organising revolts against British rule, why cannot they find money for a little development on behalf of the poor Arab people?

It is often said that the Arab case is indifferently put in this House, and that it is only the Jewish case which gets put effectively.   I cannot help thinking that there is a great deal of truth in that when I listen to the Debate which is taking place during these last two days. A number of hon. Members have made eloquent speeches which were ostensibly on behalf of the Arab case.   The hon. Member for Stretford (Mr. Crossley) told the House that he was going to deploy the Arab case.   But did he?   He did not at all.   He deployed the case of powerful feudal families in Palestine.   When I think of the Arab people whom I want to help I do not think of those powerful feudal families, and of the Mufti or the Nahashibis.   I think of the fellahin living by the hundreds of thousands on the land, and living there more prosperously, as the Royal Commission reported to us, than they were before the Jews came to establish their National Home in 1920.

I think also of the increasing number of Arab industrial workers. The hon. Member for Stretford referred rather contemptuously to the 25,000 whom he found cooped up in little shacks on the outskirts of Haifa.   He rather indicated to the House that they were wretched, unemployed, destitute people.   You have only to look at the report of the Royal Commission to find them described as living in what the Royal Commission describes as Tin Town.   It may be that their housing is bad and that it reflects discredit upon the Government of the country, but not upon the Jews who were not responsible for it. The Royal Commission also says that they are people who find employment in the industrial life of the country and are earning increasingly good wages and improving their conditions.   When a little time ago the Government set aside £250,000 to resettle the Arabs who had been turned off their land in order to make room for Jewish enterprises, only one-third of the money was used.   The other Arabs had either got into agriculture again and obtained other holdings on their own account or had entered industry and were earning good wages.

I think of the fellahin, of these people who are working in industry and improving their position, of the villagers terrorised by the bands of the Mufti and working where they can in close co-operation with the Jews.   I think of those trade unionists of whom the right Hon. Gentleman the Member for South Hackney (Mr. H. Morrison) spoke, who were also, as he pointed out, terrorised by the so-called Arab leaders. These people, with their standards of living rising and their social services improving, and the increased happiness of their families dependent upon Jewish enterprises under the protection of the Mandatory Power—these are the Arabs whom the House ought to protect against the feudal Arabs and the foreign agitators, and protect them against the loss of the spring of their own happiness which is the Jewish National Home. It is from that that their increased prosperity is derived. The benefits which the Arabs have derived from the Jewish National Home depend on the continuance of its prosperity. That is in the report of the Royal Commission. We must not ignore the mass of the Arab people whose welfare, along with that of the Jews, should be our primary consideration in Palestine. It is only if we think of that that we shall be able to reconcile the interests of the Jews and Arabs in Palestine. In concluding his eloquent speech last night the Under-Secretary of State for Foreign Affairs referred to the blessings of retirement, rest, quietness and confidence in a very eloquent passage. It is our task to confer these blessings upon the Arabs and Jewish people in Palestine, and until we have done so His Majesty's Government must forego them for themselves.

I do not want to take up too much of the time of the House today, as there are, no doubt, many other Members who want to speak, and therefore I propose to concentrate almost entirely upon one point for the rest of my speech, and it is the impropriety of asking Parliament to endorse the policy of His Majesty's Government at the present time. The Under-Secretary of State in his speech winding up the Debate last night said:

> "The Amendment of the official Opposition requests that the House should await the examination of the proposals by the Permanent Mandates Commission of the League. In the view of His Majesty's Government it will not be necessary for the House to await such a decision because there is nothing inconsistent between the Mandate and anything contained in this White Paper."—(Official Report, 22nd May, 1939; col. 2065; vol. 347.).

It is my very strong representation to the House, and especially to the Secretary of State for Dominion Affairs, who, I understand, is going to answer this Debate, that the White Paper is inconsistent with the terms of the Mandate. I am going to base myself not on my own unsupported assertions but upon the highest authorities there are available. I have first the report of the Palestine Royal Commission of 1937, and on page 39 it says:

> "Unquestionably, however, the primary purpose of the Mandate *as expressed in its Preamble and its Articles*, is to promote the establishment of the Jewish National Home."

On page 374, the same Commission say:

> "To put it in one sentence, we cannot—in Palestine as it now is—both concede the Arab claim to self-government and secure the establishment of the Jewish National Home."

And on the following page they say:

> "We do not think that any fair-minded statesman would suppose, now that the hope of harmony between the races has proved untenable, that Britain ought either to hand over to Arab rule

400,000 Jews, whose entry into Palestine has been for the most part facilitated by the British Government and approved by the League of Nations; or that, if the Jews should become a majority, a million or so Arabs should be handed over to their rule."

Perhaps the right hon. Gentleman will say that we ought to trust to the safeguards, if we hand them over to the care or supervision of self-governing institutions in which the Arabs will have a majority of two to one over the Jews. But what safeguards? We have no right to believe that the safeguards will be effective unless we are told very clearly what they are. The right hon. Gentleman the Member for South Hackney has already quoted what occurred between the Secretary of State, and myself yesterday. The Secretary of State, in answer to my interjection, said that I ought not to hurry at this stage. I ought not to ask him to lay down a time-table. I did not ask him to lay down a time-table but to tell us what the type and character of the safeguards for the five-year period of transition were going to be. Are they to be solid and real safeguards for the continuation of the Jewish National Home, so real that the Government would be ready to enforce them if necessary, as they have not been prepared to enforce the undertakings which successive Governments have given to the Jews up to now? These are questions to which we are entitled to an answer, and we ought to have an answer before we endorse the proposal which His Majesty's Government have brought before us. There could be nothing more unfair and more likely to lead to confusion and to renewed disturbance in Palestine than any uncertainty about what the new fate of either the Jewish or the Arab people is going to be under the new dispensation. Here I would call the attention of the right hon. Gentleman to the report of the Partition Commission of last year. On page 103 they say:

"The worst possible form of settlement would be one which left both Jews and Arabs in any part of Palestine uncertain whether in a few years time either of them may not be subjected against their will to the political dominance of the other."

Could there be in a single sentence a clearer summary of the situation which would arise if we endorse this White Paper? In the words of the Partition Commission this White Paper, because it leaves the uncertainty as to whether in a few years time the Jews may not be subjected against their will to the political domination of the Arabs, is the "worst possible form of settlement." That judgment prophetically condemned this White Paper. Again, if, as the Royal Commission reported, the promotion of a Jewish National Home is the primary purpose of the Mandate, and if, as they also reported, it is impossible to concede both the Arab claim of independence, as the White Paper does, and secure the establishment of a Jewish National Home His Majesty's Government's proposals are clearly contrary to the Mandate by the judgment of the Royal Commission. Let me quote from a letter written by Mr. Ramsay MacDonald to the Prime Minister in February, 1931. This is what he wrote:

"The words (in the Mandate) are not to be read as implying that existing economic conditions in Palestine should be crystallised. On the contrary, the obligation to facilitate Jewish immigration"—

the obligation was to facilitate, not to stop, Jewish immigration if the Arabs objected—

"and to encourage the settlement by Jews on the land remains a positive obligation of the Mandate."

If it remains "a positive obligation of the Mandate," to discourage and stop Jewish immigration must be contrary to the Mandate:

"and it can be fulfilled without prejudice to the rights and positions of other sections of the population in Palestine."

I cannot imagine that the Government can disavow the opinion expressed by the Royal Commission, by the Partition Commission, and by Mr. Ramsay MacDonald when he was Prime Minister, and if it is true then it is my submission that this White Paper is contrary to the Mandate. Indeed, less than two years ago, when the Government went to the Mandates Commission to consult them about the proposals of the Partition Commission, the Mandates Commission said:

"The (Mandates) Commission does not question that the Mandatory Power, responsible as it is for the maintenance of order in the territory, may on occasion find it advisable to take such a step (as to restrict immigration), and is competent to do so, as an exceptional and provisional measure; it feels, however, bound to draw attention to this departure from the principle, sanctioned by the League Council, that immigration is to be proportionate to the country's absorptive capacity."

The right hon. Member for Warwick and Leamington (Mr. Eden), who was then Secretary of State for Foreign Affairs, said at the meeting of the League Council the following month that this reduction of Jewish immigration was

"a purely temporary measure designed to meet temporary and exceptional conditions."

Not only was the then Foreign Secretary most anxious to prove that it was "temporary and exceptional," but the Mandates Commission pointed out that unless it was temporary and exceptional it would be contrary to the Mandate. As it is suggested in the White Paper that immigration is to be restricted and finally made subject to the approval—"acquiescence" is the word used in the White Paper—of the Arabs, I say that it is, in fact, a departure from the principles of the Mandate as recognised by the Royal Commission, the Partition Commission, Mr. Ramsay MacDonald, the Mandates Commission, and the right hon. Member for Warwick and Leamington when he was representing His Majesty's Government only two years ago. It may be argued—although it is not my argument—that circumstances make it impossible to carry out the terms of the Mandate in Palestine at the present time and that His Majesty's Government cannot be under obligation to perform the impossible. But it is clearly under the obligation to report such circumstances if they exist to the Mandates Commission; it cannot brush it aside as the Under-Secretary of State suggested in his speech last night.

*   *   *   *   *   *   *

If we now follow His Majesty's Government in yielding to violence in Palestine we shall create confusion in that country, we shall incur the scorn of Europe, we shall not propitiate either the Palestinian agitators or the Governments of Egypt and the Arab States, all of whom have rejected these proposals, and we shall anger public opinion in the United States of America. For generations the hostility of the Irish people has poisoned our relations with the people of the United States of America. For that hostility, now so happily allayed, we should, if we accept these proposals, substitute the hostility of 5,000,000 Jews and their Protestant sympathisers in the United States of America.

This White Paper is a spring not of healing but of bitter waters. There comes to my mind a saying of Prince Max of Baden, that Great Britain has two great sources of strength—her fleet and her good name. The good name of Great Britain will be tainted if Parliament accepts this White Paper and endorses it before obtaining the impartial judgment of the Hague Court and the Mandates Commission. It is a repudiation of solemn pledges which Parliament and the people of Great Britain have given to the Jews. If His Majesty's Government really think otherwise, let them fortify themselves by the impartial judgment of the Hague Court and the Mandates Commission. Until they do so I, for my part, shall refuse, and I hope Parliament will refuse, to endorse their policy.

RT. HON. WINSTON CHURCHILL
HOUSE OF COMMONS, MAY 23, 1939

---

*   *   *   *   *   *   *

I say quite frankly that I find this a melancholy occasion. Like my right hon. Friend the Member for Sparkbrook (Mr. Amery), I feel bound to vote against the proposals of His Majesty's Government. As one intimately and responsibly concerned in the earlier stages of our Palestine policy, I could not stand by and see solemn engagements into which Britain has entered before the world set aside for reasons of administrative convenience or—and it will be a vain hope—for the sake of a quiet life. Like my right hon. Friend, I should feel personally embarrassed in the most acute manner if I lent myself, by silence or inaction, to what I must regard as an act of repudiation. I can understand that others take a different view. There are many views which may be taken. Some may consider themselves less involved in the declarations of former Governments. Some may feel that the burden of keeping faith weighs upon them rather oppressively. Some may be pro-Arab and some may be anti-Semite. None of these motives offers me any means of escape because I was from the beginning a sincere advocate of the Balfour Declaration, and I have made repeated public statements to that effect.

It is often supposed that the Balfour Declaration was an ill-considered, sentimental act largely concerned with the right hon. Member for Carnarvon Boroughs (Mr. Lloyd George), for which the Conservative party had no real responsibility, and that, as the Secretary of State said yesterday, it was a thing done in the tumult of the War. But hardly any step was taken with greater deliberation and responsibility. I was glad to hear the account which my right hon. Friend the Member for Sparkbrook gave, derived from the days when he was working in the Secretariat of the War Cabinet, of the care and pains with which the whole field was explored at that time. Not only did the War Cabinet of those days take the decision, but all Cabinets of every party after the War, after examining it in the varying circumstances which have arisen, have endorsed the decision and taken the fullest responsibility for it. It was also endorsed in the most cordial and enthusiastic terms by many of the ablest Conservative Private Members who came into the House when a great Conservative majority arrived after the General Election at the end of 1918. It was endorsed from the very beginning by my right hon. Friend the Prime Minister.

I make him my apologies for going back as far as 20 years, but when you are dealing with matters which affect the history of two or three thousand years, there is no reason why the continuity of opinion should not be displayed. My right hon. Friend, on 13th October, 1918, said:

"The sympathy of the British Government with Zionist aspirations does not date from yesterday. . . . My father was anxious to find such a territory within the limits of the British Constitution. . . . Today the opportunity has come. I have no hesitation in saying that were my father alive to-day he would be among the first to welcome it and to give it his hearty support."

Then other members of the Government, most distinguished members, who were then Private Members in the House—a brilliant crop, if I may say so, in their young first fresh flight—made a strong effort. The Dominion Secretary, quite a slim figure on the benches up here was heavily engaged. There were also the Minister of Health, the Home Secretary and, above all, the Prime Minister; and this is the memorial they sent us. I abridge it, but not in such a way as to alter its sense. I may in abridging it diminish its force, but its force is evident from the extract:

"We, the undersigned, having cordially welcomed the historic Declaration made on 2nd November, 1917, by His Majesty's Government"—

that is, the Balfour Declaration—

"that it would use its best endeavors to facilitate the establishment of a Jewish National Home in Palestine . . . now respectfully and solemnly urge upon His Majesty's Government the necessity of redeeming this pledge by the acceptance of a Mandate under the League of Nations."

Here was this statement which was made and which was put forward, and while I say I do not compare the responsibility of private Members with that exercised by Ministers of the Crown or by the head of the Government, nevertheless I think, when all is said and done, that Zionists have a right to look to the Prime Minister to stand by them in the days of his power. They had a special right to look to him because he was not only giving effect to his own deep convictions, but was carrying forward the large conceptions of his father whose memory he reveres and whose renown he has revived. I was not a member of the War Cabinet in the days when this pledge was given. I was serving under it as a high functionary. That was the position of the Secretaries of State. I found myself in entire agreement with those sentiments so well expressed by the Prime Minister and his friends when they were sending in their memorial.

When I went to the Colonial Office it was in this spirit that I wrote this dispatch, under the authority of the Cabinet, which is quoted so much in the White Paper now before us. Great use is made of this dispatch of 1922 in the White Paper. It is sought to found the argument of the White Paper largely upon it. I stand by every word in those lengthy quotations which have been made from what I wrote. I would not alter a sentence after the 16 years that have passed, but I must say I think it rather misleading to quote so extensively from one part of the dispatch without indicating what was its main purpose. The particular paragraph would do little to cool down the ardour of the Zionist and little to reassure the apprehensions of the Arabs. The main purpose of the dispatch was clear. This is what I said in paragraph (1):

> "His Majesty's Government have no intention of repudiating the obligations into which they entered towards the Jewish people."

I then proceeded to say that the Government would refuse to discuss the future of Palestine on any basis other than the basis of the Balfour Declaration. Moreover, the whole tenour of the dispatch was to make it clear that the establishment of self-governing institutions in Palestine was to be subordinated to the paramount pledge and obligation of establishing a Jewish National Home in Palestine. In taking up this position on behalf of the Government of the day I really was not going any further than the views which were ardently expressed by some of the ablest and most promising of our back-benchers at that time. The fact that they are leading Ministers to-day should, I think, have gained for the problem of Palestine a more considered and more sympathetic treatment than it has received.

Last night the Under-Secretary of State for Foreign Affairs used a surprising argument. He suggested that the obligation to introduce self-governing institutions into Palestine ranked equally with the obligation to establish a Jewish National Home. In this very dispatch of mine, which represented the views of the entire Government of the day, the greatest pains were taken to make it clear that the paramount duty was the establishment of a National Home. It was said on page 6:

> "The position is that His Majesty's Government are bound by a pledge which is antecedent to the Covenant of the League of Nations, and they cannot allow a constitutional position to develop in a country for whch they have accepted responsibility to the principal Allied Powers which may make it impracticable to carry into effect a solemn undertaking given by themselves and their Allies."

There is much more to the same effect. It seems to me that the Under-Secretary of State had some reason to complain of the manner in which he had been briefed on this subject, because his argument was exactly contrary to the tenour of the dispatch from which the Government have quoted with a strong expression of approval and agreement wherever they have found it possible to assist their case.

Now I come to the gravamen of the case. I regret very much that the pledge of the Balfour Declaration, endorsed as it has been by successive Governments, and the conditions under which we obtained the Mandate, have both been violated by the Government's proposals. There is much in this White Paper which is alien to the spirit of the Balfour Declaration, but I will not trouble about that. I select the one point upon which there is plainly a breach and repudiation of the Balfour Declaration—the provision that Jewish immigration can be stopped in five years' time by the decision of an Arab majority. That is a plain breach of a solemn obligation. I am astonished that my right hon. Friend the Prime Minister, of all others, and at this moment above all others, should have lent himself to this new and sudden default.

To whom was the pledge of the Balfour Declaration made? It was not made to the Jews of Palestine, it was not made to those who were actually living in Palestine. It was made to world Jewry and in particular to the Zionist associations. It was in consequence of and on the basis of this pledge that we received important help in the War, and that after the War we received from the Allied and Associated Powers the Mandate for Palestine. This pledge of a home of refuge, of an asylum, was not made to the Jews in Palestine but to the Jews outside Palestine, to that vast, unhappy mass of scattered, persecuted, wandering Jews whose intense, unchanging, unconquerable desire has been for a National Home—to quote the words to which my right hon. Friend the Prime Minister subscribed in the Memorial which he and others sent to us:

> "the Jewish people who have through centuries of dispersion and persecution patiently awaited the hour of its restoration to its ancestral home."

Those are the words. They were the people outside, not the people in. It is not with the Jews in Palestine that we have now or at any future time to deal, but with world Jewry, with Jews all over the world. That is the pledge which was given, and that is the pledge which we are now asked to break, for how can this pledge be kept, I want to know, if in five years' time the National Home is to be barred and no more Jews are to be allowed in without the permission of the Arabs?

I entirely accept the distinction between making a Jewish National Home in Palestine and making Palestine a Jewish National Home. I think I was one of the first to draw that distinction. The Government quote me, and they seem to associate me with them on this subject in their White Paper, but what sort of National Home is offered to the Jews of the world when we are asked to declare that in five years' time the door of that home is to be shut and barred in their faces? The idea of home to wanderers is, surely, a place to which they can resort. When grievous and painful words like "breach of pledge," "repudiation" and "default" are used in respect of the public action of men and Ministers who in private life observe a stainless honour—the country must discuss these matters as they present themselves in their public aspect—it is necessary to be precise, and to do them justice His Majesty's Government have been brutally precise. On page II of the White Paper, in Sub-section (3) of paragraph 14 there is this provision:

> "After the period of five years no further Jewish immigration will be permitted unless the Arabs of Palestine are prepared to acquiesce in it."

Now, there is the breach; there is the violation of the pledge; there is the abandonment of the Balfour Declaration; there is the end of the vision, of the hope, of the dream. If you leave out those words this White Paper is no more than one of the several experiments and essays in Palestinian constitution-making which we have had of recent years, but put in those three lines and there is the crux, the peccant point, the breach, and we must have an answer to it.

My right hon. Friend the Secretary of State for Dominion Affairs may use his great legal ability. He is full of knowledge and power and ingenuity, but unless this can be answered, and repulsed, and repudiated, a very great slur rests upon British administration. It is said specifically on page 10 of the White Paper that Jewish immigration during the next five years will be at a rate which, if the economic absorptive capacity allows, will bring the population up to approximately one-third of the total population of the country. After that the Arab majority, twice as numerous as the Jews, will have control, and all further Jewish immigration will be subject to their acquiescence, which is only another way of saying that it will be on sufferance. What is that but the destruction of the Balfour Declaration? What is that but a breach of faith? What is it but a one-sided denunciation—what is called in the jargon of the present time a unilateral denunciation—of an engagement?

There need be no dispute about this phrase "economic absorptive capacity." It represented the intentions of the Government and their desire to carry out the Palestinian Mandate in an efficient and in a prudent manner. As I am the author of the phrase, perhaps I may be allowed to state that economic absorptive capacity was never intended to rule without regard to any other consideration. It has always rested with the Mandatory Power to vary the influx of the Jews in accordance with what was best for Palestine and for the sincere fulfilment—one must presuppose the sincere fulfilment—of our purpose in establishing a Jewish National Home there. It was never suggested at any time that the decision about the quota to be admitted should rest with the Jews or should rest with the Arabs. It rested, and could only rest at any time, with the Mandatory Power which was responsible for carrying out the high purpose of the then victorious Allies. The Mandatory Commission of the League of Nations, as was mentioned by the spokesman for the Opposition when he opened the Debate this afternoon, has recognised fully that the Mandatory Power was entitled to control the flow of immigration, or even to suspend it in an emergency. What they are not entitled to do, at least not entitled to do without reproach—grave, public and worldwide reproach, and I trust self-reproach as well—is to bring the immigration to an end so far as they are concerned, to wash their hands of it, to close the door. That they have no right whatever to do.

I cannot feel that we have accorded to the Arab race unfair treatment after the support which they gave us in the late War. The Palestinian Arabs, of course, were for the most part fighting against us, but elsewhere over vast regions inhabited by the Arabs independent Arab kingdoms and principalities have come into being such as had never been known in Arab history before. Some have been established by Great Britain and others by France. When I wrote this despatch in 1922 I was advised by, among others, Colonel Lawrence, the truest champion of Arab rights whom modern times have known. He has recorded his opinion that the settlement was fair and just—his definite, settled opinion. Together we placed the Emir Abdulla in Transjordania, where he remains faithful and prosperous to this day. Together, under the responsibility of the Prime Minister of those days, King Feisal was placed upon the throne of Iraq, where his descendants now rule. But we also showed ourselves continually resolved to close no door upon the ultimate development of a Jewish National Home, fed by continued Jewish immigration into Palestine. Colonel

Lawrence thought this was fair then. Why should it be pretended that it is unfair now?

I cannot understand what are the credentials of the Government in this matter of Palestine. It is less than two years—about 18 months if I remember aright—since they came forward and on their faith and reputation, with all their knowledge and concerted action, urged us to adopt a wholly different solution from that which they now place before us. The House persuaded them then not to force us into an incontinent acceptance of their partition plan, and within a few months, though they did not thank us for it, they had themselves abandoned and discarded it as precipitately as they had adopted it. Why, now, should they thrust this far more questionable bundle of expedients upon us? Surely it would only be prudent and decent for the Government, following the advice given by the Chancellor of the Exchequer when he was a private Member in 1930, following the opinion of the jurists of those days, to ascertain the view taken by the Mandates Commission of the League of Nations, before whom these proposals are to go, before claiming a parliamentary decision in their favour.

I cannot understand why this course has been taken. I search around for the answer. The first question one would ask oneself is foreshadowed in a reference made in the speech of my hon. Friend, and is this: Is our condition so parlous and our state so poor that we must, in our weakness, make this sacrifice of our declared purpose? Although I have been very anxious that we should strengthen our armaments and spread our alliances and so increase the force of our position, I must say that I have not taken such a low view of the strength of the British Empire or of the very many powerful countries who desire to walk in association with us; but if the Government, with their superior knowledge of the deficiencies in our armaments which have arisen during their stewardship, really feel that we are too weak to carry out our obligations and wish to file a petition in moral and physical bankruptcy, that is an argument which, however ignominious, should certainly weigh with the House in these dangerous times. But is it true? I do not believe it is true. I cannot believe that the task to which we set our hand 20 years ago in Palestine is beyond our strength, or that faithful perseverance will not, in the end, bring that task through to a glorious success. I am sure of this, that to cast the plan aside and show yourselves infirm of will and unable to pursue a long, clear and considered purpose, bending and twisting under the crush and pressure of events—I am sure that that is going to do us a most serious and grave injury at a time like this.

We must ask ourselves another question, which arises out of this: Can we—and this is the question—strengthen ourselves by this repudiation? Shall we relieve ourselves by this repudiation? I should have thought that the plan put forward by the Colonial Secretary in his White Paper, with its arid constitutional ideas and safety catches at every point, and with vagueness overlaying it and through all of it, combines, so far as one can understand it at present, the disadvantages of all courses without the advantages of any. The triumphant Arabs have rejected it. They are not going to put up with it. The despairing Jews will resist it. What will the world think about it? What will our friends say? What will be the opinion of the United States of America? Shall we not lose more—and this is a question to be considered maturely—in the growing support and sympathy of the United States than we shall gain in local administrative convenience, if gain at all indeed we do?

What will our potential enemies think? What will those who have been stirring up these Arab agitators think? Will they not be encouraged by our confession of recoil? Will they not be tempted to say: "They're on the run again. This is another Munich," and be the more stimulated in their aggression by these very unpleasant reflections which they may make? After all, we were asked by the Secretary of State to approach this question in a spirit of realism and to face the real facts, and I ask seriously of the Government: Shall we not undo by this very act of abjection some of the good which we have gained by our guarantees to Poland and to Rumania, by our admirable Turkish Alliance and by what we hope and expect will be our Russian Alliance? You must consider these matters. May not this be a contributory factor—and every factor is a contributory factor now—by which our potential enemies may be emboldened to take some irrevocable action and then find out, only after it is all too late, that it is not this Government, with their tired Ministers and flagging purpose, that they have to face, but the might of Britain and all that Britain means?

* * * * * * *

It is hoped to obtain five years of easement in Palestine by this proposal; surely the consequences will be entirely the opposite. A sense of moral weakness in the mandatory Power, whose many years of vacillation and uncertainty have, as the right hon. Gentleman admitted yesterday, largely provoked the evils from which we suffer, will rouse all the violent elements in Palestine to the utmost degree. In order to avoid the reproach, the bitter reproach, of shutting out refugees during this time of brutal persecution, the quota of immigration may be raised, as we were told by the Secretary of State, and may be continued at an even higher level in the next five years. Thus, irritation will continue and the incentive to resist will be aggravated. What about these five years? Who shall say where we are going to be five years from now? Europe is more than two-thirds mobilised tonight. The ruinous race of armaments now carries whole populations into the military machine. That cannot possibly continue for five years, nor for four, nor for three years. It may be that it will not continue beyond the present year. Long before those five years are past, either there will be a Britain which knows how to keep its word on the Balfour Declaration and is not afraid to do so, or, believe me, we shall find ourselves relieved of many oversea responsibilities other than those comprised within the Palestine Mandate.

Some of us hold that our safety at this juncture resides in being bold and strong. We urge that the reputation for fidelity of execution, a strict execution, of public contracts, is a shield and buckler whic the British Empire, however it may arm, cannot dispense with and cannot desire to dispense with. Never was the need for fidelity and firmness more urgent than now. You are not going to found and forge the fabric of a grand alliance to resist aggression, except by showing continued examples of your firmness in carrying out, even under difficulties, and in the teeth of difficulties, the obligations into which you have entered. I warn the Conservative party—and some of my warnings have not, alas, been ill-founded—that by committing themselves to this lamentable act of default, they will cast our country, and all that it stands for, one more step downward in its fortunes, which step will later on have to be retrieved, as it will be retrieved, by additional hard exertions. That is why I say that upon the large aspect of this matter the policy which you think is a relief and an easement you will find afterwards you will have to retrieve, in suffering and greater exertions than those we are making.

I end upon the land of Palestine. It is strange indeed that we should turn away from our task in Palestine at the moment when, as the Secretary of State told us yesterday, the local disorders have been largely mastered. It is stranger still that we should turn away when the great experiment and bright dream, has proved its power to succeed. Yesterday the Minister responsible descanted eloquently in glowing passages upon the magnificent work which the Jewish colonists have done. They have made the desert bloom. They have started a score of thriving industries, he said. They have founded a great city on the barren shore. They have harnessed the Jordan and spread its electricity throughout the land. So far from being persecuted, the Arabs have crowded into the country and multiplied till their population has increased more than even all world Jewry could lift up the Jewish population. Now we are asked to decree that all this is to stop and all this is to come to an end. We are now asked to submit—and this is what rankles most with me—to an agitation which is fed with foreign money and ceaselessly inflamed by Nazi and by Fascist propaganda.

It is 20 years ago since my right hon. Friend used these stirring words:

> "A great responsibility will rest upon the Zionists, who, before long, will be proceeding, with joy in their hearts, to the ancient seat of their people. Theirs will be the task to build up a new prosperity and a new civilization in old Palestine, so long neglected and mis-ruled."

Well, they have answered his call. They have fulfilled his hopes. How can he find it in his heart to strike them this mortal blow?

MEMORANDUM OF
THE JEWISH AGENCY FOR PALESTINE
ON THE LEGAL ASPECTS OF
THE BRITISH WHITE PAPER ON PALESTINE

1. At the recent Palestine Conferences in London the Jewish and Arab Delegations respectively were invited to express their views on certain suggestions laid before them by His Majesty's Government. After the conclusion of the Conferences, consultations took place between His Majesty's Government and representatives of Arab interests, and His Majesty's Government have now announced their intentions in a White Paper,[1] which supersedes the Statement of Policy of July 1937 [2] and substitutes proposals of an entirely different order. The object of this memorandum is to examine these proposals in the light of the Palestine Mandate, it being assumed that there will be no dissent from the proposition that the Mandatory Power, having been entrusted with the administration of Palestine on behalf of the League of Nations,[3] is authorised to take such measures, and such measures only, as can be shown to be consistent with the Mandate according to its true intent and purpose. Since the Mandate incorporates the Balfour Declaration, the Declaration must also be taken into account. It is further assumed to be common ground that the Declaration and the Mandate must be fairly construed, without resort to sophistical glosses or verbal jugglery, in conformity with the principle that international engagements must be interpreted and carried out in good faith. His Majesty's Government have on many occasions made clear their determination (which could, indeed, be taken for granted) to discharge their mandatory obligations not only in the letter but in the spirit.

2. The question to be considered is whether the proposals now made are consistent with the terms upon which His Majesty's Government undertook to administer Palestine on behalf of the League. As between His Majesty's Government and the League, nothing can turn on any undertakings given by His Majesty's Government to third parties without the knowledge of the League and not disclosed to it before the Mandate was confirmed. This remark is relevant to the passage in the White Paper [4] in which His Majesty's Government, after drawing attention to "their obligations to the Arabs under the Mandate," refer, in addition, to "assurances which have been given to the Arab people in the past," thus distinguishing those assurances from their mandatory obligations. Unless the Council of the League, in confirming the Mandate, can be shown to have been invited to take note of these assurances, it is not clear how they can

---

[1] Cmd. 6019.
[2] Cmd. 5513.
[3] See Preamble to Mandate: "Whereas His Britannic Majesty's Government has accepted the Mandate in respect of Palestine and undertaken to exercise it on behalf of the League of Nations in conformity with the following provisions . . ."
[4] para. 4, page 4.

be introduced into a discussion of the new proposals in relation to
the terms on which His Majesty's Government were entrusted with
the Mandate. It is, therefore, material to enquire what assurances
are meant. They are not specified in the White Paper, and it is
necessary to turn for enlightenment to the speech in which the White
Paper was explained to the House of Commons by the Secretary of
State for the Colonies. Having stated that promises touching Palestine were made by His Majesty's Government during the World War
to the Arabs as well as to the Jews,[5] Mr. MacDonald went on to
make it clear that he was not speaking of the McMahon Correspondence, which was once more declared to have no application to
Palestine, but of a message conveyed in January 1918 by Commander
Hogarth, on behalf of His Majesty's Government, to the Sharif of
Mecca.[6] Since there is no suggestion in Mr. MacDonald's speech
that there were any other assurances to the Arabs worth mentioning
in this connection, it seems clear that in speaking in general terms
of "the assurances which have been given to the Arab people in
the past," the White Paper must in fact be referring to Commander
Hogarth's message, which Mr. MacDonald summarised as follows:[7]

"He [Commander Hogarth] explained very frankly that His
Majesty's Government looked with favour upon a return of
Jews to Palestine, and that His Majesty's Government were
determined that no obstacle should be put in the way of this
return. But Commander Hogarth was instructed to say also,
and he did say, that this would be allowed only in so far as it
was compatible with the economic and political freedom of the
existing population. He also added, on instructions, that the
British Government were determined that no people in Palestine
should be subject to another."

3. The construction now placed by His Majesty's Government
upon the contents of the Hogarth Message may require to be borne
in mind in interpreting the new proposals as they affect the Jews.
But in considering whether these proposals are consistent with the
terms on which His Majesty's Government were entrusted with the
Mandate, the Hogarth Message, whatever construction His Majesty's
Government may think fit to put upon it, can clearly not be invoked
as embodying obligations towards the Arabs. Unlike the Balfour
Declaration, to which His Majesty's Government were at pains to
give immediate publicity throughout the world, the Hogarth Message
played no part whatever in the international discussions regarding
the future of Palestine which took place after the close of the War.
It was not until the message was excavated after the lapse of twenty
years that it first occurred to His Majesty's Government to mention
it in relation to the shaping of British policy in Palestine. Even
now, His Majesty's Government seem themselves to be doubtful as
to what significance is really to be attached to the message, for, in
replying to a question on the subject in the course of the recent
debate in the House of Commons, Sir Thomas Inskip, speaking for
the Government, observed that "it [the Hogarth message] is not
of sufficient importance for my Rt. Hon. Friend and myself to spend

[5] House of Commons, May 22nd, 1939, Official Report, Col. 1948.
[6] ib. col. 1951. The text of the Hogarth Message is printed in Cmd. 5964, where the date is given as January 4th, 1918.
[7] House of Commons, May 22nd, 1939, Col. 1951.

much time on it".[8] How deep an impression was made by "this
solemn pledge to the Arabs" upon the minds of the Arabs themselves, may be judged from the fact that not the slightest allusion
is made to it by the Palestine Arab Delegation in presenting its case
to His Majesty's Government in the lengthy communications reproduced in the White Paper of 1922.[9] It seems clear that the Delegation
had never heard of the Hogarth message. What is more important
for the present purpose is that neither had the League of Nations ever
heard of it. The League Council confirmed the Mandate without
being given the slightest reason to suppose that His Majesty's Government considered themselves to be under obligations towards the
Arabs other than and in excess of those contained either in the Mandate itself or in the authoritative Statement of British Policy in
Palestine [10] communicated to the League of Nations immediately
before the Mandate was confirmed. Hence, for the purpose of
determining whether the new proposals are consistent with the Mandate, the reference in the White Paper to the "assurances which
have been given to the Arab people" (meaning, as would now appear,
assurances given to them without the knowledge either of the Jews
or of the League of Nations), as distinct from His Majesty's Government's "obligations to the Arabs under the Mandate," is either
irrelevant or superfluous. If it is suggested that the "assurances"
add something not contained in the "obligations," they can have no
effect as between His Majesty's Government as Mandatory and the
League as the body on whose behalf the Mandate is exercised. If
this is not suggested, the position is the same as though the "assurances" had not been mentioned.

4. Before the new proposals are more closely approached, it will be
convenient at this stage to draw attention to a passage in the White
Paper which might, if left without comment, give rise to misunderstanding. In the opening sentences of Part I of the White Paper,
which deals with constitutional questions, His Majesty's Government
state that

> "they do not wish to contest the view, which was expressed
> by the Royal Commission, that the Zionist leaders at the time
> of the issue of the Balfour Declaration, recognised that an ultimate
> Jewish State was not precluded by the terms of the Declaration."[11]

By what can only be an oversight, the White Paper omits to make it
clear that it was not only the Zionist leaders who, in the view of the
Royal Commission, "recognised" that a Jewish State was "not precluded." The reference in the White Paper is to a passage at pages
24–25 of the Peel Report.[12] The Royal Commission first quote Mr.
Lloyd George, whose evidence is reproduced as follows:

> "The idea was, and this was the interpretation put upon it
> at the time, that a Jewish State was not to be set up immediately
> by the Peace Treaty, without reference to the wishes of the
> majority of the inhabitants. On the other hand, it was con-
> templated that, when the time arrived for according representa-
> tive institutions to Palestine, if the Jews had meanwhile responded
> to the opportunity afforded them by the idea of a national

---

[8] House of Commons, May 23rd, 1939, Official Report, Col. 2194.
[9] Cmd. 1700.
[10] See Cmd. 1708.
[11] Cmd. 6019, para. 4, page 3.
[12] Comd. 5479, Chapter II, paras. 20–21.

home and had become a definite majority of the inhabitants, then Palestine would thus become a Jewish commonwealth."

The Report then proceeds:—

"His Majesty's Government evidently realised that a Jewish State might in course of time be established, but it was not in a position to say that this would happen, still less to bring it about of its own motion. The Zionist leaders for their part recognised that an ultimate Jewish State was not precluded by the terms of the Declaration, and so it was understood elsewhere. 'I am persuaded,' said President Wilson on the 3rd March, 1919, 'that the Allied Nations, with the fullest concurrence of our own Government and people, are agreed that in Palestine shall be laid the foundations of a Jewish Commonwealth.' "

Then follow references to speeches or writings in the same strain by General Smuts, Lord Cecil, Lord Samuel and Mr. Winston Churchill. It will be seen that the authors of the White Paper have inadvertently omitted to notice that the reference in the Peel Report to the Zionist leaders is both preceded and followed by references to eminent British and other statesmen to whom substantially the same views are attributed. It may be added that, as to Lord Balfour himself, Lord Harlech,[13] addressing the Permanent Mandates Commission as Accredited British Representative in 1937, stated that "the establishment of an independent sovereign Jewish State . . . certainly was the conception in Lord Balfour's mind—it was challenged by others at the time—and the Balfour Declaration was the reflection of that conception so far as it could then be carried." [14]

5. By what appears to be a similar oversight, the White Paper states [15] that a passage which it quotes from the 1922 Statement of Policy "might be held" to imply that Palestine was not to be converted into a Jewish State, but omits to add that, referring to the definition of the Jewish National Home in the same Statement of Policy—a definition emphatically described in the White Paper [16] as "authoritative and comprehensive"—the Royal Commission remarks [17] that "there is nothing in it to prohibit the ultimate establishment of a Jewish State, and Mr. Churchill [18] has told us in evidence that no such prohibition was intended."

6. His Majesty's Government are at pains to make it clear that whatever may have been contemplated by Mr. Lloyd George or Lord Balfour in 1917 or by Mr. Churchill in 1922, they would regard themselves as unfaithful to their obligations towards the Arabs under the Mandate if they allowed Palestine to become a Jewish State. The emphasis with which they repudiate that conception suggests that they are under the impression that, if the Jewish State can once be got out of the way, the road is clear for their own proposals. This appears to involve a complete *non sequitur*. The same may be said of the contention that Palestine ought not to be kept "for ever

---

[13] Then Mr. Ormsby-Gore.
[14] XXXII P. M. C., page 180.
[15] Para. 4, page 4.
[16] Cmd. 6019, para. 6, page 4.
[17] Cmd. 5479, Chapter II, paras. 38–39, pp. 32–33.
[18] Mr. Churchill was Secretary of State for the Colonies at the time of the publication of the 1922 Statement of Policy.

under mandatory tutelage," and the similar contention advanced with reference to immigration, that the Mandate cannot be supposed to require that Jewish immigration shall be "allowed to continue indefinitely." It is not the case—and his Majesty's Government do not seriously attempt to show that it is—that either Jewish immigration must continue "indefinitely," or it must be restricted for five years to an annual average of not more (and possibly less) than 15,000, and then, in effect, be brought to an end. It is not the case that, if Palestine is not be become a Jewish State either the Mandate must go on "for ever," or an undivided Palestine must within ten years be made into an independent State with a guaranteed Arab majority of at least two to one. By selecting certain alternatives for rejection, His Majesty's Government do not make it superfluous to enquire whether their own policy is consistent with their mandatory obligations. That policy requires to be justified on its merits, and the test to be applied is whether it is calculated to give effect to the true intent and purpose of the Mandate which his Majesty's Government have undertaken to carry out both in the letter and the spirit. The Palestine Royal Commission affirms in its Report that "unquestionably the primary purpose of the Mandate, as expressed in its preamble and its Articles, is to promote the establishment of the Jewish National Home."[19] That preamble and those Articles were framed by the British Government itself. Unless the unaminous view of the Royal Commission is to be brushed aside, there can be no doubt as to the footing on which the Mandate was accepted by Great Britain. The question is, then, whether the proposals now made are consistent with the provisions of the Mandate, fairly construed in the light of their primary purpose as authoritatively defined.

7. It will be convenient to begin with the proposals relating to immigration, since the arbitrary restriction of Jewish immigration, and its subsequent suppression unless sanctioned by the Arabs, are indispensable preliminaries to the object ultimately in view, viz:— the creation of an independent State in which the Arabs will be permanently assured of preponderance. It may be observed in passing that, while the Arabs are intended to be guaranteed, in any event, a majority of two to one, the immigration restrictions are so devised that their preponderance may be still greater. On the one hand, there is no certainty that Jewish immigration will even be allowed to reach the prescribed maximum of 75,000 for the five years' period leading up to the coming into force of the Arab veto. As to 50,000 of the 75,000, admission will be granted or refused according to the economic absorptive capacity of the country at the time, as it may happen to be estimated by the High Commissioner, who is to be assisted in coming to a decision by Arab as well as Jewish representatives, and who will, moreover, be in a position to reduce the absorptive capacity by the exercise of his discretionary powers with regard to the acquisition of land. As to the 25,000 refugees, making up the balance of the 75,000, it will rest with the High Commissioner to decide, with the assistance of his advisers, who will include, as time goes on, an increasing proportion of Arabs, whether adequate maintenance can be considered to be ensured, it being only to the extent to which that question is answered in the affirmative that the refugees

---

[19] Cmd. 5479. Chapter II, para. 42, page 39.

will be admissible. On the other hand, the *numerus clausus* to be enforced against Jews during the five years' period will have no application to Arabs, nor will there be anything to prevent Arabs from outside from being admitted to fill, in their entirety, whatever openings for immigrant labour may arise after Jewish immigration has become subject to Arab veto. It follows that the Arabs may well have, in the end, a preponderance considerably exceeding their guaranteed majority of two to one.

8. This being the effect of the proposals, the question to be answered is whether they can fairly be held to be consistent with the Mandate, due regard being had to its "primary purpose" [20] viz:—to promote the establishment of the Jewish National Home—to the Royal Commission's finding (from which His Majesty's Government has indicated no dissent) that "Jewish immigration is not merely sanctioned, but required, by solemn international agreements," [21] and to the British Government's assertion in 1922 that the immigration of Jews is among the "integral and indispensable factors in the execution of the charge laid upon the mandatory of establishing in Palestine a national home for the Jewish people;" [22] it will be observed that it is not said that the stoppage of Jewish immigration is, or may become, an integral and indispensable factor in the charge laid upon the Mandatory of converting Palestine into a predominantly Arab independent State. In considering whether the present proposals can be reconciled with the Mandate, there are three distinct points to be discussed, viz:—

(1) Discrimination against Jewish as distinct from other immigration; the restrictions described in paragraph 14 of the White Paper being expressly stated to relate to *Jewish* immigration.[23]

(2) The arbitrary restriction of immigration during the five year period.

(3) The emergence of an Arab veto at the close of that period.

9. Article 15 of the Mandate requires that no person shall be excluded from Palestine on the sole ground of his religious belief. It can never have occurred to the framers of the Mandate that a person might be sought to be excluded from Palestine on the sole ground that he was a Jew. Such, however, would be the effect of the present proposals in any case in which admission was refused to a Jew as such, on the ground that the Jewish quota was exhausted, or, after the five years' period, by reason of the Arab veto. Let it be supposed, for example, that after the close of the five years' period, an individual possessing ample means desires to settle in Palestine. The question will immediately arise whether he is a Jew. How that question is to be decided is not clear. It can plainly not be decided by reference to the applicant's religious belief, for if it depended upon his religious belief whether the Arab veto was applicable or not, it would be difficult to reconcile the proceedings with Article 15 of the Mandate, which requires that no person shall be excluded from Palestine on the sole ground of his religious belief. It will, therefore,

[20] See Report of the Royal Commission, cited above, p. 7.
[21] Ibid. Chapter IV, para. 76, p. 147.
[22] Cmd. 1708, p. 4.
[23] Cmd. 6019, para. 14 (1) and (3), pp. 10–11.

be necessary to decide whether the applicant is to be classified as a Jew otherwise than by reference to his religious belief—a question on which the authorities administering the immigration laws (who may by this time be Arab authorities) will have the guidance of well-known contemporary precedents. If the applicant is held to be a Jew, his admission will only be permissible if it is found that "the Arabs" are "prepared to acquiesce." If, on the other hand, he is held not to be a Jew, the Arab veto will not affect him, and the ordinary regulations will apply. An immigration law which, both during and after the five years' period, will impose restrictions upon Jews as such may or may not be capable of being framed without violating the letter of the Mandate, but will, in any case, be clearly inconsistent with its spirit. Jewish immigration is singled out in Article 6 of the Mandate as the immigration to be facilitated. It is now proposed to be singled out as the immigration to be subjected to special restrictions, and eventually to an Arab veto, from which immigration of other types is apparently to be exempt.

10. The discrimination aggravates the offence and accentuates the indignity. But even if formal discrimination were avoided, the proposals, considered by reference to their real purpose and substantial effect, would remain irreconcilable either with the spirit or—on a fair construction—the letter of the Mandate. Reasons will be given in due course for the view, supported by high authority, that, if the Mandate be fairly construed in the light of all the relevant circumstances, the only principle on which immigration can properly be regulated will be found to be that of economic absorptive capacity, or, in other words, that immigrants ought to be admitted up to, though not beyond, the economic capacity of the country to absorb them. But the proposals now made go far beyond the repudiation of that principle. Not only is its application to be qualified during the next five years by the introduction of a fixed upper limit, but once that period has expired, it is to have no application at all, political and not economic considerations being thenceforth required to be treated as having decisive and exclusive weight. More than that, on the expiration of the five years' period, no further discretion is to be exercised by the Mandatory authorities, but it is thenceforth to be left to the Arab section of the population to decide for itself whether its "rights and position" would be "prejudiced" by further Jewish immigration, and, if so, to veto it. These arrangements are to take effect halfway through the ten years' period provisionally fixed by the White Paper for the continuance of the Mandate. The Mandate will, therefore, still be in force, and with it the provisions of Article 6. The question which arises is, then, whether such arrangements as have just been described can be said to represent a *bona fide* compliance with those provisions. In construing Article 6, due weight must be given to the distinction drawn in the terminology of the Mandate between the Mandatory and the Administration of Palestine—a distinction well brought out by Article 15, and further illustrated by other Articles, as for example, Article 11. The choice of words is not fortuitous. The scheme of the Mandate is to propound the main principles in terms of injunctions to the Mandatory, while assigning certain specific duties to the Administration of Palestine. The duty imposed upon the Administration by Article 6 must therefore be taken to be a duty imposed upon it for the purpose of enabling the

JEWISH NATIONAL HOME IN PALESTINE

Mandatory to carry out the main objects of the Mandate, as defined in Article 2, and further indicated in the Preamble. It is to be noted that the provisions of Article 6 do impose a duty. They do not merely authorise the Administration to permit immigration; they require the Administration to facilitate it. The duty is an active duty—it constitutes, as it was put by His Majesty's Government in 1931,[24] a "positive obligation," and such it remains so long as the Mandate is in force. In carrying out that obligation, the Administration is at the same time to ensure that the "rights and position" of "other sections of the population" are not prejudiced, but on no reasonable construction of Article 6, looking at it, as it must be looked at, in the light of the Mandate as a whole, can this be taken to authorise—much less require—the Administration to bring immigration to an end on the sole ground that "other sections of the population" are opposed to it. The duty thus imposed upon the Administration is not one which can properly be discharged by the announcement of a decision to take the orders of the Arabs as to the extent (if any) to which immigration is to be permitted after a fixed future date. To say that, the Mandate being *ex hypothesi* still in force, this represents a *bona fide* compliance with the requirements of Article 6, giving full weight to its true intent and purpose, amounts to saying that there is no real difference between facilitating immigration and putting a stop to it. Much has been made in various statements of what has been described as the double undertaking contained in the Mandate—the two sets of obligations which, it is customary to emphasise, are of equal weight. It might have been thought that an example of what is meant is to be found in Article 6, which couples a positive obligation to the Jews with a qualifying proviso for the benefit of "other sections of the population." If there is any substance in the doctrine of equal weight, it is not clear why it should be supposed that, once another five years have elapsed, Article 6 of the Mandate, which will still be in force, can be applied on the footing that the undertaking to the Jews need be given no weight at all.

11. The views expressed above are not without authoritative support. In a Statement of Policy on Palestine[25] published in 1930, the British Government then in office proposed restrictions on immigration which, though severe, fell far short of those foreshadowed in the recent White Paper. On that occasion, English lawyers of the highest eminence[26] expressed the considered opinion that those restrictions "clearly involve the prohibition—or, as the White Paper calls it, the 'suspension'—of all that Jewish immigration and settlement which Article 6 of the Mandate expressly directs the Mandatory to facilitate and encourage." Their conclusion was that "the White Paper[27] appears to us to involve a departure from the obligations of the Mandate." If this was their view of the White Paper of 1930, it is not difficult to infer what their comments would have been if the proposals before them had been those now announced.

[24] Mr. Ramsay MacDonald's letter to Dr. Weizmann, February 13, 1931, paragraph 7, printed in Hansard, February 13, 1931, Vol. 248, cols. 751–757.
[25] Cmd. 3692.
[26] See letter from Lord Hailsham and Sir John Simon, *The Times*, November 4, 1930.
[27] i. e. The White Paper of 1930.

12. The contentions advanced by His Majesty's Government in justification of their immigration policy [28] may at this point be considered in their bearing on the question of the Arab veto. After quoting Article 6 of the Mandate, His Majesty's Government proceed to point out that "beyond this, the extent to which Jewish immigration into Palestine is to be permitted is nowhere defined in the Mandate." But, general as are the terms in which Article 6 is expressed, on one point it is clear—Jewish immigration is to be "facilitated." Because the scale on which Jewish immigrants are in practice to be introduced is not precisely indicated, it is clearly not arguable that, that being so, the Mandatory is under no obligation to admit any immigrants at all, and, far from facilitating Jewish immigration, is free to prohibit it. Next comes a reference to the test of economic absorptive capacity, on which the White Paper observes that "His Majesty's Government do not read either the Statement of Policy of 1922 or the letter of 1931 as implying that the Mandate requires them, for all time and in all circumstances, to facilitate the immigration of Jews into Palestine subject only to consideration of the country's economic absorptive capacity." What is, however, required to be shown, in order to justify the Arab veto, is that the Mandate *does* entitle His Majesty's Government to lay it down that after the lapse of another five years Jewish immigration shall "for all time and in all circumstances" be prohibited, subject only to any wishes to the contrary which may be expressed by the Arabs. Next follows a rejection of the view that the establishment of a Jewish National Home cannot be effected unless Jewish immigration is allowed to continue "indefinitely." On this it may be observed that the question now at issue is not whether Jewish immigration must continue indefinitely, but whether, so long as the Mandate is in force, His Majesty's Government are free to disregard the injunction that Jewish immigration shall be facilitated. Finally, His Majesty's Government draw attention to the consequences which, in their opinion, will follow if "immigration is continued up to the economic absorptive capacity of the country, regardless of all other considerations." If this is intended as a justification of the Arab veto, it is left to be inferred, but no attempt is made to demonstrate, that either Jewish immigration must be kept up to the full limits of economic absorptive capacity, regardless of all other considerations, or else that, regardless of all other considerations, an Arab demand for the total cessation of Jewish immigration must, so long as it is maintained, be regarded as conclusive.

13. It remains to mention certain points, which, though not raised in the White Paper itself, played a prominent part in its exposition by the Secretary and Under-Secretary of State for the Colonies in the House of Commons and the House of Lords respectively. It was urged by Mr. MacDonald [29] that a continuance of Jewish immigration beyond the limit now proposed to be set would prejudice the "rights and position of other sections of the population" within the meaning of Article 6 of the Mandate. In construing Article 6, due weight must be given to the fact that it speaks not of the Arabs or of the non-Jewish inhabitants collectively, but of "other sections of

[28] See Paragraph 12 of the White Paper, Cmd. 6019, pp. 8–9.
[29] House of Commons, May 22, 1939, Official Report, Col. 1955.

the population" in the plural. The choice of words can hardly have been fortuitous and suggests that the draftsman was thinking of separate groups of the population rather than of the Arabs as a whole. Those who framed the 1922 Statement of Policy [30] had the draft Mandate before them, and it may reasonably be conjectured that the words "other sections of the population" are reflected in the language of that Statement in laying it down that the immigrants are not "to deprive any section of the present population of their employment." Be that as it may, Mr. MacDonald did not clearly explain what "rights" were considered to be involved. Even if the reference be assumed to be to the Arab population as a whole, its "rights" could hardly be said to include the right to retain a crushing numerical preponderance— still less, when the context is considered, the right to decide for itself whether Jewish immigrants should be admitted or not. The point may be made that it is a question not only of "rights" but of "position." But the word "position," fairly construed in its context, cannot bear the weight which must be put upon it if it is to yield the desired result. In the French text of Article 6 the word "position" appears as "situation," and in ordinary usage the French word "situation" connotes financial or economic position. That "position" is to be interpreted in an economic sense is suggested by the relevant passages in the Statement of Policy of 1922, which, without indicating any other tests, explains that "immigration cannot be so great in volume as to exceed whatever may be the economic capacity of the country to absorb new arrivals," and that "it is essential to ensure that the immigrants should not be a burden on the people of Palestine as a whole, and that they should not deprive any section of the present population of their employment." The passages in the White Paper relating to immigration, which must clearly have been drafted in the light of and with reference to the provisions of the Mandate, support the view that it is the economic position of "other sections of the population" which is referred to in Article 6. There is, indeed, in another part of the 1922 Statement of Policy an assurance to the Arabs that His Majesty's Government have never contemplated "the disappearance or the subordination of the Arabic population, language or culture in Palestine," nor do they contemplate "that Palestine as a whole should be converted into a Jewish National Home." [31] But the very fact that assurances in these terms were so specifically given in 1922 is of itself a reason against reading into Article 6 of the Mandate assurances of a different and much more sweeping character. In the 1922 Statement of Policy, His Majesty's Government were publicly declaring their intentions on the eve of the confirmation of the Mandate. If it was part of their duties under the Mandate, as they understood it, to guarantee the Arabs not only equality of status, but a heavy and perpetual preponderance in numbers, the language they selected was singularly inadequate to convey this conception. It was more particularly incumbent upon them to keep nothing back because, in order "to remove any misunderstandings that may have arisen," [32] they invited the Zionist Organisation to intimate its acceptance of the policy set forth in the Statement. It is inconceivable that they would have done so with the knowledge that its silence on a point of the highest importance made it incomplete and misleading.

[30] Cmd. 1700.
[31] Cmd. 1700, p. 18.
[32] Cmd. 1700, p. 17.

14. There is another line of argument which, though not mentioned in the White Paper itself, was favoured by the Government spokesmen in Parliament. Article 6 of the Mandate requires the Administration of Palestine, while ensuring that the rights and position of other sections of the population are not prejudiced to "facilitate Jewish immigration under suitable conditions." From the words "under suitable conditions" it was sought to extract a restriction independent of, and additional to, that contained in the words "while ensuring that the rights and position of other sections of the population are not prejudiced." It was contended,[33] in effect, that the real meaning of the injunction to facilitate immigration under suitable conditions was that the Mandatory was to facilitate immigration to the extent, and only to the extent, to which the conditions were suitable, and that whether conditions were suitable or not was for the Mandatory to decide as it thought fit. It is to be observed that this construction of Article 6 is clearly an afterthought on the part of His Majesty's Government. The White Paper of 1930[34] states that "the obligation contained in Article 6 to facilitate Jewish immigration and to encourage close settlement by Jews on the land is qualified by the requirement to ensure that the rights and position of other sections of the population are not prejudiced." There is no suggestion of any other qualification. It clearly never occurred to the authors of the 1930 White Paper that a further, and much more extensive, because much more vaguer, qualification was contained in the words "under suitable conditions." Again, Mr. Ramsay MacDonald's letter of 1931 states that "in the one aspect, His Majesty's Government have to be mindful of their obligations to facilitate Jewish immigration under suitable conditions and to encourage close settlement by Jews on the land; in the other aspect they have to be equally mindful of their duty to ensure that no prejudice results to the rights and position of the non-Jewish community."[35] It will be seen that the obligation to the non-Jewish community is set against the obligation to the Jews "to facilitate Jewish immigration under suitable conditions," with no suggestion that the words "under suitable conditions" connote an obligation, not towards the Jews, but towards the Arabs. It is evident that both those who framed the White Paper of 1930 and Mr. Ramsay MacDonald in 1931 took it for granted that the words "facilitate Jewish immigration under suitable conditions" were to be read as a whole, and that, the qualifications having been disposed of by the words "while ensuring . . . are not prejudiced," Article 6 then passes to the positive obligation. This construction seems clearly to be correct. Article 6 does not say—though it could easily have been said had it been meant—that Jewish immigration is to be permitted subject to such conditions as the Mandatory may think fit to impose, or that it is to be permitted to such extent (if any) as the Mandatory may think suitable. A duty to "facilitate Jewish immigration under suitable conditions" is a duty to facilitate Jewish immigration coupled with a duty to see that the immigrants come in under suitable conditions, as, for example, by making administrative arrangements ensuring that the flow of immigration is orderly and that the immigrants are properly selected. On

[33] See Mr. Malcolm MacDonald's speech in the House of Commons, May 22, 1939, Official Report, Cols. 1954–1955, and Lord Dufferin's speech in the House of Lords, May 23, 1939, Official Report, Col. 86.
[34] Cmd. 3692.
[35] See paragraph 15 of the letter, Hansard, February 13, 1931, Vol. 248, cols. 751–757.

no fair construction of the Mandate, read as a whole, is it possible to torture the words "under suitable conditions" in Article 6 into a justification for subjecting Jewish immigration to an Arab veto.

15. For the purpose of enquiring whether the Arab veto can be justified in the light of the Mandate by what has been said by His Majesty's Government in defence of their immigration policy, it has not been necessary to enter closely into the questions raised in Part II of the White Paper with regard to the principle of economic absorptive capacity. Even if all that is said on the subject were admitted, the Arab veto would still require, for its justification, more cogent arguments than any which His Majesty's Government have been able to advance. But in fact no such admission is made. On the contrary, there are ample grounds, both in reason and in authority, for the view that the principle of economic absorptive capacity is implicit in the Mandate, and that on no other principle can the duty to facilitate Jewish immigration be properly discharged.

16. So far as can be ascertained, the expression "economic absorptive capacity" was first used in an official statement in a speech in the House of Lords by the Duke of Sutherland, speaking for the Government, on February 14, 1922.[36] The Government had been asked a question with regard to "the introduction into the country [Palestine] of more than 20,000 aliens against the wishes of more than 90 per cent. of the people, and in violation of enemy [37] law." The Government's reply was as follows:—

"As regards immigration, the obligations imposed on His Majesty's Government by the conditions under which Palestine was entrusted to them made it necessary for them to initiate a policy of strictly controlled and selected Jewish immigration up to the economic absorptive capacity of the country."

It will be observed that the words are "up to the economic absorptive capacity." No doubt can exist as to what was meant when it is remembered that what the Government had been invited to explain was why so many immigrants had been admitted. Thus, as early as February, 1922, when economic absorptive capacity was first mentioned in an official statement in connection with immigration, it was mentioned in language which implied that it was regarded as providing a criterion, and not merely as fixing an upper limit.

17. In the Statement of Policy contained in the White Paper of 1922 the material passage is that which lays it down that "Jewish immigration cannot be so great in volume as to exceed whatever may be the economic capacity of the country at the time to absorb new arrivals." [38] Attempts have been made to extract support for the proposals now put forward from the words "cannot be so great as to exceed." [39] It has been pointed out that all that is actually announced is a restriction, the inference sought to be drawn being that, while the 1922 Statement of Policy strengthens the negative obligations contained in the qualifying proviso to Article 6 of the Mandate, it leaves His Majesty's Government free to give effect to the positive obligation in such manner and to such extent as they may think fit. The passage relating to economic absorptive capacity

[36] House of Lords, February 14, 1922, Official Report, Col. 149.
[37] i. e. Ottoman.
[38] Cmd. 1700, p. 19.
[39] See, for example, Mr. MacDonald's speech in the House of Commons, May 22, 1939, Official Report, Col. 1954.

in the White Paper of 1922 does announce a restriction, but its real significance cannot be appreciated by looking at the restrictive words in the abstract and without reference to the circumstances in which they were used. When the Balfour Declaration was published, the impression made upon the mind of the average Zionist was that Palestine was to be thrown open to Jews as freely as England is open to home-coming Englishmen, or at the least, that there was to be mass immigration controlled and organized by the Jews themselves. These expectations were cut down by the announcement that immigration could not be permitted to exceed the economic capacity of the country to absorb new arrivals. In making it clear that that limit must be respected, His Majesty's Government were, indeed, imposing a restriction, but a restriction which cannot be properly understood without considering its antecedents and background. Let it be supposed that a person who was under the impression that he was to receive ten pounds is told that he is not to have more than five. He would have some reason for feeling aggrieved if, on asking for the five pounds, he were told that no such sum had been promised him—he had merely been informed that he was not to have ten.

18. But the Jewish case is, in fact, much stronger than this. On June 3rd, 1922, a copy of the 1922 Statement of Policy was sent by the Colonial Office to the Zionist Organisation with a request for a formal assurance that it accepted the policy.[40] In giving this assurance on June 18th, 1922, the Zionist Organisation commented as follows on that part of the Statement which related to immigration:—[41]

> "The Executive further observe that His Majesty's Government acknowledge . . . that it is necessary that the Jews shall be able to increase their numbers in Palestine by immigration, and understand from the Statement of Policy that the volume of such immigration is to be determined by the economic capacity of the country from time to time to absorb new arrivals."

This was plainly intended to exclude the possibility of the passage in question being construed as merely imposing an upper limit. The Zionist Executive were at pains to make it clear that what they understood the Statement to mean was that Jewish immigration was to proceed up to, though not beyond, the limit fixed by economic absorptive capacity. This letter did not elicit any indication of dissent on the part of His Majesty's Government. The assurance which the Zionist Organisation had been invited to give had been asked for, as explained in the Colonial Office letter of June 3rd, 1922,[42] with a view to the removal of misunderstandings. It is clear that misunderstandings would have been created rather than removed if, on one of the main points touched upon in the Statement of Policy, His Majesty's Government and the Zionist Organisation had been at variance in their construction of the Statement. If His Majesty's Government did not agree with the construction placed by the Zionist Executive on the passage relating to immigration, they might reasonably have been expected to make this clear. Shortly before the confirmation of the Mandate, copies of the Statement of Policy, the Colonial Office letter of June 3rd, 1922, and the Zionist Organisation's

[40] Cmd. 1700, No. 5, p. 17.
[41] Ibid. No. 7, pp. 28–29.
[42] Ibid. No. 5, p. 17.

reply of June 18th, were sent by His Majesty's Government to the Secretary General of the League of Nations for the information of the Council.[43]   This was plainly an invitation to the Council to take note of these documents in confirming the Mandate.   The Council was entitled to treat the Statement of Policy as an authoritative exposition of the principles which His Majesty's Government proposed to apply in giving effect to the Mandate so far as it related to the Jewish National Home.   In the absence of any indication to the contrary, the Council was also entitled to assume that the construction placed by the Zionist Organisation upon what was said in the Statement on the subject of absorptive capacity was accepted by His Majesty's Government as correct.   Let it be supposed that A sends a document to B with a request for his assent.   On one vital point the document is not free from ambiguity.   B, in assenting, explains the construction which he places on the document.   A makes no comment.   He then sends the document and the correspondence to C, still without comment.   For a period of years, A, B, and C all act in harmony with B's construction.   It would hardly be suggested that, either as between A and B, or as between A and C, it would still be open to A to insist that B's construction, though left uncontradicted at the time, and subsequently acted upon by all parties for a period of years, must be set aside in favour of precisely the construction which B had quite plainly intended to exclude.

19. That the economic absorptive capacity principle was for a long period of years applied in practice in the sense of the Zionist Organisation's letter of June 18th, 1922, is a fact which is not in dispute, though the White Paper appears to under-estimate its relevance.   But, quite apart from this, there is ample authority for the view that the construction contended for by the Jewish Agency is correct.   There is first the authority of British Ministers.   In 19 , for example, more than ten years after the publication of the White Paper, and the confirmation of the Mandate, the then Colonial Secretary (Sir Philip Cunliffe-Lister) stated in the House of Commons:—

"It has always been the policy followed by the Mandatory Power—and no other policy could possibly be pursued in Palestine in carrying out the idea of a national home—that the economic conditions of the country must govern the number of immigrants." [44]

In the light of the opening words of this statement, there can be no doubt as to what was meant by the expression "govern."   But of greater significance are the more considered statements made on behalf of His Majesty's Government at the Seventeenth (Extraordinary) Session of the Permanent Mandates Commission in 1930, when the Accredited British Representative was the then Under-Secretary of State for the Colonies, Dr. Drummond Shiels.   Speaking of immigration policy, Dr. Shiels said that

"there had been no want of guiding principle.   The guiding principle had been specifically stated in the Command Paper of 1922, where the principle was laid down that immigration into Palestine must be effected according to the economic capac-

43 Cmd. 1708, communication dated July 1, 1922.
44 House of Commons, April 3rd, 1933, Official Report. Col. 1419.

ity of the country to absorb new immigrants. That was a very definite guiding principle." [45]

The proposition that immigration must not exceed economic absorptive capacity, interpreted in a purely restrictive sense, would plainly not answer to the description of "a very definite guiding principle," since it would merely fix a point beyond which immigration must not go, without affording any positive guidance as to how many immigrants were in fact to be brought in. When Dr. Shiels said that the White Paper of 1922 laid down the very definite guiding principle that immigration must be effected "according to the economic capacity of the country to absorb new immigrants," the principle to which he was alluding was clearly that immigration was to be permitted up to, but not beyond, the point at which the country was economically capable of absorbing it. A similar inference is to be drawn from Dr. Shiels' remark, at a later stage of the proceedings,[46] that the Jewish Agency

"had always accepted the provision laid down in 1922 that the number of immigrants was to be according to the economic capacity of the country to absorb them."

Dr. Shiels can have been in no doubt as to the nature of the principle which had, in fact, been accepted by the Jewish Agency and had in practice formed the basis of all its dealings with the Palestine Government on the subject of immigration. It is true that Dr. Shiels was stating the effect of the White Paper of 1922, and was not referring to any express provision of the Mandate, but reasons have already been given for the view that the 1922 White Paper is binding on His Majesty's Government in relation to the construction of the Mandate, on which it was designed to serve as an authoritative commentary. As late as January, 1936, the High Commissioner, in summarising the reply of the Secretary of State for the Colonies to a memorandum from Arab leaders, said:

"The guiding principle as regards the admission of immigrants *is a policy of economic absorptive capacity*, and His Majesty's Government contemplate no departure from that principle." [47]

20. The economic absorptive capacity principle, as thus interpreted, was approved by the Permanent Mandates Commission, which in its Report to the Council on the work of its Seventeenth Session, stated that

"The Commission views with approval the Mandatory Power's intention of keeping Jewish immigration proportionate to the country's capacity of economic absorption, as clearly intimated in the White Paper of 1922." [48]

The Report was approved by the Council of the League,[49] which must therefore be taken to have endorsed the views expressed by the Mandates Commission on the subject of immigration. Another passage from the same Report, but on a different subject, is quoted in the 1930 Statement of Policy,[50] with the comment that "it is

[45] XVII P.M.C., page 54.
[46] XVII P.M.C., page 82.
[47] Official Communique of the Palestine Government, January 30th, 1936.
[48] XVII P.M.C., page 142.
[49] League of Nations Official Journal, Nov. 1930, page 1292.
[50] Cmd. 3692, paragraph 8, page 11.

a source of satisfaction to them [His Majesty's Government] that it has been rendered authoritative by the approval of the Council of the League of Nations." The Council's approval was given at the same time and in the same manner as it was given to that part of the same Report which dealt with immigration. The recent White Paper [51] refers to "resolutions of the Permanent Mandates Commission," but refrains from adding that they have been rendered authoritative by the approval of the Council of the League.

21. The principles governing immigration into Palestine were further discussed by the Permanent Mandates Commission at its 32nd Session (1937). The Chairman's remarks leave no doubt as to what the Commission meant to convey by its observations on the subject in its 1930 Report:—

> "The Chairman...recalled that in 1930 the Council, on the advice of the Mandates Commission, had accepted the principle put forward by the Mandatory Power itself—namely that Jewish immigration should be authorised to the extent allowed by the country's capacity of economic absorption." [52]

The discussion on this occasion arose from the decision taken by His Majesty's Government to fix an arbitrary quota for Jewish immigration, pending a decision on the question of partition.[53] The Commission made the following observations in its report to the Council:— [54]

The Commission does not question that the Mandatory Power, responsible as it is for the maintenance of order in the territory, may on occasion find it advisable to take such a step, and is competent to do so, as an exceptional and provisional measure; it feels, however, bound to draw attention to this departure from the principle, sanctioned by the League Council, that immigration is to be proportionate to the country's economic absorptive capacity.

In September, 1937, a resolution taking note of this Report was adopted by the Council.[55] In a later resolution on the question of partition, the Council took occasion to recall "the assurances given . . . by the Representative of the United Kingdom on the subject of immigration"—the allusion being to Mr. Eden's assurance that the imposition of the arbitrary quota was to be regarded as a "purely temporary measure designed to meet temporary and exceptional conditions. If, as the Commission said, it were a departure from a principle sanctioned by the Council on a former occasion, Mr. Eden's colleagues on the Council would, he was sure, appreciate the special circumstances in which that decision had been taken." [56] It is clear that both the Mandates Commission and the Council viewed with misgiving even the temporary substitution of an arbitrary quota for the principle of economic absorptive capacity. What is now announced is not a temporary departure from the principle but its total repudiation.

22. Article 6 of the Mandate, which requires the Administration of Palestine to facilitate Jewish immigration, requires it also to encourage close settlement by Jews on the land, special reference being

[51] Cmd. 6019, paragraph 12, pp. 8–9.
[52] XXXII P.M.C., page 112.
[53] See Cmd. 5513, paragraph 6.
[54] XXXII P.M.C., page 233.
[55] See Minutes of Ninety-Eighth Session, para. 3937.
[56] ib. p. 16.

made to State lands and waste lands not required for public purposes. Just as the White Paper proposes to bring Jewish immigration to an end, so also it proposes to obstruct the acquisition of land for Jewish settlement by restrictions which, though vaguely described, are clearly intended to be sweeping. Any measures interfering with sales by Arabs as such, or with purchases by Jews as such, would, in so far as they affected inhabitants of Palestine, infringe the principle of non-discrimination implicit in Articles 2 and 15 of the Mandate. But even if in form discrimination is avoided, what is clearly intended is a drastic reduction of the area available for Jewish settlement. His Majesty's Government refer, in defence of their policy, to "the reports of several expert Commissions," but the Commissions which have visited Palestine of recent years were not primarily composed of agricultural experts qualified to express an authoritative opinion on the matters with which Part III of the White Paper is concerned. Much clearer evidence than any which has yet been produced would be required to show that the far-reaching restrictions which are evidently contemplated are genuinely required to ensure that the rights and position of the Arab rural population shall not be prejudiced, within the meaning of Article 6 of the Mandate. It is to be observed that the duty of ensuring that the rights and position of other sections of the population shall not be prejudiced is coupled in Article 6 with a positive obligation, not only to facilitate the immigration of Jews, but to encourage close settlement by Jews on the land. The White Paper contains nothing to suggest that His Majesty's Government propose to take any steps to carry out this obligation, or indeed, that they recognise its existence.

23. Attention was drawn in the preceding paragraph to the reference in Part III of the White Paper to "the reports of several expert Commissions" with regard to land settlement and agriculture. But there are other matters on which both the Royal Commission and the Woodhead Commission were qualified to speak with much greater authority, and if His Majesty's Government rely unreservedly upon their Reports in Part III of the White Paper, their views are clearly entitled to at least equal weight in relation to the matters discussed in Part I. The foregoing excerpts may, therefore, be apposite:

"At any given moment there must be either an Arab or a Jewish majority in Palestine, and the Government of an independent Palestine, freed from the Mandate, would have to be either an Arab or a Jewish Government." (Royal Commission Report, p. 362.)

"The worst possible form of settlement would be one which left both Jews and Arabs in any part of Palestine uncertain whether in a few years' time either of them may not be subjected against their will to the political dominance of the other." (Partition Commission Report, p. 103.)

"If the projected measure of self-government was to have any reality, if it meant any real increase of Arab power or influence in legislation and administration, then the Jews believed—and in our opinion the belief was justified—that such power or influence would be used against the interests of the Jewish National Home." (Royal Commission Report, pp. 359–360.)

24. The reports of the "expert Commissions" relied upon in Part III of the White Paper will be found, properly understood, to offer the plainest warnings against proposals of the nature outlined in Part I. The essence of these proposals is that, at the end of a transitional period, Palestine shall become an independent State, in which, by means of the artificial restriction and eventual stoppage of Jewish immigration, the Arabs are to be assured of a preponderance of at least two to one. During the transitional period, the majority status of the Arabs is to be reflected in a two to one representation among the heads of Departments—a clear indication of the principles on which the Constitution of the independent State may be expected to be framed. It is by these means that His Majesty's Government propose to carry out their obligation under the Mandate to create such political, administrative and economic conditions as will secure the establishment of the Jewish National Home.

25. In paragraph 4 of the White Paper His Majesty's Government state that "they would regard it as contrary to their obligations to the Arabs under the Mandate, as well as to the assurances which have been given to the Arab people in the past, that the Arab population of Palestine should be made the subjects of a Jewish State against their will." It is difficult to understand how His Majesty's Government can have persuaded themselves that it would not be contrary to their obligations to the Jews under the Mandate, and to the assurances given to the Jewish people in the past, that the Jewish population of Palestine should be made the subjects of an Arab State against their will. It is no answer to say that the State will not be an Arab State but a Palestinian State. It is not names that matter, but realities. The authority of the Royal Commission has already been quoted for the proposition that "at any given moment there must be either an Arab or a Jewish majority in Palestine, and the Government of an independent Palestine, freed from the Mandate, would have to be either an Arab or a Jewish Government." It can make little difference to the Jews whether the State into which they are forced is an Arab State so described or a "Palestinian" State with an Arab Government. "Forced" is the correct expression, for it has been made clear that the independent State is to be formed, and the Jews included in it, with or without Jewish consent.[57] It is true that it is stated to be the desire of His Majesty's Government that the independent State "should be one in which Arabs and Jews share in government in such a way as to ensure that the essential interests of each community are safeguarded."[58] There was some talk of safeguards in the Parliamentary Debate, but, pressed for more precise information, Mr. MacDonald could only state vaguely that "those are matters for consideration when the time arrives."[59] Here again it may be apposite to quote the Royal Commission:

> "We are not questioning the sincerity or the humanity of the Mufti's intentions or those of his colleagues; but we cannot forget what recently happened, despite treaty provisions and explicit assurances, to the Assyrian minority in Iraq; nor can we forget that the hatred of the Arab politician for the National Home has never been concealed."[60]

[57] See House of Lords, May 23, 1939, Official Report, Cols. 104-105.
[58] Cmd. 6019, paragraph 10, p. 6.
[59] House of Commons, May 22, 1939, Official Report, Col. 196
[60] Cmd. 5479, Chapter V, par. 58, p. 141.

25. But it is not only a question of security; it is a question of status. Mr. MacDonald, though unable to be more specific on the question of safeguards, declared that "the whole spirit of this arrangement . . . is that the interests of the minority and majority in Palestine shall be adequately secured." [61]   The status of a minority in the nominal enjoyment of minority rights is not the status which was contemplated for the Jews when His Majesty's Government promised them to facilitate the establishment in Palestine of a National Home for the Jewish people, or when that promise was subsequently incorporated in the Mandate. Addressing the Permanent Mandates Commission as the Accredited British Representative in 1937, Lord Harlech [62] stated, with reference to the Jews, that "he agreed . . . that the fundamental question was that of status . . . From the Jewish point of view, status was all important." [63]   In the White Paper of 1937 [64] His Majesty's Government point out, as one of the advantages of the partition scheme, that "the Jews would at last cease to live a 'minority life,' and the primary objective of Zionism would thus be attained." It is now proposed to fulfil the British Government's "declaration of sympathy with Zionist aspirations" by imposing upon the Jews in Palestine precisely the status of which Zionism is designed to relieve them.

26. It is characteristic of the spirit in which the constitutional proposals are conceived that they tacitly brush aside the connection, repeatedly acknowledged by British statesmen in the past and expressly recognised in the preamble to the Mandate, between Palestine and the Jewish people as a whole. The symbol of that connection, the Jewish Agency, is studiously ignored. The "appropriate body" to be set up under paragraph 10 (6) of the White Paper for the purpose of reviewing the constitutional situation is to be representative of "the people of Palestine." The Jewish Agency is not mentioned and seems clearly intended to be excluded, notwithstanding that in the White Paper of May, 1930, [65] the question of self-government was described by His Majesty's Government as "one which deeply concerns the Jewish Agency." As though to make it clear that the Arab people as a whole is henceforth to be brought into the affairs of Palestine, and the Jewish people as a whole kept out, the White Paper proceeds to announce that if, at the end of ten years, His Majesty's Government should desire to postpone the creation of the independent State, they will first consult with representatives of the people of Palestine, the Council of the League of Nations, and the neighbouring Arab States, and that if they should still think that postponement is unavoidable, the Arab States will be included among the parties to be consulted as to plans for the future. The Jewish Agency, with all that it stands for, recedes from the scene, and in its place are brought forward the Arab Kings. It was not in this spirit nor with these intentions that the British Government published the Balfour Declaration and accepted the Mandate.

London,
1.6.39.

---

[61] House of Commons, May 22, 1939, Col. 1962.
[62] Then Mr. Ormsby-Gore.
[63] XXXII P. M. C. p. 180.
[64] Cmd. 5513, para. 7.
[65] Cmd. 3582, para. 7, page 9.

STATEMENTS RELATING TO THE EFFORTS

OF

HON. SOL BLOOM, CHAIRMAN

COMMITTEE ON FOREIGN AFFAIRS

CONCERNING

THE JEWISH NATIONAL HOME IN PALESTINE

(Excerpts from hearings by Committee on Foreign Affairs on H. J. Res. 418 and H. J. Res. 419)

STATEMENT OF HON. JOHN W. McCORMACK, MAJORITY LEADER, HOUSE OF REPRESENTATIVES

May I at this time to you, Mr. Chairman, and to the committee express my congratulations and my thanks for this fine, historical compilation, and to the chairman, Congressman Bloom, whom we all admire and respect, a man who enjoys the deep respect of every colleague of his, a great American, may I express my appreciation for your courtesy, and may I compliment you for this fine publication of the documents which are of great value and which will remain a source of intelligent information.

STATEMENT OF HON. CHARLES A. EATON, A REPRESENTATIVE IN CONGRESS FROM THE STATE OF NEW JERSEY, AND RANKING MINORITY MEMBER OF THE COMMITTEE ON FOREIGN AFFAIRS

Mr. EATON. I would like to call the attention of the members of the committee to a very constructive and useful compilation on the history of this proposition which has been prepared by the chairman, and which, as I understand, is, and ought to be before us. Note this little book. It is a very concise and comprehensive statement, and I want to thank the chairman for preparing it for us. I have read it carefully, and it is filled with information which we will need in order to intelligently discuss these resolutions. Thank you, Mr. Chairman.

STATEMENTS OF HON. HERMAN P. EBERHARTER, A REPRESENTATIVE IN CONGRESS FROM THE STATE OF PENNSYLVANIA, AND HON. LUTHER A. JOHNSON, REPRESENTATIVE IN CONGRESS FROM THE STATE OF TEXAS, AND RANKING MAJORITY MEMBER OF THE COMMITTEE ON FOREIGN AFFAIRS

Mr. EBERHARTER. The chairman, of course, I feel is to be commended very highly for his wisdom and foresight in having prepared in advance for study by members of the committee this pamphlet which contains the important and relevant facts relative to this very difficult problem, and yet it is not so difficult but that if it were tackled in the right way I believe it could be solved to the satisfaction of the world and all mankind.

Mr. JOHNSON. Will the gentleman yield for a question?

Chairman BLOOM. Mr. Johnson.

Mr. JOHNSON. I want to concur in what you said with reference to the chairman's compilation of these documents in this pamphlet, and it is not only valuable for the use of this committee, but it has hisotrical data and knowledge in it which will cause many of us to want to preserve it.

STATEMENT OF HON. JOSEPH L. PFEIFER, A REPRESENTATIVE IN CONGRESS FROM THE STATE OF NEW YORK

Mr. PFEIFER. Mr. Chairman, your fairness at all times has again been exemplified in these hearings on Resolutions 418 and 419. From what we have learned from the witnesses confirms my opinion of long ago, that drastic action should be taken immediately to give all aid possible to this group of suffering humanity.

STATEMENT OF DR. ISRAEL GOLDSTEIN, PRESIDENT OF THE ZIONIST OR-
GANIZATION OF AMERICA, AND OF THE SYNAGOGUE COUNCIL OF AMER-
ICA, COCHAIRMAN OF THE INTERIM COMMITTEE OF THE AMERICAN
JEWISH CONFERENCE, AND HONORARY PRESIDENT OF THE JEWISH NA-
TIONAL FUND OF AMERICA

Dr. GOLDSTEIN. Mr. Chairman and members of the committee, I am deeply
gratified for the courtesy extended me to appear before this committee. I am
especially grateful to my friend, Mr. Bloom, whom perhaps I may in a sense
claim as a communicant, because I happen to be administering to the community
in which he is a resident.

STATEMENT OF THE HONORABLE TOM ROLPH, A REPRESENTATIVE IN
CONGRESS FROM THE STATE OF CALIFORNIA

Mr. ROLPH. Mr. Chairman, and members of the committee, I want to say that
it is a decided privilege and a pleasure to be here today and to attend a meeting
that is under the chairmanship of a former San Franciscan. There are people who
do not know that Sol Bloom lived in San Francisco years ago. The people of San
Francisco are very proud of the job he has been doing here in the House of Representatives, and it is an honor and a privilege to serve with him.

STATEMENT OF RABBI JAMES G. HELLER, FORMER PRESIDENT, CENTRAL
CONFERENCE OF AMERICAN RABBIS AND CHAIRMAN OF THE UNITED
PALESTINE APPEAL

First of all, may I have the privilege of saying, Mr. Chairman, that although
an American citizen for many years, this is the first time in my life I have ever
attended a hearing of the Committee on Foreign Affairs, and I have been tremendously interested in the conduct of the hearing—I hope this will be included
in the record, Mr. Chairman—and greatly impressed with the conduct of the
meeting, and with the participation of the members of the committee in attempting
to formulate their opinion in regard to what is a very difficult question.

STATEMENT OF HON. CHARLES A. PLUMLEY, MEMBER OF CONGRESS FROM
THE STATE OF VERMONT

I believe that a careful study of the documents compiled in the pamphlet
arranged by Chairman Bloom, which contains the remarks in opposition to the
British white paper on Palestine which were made in the British Parliament in
1939, will show that House Resolutions 418 and 419 merit the support of the
Congress.

ARTICLE FROM THE VOICE, FEBRUARY 1944, SAN FRANCISCO, CALIF.

VETERAN CONGRESSMAN SOL BLOOM SPEAKS OUT FOR PALESTINE

Veteran Congressman Sol Bloom, chairman of the House Foreign Affairs takes
a stand against the Council for Judaism and the American Jewish Committee in
an interview with the reporters of the Jewish Morning Journal, a national Jewish
daily newspaper. In his interview Congressman Bloom declared that if it were
not for the Council for Judaism the resolution for Palestine would have been
recommended to the House without any discussion.

He further stated with pride: "I want you to know that I am not a reform
Jew; I am an orthodox Jew; I have never prayed without a hat; I follow Judaism
in the footsteps of my father and mother, and they were orthodox Jews. During
the interview he took out an Agada and he said: "For the last 40 years I repeated
with my parents the age-old saying "L'shono habo b'yerusholayim" i. e., "Next
year in Jerusalem," that means that Jerusalem was always our hope and Why
not now?"

Mr. Bloom has presented for the enlightenment of the Congress a document
concerning the Jewish National Homeland.

EXCERPT FROM LETTER WRITTEN TO HON. SOL BLOOM BY RABBI ABBA HILLEL SILVER, CHAIRMAN OF EXECUTIVE COMMITTEE, AMERICAN ZIONIST EMERGENCY COUNCIL, FEBRUARY 19, 1944

I have just returned home and I regard it as my first pleasant duty to write to you and to tell you how grateful I and my friends are to you for the superb manner in which you conducted the historic hearings on the Palestine resolution. No one who attended those hearings could fail to be impressed by your unfailing fairness, courtesy, and good humor. I know that some of the opinions which were expressed by some of the witnesses were distinctly distasteful to you, nevertheless you gave each one his day in court. Friend and foe alike of the resolution departed with a sense of having been given a square deal at your hands. You brought high honor to your distinguished office and you reflected credit upon your people.

EXCERPTS FROM WASHINGTON NEWS LETTER BY MURRAY FRANK, FROM THE NATIONAL JEWISH LEDGER OF MARCH 10, 1944

For 4 days the House Foreign Affairs Committee conducted public hearings on House Resolutions 418 and 419 relative to the establishment of a Jewish commonwealth in Palestine. The committee is composed of 25 Members of the House of Representatives, 14 of whom are Democrats and 11 Republicans. The chairman of the committee is the Honorable Sol Bloom, of New York, the only Jewish member of the committee, in whose office the hearings took place.

Throughout the hearings the small room in the Capitol was crowded beyond capacity. In the center of the room the members of the committee occupy their assigned places around the table. To the right of the chairman, a section is designated for witnesses, while to his left a section is reserved for the press. Every inch of the remaining space had been occupied long before the daily sessions were under way.

Many outstanding personages of American Jewry are present, some are seated among the audience, others among the witnesses. There are prominent rabbis here, well-known Zionist leaders and leaders of many nations, Jewish organizations, and outstanding Jewish journalists and many writers of note, among the latter the biographer Emil Ludwig.

Congressman Bloom was a very pleasant surprise to us of the Jewish press, who had heard many rumors prior to the hearings that he was opposed to the resolution. These rumors we are happy to state were utterly unfounded and entirely untrue. On the contrary Mr. Bloom not only supported the resolution, but on numerous occasions he was able to use his prerogative as chairman in ironing out an embarrassing situation, or in reminding a procommonwealth witness of a particularly helpful document, or in directing the discussion or cross-examination into the proper channels dealing directly with the resolution.

Congressman Bloom also deserves a great deal of credit for his painstaking job of collecting the most important documents concerning the problem under discussion which were published under the title "The Jewish National Home in Palestine" in a booklet of over 100 pages. In it are included among other excerpts from State Department records on the Palestine mandate, the 1924 convention between the United States and Great Britain regarding Palestine, the Palestine mandate, the British White Paper and remarks of British statesmen opposing the White Paper, the memorandum submitted to the Permanent Mandates Commission of the League of Nations by the Jewish Agency for Palestine regarding the legal aspects of the White Paper, etc. Even if Congressman Bloom had done nothing more than just the compilation and publication of these documents, which were constantly used and referred to by committee members, he deserves the praise and gratitude of American Jewry.

EDITORIAL FROM THE JEWISH REVIEW, FEBRUARY 24, 1944

The initial hearings on the Palestine resolution before the Foreign Affairs Committee of the House of Representatives constitute yet another milestone in our struggle for a Jewish Palestine. The hearings have shown unmistakably that the pending resolution commands very strong support both in the committee and the House. This was indicated by the attitude of the chairman, Mr. Sol Bloom, by the emphatic expression of support made in committee by the majority and minority leaders of the House and by the long line of Congressmen who appeared and asked to be heard in favor of the resolution.

EDITORIAL FROM THE NEW YORK DAILY MIRROR, FEBRUARY 1, 1944

Representative Sol Bloom, of New York, chairman of the Foreign Affairs Committee, told the House the British Government has agreed to this suspension of the White Paper until 30,000 Jews seeking entry into Palestine are so accommodated—"even if it does not occur until March of 1945."

Mr. Bloom, however, in conjunction with the leaders of both the Democratic and Republican Parties in the House, urges the passage of a resolution petitioning Britain to scrap the White Paper in its entirety.

EXCERPT FROM LETTER TO HON. SOL BLOOM FROM MR. LOUIS LIPSKY, ZIONIST ORGANIZATION OF AMERICA, AND THE AMERICAN JEWISH CONFERENCE, DATED FEBRUARY 23, 1944

I need not say how deeply all of us appreciate—and especially myself—the admirably fair and genial way you conducted the hearings during the entire proceedings. You have created a tremendous amount of good will toward you which you earned during these trying days.

EXCERPT FROM LETTER TO HON. SOL BLOOM FROM RABBI MORRIS S. LAZARON, 7401 PARK HEIGHTS AVENUE, BALTIMORE 8, MD., DATED FEBRUARY 21, 1944

It was pleasant to see you again and also to witness your fine bearing under a very difficult and trying situation.

EXCERPTS FROM LETTER TO HON. SOL BLOOM FROM MR. LOUIS SEGAL, GENERAL SECRETARY, JEWISH NATIONAL WORKERS' ALLIANCE, 45 EAST SEVENTEENTH STREET, NEW YORK 3, N. Y.

I wish to express to you on my behalf and on behalf of the membership of my organization, our deepest appreciation for the fine humane attitude that you have demonstrated in connection with the hearings held on the Palestine resolution.

The Jewish people the world over feel a deep gratitude for your kind cooperation for their liberation as a people through the establishment of Palestine as the Jewish commonwealth.

EXCERPTS FROM LETTER TO HON. SOL BLOOM FROM RABBI LOUIS WOLSEY, THE AMERICAN COUNCIL FOR JUDIAISM, INC., 615 NORTH BROAD STREET, PHILADELPHIA, PA., DATED FEBRUARY 10, 1944

I cannot tell you how much I am grateful to you for all of your kindness, fairness, and hospitality yesterday. Your presiding over the sessions of your committee was impeccable in every way, and it was a pleasure to testify before your authoritative committee on a subject of such pressing interest. I can only thank you for your kindness.

I was deeply impressed by your committee. Its questions were distinguished by fine intelligence and discernment, and I was very deeply impressed by the genuine seriousness with which all of the members dealt with the question, whether they were for or against the position Mr. Rosenwald and I represented.

EXCERPT FROM LETTER TO HON. SOL BLOOM FROM MR. HERMAN SHULMAN, 39 BROADWAY, NEW YORK CITY, DATED FEBRUARY 21, 1944

I want you to know how grateful I am for the opportunity you were kind enough to give me to testify before the Foreign Affairs Committee on the Wright and Compton resolutions and how much I appreciate the courtesies which you and the members of the committee extended to me.

EXCERPTS FROM LETTER TO HON. SOL BLOOM FROM RABBI MAX KIRSH-BLUM, EXECUTIVE SECRETARY, MIZRACHI ORGANIZATION OF AMERICA, 1133 BROADWAY, NEW YORK CITY, DATED FEBRUARY 17, 1944

As the American secretary of His Eminence, Dr. Isaac Halevi Herzog, Chief Rabbi of the Holy Land, and as secretary of the Mizrachi Organization of America, I have had numerous opportunities to accompany the distinguished men who had come to see you on matters vital to the American Jewish community. As a result of these conversations, I have learned to admire you for your vision and astuteness. Never before, however, have I seen you in your full glory and statesmanship as during the hearings of last week on the resolutions in behalf of the Jewish Commonwealth in Palestine, at which I was a "neutral observer."

MEMORANDUM SUBMITTED
BY
CHAIRMAN SOL BLOOM, COMMITTEE ON FOREIGN AFFAIRS
HOUSE OF REPRESENTATIVES

ON EVENTS RELATING TO
THE JEWISH NATIONAL HOME IN PALESTINE

THE BALFOUR DECLARATION

On November 2, 1917, the Principal Secretary of State for Foreign Affairs of Great Britain issued what has since become known as "The Balfour Declaration," reading as follows: "His Majesty's Government view with favour the establishment in Palestine of a national home for the Jewish people, and will use their best endeavours to facilitate the achievement of this object, it being clearly understood that nothing shall be done which may prejudice the civil and religious rights of existing non-Jewish communities in Palestine, or the rights and political status enjoyed by the Jews in any other country."

JOINT RESOLUTION OF CONGRESS SIGNED BY PRESIDENT HARDING

President Warren G. Harding on September 21, 1922, signed Public Resolution Numbered 73, Sixty-seventh Congress, in which the Congress of the United States resolved, "That the United States of America favors the establishment in Palestine of a national home for the Jewish people, it being clearly understood that nothing shall be done which may prejudice the civil and religious rights of Christian and all other non-Jewish communities in Palestine, and that the holy places and religious buildings and sites in Palestine shall be adequately protected."

BRITISH MANDATE OVER PALESTINE

The British mandate over Palestine came into force on September 29, 1923, and the preamble of the mandate contained the following statements: "The Principal Allied Powers have also agreed that the Mandatory should be responsible for putting into effect the declaration originally made on the 2nd November 1917 by the Government of His Britannic Majesty, and adopted by the said Powers, in favour of the establishment in Palestine of a national home for the Jewish people, it being clearly understood that nothing should be done which might prejudice the civil and religious rights of existing non-Jewish communities in Palestine, or the rights and political status enjoyed by Jews in any other country; and whereas recognition has thereby been given to the historical connection of the Jewish people with Palestine and to the grounds for reconstituting their national home in that country."

ESTABLISHMENT OF THE JEWISH NATIONAL HOME IN PALESTINE

Article 2 of the British mandate over Palestine reads as follows: "The Mandatory shall be responsible for placing the country under such political, administrative, and economic conditions as will secure the establishment of the Jewish national home, as laid down in the preamble, and the development of self-governing institutions, and also for safeguarding the civil and religious rights of all the inhabitants of Palestine, irrespective of race and religion."

502

FACILITATION OF JEWISH IMMIGRATION INTO PALESTINE

Article 6 of the British mandate over Palestine reads as follows: "The Administration of Palestine, while ensuring that the rights and position of other sections of the population are not prejudiced, shall facilitate Jewish immigration under suitable conditions and shall encourage, in cooperation with the Jewish agency referred to in article 4, close settlement by Jews on the land, including State lands and waste lands not required for public purposes."

CONVENTION BETWEEN UNITED STATES AND GREAT BRITAIN SIGNED BY PRESIDENT COOLIDGE

The United States as one of the Allied Powers consented to the British mandate over Palestine, and to the terms and conditions of such mandate, in a convention between the United States and Great Britain, ratification of which was advised by the Senate on February 20, 1925, and which was proclaimed by President Calvin Coolidge on December 5, 1925.

In such convention the terms of such mandate were quoted in full and consent given to British administration of Palestine only pursuant to such mandate.

In the provisions of article 7 of said convention it was provided: "Nothing contained in the present convention shall be affected by any modification which may be made in the terms of the mandate, as recited above, unless such modification shall have been assented to by the United States."

BRITISH WHITE PAPER ON PALESTINE

Although no modification has been assented to by the United States, there were put into effect in May 1939 certain policies contained in a statement of policy presented to the British Parliament in May 1939, known as the British White Paper on Palestine.

STATEMENT IN PARLIAMENT BY RIGHT HONORABLE SIR ARCHIBALD SINCLAIR

During the debate in the British Parliament on the British White Paper on Palestine the Right Honorable Sir Archibald Sinclair declared, "It is a repudiation of solemn pledges which Parliament and the people of Great Britain have given to the Jews."

STATEMENT IN HOUSE OF COMMONS BY RIGHT HONORABLE WINSTON CHURCHILL

In the Parliamentary debate in the House of Commons on the British White Paper on Palestine, the Right Honorable Winston Churchill stated, "I regret very much that the pledge of the Balfour Declaration, endorsed as it has been by successive Governments, and the conditions under which we obtained the Mandate, have both been violated by the Government's proposals".

FURTHER STATEMENT IN HOUSE OF COMMONS BY RIGHT HONORABLE WINSTON CHURCHILL

The Right Honorable Winston Churchill further stated in the Parliamentary debate on the British White Paper on Palestine, "We are now asked to submit—and this is what rankles most with me—to an agitation which is fed with foreign money and ceaselessly inflamed by Nazi and by Fascist propaganda".

STATEMENT BY MR. LLOYD GEORGE ON JEWISH COMMONWEALTH

In speaking of Palestine, Mr. Lloyd George stated, "The idea was, and this was the interpretation put upon it at the time, that a Jewish State was not to be set up immediately by the Peace Treaty, without reference to the wishes of the majority of the inhabitants. On the other hand, it was contemplated that, when the time arrived for according representative institutions to Palestine, if the Jews had meanwhile responded to the opportunity afforded them by the idea of a national home and had become a definite majority of the inhabitants, then Palestine would thus become a Jewish commonwealth".

STATEMENT BY PRESIDENT WILSON ON JEWISH COMMONWEALTH

President Woodrow Wilson, stating the case for America, said: "I am persuaded that the Allied nations, with the fullest concurrence of our Government and our people, are agreed that in Palestine shall be laid the foundations of a Jewish Commonwealth".

DECLARATION BY MEMBERS OF COMMITTEE ON FOREIGN AFFAIRS

A majority of the members of the Committee on Foreign Affairs issued a declaration in May 1939 reading as follows: "We, the undersigned members of the Committee on Foreign Affairs, desire to call to the attention of the House and the State Department a declaration of the British Government announced last Wednesday, May 17, which is a clear repudiation of the convention between the United States and Great Britain with respect to Palestine, dated December 3, 1924", which was signed by Sol Bloom, of New York; Luther A. Johnson, of Texas; John Kee, of West Virginia; James P. Richards, of South Carolina; James A. Shanley, of Connecticut; Edward V. Izac, of California; Robert G. Allen, of Pennsylvania; W. O. Burgin, of North Carolina; Hamilton Fish, of New York; George Holden Tinkham, of Massachusetts; Edith Nourse Rogers, of Massachusetts; Bruce Barton, of New York; Robert J. Corbitt, of Pennsylvania; John M. Vorys, of Ohio; and Andrew C. Schiffler, of West Virginia.

THE COMMITTEE ON FOREIGN AFFAIRS
HOUSE OF REPRESENTATIVES
SEVENTY-EIGHTH CONGRESS
SECOND SESSION

ON

HOUSE RESOLUTION 418 AND HOUSE RESOLUTION 419
RELATIVE TO
THE JEWISH NATIONAL HOME IN PALESTINE

At an executive meeting held on March 17, 1944, by the Committee on Foreign Affairs on House Resolution 418 and House Resolution 419, relative to the Jewish National Home in Palestine, and following the receipt of a letter from the Secretary of War, the committee approved the issuance of the following statement:

"Advice and information given to us by those responsible for the conduct of the war have convinced the committee that action upon the resolutions at this time would be unwise."

(Letter from the Secretary of War:)

WAR DEPARTMENT,
Washington, D. C., March 17, 1944.

Hon. SOL BLOOM,
    Chairman, Foreign Affairs Committee,
        House of Representatives, Washington, D. C.

DEAR MR. BLOOM: Concerning our conversation with respect to House Resolutions 418 and 419, it is the considered judgment of the War Department that without reference to the merits of these resolutions, further action on them at this time would be prejudicial to the successful prosecution of the war.

Faithfully yours,

HENRY L. STIMSON,
Secretary of War.

INDEX

X